Guide to Pan Sizes

When measuring pan sizes, always measure from inside edge to inside edge.

Common Pan Size	Type of Pan	Approximate Total Volume
1¾" × ¾"	Mini muffin cup	⅛ cup
2¾" × 1⅛"	Muffin cup	¼ cup
3" × 1¼"	Jumbo muffin cup	Scant ⅔ cup
1-quart	Casserole	3 cups
8" × 1½"	Pie or round cake	4 cups
11" × 1"	Tart	4 cups
9" × 1½"	Pie	5 cups
8" × 2"	Round cake	6 cups
9" × 1½"	Round cake	6 cups
8" × 8" × 1½"	Square	6 cups
10" × 1½"	Pie	6 cups
11" × 7" × 2"	Rectangular	6 cups
7½" × 3"	Bundt	6 cups
8½" × 4½" × 2½"	Loaf	6 cups
2-quart	Casserole	6 cups
9" × 5" × 3"	Loaf	8 cups
9" × 2"	Pie (deep dish) or round cake	8 cups
8" × 8" × 2"	Square	8 cups
9" × 9" × 1½"	Square	8 cups
9¼" × 2¾"	Ring mold	8 cups
9" × 3"	Bundt	9 cups
8" × 3"	Tube	9 cups
9" × 9" × 2"	Square	10 cups
15" × 10" × 1"	Jelly roll pan	10 cups
3-quart	Casserole	10 cups
10" × 2"	Round cake	11 cups
10" × 3½"	Bundt	12 cups
10" × 2½"	Springform	12 cups
13" × 9" × 2"	Rectangular	15 cups
10" × 4"	Tube	16 cups
14" × 10½" × 2½"	Roasting	18 cups

Common Temperatures and Conversions

To convert Fahrenheit into Celsius, subtract 32, multiply by 5, then divide by 9. To convert Celsius into Fahrenheit, multiply by 9, divide by 5, then add 32. The equivalents below have been rounded slightly.

Temperature Notes	Fahrenheit	Celsius	Gas Mark
Freezer storage	0°	-18°	N/A
Water freezes	32°	0°	N/A
Ideal temperature of butter for creaming	67°	19°	N/A
Room temperature	68°–72°	20°–22°	N/A
Ideal temperature for rising yeast dough	85°	29°	N/A
Poaching temperature	160°–180°	71°–82°	N/A
Water simmers	185°–205°	85°–96°	N/A
Water boils	212°	100°	N/A
Very cool oven	225°–250°	107°–121°	¼–½
Cool oven	275°–300°	135°–149°	1–2
Very moderate oven	325°	163°	3
Moderate oven	350°–375°	177°–191°	4–5
Moderately hot oven	400°	205°	6
Hot oven	425°–450°	218°–233°	7–8
Very hot oven	475°	246°	9

Container Size Equivalents

Size	Approximate Total Volume
8 oz can	1 cup
10½–12 oz can	1¼ cups
12 oz vacuum-packed can	1½ cups
14–17 oz can	1½–2 cups
29 oz can	3½ cups
46 fluid oz can	5¾ cups
6 oz can frozen juice concentrate	¾ cup
10 oz package frozen vegetables	1½–2 cups
16 oz package frozen vegetables	3–4 cups

THE CLEVER COOK'S KITCHEN HANDBOOK

5,037

Ingenious Hints, Secrets, Shortcuts, and Solutions

DAVID JOACHIM

with

Andrew Schloss, Jan Newberry,
Maryellen Driscoll, and Paul E. Piccuito

RODALE

For Christine and August

© 2002 by Rodale Inc.
Illustrations © by Judy Newhouse
Cover photograph © by Thom DeSanto

Printed in the United States of America
Rodale Inc. makes every effort to use acid-free ∞, recycled paper ♻ .

The Healthy Substitutions chart on page 570 is adapted from *More Healthy Homestyle Cooking* (Rodale, 2000), by Evelyn Tribole, M.S., R.D.

Cover Designer: Christopher Rhoads
Interior Designer: Carol Angstadt
Cover Photographer: Thom DeSanto
Interior Photographer: Kurt Wilson
Illustrator: Judy Newhouse

Library of Congress Cataloging-in-Publication Data

Joachim, David.
    The clever cook's kitchen handbook : 5,037 ingenious hints, secrets, shortcuts, and solutions / by David Joachim.
        p.   cm.
    Rev. ed. of: Brilliant food tips and cooking tricks, 2001
    Includes index.
    ISBN 1–57954–549–1   hardcover
    1. Cookery—Encyclopedias.   2. Food—Encyclopedias.   I. Joachim, David. Brilliant food tips and cooking tricks.   II. Title.
    TX349 .J3223   2002
    641.3'003—dc21   2001005876

Distributed to the book trade by St. Martin's Press

   4 6 8 10 9 7 5 3   hardcover

In all Rodale cookbooks, our mission is to provide delicious and nutritious recipes. Our recipes also meet the standards of the Rodale Test Kitchen for dependability, ease, practicality, and, most of all, great taste. To give us your comments, call (800) 848-4735.

FOR MORE OF OUR PRODUCTS

WWW.RODALESTORE.COM
(800) 848-4735

Contents

Acknowledgments

THIS BOOK HAS BEEN A LABOR OF LOVE. I am lucky to have worked with such a talented group of cooks, colleagues, contributors, writers, researchers, tip testers, and friends. Without them and many other behind-the-scenes people, this book would never have made it into print.

My sincere thanks to the contributing writers, including:

Andrew Schloss, for his inimitable expertise in how to do everything in the kitchen faster. I'll never look at leftovers the same way again.

Jan Newberry, for her rock-solid knowledge of essential cooking techniques.

Maryellen Driscoll, who swiftly resolved hundreds of common cooking problems with inspired ingenuity.

And **Paul E. Piccuito**, an inventive cook who knows how to get the most nutrients as well as the most flavors from food.

Thanks also to:

Neil Wertheimer, **Susan Clarey**, and **Anne Egan** at Rodale Books, who lit the way for this project and guided it with gentle hands.

Carol Angstadt, a gifted designer who made a very complicated book look easy.

The Rodale Test Kitchen staff, who spent countless hours making sure that these tips and recipes work.

Kathleen Hanuschak, for her help in organizing this sometimes unwieldy volume of information.

Kathy Everleth, a terrific recipe editor whose special touch made many of the recipes easier to follow.

Susannah Hogendorn, for her dogged copyediting and attention to accuracy.

Barbara Thomas-Fexa, for verifying hundreds of food facts.

Julie Kehs Minnix, who phoned, faxed, mailed, typed, and helped process hundreds of thousands of words into electronic form.

Donna Rossi, whose knack for crystal-clear layouts made these pages more user-friendly.

Judy Newhouse, for her clean illustrations that helped many hard-to-visualize tips see the light of day.

And **Janine Slaughter**, **Sindy Berner**, **Cindy Ratzlaff**, and the rest of the staff at Rodale Books, who worked tirelessly to bring this book into your hands.

How to Use This Book

A GOOD REFERENCE BOOK IS LIKE A KALEIDOSCOPE OF INFORMATION. At every turn, it sparkles with new and interesting perspectives. And, hopefully, it provides some insight that is truly useful.

My goal in these pages was to create such a book. Everything here is designed to help you develop a keener sense of food and cooking by revealing the little details that most cookbooks don't tell you. This book shows you how to buy, store, and prepare hundreds of common (and not-so-common) foods; how to fix food that goes kaflooey in the kitchen; how to cook smarter and faster; how to create and balance flavors; and how to cook more healthfully. Step-by-step illustrations demonstrate essential as well as lesser-known techniques such as the best way to crack an egg, how to seed a chile pepper without touching it, and two ways to carve a turkey. There are even tips on how to read a recipe, set up an efficient kitchen, and plan a party.

And, of course, the book contains a broad selection of recipes—over 950 in all. The recipes are meant to address nearly every cooking occasion you may be faced with, from simple breakfasts and weeknight meals to more elaborate holiday meals and special occasions. Each recipe has been developed in a home kitchen and streamlined for home cooks.

This book is organized from A to Z. Each entry (Apples, for instance) begins with a brief description followed by tips, recipes, illustrations, and other useful information.

The tips within each entry are further organized under five categories: Basics, Problem Solvers, Time Savers, Flavor Tips, and Healthy Hints.

All entries are alphabetized by letter rather than by word. This means that if a space occurs between two words in an entry, it is alphabetized as if there were no space. For example, Cake Pans appear before Cakes.

If you don't find what you're looking for, check the index. The information you're after may be in another entry. For instance, a tip on how much acid to add to a marinade is listed under Marinades rather than under Acidity. Likewise, the index is the best place to search for recipes because not every recipe will appear under its likely entry. Simple Red Pepper Sauce, for example, appears under Peppers, Sweet rather than under Sauces.

Most of this book's recipes appear in a shorthand paragraph form, in which the ingredients and directions are mixed together, and the ingredients appear in boldface type for easy reference. Notice that a few dozen recipes *do* appear in a more traditional recipe format with an ingredient list followed by a set of cooking directions. These recipes have been given special treatment because they demonstrate the book's most practical tips.

I've found that knowing your way around a kitchen comes mostly with practice. But good guidance helps. My hope is that these recipes and tips will make your life in the kitchen easier and more enjoyable; and that the little-known food facts will delight and surprise you along the way.

1

a

A

Acidity

Acidity in food imparts a sour (tart) taste on the tongue that is one of the four basic flavors. The most common forms are citrus juice, vinegar, wine, and tomatoes. Acidic ingredients (yogurt and buttermilk included) also affect the texture, color, and shelf life of foods. A bit of acid can make a pie crust more tender, stabilize whipped egg whites, and bring a shine to copper cookware.

BASICS ▼ **To make acidulated water** • For each quart (4 cups) of cold water, add 4 tablespoons lemon juice. Or add a different acidic ingredient, such as 2 teaspoons vinegar or ½ cup white wine.

PROBLEM SOLVER ▼ **To prevent discoloration of low-acid foods** • Toss the cut food with lemon juice or vinegar. This method will keep cut apples, potatoes, bananas, and other low-acid foods from turning brown. Or place the cut food in acidulated water until needed.

FLAVOR TIPS ▼ **To enhance flavors** • A bit of citrus juice or vinegar enhances the flavors of fruits, vegetables, poultry, and seafood by complementing natural sweetness.

To decrease acidity • Add a sweet ingredient such as sugar, honey, or syrup. Start with a ratio of 1 part sweetener to 3 parts acidic ingredient (say, 1 teaspoon sugar to 1 tablespoon lemon juice). Increase the ratio as desired. Equal amounts give a pleasant sweet-and-sour flavor.

Alcohol *see also* Beer; Flambé; Sherry; Wine

An important ingredient in many recipes, alcohol adds flavor to sauces, soups, marinades, and even ice cream. When heated, some but not all of the alcohol evaporates.

BASICS ▼ **To select** • Match the type of alcohol to the food. For instance, flavor a raspberry sorbet with raspberry liqueur. There is no reason to use very expensive spirits for cooking, but keep in mind that if it's not worth drinking, it's not worth cooking with either. Avoid products labeled "cooking wine." These often contain salt, are of poor quality, and taste awful.

To cook with alcohol • Be careful not to add too much. Many alcohol spirits have strong flavors that can easily overpower a dish. Begin by adding just a teaspoon or tablespoon, then taste the dish and add more if desired.

To safely add alcohol to a hot pan • Remove the pan from the heat and slowly

SUBSTITUTES FOR ALCOHOL

Liqueur extracts are mighty handy for replacing liqueurs. You can find extracts of Grand Marnier, Chambord, and other liqueurs in the spice aisle of many supermarkets.

Instead of This . . .	Use This . . .
1 cup wine or beer	1 cup nonalcoholic wine or beer
1 Tbsp rum or liqueur	1 tsp rum extract or liqueur extract + 2 tsp water
1 Tbsp coffee-flavored liqueur	1 Tbsp coffee
1 Tbsp orange-flavored liqueur	1 Tbsp orange juice + ½ tsp grated orange zest
1 Tbsp sherry or Madeira	1 Tbsp apple juice

pour in the alcohol, swirling the pan to help keep the alcohol from heating too quickly. Return the pan to low heat and continue cooking as necessary.

To give frozen desserts a smooth, creamy texture • Add 1 to 2 teaspoons alcohol to the base. Alcohol prevents ice crystals from forming, which helps keep frozen desserts creamy. But be careful. Too much alcohol will prevent your dessert from freezing at all, and you may end up with something best enjoyed with a straw rather than with a spoon.

To boil off alcohol • Remove a hot skillet from the heat and add ½ to 1 cup liquor, wine, liqueur, or beer. Let the liquid in the pan boil until the vapors do not sting the inside of your nose when inhaled, about 1 minute for liquor, wine, or liqueur and 30 seconds for beer.

Al Dente

This Italian term translates to "to the tooth" and is used to describe the preferred texture for cooked pasta and some vegetables.

BASICS **To check for al dente texture** • Take a bite and look at the center of the food. Pasta should be completely cooked through with no white core but should still offer a bit of resistance. Vegetables should be tender yet crisp.

Anchovies; Anchovy Paste

These tiny, bold-flavored fish are most often available in their preserved form in tins. Anchovy paste is available in tubes.

BASICS **To select** • Go for whole anchovies packed in salt. They have the best flavor and are usually bigger and meatier than oil-packed anchovies. If you can't find salt-packed anchovies, glass jars of oil-packed fillets are the next best choice. Choose the jar with the meatiest fillets. Tins of oil-packed anchovies, which don't allow you to see what you're buying, are a poor third choice. Finally, buy anchovy paste only as a last resort for convenience. Anchovy paste is essentially the leftovers of the anchovy production plant packed into tubes.

a

To store • After opening, transfer any unused anchovies to a container, cover with at least 1" of olive oil, seal the container, and refrigerate for up to 1 year.

To fillet whole, salt-packed anchovies • Rinse off the salt with cold water. Working over a colander in the sink under slow running water, hold the fish belly-up and run a finger from the head down through the tail to separate the fillets and expose the backbone. Lift the backbone away from the fillet and discard. Soak the fillets in cold water for 20 to 30 minutes to reduce saltiness. Dry on paper towels before using or storing. Store as you would unfilleted anchovies.

To cook • Keep the heat low and cook anchovies slowly, so that they dissolve gradually. Avoid high heat, which hardens anchovies and gives them a harsh, bitter flavor.

TIME SAVER
▼

To replace anchovies • For pure convenience, substitute anchovy paste for mashed anchovies. It saves mashing time and cleanup. Use ½ teaspoon anchovy paste in place of each anchovy fillet. Refrigerate unused anchovy paste in its tube for up to 6 months. For a vegetarian substitute, use ½ teaspoon soy sauce or vegetarian Worcestershire sauce mixed with ½ teaspoon dried dulse sea vegetable flakes (see page 456) in place of each anchovy fillet.

QUICK ANCHOVY SAUCE Combine **2 ounces anchovy paste, 5 tablespoons olive oil,** and **4 minced garlic cloves.** Use as a sauce for 1 pound pasta, 2 pounds potatoes, or 3 cups cooked rice. Also adds a quick flavor shot to fish soups, salad dressings, and pan sauces. *Makes about ½ cup.*

Angel Food Cake

A type of sponge cake, angel food cake requires no other leavening than egg whites. It also contains no butter and no egg yolks, so it is extremely low in fat.

PROBLEM SOLVERS
▼

To invert the pan during cooling • Place the pan tube over the neck of a tall, sturdy bottle. Or prop the pan edges on 4 cans of equal height.

To slice easily • Freeze the cake, then thaw before cutting.

To use leftover egg yolks • Hard-cook the yolks in a microwave oven, then press through a sieve. Use in a salad or as a garnish. (To hard-cook 3 to 4 yolks, stir to blend, loosely cover in an oiled, microwaveable bowl, and cook on medium power for 60 seconds.) Or, if you're really ambitious, use leftover yolks to make Classic Hollandaise Sauce (see page 439).

Appetizers

Meant to stimulate the palate, appetizers differ from hors d'oeuvres in only one respect: They may be served with utensils, whereas hors d'oeuvres are usually served as finger food. (See page 6 for a party's worth of easy appetizers.)

Apples *see also* Pies

New York might be the Big Apple, but Washington State is the largest apple-producing state in America. The apple itself is native to central Asia.

BASICS
▼

To select • The flesh should be firm; the skin should be smooth, tight, and free of blemishes and bruises; and the scent should be full and fresh. Don't judge an

a

Angel Food Cake

This recipe calls for superfine sugar. If you can't find it in a store, process granulated sugar in a blender or food processor until fine in texture, about 1 minute.

1 **cup sifted cake flour**

¼ **teaspoon salt**

1½ **cups superfine sugar, divided**

12 **egg whites**

1 **tablespoon water**

1½ **teaspoons cream of tartar**

1½ **teaspoons vanilla extract**

¼ **teaspoon almond extract**

1. Preheat the oven to 350°F. Adjust an oven rack to the lower-middle position. Have ready 1 ungreased 9" or 10" tube pan, preferably with a removable bottom. If the bottom is not removable, line the pan bottom with parchment or waxed paper.

2. In a small bowl, combine the flour, salt, and ½ cup of the sugar.

3. In a large bowl, beat the egg whites on low speed, 1 minute. Increase the speed to medium and continue beating until foamy. Add the water and cream of tartar. Beat on medium speed until the egg whites are billowy but not yet forming soft peaks when the beaters are lifted. Continue beating on medium speed, and begin to gradually add the remaining 1 cup sugar, 1 tablespoon at a time. After you add the sugar, the egg whites should soon develop soft, glossy

peaks. Blend in the vanilla extract and almond extract.

4. Sift the flour mixture over the whites, ¼ cup at a time, gently folding each batch of flour into the whites until the flour just disappears. Do not stir or mix.

5. Pour into the cake pan. Using a rubber spatula, gently even out the foam in the pan. Bake until the top is golden brown and lightly springs back when touched, 40 to 45 minutes. Cool upside down 1½ hours, propping the pan tube on a bottleneck or the edges of 4 cans of equal height.

6. To unmold, slide a thin knife around the perimeter, pressing firmly against the pan to prevent tearing the cake. Repeat around the center tube. If the pan has a removable bottom, push it up to remove. If the bottom is not removable, invert the pan.

Makes 16 servings

Lemon Angel Food Cake: Omit the almond extract. Replace the water with 2 tablespoons lemon juice. Add 2 teaspoons grated lemon zest to the flour mixture.

Mocha Angel Food Cake: Reduce the flour to ½ cup sifted flour and mix with ½ cup unsweetened cocoa powder, sifted, and 2 tablespoons finely ground instant coffee.

a

APPETIZERS THAT LET YOU ATTEND YOUR OWN PARTY

The following 5 master appetizer ideas are as quick and easy as they are bright and delicious. Use the variations to create 20 different appetizers. Each makes about 8 servings.

Hot-Pepper Olives: Toss **1 pint assorted olives (pitted or unpitted)** with **1 tablespoon extra-virgin olive oil, 1 minced garlic clove,** and **½ teaspoon red-pepper flakes.** *Variations:* Use green olives and add ½ cup chopped roasted peppers and ¼ cup small capers. Or use kalamata olives and add ½ cup chopped toasted walnuts and 1 minced garlic clove. You can also use mixed olives and add 1 cup chopped preserved lemon and ¼ cup chopped fresh parsley.

Lemon Cheese: Mix **½ pound farmer cheese, 1 tablespoon lemon juice, 1 table-spoon lemon zest,** and **1 teaspoon sugar.** Serve on **pumpernickel bread,** with some of the **Hot-Pepper Olives** above if you have them. *Variations:* Replace the lemon juice with balsamic vinegar and replace the lemon zest with 1 teaspoon cracked peppercorns. Or replace the lemon juice with wine vinegar and replace the lemon zest with 1 minced garlic clove.

Roasted Peppers Four Ways: Toss the **sliced, roasted peppers from a 12-ounce jar** with **4 ounces fresh mozzarella** cut into fingers, **2 tablespoons chopped fresh basil, 1 minced garlic clove,** and **1 tablespoon extra-virgin olive oil.** *Variations:* Toss the peppers with 1 cup pitted black olives and 2 tablespoons chopped fresh oregano. Or toss them with 2 tablespoons orange zest, 1 minced garlic clove, and ¼ cup chopped toasted hazelnuts. Or toss them with 6 ounces slivered, smoked ham and 2 table-spoons capers.

Prosciutto: Paper-thin slices of prosciutto di Parma make an elegant appetizer that requires no work and no time (ask the store to slice it for you). Plan on **½ pound prosciutto** for 16 to 20 portions. You can also serve prosciutto with bread. It is even better with about **½ cup shaved Parmesan cheese,** and better still surrounded by bunches of **grapes, melon slices,** or **halved fresh figs.** You can continue to gild the piggy with **¼ cup chopped toasted nuts** (hazelnuts are wonderful), **¼ cup chopped fresh mint leaves,** or **4 to 6 ounces high-quality candied fruit** cut into slivers.

Marinated Shrimp: Heat **3 cups water,** the **juice of ½ lemon,** and **¼ teaspoon** *each* **salt and ground black pepper** to boiling. Add **1 pound peeled and cleaned large shrimp.** Stir until shrimp begin to turn pink, 1 minute. Remove from heat, cover, and set aside 30 seconds. Drain. While they're still warm, toss shrimp with **1 cup Italian salad dressing,** and chill. Serve with toothpicks for spearing. *Variations:* Add 2 tablespoons Dijon mustard, 2 minced garlic cloves, and/or ¼ cup chopped fresh parsley to the dressing.

apple by its looks alone; the best tasting are often not the most beautiful.

To tell when an apple is ready to eat • As an apple ripens, its texture, color, flavor, and aroma all change. The flesh softens slightly, the color deepens, the sweetness intensifies, and the acidity drops as the aroma becomes stronger.

a

To store • Store unripe apples at room temperature until they are ready to eat. Keep apples that are ready to eat in the refrigerator. To make apples last as long as possible, store them so that they aren't touching each other. Keep apples away from strong-smelling foods such as onions, as apples easily absorb odors.

To peel • Use a vegetable peeler (a knife takes too much of the fruit with the peel). Remove the stem. Hold the peeler at the stem end and begin turning the apple into the blade of the peeler. Angle the peeler at about 60 degrees so that each rotation moves you farther along the circumference of the apple, resulting in a spiral of apple peel. With practice, you should be able to peel an apple in about 20 seconds.

To core and keep whole • Use an apple corer made especially for the job. If you don't have a corer, carefully push a small paring knife down through the top of the apple just off-center from the core, and cut around the core.

To core for baked apples • Hollow out the core using a melon baller, without going all the way through the bottom.

To preserve • Peel, core, and cut the apples into wedges. Toss in lemon juice, then sugar. Spread on a baking sheet and freeze until firm. Transfer to a zipper-lock freezer bag and freeze for up to 6 months.

PROBLEM SOLVERS ▼ **To keep cut apples from turning brown** • Drop the fruit into a bowl of acidulated water (see page 2).Or toss the fruit with lemon juice or orange juice. If the sliced apples are to be baked, such as in a crisp or a pie, the browning reaction will be reversed as the apples cook, so no such precautions are necessary.

To revive slightly overripe apples • Chop them, immerse them in apple cider or apple juice, and refrigerate for at least 30 minutes. Or peel and cut the apple and add as is to muffin or pancake batter, where a softer texture is preferred.

CARAMELIZED APPLE WEDGES Core **1 overripe apple** (peel if desired), slice into very thin wedges, and place wedges on a foil-lined baking sheet. Brush with **1 tablespoon melted butter,** or dot with **butter pieces.** Sprinkle with **1 tablespoon brown sugar** or **maple syrup** and a **pinch of ground cinnamon.** Broil until rich golden brown and caramelized, about 3 minutes. Serve with **vanilla ice cream** for a simple dessert. *Makes ½ cup.*

Fascinating Fact: A bruise on an apple is no different from the browning that occurs when a sliced apple is exposed to air. In both cases, phenolic compounds and enzymes in the apple's cells react with air, turning the apple brown. In the case of bruising, however, the skin is not broken. It is the air pockets within the apple itself that are reacting with the damaged cells. Either way, the browned part is safe to eat.

TIME SAVERS ▼ **To core quickly** • Slice the apple in half from top to bottom. Scoop out the core with a melon baller. Or, if the shape of the final apple slices is not important, use a paring knife to make two deep cuts angled inward—one along each side of the core on each apple half. This cuts out the core in a V shape.

To peel and core large amounts quickly • Use a peeling-coring-slicing machine. These nifty contraptions attach to the edge of a countertop and cut prep time almost in half.

a

CHOOSING THE RIGHT APPLE

There are currently more than 3,000 varieties of apples, which range from mouth-puckeringly tart to candy-sweet in shades of green, gold, pink, and red. Here are the most popular varieties and how to use them (the best uses for each apple are listed first). Some apples are recommended specifically for salads because their flesh is slow to brown. For baked apples, Rome Beauty is the best choice.

Apple	Characteristics	Best Uses
Arkansas Black	Crisp, juicy	Eating, sauce
Baldwin	Crisp, juicy	Baking, eating
Braeburn	Crisp, sweet/tart	Eating, sauce, pie
Bramley	Sweet, tangy	Baking, sauce
Cortland	Fragrant, tangy	Salads, baking, sauce, eating
Empire	Super-crisp, sweet, juicy	Eating, salads
Fuji	Sweet, juicy	Eating
Gala	Crisp, fragrant, mildly tart	Eating, baking, sauce
Golden Delicious	Juicy, sweet	Sauce, baking, salads, eating
Granny Smith	Tart, crisp	Baking, eating
Gravenstein	Crisp, tart	Baking, sauce
Idared	Juicy, fragrant, tart	Baking
Jonagold	Tart, juicy, crisp	Eating, baking
Jonathan	Crisp, juicy	Eating, sauce, pie
Lady Apple	Juicy, intensely sweet	Eating, baking
Macoun	Firm, fragrant, very flavorful	Eating, baking
McIntosh	Tart, juicy, slightly spicy, very soft	Eating, sauce
Mutsu	Crisp, juicy	Eating
Northern Spy	Full-flavored, very firm	Baking, eating
Red Delicious	Crisp, mildly tart	Eating
Rome Beauty	Slightly tart, firm	Baking
Spartan	Well-balanced, sweet, tart	Eating
Winesap	Sweet, juicy with a slightly fermented, winey flavor	Eating, sauce

a

MICROWAVE BAKED APPLES Remove cores of **1 to 6 Rome Beauty apples** through stem ends with an apple corer or melon baller, without going all the way through blossom ends. Cut a slice off bottom of each apple to help it sit stably. Remove a strip of peel from top of apple to keep skin from bursting. For each apple, mix **2 teaspoons honey or maple syrup** and **½ teaspoon apple juice or brandy.** Brush hollowed core and all cut surfaces with this syrup. Stuff each hollowed core with **2 teaspoons** *each* **raisins, chopped walnuts, and brown sugar.** (Or use **2 teaspoons chutney** and **1 teaspoon chopped fresh thyme or fresh lemon balm**). Place apples in an equidistant circle on a round microwaveable plate, cover loosely with plastic, and microwave on high power, 3 minutes for 1 or 2 apples, 5 minutes for 4 apples, or 9 minutes for 6 apples. Puncture plastic and allow apples to rest 5 minutes to finish cooking. *Makes 1 to 6 servings.*

FLAVOR TIP ▼ **To flavor** • Cinnamon and nutmeg are perfect flavorings for apples, but try these other combinations: ground cardamom (which is strong, so use just a little); ground ginger (could be combined with cardamom); ground allspice; pumpkin pie spice; or grated lemon, lime, or orange zest.

FRAGRANT STUFFED BAKED APPLES Working from the stem ends of **4 Rome Beauty apples,** remove cores but don't cut all the way through to bottoms. Remove a strip of peel from top of each apple to keep skin from bursting. Mix together **⅓ cup** *each* **finely chopped walnuts and brown sugar, 3 tablespoons butter, 1 tablespoon flour, 1 teaspoon ground cinnamon,** and **½ teaspoon ground nutmeg.** Stuff into apples, mounding over tops. Place in an 8" × 8" baking pan, pour 1 cup apple cider around apples, and bake at 350°F, basting several times, until tender, 45 to 60 minutes. Serve hot or cold. Crème Anglaise (page 446) makes a wonderful adornment. *Makes 4 servings.*

CIDER-GLAZED BREAKFAST SAUSAGES Lightly brown **½ pound breakfast sausage links** in a skillet. Discard fat, leaving sausages in the pan. Add **1 cup apple cider** and simmer until cider reduces to a glaze and sausages are no longer pink inside, about 10 minutes. *Makes 4 servings.*

EASY ICEBOX APPLE CAKE Slice **1 pound cake** into 10 thick slices. Spread each slice with **apple butter** (about ¾ cup total). Place a layer of coated cake slices in a loaf pan or terrine, buttered side up. Spoon on a layer of **lightly sweetened whipped cream (about ½ cup)** and sprinkle with **a pinch or two of ground cinnamon.** Repeat layering twice more with cake, whipped cream, and cinnamon. Chill for 20 minutes. *Makes 10 servings.*

Applesauce

If you've never made fresh applesauce at home, give it a try. It's really simple. Serve it alongside roast pork or as a dessert served warm with vanilla ice cream. Applesauce is also a key ingredient for great-tasting, low-fat quick breads and muffins (see "To reduce fat using fruit purees" on page 22).

BASICS ▼ **To make smooth and creamy applesauce** • Use a soft-textured apple, such as McIntosh. Add the sugar after the apples have softened, and pass the finished sauce through a food mill or sieve.

To make chunky applesauce • Use a firm apple, such as Northern Spy or Granny Smith. Add the sugar at the beginning of the cooking time, and mash the finished sauce with a wooden spoon or a potato masher.

To tint applesauce pink • Include apples with red skins, such as McIntosh or Cortland, and do not peel before cooking. Pass the cooked sauce through a food mill or a fine-mesh sieve to separate out the skins. The sauce will remain a lovely shade of pink. Or make apple-cranberry sauce by replacing some of the apples with cranberries (3 cups cranberries replaces 1 pound apples). Add ½ cup sugar to balance the tartness of the cranberries.

FLAVOR TIP ▼ **To flavor curried dishes** • Add ½ cup applesauce to each 1 cup of curry sauce (or broth) when making a curried dish. Simmer as the recipe directs.

SPICY APPLESAUCE In a large saucepan, combine **1 cup apple cider, ¼ cup sugar, 2 tablespoons lemon juice, 1 cinnamon stick,** and **5 whole cloves.** Add **3 pounds peeled, cored, and chopped McIntosh apples.** Bring to a boil over high heat. Reduce heat to low and simmer about 20 minutes. Taste for sweetness and add more sugar if desired. Simmer until desired thickness is reached. *Makes about 8 cups.*

Arrowroot *see also* Gravy; Sauces

You couldn't ask for a better thickener. This silky white powder is a pure starch derived from a tropical American plant. It's fat-free, easy to digest, and flavorless (so it won't in-terfere with delicate sauces); it thickens at low temperatures (perfect for heat-sensitive egg-based sauces and custards); it has twice the thickening power of wheat flour and doesn't get cloudy upon thickening (so it makes beautiful fruit sauces and gravies); and it has none of the chalky taste associated with cornstarch.

BASICS ▼ **To store** • Keep in an airtight container marked with the date that you bought it. Use within 2 months because its thickening properties diminish with age.

To use • Dissolve 1½ teaspoons arrowroot in 1 tablespoon cold liquid. Stir or whisk the cold mixture into 1 cup hot liquid at the end of cooking time. Stir until thickened, about 5 seconds. These proportions will make about 1 cup of medium-thick sauce, soup, or gravy. For a thinner sauce, use 1 teaspoon arrowroot. For a thicker sauce, use up to 1 tablespoon arrowroot.

To replace cornstarch • Use 1 tablespoon arrowroot in place of 2 teaspoons cornstarch.

To replace flour • Use half as much arrowroot as flour. If the recipe calls for 1 tablespoon flour, substitute 1½ teaspoons arrowroot.

Fascinating Fact: The word *arrowroot* is believed to originate with Native Americans, who used the root to draw out poison from arrow wounds. Another possible origin is a Native American word for flour, *araruta*. Its scientific name is *Maranta arundinacea*.

PROBLEM SOLVER ▼ **To keep an arrowroot-thickened sauce thick** • Stir until just combined. Overstirring can make it thin again.

Artichoke Hearts

Marinated artichoke hearts are one of the greatest convenience foods ever made.

a

SIMPLE ARTICHOKE SALSA Combine **1 jar (6 ounces) finely chopped marinated artichoke hearts,** drained; **1 finely chopped canned jalapeño chile pepper; 1 minced garlic clove;** and the **juice of 1 small lime.** Serve with fish, grilled turkey, or chicken. *Makes about ½ cup.*

FLAVOR TIPS
▼

To use in potato salad • Drain a jar of marinated artichoke hearts; chop coarsely and fold into your favorite potato salad.

To flavor casseroles • Drain a can of water-packed artichoke hearts. Quarter them and fold into your favorite chicken or rice casserole.

BOLD SANDWICH RELISH Drain **1 jar (6 ounces) marinated artichoke hearts** and **1 can (6 ounces) pitted black olives.** Place in a food processor with **½ cup sliced stuffed green olives, 8 anchovy fillets, 2 tablespoons lemon juice, 1 tablespoon capers, 1 garlic clove** (optional), and **a pinch *each* dried oregano, ground red pepper, and ground black pepper.** Process to a coarse puree. Refrigerate for up to 1 week. *Makes about 1 cup.*

Artichokes

Originally from the Mediterranean but now cultivated mainly in California, artichokes are the buds of a large thistle in the sunflower family. The edible portions include the base of the green leaves, the tender inner heart, and the base of the choke itself. Artichoke season is at its peak from March to May.

BASICS
▼

To select • Rub an artichoke with your fingers and listen carefully. If it's tender, the leaves will squeak. A hollow and dry sound indicates a tough, overdeveloped heart. Hold the artichoke in the palm of your hand. Tender ones have a heavy, solid feel. Those with more mature and tougher chokes will feel light and less substantial because they have begun to dehydrate. Keep in mind that size doesn't matter. Size is an indication of where an artichoke grew on the plant, not its age or tenderness. Large ones grow at the top of the plant; smaller ones sprout from the sides of the stalk. And look kindly on artichokes with brown streaks or scars. These marks are known as the "kiss of the frost" and often indicate a delectable nutty flavor.

To store • Keep raw artichokes in a plastic bag in the coldest part of the refrigerator. They should last for at least 1 week.

To wash • Plunge artichokes up and down in a sink full of cold water to dislodge any debris trapped between the leaves.

To steam • Put artichokes, stem end up, in a steamer basket set over 3" of boiling salted water. (This method gets steam to the leaves faster.) Cover and cook until tender, about 15 minutes for baby artichokes and up to 45 minutes for large ones. To test for doneness, tug on one of the leaves. If it comes off easily, the artichoke is ready to eat. Drain by setting the artichokes upside down on a rack; let stand for several minutes before serving.

To cook artichoke stems • Peel and cook in salted, acidulated water. Though often discarded, artichoke stems can be as tender and delicious as the heart.

To serve with wine • Wine enthusiasts agree that artichokes can ruin the flavor of a fine wine because artichokes make other foods taste sweeter (see "Fascinating Fact" on page 13). Experts recommend skipping wine when eating a healthy dose of artichokes. If, however, you have your heart

HOW TO PREP AND EAT AN ARTICHOKE

1 Cut off the stem at the base of the artichoke, then turn it around and cut off the upper third of the leaves. To prevent browning, rub all cut edges with lemon juice or dip frequently into acidulated water (see page 2).

2 If the spiny tips of the leaves bother you, cut them off with stainless steel scissors. (These tips will soften when cooked, so, instead, you could hold the artichoke in a towel during handling to protect your hands.) Peel away the loose bottom leaves, which can have a bitter taste. If you don't plan to stuff the artichoke whole, at this point you can steam, boil, or microwave it and remove the choke after cooking. Or place it in a bowl of acidulated water until ready to cook.

3 To eat a whole cooked artichoke, pull off one leaf at a time and place it between your teeth. Bite gently and pull the leaf away from your teeth to scrape off the meat. Continue with the remaining leaves. Use the point of a spoon to scrape out and discard the fuzzy choke, then enjoy the very tender artichoke heart.

4 If you plan to stuff the artichoke, use your hands to gently spread the leaves apart and pull out the central core of spiky leaves, exposing the choke. Use the point of a spoon (a grapefruit spoon works great) to scrape out and discard the fuzzy choke.

set on it, select a white wine with high acidity, such as Chenin Blanc or dry Riesling, to counteract the sweetening effect.

Fascinating Fact: Eating artichokes creates a chemical reaction in the mouth that makes other foods or beverages taste sweeter. This is due to a compound called cynarine, which stimulates the sweetness receptors on your tongue. Since artichokes have this effect, it's best to serve them on their own or to pair them with neutral-tasting foods such as pasta.

PROBLEM SOLVER ▼ **To prevent discoloration** • Use only stainless steel knives or scissors when cutting artichokes. Carbon knives cause discoloring. Immediately rub the cut surfaces with lemon juice, or keep cut artichokes in acidulated water until you are ready to cook them. To cover cut, raw artichokes until cooking time, use parchment paper or plastic wrap, but not aluminum foil. For cooking, use stainless steel, nonstick, or enamel-coated pans. Avoid cooking artichokes in cast-iron or aluminum pots, as these metals will discolor artichokes. Also, add lemon juice, vinegar, or white wine to the cooking water.

TIME SAVERS ▼ **To speed trimming and cooking** • Smash each artichoke facedown against a counter. This will loosen the leaves and spread them apart slightly, making the leaves easier to trim. It also allows heat to permeate the interior of the artichoke faster.

To microwave • Trim the artichokes, wrap each tightly in microwaveable plastic, and arrange in a circle on a carousel or plate. Microwave 4 to 6 large artichokes on high power until the stem ends can be easily pierced with a fork or small knife, about 15 to 20 minutes. Increase or decrease the time depending on the size and number of artichokes.

THREE ARTICHOKE DIPPING SAUCES

Each of these recipes makes enough dip for 4 whole steamed artichokes.

Creamy Lemon Sauce: Mix **1 cup ranch dressing, 1 crushed garlic clove,** and the **juice of 1 lemon.**

Mint-Yogurt Sauce: Mix **½ cup plain yogurt,** the **juice of 1½ lemon, 1 tablespoon chopped fresh mint,** and **1 small minced garlic clove.**

Sun-Dried Tomato Pesto with Goat Cheese: Mix **2 tablespoons** *each* pureed marinated **sun-dried tomatoes** and prepared **pesto** with **2 ounces fresh goat cheese** and **1 tablespoon olive oil.**

To pressure-steam • Place the artichokes, right side up, in a basket in a pressure cooker. Add a few inches of water, lock on the top, and heat to high pressure. Pressure-steam at high pressure for 10 minutes for large artichokes, 7 minutes for medium. Release the steam immediately.

FLAVOR TIP ▼ **To use in scalloped potatoes** • Trim 3 fresh artichokes down to the hearts, rubbing with half a lemon as you work to prevent darkening. Remove and discard the fuzzy chokes. Slice the fresh artichoke hearts ⅛" thick and layer with potatoes.

SAUTÉED BABY ARTICHOKES WITH WALNUTS Baby artichokes (the size of golf balls) are so young and tender that they need no trimming. Cut **1 pound baby artichokes** lengthwise into quarters and sauté in a skillet with **1 minced**

a

garlic clove in **2 tablespoons olive oil** until tender, about 10 minutes. Add **2 tablespoons chopped walnuts** and cook just until walnuts begin to toast, about 1 minute. Swirl the **juice of 1 lemon** around the pan. Season with **½ teaspoon salt** and **¼ teaspoon freshly ground black pepper.** *Makes 4 servings.*

Asparagus

A subtly sweet, fresh grassy taste makes asparagus one of the most anticipated arrivals of spring. White asparagus is simply green asparagus that's grown beneath a cover of soil or hay, which prevents photosynthesis and gives white asparagus a crunchier texture. Purple asparagus tends to have a somewhat sweeter taste than green. The purple pigment turns green when heated.

BASICS ▼ **To select** • Look for spears with a vivid color and no blemishes and bruises. The buds at the tip should be tightly closed, and the base of each stalk should appear freshly cut. Whether you choose pencil-thin, standard, or jumbo is a matter of personal preference. All can be equally tender as long as they are fresh. For the best flavor, enjoy asparagus at the peak of its season from March to May. At other times of year, the asparagus in your market has likely been flown in from a distant country.

To store • Remove any bands that bind the spears together, and put the bases of the stems in a glass filled with about 2" of water. Cover loosely with a plastic bag and refrigerate for up to 3 days. Changing the water daily will help the asparagus stay fresh longer, but for the best flavor, enjoy asparagus soon after you buy it.

To trim • Hold one end of the asparagus spear in each hand and bend the stalk. The spear will naturally break at the point where it becomes tough.

To peel • Thick, tough-skinned asparagus may need peeling with a vegetable peeler. To avoid breaking the spears, lay each flat on a work surface with the tip away from you and the stem end near you. Using a vegetable peeler, peel from tip to stem end, working in that direction only.

To blanch • Blanching or parboiling asparagus makes it perfect for a platter of crudités (fresh vegetables) and dips. Trim the asparagus and place in boiling water for 15 seconds (for small spears) to 30 seconds (for large spears). Transfer to paper towels, pat dry, and let cool.

To steam upright • Trim asparagus and cut the stem ends level with a knife. Using kitchen string, tie the asparagus together in a bundle. You may need two separate bands of string to secure the bundle. Place 1" of water in a tall, covered saucepan and bring to a simmer. If needed, trim the asparagus to fit in the covered saucepan. Stand the asparagus upright in the saucepan, cover, and cook for 5 to 10 minutes, depending upon thickness. If you don't have a tall saucepan, use another saucepan or a metal bowl of the same diameter to invert over the asparagus.

To boil evenly • Use a large, wide skillet. Add 1" of water and heat to boiling. Add trimmed asparagus so that all the spears face the same direction. Move the pan so that the stem ends are directly over the heat and the tips are well off the burner. Boil just until crisp-tender, about 4 to 6 minutes for 1 pound of asparagus.

To grill • Preheat the grill and spray the grill grate or a grilling screen with oil. Toss the spears in olive oil and put them on the grilling screen, or thread them onto wooden skewers so that they don't fall between the grate. Place the spears perpendicular to the bars of the grate and grill 20 to 40 seconds per side (for thin spears) or 40 to 60 seconds (for thick spears) over a medium-hot fire. There will be grill marks on the spears, but the asparagus may not look completely cooked. That's okay. Transfer the spears to a plate; within 20 seconds, they will soften and turn bright green. Season with salt, pepper, and other seasonings if desired.

To roast • Spread the spears on a baking sheet and toss with olive oil. Roast at 425°F about 2 minutes, then shake the pan to turn over the spears and roast until tender, 2 to 3 minutes more. Season with salt, pepper, and other seasonings if desired.

To test for doneness • Pierce the stalk with the tip of a knife. Consider asparagus done when the stalk is just tender and meets the knife with a bit of resistance. Asparagus will continue cooking with residual heat once it has left the heat, so cook it until crisp-tender.

To cool cooked asparagus • Spread the spears in a single layer on a rack or a towel. Avoid plunging them into a bowl of cold water, which dilutes the flavor.

PROBLEM SOLVERS ▼ **To revive limp asparagus** • Cut a small slice off the stem ends and place upright (stem ends down) in a glass containing 1" of ice water. Cover loosely with a plastic bag and refrigerate for 1 to 2 hours.

To salvage overcooked, limp asparagus • Cut into 1" lengths to mask their floppiness.

To make asparagus servings look bigger • If you are short on supply, cut spears on a sharp diagonal into 1" pieces to make them look less scant.

TIME SAVERS ▼ **To quick-cook thick asparagus** • Cut diagonally into 2" pieces to increase the surface area exposed to the heat.

To microwave • Place trimmed asparagus in a microwaveable dish with the tips pointing inward. The tips can overlap, if needed. Add 1/8" of water, cover, and microwave on high power until just tender, 3 to 6 minutes (depending on thickness).

To stir-fry • Cut 1 pound trimmed asparagus into 2" lengths. Heat 1 teaspoon oil in a wok or large skillet over high heat. Add asparagus and toss until the spears start to turn bright green, about 45 seconds for thin spears. For thicker spears, add 1/4 to 1/2 cup broth or water and immediately cover the pan. Steam for 30 seconds to 1 1/2 minutes, depending on the thickness. Season with salt and pepper, if desired.

Chef's Tip: Only the thickest, woodiest asparagus spears need peeling. Even then, it isn't necessary to remove all of the skin, because it is not the skin itself that makes the asparagus tough. Rather, the skin forms a barricade around the interior fibers that need to be softened. Once the skin is opened, even partially, the asparagus will cook through more evenly. Save time by peeling just 2 strips on opposite sides of each spear with a vegetable peeler. This will allow the heat to permeate the tougher fibers faster.

SIMPLE LEMON ASPARAGUS Grate the **zest from 1 lemon,** then squeeze the **lemon juice** into a bowl. Add zest and whisk in 1/4 **cup olive oil.** Toss with about **1 1/2 pounds trimmed and roasted or steamed asparagus.** Optional seasonings include minced garlic and shards of Parmesan cheese. *Makes 4 to 6 servings.*

ASPARAGUS PARMIGIANA In a large, wide skillet, heat 1" of water to boiling. Add **1 pound trimmed asparagus** so that all spears face the same direction.

a

Move the pan so that stem ends are directly over heat and tips are well off the burner. Boil just until crisp-tender, 4 to 6 minutes. Drain. Butter a shallow baking dish and add asparagus. Dot with **2 tablespoons cut-up butter** and sprinkle with **¼ teaspoon salt** and **⅛ teaspoon ground black pepper.** Sprinkle **⅓ cup freshly grated Parmesan cheese** over top. Brown in the top of a 450°F oven, about 12 minutes. *Makes 4 servings.*

HEALTHY HINT ▼ **To preserve nutrients** • Cook asparagus in an upright position. Most of the nutrients are found in the tips. Cooking asparagus upright also gently steams the tender tips while the thicker stalks cook in the simmering water, resulting in even cooking from top to bottom.

Avocados *see also* Guacamole

These pear-shaped fruits crop up mostly in Mexican and South American cooking. They are best known as the base for guacamole.

BASICS ▼ **To choose** • Cradle each avocado in the palm of your hand and take home those that feel heavy for their size. Most avocados are sold unripe and are firm. Fruit that yields slightly to a gentle squeeze is further along in the ripening process. To test for ripeness, pry the small stem off the tapered end with your thumb. If it comes off easily and is green, it is ripe. If it comes off easily but is brown, it is overripe. If it does not come off, it is underripe. Never buy avocados with soft spots or that rattle when you shake them (which means that the pit has pulled away from the flesh).

To store • Keep unripened avocados at room temperature. Store ripe avocados in the refrigerator, where they can last for as long as 10 days.

To cut an avocado • With a chef's knife, cut it in half from top to bottom through the peel and around the pit. Twist the halves apart. Place the half containing the pit face up in your hand or on a cutting board (nest it in a towel if it falls to the side). Whack the pit with the blade of the knife. Twist the knife and lift out the pit.

To get the pit off the knife blade • Bang it smartly on a cutting board. The knife will cut the pit in half, releasing itself. Or knock the pit off with a wooden spoon.

To slice or cube • Cut it in half lengthwise and remove the pit. Place a

---

AVOCADOS: CALIFORNIA VERSUS FLORIDA

Though odd varieties sometimes appear in markets, the two most popular types are California Haas and Florida Fuerte. Haas avocados have dark, pebble-textured skin, a buttery flavor, and ultra-rich, creamy flesh. These are best for guacamole and other spreads, and in blended dressings and cold soups. The Florida Fuerte avocado has smooth green skin and firmer flesh. Fuerte avocados work well in vegetable, pasta, and grain salads as well as in sandwiches, roll-ups, and salsas because the avocado flesh will hold its shape. Although Fuerte avocados contain about half the fat of Haas avocados, most of the fat in any avocado is the health-friendly monounsaturated kind.

a

doubled-up kitchen towel in the palm of one hand. Cradle one of the avocado halves, flesh side up, in the towel. With a paring knife, slice the flesh inside its skin in parallel slices. To cube, cut across the slices you have already made. Be careful to not cut through the skin. With a large spoon, scoop the sliced or cubed avocado from its skin starting at the wide end.

To cut wedges • Trim off the avocado's top and bottom. Using a chef's knife, cut it in half from top to bottom through the peel and around the pit. Turn the fruit and cut it in half again from top to bottom. Repeat to make 2 more cuts, creating slim segments. Peel off the skin and separate the wedges from the pit.

To mash • Remove the flesh from the skin and place it in a bowl. For a silky-smooth consistency, mash with an old fashioned potato ricer. For a coarser texture, mash with a fork or pastry cutter.

PROBLEM SOLVERS ▼

To prevent browning • Drizzle with lime or lemon juice. Or store halved avocados, cut side down, in a bowl of acidulated water (see page 2). The avocados will keep well without browning for several days. For slices or cubes, place in acidulated water for up to 3 hours. Forget what you may have heard about leaving the pit in mashed avocado. It will only protect the small portion that surrounds the pit.

To avoid bitterness • Never cook avocados, as they will turn bitter. Eat them raw or add them to a cooked dish after the dish is taken off the heat.

TIME SAVER ▼

To speed ripening • Put firm, unripe avocados in a brown paper bag. The bag will trap the ethylene gas that naturally emits from the fruit and hasten the ripening process. Crimp the bag closed and set it aside at room temperature, and the avo-

FOUR WAYS TO USE AN AVOCADO

• *Instant Avocado Sauce:* Mash ½ ripe avocado with ½ cup Italian salad dressing. Use on 1 pound grilled poultry, meat, or fish. Add another ½ cup dressing and you have 1½ cups of *Creamy Avocado Dressing* for a summer salad.

• *Chopped Cobb Salad:* Toss 1 chopped avocado, 1 chopped tomato, 1 chopped cucumber, 1 cup corn kernels, and 2 crumbled strips cooked bacon with ½ cup Italian dressing. Makes 4 servings.

• Add chopped avocado to salsa, or try mixing it into a tuna or chicken salad.

• For a beautiful appetizer, fan avocado slices alternately with grapefruit sections and a garnish of fresh tarragon leaves.

cados will ripen in 1 to 3 days. Or, for a single avocado, add a few strips of banana peel, a whole banana, or a whole apple to the bag. The extra fruit will increase the amount of ethylene gas and speed ripening. In a real time crunch, you can pretend to ripen an avocado in a microwave oven. Prick the fruit with a fork and microwave on medium power for 30 to 90 seconds, stopping to check the fruit every 30 seconds. This will soften a hard avocado to a point where it is edible (fine for guacamole), but to call it ripe is just a benign form of self-deception.

b

Bacon *see also* Ham; Pancetta; Pork

Cut from the sides of pork belly, bacon is then brined and smoked, sometimes double-smoked. This technique intensely flavors the meat but only partially cures it. All bacon must be cooked before eating.

BASICS ▼

To choose • Look for bacon with a healthy ratio of fat to meat. The ideal proportion of fat is about one-third to one-half of the total weight. To get thick sliced bacon or unsliced bacon (slab bacon) check the supermarket deli department or your local butcher.

To store uncooked • Unopened packages of bacon should be refrigerated and used within 1 week of the sell-by date. Opened packages of bacon can be kept in the refrigerator for up to a week. You can also freeze bacon for up to 2 months. To avoid defrosting the entire package, separate every few slices with parchment paper or plastic wrap, then seal in a zipper-lock freezer bag.

To defrost • Wrap in plastic wrap and submerge in warm water for 10 minutes. Or microwave on medium-low power for 2 to 3 minutes, flipping halfway through.

To easily cut uncooked bacon • Freeze for 30 minutes before cutting.

To fry • For the best flavor, start bacon in a cold pan and cook over medium heat until cooked through.

To bake • Lay the slices in a single layer on a rimmed baking sheet. Bake at 375°F until cooked through, about 15 minutes, rotating the pan halfway through. Baked bacon will remain flat.

To microwave neatly • Place strips of bacon between sheets of white paper towel; use 1 thickness of towel for every slice being cooked (you can fold a single sheet over several times for a few strips). Microwave on high power until cooked through, 1 minute per strip of bacon. Discard the towels. Microwaved bacon will also cook without curling.

To make extra-crispy • Use a bulb baster to remove excess fat from the pan as the bacon cooks. To drain, set the bacon on a rack set over a plate lined with paper towels. The fat will drain off and the bacon will stay crisp. If you set it directly on paper towels, the bacon sits in its own fat and won't be as crisp.

To store cooked bacon • Cool the bacon and wrap in paper towels, then wrap again tightly in plastic. Refrigerate for up to 1 week or freeze for a month. To reheat: Unwrap refrigerated or frozen bacon and microwave on high power until heated through, 45 to 60 seconds for a few strips.

Or warm it in a skillet over medium-high heat for 2 to 3 minutes.

To separate bacon slices easily • Roll packages of bacon lengthwise and secure with a rubber band before refrigerating. When the package is unrolled, the spaces between the slices will be enlarged, making it easier to separate each slice. Or let the package stand at room temperature for 30 minutes before separating the slices.

To prevent curled edges • Pierce the bacon slices with the tines of a fork before frying. Or place a heavy weight such as a skillet over the bacon. You can also bake or microwave the bacon as described on the opposite page.

To neatly dispose of bacon fat • Pour cooled fat into an empty frozen juice container, a cardboard milk or cream container, or an aluminum can. If you don't have a container on hand, pour the hot fat into a small bowl lined with foil. When the fat cools and solidifies, fold up the foil and throw it away.

To quickly chop uncooked bacon • Use kitchen shears or scissors. For short strips, snip the bacon across its length. To dice bacon, snip it in half lengthwise first and then snip into squares from each length. Bacon will shrink by a factor of 5 during cooking, so don't cut it too small; $\frac{1}{4}$" squares will reduce to just $\frac{1}{20}$" after cooking.

To more easily cook larger amounts (1 pound or more) • Lay the bacon in a single layer on a metal rack set over a rimmed baking sheet. Bake at 400°F until cooked through and crisp, 12 to 15 minutes.

To quick-cook bacon that will be crumbled • Chop it first. Chopped bacon cooks much faster than bacon in strips.

To baste roasted meats, poultry, or fish • Lay strips of bacon over the roast to baste and add flavor. When finished, the bacon can be served along with the roast.

To flavor poultry stuffing • Chop $\frac{1}{2}$ pound bacon and cook until crisp. Drain off and reserve the fat for sautéing onions and celery for the stuffing. Add the bacon to the stuffing.

To use in cornbread • Cook 6 to 8 slices of bacon until crisp. Drain, cool, and crumble into your favorite cornbread batter. Use the bacon drippings to replace the fat called for in your recipe.

b

GRILLED SHRIMP WITH BACON In a zipper-lock plastic bag, combine **¼ cup lime juice, 3 tablespoons olive oil, 3 sliced garlic cloves,** and **½ cup chopped fresh cilantro.** Add **1 pound peeled and deveined jumbo shrimp,** shake to coat, seal the bag, and refrigerate 30 to 45 minutes. Meanwhile, preheat a grill. Cut **½ pound meaty bacon slices** in half crosswise and cook in a skillet over medium heat, 2 minutes per side. Drain and wrap a piece of precooked bacon around each shrimp. Secure with a wooden skewer and grill over a medium-hot fire until shrimp are opaque, about 3 minutes per side. *Makes 6 servings.*

RUMAKI In a zipper-lock plastic bag, combine **¼ cup** *each* **dry sherry, soy sauce, and water; 2 tablespoons** *each* **brown sugar and canola oil; ¼ teaspoon garlic powder;** and **⅛ teaspoon ground ginger.** Cut **¾ pound chicken livers** in half (or quarters for large livers) and add livers to the bag. Shake to coat, then seal the bag and refrigerate 4 hours or overnight. Drain and discard marinade.

b

Drain **1 can (8 ounces) sliced water chestnuts.** Cut **12 slices uncooked bacon** in half crosswise. To make each rumaki, place 1 chicken liver and slice of water chestnut together, then wrap 1 piece bacon around them. Secure with a wooden toothpick. Place on a baking sheet and broil until livers are no longer pink, about 8 to 10 minutes, turning halfway through cooking. Serve warm.

Makes 8 appetizer servings.

HEALTHY HINTS ▼

To reduce fat • Instead of frying bacon, bake it on a rack set over a rimmed baking sheet (see "To bake" on page 18).

For smoke flavor with less fat • Use turkey bacon, a combination of ground white and dark turkey meat that is seasoned and preserved. Cook and use turkey bacon as you would pork bacon.

Baking *see also* Breads, Quick; Breads, Yeast; Brownies; Cakes; Convection Oven; Cookies; Creaming; Ovens; Pie Crusts; Pies; Roasting

One of the most basic cooking methods, baking cooks food by surrounding it with dry heat in an oven.

PROBLEM SOLVERS ▼

To adjust baking temperature for cookware used • When using glass bakeware, reduce the oven temperature by 25°F because glass conducts heat better than metal.

To adjust baking time for cold foods • For casseroles, add 45 minutes to 1 hour if frozen or 15 to 20 minutes if refrigerated. For cookie dough, add 3 to 5 minutes if frozen or 1 to 2 minutes if refrigerated. For bread dough, always thaw first; add 7 to 8 minutes if refrigerated. Meats, poultry, and seafood should always be thawed first;

no change is necessary to baking time if refrigerated. Frozen or refrigerated vegetables can go straight from the freezer or fridge to the oven with no change to baking time.

To ensure even baking • Ovens cook by surrounding food with hot air, so be sure to leave ample space around the food. Avoid placing one item directly over another. If necessary, stagger the pans and rotate them during baking. If you must crowd an oven, opt for a convection oven, which is equipped with a fan that circulates air for more even cooking.

To aid browning in baked goods • Use a higher-protein flour than the recipe usually calls for. For example, use all-purpose flour instead of cake flour, bread flour instead of all-purpose flour, or unbleached flour in place of bleached flour. Or substitute 2 tablespoons milk or an egg yolk for 2 tablespoons of the liquid in the recipe.

TIME SAVERS ▼

To speed baking time • Use a convection oven.

To easily dust greased pans with flour • Keep some flour in a small shaker jar, such as a clean spice jar with a shaker top. Grease your baking pans, then sprinkle the flour over the coated surfaces and tap out any excess flour.

Chef's Tip: If you bake a lot, save time greasing and flouring pans by whisking together ½ **cup** *each* **of flour, vegetable oil, and solid vegetable shortening** until smooth. Brush the mixture onto baking pans to substitute for greasing and flouring. Refrigerate the mixture in a covered container for up to 4 months.

To mix dry ingredients quickly • Use a whisk instead of a spoon. A whisk combines dry ingredients more evenly, more thoroughly, and more quickly.

HOW BAKING WORKS

Baking is a fine science. Every ingredient plays a distinct, carefully balanced role. For example, let's look at chocolate chip cookies.

Flour: The Basis of Structure

There would be no substance to a chocolate chip cookie without flour. When mixed with liquid, the protein in flour forms elastic, web-like sheets of gluten. These create the structure of the cookie. The more you mix, the stronger this structure becomes (and the chewier your cookies will get). The kind of flour you use also defines how much structure you'll end up with. All-purpose flour holds the middle ground in protein content, which is why it's popular for cookies. Cake flour is low in protein, which makes it ideal for delicate baked goods such as—you guessed it—cakes. On the opposite spectrum is high-protein bread flour, which creates the firm structure needed for yeast breads.

Sugar: Flavor, Texture, and Browning

Of course, sugar adds the sweet taste expected in cookies and other baked goods. But it also affects tenderness, crispness, and browning. If you cut back on the granulated sugar in a chocolate chip cookie recipe, the texture will be more soft, dry, and chewy, almost bready like a scone. The color will be more pale than golden brown. If you cut back on the brown sugar, you are also apt to get less puff. Brown sugar contains molasses, which is acidic and reacts with baking soda to help give the cookie its lift. If you increase the sugar (any type), your cookie may become cloyingly sweet and overly moist. It is also likely to spread more since the sugar is binding up the liquid that would otherwise interact with flour proteins to form structure-building gluten.

Leavener: The Rise

That brings us to the leavener, which is usually baking soda and/or baking powder. In baked goods such as cookies, the leavener is a carefully balanced measurement designed to give the cookie its maximum rise. If you decrease the baking soda and/or baking powder, your cookie may not rise at all. If you increase it, your cookie may rise so high that it falls. Additional leavener may also introduce off flavors to the cookie. (See page 24 to read about the important differences between baking powder and baking soda.) Eggs also contribute to leavening as well as to tenderness and structure.

Fat: Tenderizer and Flavor Carrier

Finally, there is the fat. In baking, fat contributes to tenderness by helping coat some of the flour and protect it from liquid, which in turn limits gluten development. In a cookie recipe, this helps prevent the cookies from becoming overly chewy. Lower the fat, and you are likely to create a chewier cookie. Increase the fat, and you will create a more tender cookie. For flavor, butter is the best. But butter has a low melting point, so it tends to cause cookies to spread. For less spread, cut back on the butter and replace it in part with vegetable shortening. This will create a more tender, slightly chewy cookie.

b

b

To avoid dairy products in baking • Replace milk with an equal amount of soy milk. Replace ½ cup butter with ⅛ cup soy milk mixed with ⅛ cup vegetable oil.

To bake with less fat • You can generally reduce fat by 25 percent in traditional baked goods, replacing the fat with an equal amount of a moist ingredient such as reduced-fat sour cream or cream cheese, fruit puree, fruit juice, or corn syrup. You can also cut back on the total amount of high-fat add-ins, such as chocolate chips and nuts, and put them on top of the product so that they are the first thing you taste. And you can use cooking spray instead of butter to grease pans.

To reduce fat using fruit purees • Replace 25 percent of the fat with drained, unsweetened applesauce or another fruit puree, such as baby-food prunes, which work well with chocolate. Fruit purees work best when buttermilk is the liquid in the recipe.

To reduce fat from egg and dairy ingredients • Replace butter with chilled light butter and omit 1 or 2 eggs from the recipe to make up for light butter's extra moisture content. Or replace each whole egg with 2 egg whites. In many recipes, it helps to leave in at least 1 whole egg. Whole milk can be replaced with low-fat buttermilk, fat-free milk, 1% milk, or 2% milk. And sour cream can be replaced with fat-free or reduced-fat sour cream, or yogurt cheese. When a recipe calls for cream cheese, start by using equal amounts reduced-fat and fat-free cream cheese.

To reduce fat from chocolate ingredients • Replace half of the unsweetened baking chocolate called for with unsweetened cocoa powder. Use 1½ tablespoons unsweetened Dutch process cocoa powder or 3 tablespoons unsweetened cocoa powder. You can also use mini chocolate chips instead of the full-size variety and reduce the amount you add to baked goods, since small chips distribute flavor more evenly.

To reduce fat from nuts • Toast and finely chop a smaller amount of nuts. Toasting intensifies flavor so you can use less nuts, and finely chopping the nuts distributes the flavor more evenly. Also reduce the use of macadamia nuts and coconut, which are loaded with saturated fat. Substitute a lesser quantity of pecans, walnuts, almonds, or hazelnuts, which contain mostly unsaturated fats.

To reduce fat in pies • Make open-faced fruit tarts, as opposed to double-crust pies. Or use an oil-based pie crust (see Low-Fat Two-Crust Pastry on page 364). For cream pies, use a cookie crumb crust instead of pastry crust (see Cookie Crumb Crust on page 361).

To choose the right flour for reduced-fat baking • Use a low-protein flour, such as cake flour or pastry flour, especially when reducing the fat in cakes, quick breads, and cookies. Low-protein flour will allow less gluten to develop, giving the final baked good a softer, more tender crumb, which is normally achieved by the addition of fat. You can also tenderize low-fat baked goods by replacing half of the all-purpose flour (or other flour) with soy flour, which has a slightly higher fat content and helps create a tender crumb.

Baking Powder

This leavener is made from a combination of baking soda and one or more acids, such as cream of tartar or sodium aluminum sulfate. Cornstarch is also added to absorb moisture and keep the ingredients powder-dry.

BASICS ▼ **To choose** • Check the date on the bottom of the can to make sure that what you're buying is fresh. Buy in small quantities, as baking powder loses effectiveness with age.

To store • Keep baking powder in a cool, dry place. To keep track of the expiration date after opening, write the date on the lid. Baking powder begins to lose effectiveness about 3 months after opening.

To keep baking powder active • Never dip a wet spoon into the can. Moisture will deactivate the powder.

To test baking powder for freshness • Stir 1 teaspoon powder into ⅓ cup hot water. If it bubbles vigorously, the baking powder has plenty of leavening power.

To make your own baking powder • Combine 1 tablespoon baking soda, 2 tablespoons cream of tartar, and 1½ tablespoons cornstarch.

Baking Sheets

Cookies and biscuits are almost always baked on flat baking sheets. Rimmed baking sheets can also be used for cookies and biscuits, but the 1" rims on those pans are designed for making sheet cakes or sponge cakes such as jelly rolls. Whether flat or rimmed, heavy-gauge aluminum baking sheets that don't warp are the hands-down favorite among professional bakers.

BASICS ▼ **To help prevent burning** • Bake cookies, biscuits, or breads on baking sheets with a shiny finish that will deflect heat.

To help ensure even browning • Use a baking sheet that allows at least 2" of space between it and the sides of your oven.

To line • When making cookies, much of the hassle is relieved by lining pans. The cookies won't stick; the liners minimize hot spots and burning; they allow you to set up batches on separate liners ahead of baking; and they make cleanup effortless. You can use baking parchment, foil, or special baking paper with a nonstick coating (available in cookware stores). Tear sheets large enough to cover the bottom of the pan without hanging over the edges. For the first batch, place the liner on the pan before arranging cookies on it. While the first batch bakes, arrange another batch of cookies on a separate liner. When the first batch is done, slide the liner and its cookies onto a rack. Slide the prepared liner onto the baking sheet and start baking that batch. Wait 5 minutes for the hot cookies to cool before removing them from their liner.

To remove burned bits of sugar and crust from rimmed baking sheets • Put the pan on top of the stove and fill with boiling water from a kettle. Add 1 teaspoon baking soda per cup of water, then boil until the crust begins to loosen.

Baking Soda *see also* Burnt Foods; Cookware; Odors; Stains

Also known as sodium bicarbonate or bicarbonate of soda, baking soda is an alkaline compound used for leavening baked goods that contain acidic ingredients such as buttermilk, yogurt, cocoa, chocolate, honey, molasses, or lemon juice. Baking soda is also useful in the kitchen for cleaning and deodorizing. As a mild alkali, it helps dirt and grease dissolve in water for easy removal. And it neutralizes odors all around the house.

BASICS ▼ **To choose** • Buy in small quantities, as baking soda becomes less effective with time.

b

BAKING SODA VERSUS BAKING POWDER

They look almost identical. They're both used to leaven baked goods. Is there any difference between baking soda and baking powder? Yes. A crucial difference.

Tiny Bubbles

Baking powder and baking soda are both powders that react chemically to release a profusion of tiny carbon dioxide bubbles. When heated, these bubbles expand, working to lift and lighten all kinds of batters—including muffins, quick breads, pancakes, cakes, cookies, brownies—before the batter sets in the oven. Such baked goods cook quickly and tend to be relatively delicate in texture. The style of recipes in which these two leaveners are used, however, is about as far as the similarities go.

Baking Soda Basics

Just as an experiment, try dropping ¼ teaspoon baking soda into a drinking glass. Mix in ¼ cup water. Nothing happens. Add 1 tablespoon lemon juice and it will immediately begin to fizz and bubble like carbonated water. Baking soda is an alkali, or base, made of a naturally occurring compound known as sodium bicarbonate. As the experiment demonstrates, for baking soda to release carbon dioxide bubbles, it needs to react with an acidic ingredient. Some common acids in baking are buttermilk, cream of tartar, brown sugar, lemon juice, sour cream, and chocolate. The catch with baking soda is that it must be properly balanced with the acidic ingredient so that it is fully neutralized. If not, the leftover baking soda will leave a soapy, bitter flavor.

The Power of Baking Powder

Baking powder works on the same principle as baking soda. An acid and an alkali react to release carbon dioxide bubbles. The difference: Baking powder contains both components. It consists of baking soda and one or two acids. Just add something wet, even water, and bubbles will start to form. Most supermarkets carry "double-acting" baking powder, which contains two acids that react at different times in the baking process. The first acid reacts with the baking soda when a liquid is mixed in. The second acid reacts with the baking soda when exposed to heat. Single-acting baking powder contains only one acid and is not often found in supermarkets. Most contemporary recipes are developed with double-acting baking powder.

Mix and Mismatch

While you can't swap baking soda for baking powder, or vice versa, you can make baking powder at home (see "To make your own baking powder" on page 23). Homemade baking powder is single-acting, so use it for doughs or batters that will be baked right away. You may wonder why some recipes call for both baking powder and baking soda. Usually, the amount of baking soda used to neutralize the recipe's acid is not enough to sufficiently leaven the baked good. So, baking powder is added as a backup leavener. Another often-asked question: How come a favorite recipe, such as a muffin or cake, turns out light and airy one time and heavy and deflated another? The culprit just might be the baking powder, which loses its effectiveness about 3 months after opening.

To store • Transfer to an airtight container before storing to extend baking soda's shelf life.

To test baking soda for freshness • Pour a few tablespoons of vinegar into a small dish and stir in 1 teaspoon baking soda. A burst of froth indicates that the baking soda still has plenty of leavening power. If it doesn't fizz, use the baking soda for neutralizing odors around the house.

To maximize baking soda's deodorizing effectiveness • Periodically turn over the contents in the box, and replace the box after a few months.

Household Hint: If a grease fire ever erupts on your stove top, scatter baking soda over the fire to douse the flames.

Bananas

These popular fruits are actually the berries of a large tropical herb.

BASICS
▼

To choose • Look for plump fruits with an even color. A green tinge indicates an underripe banana; those with brown spots are edging toward overripeness.

To store • Store bananas at room temperature. you can also seal ripe bananas in a zipper-lock plastic bag and refrigerate until ready to use.

PROBLEM SOLVERS
▼

To delay ripening • Store bananas in the refrigerator. The peel will turn black but the banana will not ripen any further.

To prevent browning • Toss sliced bananas with citrus juice.

To salvage overripe bananas • Never throw out over-the-hill bananas. Puree them and freeze them to use in banana bread, muffins, waffles, pancakes, pudding, desserts, or blended drinks. For every cup of banana puree, add ¼ teaspoon lemon juice or 1 tablespoon sour cream to keep the puree from browning. Freeze in ½-cup amounts for up to 6 months. Or, mash overripe bananas and add them to oatmeal as a natural sweetener. Or, peel them, wrap them in plastic, and freeze for up to 6 months. Use them later for banana cream pie or blended drinks.

TIME SAVERS
▼

To speed ripening • Store green bananas in a brown paper bag.

To ripen quickly for quick breads • Put the peeled fruit on a baking sheet and warm in a 450°F oven until very soft, about 10 minutes.

BANANA-NUT MUFFINS Preheat oven to 350°F. In a saucepan, melt **1 stick (½ cup) butter.** Remove from heat and mix in **1 cup sugar, 1 teaspoon vanilla extract, 1½ cups mashed bananas (about 3 bananas), ¼ cup sour cream, 2 eggs, 1 teaspoon baking soda,** and **½ teaspoon baking powder** until smooth. Mix in **2 cups flour** and ⅔ **cup walnut pieces** until just blended. Spoon into a greased nonstick 12-cup muffin pan and bake 18 minutes. Cool in the pan on a rack 5 minutes. To help keep moisture from forming at muffin bottoms, loosen each muffin from its cup and return it to the cup on its side. Let cool again briefly. *Makes 12.*

EASY BANANA ICE CREAM Wrap **2 peeled bananas** in plastic and place in the freezer. Unwrap frozen bananas and place in a food processor with ½ **cup cream, plain or flavored yogurt, or milk.** Puree just until smooth. For more flavor, add ½ **teaspoon ground cinnamon**

and/or vanilla extract, and/or ½ **cup fresh blueberries or strawberries.** For a tropical twist, use ½ **cup coconut milk** in place of cream, yogurt, or milk.
Makes about 1½ cups.

Barbecue *see also* Grilling

Though the terms *grilling* and *barbecuing* are often used synonymously, the two techniques are actually quite distinct. Grilling refers to cooking relatively tender foods quickly over high heat. Barbecuing is just the opposite: cooking relatively tough foods for a long period of time with the gentle heat and smoke of a very low fire. Barbecuing is really a form of braising, in which large cuts of tough meat are basted with sauce and slowly cooked until their fibers soften to the point of meltdown.

BASICS ▼ **To get the most flavorful barbecue** • Use a combination of hardwood charcoal and wood, such as apple or hickory.

To sustain the low temperatures required for proper charcoal barbecuing • Use the indirect method. Push the hot coals into parallel rows out on the sides of the grill and set your food in the center of the grill grate so that it's not directly over the coals. If using a gas grill with separate heat controls, heat only one side of the grill and place the food on the other side. Rotate the food occasionally so that all sides are heated. If your grill has vents, close them partially.

To prevent flare-ups from dripping fat • Place a disposable aluminum pan between the coals directly underneath the food. This drip pan makes cleanup a snap.

To test barbecued meats for doneness • Stick a large fork directly down into the meat and try to pick it up. If it's impossible to pick up because the meat is so tender that it won't hold the fork, the meat is done.

FAST FAUX BARBECUE Rub ¼ **cup barbecue seasoning** over the surface of **2 pounds pork butt or beef chuck.** Place meat in a pan and brush all over with **2 tablespoons hickory-flavored oil (made from 2 tablespoons oil mixed with 1 to 2 drops Liquid Smoke hickory seasoning).** Add **1 cup beer or water** to the pan and wrap the pan with foil, covering completely. Place in a 275°F oven and roast until the meat is fork-tender, 1½ to 2 hours. Slice and serve with barbecue sauce for dipping.
Makes 6 servings.

Beans, Canned

Although cooked dried beans have a more resilient consistency and a cleaner flavor, canned beans are much more convenient, especially when you're in a hurry, and provide similar nutrients in a fraction of the time. Unfortunately, the canning process tends to overcook beans, causing many brands to be overly mushy. For less mush, look for organic canned beans.

BASICS ▼ **To estimate amounts** • One 15-ounce can of beans equals about 1¾ cups drained.

To reduce gassinesss • Pour off the canning liquid and rinse the beans well before using. Rinsing washes away some of the oligosaccharides (complex sugars) that contribute to gassiness. Rinsing also removes up to 40 percent of the sodium. Black-eyed peas, lima beans, and chickpeas are the least gassy beans.

Baked Tex-Mex Bean Dip

b

Cream cheese and Cheddar cheese add creamy texture and rich flavor here. This dip also gets a blast of spicy flavor from chile peppers and hot-pepper sauce. To roast and peel chile peppers, see page 113.

3	**cans (16 ounces each) pinto beans, rinsed and drained, divided**
6	**ounces cream cheese**
1¼	**cups shredded sharp Cheddar cheese, divided**
1	**can (8 ounces) tomato sauce**
1	**teaspoon hot-pepper sauce**
1	**teaspoon salt**
½	**teaspoon ground cumin**
½	**teaspoon dried oregano, crumbled**
⅛	**teaspoon ground black pepper**
½	**pound fresh poblano chile peppers, roasted and peeled, or 1 can (4 ounces) whole, mild green chile peppers, drained and chopped**
	Corn tortilla chips

1. Preheat the oven to 375°F. Lightly grease a shallow 2-quart baking dish.

2. In a food processor, combine 2 cans of the beans, the cream cheese, 1 cup of the Cheddar, the tomato sauce, hot-pepper sauce, salt, cumin, oregano, and black pepper. Process to puree. Transfer to a large bowl. Add the remaining beans and the chile peppers to the bowl. Stir to combine. Turn into the prepared baking dish. Top with the remaining ¼ cup Cheddar. Bake until hot and bubbly, 35 minutes. Serve hot with the corn chips.

Makes 12 appetizer servings

TIME SAVER ▼ **To save prep time** • Buy preseasoned canned beans. These make quick work of throwing together black bean soup, chili, burrito fillings, and side dishes.

ROASTED CHICKPEAS Toss **1 can (15 ounces) chickpeas,** rinsed and drained, with **2 teaspoons olive oil** and **½ teaspoon *each* ground cumin, ground coriander, and ground white or black pepper.** Bake in a single layer on a greased baking sheet at 400°F until golden, about 35 minutes. *Makes 8 appetizer servings.*

EASY COLA BAKED BEANS Drain and rinse **3 cans (16 ounces each) assorted beans** (kidney, black, and pinto work well). Mix with **½ cup tomato puree, 2 tablespoons spicy brown mustard, 1 tablespoon cider vinegar, ½ teaspoon salt, ⅛ teaspoon ground black pepper,** and **1½ cups cola soft drink.** Turn into a greased 8" × 8" pan. Top with 6 slices bacon, cut into quarters. Bake at 375°F until bacon is crisp and cooked through and beans are hot and bubbly, about 1 hour. *Makes 6 servings.*

Beans, Dried *see also* Lentils;
Lima Beans; Peas, Dried

Beans are a member of the legume family, which also includes lentils, peas, peanuts, and even clover and alfalfa.

BASICS **To choose** • Buy beans from a busy market with a steady turnover. Freshness counts, even for dried beans. Older ones will take longer to cook.

To store • Transfer dried beans to a glass jar and stick a couple of dried chile peppers in with them. The chiles will keep any pantry bugs from invading your beans.

To sort and rinse • Spread the beans out in a single layer on a baking sheet and pick out any stones and shriveled or discolored beans. Dump the beans into a large bowl of water and swish around. Discard any beans that float to the top. Transfer to a sieve and rinse, then transfer into a pan for cooking.

Fascinating Fact: Raw beans contain small amounts of toxins, which are destroyed when cooked.

To soak beans • Cover rinsed and sorted dried beans with 4 times the volume of cold water (about 4 cups water for each cup of beans). Cover and set aside for 6 to 8 hours or overnight, until the beans have doubled in size. When one is cut open, it should be moist all the way through. Drain the beans and discard the soaking water. Cook as desired. Note that lima beans and pinto beans generally do not need soaking.

To "quick-soak" beans • In a large saucepan, cover rinsed and sorted dried beans with 4 times the volume of cold water (about 4 cups water for each cup of beans). Bring to a boil. Reduce the heat to medium-low and simmer about 10 minutes. Cover, remove from the heat, and let stand about 1 hour.

To cook • Place soaked beans in a large pot of water or broth, allowing enough room for them to swell at least 3 times their original volume. Bring to a boil, reduce the heat to medium-low, and simmer, uncovered, stirring occasionally. Cook until the beans are tender (1 to 2 hours for most beans).

To store cooked beans • Cool cooked beans quickly and refrigerate. Don't let cooked beans stand at room temperature for too long; they can ferment and turn sour.

To remove the skins from cooked chickpeas • Remove partially cooked chickpeas from their cooking liquid and roll them in a rough cloth until the skins come off. Then, return the peeled chickpeas to the pot and finish cooking.

PROBLEM SOLVERS **To soften beans for better texture** • Add salt to the soaking water. Forget what you might have heard about salt toughening beans. Although salt toughens beans during cooking, it actually has the opposite effect during soaking. Before cooking, drain the soaking water and add fresh water for cooking.

To prevent beans from toughening as they cook • Hold off on adding acidic ingredients, such as tomatoes, vinegar, or wine, until after the beans have cooked through. Acids react with the starch in beans and prevent them from swelling. Also hold off on adding salt during cooking, which inhibits the absorption of water into the beans. After the beans are cooked through, add the salt and/or acids and allow the beans to cook for 10 to 15 minutes longer so that the flavors can blend.

b

BEAN DISHES IN MINUTES

Some of the most versatile and convenient bean products are dehydrated bean powders, or "instant" beans. They come in both smooth and whole bean styles and require nothing more than the addition of boiling water to transform them into full-flavored low-fat bean pastes and dips in minutes.

Spicy Black Bean Soup: In a medium saucepan over high heat, combine **1 can (15 ounces)** *each* **chicken or beef broth, crushed tomatoes, and black beans** and **1 can water.** Bring to a boil. Stir in **1 box (7 ounces) instant black beans, ⅛ teaspoon salt,** and **⅛ teaspoon hot-pepper sauce.** Cook until slightly thickened, 2 minutes. Adjust seasoning to taste. *Makes 4 to 6 servings.*

Poached Fish with Bean Sauce: In a large skillet, combine **1 bunch thinly sliced scallions, 2 tablespoons grated fresh ginger, 2 to 3 tablespoons soy sauce, 1 tablespoon rice vinegar,** and **2 cups water.** Boil for 1 minute. Add **2 pounds salmon fillets,** cover, and cook over very low heat until fish is opaque, 10 minutes. Remove fish to warm platter. Bring liquid to a boil. Add **⅓ cup instant hummus** (chickpea dip mix) and stir until lightly thickened, about 1 minute. Add **1 chopped tomato** and heat through. *Makes 4 servings.*

Grilled Shrimp with Smoky Bean Sauce: Preheat a grill. Puree **⅓ cup jarred roasted red peppers** and mix with **¼ cup jarred chipotle bean dip** and **1 small minced garlic clove.** Toss **1 pound peeled and deveined large shrimp** in **1 tablespoon olive oil** with **1 small minced garlic clove.** Grill over a hot fire 1 minute, turn and grill until opaque, another minute. Serve with the pepper-bean sauce. *Makes 4 main dish or 6 appetizer servings.*

To cook beans without bursting their skins • Keep the heat low and the pot uncovered.

To keep long-cooked beans from turning to mush • Add a bit of sugar to the recipe. Brown sugar, molasses, or maple syrup can flavor a pot of beans and help them retain their shape. Baked beans are a perfect example.

To soften up tough, slow-to-cook beans • Add baking soda to the cooking water, starting with ½ teaspoon and increasing as needed.

To salvage slightly overcooked beans • Add an acid such as vinegar, tomato juice, or citrus juice. Start with about 2 teaspoons acid per quart of beans. Remove from heat and stir to blend. For the least obtrusive vinegar flavor, use rice vinegar. Lemon juice works well with chickpeas. Lime juice works well with Latin dishes. You can also use orange juice. If your beans are substantially overcooked, mash them to make bean dip.

To rescue burnt beans • Do not stir. Transfer the unburnt beans to another pan.

TIME SAVERS ▼ **To cool cooked beans quickly** • Dump the cooked beans into a shallow pan. The broad surface area allows the steam to evaporate more quickly.

b

PRESSURE COOKING BEANS

By far, the fastest method for cooking dried beans is in a pressure cooker. That's in part because you can skip the soaking step. But if you do soak the beans first, the cooking time will be reduced even more. Here's the method: For every cup of dried beans you cook under pressure, add 3 cups water and 1 teaspoon oil (to prevent foaming). Follow the chart for cooking times. When the prescribed time is up, release the steam immediately. Note that lentils and split peas cook so quickly that there's no time saved by soaking them.

Beans (1 cup dry)	Soaked (min)	Unsoaked (min)
Black (Turtle)	14	20
Chickpeas	18	30
Fava	17	24
Great Northern	13	25
Lentils	N/A	7
Lima	7	13
Navy	10	17
Peas, split	N/A	7
Pinto	7	22
Red kidney	12	20
Soybeans	17	30
White kidney	12	22

To cook beans in a slow cooker • Cooking with a slow cooker such as a Crock-Pot actually takes more time than stove-top cooking, but it's all unattended time, so you are free to leave the house and do other things. In a slow cooker, cover soaked beans with 3 times their volume in water or broth (for unsoaked beans, use 4 times the volume). Add sautéed onions and/or smoked meat for flavor, if desired. Cook on high for 2 hours or on low for 6 to 8 hours.

FLAVOR TIPS ▼ **To get the best flavor and texture •** Cook beans the day before you serve them and let them cool in their cooking liquid.

To add flavor during cooking • Add dried herbs, sautéed onions and/or garlic, or smoked meat about halfway through the cooking process.

HEALTHY HINT ▼ **To make healthier baked beans •** Substitute ¼ pound Canadian bacon and 6 sun-dried tomato halves for the salt pork called for in most recipes. Or add a few drops of bottled smoke flavoring and 2 slices crispy, cooked turkey bacon.

Beans, Fresh *see also* Lima Beans

Fresh beans are usually sold in their pods. These include green beans, lima beans, and fava beans.

BASICS ▼ **To choose •** Dig to the bottom of the green bean bin, where the smallest beans inevitably wind up. These littlest beans are almost always the most tender. Hold a bean lengthwise between your index finger and thumb. It will snap under light pressure if it is fresh. If old, it will bend. Also, the best shell beans have full, slightly soft pods.

To store • Keep green beans in a zipper-lock plastic bag in the refrigerator for up to 4 days. Keep shell beans at room temperature for a few days, or put them in a brown paper bag and refrigerate for up to a week.

To trim green beans • Gather the beans into a bunch and line up the stem ends. Cut off the stems with a sharp knife and repeat on the other end, if desired.

To french-cut green beans • Trim off both ends. One at a time, place a bean, flat side down, on a cutting board. With a sharp paring knife, cut in half lengthwise between the seams. This creates the most amazing texture but requires time and patience. Steam or boil the beans in a small amount of water just until tender, 3 to 5 minutes. Dress with butter if desired.

PROBLEM
SOLVERS
▼ **To prevent discoloration of green beans during cooking** • Cook them in an uncovered pot and reserve any acidic ingredients such as tomatoes or lemon juice to use as a seasoning after the beans are cooked.

To retain color of green beans after cooking • Drain and toss in ice water to cool quickly. Serve cold in salads or reheat with 1 tablespoon hot water.

Fascinating Fact: The fibrous string that once ran down the seam of the string bean's pod is what gave this vegetable its name, but it has since been bred out of the species.

FLAVOR
TIP
▼ **To bring out the flavor of green beans** • Add a pinch of sugar to the cooking water.

▪▪▪▪▪▪▪▪▪▪▪▪▪▪▪▪▪▪▪▪▪▪

ASIAN GREEN BEANS Steam **1 pound fresh, trimmed green beans** until tender, 6 to 8 minutes. Toss with **2 tablespoons light soy sauce** and **2 teaspoons toasted sesame oil.** Top with **1 teaspoon sesame seeds** or **1 tablespoon sliced almonds**. *Makes 4 servings.*

Beef *see also* Burgers; Filet Mignon; Meat Loaf; Meat; Meatballs; Pot Roast; Doneness Tests and Temperatures (page 572)

Since the mid-1900s, beef has been one of America's most popular meats. Cuts range from the elegant and pricey filets, tenderloins, and prime rib to the popular and versatile ground chuck.

BASICS
▼ **To choose** • Look for the grade. USDA inspectors grade beef into 8 quality grades, but only the top 3 are available to consumers: Prime, Choice, and Select. Prime cuts are the very best. They're tender, juicy, and full of flavor, partly due to their high degree of marbling (streaks of fat). Prime cuts make up less than 2 percent of all graded beef and are the most expensive. Most Prime cuts go to high-end restaurants and some finer butchers. Choice cuts of beef are the next best. These cuts are readily available from butchers and supermarkets, but quality tends to vary. For the best Choice beef cuts, look for pieces with the most marbling. Select cuts of beef are the least expensive and have the least marbling. Very little fat makes Select cuts the healthiest choice, but they are also the least tender and are best prepared with moist-heat cooking methods such as braising.

Whatever grade you choose, look for a bright red color. Beef that is beginning to darken has been sitting in the butcher case too long. One exception: vacuum-packed beef looks darker and purplish red because it is not exposed to oxygen. It will turn bright red when removed from the package and exposed to air. Also, if judging by touch, choose beef that is firm to the touch, neither soft nor mushy. And always be sure to buy beef before the sell-by date and make sure that it is tightly wrapped.

b

b

To grind at home • The colder the beef, the better the grind. Cut the beef into 1" cubes and set in the freezer just until firm but not frozen. Place about ½ pound of cubes in a food processor and use the pulse button to grind (not too fine). Or put the beef through a meat grinder. Chuck, round, and sirloin roast or steak, trimmed of fat, all grind well.

To refrigerate • Chill meat in its original packaging if you plan to cook it within 8 hours. If you need to refrigerate it longer than that, remove the packaging and rewrap the beef in waxed paper. This will keep the surface of the meat dry and inhibit the growth of bacteria. Stored this way, steaks and roasts should keep 3 to 4 days; chunks of stewing beef, 2 to 3 days; and ground beef, 1 to 2 days.

To freeze • Any beef that you don't plan to use within 3 days should be wrapped airtight in freezer wrap, labeled and dated, and frozen at 0°F or colder. You can freeze steaks, roasts, and chunks of stewing beef for 6 to 12 months, and ground beef for 3 to 4 months. Cooked beef can be frozen for about 3 months.

To thaw frozen beef • Thaw beef in the refrigerator to reduce any chance of contamination. Also, the ice crystals will melt slowly, allowing the beef to reabsorb the liquid, so that the thawed meat is less likely to be dry. Place the meat on a tray to catch any liquid. Thaw large roasts for 4 to 7 hours per pound; smaller roasts and steaks for 3 to 5 hours per pound; and ground beef, in a 1½"-thick package, for 24 hours. It is not safe to thaw at room temperature or to refreeze thawed meat.

To slice against the grain • Look for natural striations in the meat, which resemble lines running in the same direction (the grain). Cutting across the grain helps to tenderize the meat (especially tougher cuts such as flank steak) by breaking down the meat's natural structure. For the easiest against-the-grain slicing, place the meat in the freezer for 30 minutes beforehand.

To choose the best cooking technique • Cuts of meat from the center of the animal, such as loin and rib portions, and premium roasts, are exercised very little and therefore are most tender. Cuts from the front and rear, such as chuck, round, brisket, and shank, are heavily exercised and therefore tougher. Generally, dry-heat cooking techniques such as broiling, pan-frying, stir-frying, roasting, and grilling are best for tender cuts of beef. Moist-heat cooking methods, such as braising, stewing, and simmering, are generally best for tougher cuts because it makes them more tender. But some tough cuts, such as chuck shoulder steak, top round, and flank, can be cooked by dry-heat methods if they are first marinated in liquid with acidic ingredients (such as lemon juice, vinegar, wine, or plain yogurt) or marinated with foods (such as papaya, pineapple, and ginger) that have natural tenderizing enzymes.

PROBLEM SOLVERS ▼
To prevent a steak from curling as it cooks • Slash through the edge of the steak every ¾". If it's already begun to curl, slash the steak, then flip it so that the curled side is now facing down. If necessary, cover with a heavy weight such as a cast-iron skillet or a foil-wrapped brick.

To serve an overdone steak • Slice it very thinly across the grain so that it is easier to chew. Fan out the slices and top with salsa, relish, barbecue sauce, or First-Aid Pan Sauce for Meats (page 443).

To get an extra-brown sear on a steak • Let it come to room temperature and blot with paper towels before searing.

STEAK DONENESS: THE TOUCH TEST

Nature's best tool is only an arm's length away: It's your hand. While temperatures are crucial for warding off foodborne illness, the texture of beef is key for great taste. And the best way to test the texture of meat is by touching it. If it feels very tender, it's rare; if it resists your finger slightly, it's medium-rare; firm meat is well-done. To get a better feel for *tender*, *resists slightly*, and *firm*, try the dry run illustrated below. If the touch test isn't your style, go ahead and cut into the steak. You might lose some juice, but it's better than overcooking it and losing the whole steak. For doneness temperatures, see the chart on page 572.

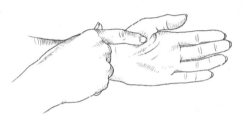

1 Hold out your hand, palm up. With the forefinger of your other hand, gently press the fleshy part of your palm at the base of your thumb on the outstretched hand. Feels kind of soft and squishy, right? That's the feel of tender meat or meat cooked rare.

2 Then, on your outstretched hand, bring your thumb and middle finger together. Poke the fleshy part again. It will be a bit firmer, resisting slightly, yet still tender. That's the feel of beef cooked medium. (If you touch your thumb to your forefinger and poke the fleshy part, that's the feel of medium-rare meat; touch your thumb to your ring finger and poke the fleshy part for medium-well.)

3 Then, bring your thumb and pinkie finger together. Feel the fleshy part again. It should feel quite firm with only a little "give." That's the feel of well-done meat.

TIME SAVERS ▼ **To shorten marinating time** • A few minutes in a marinade are sufficient for thin strips of beef. For large cuts, the surface will pick up flavors from a marinade in an hour or less. For tough cuts of meat, you can shorten marinating time by adding more acid to your marinade, which will help break down the meat's fibers faster. Some possible acids: citrus juices, soy sauce, vinegar, wine, fruit juice, tomato

b

HOW TO GRILL A STEAK

Sitting down to a perfectly grilled steak is one of life's great pleasures. Here's how to get grilled steak that's crisp and brown on the surface, yet juicy and pink on the inside.

1. Choose the right cut. Tenderloin, T-bone, porterhouse, and sirloin are all excellent candidates. Look for steaks that are well-marbled with fat, which melts as the steak cooks and helps keep the meat moist. Steaks for grilling should be at least 1" but no more than 3" thick.

2. Trim the steak of excess fat at its edges to help prevent flare-ups.

3. Nick the border of the steak with the tip of your knife at ¾" intervals to help prevent the steak from curling as it cooks. If the steak has a thin "tail," wrap it around the steak and secure it with toothpicks or a wooden skewer that has been soaked in water for 10 minutes.

4. Rub a few drops of oil into both sides of the steak and season well with salt and freshly ground black pepper.

5. Coat the grill rack with oil (or spray) and set the rack 4" to 6" over the heat for a few minutes to get it nice and hot. This will help sear the meat properly.

6. Put the steak on the rack, directly over the hottest part of a medium-hot fire. When small beads of juice rise to the surface, turn the steak over and cook the second side until the juices rise to the top again.

7. Using a pair of long-handled grilling tongs, hold the steak on its side and turn to sear all the edges until brown.

8. Move the steak to one side of the grill where the heat is less intense and continue cooking, turning once until it's done to your liking. Total grilling time will depend on the thickness of the steak and the temperature of the fire. Generally, for each 1" thickness of steak, allow 8 to 10 minutes for rare, about 12 minutes for medium, and 15 minutes for well-done. Test for doneness by pressing the steak with your fingertip and/or checking the internal temperature with an instant-read thermometer. If it's soft, the meat is medium-rare (145°F); a bit of spring to the meat indicates that's it cooked medium (160°F); and if the meat feels stiff, it's well-done (165°F). For the juiciest steak, let it stand 10 minutes before slicing.

---

juice, honey, and plain yogurt. Use about ½ cup marinade for each pound of meat.

To speed cooking • Bring steaks to room temperature before cooking.

To use leftover cooked beef • Think of leftovers as prepared beef that can save time when whipping up your next meal.

Use cooked hamburger as the base for a pasta sauce, a taco filling, or a stuffing for cabbage leaves or peppers.

PRESSURE COOKER POT ROAST
Season a **3-pound brisket, bottom**

round, or **chuck roast** with **½ teaspoon salt** and **¼ teaspoon ground black pepper.** Brown on both sides in a pressure cooker in **1 tablespoon oil.** Add **2 chopped onions, 1 pound quartered carrots, 4 thickly sliced celery ribs, 4 minced garlic cloves, ½ cup cider vinegar, 6 tablespoons brown sugar, 1 cup ketchup,** and **1 cup water.** Lock on the lid and heat to high pressure. Adjust heat to maintain the pressure and cook until fork-tender, 50 minutes. Turn off the heat and allow to rest 10 minutes. Release the pressure. (For more on pressure cookers, see page 394.) To vary the flavor, substitute 2½ cups vegetable juice cocktail for the vinegar, sugar, ketchup, and water. *Makes 8 servings.*

7-MINUTE CHILI In a large nonstick skillet over medium-high heat, cook **1 pound ground beef** until no longer pink, 5 minutes, stirring often. Add **1 can (16 ounces) chili beans** and **½ cup salsa.** Simmer 2 minutes. *Makes 4 servings.*

QUICK BARBECUE BEEF SANDWICH In a saucepan, bring **¼ cup bottled barbecue sauce** to a simmer. Add **¼ pound sliced deli roast beef** and heat through 5 minutes. Place on a roll with your favorite toppings. *Makes 1 serving.*

GRILLED SHORT RIBS OF BEEF Coat a grill rack with cooking spray and preheat the grill until very hot. Strip the meat from **3 pounds beef short ribs.** It will come off in one piece. Thinly slice meat against its grain (30 minutes in the freezer facilitates slicing) and toss with **½ cup bottled** teriyaki sauce. Grill meat slices just until no longer pink, about 1 to 2 minutes per side (turn meat carefully to prevent it from falling through the grill rack). Serve garnished with **3 tablespoons chopped scallions.** *Makes 6 servings.*

GRILLED FLANK STEAK Marinate **2 pounds flank steak** in **1 cup bottled salad dressing or barbecue sauce,** 20 minutes to 1 hour, and preheat a grill. Grill over a hot fire until no longer pink outside but still medium-rare inside (145°F internal temperature), about 5 to 7 minutes per side. Let stand 10 minutes before slicing. Cut against the grain into ⅛"- to ¼"-thick slices. *Makes 6 servings.*

ROAST BEEF SALAD Slice **leftover roast beef** about ¼" thick and cut into strips to equal 2 cups. Toss with **⅓ cup Italian vinaigrette, 2 tablespoons** *each* **capers, chopped fresh parsley, and other fresh herbs** (such as basil, oregano, or tarragon). Add **1 thinly sliced medium-size sweet onion** and **3 chopped celery hearts with leaves.** Serve over **4 cups assorted salad greens** or **arugula.** *Makes 4 servings.*

SHREDDED BEEF TAQUITOS Make Simple Beef Taco Filling (page 499). Pour **⅛" to ¼" vegetable oil** into a large skillet and place over medium-high heat. Warm **1 corn tortilla** in the microwave oven on high power until softened, 15 seconds. Remove it and arrange **2 tablespoons filling** in a line across the lower third of the tortilla. Fold about 1" of the tortilla up over the filling, then roll it up tightly like a cigar. Do not let go or it may unroll or loosen. Carefully place, seam side down, in the hot oil and hold in place with tongs until seam is set before letting go. Fry until crisp and golden, turning once, 3 to 4 minutes. Repeat with **15 more tortillas** and remaining filling, adding oil to the pan if necessary. Serve with **guacamole** or **sour cream.** *Makes 16.*

ROAST BEEF HASH Chop leftover roast beef to equal 2 cups of ¼" cubes. Chop 1 leftover boiled potato into ¼" cubes. In a large nonstick skillet, sauté **1 chopped onion** in **2 teaspoons vegetable oil** to soften. In a large bowl, combine **beef, potatoes, sautéed onion, ¼ cup chopped fresh parsley, 2 teaspoons flour, ¾ teaspoon salt, ½ teaspoon thyme,** and ¼ **teaspoon ground black pepper.** Toss to mix. Add ½ **cup heavy cream** and toss again. Place the skillet used to cook onion over medium-high heat. Add **1½ tablespoons vegetable oil.** Turn the hash into the pan and press gently with a spatula to flatten. Cook over medium heat until browned, about 20 minutes. Turn in pieces with a spatula. (To turn the whole cake, invert a plate over the pan, invert the pan, then slide the cake from the plate back into the pan.) Drizzle a little oil around the hash and brown 5 to 10 minutes longer. Sprinkle with **1 tablespoon chopped fresh parsley** and serve hot. *Makes 4 servings.*

BEEF BLINTZES In a large nonstick skillet, sauté **1 chopped onion** in **1 tablespoon vegetable oil** until tender. Add **2 cups chopped leftover pot roast,** ½ **teaspoon salt,** and ⅛ **teaspoon** *each* **grated nutmeg and ground black pepper.** Stir in **2 eggs.** Arrange ¼ cup of this filling in a line across the lower third of **1 store-bought crepe.** Fold crepe edge over filling, then roll up loosely and fold crepe ends under to seal. Repeat with **7 more crepes** and remaining filling. Wipe out skillet used to cook filling, add **1 tablespoon chicken fat** or **vegetable oil,** and warm over medium heat. Cook blintzes in batches until browned on the bottom, 5 minutes. *Makes 8.*

FLAVOR TIP ▼ **To flavor corned beef with cloves** • Most recipes for corned beef call for just a clove or two, but it's best to use more. Add 25 whole cloves to a pot when cooking a 3- to 4-pound corned beef. Cover generously with water and cook until tender, 2½ to 3 hours. The water will taste strongly of cloves, but it takes this many to add just a tinge of clove flavor to the meat.

PEPPERED RIB STEAKS WITH WATERCRESS Take **4 small, trimmed boneless rib steaks** (4 to 6 ounces each) and rub in **2 teaspoons coarse black pepper** (½ teaspoon for each steak). Warm **1 tablespoon olive oil** in a large, heavy skillet over medium-high heat. Add steaks and brown well, 3 to 4 minutes. Turn and cook to desired degree of doneness, about 2 minutes longer for medium (160°F internal temperature), about 4 minutes longer for well-done (165°F internal temperature). Transfer to a warm platter. Add ¼ **cup dry red wine** to the skillet and stir, scraping up browned bits. Cook until reduced by half, about 1 minute. Pour over steaks. Wipe out the skillet and add **2 tablespoons butter.** Trim off 1" from stems of **2 bunches watercress.** Add watercress to the skillet and cook over high heat until wilted, about 1 minute. Serve alongside steaks. *Makes 4 servings.*

37

b

Beef Stew

This recipe has multiple layers of flavor: woodsy porcini mushrooms, hickory-smoked bacon, and slow-simmered beef, to name a few. For more mushroom flavor, add 1 pound sliced, sautéed mushrooms along with the potatoes and carrots.

1 **ounce dried porcini mushrooms**

¾ **cup very hot water**

6 **slices hickory-smoked bacon, chopped**

2 **pounds beef chuck, trimmed of fat and cut into 1½" chunks**

⅓ **cup all-purpose flour**

4 **cups beef broth**

1 **cup red wine**

6 **large fresh thyme sprigs**

2 **strips (1" × 3" each) orange zest**

1 **teaspoon salt**

¼ **teaspoon ground black pepper**

2 **pounds tiny new potatoes, peeled, or larger ones cut into chunks**

1 **pound carrots, peeled and cut into chunks**

1. In a glass measuring cup, soak the mushrooms in the water until soft, 20 minutes. Remove the mushrooms from the liquid and chop, setting them aside. Strain the liquid into a small bowl and set aside.

2. In a 5-quart Dutch oven over medium heat, brown the bacon until crisp and golden, 5 minutes. Remove with a slotted spoon. Spoon off and set aside all but 1 tablespoon of the fat. Working in batches without crowding the pan, add the beef and cook, turning often, to brown all the pieces. Remove the pieces as they brown, adding the reserved fat as necessary to keep the meat from sticking to the pan.

3. When all the meat is browned, stir the flour into the pan and cook 1 minute (the mixture will be dry). Add the broth, wine, and reserved mushroom liquid, stirring until boiling and thickened. Reduce the heat to low and return the beef and bacon to the pan. Add the thyme, orange zest, salt, and pepper. Cover and simmer until the beef is tender, 2 hours.

4. Add the potatoes, carrots, and reserved mushrooms. Cover and simmer until the vegetables are tender, 50 to 60 minutes. Remove and discard the orange zest and thyme sprigs before serving.

Makes 6 servings

BEEFY NACHOS Heat **2 teaspoons vegetable oil** in a large skillet. Crumble in ½ **pound lean ground beef** and cook over medium-high heat until no longer pink. Add **1 or 2 fresh or pickled jalapeño chile peppers, minced,** and ½ **teaspoon** *each* **ground cumin,**

b

oregàno, and salt. Cook 1 minute. Stir in **1 teaspoon** *each* **chili powder and flour.** Cook 30 seconds. Stir in **¾ cup drained diced canned tomatoes, 3 tablespoons raisins, 1 tablespoon cider vinegar,** and **2 teaspoons sugar.** Cook until thickened, 2 to 3 minutes. Stir in **1 can (16 ounces) black beans, pinto beans,** or **pink beans,** rinsed and drained. Arrange **1 bag (10 ounces) corn tortilla chips** on each of 2 baking sheets or heatproof platters. Spoon on the beef in dabs all over and top with **1½ cups shredded Cheddar cheese.** Bake in the top third of a 450°F oven until lightly browned, about 5 minutes. Add dabs of salsa to each sheet. If desired, add **shredded lettuce, chopped fresh cilantro,** and **dabs of sour cream.** It's a good idea to bake one sheet at a time and serve them hot. *Makes 8 servings.*

HEALTHY HINTS ▼ **To get the leanest stew beef** • Although it's more convenient to buy cubed stew meat, consider purchasing a lean piece of beef and cutting it yourself. Most prepackaged, cubed stew meat contains higher amounts of fat. By cutting your own, you'll get the leanest possible beef. Single, uncut pieces of meat also have less surface area exposed to air and bacteria.

To get the leanest, freshest ground beef • Buy round steak; have the butcher trim off visible fat and grind it fresh.

To remove excess fat from store-bought ground beef • Cook the ground beef and set it on paper towels to absorb excess fat. Then, place the beef in a colander under running hot tap water to rinse off any surface fat.

To avoid *E. coli* bacteria in ground beef • Unlike a solid piece of meat, ground meat creates all sorts of miniscule spaces for pathogens to hide and multiply. To avoid the possibility of contamination,

---

COOKING LEAN CUTS OF BEEF

These beef cuts have the least fat. In many cases, moist-heat cooking methods are best for tenderizing them.

Cut of Beef	Best Cooking Method
Bottom round roast	Roast or braise large pieces
	Broil or pan-grill steaks
Brisket	Braise
Chuck roast	Braise or stew
Eye of round	Roast large pieces
	Braise chunks
	Broil or pan-grill steaks
Flank steak	Broil or pan-grill
Round tip	Roast or braise large pieces
	Broil or pan-grill steaks
	Sauté thin strips
Shank cross cuts	Braise
Sirloin steak	Broil or pan-grill (whole or cubed)
Top round	Roast large pieces
	Broil or pan-grill marinated steaks

---

ground beef in loaves or patties should always be cooked to 160°F internal temperature on an instant-read thermometer. Visually, the meat should no longer be pink and the juices should run clear when the meat is pierced.

To avoid cross-contamination • Be aware that any utensils, bowls, boards, and work surfaces that have come in contact with raw ground beef can retain bacteria and pass them on. For safety's sake, clean

Stuffed Flank Steak Spirals

Flank steak is among the leanest cuts of beef. Here, it's tenderized with a balsamic marinade, then stuffed with sun-dried tomatoes, corn, scallions, and pine nuts.

¾ **cup dry-packed sun-dried tomato halves (about 16 halves)**

1 **flank steak (about 1½ pounds), trimmed**

2 **tablespoons balsamic vinegar**

1 **large garlic clove, crushed**

¼ **teaspoon ground black pepper**

¾ **cup frozen corn**

3 **large scallions, sliced**

⅓ **cup grated Parmesan cheese**

1 **egg or 2 egg whites**

3 **tablespoons pine nuts, toasted**

1 **tablespoon chopped fresh oregano**

⅔ **cup dried bread crumbs**

½ **teaspoon salt**

1. Place the tomatoes in a small bowl and cover with boiling water. Let stand at least 20 minutes, or until softened.

2. Meanwhile, pound the steak between sheets of plastic wrap to about ¼" thickness.

3. In a small bowl, combine the vinegar, garlic, and pepper. Brush onto both sides of the steak and place the steak in a large, shallow baking dish. Cover with plastic wrap and marinate 30 to 60 minutes.

4. Preheat the oven to 400°F. Drain the tomatoes and chop. In a medium bowl, combine the tomatoes, corn, scallions, cheese, egg or egg whites, pine nuts, and oregano. Stir in the bread crumbs.

5. Place the steaks on a large cutting board or clean surface and sprinkle with the salt. Spread the filling evenly over the top, leaving a 1" border on the long side. Roll up from the long side without the border, shaping into a log.

6. Cut fourteen 12" pieces of kitchen twine. Starting ¾" from one end, tie the meat at 1½" intervals. Return the meat to the baking dish.

7. Bake until a thermometer inserted in the center registers 145°F for medium-rare, 16 to 18 minutes. (Add an additional 2 to 4 minutes for medium doneness, 160°F.) Let rest 10 minutes. Cut between the strings to make about 14 spirals. Remove the strings and serve.

Makes about 14

b

up with a mild bleach solution or an antibacterial kitchen cleaner and hot water.

To avoid hormones and antibiotics in beef • Cows and pigs are often injected with growth hormones and antibiotics, raising concerns about the residues of these additives in purchased meat. The FDA claims that the amounts of these residues are miniscule and not harmful to the consumer. For those still concerned, choose organic beef and pork that have been raised without the use of these additives.

Beer *see also* Alcohol; Wine

Not only is beer the perfect accompaniment to many foods, it's also an important ingredient in many recipes. Beer can be used to add flavor to chili, as a steaming liquid for clams and mussels, or to cook rice instead of using water. It's essential to the classic Belgian beef stew *carbonnade à la flamande* and can be found in recipes for yeast breads and even cakes.

BASICS ▼ **To choose the best-tasting beer** • Drink it as fresh as possible. Unlike wine, beer does not age gracefully. The first 90 days are the best of a beer's life, though most will be drinkable for up to a year. Many beers are now marked with sell-by dates. Check them before you buy.

To store • Keep beer bottles and cans upright. Laying them on their sides increases the surface area of the beer and exposes more of it to the air in the bottle, which weakens the beer's flavor.

To pour • Start pouring vigorously straight down the center of the glass. Once the foam or "head" starts forming, slow the rate of the pour or tilt the glass slightly to pour the beer onto the side of the glass. Proper pouring brings out the best characteristics of a beer.

To pair with food • Serve lagers, which are light in both body and color, as you would serve white wine. Likewise, serve ales, which are more robust and full-bodied, as you would serve red wine. For example, pair lagers with chicken, fish, pork, and spicy foods. Darker ales are a good match for duck, lamb, and beef.

TIME SAVER ▼ **To flatten beer quickly** • Heat the beer in a saucepan until warm, about 160°F. Stir vigorously with a whisk for 1 full minute. When the foam clears, the beer is flat.

BEER-KISSED CORN Warm **1½ tablespoons olive oil** or **butter** in a skillet over medium-high heat. Add **2 cups fresh corn kernels** (cut from 4 to 5 medium ears) and cook 5 minutes, tossing once or twice. Stir in **½ cup beer** and ½ **teaspoon** *each* **ground cumin and salt.** Bring to a boil. Turn off the heat, drain, and serve. *Makes 4 servings.*

BEER BATTER Into a large bowl, sift together **1 cup all-purpose flour, ½ cup cornstarch,** and **1 teaspoon salt.** Pour in **1½ cups beer** (one 12-ounce can or bottle) all at once and whisk rapidly until smooth. Chill 1 hour and whisk before using. *Makes about 3 cups.*

BEER-BATTERED ONION RINGS In a deep fryer, heat about **2" vegetable oil** to 375°F. Cut **3 medium onions** into ¼"-thick slices. Separate into rings and drop into **Beer Batter** (above). Working quickly, use tongs to place rings one by one into hot oil and fry until golden brown, 1 minute. Drain on paper towels and sprinkle with salt. *Makes 6 servings.*

Beets

These edible roots come in a range of colors, including pink, crimson, white, and gold, and there are even two-tone striped beets called Chioggia. Used in salads, pickles, and the brilliant pink soup known as borscht, beets have an earthy, sweet flavor that is best when tempered with a bit of acid, such as lemon or orange juice, vinegar, or wine.

BASICS ▼

To choose • Buy beets at the peak of their season from June through October. Spring beets tend to be woody and tough. Look for beets with firm, regularly shaped roots. Misshapen roots indicate that beets may have struggled to grow and their flesh will be bitter and tough. Also, purchase beets with the greens or tops still attached. Fresh beet tops should be bright green with no signs of wilting or yellowing.

To store • Cut off the greens, which drain moisture and nutrients from the beets, leaving about 1" of the stem attached to the beet (to minimize "bleeding" during cooking). Wrap the greens in moist paper towels and refrigerate in a zipper-lock plastic bag for up to 3 days.

To use beets raw • Beets can be eaten raw and are quite flavorful and slightly sweet. Pare off the skins with a swivel-blade vegetable peeler before using. Then, grate raw beets into salads or use as a topping for cold soups. Or slice them paper-thin and use on a platter of crudités as a fun and colorful dipper.

To peel easily • If you plan to cook beets, leave the skins on. They are much easier to remove when cooked. Leaving the skins on during cooking also helps preserve color and retain nutrients. After cooking, let the beets cool enough to handle, then rub off the skins with a paper towel or under warm, running water.

To boil • Boil scrubbed beets (with 1" of the stem still attached) in water to cover until tender, 30 to 50 minutes, depending on the size of the beets.

To roast • Roasting beets concentrates their sugar and intensifies their flavor. Individually wrap scrubbed beets (with 1" of the stem still attached) in a double layer of foil, place in a shallow pan, and roast at 400°F until tender to the center when tested with a fork, 45 to 70 minutes. When beets are cool enough to handle, cut off the root tips and stem ends and slip off skins by rubbing.

To cook beet greens • The greens are the most nutritious part of the beet. To cook them, cut into 2" lengths, keeping the stems and greens separate. Bring ½" of stock, broth, or water to a boil in a wide skillet, add the stems, cover, and cook for 4 minutes. Then, add the leaves and cook both stems and leaves for 4 to 8 minutes more, or until just tender.

Fascinating Fact: Despite their high sugar content, beets are actually low in calories, at only 70 calories per cup.

PROBLEM SOLVERS ▼

To save not-so-fresh beets • Boil and add ½ teaspoon *each* sugar and salt per quart of water to help revive flavors.

To minimize "bleeding" • Cook beets with skins intact. Also, leave the root and 1" of the stem attached during cooking. This minimizes loss of both color and nutrients. Steaming or roasting are best for minimizing bleeding.

To preserve color when boiling beets • Add 2 tablespoons lemon juice or vinegar to each quart of cooking water.

To prevent beets from staining a salad • Toss them separately in vinaigrette and add to the salad at the last minute before serving.

b

To remove beet stains • Rub the surface with salt, rinse, scrub with soap, and repeat until stains disappear. This works on hands as well as cutting surfaces.

To quick-roast beets • Slice scrubbed, unpeeled beets about ½" thick. Toss with olive oil, salt, and pepper, and spread on a baking sheet in a single layer. Roast at 450°F until tender, 15 to 20 minutes.

To microwave beets • Individually wrap scrubbed, unpeeled beets in microwaveable plastic wrap. Place 4 to 6 wrapped beets in a circle on a plate. Microwave on high until tender to the center when tested with a fork, 12 to 15 minutes. Cool a few minutes before peeling.

INSTANT BEET BORSCHT Refrigerate **1 jar (16 ounces) pickled beets.** In a blender, puree the beets and their juices with **2 cups cold buttermilk, 1 cup ice water,** and **⅓ cup chopped fresh dill.** *Makes 4 servings.*

RED FLANNEL HASH In a skillet, combine **½ pound leftover corned beef, 1 large cooked potato, ½ sautéed onion, 2 tablespoons chopped fresh parsley,** and **6 ounces grated or chopped cooked beets.** *Makes 4 side-dish servings.*

GLAZED BEETS Roast or boil **1 pound medium beets,** then peel and cut into ¾"-thick wedges. Melt **2 to 3 tablespoons butter** in a skillet. Add beets and **¼ cup chicken broth, 2 tablespoons red wine vinegar,** and **1 to 2 tablespoons honey** or **sugar.** Cook 2 minutes. Remove beets to a warm platter.

Reduce liquid to ⅓ cup by boiling about 2 minutes. Remove from heat and swirl in **2 teaspoons butter;** pour over beets to glaze. Top with ½ **teaspoon cracked green peppercorns,** if desired, or ⅛ **teaspoon ground black pepper.** *Makes 4 servings.*

PICKLED BEETS Heat ½ **cup water, 3 tablespoons red wine vinegar, 2 tablespoons honey, 3 whole cloves, ½ teaspoon salt,** and ¼ **teaspoon** *each* **allspice and ground black pepper** to boiling in a small saucepan. Pour over **1 pound cooked, chopped beets** and **2 slices red onion.** Cool and refrigerate at least 3 hours. *Makes 4 servings.*

Belgian Endive

Related to chicory, Belgian endive looks like a thick, cream-colored cigar of tightly packed leaves that are about 6" long. The crisp leaves have a slightly bitter taste and a canoelike shape that allows their hollows to be stuffed with cream cheese as an appetizer.

To grill • Cut tight heads of Belgian endive in half lengthwise through the root end. Soak in water 5 minutes. Brush with olive oil and grill over a medium-hot fire, cut side down, until browned, then turn every 2 minutes until tender, 10 to 15 minutes.

BRAISED BELGIAN ENDIVE Choose **2 to 4 tight, firm heads Belgian endive.** Trim off a sliver from the stem ends, then cut in half lengthwise. Warm **1 tablespoon olive oil** or **butter** in a skillet. Arrange endive halves, cut side down, in the pan, raise heat to medium-high, and cook until deep brown, about 4 minutes. Turn the halves over and add ⅓ **cup water** or **chicken broth.** Cover and braise until tender, 2 to 3 minutes. Sprinkle with ¼ **teaspoon salt** and ⅛ **teaspoon ground black pepper.**

Berries *see also* Strawberries

A huge range of fruits fall under this category. Strawberries, blueberries, and raspberries are some of the best-known ones. Lesser-known berries include gooseberries, currants, and Sylvan berries.

BASICS
▼ **To choose** • Shop for berries with your nose. A heady perfume indicates a berry that is ripe and bursting with flavor. Also, if buying berries in a box, turn it upside down. Excessive stains signal overripe berries that are well on their way to mush.

Try to buy locally grown berries. Ripe berries don't travel well, and once picked, berries don't continue to ripen.

To store • Gently spill the berries onto a paper towel. Remove any that are mushy or show signs of mold. Spread the rest in a single layer on a plate or a small baking sheet lined with paper towels. Cover with another layer of paper towels and refrigerate until ready to use.

To wash • Wait to wash berries until just before using. This helps prevent mushy berries. Rinse them gently with cool water and then pat dry with paper towels. To keep strawberries from getting soggy, leave the hulls intact until after washing. The hulls work as a cork and keep the berries from absorbing water.

To freeze • Wash the berries and pat dry, then spread them on a waxed paper–lined baking sheet, making sure that they don't touch. Freeze for several hours until

THREE WAYS WITH FROZEN BERRIES

Use home-frozen or commercially frozen berries in the following recipes.

Berry Smoothie: In a blender, mix **1 tablespoon honey** and ½ **cup milk** for 30 seconds. Add **6 to 8 frozen strawberries,** one at a time, or ½ **cup frozen raspberries** or **blueberries** in two additions, and blend until thick and smooth. *Makes 1 serving.*

Berry Sorbet: In a small saucepan or using a microwave oven, heat ¼ **cup honey** in ¼ **cup milk** until dissolved. In a food processor, pulse **30 frozen strawberries** or **2 cups frozen raspberries** until finely chopped. Add warm milk mixture and

process until smooth, scraping the work bowl as necessary. *Makes 4 servings.*

Warm Berry Sauce: In a food processor, pulse **2 cups frozen berries** until finely chopped. In a skillet, melt **2 tablespoons butter.** Add chopped berries and heat until bubbling vigorously, about 1 minute. Add **2 tablespoons of the liqueur of your choice** and ½ **teaspoon vanilla extract.** Match the liqueur to the berry used (Chambord with raspberries, for instance) or choose a liqueur with complementary flavor (Grand Marnier with blueberries, for example). *Makes about 1 cup.*

b

solid, then loosen from the paper, using a spatula if necessary. Transfer the berries to a zipper-lock freezer bag and freeze for up to 9 months. This freezing method prevents the berries from freezing together and allows you to remove just the amount needed from the bag.

To use frozen berries in muffins or cakes • Simply add them to the batter without bothering to defrost them. The berries will warm in the heat of the oven.

Fascinating Fact: Each raspberry and blackberry has a delicate cluster of 75 to 125 plump, juicy *drupelets,* each of which holds a berry seed.

PROBLEM SOLVERS
▼
To save softened berries that are not moldy or rotten • Place in a single layer on a baking sheet and freeze for 20 min-

utes to firm. If desired, roll in sugar to create a frosted look, and serve. Or mash the berries with a fork and serve spooned over vanilla ice cream, cake, or biscuits. You can also stir them into yogurt.

To remove seeds from fresh berry puree • Press the berries through a fine-mesh sieve. If you have only a large-mesh sieve, line a strainer with cheesecloth.

To prevent "bleeding" into baked goods • Quick-freeze the berries on a baking sheet for 10 minutes, then gently fold them into the batter. Or use dried fruit instead of fresh.

Chef's Tip: Wild blueberries, which are small, tender berries about one-third the size of cultivated blueberries, are available in frozen loose packs. Wild blueberries have a more intense flavor and hold up better in baking.

FOUR FAST BERRIED TREASURES

With fresh berries, the best thing a cook can do is handle them as little as possible. Each recipe below makes about 4 servings.

Blueberries with Rum and Lemon: In a saucepan or microwave oven, heat **1 tablespoon sugar** in **¼ cup rum** until sugar dissolves. Add **grated zest and juice of ½ lemon.** Cool and serve over **1½ pints blueberries.**

Raspberries in Peach Schnapps: In a saucepan or microwave oven, heat **2 teaspoons sugar** with **3 tablespoons peach schnapps** and **¼ teaspoon lemon juice.** Serve over **1½ pints raspberries.**

Strawberries in Easy Chocolate Fondue: In a 4-cup glass measure, combine **2 ounces chopped unsweetened choco-**late, **⅓ cup sugar,** and **¼ cup *each* strong brewed coffee and milk.** Cover and microwave on high power just until the chocolate is melted, about 3 to 5 minutes, stopping every 45 seconds to stir. Remove the cover, whisk until smooth, and blend in **1 tablespoon of any liqueur** (Grand Marnier works well). Cool 5 minutes and serve with toothpicks and **1½ pints strawberries for dipping.**

Strawberries with Walnut Mascarpone: In a food processor, process **½ cup walnuts** with **1 teaspoon sugar** to a paste. Scrape down the work bowl. Add **½ cup mascarpone cheese** and **1 tablespoon coffee liqueur.** Process until smooth. Serve as a dip with **1½ pints strawberries.**

To prevent berries from sinking to the bottom of baked goods • Toss in flour before folding into the batter.

To avoid discoloration in baked goods • Blueberries will sometimes discolor the surrounding crumb of baked goods, turning it a distasteful gray/green. This is due to a chemical reaction between the blueberries and baking soda. To avoid this reaction, select a recipe without baking soda. To adapt a recipe with baking soda, replace the acidic liquid in the recipe (usually buttermilk or yogurt) with milk and eliminate the baking soda. If there is no leavener other than baking soda, replace it with 1 tablespoon baking powder for every 2 cups flour.

To separate berries that are frozen together • Run them under cool water.

To adjust recipes when using frozen berries in pie recipes that call for fresh • Slightly increase the thickeners (flour, cornstarch, or tapioca) in the recipe to offset the additional liquid that will accumulate with frozen berries.

To remove berry stains • Rub them with a wedge of lemon.

FLAVOR TIPS **To sweeten bland-tasting berries** • Toss in granulated sugar (2 teaspoons sugar per cup of halved berries) and let stand at room temperature for 30 minutes.

To make fresh berry sauce • Sprinkle fresh berries with sugar and mash with a potato masher.

Fascinating Fact: Blueberries are the number one source of antioxidants found in the produce aisle. Antioxidants fight free radicals, helping to prevent cancer, high blood cholesterol, and aging skin. Genetically from the same plant family as cranberries, blueberries and their juice also contain condensed tannins, which help fight urinary tract infections.

Biscuits *see also* Breads, Quick

One of the most popular and easiest to make of all quick breads, biscuits are the subject of much baking lore and mystique. Though the ingredients are simple—just flour, salt, leavener, fat, and liquid—the quality of those ingredients and the care with which they are combined are the keys to making biscuits that are high-rising, tender, and flaky.

BASICS **To avoid mixing in excess flour when rolling the dough** • Handle the dough as little as possible. Knead it gently just until the dough forms a mass.

To mix biscuit dough without a pastry blender • Use 2 table knives, a fork, or just your fingertips to cut in the fat. The palms of your hands are too warm and can cause the fat to melt.

To roll to an even thickness • Place the dough between two ½"-high jelly-roll pans set side-by-side. Roll the rolling pin over the dough and the pans at the same time.

To shape without a rolling pin • Gently pat the dough to an even thickness with your fingertips.

To cut • Punch a metal biscuit cutter straight down onto the dough with a quick motion. Try not to twist the cutter or press the dough, which seals the edges and prevents the biscuits from rising.

To keep a biscuit cutter from sticking to dough • Dip the cutter in flour while using.

To cut without a biscuit cutter • Cut biscuits into squares with a long, sharp knife, cutting straight down (a cleaver works well). Avoid using an overturned glass, which can seal the edges of the biscuits and prevent them from rising.

To make biscuits without rolling • Just drop the dough from a tablespoon onto ungreased baking sheets.

b

To store • Wrap in foil and keep at room temperature for up to 3 days or freeze for up to 3 months.

To reheat frozen biscuits • Put them directly from the freezer into a 300°F oven for about 25 minutes.

To prevent brown spots and a bitter, salty taste • Mix the dry ingredients with a whisk to make sure that the baking powder is evenly distributed.

To rescue burnt biscuits • Rub the burnt bottom gently over a grater to remove it.

To make tender, flaky biscuits • Use soft Southern flour if available. Otherwise, use equal amounts of all-purpose flour and cake flour (or pastry flour). Mix only until the ingredients just hold together. Overworking the dough will develop the gluten in the flour and toughen the biscuits.

To make biscuits with a crisp crust • Brush the biscuits lightly with water before baking and set them 1½" apart on the baking sheet.

To make biscuits with a soft crust • Brush the biscuits with milk before baking

Buttermilk Biscuits

A combination of cake flour and all-purpose flour makes for an exceptionally tender biscuit. In a pinch, you can make these biscuits with just all-purpose flour.

- 1⅓ **cups cake flour**
- ⅓ **cup all-purpose flour**
- 2 **teaspoons baking powder**
- ½ **teaspoon baking soda**
- ½ **teaspoon salt**
- 3 **tablespoons chilled butter, cut into small pieces**
- 3 **tablespoons chilled vegetable shortening, cut into small pieces**
- ¾ **cup buttermilk**

1. Preheat the oven to 425°F.

2. In a large bowl, whisk together the cake flour, all-purpose flour, baking powder, baking soda, and salt. With a pastry blender or 2 knives, cut in the butter and vegetable shortening until it is evenly mixed and there are no large clumps. Quickly fold in the buttermilk until it is just blended. Do not overmix.

3. On a work surface lightly dusted with flour, briefly and gently knead the dough with your fingertips until it just holds together. Do not overknead. Press or roll out the dough to a thickness of 1". Using a 2" biscuit cutter, cut out 8 biscuits. Gather up the scrap pieces of dough, gently roll them out, and cut 4 more biscuits.

4. Place the biscuits on an ungreased baking sheet. Bake until the tops are a light golden brown, 18 to 20 minutes. Serve hot.

Makes 12

and put them on the baking sheet so that their edges touch.

To flavor with fresh herbs • Stir 1½ to 2 tablespoons chopped fresh herbs (such as oregano, thyme, or basil) into the milk before adding to dry ingredients.

To make cocktail sandwiches • Split or slice small biscuits in half horizontally. Spread honey mustard lightly on both halves. Add folded slices of smoked ham to one half and top with the other. Secure with a toothpick and an olive.

Blanching

A method of partially cooking ingredients in boiling water, blanching is usually done as a precursor to some later preparation. Peaches, tomatoes, and almonds are blanched in preparation for peeling. Broccoli, green beans, and cauliflower are sometimes blanched to soften their fibers before baking, frying, or sautéing. Blanching is often used to heighten and set the color and flavor of vegetables, usually before freezing or before serving in salads or as crudités.

BASICS ▼ **To blanch** • Bring a pot of water to a boil. Add the food to the water and boil about 30 seconds for most foods. Remove the food from the pot and immediately plunge it into ice water to stop the cooking process. Note that some vegetables, such as asparagus and broccoli, can suffer in an ice water bath. To preserve their flavor and texture, spread them out in a single layer and let them cool to room temperature.

To blanch a large amount of food • Blanch in batches. Too much food will bring the boiling water to a halt and slow-cook rather than blanch the vegetables.

THE BLANCH-AND-PEEL METHOD

When blanched, the skins of tomatoes and peaches slip off easily.

1 For tomatoes, core the tomato with a paring knife, removing the stem and white middle. For peaches, just remove the stem.

2 Cut an X in the bottom of the tomato or peach, cutting only the skin. Then, immerse in boiling water for 20 to 30 seconds, depending upon the size and amount of fruit. Remove and plunge into ice water.

3 When the fruit is cool enough to handle, use the edge of the knife to slip off the skin.

b

PROBLEM SOLVER ▼ **To minimize ice formation when freezing blanched vegetables** • Spread vegetables on a rack or a towel to thoroughly dry before sealing in a zipper-lock freezer bag. If possible, also place in front of a fan to speed the process.

Fascinating Fact:
Blanching is also a horticultural term for a labor-intensive technique in which the leaves of plants are not permitted to photosynthesize and turn green, by growing them in complete darkness. Belgian endive is grown in this manner.

TIME SAVERS ▼ **To blanch faster** • Use a pot with a pasta insert, or use a steamer basket. This makes it much easier to retrieve blanched ingredients from the boiling water and plunge them into ice water to stop their cooking.

To avoid unnecessary blanching • Almonds are often blanched for baking. But really, the only reason to blanch an almond is if you object to brown specks in your cake or cookie. The same holds true for some tomato recipes. Blanching tomatoes is ubiquitous in recipes for fresh tomato sauce, but if a sauce is cooked minimally and the fresh tomato is predominant, the skin is unnoticeable. It is only when a tomato sauce is cooked for hours that the skins will separate from the tomato and become texturally unpleasant.

Blenders

Originally designed as a bar accessory, blenders are a great help in the kitchen. Use them to crush ice, puree soups, smooth lumpy custards, and make no-cook sauces.

FOUR NO-COOK BLENDER SAUCES

Tomato and Red Pepper Sauce: In a blender, combine **4 peeled and seeded tomatoes** with **1 peeled roasted red pepper, 2 tablespoons extra-virgin olive oil, 1 mashed garlic clove, ½ teaspoon salt,** and **a pinch of ground red pepper.** Blend until smooth. Toss with pasta or use as a sauce for grilled shrimp.
Makes about 2 cups.

Parsley and Caper Sauce: In a blender, combine ⅔ **cup parsley leaves, ½ cup extra-virgin olive oil, 2 anchovy fillets, 2 table-spoons capers, 1 tablespoon lemon juice, 1 mashed garlic clove,** and **½ teaspoon** *each* **Dijon mustard and salt.** Blend until smooth. Serve with poached beef or grilled fish.
Makes about 1¼ cups.

Pesto: In a blender, combine **2 cups tightly packed fresh basil, ½ cup extra-virgin olive oil,** and **3 tablespoons lightly toasted pine nuts.** Blend until smooth. Transfer to a bowl and stir in **1 minced garlic clove** and **½ cup freshly grated Parmesan cheese.** Taste and add salt if needed. Serve with pasta, spread on a pizza, or use as a dressing for potato salad. *Makes 1 cup.*

Simple Raspberry Sauce: In a blender, puree **1½ cups ripe raspberries** with **¼ cup sugar.** Pass sauce through a fine-mesh sieve to remove seeds. Add **3 tablespoons lemon juice** and **1 tablespoon raspberry liqueur,** if desired. Serve over angel food cake, vanilla ice cream, or slices of dense chocolate cake. *Makes about 1½ cups.*

BASICS ▼ **To choose** • First, consider how you'll be using your blender—290 watts is fine for most blending jobs. If you plan on crushing ice often, go for a 330- to 400-watt blender. Look for a blender with a removable bottom for easy cleaning.

To keep your kitchen walls clean • Blend quantities larger than 3 to 4 cups in a food processor instead of a blender.

To blend hot liquids • Start on low speed and gradually increase the speed as needed. Remove the center of the lid so that steam can escape.

To clean a blender quickly • Add warm water and dish soap and blend for a few seconds. Then, rinse in the sink and dry. If you need to wash the jar, do so by hand. Plastic jars don't hold up well in the dishwasher.

Braising

This classic cooking technique calls for food to be browned in hot fat, then covered and slowly cooked in a small amount of liquid over low heat. Braising is ideal for preparing tough cuts of meat, such as beef short ribs and pork shoulder, and firm-textured vegetables, such as cabbage, leeks, and turnips.

BASICS ▼ **To braise vegetables evenly** • Cut the vegetables to a uniform size.

TIME SAVERS ▼ **To brown meat faster** • For meat that will be braised, save time by browning it on a grill or under a broiler while you use the braising pot to sauté the vegetables. After browning, combine everything in the braising pot without skipping a beat.

To braise in a pressure cooker • Pressure cookers cut braising time in half without sacrificing flavor or tenderness. To convert a braised recipe for the pressure cooker, cut both the liquid and cooking time in half. See, for example, Pressure Cooker Pot Roast on page 34.

To save time by stir-braising • If you thinly slice tough cuts of meat, stir-frying techniques can be used to speed recipes for braising and stewing. Because the timing is shorter, flavors come from the addition of sauces, seasonings, and broths rather than from long simmering.

STIR-BRAISED CHINESE CHICKEN STEW Rehydrate **8 dried shiitake mushrooms** in hot water for 20 minutes. Pluck out mushrooms and reserve liquid. In a hot wok or large skillet, cook **1½ pounds skinless chicken thighs** in **2 tablespoons peanut oil** until lightly browned. Add about ½ **sliced fennel bulb, 2 minced garlic cloves, 1 tablespoon minced fresh ginger, 1 teaspoon ground aniseed,** and ½ **teaspoon red-pepper flakes.** Cook another minute. Add **3 tablespoons light soy sauce, 1¼ cups chicken broth, ¼ cup dry sherry** or **rice vinegar, 2 tablespoons sugar, reserved mushroom liquid,** and **rehydrated mushrooms.** Cover and simmer until thickest thigh portion registers 170°F on an instant-read thermometer and juices run clear, 10 minutes. Add **2 tablespoons cornstarch** dissolved in **1 tablespoon water** and stir until thickened. Stir in **1 teaspoon toasted sesame oil.**
Makes 4 servings.

FLAVOR TIPS ▼ **To add flavor** • Use broth, stock, or vegetable juice, or a combination, instead of water. Fruit juices can also be used, and their sweetness may help balance the acidity of tomatoes or wine. Apple cider goes well with poultry or pork.

b

BRAISING MEATS, STEP BY STEP

1. Choose a cut of meat from the animal's working muscles: Beef short ribs, brisket, rump roast, and some of the less expensive cuts of veal (such as the breast, shoulder, and shank) are ideal. Chicken drumsticks and thighs are other good choices. Use about 1 to 1½ pounds for 4 servings.

2. Use a heavy casserole pot with a tight-fitting lid. The pot should hold all of the ingredients snugly in order to minimize the amount of cooking liquid needed.

3. Heat about 1 tablespoon of fat in the pan over medium-high heat. Add the meat, taking care not to crowd the pan, and brown well on all sides. Don't rush the browning process. It's essential to the flavor of the dish.

4. Remove the browned meat from the pan and add any aromatic vegetables. Let these cook over medium heat until softened, stirring occasionally.

5. Return the browned meat to the pan with the softened vegetables and add your braising liquid. Choose veal stock for both veal and beef. Use beef stock only for hearty beef braises. Chicken stock goes well with poultry. For more flavor, add wine along with the stock. Tomatoes are another popular braising medium. They complement the flavor of beef and chicken dishes and help thicken the braising liquid. Be sure to keep the quantity of liquid to a minimum. The less liquid you add, the more concentrated the flavors will be.

6. Once all the ingredients are combined, bring them to a boil over high heat. As soon as the liquid begins to boil, reduce the heat to barely a simmer, cover tightly, and cook over low heat. Gentle heat is vital to dissolve the tough tissues in the meat. If allowed to boil unchecked, braised meats will become unpleasantly tough. Braised meats can be cooked on top of the stove or in an oven at about 300°F. Cook until the meat is fork-tender.

7. When the meat is tender and the liquid is still hot, skim the fat from the surface. Most braised dishes taste better when they're allowed to chill overnight and reheated the next day. If you choose to do this, don't bother to degrease before cooling. The fat in the dish will congeal on the surface as it cools and can then be easily lifted away.

To get creative with braising juices • Combine ingredients such as carrots, celery, and leeks and run through a juicing machine. If you don't have a juicer, a health food store can juice the ingredients for you. Bottled vegetable juices are also available in health food stores.

Bread Crumbs *see also*
Breading; Gratin

Used as a crisp topping for casseroles or as a thickener to add body to sauces, bread crumbs are an economical way to use yesterday's bread. Use dried bread crumbs as a

coating for fried fish or as a crust for vegetable gratins. Fresh bread crumbs are perfect for lighter crusts such as the classic coating for a roasted rack of lamb. It's a good idea to keep store-bought bread crumbs on hand, but it's simple to make your own.

BASICS **To make dried bread crumbs •** Use completely dry or stale bread, tear it into small pieces, and grind it into crumbs in a food processor. If your bread is still somewhat soft, slice it thin and place in a 250°F oven until completely dry. You can also season the bread at this point by spraying with cooking spray and coating with herbs.

To make bread crumbs without a food processor or blender • Place slices of very dry, stale bread in a sturdy plastic bag and crush with a rolling pin.

To make light, flaky bread crumbs • Grate dried bread on a grater.

To store dried bread crumbs • Keep dried bread crumbs in a zipper-lock plastic bag or an airtight plastic container at room temperature for about 2 weeks or in the freezer for a few months.

To make fresh bread crumbs • Use fresh bread and grind it in a food processor or blender, but make sure that it is not too soft or it will clump into balls rather than separating into crumbs. To ensure fresh crumbs of a uniform size, remove any thick crust from the bread before grinding.

To store fresh bread crumbs • Don't. Use them the day that you make them. Or dry them on a baking sheet at 250°F and use as dried bread crumbs.

SEASONED DRIED BREAD CRUMBS Brown **1 cup homemade dried bread crumbs** in ⅓ **cup butter** or **olive oil** with ½ **teaspoon salt**. If desired, stir in **1 tablespoon finely chopped fresh herbs** such as rosemary, thyme, sage, and/or parsley and **1 tablespoon freshly grated Parmesan cheese** while browning the crumbs. *Makes about 1 cup.*

Chef's Tip: The next time you make a crumb coating mix for oven-frying or sautéing, reach for a different base to make your crumbs. Try one or a combination of the following to crush into crumbs: flavored melba toasts, tortilla chips, crackers, dry bagged stuffing mixes, pretzels, or gingersnaps.

Breading *see also* Bread Crumbs

Crisp coatings help keep delicate foods such as fish fillets and chicken cutlets moist while they cook. Two elements are essential: something dry for the coating and something wet to hold the coating in place. The dry element could be bread or cracker crumbs, flour, cornmeal, crushed nuts, dried herbs, or dried cheese. The wet mixture should be some form of fluid protein, such as beaten egg or egg white, buttermilk, thinned plain yogurt or a creamy salad dressing.

BASICS **To help breaded foods brown evenly •** Pat the food dry before breading to prevent trapped moisture from steaming and blistering the coating. Before adding a coat of crumbs, roll the food in flour or cornstarch and then in the wet mixture.

To keep breadings from becoming too thick • Add 1 tablespoon water or milk to the wet mixture.

For a richer, more tender crust • Add 1 tablespoon oil to the wet mixture.

For the lightest crust • Use finely ground fresh bread crumbs.

For a crisp, sturdy crust • Use a meal coating such as cornmeal or finely ground cracker crumbs.

b

To distribute seasonings evenly in a breading • Add them to the wet mixture.

To help breadings adhere better to food • Let the coated food sit on a rack for 15 minutes before cooking.

TIME SAVER ▼ **To bread ahead of time** • Coat the food well, then cover tightly and refrigerate for several hours.

FLAVOR TIPS ▼ **To make a cheese breading** • Add ¼ cup grated Parmesan cheese to each ¾ cup or 1 cup dry bread crumbs.

To make a nut breading • Add finely ground nuts to the bread crumbs.

To make a seasoned breading • Add finely chopped herbs or ground spices.

To make an *alla Francese*–style breading • Originally created as a coating for veal cutlets, this breading method works well on chicken cutlets too. For most breadings, you dip the food first into flour, then into egg, then into crumbs, each layer holding on to the next. For *alla Francese* coating, the final dip is into egg, which sort of explodes upon hitting the hot oil in a skillet. This makes the coating fluffy and spongy, so it will eagerly soak up more of the sauce that it is served with.

Bread Machines

These computerized bread makers combine the functions of a mixer, a dough kneader, a proofing box, and a miniature oven. Some models even bake cakes and cook jams.

BASICS ▼ **To choose** • Decide whether you want a basic or multifunctional model. If you're still learning how to program your VCR, you may want to skip the models that require a lot of programming and opt for a basic model instead. Just make sure that your machine has a dough or manual cycle that al-

lows you to remove dough after it rises, so that you can shape it as you wish or bake it in a conventional oven. Multifunctional models have preprogrammable baking cycles and settings for different types of bread. If you're a fan of whole wheat bread, look for a heavy-duty machine with a whole wheat cycle or at least one that can be programmed for a longer knead and rise cycle.

For successful breads from a bread machine • Measure carefully. Bread machines are not as forgiving of casual measuring as conventionally made loaves. Too much yeast could cause the loaf to collapse or to fuse itself to the lid of the machine, while too much sugar or fat could make a loaf cave in. Also, since bread machines vary, add the ingredients in the order specified for your model.

To clean • Use a dishcloth or sponge on the paddle and pan. Avoid the dishwasher, knives, and other sharp or abrasive objects that may scratch the nonstick surface.

Breads, Quick *see also* Baking Powder; Baking Soda; Biscuits; Muffins; Pancakes; Scones

Made without yeast, quick breads encompass a remarkably wide variety of baked goods. Pancakes, muffins, crackers, and fried doughs all fall under this category. These breads are relatively quick to make, requiring none of the rising time that yeast breads need. Heat, eggs, and fast-acting chemical leaveners such as baking powder and baking soda are the most common leavening agents for quick breads.

BASICS ▼ **To make tender quick breads** • Mix just until the wet and dry ingredients are combined. A few patches of dry flour are okay;

they will moisten during cooking. Avoid overmixing, which develops the gluten in the flour, and will make the quick bread tough and chewy.

HONEY ORANGE LOAF Preheat oven to 350°F. Place ¼ cup **currants** or **chopped raisins** in a small bowl. Cover with **boiling water** and let soak 15 minutes. In a large bowl, mix ¾ **cup** *each* **whole wheat flour and all-purpose flour, 1¼ teaspoons baking powder,** and ½ **teaspoon** *each* **salt and baking soda.** Make a well in the center and add ¾ **cup milk** (any kind), ¼ **cup honey, 2 teaspoons grated orange zest,** and **2 tablespoons orange juice.** Stir wet ingredients to blend. Add currants or raisins and stir all together just until blended. Spoon into a greased 8" × 4" loaf pan. Bake until a tester inserted in the center comes out clean, about 45 minutes. Cool in the pan on a rack 15 minutes. Remove to the rack and cool completely. Slice thin. *Makes 10 to 12 servings.*

APRICOT COFFEE CAKE Preheat oven to 325°F. Drain **1 can (16 ounces) apricots** packed in syrup. Pat apricots dry on paper towels. In a 1-cup measure, combine ½ **cup chopped walnuts** and ¼ **cup brown sugar.** In a medium bowl, stir together **2 large eggs,** ½ **cup sugar, 3 tablespoons melted butter, 2 tablespoons milk,** and **2 teaspoons vanilla extract.** In a large bowl, stir together **1 cup all-purpose flour,** ½ **teaspoon baking powder,** and **a pinch of salt.** Pour egg mixture into flour mixture and stir just to blend. Spread half the batter evenly over the bottom of a greased 9" cake pan (can be a pan with a removable bottom). Arrange apricots, cut side up,

over batter and sprinkle with walnut mixture. Drizzle remaining batter over top but do not spread. Bake until edge begins to pull away from the pan, about 45 minutes. Cool 15 minutes. *Makes 8 servings.*

PROBLEM SOLVERS ▼ **To salvage overcooked quick breads** • Poke deep holes through the top with a skewer and drizzle fruit juice or a liquid sweetener (maple syrup or honey) over the holes to penetrate into the bread.

To cook an underbaked quick bread through • If the bread has already cooled, lay slices across a baking sheet, cover with foil, and bake at 300°F until cooked through. If the bread is still hot, put it back in the oven until done.

To retain moistness in quick breads that include dried fruits • Dried fruits such as raisins, apricots, and apples absorb moisture in quick breads. To retain moisture, replace up to one-third of the liquid in the recipe with low-fat plain yogurt. Also, plump the dried fruit before adding it to the batter. Cover with boiling water and let soak 15 minutes. Cool and pat dry with paper towels. Or substitute some honey for the sugar in the recipe (see page 235 for substitution adjustments). The hydroscopic quality of honey (drawing moisture from the air) helps retain moisture in the finished product.

TIME SAVER ▼ **To make ahead** • If you want fresh, hot quick breads in the morning, prepare the ingredients the night before, keeping the dry and wet ingredients in separate bowls. Come morning, preheat the oven, combine the 2 bowls of ingredients, turn the batter into a pan, and bake.

HEALTHY HINTS ▼ **To reduce fat** • In many traditional quick-bread recipes, you can use 25 percent less fat than is called for in the recipe with no other changes.

b

To improvise a more healthful doughnut • When preparing any quick bread, make up an extra batch of plain batter, adding a pinch of nutmeg. Bake in mini Bundt pans according to the recipe directions. Cool and coat with a glaze made from 1 cup confectioners' sugar thinned with 3 to 4 tablespoons milk or orange juice. Wrap well and freeze up to 2 months. Reheat briefly in the microwave oven for those moments when you crave a glazed doughnut.

Breads, Yeast *see also* Flour

Perhaps the most essential of all foods, bread is extremely gratifying to make and to eat. The basic ingredients of flour, water, salt, and yeast can yield an enormous variety of loaves with a huge range of flavors, textures, and shapes. Bread has a reputation for being time-consuming and difficult to make, but almost anyone can make a satisfying loaf. In fact, the actual hands-on time spent making bread is less than the average prep time for a meal.

BASICS
▼

To knead yeast dough • Pulling and stretching dough helps develop its gluten and incorporate air, both necessary for the chewy texture and proper rise of good yeast bread. Don't be too gentle during initial kneading; the harder you work dough, the better the gluten develops.

Place your hands side by side on the dough and press firmly down with the heels, flattening the dough to about ½" thick ❶.

With your hands still side by side, grasp the far end of the dough and fold it back on itself, flattening again. Rotate the dough ¼ turn and repeat. Continue kneading and rotating until the dough feels elastic, pliable, and somewhat sticky ❷.

To clean sticky scraps of dough from a work surface • Scrape off with a plastic or metal pastry bench knife. Or use warm water and a woven mesh scrubbie. Avoid hot water, which "cooks" the dough and leaves a sticky mess. Also avoid using a sponge, which will quickly become clogged with dough.

To rise yeast dough • Dough rises best in a warm, moist, draft-free spot. The ideal temperature is 85°F. This is warmer than most homes, but there are several ways to create the right environment. Fill a heat-proof bowl with boiling water and let it stand while you prepare the dough. Throw out the water, dry the bowl, and let the dough rise in the warm bowl. Or fill a large stockpot with a couple of inches of tepid (not hot) water. Place the covered bowl of dough inside and cover the pot. You can also boil a cup of water in a microwave oven for 2 minutes, place it in a corner of the microwave oven, then put in the covered bread dough and close the door. Or run the dishwasher on the rinse cycle, wait a few minutes, then place the covered dough inside. You can even preheat your oven for 2 minutes, then turn it off and place the covered dough inside. For steam, place a baking pan on the bottom shelf of the oven and pour a teakettle of boiling water into the pan. (When using these microwave oven, dishwasher, or conventional oven techniques, it's best to tape over the controls or knobs so that no one accidentally turns the appliances on.) Another option: Place the bowl of dough on a warm radiator, using a towel as insulation under the bowl, and cover the bowl with another towel. Or place the bowl on top of your refrigerator, toward the back, where the running motor gives off a bit of heat. For a food processor dough, after it is kneaded in the machine, simply replace the cover and set the covered work bowl in a warm place to rise.

To accurately monitor a dough's rise • Use a straight-sided container so that the dough is only rising up, not out. If the container is transparent, mark the height of the dough on the outside of the container when you first lay it in. Use this mark to gauge the rise of the dough. If your straight-sided container is not transparent, insert a large skewer straight down into the dough. Mark the dough's height on the skewer, then mark the point on the skewer where the dough should be once doubled.

To slow a dough's rate of rising • Store it in the refrigerator for as long as overnight. Remove from the refrigerator and let the dough rest at room temperature for an hour before baking.

To test whether a yeast dough is sufficiently risen • Give the dough a good poke with your finger. If the indentation slowly but resolutely rises back, your dough is ready for shaping. If the indentation springs back very quickly, the dough needs more rising time. If it doesn't spring back at all or the indentation stays put, your dough has risen too long.

To freeze yeast dough • Prepare the dough at least through its first rise. Punch out all of the air and seal in a zipper-lock freezer bag, leaving a little room for expansion. Freeze as quickly as possible in an empty section of the freezer. When dough is frozen solid, remove any air space in the bag, reseal, and store for up to 2 months.

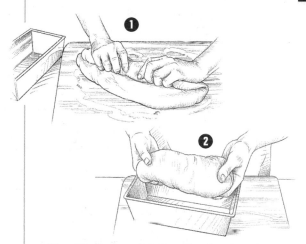

To shape dough into a loaf • Punch down the risen dough. Gently form it into an oval shape, then roll it into a thick cylinder slightly longer than the bread pan ❶.

Fold the ends under, then lower the loaf into the pan, seam side down ❷.

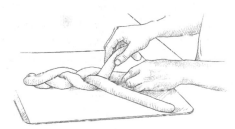

To make a braided loaf • Divide the dough into 3 equal parts and roll each into a cylinder. (At this point, you could just bake the 3 cylinders to make baguettes). Line up the cylinders so that the ends face you. Braid from the middle to the ends, slightly stretching each cylinder as you go, so that the loaf tapers at the ends. Pinch the ends together.

b

b

To freeze shaped, unbaked bread dough • After the first rise of the dough, punch down and shape as directed, lining the pan with foil. Spray the foil with cooking spray, add the dough, and freeze until solid. Remove dough and foil, wrap airtight, and freeze up to 3 months. To use, remove from the freezer and return to the pans, thawing, covered, in the refrigerator overnight. Remove, cover with a towel, and let rise in a warm place until doubled. Then bake as directed.

To roll out stiff dough • Set the dough aside for 5 minutes and try again. Often, the gluten in the dough simply needs to "rest" in order to relax.

To slash the tops of formed dough just before baking • Use a single-edge general household razor blade. The special tools for this task are overrated. You can

THE FUNDAMENTALS OF YEAST BREAD

Making bread is not an instant process by any means, but the actual hands-on time involved is minimal. All it really takes is a series of pauses throughout an afternoon.

The Science Behind It: The structure of yeast-leavened breads is formed by wheat flour. When water is stirred into wheat flour, two unique proteins in the flour connect with each other and overlap, forming elastic sheets known as gluten. If you've ever watched someone spin a ball of dough into a flat disc for pizza, you've witnessed the magic of gluten. One type of protein in the gluten allows the dough structure to stretch, while the other provides the snap, so that the dough doesn't just fly out into the room. To give it lift, the dough needs yeast, a living, single-celled organism that releases carbon dioxide as it feeds on the dough. As it feeds, it multiplies. As it multiplies, more and more gas is released into the dough, pushing against the gluten mesh so that the dough's volume expands. Yeast also releases alcohol and organic substances that lend flavor to bread.

Getting Started: Typically, the first step to making yeast bread is activating or "proofing"

the yeast. (The exception is quick-rising yeast, which does not need proofing.) This is done by dissolving the yeast in warm water and sometimes in sugar or in with the flour. Avoid hot water, which will kill the yeast. The water needs to be only about 98°F, the same as human body temperature, so if it feels hot to the touch, the water is probably too hot. Proofing takes only 5 to 6 minutes, at which time the yeast will wake up, bubble, and start to smell yeasty. If your yeast shows no signs of life, try adding a scant tablespoon of sugar per tablespoon of yeast. If, after 5 minutes, the yeast still shows no signs of life, you likely need to purchase new yeast.

Working the Dough: Once the basic ingredients of flour, water, salt, and yeast are mixed, you can knead bread dough by hand or with a standing mixer or food processor. Kneading is vital to developing the gluten in the dough as well as to incorporating air into the dough. But take care not to add too much flour while kneading. The goal is to create a dough that is somewhat sticky. If you need to add flour, dust the dough and work surface with no more than a tablespoon at a time, and knead it into also snip slashes with kitchen shears or use a sharp knife.

To maintain the shape of breads made with soft doughs • Poke a series of holes in the top of each loaf with a metal skewer before baking.

To bake breads with thick, crisp crusts • Use bread flour with 12 percent to 13 percent protein. And don't forget the salt in the dough. Salt tempers the conversion of starch to sugar and plays a role in the color and crisping of the bread, not to mention adding flavor. When handling the dough, use as little additional flour as possible. Too much flour on the surface of the dough can interfere with the formation of the crust. It also helps to slash the top of the loaf just before putting it in the oven. An uncut crust will rip at random as it expands in the first few minutes of baking.

the dough. To keep your hands from sticking to the dough, oil your hands rather than adding more flour. Knead the dough until it is smooth and elastic. Pull on it every so often to test its elasticity. Also, press your fingers into it. If your finger indentations rise slowly, the gluten has been properly developed.

Rising: Form the dough into a ball and place it in a bowl or container large enough to hold the dough once it has doubled in size. Misting oil on top of dough will keep it soft and moist so that it doesn't resist expansion. Cover the container with a warm, damp dish towel or loosely with plastic wrap. Place it in a warm, draft-free spot. The dough should rise until it is no more than double in size. This takes about 2 hours. If you press your fingers into the dough and the indentation comes back slowly, the dough has amply risen.

Punching and Pulling: Once risen, bread dough is bloated with large pockets of carbon dioxide. By punching down the dough, you will break the large gas pockets down into numerous smaller pockets for a more even rise. Often, recipes will direct you to then briefly knead the dough, which further works out any stray bubbles and evenly distributes the multiplied yeast in the dough. Some recipes may also call for a second rise, which helps develop numerous little pockets of gas that contribute to an even, tender crumb in the finished bread.

Shaping, Slashing, Stones, and Steam: The next step is to let the dough rest for 5 to 10 minutes to relax the gluten so that it is easy to shape. Then, divide the dough and shape as desired. Once shaped, let the dough rise briefly to regain some of the volume lost through shaping. Then slash the top with a serrated knife or razor blade to relieve some tension on the top crust during baking. Many recipes call for placing the bread on a preheated bread or pizza stone. While it's not absolutely necessary, a stone provides a hot surface to speed the warming of the dough as well as help develop a crisp bottom crust. Some recipes may call for steam within the first 5 minutes of baking. Steam delays the setting of the crust and gives the bread time to rise to its full expansion, which occurs mostly within the first 15 minutes of baking.

b

Another trick: Brush or spray the dough with water just before putting it in the oven and use a baking stone to disperse heat evenly. Or, create steam: Preheat a metal pan on the floor of the oven or on the bottom rack. Add the bread to the oven, then pour water into the hot pan.

To keep the crust crisp longer • Store the cooled loaf in a paper bag at room temperature. Completely cooling the bread before storage also prevents condensation and discourages mold.

Chef's Tip: Using different glazes when baking breads will produce crusts of varying colors and textures. An egg yolk will brown the crust. An egg white glaze will produce a shiny crust. Whole eggs give both sheen and color. Milk mixed with melted butter or oil creates a soft crust. Water will produce a crisp crust (brush or spray prior to baking and, for an extra-crisp crust, 10 minutes before removing from the oven.) Mixing water and whole eggs will produce a shiny brown, crisp crust. Honey or molasses makes a soft, sweet crust.

To coat bread with seeds and a shiny glaze • For 2 loaves, mix 3 tablespoons of seeds (such as sesame, poppy, or sunflower) with 1 egg (or 2 egg whites) beaten with 1 tablespoon of water. After forming the loaves but before they begin their final rise, brush the tops with the seed mixture.

To coat bread or rolls with seeds but no glaze • Cover the bottom of a pie plate with seeds. When loaves or rolls are formed, spray them with a light mist of water. Roll them in seeds and place in the pan for the final rise.

To determine whether a loaf of bread is done • You can't always rely on the old trick of tapping the loaf's bottom. To be sure, insert an instant-read thermometer into the loaf's center (through the bottom

if possible). The bread is done when it reads between 190° and 200°F (unless the recipe indicates otherwise; some breads finish at different temperatures).

To evenly slice a large, round loaf with a thick crust • Cut the loaf in half. Then place it, cut side down, on the cutting board. Grip the bread by its crust and slice through the crust.

To prevent acceleration of the staling process • Store yeast bread at room temperature or freeze it. Only refrigerate bread that's very moist or that contains fruit pieces.

To freeze • Freeze whole loaves or slice first so you can pull out only as much as you need. Seal in a zipper-lock freezer bag and freeze for up to 3 months. The taste and texture will remain intact. Toast frozen bread to thaw and reheat in one step.

To get a crisp crust from frozen whole rolls or breads • Thaw in a 200°F oven until warmed through (a thick, rustic loaf of bread may take up to 1 hour).

Chef's Tip: Since flour can act like a sponge, absorbing moisture from the air, be aware that atmospheric conditions can have an effect on baking. In really humid weather, a 6-cup bread dough recipe may require the addition of as much as an extra cup of flour.

PROBLEM SOLVERS ▼ **To avoid sticking when working with dough** • When kneading dough by hand, coat your hands with oil or cooking spray. When kneading with a standing mixer, oil or spray the top part of the dough hook. When rolling out dough, coat the rolling pin too. And when punching down dough, make a fist and lightly coat your knuckles. Or, to avoid the mess of oil or oily sprays, try cold water instead.

TROUBLESHOOTING YEAST BREADS

Even for the experienced home baker, bread holds a certain mystique. Here is how to come ever closer to the perfect loaf.

Problem	Possible Causes	Solutions/Suggestions
Dough is not rising	Yeast is old Yeast was dissolved in too-hot or too-cold water Dough was kneaded too stiff; gluten was overdeveloped Rising location was too cold	Try proofing new yeast and kneading it into the dough; additional flour might be necessary
Dough is bloated and blistering	Dough has over-risen Rising place is too warm	Punch down, reshape, and let rise again
Bread rises and bakes unevenly	Dough was shaped unevenly Dough was not scored or scored unevenly Oven heats unevenly	Try rotating the loaf; there is little more you can do at this point
Bread browns unevenly on top	Loaf is or was too close to the oven top Oven heats unevenly	Rotate loaf if browning unevenly Lower the rack on which the bread sits if browning too quickly
Bread is too brown on bottom	Baking stone or oven is too hot	Place a rack or wire cake stand between loaf and stone; check that oven is calibrated correctly
Bread is too brown all over	Oven is too hot	Lower heat; check that oven is calibrated correctly
Bread interior has gaping holes	Too much yeast was used in dough Too little flour was used Too little kneading Dough over-rose Oven was too cool	Use the bread for toast; the uneven texture is desirable in certain breads such as sourdough and French bread
Bread didn't rise high enough	Water was too hot for yeast Too little flour was used Too little kneading Dough was under-risen Pan was too large	Slice thin and serve small pieces
Bread is heavy and dense	Too much flour was used Too little kneading Dough was under-risen	Slice thin and serve small pieces
Bread has a yeasty taste	Dough over-rose Temperature was too high during rise	Let the bread dry 1 day and use to make bread crumbs

b

b

To prevent rising dough from sticking to the plastic wrap used to cover a bowl • Spray the plastic with cooking spray. To do this, spool out the plastic, hold it taut, then spray it before tearing from the roll. Or drape the torn plastic over the bowl, spray the top side, then flip.

To correct for over-risen dough • Punch it down and let it rise again just until doubled. The texture of the loaf may suffer and be a bit denser, but the flavor should be fine.

To salvage dense, under-risen bread • Slice it thin to serve. You can also quarter the thin slices and dry them out in a 200°F oven to make melba toast.

To revive stale bread • Wet your hands and rub them over the surface of the bread before baking at 400°F for about 15 minutes. Or place the bread in a steamer insert or colander set over a pan of boiling water. Cover and steam the bread until softened and warmed through.

Money Saver: Instead of buying a $30 baking stone, purchase $5 unvarnished quarry tiles at your local home-supply store.

TIME SAVERS ▼ **To speed rising** • Use a microwave oven. Place a glass of hot water in the microwave oven with a loosely covered bowl of bread dough. Heat on low power 3 minutes. Allow to rest 2 minutes. Heat 3 minutes more and rest 8 minutes. At this point, the dough should be doubled in bulk. Total rising time: 16 minutes.

To bake bread faster • Baking bread on a baking stone transfers heat to the bottom of the loaf faster, giving it a thicker crust and faster baking time. Heat the stone in the oven for 45 minutes to 1 hour before placing the loaf on it.

To use store-bought frozen bread dough • One of the great convenience foods is frozen, unbaked bread dough. It allows you to quickly make pizza "from scratch," to assemble fresh soft pretzels in minutes, and to make fancy stuffed breads without waiting for the dough to rise. Thaw the dough overnight (about 8 hours) in the refrigerator. The dough will rise as it thaws and be ready to use.

FLAVOR TIPS ▼ **To flavor with herbs or olives** • Knead ⅓ cup chopped fresh herbs or ½ cup pitted, chopped oil-cured black olives into bread dough after the first rise. Shape and rise again before baking.

To flavor breadsticks • Add 2 to 3 teaspoons whole caraway seeds to bread dough after the first rise. Shape and rise again. Brush with beaten egg white and sprinkle with coarse salt before baking.

To make a tricolor dough • Take enough homemade or thawed frozen bread dough to make 1 loaf and divide it into thirds. Take one-third and, using a food processor, knead in 4 tablespoons tomato paste and 2 teaspoons flour (to prevent sticking). To another third, knead in ½ cup thawed, frozen spinach (squeezed very dry), adding flour if needed. Into the remaining third, knead ¼ cup grated Parmesan cheese. Shape into ropes and braid, then bake on a baking sheet or in a loaf pan as directed.

To add flavor and retain moisture • Sauté your favorite vegetable combination, such as finely chopped red onions, bell pepper, chopped garlic, and chopped fresh basil. Cool and knead ¾ cup sautéed vegetables into enough bread dough to make 1 loaf. Bake as directed.

To make stuffed breads • Roll 1 pound yeast dough into a rectangle ½" thick. Sprinkle on a filling, such as fresh sliced spinach and shredded cheese or lay-

Whole Wheat Bread

Great for toasting, this basic bread can be made by hand or in a bread machine.

1⅔ **cups whole wheat flour**

1½ **cups bread flour, divided**

3 **tablespoons packed brown sugar**

1½ **teaspoons active dry yeast**

1 **teaspoon salt**

½ **cup milk**

½ **cup water**

1 **tablespoon vegetable oil**

1. Coat a medium bowl and a 9" × 5" loaf pan with cooking spray.

2. In a large bowl, combine the whole wheat flour, 1 cup of the bread flour, the brown sugar, yeast, and salt.

3. In a small saucepan over medium heat, heat the milk, water, and oil until warm (125° to 130°F). Pour slowly into the flour mixture and beat well. Add enough of the remaining ½ cup bread flour to form a soft dough.

4. Lightly sprinkle a work surface with all-purpose flour. Turn the dough out onto the work surface and knead until smooth and elastic, 8 to 10 minutes, incorporating a little flour if the dough becomes too sticky. Form into a ball and place in the prepared bowl, turning to coat with the cooking spray.

5. Cover the bowl with a damp kitchen towel. Place in a warm spot (80°–90°F) until

doubled in size, 1 hour. Punch down the dough and let it rest 5 minutes.

6. Turn the dough onto the floured work surface, and gently stretch and press into a rectangle roughly 20" × 12". Starting at a narrow end, roll up the dough. Pinch the seams closed on each side and turn them underneath. Place in the prepared pan. Cover with plastic wrap and a towel. Let rise until about ½" above the top of the pan, 30 minutes. Remove the plastic wrap and towel.

7. Preheat the oven to 400°F. Bake until golden brown, 20 to 25 minutes. Remove from the pan and cool on a rack.

Makes one ½-pound loaf (12 slices)

Cinnamon-Raisin Wheat Bread: Stir ¾ cup raisins in with the second addition of bread flour. After rolling the dough into a rectangle, sprinkle with 3 tablespoons sugar and 1 teaspoon ground cinnamon. Roll up and proceed as directed.

Fresh Herb Wheat Bread: Stir 3 tablespoons chopped fresh herbs in with the second addition of bread flour (use one herb, such as rosemary, or a combination, such as 1 tablespoon chopped fresh chives, 1 tablespoon chopped fresh sage, and 1 tablespoon chopped fresh thyme). Roll up and proceed as directed.

b

b

ered cold cuts and chopped artichokes, being careful not to overfill. Roll up, pinch the seams to seal, and let rise again. Make a few steam vents in the top and bake as directed.

To guarantee a soft crumb in sweet yeast breads • For coffee cakes and other sweet yeast breads, use all-purpose flour instead of bread flour. All-purpose flour has more starch and less gluten, which will produce a more tender crumb.

CHEESE BREAD Into **1 pound homemade or thawed frozen bread dough,** knead **1 cup grated sharp cheese** (such as Cheddar, provolone, or even smoked Gouda). Then, work in **½ cup of the same cheese cut into small cubes.** Shape into loaf or rolls and let rise until doubled before baking. Bake as directed. *Makes 1 loaf.*

BROCCOLI RABE AND PEPPERS BAKED IN BREAD Preheat oven to 350°F. Slice hard stem ends from **2 bunches broccoli rabe** and cut rest of stalks in 1"-long sections. Wash thoroughly. Add washed rabe, along with any water still clinging to it, to **2 tablespoons olive oil,** heated in a large nonstick skillet. Add **a large pinch of red-pepper flakes** and season with **¾ teaspoon salt** and **¼ teaspoon ground black pepper.** Cover and simmer over medium heat for 10 minutes. Stir in **1 minced garlic clove** and **1 chopped, roasted red pepper.** Cut top off of a **1-pound round loaf of crusty whole grain bread.** Hollow out interior and fill with broccoli rabe and peppers, layered with **1 cup shredded smoked cheese.** Place top on bread and bake 40 minutes. Serve in wedges. Cool 5 minutes. Serve warm. *Makes 6 servings.*

NEW LIFE FOR OLD BREAD

Here's how to revive yesterday's loaf.

Bread Salad: Tear **½ pound stale Italian bread** into 1" pieces and combine in a large serving bowl with **4 seeded and chopped tomatoes; 1 peeled, seeded, and chopped cucumber; 1 chopped red onion;** and **½ cup torn basil leaves.** In a small bowl, whisk together ½ cup extra virgin olive oil, ¼ cup red wine vinegar, **1 teaspoon salt,** and ¼ teaspoon ground black pepper. Pour onto the salad and toss well. Let stand about 20 minutes before serving. *Makes 4 servings.*

Parmesan Croutons: Cut **1 old baguette** diagonally into ¼"-thick slices. Brush each slice with **melted butter** and sprinkle with **grated Parmesan cheese.** Toast under the broiler until cheese is melted and golden. Serve alongside salads and soups. *Makes 6 servings.*

French Toast: Day-old brioche and white bread is ideal for making French toast. Beat **4 eggs** with **2 cups milk, 1 tablespoon sugar,** and ¼ teaspoon *each* vanilla extract and ground nutmeg. Melt **2 tablespoons butter** in a large skillet over medium heat. Dip 1"-thick slices cut from **1 pound bread** into the egg mixture and fry in hot butter until golden brown, 5 minutes on each side. *Makes 4 servings.*

MAKING FAST FLATBREAD

Flatbreads bake in minutes. The dough need not be special because the crucial factors of making flatbread are how the loaf is rolled and the speed at which it bakes.

How Flatbreads Work: To create the blistered surface and inflated pocket of a classic flatbread, roll the dough to no thicker than ¼". At this thickness, most of the air bubbles in the dough are dispersed horizontally. When the flat loaf is laid on a hot surface, such as the floor of a preheated oven, or an inverted baking sheet, the bottom surface sets up instantly. Air trapped in the dough expands, and all of the bubbles sitting side by side flow into one another, forming one big air pocket. The air pocket begins to grow, causing the still-flexible top of the loaf to separate from the bottom. This is the principle behind pita pockets. Flatbread loaves are baked one or two at a time and then cooled and stacked. As they cool, the air pockets deflate and the breads become flat, but the pockets are still there, allowing each flatbread to be opened up into a vessel that can hold any number of fillings.

To Make Flatbread at Home: Divide 1 pound of bread dough into 4 equal portions and roll each portion into a ball. On a floured board, flatten the balls with your hands and roll with a rolling pin into flat rounds, approximately 8" in diameter and ⅛" thick. Place the flattened bread rounds on a lightly floured cloth. Cover this with another floured cloth and set in a warm spot to rest about 15 minutes. Meanwhile, preheat the oven to 500°F. Place a baking sheet, upside down, in the oven and preheat 5 minutes. Place one or two rounds at a time on the back of the hot, dry pan. Cook 3 to 4 minutes. The bread will swell in the middle and color lightly; do not overcook to reach a dark brown color. Remove from the oven and wrap in a clean cloth to keep moist. The swelling will disappear when the bread is removed from the oven. Continue with the remaining rounds.

b

To make whole grain breads • To convert an all-purpose flour recipe to whole grain, use at least 50 percent high-gluten wheat flour such as bread flour, since non-wheat-grain flours (such as rye and oat flour) lack gluten.

To increase gluten in whole grain breads • When making bread using low-gluten flours such as rye, increase the gluten content by adding gluten flour. This is a high-protein flour treated to remove most of the starch, leaving behind a concentrate of gluten. Add 2 to 3 tablespoons gluten flour to a standard 4-cup bread dough made with low-gluten flour.

To deepen the flavor of whole grain bread • Substitute beer for half of the water in the recipe. The beer will add a deeper, richer, slightly sourdough flavor.

To adjust yeast when reducing fat in bread dough • If you drastically reduce the amount of fat in a bread dough, you may need to reduce the yeast as well. Typically, you should use 1 package yeast for a standard bread loaf using 4 cups flour and 1 to 2 tablespoons fat. Use ½ package yeast if reducing the fat to 2 teaspoons or less.

b

Brines

Concentrated solutions of salt water or salt and sugar water, brines are used to cure, preserve, and flavor a wide variety of foods, including olives, pickles, cheeses, meats, and fish. Homemade brining solutions are one of the best ways to enhance the flavor and texture of meats that tend to be dry, such as turkey and lean cuts of pork. Brining actually makes meat juicier by increasing the amount of liquid inside the meat cells.

BASICS **To brine meat** • Choose a large container made from a nonreactive material such as porcelain, stoneware, or enameled cast iron. It's important that the container be large enough that the meat is completely submerged in the brine. Submerge the meat in the brine and prevent it from floating to the surface by putting a plate on top of it. Weight the plate with a water-filled jar or other heavy object. Avoid using a metal weight, which can react with the brine. If the cut of meat is particularly thick, such as a pork shoulder or fresh ham, pierce it in several places with a sharp skewer to help the brine penetrate the meat. Cover and refrigerate for 3 to 7 days depending on the thickness of the meat. The flavor will become stronger the longer the meat stays submerged in the brine.

BASIC BRINE FOR MEAT In a saucepan, combine **4 cups water** and ¾ **cup** *each* **sugar** and **kosher salt.** Bring to a boil over high heat, stirring until sugar and salt are completely dissolved. Let cool and combine with **3 quarts cold water.** Add **1 teaspoon cracked black peppercorns, 1 thinly sliced celery rib, 1 thinly sliced carrot, ½ small onion cut into thin slices, 3 sprigs** *each* **fresh thyme and fresh parsley,** and **3 bay leaves** to the water. Use as a brine for **1 pound pork** or **poultry.** Proportions can be divided or multiplied as needed. *Makes about 4 quarts.*

Broccoli

Though available year-round, broccoli is a cool-weather vegetable, and its flavor is best from late fall through early spring. Warm-weather broccoli is less tender and lacks the flavor and bright green color of broccoli grown in cooler months.

BASICS **To choose** • Look for firm stalks and firm, tightly bunched heads. Tiny yellow buds on the head signal that broccoli is over the hill. Also, hold a bunch up to your nose and breathe deeply. If it has an odor, leave it behind. For more beta-carotene, choose broccoli with darker tops and a purplish hue. (Don't worry; the purple tinge will turn to green when the vegetable is cooked.) Beta-carotene, which the body converts to the antioxidant vitamin A, has been linked to lower rates of heart attack and lower rates of cataracts and certain cancers.

To remove dirt from a head of broccoli • Soak it upside down in a bowl of cold water for 20 minutes.

To store • Cut a slice off the bottom of the stalk and put the head of broccoli, stem end down, in a large glass of water. Cover the top loosely with a plastic bag and refrigerate for up to 1 week.

To use the stems • After you've chopped off the florets, peel the stems and cut them into coins or batons to use in stir-fries or as a raw vegetable for dipping.

PROBLEM SOLVERS **To revive limp, uncooked broccoli** • Trim ½" from the base of the stalk and set the head in a glass of cold water in the refrigerator overnight.

THREE QUICK DISHES WITH FROZEN BROCCOLI

Frozen broccoli saves loads of time without sacrificing quality.

Broccoli-Tarragon Soup: In a saucepan over medium heat, combine **2 boxes (10 ounces each) frozen broccoli pieces, a large pinch of dried tarragon,** and **4 cups chicken broth.** Simmer 7 minutes. Puree until smooth in a food processor or blender. Season with **¼ teaspoon salt** and **⅛ teaspoon ground black pepper.** Reheat over low heat and serve. *Makes 4 servings.*

Pasta with Broccoli, Garlic, and Cheese: In a large pot of salted boiling water, cook **1 pound shaped pasta** (such as ziti or radiatore) until tender yet firm to the bite, 7 to 9 minutes. Three minutes before pasta is finished cooking, add **1 box (10 ounces) thawed frozen broccoli pieces.** At the end of the cooking time, drain pasta and broccoli. Toss with **1 minced garlic clove, 3 tablespoons extra-virgin olive oil, ½ cup freshly grated Romano cheese, ¼ teaspoon salt,** and **⅛ teaspoon ground black pepper.** *Makes 4 servings.*

Stir-Fried Broccoli with Hoisin Almonds: In a wok or large skillet, stir-fry **1 whole garlic clove** in **2 tablespoons oil** over medium-high heat until browned. Remove and discard. Add **½ chopped onion** and stir-fry until soft. Add **⅛ teaspoon red-pepper flakes** and **2 thawed packages (10 ounces each) frozen broccoli stalks.** Cover until heated through, about 2 minutes. Add **⅓ cup sliced toasted almonds, 1 tablespoon hoisin sauce,** and **1 teaspoon sugar.** Heat through. *Makes 4 servings.*

To cook limp broccoli • Steam-boil in a shallow pan of water, adding a pinch *each* salt and sugar per cup of cooking water.

To brighten the color • Blanch (see page 47) or quick-cook over high heat.

To avoid gray-green broccoli • Do not add acids, such as lemon juice or vinegar, to the cooking water. If desired, add them after cooking instead.

To prevent a sulfurous smell or taste • Avoid overcooking. If steaming, only partially cover the broccoli, and if boiling, don't cover it, so that the vegetable's natural sulfur compounds can escape. You can also place a piece of bread on top of the cooking broccoli to absorb some of the odor. Never cook broccoli in an aluminum pan, or the odor will worsen.

To rescue overcooked broccoli • Chop it fine and toss it with rice and seasonings, sprinkle over baked potatoes, and top with melted cheese.

To prevent slightly overcooked broccoli from cooking further • Drain immediately and rinse with cold water.

TIME SAVERS ▼

To quickly cut a head of broccoli into florets • Cut off the stalk crosswise as close

b

to the florets as possible, cutting through the small stems that attach the bottom layer of florets to the stalk. The bottom layer of florets will fall away from the stalk. Continue cutting across the stalk through the stems on the next layer of florets. Repeat until all florets have been removed.

To save time when cooking with pasta or rice • Like all vegetables, broccoli can be cooked along with pasta or rice. Add trimmed and cut broccoli to cooking pasta or rice 3 minutes before it is scheduled to be done.

To avoid peeling and slicing stems • Buy packaged broccoli slaw. It makes an easy addition to stir-fries.

FLAVOR TIPS
▼

To use broccoli in a stir-fry • Blanch it first. The texture and flavor will be much improved. Drop into a large pot of boiling, salted water and cook until the stems can be pierced with the tip of a knife but before the bright green color starts to fade.

To preserve the flavor and texture of blanched broccoli • Don't plunge it in a bowl of cold water. Instead, lay it on a plate or tray in a single layer and let it come to room temperature.

To dress with vinaigrette • Cut florets from a large head of broccoli. Blanch or steam florets. Toss with ½ cup vinaigrette (see page 422). To serve cold, cool broccoli first, then toss with dressing.

BROCCOLI "MOPS" WITH GINGER SAUCE Cut florets from **1 large head broccoli** (you'll have about 40); drop into a large pot of boiling salted water. Cook over high heat just until tender, about 3 minutes after boil returns. Drain and cover to keep warm. In a small saucepan, combine **1 tablespoon** *each* **vegetable oil**

FOUR IDEAS FOR STEAMED BROCCOLI

Toss these dressings with steamed florets from a large head of broccoli.

Chinese Broccoli: Combine ¼ cup bottled stir-fry sauce, 2 teaspoons rice vinegar, and 1 teaspoon grated fresh ginger. Sprinkle with ½ teaspoon toasted sesame seeds.

Orange-Fennel Broccoli: Combine ½ cup orange juice, 1 tablespoon extra-virgin olive oil, 1 teaspoon grated orange zest, and ½ teaspoon crushed fennel.

Broccoli with Blue Cheese: Combine ⅓ cup bottled blue cheese dressing, 3 tablespoons plain yogurt, 2 tablespoons chopped fresh chives, and ½ teaspoon lemon juice.

Mediterranean Broccoli: Combine ½ cup vinaigrette and 1 tablespoon *each* chopped, rehydrated sun-dried tomatoes and pitted kalamata olives.

---

and minced fresh ginger, and **1 minced garlic clove;** sauté gently over low heat. In a bowl, stir together **1 tablespoon** *each* **cornstarch, dry sherry, and soy sauce;** stir in **1 cup chicken broth, 2 teaspoons rice vinegar,** and **1 teaspoon sugar.** Add to ginger mixture and cook, stirring, until thickened and simmering. Stir in **1 teaspoon toasted sesame oil** and **2 thinly sliced scallions.** Pour sauce onto a warm platter and arrange broccoli mops, stem ends up, in sauce. Serve hot or warm. Great appetizer or side dish. *Makes 4 servings.*

BATTERED BROCCOLI Cut **1 head broccoli** into 1" to 1½" florets. Drop several florets into chilled **Beer Batter** (page 40) to coat. Place in a deep fryer with about 2" of vegetable oil at 365°F and fry until golden brown, about 3 minutes. Drain on paper towels and sprinkle lightly with salt. Repeat with remaining broccoli and serve hot. If desired, serve with lemon wedges or flavored mayonnaise such as **Lemon-Basil Mayonnaise** (page 273). *Makes 6 servings.*

HEALTHY HINT ▼ **To preserve nutrients** • Avoid overcooking, which destroys broccoli's protective compounds. Gentle cooking helps preserve the beta-carotene. For maximum nutrient retention, lightly steam or microwave broccoli until tender-crisp.

Broccoli Rabe

This slightly bitter, peppery green (also called broccoli raab or rapini) is a classic Italian vegetable in many pasta dishes.

FLAVOR TIPS ▼ **To miminize bitterness** • If you are a newcomer to broccoli rabe, try blanching it in salted, boiling water for 2 to 3 minutes to minimize its bitter flavor. Once blanched, it can be sautéed in olive oil with garlic, red-pepper flakes, or other seasonings of your choice.

To retain bitterness • Many people enjoy the peppery bite of broccoli rabe. If that's you, sauté the vegetable in olive oil, adding the seasonings of your choice.

To use young leaves • When broccoli rabe is young, the leaves can be used uncooked, like arugula, adding a slightly sweet, mustardy bite to salads and sandwiches. You can also add young leaves to stir-fries. As the vegetable ages, the leaves develop a more bitter flavor.

Fascinating Fact: Broccoli rabe is actually a member of the turnip family (*rapa* is Italian for "turnip").

Broiling

Defined as cooking directly beneath a heat source, broiling is a high-heat, quick-cooking method that produces browned food with a juicy, tender interior. The intense heat causes the natural sugars in foods to caramelize more quickly. That's why broiled steaks, poultry, and other meats are so flavorful. That's also what creates the delectably brittle caramel atop crème brûlée.

BASICS ▼ **To choose foods for broiling** • Select lean, tender foods that are not too thick. Thin cuts of meat, such as chicken breasts, veal or pork cutlets, hamburgers, or steaks, and fish fillets are ideal.

To get a crisp crust using a broiler • If your oven-baked gratin is cooked through but the surface has not developed a crisp crust, put the dish under a hot broiler until the top is browned and crisp. You can also use the broiler to melt cheese on a pizza or frittata.

PROBLEM SOLVERS ▼ **To reduce the risk of flare-ups** • Trim excess fat from meats before broiling.

To prevent foods from drying out • Brush or spray them with oil.

To soak up grease and prevent possible fires • Scatter pieces of bread in the pan under the broiler rack.

To prevent broiled fish or meat from steam-cooking • Leave the oven door ajar so that steaming juices can escape.

To prevent burning thick foods • When broiling foods that take time to cook through, such as butterflied chicken, move them farther from the heat source by lowering the oven rack.

b

To save preheating time • If broiling something for longer than 5 minutes, there is no need to preheat the broiler. Just allow a bit more time for the top side of the food to cook. For instance, a steak that broils for 7 minutes per side will take 8 minutes for the first side and 6 minutes for the flip side when placed under a broiler that has not been preheated.

To make cleanup easy • Line the broiling rack with foil, cutting through the foil to correspond with the drain slits.

Broth *see also* Stock

Let's face it: Most home cooks don't make stock anymore. Instead, we turn to the supermarket for this essential liquid used to make soups, sauces, braised dishes, and stir-fries, or for cooking grains. Most store-bought broth is riddled with additives, heavy on the salt, and not very flavorful. Here's how to make the most of broths, bases, and bouillons, whether they be canned, frozen, or aseptically packaged.

BASICS **To get the best flavor** • Choose broths sold in aseptic packaging. These undergo a flash heating and cooling process that helps preserve what little flavor commercial broths have. Also, look for reduced-sodium broths, which taste more like homemade than fully salted products. Reduced-sodium broth is particularly important if the broth will be reduced or simmered for extended periods, as in many sauces and soups. Starting with reduced-sodium broth ensures that, after extended cooking, the broth doesn't become unpleasantly salty. It's easier to add salt than to remove it.

To avoid monosodium glutamate (MSG) • Avoid bouillon cubes. They are almost certain to contain MSG and tend to taste like little more than salt and dried onion powder.

To avoid watery broth • It's best not to use frozen broth products, which are expensive yet taste remarkably watery.

To store unused portions of canned broth • Transfer to an airtight plastic container so that it doesn't pick up a metallic taste from the can. Use within 3 days.

To track the expiration date on an aseptic box of broth • After opening, mark the last possible use date in bold marker on the box (most aseptic broths last 2 weeks after opening).

**PROBLEM
SOLVER
▼** **To reduce saltiness** • If your broth (or the dish that it is used in) tastes too salty, toss in a few thin slices of raw potato during cooking and let cook until the potatoes become translucent. At that point, the potatoes will have absorbed much of the excess salt flavor.

**FLAVOR
TIPS
▼** **To doctor up flavor in store-bought broth** • Chicken bones are the ideal flavor booster. If you are in the habit of boning your chicken, keep a zipper-lock plastic bag of the uncooked bones in the freezer. Chop the bones as needed to release maximum flavor. In a saucepan, combine ½ cup chopped chicken bones and 1 quart store-bought chicken broth. Bring to a boil. Reduce the heat to low and simmer 30 minutes. Before using, strain and discard solids. For more flavor, sauté 1 chopped carrot, 1 chopped rib of celery, and 1 chopped onion in the saucepan before adding the bones. Cook the bones for 5 minutes, then add the broth. Here's another quick fix: Stir in 1 envelope (¼ ounce) unflavored gelatin per gallon of cool broth. Reheat until gelatin dissolves. This will give

the broth the flavor and mouthfeel of freshly made stock. Use immediately or freeze.

QUICK FISH BROTH In a large saucepan, combine **1 chopped carrot, 1 chopped celery rib,** and **1 chopped onion.** Cover and cook over medium-low heat until vegetables begin to release moisture, 3 minutes. Stir and add water if needed to prevent sticking. Uncover and cook until vegetables start to soften, 5 minutes. Raise the heat to high, add **1 cup white wine,** and boil vigorously 1 minute. Add **juice of ½ lemon, 2 fresh parsley sprigs, 5 cups water,** and **2 fish bouillon cubes** or **¼ cup bonito flakes** (available in Asian groceries). Reduce heat to medium and simmer 5 minutes. Strain and discard solids. *Makes 6 cups.*

HEALTHY HINT ▼ **To defat canned broth** • If using broth that's not fat-free, store the unopened can in the refrigerator for at least 6 hours. When you open the can, the fat will have congealed for easy removal. If you're in a hurry, put the can (opened or unopened) in the freezer for 15 to 30 minutes.

Brownies *see also* Chocolate;
Cocoa Powder

Part cookie, part cake, brownies are one of the best loved of all baked goods.

BASICS ▼ **To help brownies stay moist longer** • Let them cool completely before cutting. When cut too soon, brownies will release their moisture in the form of steam and dry out more quickly.

To test for doneness • Start checking the brownies 5 to 10 minutes before they are scheduled to be done. Do not insert a toothpick in the center of the brownies. Instead, insert it halfway between the center and the edge. If the brownies are done, the toothpick should come out clean. With some recipes, though, especially for fudgy brownies, you might want some moist crumbs adhering to the toothpick. Underdone brownies are always better than overdone brownies. If your brownies do come out a bit underdone, place them in the refrigerator to firm up.

To slice • Cool the brownies completely. Then, if you have removed the entire pan of cooked brownies from the pan, use a pizza cutter or thin-bladed knife.

To enjoy frozen • Cut up cooled brownies into small squares and freeze solid on a baking sheet. Transfer to a zipper-lock freezer bag and store in the freezer. These frozen treats are especially satisfying during hot summer months.

PROBLEM SOLVERS ▼ **To easily remove from the pan** • Lay a strip of heavy-duty aluminum foil (or a double layer of standard foil) across the pan before adding the batter. The strip should be wide enough to cover the base of the pan and long enough on each end to fold over the pan's edge. This creates a sling so that once the brownies have cooled, you can lift the entire pan out by grabbing each end of the foil. This also avoids wasting any precious brownies and makes the pan much easier to clean.

To save dry, overcooked brownies • Soak in hot chocolate or hot fudge for 10 minutes before serving and top with ice cream or whipped cream.

To revive slightly stale brownies • Place in a colander over boiling water and steam until softened through.

b

Fudgy, Cakey Brownies

To get both a fudgy and cakey brownie, you need to mix 2 chocolate types: unsweetened chocolate and semisweet chocolate (in the form of chocolate chips, a bar, or a block). The unsweetened chocolate drives forth a resonant chocolate flavor with a bitter edge. The semisweet chocolate adds a sugary essence that smoothes out the rough edges of the unsweetened chocolate. Just under a cup of flour gives the brownie some body and crumb without dryness. The butter, not quite a full stick, delivers a moist chew without making the brownie too dense.

5 **ounces unsweetened chocolate**

2 **ounces semisweet chocolate**

6 **tablespoons butter**

1 **cup + 2 tablespoons sugar**

3 **eggs**

1 **tablespoon vanilla extract**

½ **teaspoon salt**

¾ **cup all-purpose flour**

1. Adjust the oven rack to the lower-middle position. Preheat the oven to 350°F. Grease an 8" × 8" baking pan.

2. Fit a medium-size, heatproof bowl over a medium saucepan containing 1" of barely simmering water. Add the unsweetened chocolate, semisweet chocolate, and butter to melt. Stir frequently until completely melted and smooth. Remove the bowl from the pan to cool slightly.

3. In a medium bowl, whisk together the sugar, eggs, vanilla extract, and salt until blended. Whisk in the chocolate mixture. With a rubber spatula, stir in the flour until just blended. Spread the batter evenly into the prepared baking pan. Bake until a wooden pick inserted in the center comes out with a few crumbs on it, 35 to 40 minutes. Transfer to a rack to cool completely before cutting into squares.

Makes 16

Fudgy, Cakey Brownies with White Chocolate and Macadamia Nuts: Stir 4 ounces white chocolate chips (or chopped white chocolate) and ½ cup macadamia nuts, chopped, into the batter before spreading it into the pan.

FLAVOR TIPS ▼ **To add flavor** • Stir ¼ to ½ teaspoon ground cinnamon in with the flour and ½ teaspoon pure almond extract in with the vanilla extract in a standard recipe that makes an 8" × 8" pan of brownies. Or stir 1 teaspoon instant espresso powder in with the flour in a standard brownie recipe.

To make light-textured brownies • Increase the number of eggs and beat the batter until it forms a flat ribbon, falling back on itself when the beater is lifted. Or increase the amount of leavener.

To make firm-textured brownies • Use fewer eggs and beat lightly.

To make brownies with an ultra-smooth texture • Use cake flour instead of all-purpose flour.

HEALTHY HINT ▼ To reduce fat • Replace up to one-fourth of the fat with an equal amount of a liquid sweetener such as honey, corn syrup, chocolate syrup, molasses, or fruit jam. For example, in a recipe with ½ cup butter, use 6 tablespoons butter and 2 tablespoons liquid sweetener. Or, use half the amount of fat called for and add half that amount of drained, unsweetened applesauce. For example, to replace 1 cup butter, use ½ cup butter and ¼ cup applesauce. Or, replace each ounce of solid chocolate with 3 tablespoons unsweetened cocoa powder. For each ounce replaced, add ⅛ teaspoon instant coffee or espresso powder to deepen the flavor.

Browning *see also* Searing

The term *browning* may refer to several different processes. The most common type of browning, also known as the Maillard reaction, refers to a series of chemical reactions that makes foods from cookies to fried chicken and grilled steaks taste and look more appetizing. As the sugars in any food are heated, they change color from clear to dark brown and produce new flavor compounds. Browning is also an effective way to kill surface bacteria on meats. A similar type of browning is known as caramelization: This is what happens to white sugar at high temperatures. Another, less desirable, browning is what happens to certain fruits and vegetables when phenolic compounds in their flesh react with oxygen in the air to discolor the food.

BASICS ▼ To brown meats • Pat dry and place in a medium-hot pan and cook, turning occasionally, until browned all over.

To ensure even browning of meats • Avoid crowding the meat in the pan. Without enough room around the meat to allow for quick evaporation of moisture, the meat will steam instead of browning.

To brown roasted meats • Increase the oven temperature at the end of cooking time. By that point, the juices, which contain many sugars and proteins, will have risen to the surface and will aid in browning the surface of the meat.

To delay browning in fried foods • Use a low-protein flour or cornstarch for dusting or in a batter. Or eliminate any sugar called for in the batter. Or add a little lemon juice or vinegar to the batter to make it more acidic.

TIME SAVER ▼ To brown faster • Use a broiler, a grill, or a very hot oven. Browning ingredients this way frees you up to do other tasks in the kitchen. If the food to be browned this way is low in fat, a light coating of oil will help it brown more evenly and quickly. Also, to prevent flare-ups when browning at high heat, remove large deposits of fat from meats before browning. To brown under a broiler or on a grill, place the food about 3" from the heat (using a hot fire on a grill). To brown in an oven, preheat the oven to 500°F and roast the food until browned, usually about 15 minutes.

FLAVOR TIPS ▼ To brown for extra flavor and color • Brown the meat without a flour coating. This will develop flavors in the meat

b

b

rather than just browning the flour. After browning uncoated meat, deglaze the pan by adding liquid and scraping up the browned bits of caramelized meat juices in the pan. These browned bits will dissolve and add depth of flavor, creating the basis for a sauce.

To blacken • This technique is essentially the same as browning but more intensely so. Char the meat until dark brown or nearly black, but not burnt.

Bruschetta and Crostini

Both bruschetta (pronounced "broo-SKEH-tah" or "broo-SHEH-tah") and crostini are slices of toasted bread with some sort of topping, which can be as simple as garlic and olive oil (the original garlic bread). See "Bruschetta and Crostini Appetizers" on the opposite page.

BASICS ▼ **To distinguish and serve** • Some sources claim that bruschetta stems from the Italian verb *bruscare,* meaning "to toast or roast." Others translate the name as "little burnt ones" or as "roasted over coals." In general, bruschetta is made from thicker and larger slices of crusty bread than crostini and is often grilled until the edges are charred. Bruschetta can also be toasted in the oven or fried in a skillet with olive oil. Crostini are usually smaller, sometimes cut on an angle from long, narrow loaves of bread and sometimes with the crusts removed. They are more like toasted canapés. To confuse things a bit more, in Tuscany, bruschetta may be called *fettunta,* which means "under the oil." Indeed, olive oil is just as important as the bread, whether you are making crostini, bruschetta, or fettunta. Think of all of them as appetizers, hors d'oeuvres, or canapés.

Brussels Sprouts

Brussels sprouts have to be one of the most hated of all vegetables, but it's not the little cabbage's fault. We just take too long to cook them. The solution? Quick-cooking avoids the release of unpleasant sulfur compounds and preserves the vegetable's delicate, nutty flavor.

BASICS ▼ **To choose** • Pick the sprouts up and hold them in your hand. You want the ones that are heavy for their size. If you are lucky enough to find Brussels sprouts still on the stalk, buy the smallest stalk; it will have the sweetest sprouts.

To clean • Soak Brussels sprouts in cold salt water for 20 minutes. This will loosen any debris that may be trapped in the leaves.

To trim • Remove the stem and any loose leaves.

PROBLEM SOLVERS ▼ **To cook evenly through** • Cut an X into the stems of Brussels sprouts. Or cut the sprouts in half.

To prevent Brussels sprouts from becoming bitter • Cook within 3 days of purchasing. Also avoid overcooking, which can cause bitterness as well as destroy vitamin C.

To salvage overcooked Brussels sprouts • Cut in half, spread across a baking pan, cover in a mixture of bread crumbs and Parmesan cheese, dot with butter, and place under a broiler until bread crumbs are toasty brown.

TIME SAVER ▼ **To quick-cook Brussels sprouts and help seal in flavor** • Slice them thin and stir-fry them. Or steam individual leaves. You can also sauté individual leaves.

b

BRUSCHETTA AND CROSTINI APPETIZERS

To make any of these appetizers, take a serrated knife and slice a loaf of long, narrow bread (such as a baguette) into thin slices, about ½" to ¾" thick for bruschetta and only ¼" thick for crostini. Toast using one of the toasting methods below. Then, while the bread is still warm, rub with a cut garlic clove and brush, drizzle, or spray with olive oil. (The garlic will be juicier if you smash it first.) Finally, top the bread with one of the toppings below. Each makes enough to top the slices of 1 baguette, about 16 pieces.

Toasting Methods

Over Charcoal: Grill bread slices over a medium-hot fire until edges begin to char slightly. Turn and toast the other side.

Under the Broiler: Toast bread under the broiler, turning once, until golden.

In a Grill Pan: Heat a grill pan on the stove top for 5 minutes. Arrange bread slices all over and toast until golden with darker edges, 3 to 5 minutes, turning once.

In the Oven: Preheat the oven to 400°F. Arrange bread slices directly on the oven rack for bruschetta or on a baking sheet for crostini. Bake until golden on both sides, turning once, 5 to 6 minutes.

Toppings

Tomato-Basil: Cut **6 to 8 ripe plum tomatoes** in half lengthwise. Cut out cores and gently squeeze out seeds. Finely chop tomatoes and mix with ½ **cup shredded fresh basil, 1 to 2 tablespoons olive oil,** ½

teaspoon salt, and ¼ **teaspoon ground black pepper.**

Grilled Zucchini: Preheat a grill or broiler. Cut **2 small zucchini** lengthwise into slices about ¼" thick. Brush with **olive oil** and grill or broil over medium heat until softened and charred on both sides. Cut into lengths to match toast. Spread ½ **teaspoon pesto** over each toast and top with **1 piece zucchini** and ½ teaspoon grated Parmesan cheese.

Chicken Livers with Sage: Melt **1 tablespoon butter** in a medium skillet over medium heat. Add **1 finely chopped onion** and sauté to soften, 3 to 5 minutes. Cut ½ **pound chicken livers** in half. Sprinkle **2 tablespoons flour** on a plate. Add livers and toss to coat. Add to the skillet along with **2 tablespoons chopped fresh sage,** ½ **teaspoon salt,** and **a pinch of ground black pepper.** Cook until livers are cooked through and firm, 4 to 5 minutes, stirring occasionally. Stir in **2 tablespoons dry sherry or red wine.** Remove from the heat and add **2 tablespoons chopped fresh parsley.** Mash livers slightly with a fork. Let cool. Mound 1 tablespoon onto each toast.

Mediterranean Olive: In a food processor, combine ¾ **cup pitted kalamata olives, 4 flat anchovy fillets, 3 tablespoons olive oil, 2 tablespoons capers, 1 tablespoon** *each* **Dijon mustard and lemon juice,** and ¼ **teaspoon ground black pepper.** Process to a coarse puree and mound 1 tablespoon on each toast.

b

HEALTHY, HIGH-FLAVOR SAUCES FOR BRUSSELS SPROUTS

These simple sauces make enough for ½ pound of Brussels sprouts, trimmed and cooked (about 4 servings).

Mediterranean: In a skillet, warm **3 tablespoons light balsamic vinaigrette** with **1 tablespoon finely chopped, rehydrated sun-dried tomatoes** and **1 teaspoon chopped fresh chives or scallions.**

Swiss Cheese: Stir **¼ cup shredded reduced-fat Swiss cheese** and **1 teaspoon Dijon mustard** into **½ cup prepared Basic White Sauce** (page 439).

Creamy Tarragon: In a saucepan, warm (but do not boil) **3 tablespoons reduced-fat sour cream.** Add **1 tablespoon chopped fresh tarragon, 1 teaspoon olive oil,** and **½ teaspoon lemon juice.**

Bacon and Shallot: Sauté **2 tablespoons** *each* chopped **Canadian bacon and shallots** in **1 tablespoon olive oil** until bacon is cooked through and shallots are soft, 4 minutes. Deglaze the pan with **¼ cup white wine** or **chicken broth.**

Chef's Tip: To avoid the strong cooking odor of Brussels sprouts that are boiled or steamed, add a rib of celery or a sprinkling of caraway seeds to the cooking water.

MICROWAVED BRUSSELS SPROUTS Trim **½ pound Brussels sprouts.** Cut in quarters and place in a microwaveable dish large enough to fit sprouts in a single layer. Drizzle with **2 tablespoons milk** and season with **¼ teaspoon salt** and **⅛ teaspoon ground black pepper.** Cover and microwave on high power just until tender, 3 minutes. *Makes 4 servings.*

BRUSSELS SPROUTS SAUTÉED WITH BACON AND APPLES Trim **½ pound Brussels sprouts** and slice in half lengthwise. Place on flat sides and cut into thin shreds, starting at rounded ends. In a large skillet over medium-high heat, cook **2 slices chopped bacon** until crisp and cooked

through. Add **2 tablespoons chopped onion** and **1 peeled and chopped apple;** cook and stir until softened, about 3 minutes. Add shredded sprouts and toss until sprouts are lightly browned and tender. Season with **¼ teaspoon salt** and **⅛ teaspoon ground black pepper** anytime during cooking. *Makes 4 servings.*

Fascinating Fact: While many vegetables are destroyed by autumn's first frost, Brussels sprouts are at their sweetest after the season's first frost.

Buffalo Sauce

One of the great flavor combinations of the second half of the 20th century is also one of the easiest to prepare and most versatile. It is the elixir—fiery and tangy, lush and spare—that we call Buffalo. Though made infamous on chicken wings, Buffalo sauce is equally magical on burgers, fried fish, and roasted potatoes.

b

FOUR SPINS ON BUFFALO SAUCE

Here's a basic sauce and some novel foods to "Buffalize" (each recipe makes 4 servings).

Buffalo Sauce: Melt **1 stick (½ cup) butter** and mix in **⅓ cup mild hot-pepper sauce.** Keep warm or refrigerate for up to 2 weeks and reheat as needed. *Makes ¾ cup.*

Buffalo Spuds: Slice **4 baking potatoes** lengthwise into 8 to 10 wedges each. Toss in a large roasting pan with **1 tablespoon melted butter** and **1 teaspoon salt.** Roast in a 425°F oven, 45 minutes, turning once halfway through. Toss with **¼ cup warmed Buffalo Sauce.**

Grilled Buffalo Burgers: Preheat a grill or broiler. Mix **1 pound ground beef; ½ teaspoon** *each* **garlic powder, onion powder, and salt;** and **⅛ teaspoon ground black pepper.** Form into 4 burgers and grill close to a hot flame or broil until meat is no longer pink and registers 160°F internal temperature on an instant-read thermometer, 5 to 6 minutes per side. Place on 4 toasted buns and divide **6 tablespoons Buffalo Sauce** among the burgers and buns. Top with **1 tablespoon bottled blue cheese dressing** each (¼ cup total) and serve.

Buffalo Fins: Cook **1½ pounds breaded fish fillets** according to recipe or package directions. Drizzle fillets all over with **6 tablespoons Buffalo Sauce.**

Buffalo Drumsticks: Fry **3 pounds small chicken drumsticks** in several inches of oil at 350°F until an instant-read thermometer registers 170°F internal temperature and juices run clear, about 15 minutes. Chicken should be crisp and brown. Remove, drain on paper towels, and toss in a large bowl with **¾ cup Buffalo Sauce.**

FLAVOR TIP ▼ **To choose a hot-pepper sauce for Buffalo sauce** • Although many hot sauces recommend themselves for Buffalo, choose one that is not too hot. Mild hot-pepper sauces such as Crystal Hot Sauce and Frank's Original RedHot Cayenne Pepper Sauce have a balance of pepper and vinegary tang. Because they are not overly fiery, you can add more without worrying about going over the top.

Bulgur

Bulgur is a chopped form of the whole wheat berry. It contains all the components of the whole wheat grain: the bran, the endosperm, and the germ. The germ, or the nutritional core of wheat, accounts for only 3 percent of the berry, yet contains 23 different nutrients, making it a powerhouse of nutrition. This form of wheat is cracked and dried, giving rise to its other moniker, cracked wheat. It needs no cooking, just a soaking. But it can withstand cooking in pilafs and stuffings. It is available in fine, medium, and coarse granulation. It is a crucial part of the Middle Eastern salad known as tabbouleh.

BASICS ▼ **To use** • Place bulgur in a sieve and rinse under barely warm running water until the water runs clear. Transfer to a bowl, cover generously with barely warm water, and let soak until softened, 20 to 45 min-

b

utes. Drain any excess water. For cooked dishes such as pilaf or stuffed peppers, skip the soaking step. Just drain the bulgur in a fine sieve, pressing to squeeze out water; or wrap it in several layers of cheesecloth and squeeze out excess water. Make sure that the recipe includes a moderate amount of liquid to plump up the grains during cooking.

TABBOULEH SALAD Rinse **1 cup medium bulgur.** Soak about 1 hour, then drain and squeeze out excess water. Add **1 large chopped tomato,** ½ **chopped green bell pepper,** and **1 peeled, seeded, and chopped cucumber.** Add **4 large sliced scallions** and ⅓ **cup** *each* **chopped fresh parsley and chopped fresh mint.** Toss with ½ **teaspoon salt** and ¼ **teaspoon ground black pepper.** Drizzle **3 tablespoons lemon juice** and ¼ **cup olive oil** on salad. Toss again and chill 1 hour. *Makes 4 to 6 servings.*

HEALTHY HINT ▼ **To use in place of ground meat •** Replace up to one-fourth of the ground meat in your recipe with softened bulgur. This works in meat loaves, meatballs, burgers, chilis, and stuffings.

Burgers *see also* Beef; Grilling

Typically made of ground beef, these unfussy sandwiches are one of America's best-loved meals. The secret to making a good ground-beef hamburger is to keep it simple. Use the best quality ground beef, season it simply, handle it gently, and you can't go wrong. You can also make burgers with ground turkey or chicken, or make veggie burgers with vegetables and/or beans.

BASICS ▼ **To choose beef for burgers •** Buy the best meat you can and don't skimp on fat. Meat with 10 percent to 15 percent fat makes the most flavorful, juicy burgers. Having it ground fresh by the butcher is best. A blend of ground sirloin and chuck makes tender burgers with a rich flavor.

To make juicy hamburgers • Avoid making the burgers too big. Oversize burgers need more time to cook, which can dry out the surface of the meat before the inside is done. Five ounces of raw beef makes a perfect burger.

To shape ground beef for hamburgers • Handle the meat as little as possible. Shape each patty by lightly passing 5 ounces of meat back and forth between your cupped hands until it's about ¾" thick and about 3½" in diameter. Handle the meat just as long as it takes to make the patty. Overhandling the meat will make the burger tougher.

To cook • Let the shaped hamburger patties sit at room temperature for about 5 minutes before cooking. The meat should feel cool but not cold to the touch. If the meat is too cold, the burgers will cook unevenly. Also, cook hamburgers on a flat surface. A well-seasoned cast iron griddle is ideal. Some prefer open grills, but these allow valuable juices to escape, and the flavor of the charcoal interferes with the pure beef taste of the meat. Avoid pressing down on the burger with a spatula as it cooks. This forces out the juices that keep the meat tender and give it flavor.

Fascinating Fact: The road to the modern-day hamburger was indeed paved in Hamburg, Germany, where shredded raw meat (steak tartare) was popular. The bun was an American innovation.

Rosemary Portobello Burgers

Marinated portobello mushrooms make meaty, juicy burgers that cook perfectly on a grill or even over a wood campfire. Serve on buns with no adornments or with a bit of flavored mayonnaise, if desired.

- **4 portobello mushroom caps**
- **2 tablespoons extra-virgin olive oil**
- **2 tablespoons tamari or soy sauce**
- **2 tablespoons chopped fresh rosemary**
- **3 garlic cloves, minced**
- **1½ teaspoons toasted sesame oil**
- **1½ teaspoons pure maple syrup**
- **¼ teaspoon salt**
- **¼ teaspoon ground black pepper**
- **4 kaiser rolls or hamburger buns**

1. Brush any loose dirt from the mushrooms and set aside.

2. In a large zipper-lock plastic bag, combine the olive oil, tamari or soy sauce, rosemary, garlic, sesame oil, maple syrup, salt, and pepper. Seal the bag, shake to mix, then lay the bag flat to distribute the marinade evenly. Open the bag and slide in the mushrooms, gill side down, fitting them in 2 rows of 2. Seal the bag and quickly turn it over. Using your hands on the outside of the bag, coat the mushrooms completely with marinade. Let rest at room temperature at least 15 minutes or up to 6 hours.

3. Preheat the grill or broiler.

4. Remove the mushrooms from the bag. Place, gill side up, on the grill rack or broiler pan. Grill or broil over medium heat 5 to 8 minutes, pouring or brushing half of the marinade from the bag over the mushrooms. Turn over and cook until the centers are fork-tender, 4 to 6 minutes longer. Pour the remaining marinade over the mushrooms.

5. Toast the rolls and serve the mushrooms on the rolls.

Makes 4 servings

PROBLEM SOLVERS ▼

To form even-size burgers • Divide the total weight of the meat you are using by the number of burgers desired. Then use a scale to weigh out each burger.

To keep ground beef from sticking to your hands • Wet your hands with cold water.

To rescue a hamburger that is burnt on the outside • Gently saw off the crust with a bread knife.

To rescue an overcooked burger • Slice in half horizontally and tuck a slice of cheese in the center. At least it's a distraction.

Turkey Burgers

The appeal of turkey burgers is that they are healthful. The drawback is that they are not beefy in flavor or texture. Mushrooms and soy sauce help deepen the savory flavor of these turkey burgers, bringing the taste closer to a "real" burger. The egg white also helps bind the supple turkey meat into hearty patties.

- **5 ounces white mushrooms**
- **1 tablespoon butter**
- **1 pound ground turkey**
- **1 egg white**
- **1 tablespoon + 1 teaspoon soy sauce**
- **½ teaspoon salt**
- **½ teaspoon ground black pepper**

1. In a food processor, pulse the mushrooms until coarsely ground.

2. Melt the butter in a large skillet over medium heat. Add the mushrooms. Cook until the mushrooms begin to give up their liquid, 5 minutes, stirring occasionally. Remove from the heat to cool.

3. In a medium bowl, combine the turkey, egg white, soy sauce, salt, pepper, and cooled mushroom mixture. Form into 4 patties.

4. Wipe any mushroom juices out of the skillet. Place over medium-high heat. When the pan is hot, liberally coat it with cooking spray. Add the burgers and cook until well-browned, 3 to 4 minutes per side. Reduce the heat to medium-low and cook until a thermometer inserted in the center registers 165°F and the meat is no longer pink (another 2 minutes per side).

Makes 4 servings

Southern California Turkey Burgers: Top each cooked burger with a slice of avocado, ¼ cup alfalfa sprouts, a thick slice of tomato, and a thin slice of red onion.

Turkey Barbecue Burgers: Replace the soy sauce with barbecue sauce.

Bacon and Cheese Turkey Burgers: After flipping the burgers, top each with a slice of crisp cooked bacon (regular or turkey), halved, and 1 ounce sliced Gruyère, Cheddar, or blue cheese. If the cheese doesn't melt by the time the burger is done, shake a few drops of water into the hot pan and cover. The steam will melt the cheese very quickly.

Mediterranean Turkey Burgers: Add 1½ tablespoons minced sun-dried tomato to the burger mix. Spread 1 teaspoon prepared olive paste (tapenade) on the bun bottoms. Spread 2 teaspoons goat cheese on the bun tops. Serve with lettuce and thinly sliced red onion.

TIME SAVER ▼ **To cook hamburgers faster** • Add 1 tablespoon ice water for every 5 to 6 ounces of ground meat used. Just a tablespoon of water per burger reduces cooking time by 10 percent regardless of the degree of doneness. As the burger cooks, the water trapped in the meat steams, increasing the speed at which heat will permeate into the burger's center. Adding ice water also helps keep burgers juicier, even when cooking them through to well-done.

GREEN CHILE HAMBURGERS Mix **1 drained can (4 ounces) chopped green chile peppers** and **¼ cup chopped fresh cilantro** into **1 to 1½ pounds ground beef.** Shape into 4 patties and grill, broil, or pan-fry over medium heat until center registers 160°F on an instant-read thermometer and meat is no longer pink, 4 to 6 minutes per side. *Makes 4 servings.*

ONION HAMBURGERS Chop **1 large or 2 medium onions** and sauté in **2 teaspoons olive oil, vegetable oil,** or **butter** in a skillet until softened and translucent, about 5 minutes. If dry at any time, add **1 to 2 tablespoons water** and continue cooking. Cool, then mix onions into **1 to 1½ pounds ground beef.** Shape into 4 patties and grill, broil, or pan-fry over medium heat until center registers 160°F on an instant-read thermometer and meat is no longer pink, 4 to 6 minutes per side. *Makes 4 servings.*

HEALTHY HINTS ▼ **To make a more healthful burger** • Replace one-eighth of the ground meat with an equal amount of finely chopped and sautéed vegetables, such as onions, peppers, and/or zucchini. Or use equal amounts ground beef and ground turkey or chicken breast meat, mixing well. Or use a blend of chicken and turkey meat (see Poultry 'n' Vegetable Burgers, below). You can also soften ½ cup textured vegetable protein in 2 tablespoons hot water, and mix it into 1 pound ground beef. To go completely veggie, grill or roast a large portobello mushroom and use it in place of a burger. For an example, see Rosemary Portobello Burgers (page 77). Or try a ready-made veggie burger from the supermarket.

POULTRY 'N' VEGETABLE BURGERS Chop, sauté, and cool **¼ onion** and **½ small bell pepper.** Mix with **½ pound ground chicken, ½ pound ground turkey breast,** and **1 egg white.** Shape into 4 patties and grill, broil, or pan-fry over medium heat until center registers 165°F on an instant-read thermometer and meat is no longer pink, 5 to 6 minutes per side. *Makes 4 servings.*

Burnt Foods *see also individual food listings*

If exposed to heat long enough, almost all foods will carbonize or burn. In some cases, carbonization is desirable, as in a finely charred piece of grilled meat or the deeply browned crust on crème brûlée ("burnt cream"). In other instances, the cooking simply goes too far, resulting in accidentally burnt food.

PROBLEM SOLVER ▼ **To remove burned-on food from a pan** • Douse the burnt bits with fabric stain remover. Let the pan sit a few minutes, then wipe off the food with a scrubbie. Much quicker than soaking the pan overnight.

b

Or dribble 2 tablespoons dishwashing liquid in the bottom of the pan, add hot water to cover the bottom, then bring it to a boil on the stove top. You can also soak the pan in baking soda and water for 10 minutes before washing. Or scrub the pot with dry baking soda and a moist scouring pad. If the food is really stuck, cover it with a thick layer of baking soda, sprinkle with just enough water to moisten, and let it sit overnight before scrubbing clean.

Butter *see also* Fat Replacement; Fats and Oils

Made from churned cream, butter is favored by cooks both for its rich flavor and for the incomparable texture it gives to food.

BASICS ▼ **To store** • Wrap butter tightly in foil or plastic and freeze until needed. Butter is particularly vulnerable to spoiling as well as to picking up odors. For this reason, it turns out that your refrigerator's butter compartment is the worst place to store butter. It's too warm. If you must refrigerate rather than freeze butter, put it in the center of the refrigerator near the back.

To measure frozen butter easily • Before freezing, score sticks of butter with a table knife along the tablespoon marks on the package. Later, when the wrapper is removed, the indentations remain, making it easy to measure.

To test whether butter is at the right temperature for creaming • Insert an instant-read thermometer into it. It should be at about 67°F. Or press your finger into the butter. It is ready for creaming when it gives slightly but still holds its shape. You can also bend it. It should bend with slight resistance but not so much that it cracks or breaks.

To easily chop frozen butter into pieces • Use a metal pastry scraper (a bench knife). Or run a knife under hot water to warm it before slicing the butter.

To shred • Cut a frozen stick of butter in half. Using the wrapper to hold each piece, shred the butter, rubbing one of its long sides against the grater.

To cut cold butter into dry ingredients • Use a pastry cutter, food processor, or fork until the butter is in very small pieces throughout the dry ingredients.

To soften cold butter • Run a small, stainless steel bowl under hot water until hot, then place it, upside down, over the butter. Or, for spreading on toast, place a frozen slice of butter on the toast. Run a wide-bladed knife, such as a chef's knife, under hot water or hold over a gas burner flame for just a second or two to heat. Hold the broad side of the hot knife blade over the butter to gently soften and melt it. To soften a wrapped stick of butter, hold it in both hands and massage gently until it begins to soften, about 4 minutes.

To grease baking pans • Use the wrappers from the butter in the recipe.

PROBLEM SOLVERS ▼ **To measure butter that does not have a wrapper** • Partially fill a liquid measuring cup with water, then add butter until it reaches the measure you need. For example, for ½ cup butter, start with ½ cup water and add butter until the water line reaches 1 cup.

To prevent butter from burning when sautéing • Use half oil.

To prevent a bitter flavor and burnt taste when frying in butter • Use clarified butter, which can withstand high heat. To clarify butter, melt it in the microwave oven or over low heat on the stove top. Skim the froth from the top and pour off the yellow liquid to separate it from the white solids that are settled at the bottom. Use the yellow liquid (clarified butter) to sauté or fry at high temperatures.

To avoid baking-recipe pitfalls • Use stick butter only. Avoid using whipped butter, which has air incorporated into it that can adversely affect baking recipes.

To help prevent baked goods from sticking to the pan • Use unsalted butter rather than salted.

To save creamed butter that seems runny • Place the bowl in the refrigerator to firm. If there is no space in your refrig-erator, place the bowl in a larger bowl that's partially filled with ice.

To soften creamed butter that is slightly too cool and has a granular tex-ture • Place the bowl in a larger bowl of lukewarm water.

To cut butter into flour without a pastry cutter or food processor • Grate a frozen stick of butter over the flour. Stop periodically to toss the butter and flour to-gether to prevent sticking.

To prevent "blowouts" when melting butter in the microwave oven • Cut a

---

FIVE FLAVORED BUTTERS

Flavored butters are made by softening butter and then blending in herbs, spices, and flavorings. Use them in place of plain butter or as a sauce or basting butter.

Basic Procedure: Soften 1 stick (½ cup) butter to room temperature. In a bowl, stir until smooth. Add flavorings and stir to blend. On a sheet of waxed paper, plastic wrap, parchment, or aluminum foil, shape into a log about 5" long. Roll up to enclose, twisting the ends to hold in place. Or place the flavorings directly on the waxed paper and roll a stick of butter into them. Chill until firm. Slice as needed. Each recipe below makes ½ cup.

Basil Tomato Butter: Combine **1 stick softened butter, ⅓ cup shredded fresh basil, 1 tablespoon tomato paste, and ¼ teaspoon salt.** Great on corn, beef, and poultry.

Citrus Butter: Combine **1 stick soft-ened butter; 1½ teaspoons grated lemon, lime, or orange zest; 1½ tablespoons lemon, lime, or orange juice; and ¼ tea-spoon** *each* **salt and ground black pepper.** Delicious over seafood, poultry, or vegeta-bles. To use orange butter over pancakes, omit the salt and pepper.

Garlic Butter: Combine **1 stick soft-ened butter, 1 or 2 minced garlic cloves (raw or cooked), and ¼ teaspoon** *each* **salt and ground black pepper.** Great for garlic toast or melted over corn on the cob, or atop broiled chicken, beef, or seafood.

Hazelnut Butter: In a food processor, combine **½ cup whole toasted and peeled hazelnuts** with **2 teaspoons lemon juice.** Pulse until finely ground (but not a paste). Combine **1 stick softened butter, ground hazelnuts, and ¼ teaspoon** *each* **salt and ground black pepper.** Use over broiled or sautéed fish fillets and with chicken.

Herb Butter: Combine **1 stick softened butter and ¼ cup chopped fresh herbs.** Stir in **1 to 2 teaspoons orange** or **lemon juice** and **¼ teaspoon** *each* **salt and ground black pepper.** Great over everything from grilled chicken and steaks to seafood and potatoes.

b

stick of butter into tablespoon-size pieces, place in a microwaveable container, cover with plastic wrap, and melt at medium power for 2 minutes.

To speed softening • Cut the butter into thin slices. You'll expose more surface area and the butter will soften more quickly.

To speed the cooling process of melted butter • Place the container of melted butter in a bowl of cool water or ice cubes. This is something you would do to avoid the hot butter "cooking" something such as raw eggs when it is added to them, as in a pancake recipe.

To soften quickly for creaming • Use a handheld hair dryer. Cut butter into large cubes and put them in the metal bowl of an electric mixer. Turn the mixer on low and use a hair dryer on high setting to direct hot air around the outside of the bowl. Watch for the first signs of melting at the edge of the bowl, and stop at that point. If you don't have a hair dryer, rub the bottom of the mixing bowl with a towel dipped in hot water. Or place the butter in a metal bowl near a heat register or radiator. Check frequently to avoid melting the butter. You can also cut 1 stick (½ cup) of butter into 4 pieces, place it in a microwaveable bowl, and microwave it uncovered on medium power for 15 to 30 seconds.

To brown for flavor • When butter is browned, the milk solids toast and add flavor. Melt the butter in a small pan over medium heat. Continue to cook until it turns a medium to dark golden brown. Pour over vegetables such as steamed asparagus, green beans, or baked potatoes. Browned butter is also a classic old-fashioned American flavor for buttercream. Just chill the browned butter, let it soften to room temperature, and beat in confec-

tioners' sugar and a few drops of milk to make a fluffy buttercream for cakes, cupcakes, or cookies.

To use less butter • Try to think of butter as a condiment, using a little of it to add to a dish at the end. For example, instead of sautéing fish or chicken in butter, steam it or pan-fry with a little cooking spray. Remove the food from the pan and, while it is still hot, add a small nugget of butter on top, allowing it to melt. Your tastebuds will taste the butter coating the food, but you'll take in fewer calories and less saturated fat. You can also use a nonstick pan for sautéing and cut back to 1 to 3 teaspoons of fat. Make sure to preheat the pan before adding the food being sautéed, as the food you are cooking will absorb less fat when the fat is hot. Or use a mixture of butter and oil when sautéing.

To use light butter • This product has half the fat and calories of regular butter. It tastes terrific spread on hot muffins or melted and drizzled over steamed vegetables. It also works well in frostings, nut toppings, and streusel toppings. To use it in pastry dough, avoid overworking the dough by chilling the light butter and then shredding it on a handheld grater so that it mixes quickly and evenly into the dry ingredients. The fat in light butter is lowered primarily by the addition of water. So, to use light butter in baking recipes, reduce the amount of liquid in the recipe. For example, in cookie dough, omit an egg white or two. In muffin or pancake batter, reduce the milk or juice.

Buttermilk

Years ago, buttermilk was the liquid left in the churn after making butter. Today, it's made by adding a bacteria culture to low-fat

milk, which thickens the milk and gives it a slightly tangy flavor. Buttermilk will break when heated to a near boil, so it is used mostly in baking or in cold soups, smoothies, or ice creams.

PROBLEM SOLVERS ▼ **To substitute buttermilk for regular milk in baking recipes** • Buttermilk adds a wonderful, slightly tangy flavor to quick breads such as pancakes and muffins. Add ½ teaspoon baking soda to the dry ingredients for every cup of buttermilk. The baking soda will react with the buttermilk to lighten and aerate the baked good.

To replace buttermilk • Replace 1 cup buttermilk with ½ cup plain yogurt mixed with ½ cup milk. Or stir together 1 tablespoon lemon juice or white vinegar and 1 cup milk, and let stand 5 minutes before using. Another option is dry buttermilk powder; it can be added directly to the dry ingredients in a recipe or can be reconstituted by combining ¼ cup powder with 1 cup water.

FLAVOR TIP ▼ **To enrich soups and dressings** • For a thick and velvety texture, use buttermilk in cold soups and salad dressings in place of milk or cream. Taste and add a little sour cream for additional richness if desired.

b

Butterscotch

In general, brown sugar cooked with butter creates a butterscotch flavor. Sometimes, lemon juice and heavy cream or evaporated milk is added. You can also buy butterscotch morsels and candies to incorporate into cooking and baking.

RICH BUTTERSCOTCH SAUCE In the top of a double boiler or in a metal pan set over a saucepan of gently simmering water, combine **2 cups brown sugar,** ⅓ **cup *each* butter and heavy cream,** and **1 tablespoon lemon juice.** Cook until thick, 1 hour, stirring frequently. Excellent over ice cream or cake. *Makes about 3 cups.*

C

Cabbage *see also* Coleslaw

White, green, red, and purple: Cabbages come in many colors. While they are available in markets year-round, the best cabbages arrive at the end of summer and stay until winter's cold puts an end to the harvest.

BASICS
▼

To choose • Look for the heaviest heads with bright, firm leaves. Or check out the stem end. If it is dry and shows signs of cracking, it may have been sitting around for a while. Dry stems could also indicate that the cabbage grew in dry weather and may have a sharp, unpleasant flavor.

To wash • Slice it first. A cabbage's compact shape makes it hard to clean.

To make a clean cut through a large head • Position a cleaver over the cabbage and tap the cleaver through with a rubber mallet or a hammer padded with a potholder.

To core • Cut the cabbage into quarters through the stem end. Cut the wedge of core out of each quarter.

To core when you want whole leaves • Stick a long, thin knife (such as a boning knife) into the base of the cabbage and run it around the core. Once it's loosened, grasp the end of the core, twist, and pull it out.

To separate leaves • There are three basic ways to separate cabbage leaves without breaking them. To blanch them, submerge the cored head of cabbage in a large pot of boiling water for 1 minute. Remove and peel off as many leaves as you can. Repeat until you have the number of leaves that you need. Or, to microwave them, place a cored head of cabbage in a microwave oven and cook on high power for 3 minutes. Remove the cabbage and peel off as many leaves as you need. After removing a few leaves, microwave another minute, if needed. You can also freeze cored cabbage for 45 minutes (for ¼ head of leaves) or 4 hours (for an entire head of leaves). Allow to thaw 10 minutes (for ¼ head of leaves) or 1 hour (for an entire head of leaves). Once thawed, the leaves can be easily removed from the head. They will be soft and pliable for easy-to-roll stuffed cabbage without blanching or steaming.

To shred with a knife • Remove the dark outer leaves. Cut into quarters through the stem end. Place a quarter wedge, flat side down, on a cutting board. Hold the cabbage by its stem end and slice it in straight ⅛"-thick slices, starting at the rounded end. As the slices fall from the cabbage, they will break into thin shreds. When the slivers become too wide, stop shredding and repeat with the other quarters.

To shred in a food processor • Cut into 8 wedges through the stem end and run each wedge through the feeder tube, shredding with the slicing disk.

To salvage wilted cabbage • Peel off a few layers of leaves. It is likely still fresh on the inside.

To preserve the deep color of red cabbage • Add an acid, such as a squirt of lemon juice or a splash of vinegar, to the cooking water. If you forget the acid and the cabbage has become discolored, don't panic. Just add the acid to the water and the cabbage will turn back to its original color.

To keep wedges from falling apart during cooking • Skewer with a toothpick.

To reduce cooking odors • Cabbage has several sulfur-containing compounds, which break down when cooked and release hydrogen sulfide. We know this better as the stench of a rotten egg. The best so-lution is also the quickest: Cut the cabbage finely and cook it fast, so that the sulfur never gets a chance to emerge. Quick-cooking not only reduces odors, it also preserves the maximum amount of nutrients. You can also shred it finely and use quick-cooking methods such as stir-frying. Or, for boiling or steaming, try thin-cut wedges. If you're cooking larger pieces of cabbage, add a few chunks of bread to the cooking water to help absorb odors.

To reduce gassiness • When boiling cabbage, reduce gassiness by discarding the cooking liquid halfway through the cooking process. Reboil more water and then finish the cooking. To make ahead, refrigerate for up to 1 day after the first cooking, finishing off in fresh water.

Fascinating Fact: Legend has it that Babe Ruth wore a cabbage leaf under his cap to help him keep a cool head. He changed it every 2 innings.

THE GOOD THINGS IN CABBAGE

Some varieties of cabbage have more nutrients than others. Here's which varieties have what.

Variety	Appearance	Nutrition Benefit
Green cabbage	Grows in tight, dense heads with darker green outer leaves	Higher in vitamin C than other varieties
Red cabbage	Grows in dense heads with red or purple leaves	Higher concentration of vitamin C than other varieties
Savoy cabbage	Grows in less dense heads with frilly, ruffled leaves and yellow/green color	Higher in beta-carotene than other varieties
Bok choy	Grows in bunches like Swiss chard, on thick, white stalks with green, leafy tops	Higher in calcium than other varieties
Napa cabbage (Chinese cabbage)	Grows in dense, oblong heads, with light green leaves and wide, white, crunchy stems	Good source of vitamin A, folic acid, and potassium

C

SHREDDED CABBAGE SAUTÉ Heat **2 tablespoons oil** in a large, deep skillet or wok until very hot. Add **1 sliced onion** and **2 teaspoons dill seeds.** Sauté until tender, about 2 minutes. Add **1 small head shredded green cabbage** (about 4 cups) and cook until tender, about 3 minutes, stirring constantly. Season with ½ **teaspoon salt** and ⅛ **teaspoon ground black pepper.**
Makes 4 to 6 servings.

SWEET-AND-SOUR CABBAGE Cook **2 slices chopped bacon** in a large skillet over medium heat until cooked through or to the desired crispness. Spoon off all but 1 tablespoon fat. Add **1 small head chopped or shredded green cabbage** (about 4 cups; or use presliced coleslaw mix) and sauté, tossing, until well-browned and caramelized, 8 minutes. Halfway through, sprinkle in **1 to 2 tablespoons sugar.** Pour in **2 to 3 tablespoons cider vinegar** and sprinkle with ½ **teaspoon salt** and ⅛ **teaspoon ground black pepper.** Cook until soft and flavorful, 10 minutes. Add more or less sugar and vinegar to taste.
Makes 4 to 6 servings.

Cake Pans

Many a baking failure can be traced to using the wrong pan. So before you begin making a cake, make sure that you have the right pan for the job.

BASICS **To line** • Many recipes call for parchment paper, but any liner will do: aluminum foil, waxed paper, even a cut-up brown paper bag.

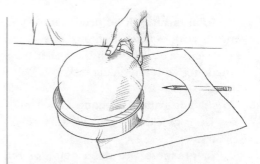

To line a round pan • Use the pan as a template. Tear off a sheet of paper or foil that is bigger than the bottom of the pan you are lining. Place the pan, right side up, on the liner. Using a pencil, draw a line around the perimeter of the bottom of the pan. Cut just inside the line to make a circular liner. Set the liner in the pan.

To line the bottom and sides of a round pan • Turn the pan upside down. Tear a sheet of foil large enough to overlap the bottom of the pan by several inches on all sides. Carefully mold the foil over the outside of the pan. Then, remove the foil, invert the pan, and insert the molded foil liner into the pan. Smooth the liner into place.

To line a tube pan • Tear off a sheet of paper or foil that is bigger than the bottom of the pan you are lining. Place the pan, right side up, on the liner. Using a pencil, draw a line around the perimeter of the bottom of the pan. Then, invert the pan and place the liner on top, lining up the pan bottom with the line you just drew. Carefully draw another line around the perimeter of the pan's inner circle (the inside of the tube). Cut just inside both lines drawn to make a ring-shaped liner. Set the liner in the pan.

To line a springform pan • Tear off a sheet of foil larger than the bottom of the pan. Place the pan bottom, upside down, onto the foil. Invert both pan bottom and foil, then loosely tuck the overhang of foil underneath the pan bottom. Secure the lined bottom in the springform ring and fold the excess foil up the outside of the ring. Lining the bottom of a springform pan this way helps the cake slide out easily, reduces leaking from an ill-fitting bottom, and protects the contents of the pan if the cake needs to be baked in a water bath.

To grease • Turn a small zipper-lock plastic bag inside out, then place it on your hand like a glove. Smear shortening or butter on the bottom and sides of the pan with your fingers. When done, seal any remaining shortening or butter in the bag and store, refrigerated, until the next time you need it. Or you can use the butter wrapper—there is always some butter that adheres to the inside of the wrapper, which makes a perfect wipe for applying butter over the sides and bottom of the pan. If greasing a pan with butter, use only unsalted butter. Salted butter will cause cakes to stick. Another alternative is to use cooking spray.

To bake heavy, dense batters such as pound cake • Use a tube pan. It's designed to conduct heat toward the center of the batter, allowing the cake to rise and bake evenly.

To make a more tender cake • Use a shiny cake pan, which will reflect the oven's heat.

To make a delicate cake with a tender crust • Avoid iron or black steel pans, which will cause a heavy crust to form on the sides of the cake.

PROBLEM SOLVERS ▼ **To keep cakes from sticking to the pan** • Grease the pan with vegetable shortening instead of butter. Unlike butter or margarine, shortening contains no water, which can cause batters to stick. Shortening can also withstand higher temperatures than butter.

To make a too-big cake pan smaller • Using foil, make a smaller pan inside the pan that you have. Line the pan with foil, folding the foil into a lip at the points where you want the pan edges to be. Fill the space between the foil edge and the pan edge with dried beans.

Cakes *see also* Angel Food Cake; Baking; Cake Pans; Cheesecake; Chocolate; Creaming; Flour; Frosting; Sifting

Pound cakes, jelly rolls, angel food, and genoise all require their own techniques and ingredients. But there are a few general guidelines for successful cakes every time.

BASICS ▼ **To help a cake rise higher** • Make sure that all the ingredients are at room temperature before you begin.

To best disperse salt and spices in batter • Add them to the butter when creaming rather than including them in the dry ingredients.

To dispel air bubbles in delicate batters • Run a knife or a metal spatula through the batter in a zigzag pattern.

To level batter in a round pan • Place the pan on a flat surface. Place a hand on each side of the filled pan and gently, but with a little snap, spin the pan. Centrifugal force will instantly level the batter.

To level batter in a square or oblong pan • Place your hands on opposite sides of the filled pan and shake it vigorously back and forth several times.

For light, airy cakes • Bake them in the bottom third of the oven.

To test for doneness • A toothpick inserted into the center should come out clean or almost clean, meaning that a few crumbs stick to the pick.

C

To keep cakes fresh • Always cover cut slices with plastic wrap; cover cakes with a cake cover, or improvise with an inverted plastic storage container or bowl and refrigerate.

To keep a cut cake moist • Place a cut apple in the storage container.

To freeze a cake • Slice it first, and place sheets of waxed paper between slices so that you can thaw slice by slice. Wrap and freeze cakes as soon as they are cooled, even if using them in 1 to 2 days. To thaw frozen cakes, unwrap and thaw at room temperature.

To make a homespun cake stand • Turn a ceramic or porcelain bowl upside down and place a matching plate on top.

To transport a frosted cake • Use a cake carrier. Or insert toothpicks into the top of the frosted cake and stick miniature marshmallows or gumdrops onto the tops of the toothpicks (to prevent them from poking through the plastic wrap). Gently cover with plastic wrap.

PROBLEM SOLVERS ▼ **To prevent a coating of white flour on chocolate cake** • When a chocolate cake recipe calls for greasing and flouring a pan, dust the pan with unsweetened cocoa powder instead of flour. To help the cocoa cling to the pan better, sift it first. For boxed cake mixes, use a bit of the box mix to coat the pan.

To keep add-ins from sinking to the bottom • Toss dried fruit, nuts, or chocolate chips in flour before adding to the batter.

To prevent a dome in the middle of a cake • Wrap a thick strip of moistened cloth or newspaper around the edge of the cake pan. Secure it with paper clips. This will slow down the baking at the edge of the pan so it doesn't set before the center of the cake does.

SPLITTING A CAKE

To cut a single layer cake into 2 thinner layers, use a serrated knife or dental floss.

❶ Chill the cake to firm it up. Make a slight vertical cut on the side of the cake layer to perfectly line up the pieces later on. Then, cut through the side of the cake layer to split it in half horizontally.

❷ If you're not steady with a knife, mark the center of the cake with toothpicks at 4" intervals in the side. Loop a long piece of dental floss (about 3 feet) around the cake, resting it on the toothpicks. Cross the ends of the floss nearest you and pull steadily to cut the cake into 2 layers.

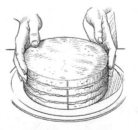

❸ To assemble split cake layers, brush off loose crumbs and place on a serving plate. Spread frosting between the layers and stack them, lining up the vertical cuts.

To prevent undercooking or over-cooking • Keep a thermostat or oven thermometer in your oven to make sure that it is properly calibrated. If your oven is slightly off, adjust the temperature accordingly. If it is way off, call for repairs.

To release from pans • Put the hot cake pan on a wet kitchen towel for about 5 minutes. The steam created will help loosen the cake from the pan. If that doesn't work, run a thin knife around the edge. Of course, the best remedy is ample greasing (about 1 tablespoon shortening for each cake pan).

To prevent from sticking to the rungs on a rack as it cools • Place a piece of parchment on the rack and poke a scattering of holes for improved ventilation. Place the cake on top.

To rescue a cake that is undercooked in the center • Cut out the center. Frost the rest and serve as a ring-shaped cake.

To salvage a fallen cake • Slice into cubes and serve with berries and flavored whipped cream.

To save a cake that's burnt on top • Lop off the burnt top with a serrated knife. Similarly, if a cake is humped on the top, shave off the top with a bread knife.

To save an overly dry cake • Cut off the sides and top of the cake and brush the cake with sugar syrup (see page 90).

To get a flat-topped cake with clean edges • Turn the cake bottom up for the top layer.

To frost if very soft or crumbly • Freeze the cake for 15 minutes, then spread a thin layer of frosting onto the partially frozen cake. Return to the freezer for 15 minutes for the frosting to set. Then, add a thicker layer of frosting to complete.

To frost without a cardboard cake round • Cut a makeshift cake round from a clean cardboard box. Or place the cake on a smooth-bottom inverted dinner plate.

TIME SAVERS ▼

To skip sifting dry ingredients • Just mix together the leavener, salt, and flour in a mixing cup and stir right into your batter. There's only one reason to sift dry ingredients, and that's to aerate the flour. But aerating flour is essential only for the most delicate sponge or angel food cakes.

To get a head start on any cake • Assemble the dry and/or wet ingredients hours or even days ahead. Then, you can easily combine them and bake them closer to serving for a fresher cake. This is especially helpful for breakfast cakes. Mix the dry ingredients up to 3 days ahead and tore in a zipper-lock plastic bag or sealed container. Wet ingredients can be assembled up to 1 day ahead and kept tightly sealed in the refrigerator. Remove 1 hour before it is time to mix them with the dry ingredients, and bring to room temperature. If the recipe includes creaming butter with sugar, do this just before baking. Add half the dry ingredients to the creamed butter, followed by all of the wet ingredients, then the remaining dry ingredients. Bake as directed.

To cool cake layers quickly • Place warm cake layers on a rack in the freezer for 15 minutes while you prepare the frosting. When they come out, they will be cool enough to decorate without melting the frosting.

FLAVOR TIPS ▼

To flavor cake batter • Add flavor extracts, such as vanilla, almond (perfect with chocolate, fruit, or nuts), or citrus (wonderful with berries). For chocolate cakes, you can also add cinnamon to the batter.

To make a more tender cake • Replace any type of milk called for with buttermilk, adding ½ teaspoon baking soda for each cup of buttermilk used.

To make a richer cake • Substitute 2 egg yolks for each whole egg.

C

Chocolate-Almond Marble Cake

It's not necessary to prepare 2 separate batters to make a marble cake. You can pour half of the light-colored batter into the pan, add the dark ingredients to the remaining batter, then swirl the batters together. This cake dirties only 2 dishes.

2　**sticks (1 cup) butter**

2　**cups sugar**

3　**eggs**

1　**teaspoon vanilla extract**

1　**teaspoon baking powder**

2½　**cups all-purpose flour**

¾　**cup milk**

¼　**cup amaretto**

3　**tablespoons unsweetened cocoa powder**

¼　**teaspoon baking soda**

1. Preheat the oven to 350°F. Grease a 12-cup Bundt pan or 10" tube pan.

2. Melt the butter in a large, heavy saucepan over medium heat. Remove from the heat. Add the sugar, eggs, and vanilla extract.

Using an electric mixer on medium speed, beat until smooth. Add the baking powder and stir well. Stir in the flour and beat until it is well-incorporated and the batter is thick. Stir in the milk and amaretto until the liquid is completely incorporated. Pour half of the batter into the prepared pan.

3. In a cup, combine the cocoa and baking soda. Beat into the remaining batter. Pour along the center of the ring of batter, creating a dark circle. Run a knife through the dark batter briefly to create a few swirls. Bake until a wooden pick inserted in the center of the cake comes out clean, 40 to 45 minutes. Cool in the pan on a rack 10 minutes. Cover with a rack and invert. Remove the pan and cool to room temperature.

Makes 12 servings

To add moisture and flavor to cake layers • Brush with a sugar syrup. In a saucepan over medium heat, simmer together ¾ cup water and ½ cup sugar. If desired, add the peel of 1 lemon or the peel of ½ orange, plus a cinnamon stick and/or whole cloves. You can also add 1 teaspoon flavor extract to ½ cup syrup. Let cool in the pan to room temperature.

To flavor jam or jelly for filling cake layers • Combine ½ cup jam, jelly, or preserves and 1 tablespoon brandy, cognac, or liqueur. Heat in a small saucepan or microwave on high until heated through, 1 minute. Brush over each of 2 cake layers before stacking, or brush onto 1 jelly roll cake before filling with a creamy filling.

To make simple ice cream cake • Split a cake layer, placing the bottom half in a springform pan. Spread evenly with softened frozen yogurt, sherbet, or ice cream. Repeat with cake and ice cream. Freeze until solid, at least 3 hours. Thaw in the refrigerator 30 minutes before using. Serve with a berry sauce.

To make cone cakes • Fill flat-bottom ice cream cones half-full with your favorite cake batter. Place in a baking dish and bake until a tester inserted into the cake comes out almost clean. Cool, then frost and decorate with sprinkles.

To reduce fat and calories • Choose cakes that are naturally low in fat, such as angel food, chiffon, and sponge cakes, as opposed to denser cakes such as pound cakes and nut tortes. In recipes, replace up to one-fourth of the butter with fat-free sour cream, or for dark cakes, use prune puree. If the recipe is leavened only with baking powder, replace ¼ teaspoon of the powder with ¼ teaspoon baking soda to complement the sour cream. Use cake flour instead of all-purpose flour for a more tender crumb. Replace half or all of the all-purpose flour with cake flour; add 2 additional tablespoons of cake flour for each cup of all-purpose flour replaced. For a chocolate cake, you can also use buttermilk instead of milk.

To reduce fat and calories in cake frosting • Replace chocolate buttercream frosting with Pudding Frosting (page 197)

ONE-POT CAKES

Traditional cake recipes begin by creaming butter with sugar until the mixture is thick and aerated. Into this mixture is blended eggs; sometimes, beaten egg whites; extracts; milk; and sifted dry ingredients. One-pot baking changes all that.

One-Pot Applesauce-Chocolate Cake: Preheat oven to 350°F. In a large saucepan over medium heat, melt **1 stick (½ cup) butter.** When half-melted, stir in **2 ounces unsweetened chocolate.** Remove from heat and stir until everything is melted. Stir in **1¼ cups applesauce, 1 cup sugar, 1 tablespoon coffee, 1 teaspoon vanilla extract,** and **2 eggs.** Mix **½ teaspoon baking soda** with **1 cup flour** in the measuring cup. Stir into batter, and beat 30 seconds. Scrape into a greased 8" layer pan and bake until a tester inserted in the center comes out clean,

45 minutes. Cool in the pan on a rack 10 minutes. Remove to the rack and cool completely. *Makes 6 servings.*

Chocolate Almond Torte: Preheat oven to 375°F. Grease an 8" layer pan and line the bottom with a round of foil. Grease the foil. In a large saucepan over medium heat, melt **1 stick (½ cup) butter** halfway. Add **4 ounces semisweet chocolate** and stir. Remove from heat and continue stirring until both are melted. Mix in **⅔ cup sugar.** Mix in **3 eggs, 1⅔ cups (½ pound) ground almonds,** and **1 teaspoon vanilla extract.** Pour batter into the prepared pan and bake 25 minutes. Cool in the pan on a rack 20 minutes. Remove from the pan and peel off the foil. Cool completely on the rack. Serve dusted with **confectioners' sugar.** *Makes 10 servings.*

EASY WAYS TO DRESS UP A CAKE

Put 2 to 3 tablespoons confectioners' sugar or cocoa powder into a sieve, then lightly tap the side of the sieve to evenly dust the top of the cake. For a fancier look, put a paper doily, small leaves, or paper cutouts over the cake first, then dust it. Carefully lift the stencil, and its design will be left on top of the cake. You can also use both confectioners' sugar and cocoa in separate dustings.

Pour melted semisweet or bittersweet chocolate into a small zipper-lock plastic bag. Cut off a small piece of one corner. Pipe the chocolate on top of the dessert in a decorative pattern.

You can also top the cake with chocolate curls, chocolate leaves (see page 117), or apricot roses (see page 208). Or dust it with finely ground nuts such as almonds or walnuts.

---

with chocolate pudding. Or spread cake layers with all-fruit preserves or jam instead of frosting. Use ¾ cup to 1 cup jam for an 8" to 9" layer cake. Or, make a self-frosting upside-down cake. Combine 1 tablespoon melted butter, 3 tablespoons brown sugar, and 1 pound sliced fruit, such as pineapple, nectarines, pears, or apples. Spread the topping in the bottom of the cake pan before adding the batter. Bake, cool in the pan 10 minutes, then invert the cake and allow it to cool completely before serving.

LEMON-CHEESE FILLING Drain **1 cup lemon-flavored yogurt** in a cheesecloth-lined colander over a bowl in the refrigerator, 1 to 2 days, to make yogurt cheese (see page 554). Blend with **3 tablespoons softened Neufchâtel cheese and ¼ teaspoon grated lemon zest.** Makes about 1 cup; enough to fill an 8" or 9" two-layer cake.

Capers

The buds of the Mediterranean caper bush are picked just before they burst into flower. Soaked in salt water and aged for several months, capers develop a sharp salty-sour flavor that can brighten a wide range of dishes, such as pasta, salads, and sauces. Capers vary in size, from the tiny nonpareilles, roughly the size of peppercorns, to the meaty gruesas, measuring 13 millimeters or more.

BASICS **To choose** • Look for salt-packed capers. They have a denser, chewier texture and a taste that's truer to the plant than brined capers. Make sure that the salt is white or pale yellow. Darker salt indicates that the capers may be rancid.

To decrease saltiness • Rinse under cold running water.

PROBLEM SOLVER **To remove from a narrow jar** • Use a melon baller. This tool will fit into the most maddeningly narrow jar, will scoop up about 1 teaspoon of nonpareil capers, and will allow the brine to naturally drain away. Or insert a long, pointed vegetable peeler into the jar. Wriggle a row of capers onto the chute of the peeler.

Caramel *see also* Browning

If you put a spoonful of sugar in a skillet and place over heat, it will turn to caramel. The sugar will melt and thicken, turning amber, then golden, then brown, and eventually, when burnt, black. Each stage develops considerably more complex flavor.

BASICS **To reach the correct temperature** • Use a candy thermometer. Insert it into the caramelizing sugar; it should be between 320°F (amber color) and 350°F (deep brown color). Once you've cooked caramel too far, there's no other choice than to start over.

To avoid crystallization • Heat the sugar over low heat, without stirring, until it dissolves completely. Boil the syrup only after it has dissolved, and avoid stirring after it has reached a boil. You can also add a squirt of lemon. Dip a pastry brush in hot water and brush down any crystals from the sides of the pan to dissolve them.

To ensure even cooking • Swirl the pan to redistribute the liquid.

To immediately halt further cooking • Transfer to a cool pan if necessary. Or remove from the heat and add butter and a liquid, such as water or cream to thin the caramel and keep it fluid when cooled.

To keep fluid and warm • Place the pan over a double boiler or in a pan of barely simmering water.

To crush hardened caramel • Place in a zipper-lock plastic bag and crush with a rolling pin.

PROBLEM SOLVERS **To prevent sticking** • Grease the container before adding caramel. The same goes if you're pouring it onto a baking sheet to harden.

To rescue an entire pan of rock-hard caramel • Break up the crystallized caramel with a spoon; continue cooking.

To avoid burning yourself when adding water • Wear long sleeves and stand back from the pan.

To easily clean pans in which caramel has been cooked • Avoid letting caramel harden in the pan. If it does, soften it over low heat in a pan of simmering water.

Carrots

These orange roots are a workhorse in the kitchen. They bring a rich, sweet flavor to soups, stews, and sauces. They also shine when cooked as a vegetable in their own right. Though available year-round, carrots have different characteristics in each season. In spring, you'll find tiny, tender baby carrots with a mild flavor. Summer carrots have a slightly stronger flavor. The very sweetest carrots are found in the fall and early winter, when the starches convert to sugar in the cold weather.

C

BASICS ▼ **To choose** • Look for carrots with a firm texture and smooth skin. Carrots sold with their green tops intact are likely to be fresher than topless ones sold in plastic bags.

To store • Keep carrots in the coldest part of the refrigerator and use within a week or two.

To slice • Cut a thin slice off the length of the carrot to give it a flat, stable base. Then, lay the carrot flat on your work surface for easy slicing.

To prepare old carrots • Remove the woody cores and use only the outer flesh.

HEALTHY HINTS ▼ **To benefit from a carrot's nutrition** • Much of the nutrition is right under the skin, so rinse and scrub carrots well, but don't peel them. Raw carrots make a healthy snack, but for maximum nutrition benefits, cook carrots for at least 3 to 5 minutes. Cooking helps free beta-carotene from the carrot's fiber cells, making it easier for your body to absorb.

To use carrot juice • Carrot juice is a delicious way to get beta-carotene into your diet. Make a blend of carrot and orange juice to start your day. Or use carrot juice in salad dressings to replace part of the oil. You can also cook couscous in a mixture of carrot juice and water. And you can steam fish using carrot juice for the liquid, seasoning the liquid and thickening with cornstarch.

Cauliflower

Like other members of the cabbage family, cauliflower tends to be most flavorful during the colder months. The familiar white heads are the most common type of cauliflower, but there are purple, green, and golden varieties as well.

BASICS ▼ **To choose** • Look for vibrant heads that are firm and dense with no bruises.

To store • Wrap heads of cauliflower in perforated plastic bags and refrigerate for several days. Use as soon as possible, as cauliflower's sweetness fades with time. Precut florets are even more perishable. Use them the day you buy them.

To clean • Soak in salted cold water for 30 minutes or more to flush out any debris lodged inside the heads.

To remove core and leaves • With a large knife, slice through the stem end close to the base of the head to remove the leaves. With a thin knife, cut around the core as close as possible to the florets to remove the core and tough stem ends in one piece.

To separate into florets • Core as described above, then break off the florets individually by hand.

To cook • Cook cauliflower quickly. To speed cooking time, divide the head into small florets. Florets can be boiled, steamed, or cooked in a microwave oven on high power. With either method, it takes about 5 minutes to cook a pound of cauliflower florets to tenderness.

To cook a large head whole • For large heads of cauliflower (1½ pounds or heavier), steaming is best. Core as described above. Then, with a large knife, slice through the stem end close to the base of the head. Insert the tip of the knife deeply into the core, making two perpendicular cuts (or a deep X), to allow steam to permeate the tough core and stem areas more quickly. Steam over boiling water, with the core end down, until a knife can pierce the core easily, 15 to 20 minutes.

To cook a small head whole • Small heads of cauliflower (less than 1½ pounds) can be cooked faster in a microwave oven.

(The microwave gives uneven results with larger heads.) Core as described on the opposite page. Then, slice through the stem end, as described for large heads. Place in a microwaveable dish (core end down), cover, and microwave on high power until the core can be easily pierced with a knife or fork, 6 to 7 minutes.

To preserve the white color • Add vinegar, lemon juice, or milk to the cooking water.

Caviar

Salted sturgeon eggs are considered one of the most luxurious foods. At their best, the tiny eggs unleash a delightful salty explosion on the tongue. There are four types of caviar; each comes from a different type of sturgeon from the Caspian Sea. The large gray eggs of the beluga are considered the best and fetch the highest price. The smaller eggs of the osetra are slightly less costly and have a fine flavor. The tiny gray eggs of the sevruga have a fine, salty taste, yet tend to clump together. The fourth type comes from the almost extinct sterlet sturgeon.

BASICS ▼ **To choose** • The eggs should be intact, uncrushed, and glistening with fat. Avoid pasteurized caviar, which is sold in vacuum-packed jars and is not refrigerated. Its flavor cannot compare to fresh caviar.

To serve • A classic way to serve caviar is with yeast-risen buckwheat pancakes (blini) and plenty of melted butter. Avoid accompaniments such as lemon juice and chopped onion, which interfere with caviar's delicate flavor and texture. Lightly toasted, buttered brioche goes well, but avoid serving caviar on crackers: Their texture is too crisp for the tender fish eggs.

To store • Put the container of caviar in a larger plastic container, pack it with ice, and store in the coldest part of the refrigerator.

Celeriac

This gnarly-looking root, also known as celery root, comes from a variety of celery that is different from the celery familiar to most people. The flavor is similar to traditional celery but softer and deeper. Celeriac makes a marvelously creamy puree, especially when combined with mashed potatoes.

BASICS ▼ **To choose** • Firm roots that are heavy for their size are the ones to take home, particularly if they still have a bit of their green attached. Large roots that feel light are likely to be spongy in the middle.

To store • Place in a zipper-lock plastic bag and refrigerate for up to several weeks.

To prepare • Trim the top and bottom of the root and peel.

To help retain its white color • Drop cut pieces of the root into a bowl of acidulated water (see page 2).

To boil • Boil the whole roots unpeeled, and they'll keep their creamy color and mellow flavor. Peel after they have had a chance to cool.

Celery

Its crunchy texture makes celery a favorite for eating raw, but celery's sweet side is best emphasized when cooked. Used as part of an aromatic base, celery lends a sweet, herbal flavor to soups, sauces, and stews. On its own, celery makes luscious braises and gratins.

C

c

BASICS ▼ **To choose** • Look for firm ribs with a bright green color. Rubbery ribs and yellow or brown leaves indicate that celery is past its prime.

To store • Wrap loosely in plastic and refrigerate. Celery will start to go limp after just 2 or 3 days, so use it soon after you buy it. To help celery last for up to 10 days, wrap it in aluminum foil.

To remove the strings • Peel away the tough, fibrous strings with a vegetable peeler. They don't become tender when cooked. Another method: With your fingers, snap off the narrow end of the celery stalk from its concave side, leaving the strings intact. Slowly pull the strings down the length of the stalk until they naturally detach at the wide end.

To keep celery sticks crisp • Stack upright in a tall glass in a couple of inches of ice water.

Chef's Tip: For the freshest-tasting celery salt, make it yourself. Combine 1 tablespoon coarse kosher salt or sea salt and 1 teaspoon celery seeds in a mortar and pound with a pestle. For a finer texture, grind in a spice grinder. For a coarser texture, pound the celery seeds with 1 teaspoon of the salt, then stir in the remaining 2 teaspoons salt.

PROBLEM SOLVER ▼ **To revive limp celery** • Trim ⅛" from the base of the stalk base and place the stalk in a glass of ice water in the refrigerator for at least 2 hours.

TIME SAVERS ▼ **To chop a large amount quickly** • Keep the whole stalk intact and slice across the entire bunch of celery ribs, starting just below the leafy tops. Transfer the chopped portion to a colander to pick out any chopped leaves and rinse clean.

To slice quickly • Use an egg slicer. Trim the celery tops and bottoms. Open the slicer, and with the slicing wires upright, guide each rib of celery lengthwise through the wires.

To julienne • Proceed as directed above for slicing, then rotate the sliced lengths one-quarter turn and pass lengthwise through the slicing wires again. Cut the resulting strips crosswise into 2" lengths.

Champagne *see also* Alcohol; Wine

Though sparkling wines are made in many regions of the world, only those made in the Champagne region of northeastern France can truly be called champagne.

BASICS ▼ **To choose** • There are several different styles of champagne. Which type you choose depends on your taste and how you plan to serve it. Brut and extra brut are very dry, with just a touch of sugar. These make wonderful aperitifs to serve with slightly salty appetizers, such as olives, caviar, or oysters. Extra dry champagnes are slightly sweeter than bruts and go well with mildly spicy foods, such as curries. Sec and demi-sec refer to sweet champagnes meant to be served with dessert.

To open a bottle of champagne • Keep the palm of your hand flat over the top of the bottle while removing the foil and the wire cage. With your palm flat on the cork, hold the bottle at a 45-degree angle away from you, making sure that you're not pointing it at anyone. With your other hand on the bottleneck, twist the bottle, not the cork, until you feel the cork begin to loosen. Then, use your thumb to pry the cork from the bottle.

To open champagne without shooting the cork • Begin opening as directed above, but keep your palm firmly positioned on top of the cork as you twist the bottle. As the cork loosens, grasp it with your palm and fingers and hold it tightly while you twist the bottle away from the cork with your other hand.

PROBLEM SOLVERS ▼ **To revive bubbles** • You can actually bring bubbles back to a bottle of champagne that's beginning to lose its effervescence. Just drop a raisin into the bottle.

To preserve bubbles in an open bottle • Invest in a special champagne stopper, sold at kitchenware stores. They do the best job of sealing the bottle and keeping the bubbles alive. The next best thing is to stick the handle of a long metal spoon into the bottle and store in the refrigerator. The bubbles should stay lively for a day or two.

Fascinating Fact: According to some estimates, you are more likely to be killed by a champagne cork than by a poisonous spider.

TIME SAVER ▼ **To chill champagne quickly** • Put it in a bucket filled with ice and cold water for 30 minutes.

Cheese, Fresh *see also* Cheese, Ripened

Unlike ripened cheeses, fresh cheeses are not cured and aged. These include cottage cheese, cream cheese, feta, mascarpone, mozzarella, and ricotta.

BASICS ▼ **To choose cream cheese** • The higher the fat content, the richer and creamier the cheese will be. Generic and cut-rate brands usually contain only the minimum of fat and lack the delicate flavor of better brands. Some U.S. cheese producers make cream cheese without the gums and thick-

eners used in commercial varieties. These more traditional-style cheeses have a better flavor and smoother texture. Whipped cream cheese spreads easily and is a good choice for spreads or dips, but avoid using it for baking; the extra air whipped into the product may alter your recipe.

To store cream cheese • Keep cream cheese in the coldest part of the refrigerator. After opening, rewrap tightly, refrigerate, and use within 1 week.

PROBLEM SOLVER ▼ **To keep mozzarella cheese from getting stringy when cooked** • Add an acid, such as lemon juice or white wine.

TIME SAVERS ▼ **To quickly soften chilled cream cheese** • Seal the cream cheese in a zipper-lock plastic bag and immerse in hot water.

To quickly slice mozzarella • Use an egg slicer. Place a ball of mozzarella in the cradle of the slicer and slice with the wires. For julienned pieces, turn the sliced cheese 90 degrees and slice again.

PENNE WITH SHRIMP AND HERBED CHEESE In a large pot of salted boiling water, cook **12 ounces penne pasta** until tender yet firm to the bite, about 7 to 9 minutes. Five minutes before pasta is done, use a large skillet to sauté **1 tablespoon finely chopped onion** in **1 tablespoon olive oil** until tender. Add **1 cup white wine** and **1 tablespoon lemon juice.** Boil 3 minutes. Add **¾ pound shelled and deveined shrimp.** Stir and cover. Remove from heat and let rest until shrimp is opaque, 1 minute. Drain pasta and add to shrimp along with **6 ounces herbed cream cheese, 2 teaspoons chopped fresh parsley, ¼ teaspoon salt,** and **⅛ teaspoon ground white or black pepper.** *Makes 4 servings.*

C

FLAVOR
TIPS
▼ **To make firm, packaged mozzarella more tender and tasty** • Grate it and marinate it in olive oil. Better yet, buy a ball of fresh, soft mozzarella cheese from an Italian grocer or cheesemaker instead.

FRIED MOZZARELLA STICKS Cut ½ **pound fresh mozzarella cheese** into sticks about 3" long and ½" thick. Place ⅓ **cup flour, 1 beaten egg,** and ⅓ **cup plain dry bread crumbs** into separate shallow bowls. Dip sticks into flour to coat, then egg to coat, then breadcrumbs to coat completely. (At this point, you can refrigerate sticks on a baking sheet for up to 8 hours.) Heat about ½" **olive oil** in a saucepan or sauté pan to 375°F. Without crowding the pan, fry sticks until deep golden, turning once, about 1 minute. Drain on paper towels. Sprinkle lightly with ¼ **teaspoon salt** and serve hot. *Makes 4 servings.*

INSTANT RICOTTA DESSERT MOUSSE Whip **1 cup ricotta cheese** and **2 tablespoons confectioners' sugar** until very smooth. Add **1 teaspoon orange juice,** ½ **teaspoon vanilla extract,** and ¼ **cup** *each* **shelled and chopped pistachios, chopped raisins, and chocolate chips.** In a separate bowl, whip ¾ **cup heavy cream** to soft peaks and fold into ricotta mixture. Spoon into individual dishes and serve immediately, or chill for up to 1 hour. *Makes 4 servings.*

HEALTHY
HINTS
▼ **To reduce fat in recipes with cream cheese** • Substitute a blend of equal amounts Neufchâtel and low-fat cream cheese. This works in baking and cheesecakes. Or substitute a combination of equal amounts blended dry-curd cottage cheese and low-fat cream cheese, adding ½ teaspoon lemon juice per ½ cup of the mixture. You can also substitute a combination of equal amounts blended dry-curd cottage cheese and yogurt cheese.

To extend ricotta cheese • Puree dry-curd 1% cottage cheese and use in combination with the higher-fat, part-skim ricotta cheese. To use as a cheese filling for stuffed pastas, season the mixture with herbs and add egg whites. Or, to use this mixture for savory dips and spreads, add fresh herbs, dried onion soup mix, and chicken or smoked salmon. You can also add a bit of sugar or fruit to use this mixture in dessert fillings for cannoli, blintzes, or cheese Danish.

Cheese, Ripened *see also*
Cheese, Fresh

Ripened cheeses can be firm, like Parmesan; semifirm, like Cheddar; semisoft, like Gouda and Monterey Jack; or soft-ripened, like blue cheese and Brie.

BASICS
▼ **To choose** • If possible, find a market that takes pride in their cheeses and allows you to taste before you buy. Look cheese over carefully. There should be no cracks or discoloration, and unless you're buying a blue cheese, there should be no signs of mold.

To store • Wrap it tightly in plastic wrap, aluminum foil, or waxed paper, and store in the refrigerator in the cheese drawer or another not-too-cold spot. Once you've unwrapped the cheese, discard the wrapping, and rewrap in fresh wrapping. In general, the harder the cheese, the longer it will stay fresh.

To serve • Bring ripened cheeses to room temperature before serving. Cold cheese right out of the refrigerator will never have the full, rich flavor of cheese at room temperature. Leave the cheese in its wrapping while it comes to room temperature. The cut surfaces will dry out if exposed to air.

To cut • Avoid buying cheese planes and other gadgets. All you need is a good, sharp knife, preferably one with a thin blade. To cut soft or semisoft cheeses, such as goat cheese (chèvre), slice through with a tautly pulled piece of dental floss.

To grate Parmesan or other hard cheeses into fluffy, light wisps • Use a cheese rasp (a long, flat cheese grater sold in kitchenware stores).

To remove mold • Rub moldy portions with salt; the mold will rub off.

PROBLEM SOLVERS ▼ **To salvage cheese that has dried out in the refrigerator** • Slice off any moldy areas and use grated in soups or to top vegetables or salads.

To avoid stringy or grainy cheese when adding to a sauce • Shred the cheese on the coarsest teeth of a box grater. Add toward the end of the cooking process, over very low heat, and whisk gently until melted.

To keep Swiss cheese from becoming stringy when cooked • Add an acid, such as lemon juice or white wine.

To keep cheese from curdling in a sauce or baked gratin • Add a little flour or cornstarch at the beginning of the recipe, before you add the cheese.

TIME SAVERS ▼ **To speed grating** • Coat the grater lightly with oil. This will prevent the cheese from sticking and make cleanup easier.

To melt quickly • If you need to melt cheese on a burger quickly, cover the burger (with a pan lid or bowl) to create steam, which will melt the cheese quickly.

FLAVOR TIP ▼ **To get the best-tasting Parmesan** • Always buy Parmigiano-Reggiano, which tastes noticeably better than domestic Parmesan cheese. Avoid buying pregrated Parmesan unless you know that it was just grated. After grating, cheese begins to lose much of its aroma and flavor. For best results, grate or shave Parmesan fresh, just before eating. To shave Parmesan, run a vegetable peeler across a block of cheese.

PARMESAN SPOON BREAD Preheat oven to 375°F. Grease a 1½-quart casserole. In a medium saucepan over medium heat, cook **2 cups milk** until bubbles just begin to form around the edge. In a bowl, whisk **1 cup cold milk** into **¾ cup coarse yellow cornmeal.** Stir into hot milk. While stirring constantly over medium heat, add **3 tablespoons butter, ¾ teaspoon salt,** and **⅛ teaspoon ground black pepper.** Cook until very thick, 3 or 4 minutes. In a large bowl, whisk **3 large eggs** until foamy. On a sheet of waxed paper, combine **¾ cup grated Parmesan cheese, 2 tablespoons all-purpose flour,** and **1 tablespoon baking powder.** Whisk into eggs. Stir in a large spoonful of hot cornmeal mixture. Add remaining cornmeal mixture and stir to blend. Turn into the prepared casserole. Sprinkle with **2 tablespoons (⅓ ounce) grated Parmesan** and **½ teaspoon paprika.** Bake until deeply golden, 35 minutes. Serve hot. *Makes 6 servings.*

Cheesecake

More custard than cake, cheesecakes are one of the best loved of all cakes. There are two main styles: those made with cream cheese, and Italian-style cheesecakes made with ricotta or other dry-curd cheese.

C

To make a simple crumb crust • Use a crisp cookie, such as graham crackers, gingersnaps, or chocolate wafers. Place in a zipper-lock plastic bag and roll with a rolling pin until crushed to medium-coarse crumbs. Dust the pan with the crumbs.

To ensure proper cooking • Use the right size pan. If the pan is too small, the filling will rise too high and the cake will take longer to cook. If the pan is too big, the cake will not rise high enough and may overcook and crack.

To make in a cake pan (instead of a springform pan) • Grease the interior of a cake pan. Line the pan bottom with a round of parchment or waxed paper.

To avoid lumps • Bring the cream cheese and eggs to room temperature. When mixing, scrape the bowl sides frequently, especially before adding eggs and liquids, so that all of the cream cheese is softened and incorporated.

To keep from curdling • Bake the cheesecake in a water bath.

To keep cheesecakes baked in a springform pan from leaking into the water bath • Wrap the exterior of the springform pan in a double thickness of aluminum foil before adding the crumb crust and filling.

To promote even cooking • Choose a pan for the water bath that is wide enough to allow at least a 1"-wide ring of water around the springform pan. Make sure that the sides of the water bath pan are not taller than the sides of the cake pan.

To avoid sloshing hot water from the water bath into the cake • Place the filled cake pan and the larger water-bath pan onto the oven rack before adding the water. Use a teakettle to pour the hot water into the pan. Before removing the cake, use a turkey baster to remove some of the water from the water bath.

To unmold a cheesecake baked in a traditional cake pan • Run a thin-bladed knife around the inside pan edges. Coat a sheet of plastic wrap with cooking spray and stretch it across the top of the cake pan. Set a metal baking sheet over the plastic wrap. Invert both pan and baking sheet, and gently rap on the inverted pan to release the cake. Remove the pan, then put a serving plate on top of the cake and invert again so that the cake is right side up. Remove the plastic wrap.

To unmold a cheesecake that clings to the pan • Wrap a hot, damp towel around the sides of the pan and wait a few minutes before releasing the cake.

To make a clean slice • Dip a long, thin knife, such as a carving knife, in hot water before slicing. Wipe and rinse under hot water again as needed.

To salvage a cracked cheesecake • Cover the surface with a layer of sweetened sour cream, fresh berries, sliced fruit, chocolate shavings, or slivered almonds.

To serve a cheesecake that is overcooked and dry • Top with a moist sauce, such as a fruit, caramel, or chocolate sauce.

To camouflage a cheesecake that has sunk in the center • Top with sliced fruit. If the cheesecake has sunk dramatically or is a total failure, scoop out servings with an ice cream scoop, roll in cookie crumbs, and serve drizzled with a sauce.

OVERNIGHT ITALIAN-STYLE RICOTTA CHEESECAKE Preheat oven to 200°F. Grease a 2-quart soufflé dish or casserole with cooking spray or butter. Press **1 cup cookie crumbs** into the bottom. Combine **1 pound room-temperature reduced-fat cream cheese, 1 container (1 pound) ricotta cheese, 1 cup sugar,**

1 tablespoon vanilla extract, ¼ cup dark rum, and ⅛ teaspoon salt. Mix until very smooth. Beat in 5 eggs and pour into the prepared pan. Bake 6 to 8 hours (the exact time is not crucial, if you decide to sleep in). Remove from oven and cool on a rack until the pan is cool enough to touch. Cover with a sheet of plastic wrap or waxed paper and an inverted plate. Invert. Remove the pan and refrigerate cake, upside down, at least 4 hours. Invert a serving plate over cheesecake and invert the whole thing. Remove the top plate and the plastic wrap or paper. Cover and store in a refrigerator up to 1 week. Cut with a long, sharp knife dipped in warm water. *Makes 16 servings.*

HEALTHY HINTS ▼ **To reduce fat in the crust** • Just use a dusting of cookie crumbs, such as reduced-fat graham crackers or gingersnaps. If using a moistened crumb crust, moisten

Overnight One-Pot Cheesecake

The slower a cheesecake bakes, the creamier it gets. Plus, when cooked at a low temperature, its surface is less likely to crack, it doesn't need a water bath, and— miracle of miracles—it bakes while you sleep!

¼ **cup graham cracker or cookie crumbs**

2 **pounds cream cheese, regular or reduced-fat, at room temperature**

1 **cup sugar**

2 **tablespoons vanilla extract**

¼ **cup brandy**

5 **eggs**

1. Just before bedtime, preheat the oven to 200°F. Grease a 9" springform pan or 2-quart soufflé dish. Dust with the cracker or cookie crumbs. Set aside.

2. In a large bowl, combine the cream cheese and sugar until smooth. Stir in the vanilla extract, brandy, and eggs until well blended. Pour the batter into the prepared pan and place in the oven overnight.

3. The next morning, 6 to 8 hours later, the cake will be set and the top will have just colored. Remove to a rack and cool in the pan until the pan is cool enough to handle, 1 hour.

4. Remove the sides of the springform pan. (Or, cover the soufflé dish with plastic wrap and an inverted plate. Turn upside down and remove the pan.) Refrigerate for at least 1 hour. (If using an inverted plate, turn right side up onto a serving plate before serving.) Cover and refrigerate until ready to serve.

Makes 16 servings

with 1 to 2 tablespoons melted better for each cup of crumbs used, adding just enough corn syrup, honey, or apple jelly that the mixture barely holds together. Press the crust into the pan.

To reduce fat in the filling • Replace the cream cheese with a combination of equal parts Neufchâtel cheese (or low-fat cream cheese) and pureed dry-curd cottage cheese (or well-drained and pureed cottage cheese). If sour cream is called for in the recipe, use reduced-fat sour cream, or vanilla yogurt drained for 45 minutes and then mixed with 1 tablespoon flour. Replace every 2 egg yolks with 1 egg white, leaving in at least 1 egg yolk for color and flavor.

Cherries

Evidence of humans enjoying cherries dates back to 300 B.C. There are two main types of these tiny stone fruits: sweet and sour. Sweet cherries, which are larger, are best enjoyed straight from the tree, but they can also be cooked. Sour cherries, usually too tart to be eaten out of hand, make delicious pies, tarts, cobblers, and preserves. The first cherries arrive in the market late in spring and they remain throughout the summer.

BASICS ▼ **To choose** • Look for plump, firm fruits with their stems intact.

To store • Keep cherries in a bag in the refrigerator. Wash just before using.

To pit • Use a cherry pitter. Stick the pitter inside a plastic bag and pit the cherries there for easy cleanup. Or use needle-nose pliers to break through the flesh, grasp the pit with the point of the pliers, and pull it out. You can also insert a sturdy drinking straw into the bottom of the cherry and push the pit out through the stem end.

PROBLEM SOLVER ▼ **To rescue bland-tasting cherries** • Marinate overnight in cherry juice or any berry juice, or in sugar-sweetened brandy. Or marinate overnight in red wine vinegar; then, warm in a saucepan and serve with pork.

Chestnuts *see also* Nuts

Lower in fat than most nuts, chestnuts have just 37 calories and less than 1 gram of fat per ounce (cooked). They add rich, earthy flavor to salads, stuffings, and rice dishes. Look for fresh, unshelled chestnuts in markets from September to February. Around the same time, you'll find chestnuts in cans, which save the time-consuming step of peeling.

BASICS ▼ **To choose** • Look for plump, firm nuts with no blemishes on the shell.

To store • Refrigerate in a zipper-lock plastic bag for up to 2 weeks. Or freeze for up to 5 months.

To roast and peel • Cut a slit in the flat part of the shell to prevent the nuts from exploding. Place on a baking sheet and roast at 400°F for 10 minutes (if peeling only) or for 20 minutes (if you want to cook them all the way through). Using a kitchen towel or oven mitts, remove and discard the shells and inner brown skins while the nuts are still hot. (If you let them cool, they are more difficult to peel). Chop or use as desired.

To boil and peel • Cut a slit in the shells, place the nuts in a saucepan with water to cover, and bring to a boil. Reduce the heat to medium and simmer for 4 minutes (to peel only), or cover and simmer for 25 minutes (to cook until tender). Peel and chop or use as desired.

TIME SAVER ▼ **To microwave** • Cut a slit in the flat part of the shell. Place the chestnuts in a shallow, microwaveable dish and cook on high power 8 minutes for 1 pound chestnuts. Peel while warm.

FLAVOR TIPS ▼ **To intensify flavor and make texture more velvety** • Cut a slit in the shells, place in a covered casserole dish with 2 tablespoons water, and bake at 425°F until tender when pierced with a knife, 30 minutes. Peel while warm.

To flavor stuffing • Add ½ cup cooked, peeled, and chopped chestnuts to your favorite 5-cup stuffing recipe.

CHESTNUT SAUCE Sauté **2 chopped shallots** in **1 tablespoon oil.** Add **2 cups beef broth** and **2 tablespoons Madeira.** Cook until reduced to 1 cup. Stir in ¾ **cup cooked, peeled, and chopped chestnuts.** Serve with **1 pound beef or game.** *Makes about 2 cups.*

Chicken *see also* Cornish Game Hens; Poultry; Turkey; Doneness Tests and Temperatures (page 572)

Chicken is the world's largest source of meat. In the United States, more than 5 billion chickens are raised annually. It is estimated that Americans consumed 81 pounds of chicken per person in 2000. The largest chicken producer in the world is Tyson.

BASICS ▼ **To estimate how much to buy** • Chicken will lose some of its weight upon cooking, so buy a little more than you intend to serve. For boneless chicken, buy 1 extra ounce for every 4-ounce cooked serving you'd like to end up with. For example, purchase a 5-ounce boneless chicken breast to equal a 4-ounce cooked serving,

C

CHOOSING CHICKEN

Choosing a bird depends on how you intend to prepare it. Chickens are classified by size, each with their own characteristics and recommended cooking methods

Bird	Weight (lb)	Characteristics	Cooking Methods
Rock Cornish hen (game hen)	1–2½	Small enough for single serving	Roast or grill
Broiler	2–3	Tender meat; usually sold cut up	Use any cooking method
Broiler-fryer	3–4	Similar to broilers; often sold whole	Roast or broil whole; grill, fry, sauté, or broil pieces
Roaster	3–5	Higher fat content than broiler-fryers	Roast, grill, or smoke whole
Stewer	3–6	More flavorful, but tougher meat	Braise or use in soups or stews
Capon	4–10	Younger roosters fattened to produce large, tender breast meat	Roast or broil whole

C

or, multiplying that figure, 20 ounces for 4 servings. For bone-in chicken, buy 3 extra ounces for every 4-ounce cooked serving of meat you'd like to end up with. For example, purchase 7 ounces chicken leg to equal a 4-ounce cooked serving, or 28 ounces for 4 servings.

To store • Keep chicken in its original packaging and store in the coldest part of the refrigerator (usually the bottom, toward the back) for no more than a day or two. If you don't plan to eat it within a day or two, freeze it in its original packaging.

To thaw frozen chicken • Put it in the refrigerator. Thaw on a plate. This will help reduce the risk of harmful bacteria developing, retain moisture, and catch any juices that seep through the packaging.

To reduce risk of contamination • Avoid storing raw chicken next to any food that you plan on eating raw, such as fruit or lettuce. Wash your hands, cutting board, counter, knives, and anything else that comes in contact with raw chicken in hot, soapy water before handling any other food. And, when preparing a meal, prep the chicken last, if possible.

To help pull off slippery chicken skin • Grab with a paper towel and pull back firmly.

To cut through raw chicken skin and bones • Use kitchen shears instead of a knife.

Fascinating Fact: There are more chickens than people in the world.

To butterfly a boneless chicken breast • Start at the thickest side of the breast and slice the breast crosswise through the side, almost in half. Open the breast up like a book and press to flatten.

Butterflied breasts can be grilled or sautéed, or pounded thinner for quicker cooking.

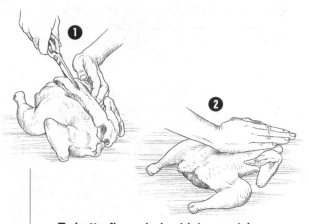

To butterfly a whole chicken • A butterflied chicken roasts in half the time and develops a crisp, golden skin. Essentially, you open the bird like a book to expose more surface area to the heat.

Cut through the ribs on each side of the backbone with a sharp knife or kitchen shears. Remove the backbone ❶.

With the bird placed skin side up, press the palm of your hand hard against the breastbone to flatten the bird ❷.

To pound boneless, skinless chicken breasts or thighs • Place the chicken on a sheet of plastic wrap on a sturdy work surface. Spray the meat with cooking spray or splash with a few drops of water to help prevent sticking, and cover with another sheet of plastic. Choose a pounder with a broad, flat face; those with raised ridges or a textured grid will tear the meat. A meat mallet, a cast-iron skillet, and the flat side of a fist-size rock all work well. Begin at the thickest section and hit the meat squarely, pounding outward to encourage the meat to spread as it thins rather than to become impacted. As you approach thinner sections of meat, lighten the force of your stroke to help produce an even thickness across the entire surface. For grilling, flatten to ½" thickness. For sautéing, flatten to ¼" or ⅛" thickness.

To evenly cook boneless, skinless breasts • Position breasts in a hot pan so that the thin, tapered ends are on the pan edges, where foods tend to cook more slowly. It also helps to remove the small tenderloin, which cooks up in just a few minutes. Or use the dull side of a chef's knife to pound the breast to an even thickness.

To reduce oil splatter when sautéing boneless, skinless breasts • Pat them dry with paper towels and lightly coat with flour before adding them to the preheated pan. Lay the breasts in the pan using tongs.

To evenly cook mixed chicken pieces • Legs and wings will cook faster than breasts and thighs, so add legs and wings halfway through the cooking time. If the legs and wings cook through before the breasts and thighs, pull them from the heat and cover in foil while the other pieces finish cooking.

To get a crisp, golden skin on roasted chicken • Rub the bird all over with mayonnaise before roasting. Or baste periodically with melted butter.

To keep breast meat moist on a roasted chicken • Set the chicken, breast side down, in the roasting pan.

To test roasted chicken for doneness • Prick the bird between the thigh bones to release some juices. If the juices are clear, the chicken is done. If they are pink, cook until the juices run clear. Also, the breast meat should register 180°F on an instant-read thermometer.

To lift a hot, roasted chicken onto a carving plate • Insert a sturdy chef's knife or a long-handled wooden spoon into the hollow of the carcass, lift, and transfer.

PROBLEM SOLVERS ▼ **To keep cut chicken pieces from drying out in the refrigerator** • Soak a large, thick kitchen towel in ice water, wring it well, and use it to line a large, rimmed baking sheet. Arrange the chicken pieces in a single layer on top of the wet towel and cover loosely with waxed paper. The chicken will remain moist in the refrigerator for up to 12 hours.

To keep boneless, skinless breasts from shrinking during cooking • Use a paring knife to strip out the white tendon that runs the length of the breast.

To prevent roasted chicken wings from stewing in their fat • Prop on a rack set inside a roasting pan. For easy cleanup, line the pan with aluminum foil.

To prevent overcooking • Insert an instant-read thermometer into the thickest portion of the meat. See page 572 for doneness temperatures.

To salvage a dry, overcooked chicken • Chop small and use to prepare a chicken salad. Or slice thin on a diagonal and serve with a quick sauce, chutney, or gravy.

To save a stew that has overcooked pieces of bone-in chicken • Shred the meat off the bone and add back to the stew just before serving.

TIME SAVERS ▼ **To thaw whole chicken faster** • Leave the chicken in its packaging and place in a bucket of cool water in the refrigerator.

To roast whole chicken faster • Butterfly it (see opposite page). Or start roasting it upside down. Coat a 3- to 3½-pound chicken with olive oil and season with salt and ground black pepper. Place on a rack in a rimmed baking pan with the breast side down. This will lift the densest part of the thighs high into the heat of the oven and protect the more tender breast, allowing it to cook gently.

C

ONE CHICKEN, MANY PARTS

To save money on chicken parts, buy a whole chicken and cut it into parts yourself. It's pretty easy. This method will result in 2 pieces each of boneless breast halves, thighs, drumsticks, and wings. If you buy a whole chicken breast and want to bone it, see just illustrations 6, 7, and 8.

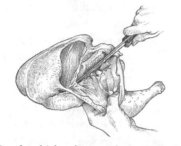

❶ Put the chicken breast side up. Pull a leg away from the body and cut between the body and thigh, bending the leg away from the body until the ball of the thigh bone pops out of the hip socket. Cut between this ball and socket to separate the leg from the body. Repeat with the other leg.

❷ To separate the drumstick from the thigh, cut firmly down between the joint.

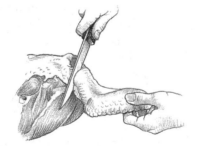

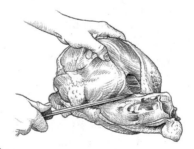

❸ Pull a wing upward until the joint pops. Cut between the ball and socket, pulling the wing away from the body and cutting through the base of the wing. Repeat with the other wing.

❹ To separate the breast from the backbone, place the bird on its back and cut from front to back just under the rib cage.

Roast at 475°F until the top surface of the chicken is golden brown, 25 minutes. Turn over the chicken and roast until the internal temperature of the breast is 180°F and the juices run clear, about 15 minutes more. Allow the chicken to rest before carving.

To barbecue chicken faster • Pre-cook it. Toss 4 pounds bone-in chicken parts in 1¾ cups barbecue sauce and place

C

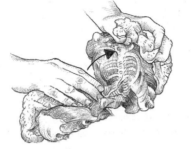

5 Pry the body apart by pushing and pulling the breast and back in opposite directions.

6 To separate the breast into halves, bend the breast halves back to pop out the keel bone.

7 Working with one breast at a time, place the knife under the rib bones and cut with steady, even pressure to trim the meat away from the bones. Cut through the shoulder joint to remove the entire rib cage.

8 Turn the breast over and trim away the wishbone. Slip the knife under the white tendons on each side of the breast, loosening and pulling them out (grasp with a paper towel if slippery). Remove the skin, if desired. Cut the breast into halves and cut each half, if desired.

in a single layer in a microwaveable dish. Reserve another ¼ cup sauce for basting. Cover and microwave on high power for 8 minutes. While the chicken is precooking, preheat the grill. Grease the rack. Remove the chicken from the baking dish. Place the chicken on the rack, about 3" from a hot fire. Grill until the surfaces are dark brown, the center of the thickest piece registers 170°F, and juices run clear, about

C

10 minutes, basting with sauce and turning at least 4 times.

To use leftover chicken • It takes no longer to roast 2 chickens than to roast 1. Save yourself work by roasting a second chicken ahead. Then, use for stir-fries, salads, sandwiches, casseroles, soups, and stews to come. Or buy a deli-roasted chicken (rotisserie chicken); eat half fresh and hot and save half for a recipe. Wherever it comes from, leftover cooked chicken is plump with possibilities.

CHICKEN À LA KING Melt **3 tablespoons butter** in a skillet over medium heat. Add **4 ounces thinly sliced mushrooms, 3 tablespoons finely chopped green bell pepper,** and **2 tablespoons minced scallion (white part) or onion.** Sauté until soft. Stir in **¼ cup all-purpose flour** and stir to moisten (mixture will be dry). Stir in **1¼ cups chicken broth, ½ cup heavy or light cream,** and **¼ cup dry sherry.** Stir constantly until thick and simmering, 2 minutes. Whisk **2 egg yolks** in a bowl and whisk in about **1 cup of hot broth mixture.** Reduce heat to low and return broth/egg mixture to pan. Stir in **½ teaspoon salt** and **⅛ teaspoon** *each* **grated nutmeg and ground black pepper.** Add **2 cups finely chopped cooked chicken, ¼ cup chopped jarred pimientos,** and **2 tablespoons chopped fresh parsley.** Serve hot over **4 split biscuits.** *Makes 4 servings.*

CHICKEN-TORTILLA CASSEROLE Stir together **2 cups chopped cooked chicken, 1 can (15 ounces) rinsed and drained black beans, 1 jar (8 ounces) drained canned chile peppers,** and **½ cup canned enchilada sauce.** Place in a 9" × 9" baking dish. Top with **¾ cup crumbled tortilla chips** and bake at 400°F until heated through, 30 minutes. Sprinkle on **½ cup shredded Jack cheese** and bake until melted, 5 minutes. *Makes 4 servings.*

CHICKEN-VEGETABLE GRATIN Combine **2 cups finely chopped cooked chicken; 1 can (15 ounces) drained water-packed artichoke hearts; 1 cup cooked, squeezed-dry spinach;** and **4 sliced scallions.** Place in a 9" round baking dish. Top with **1½ cups Basic White Sauce** (page 439). Mix **3 tablespoons grated Parmesan cheese** and **2 tablespoons dried bread crumbs.** Sprinkle over top. Bake at 350°F until bubbly and golden, 35 minutes. *Makes 4 servings.*

CHICKEN CAROLINA STEW In a saucepan over medium heat, bring to a simmer **1 can (15 ounces) chicken broth, 1 can (15 ounces) Italian-style diced tomatoes with juice, ¼ cup white wine, 2 large shredded carrots, 1 cup canned lima beans, ½ cup frozen corn, 1 teaspoon dried thyme,** and **½ teaspoon dried marjoram.** Simmer until vegetables are tender, 20 minutes. Stir in **2 cups shredded cooked chicken** and cook until heated through, 5 minutes. *Makes 4 servings.*

FLAVOR TIPS ▼ **To flavor a stewing hen** • Old hens have the biggest chicken flavor, but it takes a long time to make the tough meat tender. Put a large (5- to 6-pound) stewing hen (or 2 smaller ones) in a Dutch oven. Add 12 cups water (or half water, half chicken stock); 1 cup white wine; 2 tablespoons

Oven-Fried Chicken

For better crunch and crispness, use crushed Wheat Thins crackers or crushed plain bread sticks instead of bread crumbs.

1½ **cups buttermilk**

1 **tablespoon Dijon mustard**

3 **cups coarsely crushed Wheat Thins crackers or plain bread sticks**

½ **teaspoon ground black pepper**

¼ **teaspoon salt**

¼ **teaspoon paprika**

2 **tablespoons melted butter**

1 **cut-up chicken (about 3½ pounds bone-in chicken parts), breasts cut in half widthwise**

1. Preheat the oven to 400°F. Adjust the oven rack to the upper-middle position.

2. In a medium bowl, combine the buttermilk and mustard. Stir to blend. In a shallow, medium bowl, combine the crumbs, pepper, salt, and paprika. Sprinkle with the butter and toss to distribute evenly. Working one piece at a time, dip the chicken into the buttermilk mixture, then into the crumb mixture, pressing so that the crumbs thoroughly coat the chicken.

3. Arrange the chicken, skin side up, on a baking sheet. Bake until a thermometer inserted in the thickest portion registers 170°F, the juices run clear, and the crust is golden brown, 35 to 40 minutes.

Makes 4 to 6 servings

Barbecue Lover's Oven-Fried Chicken: Substitute 2 whole, beaten eggs diluted with 1 tablespoon water for the buttermilk, and brush the chicken with a thick layer of barbecue sauce before dipping in the egg mixture.

Oven-Fried Chicken with Garlic, Rosemary, and Lemon: Add ¼ cup lemon juice to the buttermilk mixture. Omit the paprika from the crumb mixture. Instead, combine 1 minced garlic clove, 1 teaspoon grated lemon peel, and 2 teaspoons minced fresh rosemary with the crumb mixture.

---

vinegar; 1 *each* sliced onion, carrot, and celery rib; 2 large garlic cloves; 2 bay leaves; 2 large parsley sprigs; 1 teaspoon thyme; 15 whole peppercorns; and 10 cloves. Cover and simmer over low heat until tender, 2 to 3 hours. Remove the chicken from the broth. If desired, remove all meat, then return the trimmings and

bones to the broth and simmer 1 to 2 hours longer to make chicken stock.

To add deep flavor to roasted chicken • Cut 3 tablespoons flavored butter (see "Five Flavored Butters," on page 81) into thin slices. Beginning near the large cavity of a roasting chicken, carefully slip your fingers between the skin and breast meat to separate almost to the neck cavity. Loosen the skin over both breast halves, then slide in slices of flavored butter. Roast as usual.

ROAST LEMON CHICKEN Preheat oven to 425°F. Season inside and outside of **1 whole chicken** (3 to 3½ pounds) with **¾ teaspoon salt** and **½ teaspoon ground black pepper.** Pierce **1 lemon** several times with a fork and place inside body cavity of chicken (add **2 large rosemary sprigs** and **4 peeled and smashed garlic cloves,** if desired). Tie legs together with kitchen twine, if desired, and put chicken, breast side up, on a rack set in a roasting pan. Roast until a thermometer inserted in breast registers 180°F and juices run clear, 45 to 50 minutes. Let stand 10 minutes before carving. *Makes 4 to 6 servings.*

SPICY ROASTED CHICKEN Follow the recipe for **Roast Lemon Chicken** (above). Combine **2 tablespoons olive oil, 1 tablespoon ground cumin, 2 teaspoons** *each* **dried oregano and ground black pepper, 1 teaspoon salt,** and **¾ teaspoon sweet paprika.** Brush mixture over chicken before roasting.
Makes 4 to 6 servings.

GRILLED BUTTERFLIED CHICKEN Preheat the grill. Butterfly **1 whole chicken** (about 3 pounds). (See page 104.) Rub both sides with **2 tablespoons olive oil** and season with **½ teaspoon garlic salt** and **¼ teaspoon ground black pepper.** Place, skin side down, on a greased grill rack over a hot fire. Cover with a baking sheet and weigh down with 2 bricks. Grill 12 minutes. Turn over, re-

cover with the baking sheet and bricks, and grill until skin is crisp, inside of breast registers 180°F on an instant-read thermometer, and juices run clear, another 15 minutes. Let stand 10 minutes. Cut into pieces and serve. *Makes 4 servings.*

CRISPY CHICKEN CUTLETS Pound **4 boneless, skinless chicken breast halves** to ¼" to ½" thickness. Place **¼ cup flour** in a shallow dish. In another shallow dish, combine **2 large eggs** and **1 teaspoon water.** In a third dish, combine **1 cup plain dry bread crumbs, ¼ cup (¾ ounce) grated Parmesan cheese, 1 teaspoon dried oregano,** and **¼ teaspoon salt.** In a large skillet over medium-high heat, combine **1½ tablespoons** *each* **olive oil and butter.** Dip a cutlet in flour to coat, then into egg mixture, and finally into crumb mixture, patting both sides so that crumbs adhere. Place in the hot pan and repeat with a second cutlet. Cook until crisp and golden, about 2 minutes. Turn and cook until chicken is no longer pink and juices run clear, 1 to 2 minutes. Drain on paper towels. Add more olive oil and butter if necessary and cook remaining 2 cutlets. For an appetizer, cut into strips and serve with **½ cup Lemon–Basil Mayonnaise** (see page 273). *Makes 6 to 8 appetizer servings.*

CHICKEN PARMIGIANA Make **Crispy Chicken Cutlets** (above), but don't cut into strips. Place cooked cutlets in a shallow baking dish and spoon about **½ cup chunky tomato sauce** over each. Top with **¼ cup (1 ounce) grated mozzarella cheese.** Drizzle another **2 tablespoons chunky tomato sauce** over top and sprinkle with **2 tablespoons**

FOUR TWISTS ON CHICKEN BREASTS

Boneless, skinless chicken breasts need a little flavor infusion. Yes, they're lean. Yes, they're versatile. Yes, they're easy to cook. But where's the flavor? Here it is.

The Method: In each recipe below, the chicken is marinated and then grilled, broiled, or pan-fried. The marinating instructions are included below. Whichever cooking method you choose, first remove the chicken from the marinade, then brush the chicken with oil or butter. Cook until the thickest part of the breast registers 160°F on an instant-read thermometer and the juices run clear. Each recipe makes 4 to 6 servings.

Spicy Citrus Chicken: In a zipper-lock plastic bag, combine the **grated zest from 1** *each* **orange, lemon, and lime, 1 can (6 ounces) frozen and thawed orange juice concentrate, 3 tablespoons** *each* **lemon and lime juice, ½ cup canned tomato sauce, ¼ cup honey or brown sugar, 2 large minced garlic cloves, 1 teaspoon thyme,** and **½ teaspoon** *each* **ground red pepper and ground black pepper.** Add **4 to 6 boneless, skinless chicken breast halves.** Marinate in the refrigerator 2 to 6 hours before cooking. Discard marinade.

Creamy Lemon-Dill Chicken: In a zipper-lock plastic bag, combine **1 cup plain yogurt, ¼ cup lemon juice, 3 tablespoons chopped fresh dill,** and **½ teaspoon** *each* **salt and ground black pepper.** Add **4 to 6**

boneless, skinless chicken breast halves. Marinate in the refrigerator 1 to 2 hours before cooking. Discard marinade. If broiling, **1 tablespoon crumbled feta cheese per breast** can be sprinkled over top after cooking is complete; then broil a minute or two longer to brown the feta.

Teriyaki Chicken: In a zipper-lock plastic bag, combine **⅓ cup** *each* **tamari or soy sauce, mirin (sweet rice wine), and sake (rice wine),** or use 1 cup bottled teriyaki sauce in place of all three. Add **2 tablespoons grated fresh ginger, 1 tablespoon sugar,** and **1 large minced garlic clove.** Add **4 to 6 boneless, skinless chicken breast halves.** Marinate in the refrigerator 30 minutes to 2 hours before cooking. To make a glaze for the chicken: Strain the marinade. Dissolve **2 teaspoons cornstarch** in **1 tablespoon cold water.** Stir in strained marinade and cook in a saucepan, stirring, until thickened and simmering, 2 minutes. Drizzle over the cooked chicken.

Thai Chicken: In a zipper-lock plastic bag, combine **⅓ cup** *each* **chopped fresh mint and fresh cilantro, ¼ cup Thai fish sauce, 3 tablespoons lime juice, 1 tablespoon sugar, 1 tablespoon minced or grated fresh ginger,** and **1 minced garlic clove.** Add **4 to 6 boneless, skinless chicken breast halves.** Marinate in the refrigerator 2 to 4 hours before cooking. Discard marinade.

---

grated Parmesan cheese. Bake at 400°F until chicken is hot and cheese is melted, 10 to 15 minutes. Serve on rolls or with pasta. *Makes 4 servings.*

HEALTHY HINTS ▼ **To choose a more healthy chicken •** Look for free-range, organic, or kosher chickens. Free-range chickens are allowed to roam free in a pasture and forage for seeds and grass. Some cooks believe that they are moister and more tender than commercially raised poultry. Organic chickens may only be raised on land that has not had any chemical fertilizer or pesticide used on it for at least 3 years. They also must be fed chemical-free grains and are generally free-range chickens. In some states, growers may be organically certified and inspected regularly for ecologically safe methods of raising chickens. Organic chickens may be thinner and have less fat and more flavor than commercially raised birds. Kosher chickens must meet strict standards imposed by Jewish dietary laws. They must be killed in the most humane manner possible and prepared under a rabbi's supervision. Kosher chicken is often marked with a symbol such as a U inside an O or a K for authentication. Part of the koshering process involves salting the birds, so kosher chickens will taste a bit saltier than commercially raised chickens.

To reduce calories • Removing the skin from chicken reduces calories by up to one-half. When cooking, leave the skin on to retain moisture in the meat. Remove the skin just before serving.

Chile Peppers, Dried

A popular way of preserving chiles, drying changes not only the color, texture, and flavor of chiles but sometimes even changes the name. Dried jalapeños are called chipotles, and dried poblanos are known as ancho chiles. Dried chiles are most often used for making sauces. Little ones can be pureed whole; larger ones, such as ancho chiles, are usually toasted to bring out their flavor, then reconstituted in warm water. They are then pureed and strained before using.

BASICS ▼ **To choose** • Look for dried chiles with an even color. Hold them in your hand and bend them gently. Dried chiles should be pliable, with no signs of cracking. Any light orange patches indicate that bugs got to the chiles before you did.

To clean • Wipe off any dust with a damp cloth. For very dusty chiles with deep, hard-to-reach crags, rinse briefly under running water.

To seed and devein • Using your hands or scissors, tear off the stem and then rip open the chile lengthwise. Loosen the seeds and shake them out. Tear out the light-colored veins.

To dice neatly • Using scissors, cut the seeded halves into strips. Snip across the strips into squares.

To toast • Toasting dried chile peppers intensifies their rich flavors. Tear the chile into large, flat pieces and place in a skillet over medium heat. Press the chile pieces flat with a spatula for 5 to 10 seconds. Turn over and toast the other side 5 to 10 seconds, pressing flat. The chiles will soften and turn leathery, but remove them before they have a chance to blacken and burn.

To soak • Place dried chiles (whole or pieces, toasted or untoasted) in a bowl and add boiling water to cover. Let soften 15 to 20 minutes. Drain. The soaking liquid is often discarded because it can be bitter.

Chile Peppers, Fresh

There are well over 200 varieties of chiles. These fruits of various members of the Capsicum family are best known for being fiery hot, but many chiles are quite mild and have deep, rich flavors.

BASICS **To choose** • Look for chiles with vibrant color and taut skin. Avoid those with blemishes or soft spots.

To store • Keep fresh chiles in the refrigerator.

To avoid touching when handling • You might not feel the heat of a jalapeño or other fresh chile pepper on your fingertips, but it will sear if it comes in contact with any of your mucous membranes, such as your lips, nostrils, or, the worst, your eyes. To avoid the problem, you can wear plastic gloves or use a plastic bag when handling chiles. Or, hold the chile in place with a pair of chopsticks or tweezers while slicing and cleaning out the seeds and veins. Better yet, seed and devein by holding the chile by its stem. Slice about ⅛" from the tip of the chile. Still holding on to the stem, set the pepper upright on its flattened tip. Slice downward from stem to tip, slicing the sides off of the core. Discard the core with its stem, seeds, and veins. (See the illustration on page 350.)

To seed when halved lengthwise • Hold the chile by its stem and use a toothed grapefruit spoon or melon baller to scrape out the seeds and veins.

To reduce the heat • Scrape out the veins that line the inside of the chile flesh. This is where capsaicin, the heat source in a chile pepper, is concentrated. There is no capsaicin in the seeds, but they are often quite hot because of their proximity to the veins, so remove those too if you like a milder chile. The tip of a chile pepper will always be the mildest because it is farthest from the veins. You can also reduce the heat by soaking chiles in heavily salted water for several hours.

To soothe hands irritated by handling hot chiles • Make a paste of baking soda and water. Rub over your hands and rinse with cold water.

To preserve • Rinse well and put in a glass jar filled with vinegar. They will keep indefinitely in the refrigerator.

To roast • Cook them directly over a flame, until bubbly and blackened all over, turning occasionally with a pair of tongs. You can also roast chiles with a blowtorch. Or spread them on a baking sheet and roast under a broiler. Seal roasted chiles in a paper bag until cool enough to handle, 5 minutes. Wearing plastic gloves, remove and discard the core and seeds, then peel and discard the skin.

PROBLEM SOLVERS **To put out the fire in your mouth** • Reach for a dairy product such as milk, yogurt, or ice cream. Dairy fat will intervene between the pain receptors in your mouth and the chile's hot capsaicin.

To cool down a dish that's too chile-pepper hot • Add a dairy product. Or add some sugar to help to cut the heat. You can also throw in chunks of raw potato to help absorb some of the chile's capsaicin. If the dish is so hot that none of these options work, make a second batch (minus the chiles) and combine it with the first batch to dilute the heat.

Chili *see also* Stews

This stew from the American Southwest sometimes goes by the name of chili con carne, Spanish for chili with meat. Originally a stew of beef in a red chile pepper sauce, chili has become a wildly varied dish. Some cooks leave out the beans, while others consider them essential to the dish. Tomatoes are verboten in some regions of the country and an important ingredient in others. Some chili cooks use pork instead of beef, and others leave out the meat altogether and make vegetarian chili instead. Cincinnati chili is served over pasta.

FLAVOR TIPS ▼

To doctor canned chili • Add ¼ cup beer or dry sherry and ½ teaspoon *each* ground cumin and dried oregano. Simmer 5 minutes.

To spice up chili • Most commercial chili powders are not very hot; you can add up to ⅓ cup and create great chili flavor without a lot of heat. To increase the heat, add about ½ teaspoon (or more) ground red pepper. If using a pure ground chile pepper, add just a small amount to avoid making the dish overly spicy.

To thicken • Cooking chili longer is the best way to thicken it and deepen its flavors. In a pinch, you can add 2 tablespoons cornmeal per 8 cups chili and cook 5 minutes. The cornmeal will thicken the liquid and add flavor (particularly good with chili that contains kernel corn). For really thick chili, add more cornmeal by 1-tablespoon increments.

EASY CHORIZO CHILI Remove ½ **pound soft Mexican chorizo** from its casing (or see Easy Mexican Chorizo, page 122) and sauté until crumbly and no longer pink, 5 minutes. Drain. Add **2 cans (15 ounces each) drained pinto beans** and ½ **cup tomato sauce.** Simmer 10 minutes. *Makes 4 servings.*

Chili Powder

Commercial chili powder is a blend of various ground, dried chile peppers with seasonings such as garlic and onion powder. It is fine for most traditional purposes, but for more flavor, use pure chile powder, made only from dried, ground chile peppers.

BASICS ▼

To store • Place in a tightly sealed jar in the refrigerator.

To make • If you've run out of commercial chili powder, here's a quick mix to get you by: 1 tablespoon ground cumin; 1 teaspoon *each* dried oregano, garlic powder, and onion powder; ½ teaspoon *each* ground red pepper and paprika; and ¼ teaspoon ground allspice. Makes about 2½ tablespoons.

To make pure chile powder • You can make your own pure chile powder by pulverizing dried chile skins in a clean coffee grinder. Clean any dust or dirt off the chiles. Break or slice them open and remove the stems and seeds, then grind the skins. Avoid breathing the dust that's produced by grinding.

Chocolate *see also* Brownies; Cakes; Cocoa Powder

With hundreds of varieties, chocolate ranges in flavor from mouth-puckering and bitter to cloyingly sweet. Colors range from mahogany to ivory. Even textures can vary from smooth to chalky. That's because there are so many variables in the growing, production, and manufacture of chocolate: the type of cacao bean used; the degree of roasting, grinding, and conching (a manufacturing process that gives chocolate its smooth texture); and the quality of the cocoa solids, cocoa butter, sugar, and flavorings.

BASICS ▼

Pure chocolate (unsweetened, baking, or bitter chocolate) • This is pure ground, roasted chocolate, also called chocolate liquor. Chocolate liquor is a blend of cocoa solids and cocoa butter. Pure chocolate is approximately 55 percent cocoa butter. Vanilla, ground nuts, salt, or other flavorings may be added.

Semisweet chocolate (bittersweet, extra bittersweet, or dark) • Chocolates in this category are a blend of chocolate liquor, sugar, vanilla or other flavoring, and sometimes extra cocoa butter. Bittersweet and semisweet differ only in the

MELTING CHOCOLATE TO OPTIMUM SMOOTHNESS

Here's how to make a smooth transition from solid bars or chips to silky, warm chocolate liquid.

Use small pieces. The smaller the pieces, the faster the chocolate will melt. Use uniform-size pieces when possible.

Coat the melting pan or bowl with oil. Do this before adding the chocolate, and cleanup will be a snap.

Keep the heat low and gentle. If body heat is enough to melt chocolate on our tongues, it won't take much heat on the stove. To keep chocolate from hardening and drying out during melting, heat it slowly over low heat, preferably indirect heat. The ideal method is to melt the chocolate in a double boiler over simmering water. If you don't have a double boiler, snugly fit a heatproof or stainless steel bowl into a saucepan of shallow water that's just barely simmering. Make sure the water doesn't touch the bottom of the bowl. This method works well for milk chocolate, for white chocolate, or when melting chocolate and butter together. For dark chocolate, you can simply place it in a heatproof bowl and place the bowl in an oven set on the lowest setting until melted, 8 to 10 minutes.

Beware even a drop of water. The smallest drop of water is enough to make warm, melted chocolate seize into a stiff mess. Make sure that bowls, spoons, or pans used are bone-dry. If melting chocolate in a saucepan, leave off the lid to avoid steam condensing on the lid and dripping onto the chocolate. If you are using a bowl set over a pan and the bowl is smaller in diameter than the pan, wrap a towel around the bowl and tuck it into the pan edge to prevent steam from wafting up from the pan into the chocolate.

Try the microwave method. Chop any type of chocolate into small pieces (or use chips), place in a microwaveable container, and heat on medium power: 40 seconds for 1 ounce chocolate, 1 minute for 2 ounces, 2 minutes for up to 4 ounces, and 3 minutes for up to 8 ounces. Stop halfway through to stir the chocolate, which will not lose its shape and melt completely but will soften enough to be stirred into a smooth liquid. If melting chocolate and butter together, chop the butter into tablespoon-size pieces and add during the last half of the cooking time.

Pull out the heating pad. Set a heating pad on high and place in a large bowl, preferably not metal. Put chocolate pieces into a smaller metal bowl and nestle the bowl into the heating pad. The chocolate will start to melt in about 10 minutes. Stir it briefly, then let sit until completely melted, another 5 minutes. To keep warm and melted for several hours (or if using for dipping), turn the heating pad to low.

To rescue seized chocolate: If your chocolate seizes up, blend in 1½ tablespoons vegetable oil or solid shortening for every 4 ounces chocolate. Stir constantly, and your chocolate will regain its smooth texture.

Chocolate-Brandy Pudding Cake

Pudding cakes deliver sauce and cake in one easy package. In the alchemy of the oven, the cake part rises up through the sauce (or maybe the sauce sinks down through the cake). At any rate, the exchange produces a moist, brownielike cake resting on a swamp of chocolate pudding. To serve, scoop up some cake with its pudding underneath and eat it with a spoon.

1 cup flour

1 cup sugar, divided

½ cup unsweetened cocoa powder, divided

2 teaspoons baking powder

½ teaspoon baking soda

¼ teaspoon salt

Pinch of ground cinnamon

½ cup low-fat milk

¼ cup canola oil

1 teaspoon vanilla extract

½ cup brown sugar

¾ cup boiling water

¼ cup brandy

1. Preheat the oven to 350°F. Grease a 9" × 9" baking pan.

2. In a large bowl, combine the flour, ¾ cup of the sugar, ¼ cup of the cocoa, the baking powder, baking soda, salt, and cinnamon. Add the milk, oil, and vanilla extract. Stir to make a thick batter.

3. Spread evenly into the prepared baking pan. Sprinkle the top with the brown sugar and the remaining ¼ cup cocoa and ¼ cup sugar. Pour the water and brandy over all.

4. Bake until the cake is set around the sides and the top is loose and bubbly, 30 minutes. Cool in the pan on a rack for at least 10 minutes. Slice or scoop to serve.

Makes 8 servings

amount of sugar, with semisweet being slightly sweeter than bittersweet. Sweetness and overall flavor vary tremendously from brand to brand. Chocolatiers blend various types of chocolate (roasted to different degrees) and flavorings to control for the desired taste, texture, and finish.

Milk chocolate • This type is sweeter and less chocolatey than semisweet chocolate because it contains more sugar and less choco-

late liquor. It also contains milk solids, which mellow the natural bitterness of chocolate. Because the milk solids can become rancid, milk chocolate has a shorter shelf life than other types. It is also softer and smoother than the dark chocolates. Flavor nuances range from caramel to vanilla to roasted nuts.

White chocolate • Some say that this is not true chocolate because it contains no cocoa solids. But high-quality white chocolate is made with cocoa butter, an important part of any chocolate. In general, white chocolate contains one-third *each* fat, milk solids, and sugar. In lower-quality white chocolate, the fat may be vegetable shortening instead of cocoa butter (and in this case, it cannot be rightfully called chocolate). A stark or pure white color indicates that vegetable shortening was used, while the best white chocolate will be creamy white in color. French and Swiss white chocolates tend to be very high quality. White chocolate is very sweet with a delicate structure, which makes it sensitive to heat and moisture.

German's Sweet Chocolate • Used mainly for German's (or "German") chocolate cake, these little bars of solid chocolate are sweetened dark chocolate with less cocoa butter, making them darker and more brittle.

Couverture • This is a special type of chocolate used for coating chocolate candies; it has extra cocoa butter to give it added gloss.

No-melt unsweetened chocolate • These little pouches of thick liquid chocolate are designed for convenience. The chocolate is a combination of cocoa, vegetable oil, and preservatives.

Unsweetened cocoa powder • This is pure chocolate liquor with about 75 percent of the cocoa butter extracted.

Fascinating Fact: Columbus was the first to bring the cacao bean to Europe, but it wasn't until the mid-1800s that chocolate was manufactured for eating.

To choose • Look for chocolate with a deep, rich aroma and a shiny finish. The bar should break with an audible snap and not crumble. If possible, ask for a taste. The best-quality chocolates will melt smoothly and slowly on your tongue.

To store • Wrap chocolate tightly in plastic wrap and then in foil, and store in a cool, dry place. Sometimes, no matter how careful you are, chocolate becomes mottled with a light-gray film. This is known as bloom, and though it's not pretty to look at, bloom will not affect the way chocolate performs or tastes. Properly stored, dark chocolate will keep for more than a year, milk and white chocolate for up to 6 months.

To chop • Use a heavy chef's knife and a stable cutting surface, then shave off small bits rather than large chunks. If you're working with a block of chocolate, place the knife diagonally across one corner and bear down evenly. The corner will break off in ¼" to ½" shards. Repeat at each corner.

To break coarsely chopped chocolate into fine pieces • Place chopped chocolate in a sturdy zipper-lock plastic bag and pound with a rolling pin or a cast-iron skillet. Do the same to break down a bag full of chocolate chips that has melted in the summer heat.

To make chocolate curls • Quickly draw a vegetable peeler down a block of chocolate. Chocolate curls melt at the slightest touch, so use tweezers to place them on a cake or pie.

To make chocolate leaves • Wash and dry unsprayed, nonpoisonous leaves, such as ivy, lemon, rose, or camellia. Paint the veiny side with melted chocolate. Chill 1 hour, then carefully peel away the leaf.

PROBLEM SOLVER ▼ **To fix bitter-tasting burnt chocolate** • Dissolve 1 teaspoon cocoa powder and 1 teaspoon sugar in ¼ cup hot water. Stir

Devil's Food Cake

Espresso is a fantastic flavor booster for chocolate. This recipe also features nonalkalized cocoa in combination with baking soda, which neutralizes the acidity in chocolate as the cake rises. This is the kind of old-fashioned cake that tastes great with a glass of ice-cold milk or scoops of vanilla ice cream. Start the frosting before the cake, since the frosting needs time to chill.

¾ **cup packed and leveled nonalkalized unsweetened cocoa powder**

2 **tablespoons instant espresso powder or coffee granules**

1½ **cups boiling water**

2 **cups sifted cake flour (not self-rising)**

1½ **teaspoons baking soda**

½ **teaspoon baking powder**

¼ **teaspoon salt**

1½ **sticks (¾ cup) butter, softened to room temperature**

2 **cups sugar**

3 **large eggs, at room temperature**

1 **tablespoon vanilla extract**

Fudge Frosting (opposite page)

1. Preheat the oven to 350°F. Grease and flour two 8" round cake pans.

2. Put the cocoa in a large bowl. Stir the espresso powder or coffee granules into the water and immediately pour over the cocoa. Stir to dissolve. Cool slightly.

3. In a medium bowl, stir together the flour, baking soda, baking powder, and salt.

4. In a large bowl, beat the butter with an electric mixer on medium speed, 30 seconds. Gradually beat in the sugar. Beat in the eggs, one at a time. Add the vanilla extract and beat until light, 1 minute.

5. Beat the flour mixture and cocoa mixture alternately into the butter mixture, beginning and ending with the flour mixture. Divide

into 4 ounces burnt chocolate until blended. If chocolate is extremely bitter, add 1 teaspoon instant coffee granules to make a mocha-flavored chocolate.

Fascinating Fact: Christmas is the most popular holiday for giving (55 percent) and receiving (50 percent) boxed chocolates. An esti-mated 36 percent of all boxed chocolate sales occur in December.

TIME SAVER ▼ **To save time when chopping blocks of bittersweet or semisweet chocolate for melting** • Use semisweet chocolate chips instead. These work fine in most mousse and brownie recipes.

between the prepared pans and smooth the tops. Bake until the tops spring back when lightly touched and the cake edges just begin to pull away from the pan, 35 to 40 minutes. Cool in the pans on a rack 5 minutes, then run a knife around the edges to loosen. Turn out the layers onto a rack and cool completely.

6. Brush any loose crumbs from the cake layers. Place one layer, upside down, on a serving plate. Spread with about 1 cup frosting. Center the second cake layer, right side up, on top. Frost the top and sides with the remaining frosting, making decorative swirls. Chill to set the frosting. Serve at room temperature.

Makes 16 servings

Fudge Frosting

A little cinnamon in this rich frosting enhances the chocolate in a most delightful way.

1½ **cups sugar**

1 **cup evaporated milk**

6 **ounces (6 squares) unsweetened chocolate**

4 **tablespoons butter**

1 **tablespoon corn syrup**

1½ **teaspoons vanilla extract**

½ **teaspoon ground cinnamon**

1. In a heavy, 3-quart saucepan over medium heat, combine the sugar, milk, chocolate, butter, and corn syrup. Cook until the mixture reaches a full boil, stirring constantly. Boil 1 minute. Remove from the heat. Stir in the vanilla extract and cinnamon. Cool until room temperature, 30 minutes.

2. Cover and refrigerate until very thick, 1 hour. Uncover and beat with an electric mixer on high speed until fluffy and light in color, 3 to 4 minutes.

Makes about 2¾ cups

FLAVOR TIPS ▼ **To make "freckles" in muffins** • Grate ¼ cup semiswect chocolate and fold into muffin batter.

To boost the flavor of hot chocolate • For every 2 cups hot chocolate, add 1 tablespoon Kahlúa, rum, or Frangelico; ⅛ teaspoon cinnamon; and a pinch of nutmeg.

EASY HOT CHOCOLATE Melt **4 ounces semisweet chocolate chips** in a double boiler (or use ½ cup chocolate syrup). Whisk in **6 cups milk** over medium-low heat. Stir in **2 tablespoons sugar** or more to taste.

Makes 4 servings.

Truffles

You can keep these luscious truffles in the refrigerator for up to 2 weeks, but don't count on them sticking around for more than a day.

12 **ounces bittersweet chocolate, chopped**

1 **cup heavy cream**

1 **tablespoon unsalted butter**

½ **cup Dutch-process unsweetened cocoa powder**

1. In a heatproof bowl, combine the chocolate, cream, and butter. Set the bowl over a pan of simmering (not boiling) water and stir until the chocolate has melted and the mixture is smooth. Pour into a bowl or baking dish, cover with plastic wrap, and chill until firm.

2. Line a baking sheet with parchment paper. Spread the cocoa on a plate or in a shallow bowl. Scoop out about a tablespoon of the chocolate mixture and roll between your palms to make a ball. Roll the ball in the cocoa and turn until well-coated. Transfer to the prepared baking sheet. Repeat to use all the chocolate mixture.

Makes about 36

Mocha Truffles: Add 1 teaspoon instant espresso powder to the bowl with the chocolate, cream, and butter.

Milk Chocolate Truffles: Substitute 1 pound milk chocolate for the bittersweet chocolate, and reduce the cream to ¾ cup.

Hazelnut Truffles: Substitute ½ cup finely chopped hazelnuts for the cocoa powder.

RICH HOT FUDGE SAUCE In a saucepan, combine **1 cup heavy cream,** ¾ **cup sugar, 4 ounces chopped unsweetened chocolate,** and **2 tablespoons light corn syrup.** Bring to a boil, stirring constantly. Reduce heat to low and simmer 3 to 5 minutes, stirring. Remove from heat and stir in **1 tablespoon unsalted butter** and **2 teaspoons vanilla extract.** Use warm or at room temperature.
Makes about 2 cups.

SIMPLE FRIDGE FUDGE Line an 8" × 8" metal pan with plastic wrap. Leave some plastic overhanging the edges, and smooth out most of the wrinkles on the pan bottom. In a saucepan over medium-low heat, combine **1 can (14 ounces) sweetened condensed milk** and **1 pound (two 8-ounce packages) semi-sweet chocolate,** coarsely chopped. Stir constantly until chocolate melts, 5 to 7 minutes. Remove from heat and stir in **1¼ cups chopped walnuts or pecans, 1½** teaspoons vanilla extract, and ⅛ teaspoon salt. Turn into the prepared pan, spreading evenly. Chill until firm, 3 hours. Remove from the pan, using the plastic wrap as handles. Discard plastic. Cut into 1" squares. Store in a tightly covered container at room temperature for up to 2 weeks. *Makes 48 pieces.*

HEALTHY HINT ▼ **To replace solid chocolate with cocoa powder** • Replace every 1 ounce unsweetened chocolate with 3 tablespoons unsweetened cocoa powder plus 1 tablespoon butter, shortening, or vegetable oil.

Chopping *see also* Cubing; Food Processors; Julienne; Mincing

This basic knife technique involves cutting food into irregular ¼" to 1" pieces. The pieces increase the surface area for quicker cooking, yet they are large enough to hold their shape and texture. For most chopping jobs, a sharp knife and a cutting board are your best tools. When you need to chop large amounts, or when you need to chop finely and the precise shape of the chop isn't important, a food processor saves time.

BASICS ▼

To chop • Slice the food into several strips or slabs. Line up the strips or stack the slabs and cut across them into irregularly shaped pieces. As you work, curl your fingers at the tips to protect them.

To keep foods from sticking • Coat the blade with cooking spray. This helps keep sticky foods, such as dried fruit, from adhering to knife blades and food processor blades.

To chop in a food processor • Add food in similarly sized chunks (no more than 2" diameter). Fill the work bowl a maximum of halfway. Press the pulse button for 3 to 4 seconds; release the button, then pulse another 3 seconds. Continue to press and release until the food is chopped as desired.

Chopsticks

Some people swear that Chinese food tastes better when eaten with chopsticks. That would be hard to prove, but chopsticks are more authentic than forks.

BASICS ▼

To use • Balance the thicker part of one chopstick in the crook of your thumb, with the thinner part resting on the fleshy tip of your ring finger. Pinch the second chopstick between the tip of your thumb and your index and middle fingers. Holding the first chopstick steady, flex your index and middle fingers up and down to grab your food between the two chopsticks.

Chorizo

Spain taught Mexico how to make chorizo (sausages). There are many types, but, in general, Mexican chorizo (pronounced "chor-EE-zoh") is soft and crumbly upon cooking, while Spanish varieties are often smoked and dried, making them more firm and sliceable. The Spanish chorizos are perfect for paella, while Mexican varieties are usually removed from the casing, crumbled, and cooked for tacos and such.

C

EASY MEXICAN CHORIZO In a bowl, combine ½ **pound ground pork** (or ½ pound pork cubes ground in a food processor), **2 tablespoons cider vinegar, 1 tablespoon chili powder, 2 teaspoons paprika,** and ½ **teaspoon** *each* **sugar, dried oregano, ground cumin, and salt.** If pork is very lean, add **1 tablespoon melted pork fat or vegetable oil.** Stir well, cover, and chill 24 hours. Sauté and use in place of ground beef in taco and burrito fillings or in casseroles. When using, cook until no longer pink. *Makes about 1½ cups.*

Citrus Fruits *see also* Lemons;
Limes; Oranges; Zest

This broad category of fruits includes oranges, tangerines, lemons, limes, grapefruit, pomelos, and kumquats. Citrus fruits are characterized by their segmented flesh and acidic flavors, which range from delightfully sweet to quite tart. Though some citrus fruits are available year-round, these are generally winter fruits grown in tropical and temperate climates around the world.

BASICS ▼ **To choose •** Pick the heaviest fruits. They'll be the juiciest ones. Don't depend on color as an indication of ripeness. A fully ripe, sweet-tasting orange may be green in color. You can judge ripeness by the thickness of the rind. The thinner the rind, the juicier the fruit will be.

To store • Keep citrus fruits in the refrigerator. They'll stay fresh for several weeks. For prolonged storage, sprinkle the fruits with cold water and seal in a zipper-lock plastic bag. Store refrigerated for up to 6 weeks.

To get the most juice • Bring citrus fruits to room temperature before you squeeze them. To quickly warm up cold citrus fruit, place it in a microwave oven on high power for 30 seconds per fruit. It also helps to roll the fruit on a countertop with the palm of your hand before juicing. Or use a handheld citrus reamer or fork, which will help break down the membranes and release more juice.

To use both zest and juice • Zest the fruit before juicing so that it will be easier to handle.

PROBLEM SOLVER ▼ **To avoid seeds when juicing •** Hold the tines of a fork over the center portion of the halved fruit while squeezing. Or squeeze juice into your hand. Allow the juice to run through your fingers and catch the seeds in your palm.

HEALTHY HINT ▼ **To get a nutrition bonus •** Whenever possible, remove the zest (the colorful skin) from citrus before you juice or eat the fruit. Add zest to baked goods, sauces, stews, dressings, fruit desserts, puddings, and frostings. Citrus zest contains a compound known as limonene, which helps block some of the cellular changes that can lead to cancer.

Clams *see also* Shellfish
Baked, fried, steamed, served raw, in chowders, or with pasta, clams are America's best-loved bivalves. There are dozens of varieties, but all fall roughly into two major types: soft-shell and hard-shell.

BASICS ▼ **To choose soft-shell clams •** You can recognize soft-shell clams by the necklike siphon that sticks out from the shell. When buying soft-shell clams, touch the siphon gently. It should retract slightly, a sign that the clams are fresh. If the siphon doesn't move, the clam has passed on and is not safe to eat.

To clean soft-shell clams • Soak the clams in salt water to cover (1 tablespoon salt for each 3 quarts water) in the refrigerator at least 3 hours or overnight. Soaking in salt water helps remove the sand that naturally enters through the gaping shells.

To serve soft-shell clams • Before eating, remove the black sheath covering the siphon on the side of the clam. When serving steamed soft-shell clams, let diners pull off the sheath as they eat. When serving the clams in a sauce, pull off the sheath before adding them to the sauce.

To choose hard-shell clams • Hard-shell clams are sold according to size. The smallest, known as littlenecks, weigh roughly 2 ounces each and measure about 1½" to 2½" across. Their tender meat and sweet flavor make littlenecks an excellent choice for serving raw, steaming, and using in pasta sauces. Medium-size hard-shell clams are called cherrystones and measure up to 3" across. These are good clams for baking and stuffing. Hard-shell clams that measure over 3" across are called chowder clams. Their flavor is not as delicate as littlenecks', but their low price and size make them the most practical choice for soups. Whatever size clam you buy, look for shells that are tightly closed and completely intact with no broken bits. They should have an appealing, mild ocean scent.

To clean hard-shell clams • Scrub them with a stiff brush under cold running water to remove any grit on the shell.

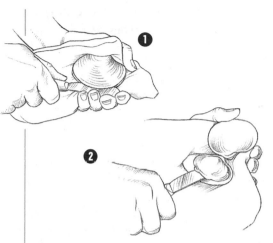

To shuck hard-shell clams with a knife • Use a clam knife (a thin knife with a dull blade designed specifically for this purpose). Working over a bowl or towel, slide the blade of the knife between the shells opposite the hinge ❶. Twist the blade to force the halves apart slightly. Run the thin edge of the knife along the inside of one shell half toward the hinge. Cut through the hinge muscle and carefully open up the shell like a book. Slide the blade beneath the clam to loosen it from the shell ❷, pouring any clam juices into the bowl.

To shuck hard-shell clams with a can opener • In the palm of your hand, hold the clam steady, with the hinge facing up. With the other hand, position the tip of a piercing can opener in the hinge so that the can opener's handle slants back over the top of the clamshell. Dig the tip of the can opener deeply into the hinge. When you feel the tip pass under the lip of the top shell, pull steadily back on the handle. The tip of the can opener will act as a lever, popping the hinge and releasing the lock of the shells. It is now easy to slip a knife between the shells, severing the muscles that hold the clam closed.

C

To serve raw clams • Shuck scrubbed hard-shell littleneck clams over a bowl to catch juices, and serve on a platter with lemon wedges and hot-pepper sauce.

To grill clams • Put cleaned hard-shell clams directly on the grill rack over a medium-hot fire. Cover and cook just until the shells pop open. Serve immediately with melted butter.

To deal with clams that don't open when cooked • Simply keep cooking the clams until they open. Contrary to popular opinion, clams that don't open readily may not be bad, just stubborn. If, however, they don't open after extended cooking (20 to 30 minutes), discard them.

STEAMED CLAMS In a large pot, bring **1 cup white wine** and **1 minced garlic clove** to boil. Add **2 dozen hardshell littleneck clams,** cover the pot, and cook until all clams have opened, 10 to 15 minutes. Transfer clams to a warmed serving bowl. Strain broth through a cheesecloth-lined sieve or colander directly onto clams. Serve in bowls. *Makes 2 dozen.*

Cleaning *see also* Burnt Foods; Stains

The best method for keeping a kitchen clean is "clean as you go."

BASICS ▼ **To clean a soiled sponge** • Run it through the dishwasher. Or soak it overnight in bleach water (1 teaspoon bleach per ½ gallon water).

To remove bread dough from countertops • Scrape with a metal bench knife or plastic pastry scraper.

To clean up honey or sticky syrups • Wipe with a hot, wet sponge. When measuring sticky liquids, coat the measuring cup or spoon with cooking spray; the sticky liquid will pour right out, making clean-up easier.

To avoid staining a plastic container • Coat the container interior with cooking spray. This helps prevent stains from tomatoes and other acidic ingredients.

To clean a box grater • Coat the grater with cooking spray before using. Or stretch a piece of plastic wrap firmly over the grater so it is punctured by the teeth. The plastic will cling to the grater so that foods such as cheese do not. Then, simply remove the plastic and throw it away.

To remove citrus zest from a grater • Scrub with a vegetable brush.

To clean water spots from stainless steel • Wipe with a paper towel dampened with vinegar.

To remove the gummy remnants of a price sticker from glass or porcelain • Rub with the peel of a citrus fruit.

To clean tarnished copper • Rub with a paste of equal parts salt and vinegar.

To clean up a spill in an oven • Sprinkle with salt as soon as possible. Wipe away once the oven has cooled.

To prevent grease from collecting in kitchen sink drain pipes • Pour a strong brine down the drain (2 tablespoons salt per quart of hot water).

To clean a blender • Add a squirt of dishwashing soap, fill halfway with hot water, cover, and turn on, pulsing occasionally. Rinse.

To clean a pan that has food stuck to it • Fill the pan with 1" hot water and bring to an active simmer over medium-high heat. Scrape with a wooden spatula or spoon to loosen. If there is a spot that is badly burnt, cover with cold water and a few tablespoons of salt and soak overnight.

C

CLEANING SAVES TIME

There is no convenience product or cooking trick that saves you more time in the kitchen than the simple habit of keeping things clean.

Clean as you go. Every minute you spend putting away used ingredients or wiping a work surface saves you at least twice as many minutes that you would waste by working in a cluttered environment.

Keep a damp towel or sponge on hand. It's much easier to wipe spills and splatters while they're "fresh" than when they've dried and caked onto your work surface or stove.

Sanitize regularly. Clean and dry surfaces are not necessarily germ-free. To safeguard your kitchen, keep a spray bottle of sanitizer near your work area. To make sanitizer, mix 1 gallon water with 2 teaspoons chlorine bleach. After cleaning a surface or a piece of equipment, spray the surface with sanitizer and allow it to sit undisturbed for at least 1 minute. It is not necessary to rinse sanitizer.

Wash hands frequently. When your hands are dirty, you are not free to crack an egg, test the texture of a batter, or make a sandwich. Keep a dry kitchen towel tucked in your apron or hip pocket to wipe your hands as you work.

Dunk dirty dishes. As soon as a dirty pot is cool enough to handle, submerge it in soapy water to loosen cooked-on food. This one move can save loads of scrubbing time.

Keep two small buckets nearby. One is for trash; the other for organic waste that can be composted. These buckets help keep your counters uncluttered as you work. Empty 1-pound ricotta cheese or yogurt containers do the job well.

Store unused equipment. Clear off counter space by storing any equipment that is used less than 3 times per week.

Use a drip cloth. When using equipment that can splatter, such as a blender, first cover your work surface with a towel or sheet of plastic. Then, just throw it away instead of spending time cleaning countertops.

Buy a bench knife. Also known as a pastry scraper, this inexpensive and versatile tool can streamline cleaning. Nothing more than a thin rectangular blade with a grip along one edge, a scraper is perfect for pushing debris from a work surface into a scrap bowl or sink, scraping up bits of dough or chopped herbs clinging to a cutting surface, or removing burnt bits from the bottom of a roasting pan.

To clean a baking stone • Avoid using soap. Remove caked-on debris or oil buildup with a piece of fine-grit sandpaper.

To clean a grill rack • Wait until the rack is warm (but not cold) and scrub it with a brass grill brush or crumpled aluminum foil. For a gas grill, turn the grill on high to burn off any residue.

Cocoa Powder *see also*
Chocolate

Like chocolate, cocoa powder is made from cacao beans that have been processed into a paste known as chocolate liquor. Using a hydraulic press, producers remove between 50 and 75 percent of the cocoa butter from the

C

chocolate liquor and then pulverize the remaining solids to make cocoa. There are two basic styles: nonalkalized (natural) cocoa and alkalized (Dutch-process) cocoa. Both are unsweetened, but natural cocoa has the natural acidity intact. Dutch-process cocoa has an alkali added during processing to neutralize the natural acidity of cocoa. The alkalizing process was perfected by the Dutch and produces cocoa with a smoother, less bitter flavor and a deep, rich color.

BASICS **To choose** • Use natural cocoa in recipes that have many ingredients or a large amount of sugar, or where the ingredients will be cooked. Dutch-process cocoa is preferred for foods where you'll taste the cocoa straight up, without much added sugar or in combination with fewer ingredients. Use Dutch-process for dusting cakes and truffles and in coffee drinks, hot cocoa, and sorbets.

To choose when a cake recipe doesn't specify type • If the cake is leavened with a good portion of baking soda, use natural cocoa.

To use natural cocoa in baking • Baking soda, an alkali, should be a part of the recipe. Baking soda neutralizes the acidity of the cocoa and creates carbon dioxide so that baked goods rise properly.

To measure • Spoon unsifted cocoa into a measuring cup and level it off without packing it. If the recipe calls for sifting, watch the wording carefully. For instance, if "¼ cup sifted cocoa" is called for, sift the cocoa first, then measure it. If "¼ cup cocoa, sifted," is called for, measure the cocoa first, then sift it.

To replace unsweetened baking chocolate • Use 3 level tablespoons cocoa and 1 tablespoon butter or oil to replace 1 ounce unsweetened baking chocolate.

PROBLEM SOLVERS **To avoid lumps when dissolving in liquid** • Stir just enough liquid into the cocoa to make a smooth paste. Gradually add the remaining liquid.

To avoid the soapy flavor sometimes found in cakes made with cocoa • Avoid substituting Dutch-process cocoa in a recipe that calls for natural. When it is not called for, Dutch cocoa will undo the balance of acid and alkali ingredients in the recipe, making the cake taste "off."

HOT COCOA In a saucepan, whisk together **⅓ cup Dutch-process cocoa powder, ⅓ cup sugar, ⅛ teaspoon salt,** and **½ cup water.** Bring to a simmer over medium-high heat, 1 to 2 minutes, whisking constantly. Cook 1 minute more. Reduce heat to medium-low and whisk in **3½ cups milk or evaporated milk.** Heat through, but do not boil. Remove from heat and whisk in **1 teaspoon vanilla extract** and **¼ teaspoon almond extract** (optional). If desired, beat with an immersion blender or electric mixer until frothy. *Makes 4 servings.*

EASY CHOCOLATE PUDDING In a saucepan, combine **¾ cup sugar, ¼ cup unsweetened cocoa powder (any kind),** and **2 tablespoons** *each* **cornstarch and all-purpose flour.** Make a well in center and add **1 large egg** and **½ cup milk.** Whisk until smooth. Whisk in **2½ cups more milk.** Whisk over medium heat until thick and simmering, 2 to 3 minutes. Cook and whisk 1 minute more. Remove from heat and stir in **1 tablespoon butter** and **1½ teaspoons vanilla extract.** Pour into dessert dishes or a bowl and cool to room temperature. Chill and serve cold. *Makes 4 servings.*

Coconut

The fruit of a tropical tree, coconuts are a popular flavoring for cakes, cookies, custards, and drinks. Fresh coconuts are at their peak of flavor from October through December.

BASICS ▼ **To choose** • Choose coconuts that are heavy for their size, and shake them to make sure that they're full of juice. Check the outer shell; it should have no cracks, which cause the meat to dry out.

To store • Store unopened coconuts at room temperature for 3 to 4 months. Once cracked, refrigerate the meat and juice for up to a week or freeze for up to 8 months.

To grate fresh • Cut peeled pieces of coconut meat into small pieces and grate on a box grater.

C

HOW TO CRACK A COCONUT

Grated fresh coconut beats the bagged stuff hands down. Here's how to get the juice and meat.

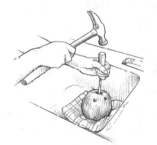

❶ Steady the coconut in the sink drain with a kitchen towel folded beneath it (or place it in a coffee can or other upright container). Using a screwdriver and hammer, pierce the dark indentations (the "eyes") at the top of the coconut. Turn the coconut upside down over a bowl to drain the juice. Taste the juice. It should be sweet with a pleasant odor. If it's sour, the coconut is rotten. Throw it out.

❷ Bake the drained, whole coconut on a baking sheet at 375°F, about 15 minutes (this will make it easier to crack). When cool enough to handle, put the coconut on a hard surface and smack it hard with a hammer to split it in half. Be careful: The coconut meat may be hot. Wearing oven mitts, break the cracked coconut into pieces and pry the meat from the outer shell, using a knife if necessary.

❸ Use a vegetable peeler to peel the dark outer skin from the white coconut meat. Rinse the meat and pat dry. You can now chop the coconut meat into chunks, grate it, or use it to make coconut milk.

C

To flake fresh • Cut peeled pieces of meat into small pieces and pulse in a food processor to make small flakes.

To toast fresh • Toast grated or flaked coconut in a nonstick skillet over medium heat until lightly golden and fragrant, stirring frequently. Or spread 1 cup grated, shredded (unsweetened), or flaked coconut over the bottom of a 10" plate and microwave on high power 3 to 4 minutes, stirring twice. The natural oils in coconut make it one of the few ingredients that brown well in a microwave oven.

PROBLEM SOLVER ▼ **To revive dry coconut flakes** • Cover the flakes with milk and refrigerate for several hours. Drain and pat dry before using.

bowl and pour **2 cups boiling water** over chopped coconut meat. Let sit 30 minutes. Add back to the processor and puree until smooth. Pour into a cheesecloth-lined bowl. Gather together the cheesecloth corners to make a bag, and squeeze milk out of puree and into the bowl. *Makes about 2 cups.*

FLAVOR TIP ▼ **To flavor Asian or Thai soups** • Combine every 2 cups chicken broth with ¼ to ½ cup coconut milk. Add chopped fresh cilantro if desired.

HEALTHY HINT ▼ **To make low-fat** • You can buy lite coconut milk. Or simply mix 1 can (16 ounces) coconut milk and ½ can water.

Coconut Milk

An essential ingredient in many Indian and Southeast Asian curries, coconut milk is a thick, creamy white infusion of coconut meat and hot water. Canned coconut milk can be found in many supermarkets, or you can make your own. Sweetened versions of coconut milk, often called cream of coconut, are used mostly for drinks. The clear liquid inside a coconut is not coconut milk but coconut juice (coconut water).

BASICS ▼ **To store** • Transfer to a glass jar, cover, and refrigerate for up to 1 week. Or freeze in an airtight container for up to 6 months. For small amounts, freeze in ice cube trays, then transfer the frozen cubes to a zipper-lock plastic bag.

COCONUT MILK Cut the **meat of 1 coconut** into small chunks and finely chop in a food processor. Transfer to a

Coffee *see also* Grinders; Instant Coffee

One of the most popular beverages in the world, coffee is also a remarkably varied drink. There are dozens of coffee bean types, plus various methods and degrees of roasting, all of which influence coffee's flavor. Brewing matters, too. Infusion and drip pots make a more mellow coffee, while steam-pressure systems such as espresso machines make a more strongly flavored drink.

BASICS ▼ **To choose** • Freshness matters most when buying coffee. Whole beans that have been roasted within the past week will have the best flavor.

To ensure the freshest beans • Order them from a mail-order source, where beans are usually shipped within a day or two of roasting.

To store • Whether coffee is ground or whole bean, it should be stored at room temperature in an airtight, opaque container just big enough to hold the coffee and allow as little air at the top as possible. Use within 2 weeks for best flavor. Both ground and whole-bean coffee can be frozen for several months, although there may be some flavor loss.

To grind whole coffee beans • For relatively quick brewing methods, such as espresso, use a fine grind. For brewing methods that require more time, such as plunger pots or drip pots, use a coarser grind.

To brew drip coffee • Use 2 table-spoons medium-grind coffee for each 6 ounces water.

To make flavorful coffee that's not too strong • Brew the coffee full-strength and dilute with hot water or milk.

To keep brewed coffee hot • Transfer the brewed coffee to a thermal carafe. Avoid leaving coffee on a hot burner, where it can develop a scorched taste.

To make iced coffee • Choose a dark roast, which will retain the most flavor when chilled. Chill the brewed coffee for at least 3 hours before serving.

To store iced coffee • Keep the chilled coffee in a covered container and use within 1 day. Coffee quickly loses its fresh flavor and can become bitter.

Fascinating Fact: Globally, coffee is the second largest traded commodity after oil.

PROBLEM SOLVERS
▼
To rescue overly strong coffee • Dilute it with water.

To save a weak pot of coffee • Stir in a teaspoon or more of good-quality instant coffee.

To diminish the bitter flavor of over-cooked coffee • Add ⅛ teaspoon salt.

To use excess brewed coffee • Freeze in ice cube trays, store in the freezer in a zipper-lock plastic bag, and add to iced coffee.

To quickly cool hot coffee when making iced coffee • Put a few stainless steel knives into the glass of ice into which you are pouring the hot coffee.

To substitute for coffee filters • Use paper towels.

To clean a coffeepot • Avoid using soap, which leaves a residue that gets trapped in the natural oils in coffee, making the coffee taste bitter or rancid. Instead, use baking soda mixed with water.

To remove coffee stains from cups • Scrub with a paste of equal parts salt and vinegar.

TIME SAVER
▼
To make quick iced coffee • Keep coffee concentrate on hand, frozen in ice cube trays. Then, dilute with water, pour over ice, and serve. To make 1 quart coffee concentrate, pour 3½ cups boiling water over 1 cup ground coffee. Let steep 5 minutes. Strain through a coffee filter and refrigerate or freeze. Combine ¼ cup concentrate with ¾ cup water for each cup full-strength coffee. Makes 3 cups coffee concentrate.

Coleslaw *see also* Cabbage

The term *coleslaw* comes from the Dutch word *koolsla*. In Dutch, *kool* means "cabbage" and *sla* means "salad."

BASICS
▼
To shred cabbage for coleslaw • Cut the cabbage into quarters, remove the core, then cut into ¼" slices.

To develop good flavor • Mix the shredded vegetables and dressing and refrigerate for at least 1 hour before serving.

C

To avoid a harsh, throat-grabbing taste • Use a less acidic vinegar, such as rice vinegar.

To avoid watery coleslaw • Toss 1 head shredded cabbage (5 cups) in 2 teaspoons salt and place in a colander in the sink. Cover with a zipper-lock plastic bag full of water. Let sit 1 hour to press out excess moisture. Rinse before using.

To make very crisp coleslaw • Soak shredded cabbage in ice water for 1 hour. Drain well, pat dry, and toss with dressing.

To boost flavor • Add the grated zest of 1 lemon plus 1 to 2 tablespoons lemon juice to the mix. Also add ¼ teaspoon celery seeds or ½ teaspoon celery salt.

To use prepared coleslaw mix in meat loaf • For 1 to 1½ pounds ground meat, sauté 2 cups coleslaw mix and 1 chopped onion in 2 tablespoons olive oil over medium heat until well-browned, about 15 minutes, stirring often. Let cool before adding to meat loaf mixture.

To use coleslaw mix for stir-fries • Sauté 1 tablespoon grated fresh ginger and 1 minced garlic clove in 1 tablespoon peanut oil. Add 2 cups coleslaw mix and stir-fry 2 minutes. Add stir-fried meat.

EASY CRISP COLESLAW Soak **1 small head (4 cups) shredded red cabbage** in ice water, 30 minutes. In a large bowl, combine **6 tablespoons cider vinegar, 3 tablespoons vegetable oil, 2 tablespoons sugar, 2 teaspoons sesame seeds, ¼ teaspoon salt,** and **⅛ teaspoon ground black pepper.** Drain cabbage, pat dry, and add to bowl. Add **2 peeled and grated carrots, 2 ribs peeled and chopped celery,** and **1 peeled, cored, and chopped Granny Smith apple.** Toss to mix. *Makes 6 servings.*

Convection Oven *see also*

Ovens

Convection ovens use fans to move hot air around, which helps speed cooking times. Generally, food prepared in a convection oven cooks 25 percent faster than it would in a conventional oven. The rapidly moving hot air also browns foods more evenly, locks in juices on roasts, and eliminates the hot spots found in conventional ovens.

To convert conventional oven recipes for a convection oven • Heat the convection oven to 25°F lower than the recipe calls for. Also, expect food to be done in 25 percent less time than it would be in a conventional oven. Start checking for doneness about 10 minutes before the food is scheduled to be done, and even sooner for foods that cook for extended periods, such as roasts.

To choose pans • No special pans are required for convection cooking, but baking sheets and roasting pans with low sides will allow food to cook more quickly and brown more evenly.

To roast meats by convection • Place the meat directly on the oven rack and position a drip pan on the lowest rack. The forced hot air will seal the outside surface of the meat to help lock in juices. Thus, the meat will drip less and brown more evenly, so you won't need to turn it or baste it as you would in a conventional oven.

To cook baked goods by convection • A convection oven will dry out the surface of food, creating a thicker crust on baked goods. As a general rule, use convection for breads, pies, or other foods where a thicker crust is desirable. When no crust is desirable, as in cakes and rich desserts that have a high moisture and fat content, it's best to stick with conventional oven cooking. Pastries and meringues cooked by convection could set at a tilt due to circulating air currents.

To keep baking parchment from being blown by the fan in a convection oven • Set a metal spoon on the parchment.

Convenience Foods

Convenience foods include everything from canned or frozen vegetables to boxed mixes such as macaroni and cheese. Almost any food that streamlines the cooking process can be considered a convenience food. See also "Convenience Recipes" below.

Cookies *see also* Baking Sheets; Brownies; Creaming

The word *cookie* comes from the Dutch *koekje,* meaning "little cake." But the first baked cookies can be traced back to 7th-century Persia. Cookies are generally categorized by the technique used to make them, such as slice-and-bake, drop, cutout, pressed, wafer, icebox, or bar cookies.

BASICS **To blend cookie ingredients evenly** • Bring all ingredients to room temperature before using, particularly fats such as butter, shortening, and eggs.

To bake cookies evenly • Rotate the baking sheet halfway through the baking time. If baking more than 1 sheet of

C

CONVENIENCE RECIPES

The pressure of daily meal preparation can either bury you in a rut of recycling the same 10 recipes ad infinitum or it can spur you to see the glazing possibilities in a can of cranberries, the stewing potential trapped in a bottle of ketchup, and the extra-crispy power in a box of cereal flakes. Here are a few recipes to get you started. Each makes enough for 4 servings.

Shanghai Sauce: Mix **1 cup plum sauce or Chinese duck sauce, ¼ cup soy sauce, and 2 tablespoons minced fresh ginger.** Use as a dip or glaze for grilled chicken, pork, beef, or fish.

Cranberry Chicken: Mix **1 can (16 ounces) whole berry cranberry sauce** and ½ cup bottled Italian dressing. Pour one-third of sauce in the bottom of a large baking dish.

Lay **4 pounds washed and dried bone-in chicken pieces** in sauce in a single layer. Top with remaining sauce. Bake at 450°F until inside of thickest portion registers 170°F on an instant-read thermometer and juices run clear, 40 minutes, turning chicken every 15 minutes.

Mushroom Pot Roast: Rub **2 pounds beef pot roast** all over with ½ teaspoon salt and ¼ teaspoon ground black pepper. In a large deep skillet or Dutch oven, brown meat on both sides over medium heat. Add **1 can (10¾ ounces) condensed cream of mushroom soup, 2 cans water,** and **1 package (1 ounce) dry onion soup mix.** Stir to mix. Reduce heat to low, cover, and simmer until meat is fork-tender, 1½ hours. Slice against the grain and hold in gravy until serving.

cookies at a time, reverse the baking sheets top to bottom and front to back halfway through the baking time. Also, make sure that cookies are the same size.

To make quick, even-size balls of dough • Use a small ice cream scoop, large melon baller, or measuring tablespoon.

To roll out dough evenly • Always roll from the center outward.

To freeze dough for drop cookies • Place balls of dough on a parchment-lined baking sheet. Leave in the freezer until hardened, then transfer to a zipper-lock freezer bag.

To freeze dough for icebox cookies • Almost any firm cookie dough can be frozen, then sliced and baked as needed. Scoop the dough onto a large sheet of plastic wrap in a column down the center. Roll the dough up into the plastic, packing it and smoothing it to form a long, solid log that's 2" in diameter. Wrap the ends tightly and wrap again in more plastic or foil. Freeze until solid. Slice frozen into ¼"- to ½"-thick slices, peel off the wrapper, and bake as directed.

To make chewy cookies • Use a high-protein flour such as bread flour or unbleached flour.

To make cookies with a chewy surface and soft center • Avoid using room-temperature dough. Chill the dough so that the surface of the dough browns and gets crisp before the interior cooks.

To make tender cookies • Use a low-protein flour such as cake flour or bleached all-purpose flour. Also, mix the fat, flour, and sugar before adding any liquid. And, don't overmix the dough; that will cause gluten to develop and create a tough cookie.

To make crisp cookies • Press the dough down flat and bake a few minutes longer than directed.

To make brown, crisp cookies • Substitute 1 tablespoon corn syrup for 1 tablespoon of the sugar called for in the recipe. You can also reduce the acidity in the batter or dough by increasing the amount of baking soda.

To store cookies • Cool the cookies completely. Then, line a canister or plastic container with a zipper-lock plastic bag, add the cookies, press out as much air as you can without crushing the cookies, and seal. Store at room temperature, or freeze. Reheat frozen cookies in a 300°F oven for 3 minutes. Avoid storing crisp and soft cookies together because the crisp cookies will become soft.

To store very delicate or very soft cookies • Put a sheet of waxed paper between each layer of cookies.

To prolong moistness • Store drop cookies, such as chewy chocolate chip cookies, in an airtight container with a slice of bread.

To ship cookies • Use a metal tin, then secure the tin inside a cardboard box. Wrap different types and flavors of cookies separately to keep flavors from mingling. To ensure the freshest cookies, pack the cookies frozen and ship them for 2-day delivery.

PROBLEM SOLVERS ▼ **To prevent parchment from slipping off baking sheets** • Sprinkle a few drops of water on the baking sheet before lining with parchment.

To make sugar cookies without a rolling pin • Form 2 tablespoons of dough into a round ball. Repeat with remaining dough. Flatten with the flat base of a measuring cup or a drinking glass that has been lightly dipped in sugar or flour.

To cut cookie dough rounds without cookie or biscuit cutters • Use a sturdy, inverted wine glass. Or roll into a log shape, freeze until firm, then slice into rounds.

Classic Sugar Cookies

These easy-to-make cookies are perfect for cutting into shapes and decorating with icing and sprinkles, especially around the holidays. Or enjoy them with a simple sprinkling of sugar. If the dough gets too soft to roll as you're working, put it back in the refrigerator for 5 minutes and roll again.

1 **stick (½ cup) butter, softened**

½ **cup sugar**

1 **egg**

½ **teaspoon vanilla extract**

1¾ **cups all-purpose flour**

½ **teaspoon salt**

¼ **teaspoon baking soda**

1. Preheat the oven to 350°F. Line 2 baking sheets with parchment paper.

2. In a medium bowl, with an electric mixer on medium speed, beat the butter and sugar until light and fluffy. Add the egg and vanilla extract. Continue beating until well-combined. Add the flour, salt, and baking soda. Mix on low speed just until combined. Wrap the dough tightly in plastic wrap and chill for at least 30 minutes.

3. Turn the dough out on a lightly floured work surface. Roll to about ⅛" thickness. Using a 2½" cookie cutter, cut out the cookies and transfer to the prepared baking sheets. Sprinkle the tops with sugar, if desired. Bake until the cookies are set but not brown, 8 to 10 minutes. Transfer to a rack to cool.

Makes 42 to 48

Lemon Sugar Cookies: Add 1 tablespoon finely chopped lemon zest and 1 teaspoon lemon juice to the butter and sugar.

Currant Sugar Cookies: Stir ¾ cup dried currants into the dough after the dry ingredients have been combined.

Nut Sugar Cookies: Stir ¾ cup finely chopped walnuts, pecans, or hazelnuts into the dough after the dry ingredients have been combined.

Sugar and Spice Cookies: Add ½ teaspoon ground cinnamon, ¼ teaspoon ground ginger, ⅛ teaspoon ground nutmeg, and a pinch of ground cloves to the dough along with the flour.

Frosted Sugar Cookies: Omit the optional sprinkling of sugar on top of the cookies. In a medium bowl, using an electric mixer on high speed, beat together 1 cup confectioners' sugar, 1 tablespoon water or 1 to 2 tablespoons half-and-half, ½ teaspoon vanilla extract, and a few drops of food coloring (optional), until smooth and spreadable. Frost the cookies after baking, while still slightly warm.

C

c

To prevent dough from sticking to your hands • Moisten your hands periodically in a bowl of cold water.

To prevent dough from sticking to a rolling pin • Chill the rolling pin in the freezer. Also, make sure that the rolling pin is clean of any dough pieces, and lightly flour it.

To prevent sticking when cutting out cookie shapes • Periodically dip the cookie cutter into flour.

To prevent a fork from sticking when pressing down balls of dough • Dip the fork into a small bowl of ice water.

To prevent cookies from spreading • Use a high-protein flour such as bread flour or unbleached flour. You can also freeze the dough before baking. Do not grease the baking sheet. Instead, prepare balls of dough on sheets of parchment so that they are ready to be slid onto the baking sheet at once. This way, the balls of dough won't melt on the hot baking sheet as others are being made. It also helps to quickly cool baking sheets between uses by running them under cold water.

To prevent cookies from burning on the bottom • Stack 2 baking sheets together, or line 1 baking sheet with a double layer of foil. This puts an extra layer of insulation under the cookies and allows for more even baking. Also, try moving the rack up a level. Or it's possible that you have too few cookies on the baking sheet and the pan is overheating. Try fitting on a few more cookies.

To remove cookies that are stuck to the baking sheet • Place the baking sheet on top of a hot, moistened towel or over a roasting pan full of simmering water. Or spray a little cooking spray on your spatula.

To soften overbaked cookies • Store slightly warm in an airtight container with a damp paper towel.

To revive stale cookies • Place on a rack set over a sauté pan of simmering water, and steam until softened.

To use stale cookies • Crush in a plastic bag with a rolling pin and use to top ice cream or add texture to pastry.

To restore the texture of crisp cookies that have softened during storage • Bake at 300°F for 5 minutes. Cool on a rack.

TIME SAVERS ▼

To save cleanup time when rolling out cookie dough • Tape a large sheet of parchment paper onto your work surface.

To save time when baking cookies • Arrange batches of cookie dough on sheets of parchment paper. Slide each batch onto a baking sheet when ready to bake. Using parchment also eliminates the need to grease baking sheets and makes it easy to transfer cookies from the baking sheet to a cooling rack.

To turn any drop cookie recipe into a bar cookie • Scrape the cookie dough into a baking pan. Eight ounces of cookie dough will make 16 thick, moist, brownielike cookies baked in a 9" × 9" pan, or 36 to 48 thin, crisp cookies baked in a 10" × 15" × 1" rimmed baking sheet.

To make meringue cookies the easy way • Preheat the oven to 400°F. Arrange 1"- to 1½"-wide meringue cookies on lined baking sheets and place in the oven. Turn off the heat and go to sleep. When you awake, you will have perfectly pale, utterly dry meringues. Remove from the liner by peeling the paper from the bottoms of the meringues.

ITALIAN ALMOND MACAROONS Look for marzipan in supermarkets, packaged in rolls or cans. Preheat oven to 325°F. Place oven racks in the two middle positions. Line 1 or 2 baking sheets with foil or parchment

THE BEAUTY OF BAR COOKIES

The bother with cookies isn't in the mixing, or in the measuring or the elaborate techniques. It's in the batches. Bar cookies end batches. And they use the same dough. Here are 4 recipes ready in less than 30 minutes.

Fire-Tongue Ginger Biscuits: Preheat oven to 375°F. In a large bowl, mix **1 stick (½ cup) softened unsalted butter, 2 teaspoons ground ginger, ⅛ teaspoon ground allspice, ½ teaspoon** *each* **ground black pepper and ground cinnamon, 1 tablespoon unsweetened cocoa powder, ¾ cup dark brown sugar, ¼ cup strong brewed coffee,** and **1 large egg.** Mix well. Stir in ½ **teaspoon baking soda.** Mix in **1½ cups flour** and beat well. Scrape batter onto a greased 10" × 15" × 1" rimmed baking sheet. Wet your hands and press dough into an even layer. Sprinkle **2 tablespoons granulated sugar** evenly over top. Bake until edges are browned and center is firm, 12 to 15 minutes. Remove from oven and cool on a rack, 10 minutes. Cut into 48 squares or diamonds (by cutting on the diagonal). *Makes 4 dozen.*

Cardamom-Pistachio Butter Cookies: Preheat oven to 375°F. In a large bowl, mix **1½ sticks (¾ cup) softened unsalted butter, 6 ounces chopped pistachio nuts, ¾ cup sugar, 2 teaspoons ground cardamom,** and ½ **teaspoon** *each* **ground ginger and vanilla extract.** Add **2⅓ cups cake flour.** Stir until a smooth, stiff dough forms, about 1 minute. Scrape dough onto a 10" × 15" × 1" rimmed baking sheet. Wet your hands and press dough into an even layer. With a fork, mark off 24 diamond-shaped bars (each about 1½"), making diagonal perforated lines that pierce through the batter. Bake 20 minutes. Cool on a rack 2 minutes. Cut along the perforated lines to separate into serving pieces. *Makes 24.*

Chocolate Exaggerations: Preheat oven to 325°F. In a large saucepan over medium heat, melt **6 tablespoons butter.** Add **8 ounces chopped semisweet chocolate** (or chips), remove from heat, and stir until chocolate melts. Stir in **1 tablespoon instant coffee granules, ¾ cup sugar, ⅛ teaspoon salt, 2 large eggs,** and **2 teaspoons vanilla extract** until well-blended. Stir in ⅓ **cup flour, 1 cup chopped nuts (any type),** and **1 bag (12 ounces) chocolate chunks or extra-large morsels.** Scrape batter into a greased and floured 9" × 9" pan. Smooth the top. Bake until top is crusty but center is soft, about 25 minutes. Remove from oven and cool on a rack to room temperature. Cut into 5 rows of 5 bars each. *Makes 25 squares.*

Coffee-Walnut Biscotti: Preheat oven to 350°F. In a large bowl, mix ¼ **cup softened unsalted butter, 2 cups walnut pieces, 2 tablespoons finely ground dark-roast coffee beans, ¾ cup sugar, 1 teaspoon vanilla extract, ¼ teaspoon almond extract,** and ⅛ **teaspoon salt.** Blend well. Mix in **2 large eggs** and ¼ **teaspoon baking powder.** Add **1 cup flour** and stir until a smooth dough forms. Wet your hands and press dough into a greased 9" × 9" baking pan. Bake 20 minutes. Remove the pan from oven, cover with a cutting board, and invert. Remove the pan, then cut cake in half with a serrated knife. Cut each half into 8 rectangular strips. Place strips back in the pan, setting each on one of its thin sides, like dominoes. Return to oven and bake until golden brown and crisp, 25 minutes. *Makes 16.*

C

paper. Set aside. In a large bowl, mix **1 roll (7 ounces) marzipan** and **1 egg white** to form a thick dough. Place ⅓ **cup confectioners' sugar** on a plate. Drop batter in heaping teaspoons into sugar. Roll into balls and place about 1" apart on prepared pans. Bake until golden brown, 18 minutes. Slide foil or parchment with its cookies onto a rack and cool for 10 minutes. Remove cookies from foil or parchment and cool on rack completely. *Makes about 20.*

FLAVOR TIPS ▼

To add flavor • Add grated citrus zest or finely minced crystallized ginger (or both) to your favorite cookie dough. Or add ½ to 1 teaspoon of your favorite flavor extract: almond, peppermint, orange, rum, or a combination.

To flavor chocolate chip cookies • Add ½ teaspoon ground cinnamon along with the flour and 1½ teaspoons vanilla extract and ½ teaspoon almond extract along with the eggs. Proceed as directed.

To make chocolate chunk cookies • Instead of using commercial chocolate chips, use the same amount of high-quality bar chocolate such as Lindt. Separate the bar into squares. If large, cut in half again on an angle.

HEALTHY HINTS ▼

To reduce fat in chocolate chip cookies • Reduce the amount of chocolate chips by one-third to one-half and replace with mini chocolate chips to better distribute the chocolate flavor. Reduce the amount of nuts by half and toast them over medium-low heat to intensify their flavor.

To make low-fat, yet crispy on the outside • Replace ¼ cup of the sugar with 2 tablespoons corn syrup. Corn syrup helps eliminate the gummy texture of many low-fat cookies.

To use less butter • Use half stick margarine and half butter. Avoid tub margarine for baking because its increased water content causes cookies to spread. If you must use tub margarine, reduce the liquid in the recipe by 1 to 2 tablespoons per ½ cup of margarine used.

To get the best texture in low-fat cookies • Avoid overbeating low-fat cookie dough. Due to reduced fat content, the dough can become tough and rubbery when overbeaten. It also helps to slightly underbake low-fat cookies. The moisture in low-fat cookies is critical to their tenderness. And for the best results, eat low-fat cookies within hours of baking or freeze cookies immediately after they have cooled.

PECAN SEAFOAM COOKIES Preheat oven to 275°F. In a small bowl, combine ¾ **cup finely chopped pecans** and **2 tablespoons flour.** In a large bowl, beat **4 egg whites** and ¼ **teaspoon cream of tartar** with an electric mixer on medium speed until soft peaks form when beaters are lifted. Gradually beat in **1¼ cups light brown sugar** and ½ **teaspoon vanilla extract.** Beat until stiff peaks form. Gently fold in nuts. Immediately drop batter onto foil-lined baking sheets by rounded teaspoonfuls, spacing 1" apart. Bake until slightly firm on top, 25 to 35 minutes. Cool on racks, remove from foil, and dust lightly with **2 tablespoons unsweetened cocoa powder.** *Makes 36.*

Cooking Ahead

Efficiency and speed in the kitchen are, more often than not, a matter of planning and cooking ahead.

TIME SAVERS ▼

To make sandwiches ahead • Make sandwich spreads ahead to have on hand for easy lunches. Tuna and chicken salad will stay fresh tightly wrapped in the refrigerator for 2 to 3 days.

To make salads ahead • When washing lettuce for a salad, wash enough for 2 salads. Store extra lettuce, slightly damp, in a zipper-lock plastic bag in the refrigerator for up to 4 days.

To make salad dressing ahead • When mixing up salad dressing, make enough for a few weeks' worth. If you serve salad to 4 people every night, 1 quart will last you about 2 weeks.

To make vegetables ahead • When cooking side-dish vegetables, make extra to be used in salads or sauces in subsequent meals. Cool the cooked vegetables, seal in an airtight container, and refrigerate up to 4 days. Then, the possiblities are endless.

To make meats ahead • Make extra, cover tightly, and store in the refrigerator up to 5 days. Roasted or grilled meats can return again in sandwiches or quick stews.

To make your own TV dinners • Commercial frozen dinners are nothing more than prepared food assembled as a meal on a plate, sealed, and frozen. Place cooled entrées and vegetables on disposable plastic plates for microwaving or disposable pie plates for reheating in an oven. Cover meats with sauces to keep the surfaces from drying, and dot vegetables with sauce or butter. Avoid mounding food higher than 1½" so that it will reheat evenly. Cover the plate with 2 layers of plastic wrap (for microwave reheating) or a single layer of heavy-duty foil (for oven heating), and press down on the cover to force out as much air as possible. Freeze in single layers. Once the food is solid, the plates can be stacked. Label the cover clearly with the date and contents. Well-sealed dinners can be frozen for up to 2 months. If reheating in a microwave oven, heat on thaw for 8 minutes, then on high power for 6 to 8 minutes more. If reheating in a conventional oven, cook covered at 350°F for 25 minutes, then uncover and bake another 10 minutes.

Cookware *see also* Baking Sheets; Cake Pans; Nonstick Pans

The type and quality of pots and pans that you use has a dramatic effect on the quality of your cooking. It's not necessary to invest a whole lot of money in an expensive matched set. A few well-chosen pieces are all you need.

BASICS ▼

To choose • Buy the heaviest-gauge cookware you can afford. Heavy-gauge pans deliver heat more evenly and last longer. Often, the best all-purpose cooking choice is stainless steel with a copper or aluminum core. Thinner-gauge materials spread and hold heat unevenly, and their bottoms are more likely to dent and warp. This means that the pans will wear out sooner and the food can scorch. As for pieces, a heavy-gauge large skillet or sauté pan is indispensible. This pan will be frequently used with high or medium-high heat to quick-cook and sear foods. For your second pan, choose a heavy-gauge medium-to-large saucepan, especially if you tend to make a lot of sauces. If you can afford it, get a couple of different sizes. When it comes to a large stockpot, however, don't worry so much about weight. Most of the time, you will use it to heat water for cooking pasta. If a soup or stew calls for browning meat in a stockpot, you can use your trusty skillet, then deglaze the pan and add the contents to the stockpot.

To decide if a pan is heavy enough • Check the thickness of the walls and base.

C

COOKING FOR THE WEEK

If artfully done, a beautiful Sunday dinner can be deconstructed and reassembled throughout the week so that no one would guess they were eating leftovers. Here's a 5-day menu to get you started. Each recipe makes 4 servings and includes amounts to be reserved and refrigerated for weeknight entrées.

The Sunday dinner is: Lemon and Olive Oil Turkey London Broil, Confetti Cornbread, and Green Beans with Smoked Almonds.

It can be transformed during the week into: Escabeche of Salmon, Warm Turkey Salad on Escarole with Salsa Vinaigrette, Stir-Fried Shrimp with Ginger Green Beans, and Trout with Cornbread Stuffing.

Sunday Dinner

Lemon and Olive Oil Turkey London Broil: In a large measuring cup, whisk together ⅔ cup **extra-virgin olive oil, 2 minced garlic cloves, finely grated zest of 1 lemon, juice of 3 lemons, ½ teaspoon salt,** and **¼ teaspoon ground black pepper.** Place a **2-pound turkey London broil** in a nonmetallic pan. (This is a butterflied boneless, skinless turkey breast. If you can't find one, ask your butcher to prepare it.) Pour ⅔ cup of marinade over top. Turn to coat completely. Refrigerate at least 20 minutes. Meanwhile, preheat the grill. Grill over a medium-hot fire until turkey breast is just barely pink in the center of its thickest section (170°F internal temperature) and juices run clear, 20 min-

utes, turning 3 times during grilling. Let meat rest 10 minutes before slicing. Slice into thin diagonal slices. Reserve remaining ⅔ cup marinade for Escabeche of Salmon. Reserve ⅔ pound (a little less than half) of Turkey London Broil for Warm Turkey Salad on Escarole with Salsa Vinaigrette.

Confetti Cornbread: Place a medium cast-iron skillet in a preheated 425°F oven. In another skillet, over medium heat, cook **1 chopped onion** in ¼ **cup corn oil** until tender. Add **1 chopped red bell pepper** and cook another minute. Add **1 teaspoon ground cumin** and **1 chopped tomato.** Stir and heat through. Remove from heat and stir in **2 tablespoons chopped fresh parsley** and **1 drained can (13 ounces) corn.** Set aside. In a large bowl, mix together ⅔ **cup flour, 1⅓ cups yellow cornmeal, 2 tablespoons sugar, ½ teaspoon salt,** and **2 teaspoons baking powder.** Mix in sautéed vegetables, **1 large egg,** and **1 cup milk** just until blended. Using a heavy pot holder, remove the skillet from oven and coat interior with cooking spray. Pour batter into hot pan and bake until puffed, brown, and firm in center, 30 minutes. Cool 5 minutes. Invert onto a plate and invert back onto a cutting board. Cut into 8 wedges. Reserve 2 wedges for Trout with Cornbread Stuffing.

Green Beans with Smoked Almonds: Boil **1¾ pounds trimmed green beans** in a large pot of water until barely tender and bright green, 3 to 4 minutes. Drain and run under cold water to stop cooking. Set aside.

Or rap the pan with your knuckles. If you hear a dull thud, you've got a heavy pan in your hands. A delicate ping signals a light-weight.

To season a cast-iron pan • Wash the pan in hot, soapy water and dry well. Using a soft cloth, rub melted vegetable shortening or oil into the entire pan,

C

Just before serving, melt **2 tablespoons butter** in a skillet over medium heat. Add **3 ounces coarsely chopped smoked almonds** and a **pinch of ground red pepper.** Cook 30 seconds. Add green beans and heat through. Reserve 3 cups green beans for Stir-Fried Shrimp with Ginger Green Beans.

Weeknight Entrées

Escabeche of Salmon: In a large skillet, sauté **1 pound deboned salmon fillet** on both sides in **1 tablespoon olive oil** until fish is just opaque. Remove to a plate. Add **1 halved and thinly sliced medium onion** to skillet and sauté over medium heat until tender. Add a **pinch of red-pepper flakes, 2 minced garlic cloves, juice of 1 orange,** and **⅔ cup reserved marinade from Turkey London Broil.** Heat to boiling, return fish to pan, and simmer 2 minutes. Remove from heat and serve.

Warm Turkey Salad on Escarole with Salsa Vinaigrette: In a large salad bowl, toss **1 head washed and dried escarole** (broken into pieces), **1 chopped red bell pepper,** and **1 bunch sliced scallions.** Set aside. In a saucepan, combine **⅓ cup olive oil** and **⅔ pound reserved grilled Turkey London Broil.** Heat 1 minute over medium heat, stirring constantly. Add **¼ cup cider vinegar** and **2 minced garlic cloves.** Heat to a boil, 2 minutes. Remove from heat, stir in **½ cup salsa,** and toss with greens in salad bowl. Scatter **2 cups croutons** over salad and serve.

Stir-Fried Shrimp with Ginger Green Beans: Wash **1 pound large cleaned and shelled shrimp** in cold water and shake off excess water. Toss in a bowl with **1 tablespoon cornstarch** until shrimp are coated. Set aside. Heat a large wok or skillet over high heat, 1 minute. Add **3 tablespoons peanut oil** and heat until very hot. Add shrimp and stir briskly until shrimp are firm, opaque, and lightly browned. Remove with a slotted spoon and transfer to a colander set over a bowl to drain excess oil. To the pan, add **1 tablespoon finely chopped ginger, 2 minced garlic cloves,** and **3 cups reserved Green Beans with Smoked Almonds.** Stir-fry 1 minute until heated through. Add **1 bunch sliced scallions, ¼ cup dry sherry, 2 teaspoons sugar, 1 tablespoon soy sauce,** and reserved shrimp. Toss and cook until heated through, 15 to 30 seconds.

Trout with Cornbread Stuffing: In a small skillet over medium heat, cook **⅓ chopped onion** and a **pinch of dried oregano** in **1 tablespoon oil** until tender. Stir in **½ to 1 teaspoon hot-pepper sauce** to taste. Remove from heat. Coarsely crumble **2 wedges reserved Confetti Cornbread** into the pan. Divide mixture into 4 equal parts and stuff into **4 deboned whole brook or rainbow trout.** Oil a rimmed baking sheet and place trout on pan. Drizzle with **2 teaspoons corn or olive oil** and **⅛ teaspoon salt.** Bake at 375°F until fish flakes easily, 20 minutes. Serve garnished with **2 lemon wedges per fish.**

coating all sides. Put the pan, upside down, over a drip pan in a 350°F oven and heat 2 hours, removing every 30 minutes to recoat with a thin layer of melted shortening or oil. Turn off the oven and let the pan cool completely in the oven.

To clean seasoned cast-iron cookware • Remove food from the pan as soon

c

as it is done cooking. While the pan is still hot, rinse it in hot water and, if necessary, rub a spoonful of salt into the pan to remove any cooked-on bits of food. Wash with hot water only. Avoid using soap, which will wash off the protective coating.

To prevent a cast-iron pan from rusting • Avoid drying with a dish towel. After washing, place the pan over low heat to evaporate the water. Before storing, rub oil into the pan with a paper towel.

To prevent corrosion in cookware • Corrosion imparts an unpleasant flavor to food. Avoid cooking high-acidity foods, such as tomatoes, citrus, vinegar, and wine, in cookware that easily corrodes, such as cast-iron and aluminum. Instead, cook highly acidic foods in stainless steel or nonstick cookware.

To improvise an ovenproof pan • If your skillet or pan is not ovenproof (if it has a plastic handle), wrap the handle in several layers of heavy-duty foil. This will protect it from the broiler for finishing dishes such as frittata in the oven.

To restore a shine to copper cookware • Mix a solution of 2 parts salt to 1 part vinegar and rub it lightly into the copper using a damp cloth or gloved hands. Rinse and dry.

To shine up stainless steel pans • Rub with a moist cloth and dry baking soda in the direction of the steel's grain. Rinse and dry.

To clean discolored aluminum cookware • Make a paste of equal parts cream of tartar and water. Use the paste with a scrub brush.

Corn *see also* Popcorn

As both a vegetable and a grain, corn is one of the most important foods we have. Whole kernels are familiar, but corn is also processed for oil, cornstarch, and corn syrup; ground to make cornmeal; turned into popcorn; and even fermented to make whiskey and beer.

BASICS ▼

To choose • For the freshest corn, your best bet is to buy directly from a farmer who grows it and who can assure you that the corn was picked the same day it is sold. Look for moist, bright green husks with tassels that are brown on top but not too dry. The cut at the stem end should look fresh. Squeeze the ears to feel whether the kernels are full, plump, and fully developed. If an ear isn't quite full of kernels all the way to the tip, don't throw it back in the bin. Slightly immature ears are likely to be more tender. Keep in mind that supersweet corn can have twice the sugar concentration of old-fashioned sweet corn. A good compromise between the two is sugar-enhanced corn.

To husk • Avoid stripping away the husks until just before preparing the corn. They are nature's own freshness seal. Once the husk is gone, the kernels quickly turn stale. If there happens to be a worm in the tip of the husked ear of corn, simply trim it away. A worm is probably an indication that the corn is coming from a field that has not been sprayed with pesticides.

To store • Refrigerate corn in its husks in a plastic bag and use it the day you buy it. Freshness is crucial because the sugar in corn begins converting to starch as soon as the ears leave the stalk.

To easily remove the silk from corn • Remove the husks, then rub the ears with a damp paper towel. The silk will stick to the towel and come right off.

To boil corn on the cob • Bring a large pot of water to a boil. Add 1 tablespoon sugar and no salt (which would toughen the kernels). Remove the husks and silks, drop the ears into the water, cover, and return to a boil. Boil 3 minutes, then turn off heat and let stand, covered, until serving.

To grill corn on the cob • Grill unhusked whole ears of corn over a medium-hot fire directly on the grill rack, 15 to 20 minutes, turning often. Cool a few minutes, then peel back the husks and enjoy (the silks will peel back with the husks). For a more caramelized flavor, peel back all but the last thin layer of husk for the last 5 minutes of grilling.

To roast corn on the cob • Hold husked ears of corn with a pair of tongs directly over a flame or under a broiler until golden all over, about 4 minutes.

To make "wheels" of corn on the cob • Remove the husks and silks from 1 or 2 ears of corn. Use a sharp, sturdy knife to cut the corn into 1" lengths. Drop into chicken broth or a stew and cook several minutes. This methods works particularly well with Southwestern dishes.

To remove corn kernels from the cob • Dip unhusked ears into a pot of boiling water for 5 seconds, then cool them under cold running water before husking. This "sets" the milk so that it doesn't spurt when you scrape the kernels off the cob. Cut off the stem end of each ear to make a sturdy base on which to stand the ear. Hold the cob upright in a wide bowl and, using a sharp knife, cut straight down, slicing the kernels from the cob in a few rows at at time. Avoid cutting too close to

the cob, or you'll end up with tough pieces in the mix. You can also remove the kernels for corn puree by running the cob along the largest teeth on a box grater.

To extract pulp from fresh corn kernels • The "milk" from fresh corn kernels makes wonderful creamed corn, spoon bread, puddings, and soup. After removing the kernels, reverse the knife and rub the dull side down the cob to extract the milk. Or, to get only the fresh pulp and juice, leaving the tougher skins of the corn kernels behind, don't remove the kernels at all. Instead, score the kernels by drawing the tip of the knife down the center of each row of kernels. Then, scrape the cob with the dull side of the knife.

To salvage bland-tasting corn on the cob • Boil it, adding ½ cup sugar to every 4 quarts of cooking water.

To make the most of old corn • Slice the kernels off the cob and add to soups, salad, salsa, or burritos. Simmer stripped leftover cobs in water or broth to use as a base for corn chowder.

To microwave corn on the cob • Place 1 to 6 unhusked ears, uncovered, in a microwave oven. Cook on high power for 2 minutes per ear of corn being microwaved. After cooking, cool 2 minutes, then remove the husk and silks.

To use cobs in vegetable broth • Add stripped corn cobs to vegetable broth. The bits of corn pulp still clinging to the cobs will add wonderful sweetness to cooking liquids.

C

To flavor frozen corn • Brown it in a little bit of butter, olive oil, or bacon fat to allow the the flavor to blossom.

CORN CHOWDER In a large saucepan, heat **2 teaspoons olive oil.** Add **4 chopped shallots** and cook 3 minutes. Stir in **2 cups frozen corn,** ¼ **cup chopped Canadian bacon, 1 chopped garlic clove,** ¾ **teaspoon crushed dried thyme,** ½ **teaspoon salt,** and ¼ **teaspoon ground black pepper.** Cook 4 minutes, stirring occasionally. Add **2½ cups milk** (any kind) and bring to a simmer. Meanwhile, stir together **1 tablespoon cornstarch** and **3 tablespoons water.** Stir into simmering soup and cook 2 minutes, or until thickened. Remove from heat. Stir in ¼ **cup sour cream** (reduced-fat or regular) and **2 tablespoons chopped fresh cilantro.** *Makes 4 servings.*

HEALTHY HINTS ▼ **To maintain optimum nutrition** • Grilling or steaming will retain the most nutrients in corn. Boiling leaches out corn's water-soluble nutrients.

To use in soups and sauces in place of fat • Pureed corn added to soups and sauces gives a rich, creamy texture.

To extend the creamy texture of cheese • You can also add pureed corn to cheese fillings such as those in casseroles and dips. Pureed corn works especially well in enchilada fillings.

Cornbread

At tables all over the American South, cornbread is served in some form at every meal.

BASICS ▼ **To make cornbread with a crisp, golden crust** • Bake it in a well-greased, preheated cast-iron skillet.

To make coarse-textured, crumbly cornbread • Use only stone-ground cornmeal and no flour.

To make lighter, cakelike cornbread • Use a combination of cornmeal and flour, an additional egg, and a combination of buttermilk and regular milk.

To serve leftover cornbread • Wrap the cornbread in foil and warm at 300°F for a few minutes before serving.

FLAVOR TIP ▼ **To make your own cornbread croutons for stuffing** • Make your favorite cornbread recipe. Cut in half through the side and allow to air-dry overnight. Cut into ½" to ¾" cubes with a serrated knife and place on a baking sheet. Bake at 350°F, tossing occasionally, until dried and toasted golden, about 30 minutes. The results are far superior to packaged croutons or stuffing mix.

Cornish Game Hens *see also* Chicken

A crossbreed of two different strains of chickens, Cornish game hens generally weigh just a little over a pound, an ideal size for a single serving.

BASICS ▼ **To choose** • Look for the smallest hens you can find. They'll be the most tender and have the best flavor.

To roast • Roast the birds at 400°F until the juices run clear and the breast meat registers 180°F on an instant-read thermometer, about 30 minutes for small birds, 40 minutes for larger ones.

To broil or grill • Cut out the backbone by cutting up each side of the backbone with kitchen shears. Remove the backbone. Lift out the sternum and open the hen up flat. Grill or broil the flattened hen until the thickest part of the thigh registers 180°F on an instant-read thermometer.

Cornstarch

Cornstarch is best known for its thickening power in sauces, gravies, soups, pies, custards, and puddings.

BASICS ▼

To store • Keep it in an airtight container. Like other starches, cornstarch loses its thickening power when exposed to air over a long period of time.

To use • Dissolve 1 teaspoon cornstarch in 1 tablespoon cold liquid (water is fine). Stir or whisk this cold mixture (known as slurry) into 1 cup hot liquid at the end of cooking time. Cook, until thickened, 30 seconds to 1 minute, stirring constantly. Cook 1 minute more to remove any "cornstarchy" taste. These proportions will make about 1 cup of medium-thick sauce, soup, or gravy. For a thinner sauce, use ½ teaspoon cornstarch. For a thicker sauce, use up to 2 teaspoons cornstarch.

To thicken a fruit pie • Combine the sugar called for in the recipe with cornstarch (use about 1 tablespoon cornstarch for each 6 cups of fruit). Toss with the sliced fruit.

To replace flour as a thickener • Use 1½ teaspoons cornstarch for each tablespoon of flour called for in the recipe.

To replace arrowroot • Use 2 teaspoons cornstarch in place of 1 tablespoon arrowroot.

PROBLEM SOLVERS ▼

To prevent cornstarch-thickened sauces from thinning • Stir gently and cook for no more than 1 minute over medium heat after the sauce has thickened. Any longer and the starch cells are apt to rupture. Also,

avoid licking the spoon. Enzymes in your saliva can break down a mixture thickened with cornstarch. Okay, you can lick the spoon—just don't put it back into the mixture. Finally, avoid freezing mixtures thickened with cornstarch.

To rescue a cornstarch mixture that has thinned upon cooling • Add a little more liquid. It seems counterintuitive, but sometimes, cornstarch does not fully swell and remain thickened if there is not enough liquid in the mixture. A higher proportion of sugar than liquid or a particularly high proportion of fat in a mixture can also be the culprit. Again, try adding more liquid to solve the problem. Lemon juice and other acidic ingredients can also reduce the thickening power of cornstarch. If you suspect that this may be the cause, slightly increase the cornstarch. To avoid this problem, add acidic ingredients after cooking.

Corn Syrup

A thick, sweet syrup derived from cornstarch, corn syrup is used for making candy, frostings, jams, and jellies. It also helps to make low-fat cookies more crisp.

BASICS ▼

To choose • Dark corn syrup has caramel flavor and color added; it's often used for making pecan pie and dark-colored candies. Choose clear corn syrup when you only want to sweeten and not add color or caramel flavor to foods.

To substitute sugar for clear corn syrup • Use 1¼ cups granulated sugar and ¼ cup water for each cup of corn syrup.

To substitute sugar for dark corn syrup • Use 1¼ cups packed brown sugar and ¼ cup water for each cup of dark corn syrup.

C

Couscous

These tiny pearls of semolina dough are a staple of the North African table. Traditionally, couscous is steamed in a perforated container that sits over a stew. Most couscous available is precooked, whether it's labeled "instant" or not.

BASICS ▼ To prepare "instant" couscous • Put 1¼ cups quick-cooking couscous in a bowl and stir in 1½ cups boiling water, stock, or canned broth (if desired, add 1 to 2 tablespoons butter or oil). Cover and let stand about 10 minutes. Fluff with a fork.

PILAF-STYLE COUSCOUS Heat **2 tablespoons butter or oil** in a saucepan over medium heat. If desired, sauté **1 cup chopped vegetables** (onion, garlic, bell pepper), **½ cup nuts** (pine nuts, pistachios), and/or **⅓ cup dried fruit** (raisins, chopped apricots, chopped figs) until soft and fragrant. Add **1½ cups instant couscous** and stir until coated with butter or oil. Add **2¼ cups hot chicken, beef, or vegetable broth** and **¼ teaspoon salt**. Bring to boil over high heat. Reduce heat to low, cover, and simmer until liquid is absorbed, about 6 minutes. Stir in **1 tablespoon butter** or **oil** and fluff couscous with a fork. *Makes 4 servings.*

HEALTHY HINT ▼ To get more nutrients • Choose whole wheat couscous, which has twice as much fiber, more protein, and many other important nutrients when compared to regular couscous.

Crabs

What type of crab you eat depends on where you live. If you live near the Atlantic Coast, you're likely a lover of blue crabs. Gulf Coast residents are aficionados of stone crab. Dungeness crabs are beloved of Pacific Coast residents, while the icy waters of Alaska and the Antarctic are home to both the huge king crabs and snow crabs.

BASICS ▼ To choose • Unless you're buying crabs that are already cooked, crabs should be alive when you buy them. Look for the liveliest ones. If you're buying cooked crabs, they should have a sweet, fresh scent. When buying cooked crabmeat, ask what grade it is. The best is called jumbo, lump, or backfin and is composed of large chunks of meat from the body. "Flake" indicates smaller bits of body meat. The lowest grade of crabmeat comes from the claw. Unpasteurized crabmeat is freshest and has a more delicate flavor than the pasteurized versions, though it has a shorter shelf life.

To tell whether a crab is male or female • Look at the small flap on the underside of the crab (known as the apron). If it's thin and pointy, the crab is male. A female crab has a rounded apron. Some crab lovers prefer males, which tend to have more meat, while others favor females for their roe (eggs).

To store live crabs • Keep live crabs covered with a damp cloth and store in the refrigerator until ready to cook. Cook crabs the same day that you buy them. Check to make sure that the crabs are still alive. The cold temperature of the refrigerator may have left them feeling groggy, but prod them gently and they should wiggle their legs and wave their claws.

To store leftover cooked crabmeat • Refrigerate the meat and keep it tightly covered. Use within 2 days.

To cook whole blue crabs • Put the crabs in a large pot of boiling water and cook until the shells turn bright red, about 6 minutes.

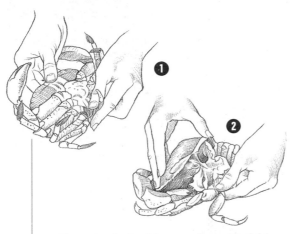

To eat whole blue crabs • Unfold, twist off, and remove the apron on the bottom of the crab ❶. Pull off the top shell and pull away the gills attached to the bottom shell ❷. Remove the meat from the body, discarding any bits of shell. Twist off the legs and claws, crack them with a nutcracker, and remove the meat.

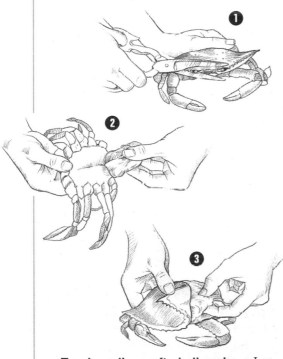

To clean live soft-shell crabs • Just before cooking, rinse the crabs under cold

running water. With kitchen shears or a sharp knife, cut off the eyes and mouth ❶. Twist off and discard the apron ❷. Then curl back one of the pointed sides on the top shell to expose the gills and pull them off ❸. Repeat on the other side.

To cook soft-shell crabs • Coat the crabs in your favorite breading and sauté them in hot oil until golden brown, about 4 minutes per side, or deep-fry them for a total of 3 to 4 minutes.

To cook Dungeness crabs • Cook the crabs in a large pot of boiling water until the shells turn red, about 10 minutes.

To remove the meat from cooked Dungeness crabs • Hold down the legs with one hand and pull off the crab's top shell. Pull off the gills and the mouth section from the inside of the crab, then scoop out the yellow fat and internal organs from the center of the body. Turn the crab over, and twist off and remove the apron. Snap off the legs and crack them with a nutcracker, then cut the body in half with a knife. See the illustrations for eating whole blue crabs.

PROBLEM SOLVER ▼ **To rid canned crabmeat of a metallic taste** • Soak the crabmeat in ice water for 10 minutes, then drain and pat dry.

Cranberries

Since cranberries show up in markets only from November through December, freeze them to use throughout the year. Toss frozen cranberries into quickbread batters and increase baking time by 5 to 10 minutes.

TIME SAVER ▼ **To halve cranberries quickly and easily** • Some recipes call for halved cranberries to keep them from bursting during cooking. Line them up in the gutter of a cutting board. Slice the whole row in half with a long knife.

▓▓▓▓▓▓▓▓▓▓▓▓▓▓▓▓▓▓▓▓▓▓▓▓▓

CHUNKY FRESH CRANBERRY SAUCE WITH PINEAPPLE Rinse and drain **1 bag (12 ounces) fresh cranberries.** Turn into a stainless steel saucepan and add **¾ cup sugar** and **1 can (8 ounces) shredded pineapple** in juice. Grate **zest from 1 large orange** and set aside. Squeeze orange juice into the pot. Bring to a boil. Reduce heat to low and simmer until thickened, 8 to 10 minutes, stirring occasionally. Remove from heat and stir in **2 teaspoons vanilla extract** and reserved orange zest. Turn in a bowl, cool, cover, then chill. *Makes about 3 cups.*

Cream *see also* Crème Fraîche; Sour Cream

Skimmed from the top of unhomogenized milk, cream is used to thicken and enrich soups and sauces, to make ice creams and custards, and to make a luscious whipped topping for desserts.

BASICS
▼

To choose • The richest cream is heavy cream, which contains a minimum of 36% milk fat. Use for custards, ice cream, and other cream-based desserts. Heavy cream whips up faster and firmer than any other cream. Whipping cream, sometimes labeled light whipping cream, has 30% to 36% fat. Use for enriching sauces and soups. Despite its name, whipping cream does not whip as easily as heavy cream. Light cream has the least fat, with only 18% to 30% milk fat; it cannot be whipped. It's the one to add to your coffee or pour over hot cereal. Half-and-half is a combination of equal parts cream and milk; it contains between 10% and 18% milk fat.

To store • Keep cream in the coldest part of the refrigerator. It will last for about a week past the sell-by date.

To cook with cream • Use heavy cream. Its high fat content makes it less likely to curdle. If using light cream for cooking, heat very gently and briefly.

To use cream in a sauce that contains wine or other alcohol • Reduce (cook down) the wine or alcohol before adding the cream. This will help keep the cream from curdling.

To whip • Whipped cream takes less than 5 minutes to make and beats the commercial stuff by a mile. The important thing to keep in mind is that the cream will turn to butter if you take it too far. For best results, keep everything cold: Use cold cream, chill the bowl and the whisk or beaters, and work in the coolest area of your kitchen. Using a whisk or an electric mixer, whisk or beat the cream steadily at medium speed and keep beating just until the cream holds soft peaks when the whisk or beater is lifted. That's all there is to it.

To get the most volume from whipped cream • Add sugar or flavorings such as vanilla extract after the cream has begun to form soft peaks.

To help stabilize whipped cream • Sweeten it with confectioners' sugar or corn syrup instead of granulated sugar.

To fold whipped cream into other mixtures such as pastry cream • Whip cream until it is light and barely holds a peak when the whisk or beater is lifted. Using a spatula, gently fold it into the other mixture.

To use whipped cream for a topping or piping • Whip the cream until it holds a stiff peak when the whisk or beater is lifted.

To hold whipped cream made a few hours in advance • Scoop into a sieve and place the sieve over a bowl. This way, it won't sit in a pool of any liquid that may separate out. Cover tightly with plastic wrap and refrigerate. Just before using, whisk gently to reincorporate any liquid that has begun to separate.

PROBLEM SOLVERS ▼ **To sweeten cream that is starting to turn sour** • Add a pinch of baking soda per cup of cream to help neutralize the natural lactic acid in cream.

To prevent overwhipped cream • Use a wire whisk instead of an electric mixer. If you are using an electric mixer for speed and ease of use, slightly underwhip the cream and finish by hand with a whisk.

To rescue whipped cream that turns yellow and begins to separate • Fold in an additional tablespoon (or more if necessary) of cream or milk until smooth.

TIME SAVER ▼ **To whip cream faster** • Use pasteurized instead, which whips quicker than ultra-pasteurized heavy cream.

FLAVOR TIP ▼ **To make flavor linger longer** • Almost anything tastes better when cream is added. That's because cream holds flavor to the tastebuds longer. Anytime you have a sauce that tastes a little sharp or too intense, a little bit of cream will usually pull it back into balance.

FRESHEST, BEST-TASTING BUTTER Pour **2 cups heavy cream** into a large deep bowl. Add ¾ **teaspoon salt** (or omit to make unsalted butter). Beat with an electric mixer until stiff, like whipped cream. Continue beating until cream looks curdled, then separates into butter and liquid whey. Pasteurized cream will take 4 to 5 minutes total; ultra-pasteurized will take 8 to 10 minutes total. Gather butter and drain it in a sieve, squeezing gently to remove excess whey. Cover and chill for up to 1 month, or use immediately. *Makes about 1 cup.*

HEALTHY HINTS ▼ **To replace cream in recipes** • For savory sauces and creamy bases, substitute fat-free evaporated milk. Remove from the heat and stir in 1 to 2 tablespoons reduced-fat sour cream to add a rich texture. Or, for cold sauces or soups, use a mixture of reduced-fat sour cream and buttermilk. For small amounts in any recipe (less than ¼ cup), use half-and-half in place of cream. For custards and pie fillings, use fat-free milk combined with nonfat dry milk.

To replace whipped cream • Instead of whipping 1 cup heavy cream, whip ½ cup light whipping cream and fold into ½ cup vanilla or plain fat-free yogurt. Or use a mixture of equal parts lightly drained vanilla yogurt (drain 30 minutes in a cheesecloth-lined colander) and fat-free sour cream. You can also beat ½ cup dry-curd cottage cheese until smooth, then fold in ½ cup fat-free sour cream, 1 to 2 teaspoons confectioners' sugar, and ¼ to ½ teaspoon vanilla extract. Or partially freeze fat-free evaporated milk and whip until fluffy; use immediately, or stir in softened gelatin to keep longer.

Creaming

The act of combining butter and sugar is one of the most important steps in baking. Poorly creamed butter can result in cakes and cookies that are disappointingly dense and coarse, especially in batters that are too thick to be leavened solely by eggs or chemical leaveners such as baking soda. Thick batters get their rising power from the air that's incorporated into butter as the butter is combined with sugar.

C

C

BASICS ▼ **To cream butter and sugar** • Begin with room-temperature ingredients. Butter that's too cold won't blend with sugar. If it's too warm, it won't hold air. The ideal creaming temperature for butter is between 65° and 70°F. Also, use a flat wooden spoon. Though electric mixers and whisks can be used, the texture of wood holds butter best and keeps it from sliding around the bowl. Begin creaming by flattening the softened butter against the sides of the bowl. Once it becomes creamy, lift the butter and fold it over on itself to incorporate air. Once the butter is light and fluffy, gradually add the sugar. After 3 to 5 minutes of vigorous beating, the butter should be pale and almost twice its original volume.

To get maximum aeration from creamed butter • Avoid overbeating it. If the mixture becomes grainy and looks curdled, it has been overbeaten. Go ahead and use it, but the mixture won't have the same leavening power that properly creamed butter would.

To keep creamed butter from deflating • If eggs are called for in the recipe, lightly beat them before adding to the mixture. Also, fold in the dry ingredients carefully.

To cream butter with an electric mixer • Use medium speed. Too much friction can melt the butter and result in a baked good that's too dense.

Crème Fraîche *see also* Cream

This cultured cream has a pleasantly tart flavor and a rich, smooth texture. In France, where cream is unpasteurized, it thickens naturally from the live bacteria that it contains. In the United States, cream is pasteurized, and the addition of an acid, such as buttermilk or sour cream, is necessary to thicken the cream and help develop the unique, tangy flavor of crème fraîche. Use crème fraîche in sauces and as a dessert topping.

BASICS ▼ **To make** • In a small saucepan over low heat, warm 2 cups heavy cream to slightly warmer than body temperature, about 100°F. Stir in ¼ cup buttermilk, then transfer the mixture to a glass or plastic container. Cover and set the cream in a warm spot, such as near a heater. Let it stand 24 hours. The cream will thicken slightly. To thicken further, refrigerate for at least 4 hours before using.

To store • Refrigerate crème fraîche, tightly covered, for up to 10 days.

HEALTHY HINT ▼ **To make a low-fat substitute** • Combine ½ cup fat-free sour cream, ½ cup 1% milk, and ¼ teaspoon sugar. Cover and let stand in a warm place overnight to thicken. Refrigerate for 4 hours before using. Cover and refrigerate for up to 2 weeks.

Crepes *see also* Pancakes

These thin, light pancakes make excellent wrappers for both sweet and savory fillings. Dessert crepes are often set ablaze with ignited liqueur such as Grand Marnier.

BASICS ▼ **To stack** • There is no need to layer sheets of plastic or paper between crepes when stacking. Simply stack them on a plate and cover tightly with plastic wrap.

To freeze • Double-wrap in plastic and foil; freeze for up to 2 months. To reheat, thaw slightly and reheat at 300°F until warm, 5 minutes.

PROBLEM SOLVER ▼ **To make lump-free crepes** • Use an instantized flour, such as Wondra. This type of fine flour has been specially formulated to eliminate lumps.

TIME SAVER ▼ **To save prep time** • Buy refrigerated crepes from the supermarket.

DESSERT CREPES Whisk together **2 cups instantized flour** and **8 extra-large eggs** until a thick, smooth batter forms. Beat in **2 cups milk, 1 tablespoon** *each* **oil and sugar,** and **⅛ teaspoon salt** until batter is smooth. Coat an 8" nonstick skillet with oil. Place over high heat until oil is very hot and shimmering. Pour 3 to 4 tablespoons batter into the pan, tilting the pan so that batter completely covers the bottom of the pan. Pour any excess batter back into the mixing bowl and cook over high heat until batter sets, about 20 seconds. Carefully flip and cook another 10 seconds. Transfer to a plate and repeat with remaining batter. Regrease the pan every 10th crepe or so. *Makes about 40.*

Croutons

Most often used to garnish soups and salads, these crisp bits of bread also make great toppings for casseroles and can be served as hors d'oeuvres.

BASICS ▼ **To make** • Choose a dense, flavorful bread. Baguettes and rustic country-style loaves work best. Supermarket white breads are too soft to stand up to a wet soup or salad dressing. Cut the bread into uniform-size cubes, diamonds, or other shapes to ensure that they cook evenly. For fun shapes, use small canapé or cookie cutters.

To toast • Toss or brush the croutons with melted butter or olive oil, and season with salt and ground black pepper. Spread them on a baking sheet in a single layer. Bake at 350°F until golden brown, about 15 minutes. For larger croutons, flip halfway through baking so that they brown on all sides.

To store toasted croutons • Cool thoroughly and store in an airtight container for up to 3 days.

To make sautéed croutons • Heat a little bit of butter or olive oil in a skillet and sauté the cubes over medium heat, tossing occasionally, until they are crisp and browned. Use immediately.

FLAVOR TIP ▼ **To flavor toasted croutons** • Before toasting, toss the cut bread with one or more of the following: chopped fresh herbs, grated Parmesan cheese, grated lemon zest, chopped fresh chives, sesame seeds, poppy seeds, coarsely ground black pepper, or seasoned salt.

HEALTHY HINT ▼ **To make low-fat croutons** • Cut crusts off stale slices of whole grain bread. Rub the bread with a cut slice of garlic and spray slices lightly with olive oil cooking spray. Cut into cubes, sprinkle lightly with crushed dried herbs, and place on a baking sheet. Bake at 325°F until lightly golden, 15 to 25 minutes.

Cubing *see also* Chopping; Julienne; Mincing

This basic cut involves chopping food into uniform ½" to 2" cubes. Larger than a dice, cubes are perfect for salads and stir-fries or other dishes where you want the food to cook quickly, yet retain its shape.

To cube • Slice the food into several wide strips or slabs, making each slice precisely the same width, usually ½" to 2". Line up the strips or stack the slabs and cut across them in precisely the same width so that you end up with uniform cubes.

Cucumbers

A popular ingredient for salads and pickles, cucumbers are available year-round but are at their best during the summer months. Though they're most often enjoyed raw, cucumbers are also delicious sautéed or roasted.

To choose • Look for small, narrow cucumbers. They're less likely to be bitter. Press the stalk end gently. If it's soft, don't bother buying it. The best cucumbers are firm all over, with no bruises or cuts. If you prefer seedless cucumbers, look for the longer, skinnier hothouse or English cucumbers.

To store • Keep cucumbers in the vegetable drawer of your refrigerator. For best flavor, use within a few days.

To seed • Cut in half lengthwise. Starting at one end, scrape the seeds down the length of the cucumber with the tip of a dinnerware teaspoon or melon baller.

To use halved cucumbers • Seeded cucumber halves will resemble boats and can be stuffed with a flavored cream cheese filling. After filling, you can also put the two halves back together, chill, and then slice into rounds to reveal the filling.

To make pretty slices • Trim the ends from a whole cucumber, then run the tines of a fork lengthwise all around, pressing firmly to score the skin. Slice crosswise into thin slices.

To make cucumber ribbons • Trim and peel a whole cucumber. Then, "peel" the cucumber flesh by running the peeler down the length of the cucumber to make long, thin ribbons. Continue "peeling" off ribbons of cucumber until you reach the seeds at the center. Then, roll the cucumber one-quarter turn and peel more ribbons. Continue until you are left with only the seedy core.

To help cucumbers stay crisp • Place 1 large, seeded and sliced cucumber in a sieve. Sprinkle evenly with 2 teaspoons vinegar, 1 teaspoon table salt, and a pinch of sugar. Using your fingertips, rub the vinegar, salt, and sugar into the cucumber slices for 1 minute. Place a zipper-lock plastic bag full of water on the cucumbers to weight them down. Let drain 15 minutes. Rinse and pat dry before using for cooking or a salad.

CRUNCHY CUCUMBER SALAD In a serving bowl, toss **1 peeled, seeded, and chopped cucumber; 2 cups peeled and chopped jicama; ¼ cup** *each* **olive oil and lemon or lime juice; ¼ to ½ teaspoon ground red pepper;** and **¼ teaspoon** *each* **salt and ground black pepper.** Add **segments from 1 orange.** *Makes 4 servings.*

Currants

There are two different fruits that we call currants: tiny dried grapes, often simply called currants, and tiny fresh berries, the true currants, which are usually named by their color—black currants, red currants, or the rarer white currants. The two different types of fruits are not related. Fresh currants are related to the gooseberry and deliver a burst of tart flavor, while tiny dried grapes taste more like raisins.

BASICS ▼ **To choose** • Fresh currants are often available in the summer months at roadside stands and local farmers' markets. They add wonderful flavor to salads.

To store • Refrigerate fresh currants in an airtight container for 2 to 3 days. Or freeze for up to 6 months.

FLAVOR TIP ▼ **To use currant jelly as a glaze** • Melt the jelly in a microwaveable dish on low power. Brush over fresh fruit to top a tart or cheesecake. Chill.

Curry

The term *curry,* which is derived from a South Indian word for sauce, refers to a wide range of East Indian dishes made with hot, spicy gravy seasoned with curry powder. In India, where spices are ground fresh just before using, curry powders vary dramatically according to the region, traditions, and tastes of the cook.

BASICS ▼ **To choose** • There are two main types of commercial curry powders: standard and the hotter Madras curry powder. Brands vary widely, so it's best to try a few and find the one that best suits your taste. Buy small quantities of curry powder, as its flavor tends to fade in just a few months.

PROBLEM SOLVER ▼ **To eliminate the raw taste of curry powder** • Sauté curry powder in a little bit of butter or oil before adding to a dish.

FLAVOR TIP ▼ **To boost the flavor of commercial curry powder** • To 1 tablespoon curry powder, add ¼ teaspoon *each* ground cumin and ground coriander.

Custards

Sometimes baked, sometimes stirred, custards are usually a combination of eggs and milk or cream. Stirred custards, such as crème anglaise, pastry cream, and lemon curd, are usually served as a sauce or filling for cakes, cream puffs, and other pastries; they're also used as a base for ice cream. Baked custards include such classic dishes as crème brûlée and flan.

C

BASICS ▼ **To prevent stirred custards from curdling** • Cook them in a double boiler to help maintain a steady, gentle heat. And keep them in constant motion by stirring gently throughout the cooking time.

To stir custard evenly • Stir in a figure-eight motion, which covers all areas of the pan. Use a flat-edge wooden spoon, which will reach into the corners of the pan better than a rounded spoon.

To make exceptionally creamy stirred custard • Use only egg yolks. Egg whites coagulate at a lower temperature than egg whites and can result in lumpy custard.

To test a stirred custard for doneness • Lift up the spoon. If it's evenly coated with the custard, remove the pan from the heat.

To quickly stop the cooking of a stirred custard to prevent curdling • Dip the pan briefly into a bowl of ice water.

To make a silky stirred custard • Strain the cooked custard through a sieve.

To keep a skin from forming on the surface of a stirred custard • Press a sheet of greased waxed paper directly onto the surface before refrigerating.

To make a baked custard that's firm enough to be unmolded • When the liquid in the recipe is ½ to 1 cup, use a ratio of 1 whole egg for each egg yolk.

To ensure successful unmolding of a baked custard • Bake custards in a container with a smooth base and sides. Porcelain and glass work fine, but metal molds work best.

To cook baked custards without curdling • Cook them in a water bath to diffuse the heat and ensure that the custards cook evenly and slowly.

To test a baked custard for doneness • Stick a thin-blade knife into the center. If it comes out clean, the custard is done. If the knife is wet, continue cooking.

Cutting Boards

A wooden or plastic board should always be used when working with a knife. Cutting directly on a marble or metal surface can dull and damage a knife blade.

BASICS ▼ **To prevent slipping while you work** • Place the cutting board on a damp towel or rubber mat.

TIME SAVER ▼ **To prepare food faster on a cutting board** • Use a wooden board. The wood absorbs some of the knife blade, making chopping steadier and faster than chopping on plastic or glass. Use the largest cutting board you can. Small boards cramp your work space, which slows you down.

HEALTHY HINTS ▼ **To avoid bacteria** • Use a wooden board, which is safer than plastic because bacteria are neutralized by the wood's natural enzymes.

To avoid cross-contamination • Use two boards: one just for meats and one for everything else. Or, if you use only one board, mark one side of the board exclusively for meats. Clean your cutting board with sanitizer each time you use it. To make sanitizer, fill a spray bottle with 2 cups water and ¼ teaspoon chlorine bleach.

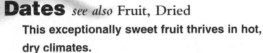

Dates *see also* Fruit, Dried

This exceptionally sweet fruit thrives in hot, dry climates.

BASICS ▼ **To choose** • The best fresh dates are plump and soft with smooth skin. Some shriveling may occur, but avoid dates with excessively shriveled skin. Dried dates are sold year-round. They can be whole, pitted, or chopped.

To store • Refrigerate fresh dates in a plastic bag up to 2 weeks. Tightly wrap dried dates and store in a cool, dry place up to 6 months, or refrigerate up to 1 year.

To separate • Microwave them on medium power for 30 to 45 seconds.

INDIO FROSTED MILK SHAKE This recipe is from the date capital of the world, Indio, California. Chop **4 large, pitted dates** and puree in a blender with **½ cup milk.** Add **large scoops vanilla ice cream** and blend to a thick milk shake. Add more ice cream for thicker shakes and more milk for thinner ones. *Makes 1 serving.*

Deglazing *see also* Sauces

When meat, poultry, fish, or vegetables are browned, roasted, or sautéed, the food's natural sugars will caramelize and stick to the bottom of the pan. These browned bits can be a mother lode of flavor. Liquids such as wine, stock, or even water are often stirred into the pan to dissolve the browned bits and release their flavor. This simple process is known as deglazing and becomes the basis for a range of sauces.

BASICS ▼ **To choose a pan for deglazing** • Make sure that it's not too large or too small for whatever you're cooking. If there's too much surface area, the juices may burn. If there's too little, the juices may not caramelize. Avoid using nonstick pans. Since juices can't stick to the surfaces of these pans, they can't caramelize. When deglazing with acidic liquids such as wine or vinegar, avoid using a cast-iron pan.

To make a quick deglazing sauce • Before deglazing, remove excess fat from the pan. Add enough liquid to cover the pan bottom: ½ to ⅓ cup for a medium sauté pan. If deglazing a roasting pan, transfer the liquid to a smaller saucepan once the caramelized bits have been dissolved.

Dicing *see also* Chopping; Cubing; Julienne; Mincing

This basic cut is similar to chopping, but the food is cut into uniform ¼" to ¾" squares

rather than irregular pieces. Dicing is often used when appearance is important.

To dice • Slice the food into several strips, making each slice precisely the same width. Line up the strips and cut across them in precisely the same width, so that you end up with uniform squares.

Dry Milk *see also* Milk

Also called powdered milk, this pantry staple makes a good stand-in for regular milk.

To choose • Stock whole dry milk, nonfat dry milk, and/or dry buttermilk.

To store • Keep unopened packages in a cool, dry place for up to 6 months, or refrigerate opened packages up to 3 months.

To replace cream • Mix 1 cup fat-free milk and ⅓ cup nonfat dry milk.

To use in low-fat custards and puddings • Add 2 tablespoons nonfat dry milk per cup of regular milk in the recipe to add richness and nutrients.

To use in low-fat baked goods • Add dry milk to improve the texture of low-fat baked goods and to help promote browning. For each cup of flour used, add

1 to 2 tablespoons nonfat dry milk to the liquid or dry ingredients.

Duck *see also* Doneness Tests and Temperatures (page 572)

Rich, succulent dark meat makes duck one of the most delicious types of poultry.

To choose • Look for light-skinned ducks with broad breasts that are plump but not too fat. The skin should be moist. Buy the heaviest ducks you can find. Most of the weight is skin, bones, and fat.

To store fresh duck • Remove any giblets from the cavity and wrap the duck in a dry, lint-free kitchen towel. Then put the bird in a zipper-lock plastic bag and refrigerate for up to 5 days. The towel absorbs any liquid that leaches from the duck, and the bird stays fresh far longer than if left to sit in its own juices.

To reduce fattiness • Trim excess skin from the duck, especially around the neck. Dry the duck extremely well inside and out to help reduce spattering. Also, pierce the skin all over with a trussing needle, taking care to pierce only the skin and not the flesh. Season the duck well with salt and pepper and set it, breast side down, on a rack in a roasting pan. Leave the duck uncovered and refrigerate it overnight to dry the skin.

To roast • Prepare as described above. Then, roast the duck in the roasting pan at 500°F, 30 minutes. Reduce heat to 425°F and roast until an instant-read thermometer registers 175° to 180°F when inserted into the thigh and juices run clear, about 20 to 30 minutes more. Let stand for 10 minutes before carving.

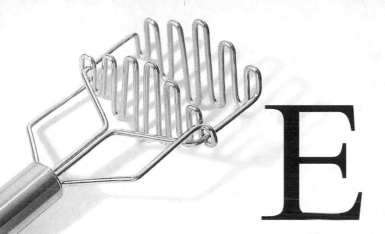

E

Eggplant

Not too long ago, the only type of eggplant in most markets was the familiar pear-shaped kind with dark purple skin. Now, markets carry eggplants in a range of sizes, shapes, and colors, thanks largely to immigrant cooks from Asia and the Middle East.

BASICS ▼ **To choose** • Buy eggplants in summer, their peak season. Fresh eggplants are less bitter and have thinner skins than eggplants sold out of season. Lift several eggplants of the same size and choose the heaviest one. Press gently on the flesh. If the eggplant is ripe, it will spring right back. If a dent remains where you pressed, the eggplant is past its prime. Look for smooth, taut skin. If the eggplant is purple, it should be glossy. White eggplants should show no hint of yellow. The green caps and stems of eggplants should be intact and free of mold. When using eggplant for a dish where you want firm-textured slices, such as eggplant rolls, choose white eggplant, which holds its shape better than other varieties.

To store • Eggplants are highly perishable. Try to use them the day that you buy them. To keep longer, place in a plastic bag and keep in a cool spot at room temperature. Refrigerating eggplants speeds their deterioration.

To salt • Place sliced or chopped eggplant in a colander, sprinkle all over with salt, and let drain in the sink for 1 hour. Rinse well and pat dry before cooking. This salting process helps to reduce bitterness in mature eggplants that are out of season. Salting also helps keep eggplant from absorbing excess oil when sautéed.

To fry eggplant slices • Salt sliced eggplant, then coat the slices in flour. In a skillet, heat ¼" of vegetable oil over medium-high heat. Add coated eggplant slices and fry until deep golden brown, about 3 minutes. Turn and brown other side, about 2 minutes longer. Drain on paper towels. Great for making eggplant Parmigiana.

To brown eggplant • When you want a firmer texture and better browning, broil eggplant slices instead of frying them. Slice, coat with cooking spray, and place under the broiler until golden brown, about 2 minutes per side.

To roast slices • Grease a rimmed baking sheet. Salt and dry slices of eggplant, then place close together on the baking sheet and roast in a 400°F oven until browned, 35 to 40 minutes.

To roast whole • Pierce whole eggplant in several places with a fork to ensure that it won't explode. Place on an oven rack or a baking sheet and roast at 425°F

e

Eggplant Rillettes

Rillettes ("ree-YEHT" or "rih-LETS") is a simple form of pâté. Here, the eggplant is roasted, but you could also char it on a grill. Serve eggplant rillettes as a spread, a dip, a sauce for vegetables, a condiment for roasted meats, a thickener for soups and stews, a flavor enhancer for mashed potatoes, a filling for quiche, a face cream . . . well, maybe not a face cream. The possibilities are *almost* endless.

2 **medium eggplants (1 pound)**

6 **anchovy fillets, finely chopped**

2 **tablespoons mayonnaise**

1 **garlic clove, minced**

Juice of 1 large lemon

1 **tablespoon capers, chopped**

1. Preheat the oven to 425°F.

2. Prick the eggplants with a fork and place, whole, on the oven rack. Bake until soft, shriveled, and black, 30 to 40 minutes. Remove and allow to cool 10 minutes.

3. Split the eggplants in half lengthwise and scoop the flesh out into a bowl. Mash coarsely with a fork. Add the anchovies, mayonnaise, garlic, lemon juice, and capers. Continue to mash until well-mixed. Do not make the mixture too smooth.

4. Serve warm or refrigerate for up to 1 week.

Makes 1½ cups

until the skin wrinkles and flesh becomes tender, 30 minutes to 1 hour, depending on size of eggplant. Cool, then halve lengthwise and scoop out the flesh for dips and spreads, or for thickening and flavoring soups, stews, sauces, and purees.

To char whole • For a smokier flavor, poke the eggplant with a fork and place directly onto the grate over a gas burner set on high or on a grill rack over a hot fire. Cook, turning, until blackened all over. When the skin is fully charred, the flesh inside will be soft and smoky tasting.

Fascinating Fact: Two-thirds of the world's eggplant is grown in New Jersey.

PROBLEM SOLVERS ▼ **To prevent eggplant from discoloring** • Brush cut flesh with lemon juice or dip in acidulated water (page 2).

To rescue overcooked eggplant • Top with grated cheese, a quick tomato sauce, or a meat sauce. Or sandwich between slices of polenta with a juicy slice of tomato and julienned fresh basil.

To rescue cooked eggplant that has a bitter taste • Mask with a vinaigrette.

BABA GHANOUSH Roast or char **2 medium eggplants.** Cool and scoop flesh from skin. Discard skin. Toast ½ **cup pine nuts or walnuts** in a dry skillet over medium heat, tossing, until lightly browned. In a food processor, combine eggplant, nuts, **½ cup tahini (sesame paste), ¼ cup lemon juice, 1 minced garlic clove, 1 teaspoon salt,** and **¼ teaspoon ground black pepper.** Process to a coarse puree, adding **¼ cup olive oil** as it blends. Serve with pita triangles, bread, crackers, or vegetables. *Makes about 2 cups.*

HEALTHY HINTS ▼

To reduce fat in breaded eggplant • Oven-fry instead of deep-frying. Dip ¼"-thick slices of eggplant in beaten egg and then in bread crumbs (fresh or dried), pressing crumbs to adhere. Place on greased baking sheets, coat with cooking spray, and bake at 400°F until fork-tender, about 15 minutes per side. Excellent for eggplant Parmigiana or roll-ups.

To use as a meat extender or substitute • The meaty texture of eggplant blends well with beef, pork, and lamb. Coat eggplant slices with oil and broil until tender, about 2 minutes per side. Use to replace some of the noodle layers in lasagna. Or cook small cubes of eggplant the same way and substitute for some of the meat in stews, casseroles or chili.

Eggs
see also Custards; Eggs, Cooking Methods; Egg Substitutes; Egg Whites; Egg Yolks; Omelettes; Quiche; Soufflé; *and other egg dishes*

Often called the perfect food, eggs are also one of the most versatile. They make a delicious dish in their own right, whether scrambled, fried, poached, boiled, or baked, but they also play essential roles in baked goods and sauce making.

BASICS ▼

To choose • Check the grade and sell-by date. Grade AA eggs are the freshest, with the firmest yolks and smallest air pockets. Also examine the shells. If they are cracked, don't buy the eggs. If you notice a crack at home, throw the egg away. And avoid buying eggs that are unrefrigerated. When it comes to shell color (brown or white) pick your favorite. Shell color has nothing to do with quality, nutrients, flavor, or cooking characteristics. It simply varies with the breed.

To store • Keep eggs in their carton, which helps protect them from cracking and prevent them from absorbing odors and losing moisture. Store the carton on a refrigerator shelf instead of on the door, which is not cold enough. Properly stored eggs will be safe to use for about 1 month. A week-old egg that's properly stored can be in better condition than a day-old egg kept at room temperature for 24 hours. For longest storage, turn the carton over so that the large, bulbous end is on top.

To store out of the shells • Separate the whites from the yolks and keep both, tightly covered, in the refrigerator. Egg whites should stay fresh for about 5 days. Egg yolks deteriorate faster and should be used within 3 days. Alternatively, you can lightly beat whole eggs and freeze them in airtight containers. Thaw overnight in the refrigerator or under cold running water. Use frozen and thawed eggs only in dishes that are thoroughly cooked. Measure 3 tablespoons thawed egg for each large fresh egg called for.

To test for freshness • Put a whole egg in a shallow glass of water. A fresh egg will sink and lie flat on the bottom of the glass. A week-old egg will sit near the bottom but will bob slightly in the water. A 3-week-old egg will stand on end, and a rotten egg will float to the surface. This happens because, as an egg ages, the air

e

pocket inside the shell expands until the egg becomes buoyant enough to float. Older eggs, with developed air pockets, are easier to peel when making hard-cooked eggs. Whites from older eggs are also easier to whip.

To avoid ruining a recipe with a bad egg • Crack eggs into a separate bowl before adding to other ingredients. Bad eggs are rare, but they are easy to detect; their odor is unmistakable.

To separate • Pour the cracked egg into a clean funnel or egg separator (available in kitchenware stores). Or wash your hands and then pour the cracked egg into your palm, with your fingers parted enough to cradle the yolk but let the whites slip through. These separation methods help avoid introducing bacteria into the egg, which can be a problem with the old method of pouring the eggs back and forth between the broken shell halves.

To clean egg-coated mixing bowls • Use warm water. Avoid hot water, which may set up the egg's protein, making it harder to wipe off the bowl.

Fascinating Fact: The egg has long been associated with fertility. Central European farmers used to rub eggs on their plows hoping to ensure a good crop. And in France, it was once customary for brides to break an egg before the threshold of her home to assure having a large family.

CRACKING AN EGG WITH ONE HAND

A sharp edge is not the best place to crack an egg; a flat surface does a better job. Cracked on a flat surface, the egg's shell is less likely to shatter, which helps avoid getting bits of shell in your egg. To make things go faster, here's how to crack an egg with one hand.

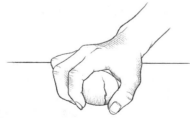

1 Grasp the egg in the upper part of your palm, between your thumb and first 3 fingers, leaving a space between your middle finger and ring finger. Give the exposed area of the egg a short, sharp crack on a flat surface rather than an edge. A countertop or the inside of a bowl works well.

2 As soon as the egg is cracked, quickly bring the egg over the bowl or pan and swiftly spread apart the two halves of the shell, pulling the lower half down with your ring finger while pushing the upper half up with your thumb and middle finger. As the shell spreads, allow the egg to gently fall into the bowl or pan.

PROBLEM SOLVERS
▼

To remove an egg that's stuck to its carton • Fill the carton indentation with cool water and let it sit for 5 minutes. The water will soften the dried egg white that is holding the egg in place.

To clean up an egg you've dropped on the floor • Sprinkle heavily with salt, cover so that no one steps on it, then wipe up after 15 minutes. The salt sets up the egg's protein so that it is easier to clean up.

To remove bits of eggshell in a bowl of cracked eggs • Use a clean wooden spoon to lift out the shell pieces. This method avoids introducing bacteria, which can result if you pick out the broken bits with an emptied eggshell half.

To avoid getting any yolk in the egg whites when separating whites that will be beaten • Crack and separate each egg over a small bowl. If it's a clean break, transfer the white to a larger bowl (which can be used to beat the whites) and transfer the yolk to a separate bowl. But if the yolk breaks, set it aside for another use and clean the bowl before cracking more eggs. The reason: Just the slightest bit of yolk or any fat in egg whites can prevent them from achieving a high volume during beating.

To remove a speck of yolk from egg whites • Lift it out with the end of a cotton swab. It is still likely, however, that the whites will not whip to their optimum volume.

TIME SAVER
▼

To quickly bring eggs to room temperature • Crack them into a metal bowl and set the bowl into another bowl of luke-warm water for 5 minutes. You can also place whole eggs in a bowl of lukewarm water, but it will take longer for the centers of the eggs to lose their chill.

HEALTHY HINTS
▼

To replace whole eggs with egg whites • In general, substitute 2 egg whites for each whole egg. When you need a very accu-rate measurement of eggs in baking recipes, replace each whole egg with 3 ta-blespoons egg white. To facilitate mea-suring, whisk the egg whites with a pinch of salt to help break down the egg protein and loosen the texture.

To replace an egg yolk with an egg white • Replace each egg yolk with half an egg white, or 1 tablespoon.

Eggs, Cooking Methods

see also individual egg dishes

Legend has it that each pleat on the classic chef's toque (traditionally 100) represents the many ways that eggs can be prepared.

BASICS
▼

To make perfect scrambled eggs • Use a heavy nonstick pan and heat it over medium heat before adding any oil or butter. Aerate the eggs with vigorous beating. For light, fluffy scrambled eggs, add 1 teaspoon water per egg while beating. Gently move a pancake turner across the eggs as they cook to help make them fluffier. Remove the pan from the heat just before the eggs are done, and let them finish cooking with just the retained heat of the pan. Add 1 tablespoon cool liquid at the very end of cooking. The cool liquid stops the cooking. Do as the French do, and add heavy cream. For lighter eggs, milk or even water works well.

To make perfect fried eggs • Grease a heavy nonstick pan. Warm over medium-high heat. Slip in the eggs and immedi-ately reduce the heat to low. Eggs fried over low heat will be moist and tender, and they absorb less fat. For basted fried eggs, after the whites have set, spoon some of the hot fat from the pan evenly over the tops of the yolks just until the tops appear light pink. For steam-basted eggs, add 1

e

teaspoon water to the pan after the whites begin to set. Cover and cook until whites are set and yolks begin to thicken.

To make perfect poached eggs • Use the freshest eggs you can find. The white will cling more strongly to the yolk and the yolk will be less likely to break. Also, use a heavy, nonstick pan. The eggs will be less likely to stick. Break cold eggs into a small dish or ramekin and add them one by one to gently simmering water. As soon as the outsides of the whites begin to set, reduce the heat to barely a simmer and cook until the whites are completely set. Remove with a slotted spoon.

To make perfect hard-cooked eggs • Place eggs in a single layer in a saucepan and cover with cold water by 1". Bring to a boil over high heat. As soon as the water begins to boil, remove the pan from the heat, cover, and let sit 15 minutes. Drain and run cold water over the eggs, or use a slotted spoon to transfer the eggs to a bowl of ice water until completely cooled.

To make soft-cooked eggs • Use the same method as for hard-cooked, but let the eggs sit, covered, 4 to 5 minutes before placing in ice water. Serve soft-cooked eggs by cutting through the shell with a knife and scooping out the egg.

To store hard-cooked eggs • Refrigerate in the shells for up to 1 week.

To peel hard-cooked eggs easily • Start with eggs that are 7 to 10 days old. These eggs have taken in a bit of air, which helps separate the membranes from the shell. After cooking, cool the eggs quickly in ice water. Roll the cooked eggs under your palm on a countertop so that the shells are thoroughly cracked into small bits all over. Then, start peeling at the rounded end of each egg near the air bubble. Work under running water to help rinse off any bits of shell.

To center the yolk in hard-cooked eggs • Before cooking the eggs, secure the egg carton with rubber bands and turn it on its side for several hours or overnight.

To tell a hard-cooked egg from a raw one • Spin it. A raw egg will wobble. A cooked egg will spin on its end.

To avoid tough scrambled eggs • Season with salt near the end of cooking. This also helps to prevent watery eggs.

To limit fried eggs from running all over the pan • Crack 1 egg into a small bowl, then carefully slide it into the hot pan. Repeat with the rest of the eggs.

To avoid rubbery fried eggs • Use a heavy skillet, which conducts high heat well. Heat the pan over a medium–high flame or burner. Turn the heat down to low as soon as you add the eggs.

To avoid overcooking the bottoms of sunny-side-up eggs • Cover with a pan lid.

To prevent poached eggs from running in the cooking water • Place small, heatproof bowls, ramekins, or cookie cutters into a pan of shallow, simmering water. Pour the eggs into the bowls, cover, and cook.

To fix untidy poached eggs • Use kitchen shears or a knife to trim any straggling pieces of white, sometimes called angel wings. For a perfectly round poached egg, use a biscuit or cookie cutter.

To prevent hard-cooked eggs from cracking • For a large amount of eggs, use separate saucepans to prevent overcrowding, which can cause the eggs to break against one another. Also, avoid placing cold eggs in hot water. Cover the eggs with cold water so that the water and eggs come to temperature together.

To rescue an egg that cracks while being hard- or soft-cooked • Add a tablespoon of salt or a teaspoon of vinegar to the water to help the white coagulate and stop seeping. Do this only if the egg is seriously cracked. A little seepage won't hurt anyone.

To prevent a green layer from forming on hard-cooked egg yolks • This happens when eggs are overcooked, causing the iron in the yolk to react with the sulfur in the white. The best remedy: Time the cooking carefully. Also, cool the eggs in ice water after cooking.

To rescue hard-cooked eggs that come out undercooked • Place the chopped yolks and whites in a bowl, cover with plastic wrap, and cook in a microwave oven using medium power until they reach the desired consistency. Start with 15- to 20-second increments. Or, if you have only peeled one of the eggs, place the other eggs back in a pan of hot water and simmer another 5 minutes.

To slice a hard-cooked egg without mashing the yolk • Use an egg slicer, a wire cheese slicer, or a piece of tautly pulled dental floss.

To keep deviled eggs from sliding on the plate • Cut a thin slice from the bottom of each egg half to make a flat base. It also helps to arrange the eggs on a bed of lettuce leaves.

To fill a deviled egg without a piping bag • Place the filling in a zipper-lock plastic bag, seal, and snip one of the bottom corners of the bag. Squeeze filling into the hollowed egg half. This method also works well for taking deviled eggs on a picnic so you can transport the eggs and filling separately.

TIME SAVERS ▼ **To poach eggs quickly** • Add 1 teaspoon salt and 1½ tablespoons vinegar to each quart of water used. Salt and vinegar help set the protein in the egg whites and keep them from feathering so they coagulate more quickly. They also flavor the egg.

To cook poached eggs in advance • Once the eggs have finished cooking, remove them from the pot with a slotted spoon, transfer to a bowl of ice water, and refrigerate until ready to use. To reheat poached eggs, transfer them to a strainer and lower them into a pot of simmering water for about 45 seconds.

FLAVOR TIP ▼ **To flavor poached eggs** • Use milk, broth, tomato juice, or wine instead of water for the poaching liquid.

BASIC FRITTATA Heat **1 tablespoon** *each* **butter and olive oil** over medium heat in a 10" nonstick skillet with a metal or heatproof handle. Add **2 to 3 cups chopped or sliced vegetables and/or meat,** and ¾ **teaspoon seasonings** (some classic combos include potato and leek; smoked fish and scallions; ham and Cheddar; and tomatoes, onions, and Swiss.) Sauté until vegetables are tender. In a bowl, beat **8 eggs** with **2 tablespoons water, milk, broth,** or **other liquid.** Add to the pan and swirl until egg is distributed all over the bottom. Cook until eggs are almost set, 3 minutes. Meanwhile, preheat broiler and set rack no more than 4" from heat. If desired, sprinkle **shredded cheese, bread crumbs,** or **crushed chips** over eggs. Slide frittata under broiler and cook until browned and puffed, 2 to 3 minutes. Cut in wedges to serve. *Makes 4 to 6 servings.*

CARAWAY DEVILED EGGS Hard-cook **8 eggs.** Cook **6 slices meaty, smoked bacon** until cooked through and crisp. Drain and crumble. In a small saucepan, combine ½ **teaspoon whole caraway seeds** and ¼ **cup water.** Simmer over

EGGS FOR DINNER

Eggs are among the easiest and fastest dinners. Each recipe below makes 4 servings.

Poached Salmon and Eggs with Lemon-Butter Sauce: Boil 2 cups *each* white wine and water, ¼ cup white wine vinegar, and ¼ teaspoon *each* salt and ground black pepper, 5 minutes. Reduce heat to medium-low and add **4 skinless salmon fillets (6 ounces each).** Poach until fish is opaque, 3 minutes. Remove from liquid and keep warm. Remove 1 cup poaching liquid to a separate saucepan, adding **2 tablespoons lemon juice** and **1 finely chopped large shallot.** Boil over medium-high heat until reduced to ¼ cup. Reduce heat to low and keep warm. Add **8 eggs** to remaining poaching liquid and poach over medium-low heat until whites are set, 3 to 5 minutes. Remove with a slotted spoon and place 2 eggs on each salmon fillet. Cut ¼ **cup butter** into pieces and whisk into reduced poaching liquid. When incorporated, spoon sauce over eggs.

Fried Egg Tostadas: Mash **1 large, peeled and pitted Hass avocado** with **1 tablespoon lemon juice, ½ teaspoon salt,** and ⅛ teaspoon ground red pepper. Heat **1 cup canned refried beans** in a saucepan or microwave oven and set aside. In a skillet, toast **8 corn tortillas (6" diameter)** in **1 teaspoon corn oil** over medium-high heat, about 30 seconds per side. Remove and keep warm. Reduce heat to medium. Add **2 teaspoons butter** to skillet and melt. Crack **8 eggs** into the pan and cook until whites are half-set. Cover and cook until whites are set but yolks are still runny, 1 to 2 minutes. Among tortillas, divide and layer refried beans, **1½ cups shredded romaine lettuce,** fried eggs, avocado mixture, and **1 chopped fresh tomato.**

Stir-Fried Shrimp and Eggs: Heat **2 tablespoons vegetable oil** in a wok or large skillet over medium-high heat. Add **1 cup cleaned and shelled baby shrimp, 3 sliced scallions,** and **1 small minced garlic clove.** Stir-fry 30 seconds. In a bowl, scramble **6 eggs** and **1 tablespoon water, 1 teaspoon hotpepper sauce, ½ teaspoon salt,** and ¼ **teaspoon ground black pepper.** Add to the pan and cook, scraping eggs toward the center of the pan until eggs are set but still moist.

medium heat until water evaporates, tilting pan so that final evaporation takes place in the corner of the pan. Remove from heat. Halve eggs and remove yolks, mashing yolks with caraway seeds and crumbled bacon. Stir in ¼ **cup mayonnaise, 1 tablespoon brown mustard,** ¼ **teaspoon ground black pepper,** and **a pinch of salt.** Mound into egg white halves and sprinkle with **paprika**. Chill and serve cold. For a more devilish filling, add ¼ **teaspoon ground red pepper.**

Makes 4 to 6 servings.

CARAMEL FLAN Preheat oven to 300°F. Place ¾ **cup sugar** in a saucepan and melt over medium heat, stirring occasionally. Continue heating until sugar caramelizes, turning medium brown, 2 to 3 minutes.

Quickly pour caramel into a 9" cake pan or 4 custard cups and rotate to cool and coat. In a large bowl, whisk **3 whole large eggs, 4 egg yolks,** and **½ cup sugar.** Whisk in **1 can (12 ounces) evaporated milk, 1 cup whole milk, ½ cup light or heavy cream, 1 tablespoon** *each* **vanilla extract and rum or brandy,** and **½ teaspoon almond extract.** Pour through a strainer into the prepared pan or cups. Place in a larger baking pan and add very hot water to come halfway up the side of the pan. Bake until set and a knife tip inserted near center emerges clean, about 40 minutes. Remove from water bath and cool on a rack 30 minutes. Run a knife around the edge to loosen flan (twirl the pan or cups to see if flan is loose). Place a large platter over the pan. Invert the pan and platter to unmold flan. Spoon loose caramel sauce over top and let cool. Chill. *Makes 4 servings.*

HEALTHY HINTS ▼ **To make more healthful egg salad** • Use twice as many egg whites as yolks. Or substitute some drained and chopped firm tofu for part or all of the egg whites. You can also replace all or part of the mayonnaise with reduced-fat mayonnaise and/or plain yogurt. Add prepared mustard to boost flavor. And you can add finely chopped vegetables, such as carrots, celery, or scallions for texture.

To eliminate the risk of salmonella when making Caesar salad • Use pasteurized egg whites.

Egg Substitutes

Found in both the refrigerated and the frozen sections of the supermarket, packaged egg substitutes usually contain egg whites, fat-free milk, food coloring, vegetable oil, and vi-tamins. Most substitutes contain no cholesterol and 1 to 4 grams of fat per serving. They can be used sparingly in baking (for yeast breads, muffins, cakes, and cookies) and in cooking (for egg-based casseroles, sauces, puddings, and custards). Avoid using egg substitutes in popovers and other delicate pastries, where they do not perform as well.**

BASICS ▼ **To thaw when frozen** • Refrigerate them until liquid.

To use in place of uncooked eggs • Since egg substitutes are pasteurized, they make a safe alternative to the uncooked, slightly cooked, or coddled eggs called for in recipes such as eggnog, homemade mayonnaise, and Caesar salad dressing. Using egg substitute in these recipes will also lower the cholesterol and saturated fat content instantly.

HOMEMADE EGG SUBSTITUTE Combine **1 egg white, 2¼ teaspoons nonfat dry milk, 1 to 2 teaspoons canola oil,** and **a pinch of ground turmeric** in a blender until smooth. Use to replace 1 whole egg. Increase recipe proportionately as needed. Refrigerate up to 1 week or freeze airtight up to 1 month. *Makes about ¼ cup.*

HEALTHY HINTS ▼ **To use non-egg substitutes** • If you do not eat eggs, there are a number of choices. Powdered egg replacer is one choice. Available in health food stores, it is made from potato starch and other leaveners. It has good binding and leavening properties for baking; it even whips up and will hold soft peaks. Whipped tofu is another option; it works well in recipes that call for a lot of eggs, such as quiches. It also works well in creamy puddings and pie fillings. Ground flaxseed is a third option. When simmered with water to form a thick mixture, it mimics the binding properties of eggs for baking, but it doesn't have nearly the leavening power of eggs. There is a bonus, however: Flaxseeds are a concentrated source of heart-healthy omega-3 fatty acids.

To replace 1 egg with tofu • Whip ¼ cup silken tofu in a blender. To use in baked goods, add 1 to 2 teaspoons water to thin the whipped tofu.

To replace 1 egg with ground flaxseed • Simmer 1 tablespoon ground flaxseed in 3 tablespoons water until slightly thickened, about 2 minutes. Cool to room temperature before using. (If you buy flaxseed whole, grind it in a clean coffee grinder.)

Egg Whites *see also* Meringue

Egg whites have the amazing ability to hold voluminous amounts of air when whipped. This makes them a key ingredient for leavening baked goods and essential for making meringues. Egg whites (known as the egg's *albumen*) also help bind ingredients together. And they can clarify cloudy stocks, broths, or coffee when added to the hot liquid by attracting minute particles like a magnet. An egg white contains no fat and is composed of mostly protein, water, and water-soluble vitamins such as riboflavin.

BASICS
▼

To store • Raw egg whites can be refrigerated in a tightly sealed container for up to 5 days. Or you can freeze egg whites in an ice cube tray, adding 1 egg white (about 2 tablespoons) to each section. When

---

THE STAGES OF WHIPPED EGG WHITES

The most important thing you need to know about beating egg whites is when to stop. Most recipes indicate a certain stage to which the foam should be beaten. Here are the stages, plus a description of overbeaten egg whites.

1. Foamy: The egg whites are just lightly whipped to a frothy but still fluid consistency. They will consist of large bubbles on the surface that readily pop. The foam will not hold any peaks when the whisk is lifted from it.

2. Soft Peaks: This means that the foam is moist, shiny, and bright white. When the whisk or beaters are lifted, the foam will form a dull peak, then pile softly or gently curl over. It will also flow when the bowl is tilted.

3. Stiff Peaks: At this stage, the foam maintains its glossy sheen and holds an upright peak when the whisk or beaters are lifted. It will not flow, or will just barely flow, when the bowl is tilted. At this point, the foam has reached its maximum volume.

4. Overbeaten: This is a common mistake, particularly when whipping with electric mixers. You will know that the egg whites are overbeaten when the foam begins to look dry and granular. To rescue overbeaten egg whites, add an extra fresh white and beat until you have a glossy foam that holds the desired peaks.

frozen, transfer to a zipper-lock plastic bag. Thaw overnight in a bowl in the refrigerator or in a tightly sealed zipper-lock plastic bag set into a bowl of cool tap water.

To choose a bowl for beating egg whites • An unlined copper bowl is ideal because it will make the whites stronger so that they can rise for a longer period of time in the oven before they dry out and set. If you don't have a copper bowl, use a glass or metal bowl. Avoid using plastic bowls, which are more porous and tend to retain a greasy film that can prevent egg whites from achieving full volume. Aluminum bowls should also be avoided because they will react with any acid added to the whites and turn them gray.

To prepare equipment for beating egg whites • Make sure that any of the equipment that might come in contact with the egg whites is absolutely grease-free, including the bowl, whisk, beaters, and scraper or spatula. Just a speck of fat can cause the whites to rise to only one-third of their potential volume, because the fat intervenes in the formation of protein bonds in the egg foam. Just to be sure, wipe everything down with a paper towel dampened with lemon juice or vinegar, then rinse and dry thoroughly. If you regularly use a whisk to beat egg whites, store it away from your stove top so that it does not collect grease.

To prepare egg whites for beating • Bring the egg whites to room temperature before beating. Warm eggs have a lower surface tension, allowing bubbles to form more easily. Most recipes call for egg whites to be beaten last, but separate the eggs first, which will give the whites time to reach room temperature as you prepare the rest of the recipe. Of course, you can beat cold egg whites; it just takes longer.

To choose eggs for beating • Any type of eggs can be beaten, but farm-fresh eggs take longer because they have thicker whites. However, they will have more structural stability. Thin, runny whites (usually found in supermarkets) beat up faster than fresh, thick whites.

To choose a beater for egg whites • If beating by hand, choose a large, well-rounded balloon whisk with many thin, flexible tines. You can also use a clean, old-fashioned rotary beater. Or use an electric mixer, making sure that the beaters move continuously around the edge of the bowl.

To beat egg whites that won't deflate • Begin by beating slowly. Beating too quickly makes large air cells, which break easily. Once an even foam forms, you can beat more vigorously until the egg whites are firm enough to hold the desired shape (soft peaks or stiff peaks). As soon as they do, stop. Overbeaten egg whites can become brittle and deflate rapidly.

To stabilize beaten egg whites • Add an acid, such as cream of tartar, lemon juice, or vinegar. The acid helps bond the protein cells together, so they beat up faster and become more stable and smooth. When beating 6 egg whites, add a pinch of cream of tartar or ½ teaspoon lemon juice after the egg whites form a foam, but before they hold a shape.

To keep beaten egg whites moist and elastic • Add sugar just when the whites reach soft peaks. If added sooner, the sugar may impede foam development. If added later, it may cause the whites to dry out and lose elasticity. To help the sweetener disperse quickly and evenly, use superfine sugar, sometimes called bar sugar, instead of granulated sugar. It also helps to add the sugar gradually, 1 to 2 tablespoons at a time, so that it doesn't decrease the foam volume. To make sure that the sugar has dissolved, rub the egg whites between your fingers. They should feel smooth. If you feel any grit, continue beating.

To fold beaten egg whites into a batter with a spatula • Use the largest rubber spatula you can find, which will cover more area in less time. Folding should be done gently but quickly, using as few strokes as possible to prevent breaking the air bubbles. Lighten the batter first by folding in about one-quarter of the beaten whites. Once they have been incorporated, add the remaining whites and fold in gently. Avoid stirring egg whites, which causes them to deflate. Instead, use a lifting and rolling motion to fold the whites into the batter.

TIME SAVER ▼ **To save time when folding in beaten whites** • Use the beater used to beat the egg whites rather than a spatula. Because a beater has many more surfaces than a spatula, it will break up the batter more easily, making more spaces into which the egg whites can flow and incorporate.

Egg Yolks

The yolk of an egg has excellent binding properties because it contains lecithin, a natural emulsifier. Egg yolks are essential for emulsifying or binding together classic sauces such as hollandaise and mayonnaise. Egg yolks are also used for their thickening properties. They are often added to custards, puddings, and other mixtures for a richer texture. One egg yolk contains 5 grams of fat (mostly unsaturated), 213 milligrams of cholesterol, and a range of beneficial B vitamins.

BASICS ▼ **To store** • Cover egg yolks with a small amount of water, seal in an airtight container, and refrigerate for up to 3 days. You can also freeze egg yolks, but they become very thick. If you must freeze them, beat in a speck of salt or a scant ½ teaspoon sugar or corn syrup per egg yolk to keep them smooth and usable. Choose salt or sugar depending on how the egg yolks will be used. Thaw overnight in the refrigerator. Use 1 tablespoon thawed egg yolk for each fresh yolk called for in the recipe.

To use leftover yolks • See "To use leftover egg yolks" on page 4.

Fascinating Fact: The thick, white, cord-like strands that hold an egg yolk in the center of the white are called chalazae. Fresher eggs tend to have more prominent chalazae. Though they don't affect an egg's cooking properties, chalazae are sometimes removed to create a smoother texture in custards.

Emulsions *see also* Mayonnaise; Salad Dressings; Sauces

An emulsion is a smooth mixture of 2 liquids that normally don't mix, such as oil and water. A vinaigrette is probably the best-known example, where fine droplets of the oil are dispersed and suspended in the vinegar. The texture of many classic sauces, notably mayonnaise, hollandaise, béarnaise, and beurre blanc, depend on emulsification.

BASICS ▼ **To make** • Start with the water or liquid portion of the emulsion and add the oil or other fat to it. For example, when making a vinaigrette, start with the vinegar and add the oil to it. Add the oil or other fat very slowly, even drop by drop, while at the same time whisking rapidly. Once the mixture begins to thicken, add the fat gradually in a thin, steady stream, continuing to whisk rapidly. This process of gradually adding fat while mixing rapidly disperses and suspends tiny droplets of the fat throughout the other liquid, creating the emulsion. If small droplets of oil begin to form on the surface of an emulsified sauce, it may be about to break. Stop adding fat and whisk in a few drops of vinegar, lemon juice, or water to thin the sauce. Then, begin adding the fat again.

To make a thick, emulsified sauce with an egg yolk base • Freeze then thaw the yolks or add salt to them.

Entertaining *see also* Timing

It's hard to pinpoint the exact moment when an evening of gracious entertaining becomes a sentence of dinner with no parole, but there are a few simple ways to make sure that the cook enjoys the party too.

BASICS **To plan a menu** • Include a variety of different types of foods. Be sure to include different textures (crispy, creamy, crunchy, tender) and flavors (sweet, sour, salty, bitter, astringent, pungent, cooling). Serve some cold items (crudités, chilled soup, ice cream or sorbet), some at room temperature (antipasto or other appetizers, cookies or cake), and some hot (stew, hot entrées, warm brownies or pies). Variety is key, but above all, rely mostly on tried-and-true dishes that are quick and easy. If you want to make a grand impression, go for it once in the meal, rather than trying for a climax at every course.

To develop a shopping and cooking plan • Think about what can be cooked ahead and what ingredients will be hard to purchase or store well. Map out a plan for what needs to be done each day leading up to the party (shopping, cooking ahead, freezing, thawing, and so on).

To manage the workload • Get help. Unless you live with a staff of four in your kitchen, you'll probably need some help, even for a small dinner party. This can be as simple as having guests help with the cooking, or deciding that you will buy the dessert rather than prepare it yourself.

To avoid last-minute disasters • Cook ahead. If you insist on cooking everything from scratch and want to be able to attend the party as well, it is essential that you prepare as much of the food ahead of time as possible. Freeze whatever you can, and plan dishes that don't require last-minute fussing. Hors d'oeuvres or appetizers that use commercially prepared frozen puff pastry are infinitely elegant and keep for weeks in the freezer. Chilled soufflés and soups can be made a day ahead and can be ready for service without so much as reheating. Pâtés can chill for weeks in the refrigerator, and marinated salads provide brilliant colors and piquant flavors that only get better after a day's sojourn in the fridge.

PROBLEM SOLVER **To cook multiple roasts** • If you do not have a double oven, prepare the roasts in batches. If you do have a double oven, you can cook multiple roasts at the same time. Halfway through cooking, switch and rotate the position of each roast to compensate for any uneven heat distribution. Keep in mind that recipes are typically written for single, modest-size roasts. Doubling up two small roasts will increase the cooking time slightly. Use an instant-read thermometer to check internal temperatures rather than going solely by cooking time.

(continued on page 170)

ESTIMATING FOOD FOR A CROWD

It's probably not often that you serve 12 guests. But when you do, you want to get the right amount of food. Amounts below are calculated for 12 guests, allowing 2 modest servings each. For 6 guests, halve the amounts.

Food	Total Amount Needed
BEEF	
Barbecued brisket	1 whole brisket, about 10 lb
Flank steak	3 steaks, 2 lb each
London broil/shoulder steak	10 lb
Rib-eye roast, boneless	6 lb
Rib-eye steak	Twelve 10-oz steaks, halved
Rib roast, bone-in	16 lb
Sirloin roast	Two 3-lb roasts
Tenderloin or filet mignon steaks	6 lb
CHICKEN	
Bone-in parts	20 lb
Breasts, bone-in	24 medium breasts
Breasts, boneless, for stir-frying	6 lb
Breasts/cutlets, boneless	20–24 boneless breast halves
Whole	Six 3-lb broilers or four 4- to 4½-lb roasters
LAMB	
Leg of lamb, bone-in	2 legs, about 6 lb each
Leg of lamb, butterflied	2 boned legs, about 4 lb each
Rack of lamb	6 racks
PORK	
Bacon	4 lb
Center-cut loin, bone-in	12 lb
Center-cut loin, boneless	6 lb
Chops, bone-in	24 chops
Chops, boneless	6 lb
Half-ham, bone-in	8 lb
Ham, boneless	6 lb
Spare ribs	24 lb
Tenderloin	6 lb

Food	Total Amount Needed
SEAFOOD	
Clams, mussels, oysters, or shrimp, fresh	144–180 pieces
Crabs, live	9–14 lb
Fish, fresh cleaned	6–8 lb
Fish, fresh fillets or steaks	4–6 lb
Fish, fresh whole	9–12 lb
Lobsters, live	12 lobsters, 1–2 lb each
Scallops or cleaned squid, raw	3–5 lb
Shrimp, crabmeat, or lobster meat, cooked	3–5 lb
TURKEY	
Whole	18–20 lb
BEVERAGES	
Coffee	8–12 oz ground beans
Soft drinks	Three 2-liter bottles
Tea, hot or iced	5–6 qt (20–30 tea bags)
SNACKS AND CRUDITÉS	
Broccoli or cauliflower florets	Four 1-lb heads
Carrot sticks	1¼ lb
Celery sticks	2–3 bunches
Chips or pretzels	1¼ lb
Olives	3–4 cups
Pickles, sliced	1 qt
MAIN DISHES	
Pizza	Six 16" pizzas
Rice	6 cups uncooked
Salad, green	6 qt
Soup	2½ gal
DESSERTS	
Cake	Two 13" × 9" cakes
Ice cream or frozen yogurt	3 qt
Pie	Three 9" pies

e

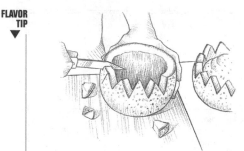

To make edible bowls • Hollowed-out edibles create a festive look for any occasion. Fill hollowed-out melons with fruit salad or sweet fruit dip; fill hollowed-out cabbage or a loaf of bread with savory dip; or fill winter squash with soup. First, cut a thin slice from the bottom of the food so that it sits flat. Then, cut off the top (if hollowing bread, cut in and around the top with a sharp knife.) Scoop out the insides, leaving at least ½" shell thickness intact. For added effect on melons, make 1" diagonal cuts around the top of the bowl to create a decorative crown.

SMOKED SALMON AND GRUYÈRE CHEESECAKE Preheat oven to 200°F. Grease a 9" springform pan or 2-quart shallow gratin dish and dust with **2 tablespoons grated Parmesan cheese.** Sauté **1 chopped onion, 1 large minced garlic clove,** and **⅔ cup chopped fresh herbs** (such as dill and tarragon) in **3 tablespoons olive oil** until onion is soft, 4 minutes. Remove from heat and stir in **½ pound coarsely chopped smoked salmon.** Beat **2 pounds good-quality cream cheese** until smooth. Beat in **¼ cup whiskey, 3 tablespoons white wine or sherry vinegar, 1 cup shredded Gruyère cheese, ¼ cup grated Parmesan cheese, 6 eggs,** and **½ teaspoon ground black pepper.** Beat until smooth. Fold in salmon mixture. Pour into the prepared pan and bake 8

hours (overnight is easiest). Let cool in the pan. Unmold (if using a springform pan) and refrigerate until cold (up to 1 week ahead). Bring to room temperature before serving. Serve with **sliced black bread**.
Makes 36 appetizer portions.

Evaporated Milk *see also* Milk;
Sweetened Condensed Milk

The silky texture of evaporated milk is created by removing 60 percent of the water from canned milk. This process imparts a slight caramel flavor to the milk, making it ideal for cooking. Evaporated milk is available in whole, low-fat, and fat-free varieties.

BASICS
▼
To replace milk • Mix equal parts evaporated milk and water.

To replace whipped cream • Remove evaporated milk from the can and freeze it briefly to chill. Then whip it with a wire whisk or mixer until it holds soft peaks.

FLAVOR TIPS
▼
To add rich flavor to mashed potatoes • Use evaporated milk in place of ½ cup of the milk called for in the recipe.

To make butterscotch flavor • When making vanilla pudding or pie filling, replace sugar with brown sugar and replace milk with evaporated milk (or replace at least half of the milk). Cook as usual.

HEALTHY HINT
▼
To use in place of cream or milk • Evaporated low-fat or fat-free milk makes rich-tasting, low-fat soups and sauces. For soups, use 1 cup evaporated milk for 4 servings. For sauces, use about ¼ cup for 4 servings. Or use evaporated milk for hot cocoa in place of milk or cream. You can also stir it into hot cereals with dried raisins or fruits. And you can use it in sherbet and ice cream recipes for a smooth texture.

Fat Replacement *see also* Baking

Fruit purees can be used successfully to replace some of the fat in baked goods. Drained applesauce, strained baby food fruit, or a puree of prunes and water all work well. You can also use a puree of water and any dried fruit, such as dried apples, apricots, or peaches. The quickest option: a product called fruit puree fat replacement, carried in most supermarkets. It's a combination of pureed fruits and lecithin, a natural emulsifier found in corn, soybeans, and egg yolks.

HOMEMADE FAT REPLACEMENT Cut **2 apples** and **2 pears** into chunks and place in a saucepan with ⅔ **cup water** and **1 tablespoon** *each* **lemon juice and lecithin granules** (available in health food stores). Bring to a simmer, cover, and cook 40 minutes, mashing occasionally. Press through a sieve or food mill. Refrigerate up to 5 days or freeze up to 6 months. To use, substitute fat replacement for about two-thirds of the total amount of oil, butter, or shortening in baked goods, adding 1 to 2 tablespoons canola oil. For example, to replace 1 stick (½ cup) butter, use 5 tablespoons fat replacement and 2 tablespoons oil. *Makes about 3½ cups.*

PRUNE PUREE Puree ½ **cup pitted prunes** (or equal amounts of **prunes** and **dried apples**) and ¼ **cup water** in a blender or processor until smooth. The dark color and strong flavor of this fat replacement make it best suited to chocolate-based or heavily spiced baked goods. To replace 1 stick (½ cup) butter, use ⅓ cup prune puree. *Makes about ⅔ cup.*

Fats and Oils *see also* Baking; Butter; Frying; Margarine; Olive Oil; Sesame

It would be impossible to overstate the role that fats play in cooking. They not only deliver enormous flavor and help transfer heat but they also contribute incredible texture to food, in everything from crispy coatings to tender cakes.

BASICS **To define solid fats and liquid oils** • The two primary categories of cooking fats are solid fats and liquid oils. Solid fats are usually derived from animal sources. Butter and cooled pan drippings are good exam-

f

ples. These fats are solid at room temperature and contain mostly saturated fat. Liquid oils come primarily from plants, including nuts, seeds, beans, and fruit (for example, peanut oil, sesame oil, soybean oil, and olive oil). They are liquid at room temperature and contain mostly unsaturated fats. The exceptions here are tropical oils such as coconut oil and palm oil, which are nearly solid at room temperature and contain mostly saturated fat, despite their plant origins.

To define hydrogenated fats • Hydrogenated or partially hydrogenated fats are a cross between the two types described above. These are liquid oils that have been chemically transformed into solid fats. The best examples are stick margarine and vegetable shortening. The hydrogenation process forces hydrogen atoms into the unsaturated fat to solidify it, creating what are known as trans fatty acids.

To store solid fats • Wrap them tightly and refrigerate for up to 2 weeks, or freeze for several months. Fats readily absorb odors, so keep them away from strongly flavored foods. Shortening can be kept at room temperature for up to 1 year, its primary advantage. Unlike other solid fats, it's also impervious to odors.

To store oils • For the longest storage, keep all oils in the refrigerator, including olive and canola oils, but especially fragile nut oils such as walnut, macadamia nut, and almond. The cool temperature may make the oil solid or cloudy. If this happens, simply bring the oil to room temperature and it will become clear again. If your refrigerator is full, store oils in the next coolest, darkest spot.

To detect a rancid oil • Sniff it. You can't miss the unpleasantly sharp odor. Or taste it: It will be bitter.

To replace butter with oil • Use 80 percent of the butter's measure in oil. Oil is 100 percent fat and butter is only 80 percent fat. For instance, replace 1 stick (½ cup, or 8 tablespoons) butter with about 6½ tablespoons oil.

To determine whether oil is hot enough for cooking • Look for a shimmering appearance on the surface. Avoid letting the oil smoke, at which point it will be overheated.

To clarify pan drippings or oil used for deep-frying • Pour into a funnel or cone-shaped sieve lined with a coffee filter, a double layer of cheesecloth, or a heavy-duty paper towel. Cool and store in the refrigerator. All vegetable oils used for deep-frying can be reused at least once if strained (clarified).

To discard oils • Sop up small amounts with paper towel and discard. For larger amounts, cool and pour into a jar with a lid. Discard in the trash.

To discard solid fats • Never pour liquefied solid fats down the drain. They can resolidify in your pipes and cause a nasty clog. While they're still hot, pour them into a small bowl lined with foil. When the fat cools and becomes solid, fold up the foil and throw it away. For large amounts, pour into a coffee can or other empty can, cool, cover, and discard.

To measure solid fat • Use the displacement method. For example, to measure ½ cup shortening or tub margarine, fill a liquid measuring cup with ½ cup water and add shortening or margarine until the water level rises to the 1-cup mark. Pour off the water before using.

PROBLEM SOLVERS ▼ **To prevent a greasy mess in your cupboard** • Place paper bags or paper towels beneath bottles of oil on your shelf. Replace when necessary.

CHOOSING THE RIGHT OIL

Vegetable oil (usually soybean oil) is the most common oil reached for by home cooks, but another oil may be a better choice, depending upon the dish you're making. Here's what to choose when, including approximate smoke points for the best frying oils. *Smoke point* refers to the temperature at which an oil will begin to smoke and impart unpleasant flavors to food.

Oil	Characteristics	Best Uses
Almond	Toasted almond flavor; breaks down with heat	Dressings, cold desserts
Avocado	Rich, buttery flavor; breaks down with heat	Dressings, sauces
Canola	Flavorless; light yellow color; fairly high smoke point (435°F)	Dressings, sautéing, frying, baking
Corn	Mild flavor; yellow color; fairly low smoke point (410°F)	Dressings, sautéing, light frying
Grapeseed	Mild flavor; high smoke point (445°F)	Dressings, sautéing, frying
Hazelnut	Aromatic hazelnut flavor; breaks down with heat	Dressings, sauces, baking
Olive	Mild to rich olive flavor; pale yellow to deep green color; fairly low smoke point (410°F)	Dressings, sautéing, light frying
Peanut	Neutral flavor; golden color; high smoke point (450°F)	Stir-frying, sautéing
Pumpkin	Roasted pumpkin seed flavor; green color; breaks down with heat	Dressings, sauces
Safflower	Mild flavor; light texture; high smoke point (450°F)	Sautéing, frying
Sesame (toasted)	Strong, nutty flavor; breaks down with heat	Dressings, sauces
Soybean	Mild flavor; light color; high smoke point (450°F)	Sautéing, frying
Sunflower	Light in flavor and color; breaks down with heat	Dressings, sautéing
Walnut	Rich walnut flavor; amber color; breaks down with heat	Dressings, sauces, baking

f

To clean up an oil spill • Thoroughly cover with a layer of flour, let sit a few minutes, then wipe up with a paper towel.

To prevent oil from splattering • Use a splatter screen. Most cookware stores and supermarkets carry them for just a few worthwhile dollars. Or, invert a wire-mesh sieve over the pan. Avoid using a colander, which can cause moisture to condense and drop back into the oil, making the oil splatter even worse.

To rid fry oil of odors • Fish, in particular, can impart its strong aroma to the oil in which it is fried. Eliminate the smell before reusing by frying a few slices of raw potato in the oil. Discard the potato before reusing the oil.

FLAVOR TIPS ▼ **To boost flavor with corn oil •** Most oils are refined, but unrefined oils have a richer flavor. Look for unrefined corn oil in health food stores. It has a golden amber color and a buttery flavor. As with high-flavor nut oils, such as hazelnut, walnut, and sesame oils, you need only 1 to 2 tablespoons of unrefined corn oil to add flavor. Try it in cornbread and corn muffins, or as an alternative to melted butter for popcorn. Store in the refrigerator.

To get the best texture in baked goods • Use a combination of butter and shortening. Unlike butter, which contains water, shortening is 100 percent fat. That lack of water means that shortening makes flakier pie crusts and crisper cookies than butter can. But shortening lacks the unique flavor of butter, so a combination of the two is the best bet.

HEALTHY HINT ▼ **To cut down on fat usage •** Measure fats and oils to be certain of the amounts you're using. Use nonstick pans and cooking spray to avoid using excess fat for sautéing. Use a pump bottle to spray olive oil or other flavorful oils instead of drizzling or pouring. Also, use lower-fat cooking techniques, such as steaming, poaching, roasting, or grilling. And use reduced-fat versions of high-fat products such as mayonnaise, sour cream, cream cheese, and other cheeses. See also the "Healthy Substitutions" chart on page 570.

GARLIC, ORANGE, AND WALNUT OIL PAN SAUCE After sautéing 1 pound of chicken breast, veal, or fish, remove the food from the pan and set aside. Add **1 minced garlic clove** and **1 cup orange juice** to the hot pan. Boil until juice re-

duces to ⅓ cup. Remove from heat and mix in **2 tablespoons walnut oil.** Pour over sautéed ingredients. *Makes about ½ cup.*

SMOKY LENTIL SOUP In a saucepan, sauté **½ chopped onion, 1 chopped carrot,** and **1 chopped celery rib** in **1 tablespoon vegetable oil** until soft. Add **1 cup chopped skinless smoked turkey, 6 cups chicken broth, ½ pound lentils, ½ teaspoon dried crumbled rosemary, ¼ teaspoon thyme,** and **1 bay leaf.** Simmer until lentils are tender, about 35 minutes. Stir in **1 chopped roasted red pepper** and **1 tablespoon** *each* **tomato paste and toasted sesame oil.** Remove bay leaf before serving. *Makes 4 servings.*

Fat Skimming

When cooking meats in liquids such as stocks, soups, sauces, and braises, the fat will rise to the surface, where it can be easily skimmed off if necessary.

BASICS ▼ **To remove fat from hot liquids •** For small amounts of fat on the surface of a stock, soup, stew, or sauce, fold a sheet of paper towel in half and pull it across the top of the liquid to absorb the fat. (When using a two-ply towel, peel it apart to get a single sheet.) Repeat until no more fat is visible, using new towels as needed. Or, use a ladle and tip it slightly to skim off the surface fat. If necessary, place the skimmed liquid in a bowl and freeze for 30 minutes to recapture any liquid that you may have skimmed off with the fat.

You can also pour the liquid into a fat separator, a type of measuring cup with a spout that pours from the base of the cup so that the fat rests on the surface and stays in the cup. These inexpensive gadgets work especially well for defatting gravy.

To remove fat from hot liquids using ice • Place a few ice cubes in a slotted spoon and drag it across the surface of the liquid. The ice will attract fat like a magnet. Discard the ice cubes before they fully melt.

Fennel

Licorice-flavored fennel, also known as anise bulb, is composed of three parts that have very different culinary uses. The most useful part is the bulb end, which looks like a cross between a peeled onion and the butt end of a bunch of celery. It can be served raw, shredded in a salad or sliced for crudités; or it can be thickly sliced and braised to tenderness in wine or broth. The stems, which ascend from the bulb, are darker and more fibrous. They don't have much use except as an addition to stocks or broth. The fronds or leaves are feathery and very delicate in flavor. They make a fanciful garnish for salad, seafood, or poultry.

BASICS ▼ **To choose** • Look for clean, firm fennel bulbs with no signs of browning. If the tops are attached, they should look bright green and fresh.

To store • Refrigerate in a zipper-lock plastic bag for up to 6 days.

To trim and slice • Chop off the stems and fronds just where the pale bulb turns darker green. Save the stems and fronds for another use, or discard them. Then, prepare the bulb like an onion, cutting it in half lengthwise (through the bottom and stem ends). Trim and discard the bottom end. Place cut side down and slice crosswise into crescent-shaped slices.

FENNEL WITH TOMATOES AND GARLIC Sauté **½ small chopped onion, 1 minced garlic clove,** and **2 trimmed and sliced fennel bulbs** in **2 tablespoons olive oil** until onion is soft. Add **2 chopped plum tomatoes** and transfer to a baking dish. Top with **¼ cup fresh bread crumbs** mixed with **¼ cup freshly grated Parmesan cheese, 1 teaspoon grated lemon zest,** and **½ minced garlic clove.** Bake at 375°F, 20 minutes. *Makes 4 servings.*

FENNEL AND ORANGE SALAD Trim and slice **1 fennel bulb** and toss with the halved sections of **2 navel oranges,** plus **½ cup walnut pieces** and **a pinch of nutmeg.** Whisk **⅓ cup extra-virgin olive oil** with **1 teaspoon ground fennel seed, ⅓ cup orange juice, 1 tablespoon lemon juice, a pinch of ground red pepper, ¼ teaspoon salt,** and **⅛ teaspoon ground black pepper.** Toss with the vegetables. *Makes 4 servings.*

Figs

A classic fruit of the Mediterranean, figs are best when eaten slowly and savored, from the soft pink flesh to the tiniest edible seeds. The peels are perfectly edible too. Look for fresh figs in markets from June through October. There are hundreds of varieties, ranging in color from pale green to golden yellow to deep purple, and in shape from round to oval to teardrop. Mission figs, one of the more popular types, migrated to North America with Spanish missionaries.

BASICS ▼ **To choose** • Hold the fig in your hand. It should be firm and unblemished, yielding slightly to very gentle pressure.

To store • Figs are highly perishable, so enjoy them as soon as you can. If you must store, refrigerate for up to 3 days.

To cut • Figs are quite sticky. If you need to cut them, refrigerate the fruit for 1 hour to reduce stickiness. Use scissors to snip the figs into bits. If using a knife, periodically dip the blade in hot water or coat the blade with cooking spray.

Fascinating Fact: Figs date back to 3000 B.C. and were used by the Assyrians as sweeteners. They were also Cleopatra's favorite fruit.

FLAVOR TIPS ▼ **To enjoy fresh** • Serve with prosciutto and melon.

To add to salad • Sprinkle ½ cup chopped figs onto your favorite mix of salad greens. Pair with a citrus vinaigrette.

DRIED FIG PUREE In a food processor, puree ¼ **pound dried figs, ½ teaspoon lemon zest, 2 tablespoons sugar,** and ⅓ **cup orange juice.** Spoon into the hollow of your favorite thumbprint cookie, or use to spread on thin, crisp cookies as a sandwich filling. *Makes about 1 cup.*

BAKED STUFFED FIGS Trim tops from **8 large black figs.** Stuff with ¼ cup *each* **chopped semisweet chocolate (or chips)** and **chopped almonds,** dividing among the figs. Bake at 350°F, 15 minutes. *Makes 4 servings.*

FIGS POACHED IN RED WINE In a stainless steel saucepan, combine **1½ cups dry red wine, 6 tablespoons sugar,** ⅓

cup **orange juice,** and **1 tablespoon lemon juice.** Add **a 1" × 3" ribbon of orange zest, 1 cinnamon stick (optional),** and **5 allspice berries (optional).** Bring to a boil. Reduce heat to low, add **8 to 10 small, slightly underripe black figs,** and simmer 5 minutes, turning occasionally. Remove with a slotted spoon and arrange on a plate. Increase heat to medium-high and boil liquid until slightly syrupy and reduced by two-thirds (to about ⅔ cup). Spoon over figs, leaving solids in pan. Serve warm or chilled. *Makes 4 servings.*

Filet Mignon *see also* Beef

Filet mignon is also called beef tenderloin. Technically, the tenderloin is the whole filet and filet mignon steaks are cut from the small end.

FLAVOR TIP ▼ **To wrap with bacon** • Partially sauté slices of bacon just to melt off some of the fat, but do not cook crisp. Wrap a slice around the outer edge of each filet mignon steak and secure with toothpicks. Grill or broil.

BLUE-CHEESE FILET MIGNON On a sheet of waxed paper or a plate, combine **1 teaspoon coarsely cracked black pepper** and **1 large minced garlic clove.** Lightly press **four 1"-thick filet mignon steaks** on both sides into mixture, to lightly coat. Heat a large, heavy nonstick skillet over medium heat, 5 minutes. Add steaks and cook until center of meat registers 145°F (medium-rare) to 160°F (medium) on an instant-read thermometer, 10 to 13 minutes, turning occasionally. Transfer to a warm platter. Into the skillet, pour ½ **cup beef broth** and ⅓ **cup dry red wine.** Increase heat and cook until reduced by half, 1 to 2 minutes, stirring. Spoon sauce over steaks and top with ½ **cup crumbled blue cheese.** Sprinkle with **chopped fresh parsley** and serve hot. *Makes 4 servings.*

Fish *see also* Doneness Tests and Temperatures (page 572) *and specific types*

Of all the fish in the sea, the most popular is canned tuna.

BASICS **To choose** • The best rule of thumb for buying fresh fish is to go to the market with an open mind. Instead of insisting on a particular fish regardless of the condition it's in, go with what is freshest. To figure that out, take a deep breath. Fish should smell like the ocean or a clean pond. If it smells fishy, it isn't fresh. Then, give the fish a poke. It should be firm, and the skin should be taut and shiny. Next, look your fish straight in the eye. The eye should be bright and protrude slightly from the head. Beware of using fish that is too fresh, though. Fish stiffen dramatically in the first few hours after they die. If the fish is cooked before rigor mortis sets in, it will contract when heated and the result will be a very mushy fish.

To choose between wild and farmed • Go wild. Its flavor is far superior.

To choose between lean and oily • Fish can be divided into two categories: lean white fish and oily fish. The type you buy is a matter of personal preference, which is why recipes often call for something vague like "any mild white fish such as flounder or sole." The flesh of white fish is lean and mild-flavored because the oil is concentrated in their livers. Lean white fish include cod, scrod, halibut, flounder, sole, hake, grouper, haddock, perch, pike, sea bass, red snapper, sea trout, and turbot. In oily fish, the oil is distributed evenly throughout the flesh, giving the fish a darker color and a stronger flavor. Oily fish (and shellfish) include anchovies, eel, sardines, mackerel, pompano, bluefish, salmon, lake trout, herring, tuna, scallops, shrimp, mussels, and swordfish. Although oily fish such as salmon and mackerel have higher fat and calorie counts, they contain beneficial omega-3 fatty acids, which may help lower heart attack risk.

To store whole fish • Rinse the fish with cold water as soon as you can. Fill a colander with ice, set it over a large bowl, put the fish on top of the ice, cover the fish with more ice, and refrigerate until ready to cook. The colander prevents the fish from sitting in a puddle, which can harm both its texture and flavor.

To store fish steaks or fillets • Leave the fish in its wrapper and refrigerate on ice in a colander as you would for whole fish (see above).

To remove scales from whole fish • Wash the fish well in cold water. With the fish still wet, place it in a large plastic bag. Working in the bag, scrape the skin with the blade of a knife as if "shaving" it of scales. The scales will fly off the skin, but they will be trapped in the bag. Wash the fish in cold water to remove any scales clinging to the skin. If you don't have a plastic bag, remove the scales under running water. If you have a fish with a lot of scales, loosen them by quickly dropping the fish into boiling water for 15 seconds and then plunging it into cold water.

To remove gills from whole fish • Your fish seller can do this for you, or it's

f

HOW TO GRILL A WHOLE FISH

Even experienced grill cooks can fumble when grilling a whole fish.

1. Choose the right fish. Firm-textured fish with assertive flavors take well to the high heat of the grill. Mackerel, bluefish, red snapper, and striped bass are good choices.

2. Use a clean, hot grill. Scrub the grill grid with a wire grill brush and give it plenty of time to heat up before adding the fish. A medium-hot fire is just the right temperature.

3. Slash and oil the fish. Make several slits about 1" deep in the sides of the fish to help it cook more evenly. These slashes will also help you judge when the flesh is cooked to the desired texture. Brush the fish very lightly with oil before you grill it, to prevent it from drying out and sticking to the grill.

4. Look, don't touch. Handle the fish as little as possible to keep it from falling apart. Set the fish on the hot grill and let it cook undisturbed until it's just shy of done, about 5 minutes. Then, gently loosen the fish from the grid with a pair of tongs and turn it just once by gently rolling it over.

5. Use 2 table knives when it's done. To check for doneness, stick a small knife or skewer into one of the slits. The flesh should be almost entirely opaque, with just a slight translucence. Slide 2 table knives beneath the fish to carefully remove it from the grill and serve. To simplify the entire handling process, use a grill basket, available in kitchen stores.

easy enough to do yourself. The gills lie right behind the head, under the gill flaps. Lift up each flap to expose the dark red, crescent-shaped gills. Using scissors, snip the cartilage at each end of the crescent. Hook a finger into the rounded side and pull the gills out in one piece.

To roast a whole fish • Remove the scales and gills. Choose a baking dish that can double as a platter. Brush the dish with oil, center the fish on it, and season the cavity of the fish with lemon slices, herbs, salt, ground black pepper, or your favorite seasonings. Rub the top of the fish with oil. Roast at 400° to 450°F (the smaller the fish, the hotter the oven) for 10 to 15 minutes per inch of thickness measured at the thickest part of the fish. To make a simple sauce, pour the juices from the platter into a small skillet. Heat to boiling;

add the juice of ½ lemon and 1 tablespoon butter. Pour over the fish and serve.

To test a roasted whole fish for doneness • Carefully stick a knife into the back of the fish and gently try to pull the top fillet away from the backbone. When the fish is done, the fillet will easily pull away from the bone. Avoid baking until the fish is very flaky and falls apart, a sign that it's overdone.

To steam-bake a whole fish • Remove the scales and gills. Run 1" of water in a roasting pan. Place the fish on a cooling rack and prop the rack in the roasting pan with balls of foil so that the rack is above the water line. Cover with foil and bake at about 425°F for 15 minutes per inch of thickness measured at the thickest part of the fish. Test for doneness as for a roasted whole fish, above.

To fillet a fish • Remove the scales. Then, use a long, sharp knife to make a diagonal cut right behind the gill flaps of the fish, angling downward toward the head. When you feel the knife hit bone, immediately make a 45-degree turn toward the tail. Cut to the tail, parallel to the center fin, in a single movement, making sure that you can feel the knife blade running along the center bone. When you reach the tail, cut through the skin to remove the fillet. Turn the fish over and repeat on the other side.

To cook fish fillets in a microwave oven • Arrange the fillets on a microwaveable dish in a single layer, with the thicker ends of the fillets around the edges of the dish. Brush with oil or butter and sprinkle with seasonings (except salt). Cook on high power 2 to 3 minutes (for ½" thick fillets) or 4 to 6 minutes (for 1" thick fillets). Let stand, covered, 2 to 4 minutes before serving; the fish will continue cooking slightly from residual heat. The fish is done when it is opaque (if it's salmon) or when it flakes easily (all other types). Add salt, if desired.

To pan-sear a fish fillet • Heat a non-stick skillet over medium-high heat until hot. Season a fish fillet with salt and ground black pepper and place it, skin side down, in the skillet. Cover and cook just until the fish is opaque (for salmon) or flakes easily (for other types), about 4 minutes for thin fillets to 8 minutes for thick fillets. Transfer to a plate. To make a simple sauce, add ½ cup white wine and 2 tablespoons chopped onion or leek to the pan.

Heat to boiling. Boil 1 minute, swirl in 1 tablespoon butter, and pour over the fish.

To neatly serve baked fish • Cook the fish in an oven-safe porcelain or glass dish that can be placed on the dinner table. That way, the presentation can wow the guests before the flaky fish is broken up into portions. Better yet, use single-serving oven-safe dishes.

To tell when fish is flaking easily • Press on the cooked flesh gently. When it is done, the fibers will separate gently. If the fibers fall apart, the fish is overcooked.

PROBLEM SOLVERS ▼ **To get a good grip when skinning a fish •** Start at the tail end and grip the skin with a paper towel.

To avoid toughening fish when cooking in a microwave oven • Hold off on seasoning with salt until after cooking.

To keep a whole baked fish from sticking to the pan • Leave the scales intact. This also helps keep the fish moist, but it means that you won't be able to eat the skin.

To keep fillets from sticking • Bake them on a bed of vegetables.

To help keep whole poached fish from falling apart • Wrap it in cheesecloth.

To whiten fish when poaching • Add an acid, such as lemon juice or wine, to the poaching liquid.

To evenly cook poached fish • Place the poaching pan over the span of 2 burners on the stove.

To prevent breading from falling off fish fillets • Dry the fish well before dipping into flour. Shake off any excess flour before dipping into egg and bread crumbs.

To keep breaded fish from turning soggy • As you bread the fish, place each fillet on a cooling rack set over a baking sheet rather than placing it on a plate.

To help prevent a fillet from falling apart while cooking • Leave the skin on.

f

To prevent a fillet from curling • Score the skin with a knife.

To evenly cook a flat fillet such as sole • Fold the thin tail end under. Or, even better, buy fillets from the thicker end of the fish so that there is no skinny tail to contend with.

To loosen fish that is stuck to a pan bottom • Drizzle a small amount of oil or other cooking fat on the pan where it is sticking, and gently loosen with a spatula.

To prevent the skin on fillets from sticking to the grill • Dip the skin side in coarse salt. Or, if you have a grill basket, by all means use that instead.

To lift or flip a grilled fish fillet without tearing it • Place a large strip of heavy-duty foil on the grill to use as a sling. Carefully slide the fillet onto the foil. Grab the ends of the foil and flip. You can also slide 2 table knives under the fish and transfer to a plate or, if flipping, transfer to a foil sling. Avoid spatulas, which tend to rip the flesh and skin.

To mute the frozen taste • Thaw frozen fish in cold milk.

To salvage fish that is dry from overcooking • Drizzle it with melted butter

HOW LONG TO COOK FISH

Recipes often direct you to cook a fish fillet "until it flakes easily with a fork" or to cook fish steaks "until just opaque." These are useful doneness tests, but they tell you nothing about the actual time required to cook the fish. To estimate how long it will take, check the thickness.

Thin fillets are no more than ½" thick. These include sole, haddock, some snapper, hake, catfish, and flounder. Thin fillets cook extremely quickly, so keep a watchful eye.

Thick fillets average about 1½" thick. Cod, some snapper, center cuts of salmon, monkfish, orange roughy, and grouper can be considered thick fillets.

Steaks are usually about 1" thick, including swordfish, tuna, mahi mahi, and salmon. Times below vary according to the fat content and density of the fish used.

	Thin Fillets	**Thick Fillets**	**Steaks**
Poach	5–7 min; medium-low heat or a bare simmer	8–10 min; medium-low heat or a bare simmer	10–12 min; medium-low heat or a bare simmer
Broil	2–6 min, depending on thickness; place 4"–6" from broiler	10 min per 1" of thickness; place 4"–6" from broiler	10 min per 1" of thickness; place very close to broiler
Grill	3–5 min; medium-hot fire	5–7 min; medium-hot fire	5–7 min; hot fire
Roast	About 6 min; 450°F	About 10 min per 1" of thickness; 450°F	About 10 min per 1" of thickness; 450°F
Sauté/Sear	4–5 min; medium-high heat	8–10 min; medium-high heat	8–10 min; high heat

THREE EASY TOPPINGS FOR FISH

Each of the following recipes will top off 1 pound of cooked fish.

Fresh Pepper and Tomato Topping: In a skillet over medium heat, sauté **½ cup chopped green bell pepper** and **½ chopped red onion** in **2 teaspoons olive oil**, 2 minutes. Add **2 chopped tomatoes, 2 tablespoons lemon juice, 1 teaspoon paprika, ½ teaspoon dried thyme,** and **⅛ teaspoon hot-pepper sauce.** Cook until vegetables are tender, about 4 to 6 minutes.

Ginger-Sesame Sauce: In a small saucepan over medium-low heat, combine **2 teaspoons sesame oil, 1 tablespoon** *each* **soy sauce and dry sherry, 1 chopped scallion, 1 teaspoon** *each* **grated fresh ginger and honey,** and **a pinch of ground red pepper.** Cook just until hot but not boiling.

Creamy Curry Sauce: Place **½ teaspoon curry powder** in a small skillet over medium-low heat. Toast, shaking pan, until fragrant. Place in a small bowl and stir in **⅓ cup low-fat plain yogurt, 3 tablespoons reduced-fat mayonnaise, 2 tablespoons chopped fresh cilantro,** and **¼ teaspoon** *each* **sugar and salt.**

and top with capers, finely chopped fresh parsley, or slivered almonds. Or top it with a quick homemade salsa. You could also use it in a soup.

To remove the stubborn odor of fish from a pan • Boil equal parts vinegar and water in the pan for 10 minutes.

TIME SAVER ▼ **To quickly thaw frozen fish** • Seal in a zipper-lock plastic bag and submerge in a container of cool water.

FLAVOR TIPS ▼ **To create a crunchy almond coating for fish** • Dust fish fillets with flour, dip them into beaten egg to coat, then dredge in a mixture of equal parts coarsely ground almonds and bread crumbs. Sauté the fillets in butter or oil.

To make a quick lunch out of leftover fish • Marinate in a vinaigrette and add to a tossed salad. Or toss with pesto sauce and pasta. You can also toss it in a mixture of hoisin and soy sauce and serve with cold noodles and sesame seeds.

LEMON-CAPER FISH FILLETS Dust **1 pound skinless mild white fish fillets** with **¼ cup flour.** Brown in a skillet with **1 tablespoon butter,** turning after first side is golden. Lower heat and cook until fish flakes easily. Remove to a warm plate. Add **1 tablespoon capers** to the skillet and cook 1 minute. Pour in **2 to 3 tablespoons white wine** and **2 teaspoons lemon juice.** Cook until mixture comes to a boil, stirring constantly. Pour over fish. *Makes 4 servings.*

CAJUN CATFISH In a shallow dish, mix **½ cup flour** and **½ teaspoon** *each* **ground red pepper and ground black pepper.** In another dish, combine **1 egg, 2 tablespoons dry white wine,** and **1 tablespoon Dijon mustard.** In a third, combine **½ cup cornmeal, 1 teaspoon dried oregano,** and **½ teaspoon ground cumin.** Lightly dust **1 pound**

catfish fillets with the seasoned flour, dip into egg mixture, then dredge in cornmeal mixture. In a large skillet, heat ⅛" **vegetable oil** over medium-high heat. Lay fillets in the skillet and cook until golden brown on undersides. Turn and cook just until fish flakes easily. Drain on paper towels. *Makes 4 servings.*

HEALTHY HINTS ▼ **To select fish that's high in omega-3 fatty acids** • An essential type of fat, omega-3 fatty acids may help protect your heart and may also be beneficial for rheumatoid arthritis, psoriasis, and hypertension (high blood pressure). The following fish are high in omega-3's, starting with the fish that is highest: swordfish, halibut, rainbow trout, canned solid white tuna, sockeye salmon, and striped bass.

To get omega-3's from canned fish • Choose canned salmon, tuna, or sardines.

To retain maximum omega-3's during cooking • Steam the fish or cook it in a microwave oven. These two gentle cooking methods don't affect the beneficial oils. High-heat methods of cooking, such as broiling or pan-frying, can destroy nearly half of the omega-3's in fish.

Flambé *see also* Alcohol

As the name suggests, flambéing is a process of "flaming" off alcohol by igniting it. As opposed to boiling off alcohol, flambéing caramelizes the sugar in the liquor slightly, producing a subtle, sweet, roasted aroma. It also makes a very dramatic presentation of dishes.

BASICS ▼ **To flambé a dish** • Make sure that your clothing, kitchen towels, and pot holders are out of the way. Have at the ready a lid that fits tightly over your pan, and use a hot pan over high heat (a pan just used for sautéing is the perfect temperature). Add ½ to 1 cup liquor, wine, or liqueur to the hot pan by first removing the pan from the heat, then pouring in the alcohol and carefully returning the pan to the heat. Stand back a bit and ignite the liquid with a long match, a fire starter, or a lighter and a quick hand. Just as the alcohol ignites, you will hear a quick "poof" and see a faint blue-orange glow on the surface. Then, just wait for the flame to subside, about 15 seconds for liquor or wine. (Beer cannot be flambéed because it doesn't have enough alcohol to support a flame; but its alcohol can be boiled off.)

To flambé a dessert • Turn that simple piece of pound cake or dish of frozen yogurt into a dramatic dessert by lighting it aflame. Warm ½ to 1 ounce (1 to 2 tablespoons) of cognac or fruit-flavored liqueur such as Grand Marnier in a small saucepan or microwave oven using low heat (it only needs to get warmer than room temperature). Quickly touch a long match, lighter, or fire starter to the edge of the liqueur so that it ignites (you'll hear a quick "poof"), immediately pulling your hand away. The alcohol will settle into an even flame. Pour the flaming liqueur over your dessert, turn off the lights, and present the dish before the flames die out.

PROBLEM SOLVER ▼ **To extinguish alcohol flames** • Immediately cover the pan and remove from the heat. Let sit for 1 minute.

Flavor *see also* Texture

The complex quality of food that affects our sense of taste is known as flavor. Most people can distinguish four basic flavors: sweet, sour, salty, and bitter. But studies have revealed that at least four more flavors exist (see "Foundations of Flavor" on page 184).

BASICS ▼ **To layer flavors** • Add a little bit more of the herbs, seasonings, or wine that was added at the start of cooking. This technique works best in dishes that simmer, stew, or braise for a long time, such as hot soup, stew, pot roast, or spaghetti sauce. Add the second layer of flavor 20 to 30 minutes before the cooking is complete.

To create big flavors • Use multiple forms of the same ingredient. For example, you could use fresh ginger, crystallized ginger, and ground ginger to boost flavor in gingerbread. Or, in a sauce, use fresh or canned tomatoes, tomato paste, and sun-dried tomatoes. Combine lemon juice and lemon zest for bigger lemon flavor. Combine dried and fresh mushrooms for deeper mushroom flavor. Each form of an ingredient has its own flavor, but when combined, two or three forms create a bolder, more exciting flavor.

TRIPLE-FLAVOR CORNBREAD Cut **6 slices smoked bacon** into small pieces. Cook in a skillet until crisp and brown. Spoon off all but 1 tablespoon of the fat. Add **1½ cups fresh or (thawed) frozen corn kernels** and **1 finely chopped jalapeño chile pepper.** Cook 2 minutes. Let cool. Preheat oven to 400°F. Grease a 9" cast-iron skillet and place it in oven to preheat. In a large bowl, combine ¾ **cup** *each* **cornmeal, corn flour (masa harina), and all-purpose flour.** Stir in **1 tablespoon baking powder, ½ teaspoon baking soda,** and **¼ teaspoon salt.** In another bowl, whisk together **3 large eggs** and ¾ **cup** *each* **plain yogurt and milk.** Stir in sautéed corn mixture, bacon, **3 tablespoons melted butter** or **corn oil,** and **1 cup coarsely grated sharp Cheddar cheese.** Add to dry ingredients and stir just until blended (batter should be slightly lumpy). Carefully remove the hot skillet and pour in batter. Bake until edges begin to pull away from pan, 30 minutes. Run a knife around the edge to loosen. Invert a plate over the skillet and carefully unmold so that crunchy side is up. Cut into wedges. *Makes 8 wedges.*

Flavor Essences

These are concentrated flavorings made by distilling fruit or other ingredients with the same process used to distill perfume. Flavor essences are much stronger and purer than flavor extracts such as vanilla extract, and a little goes a long way. In fact, if you use too much, the flavor can be intensely unpleasant. For example, ¼ to ½ teaspoon flavor essence would be enough to flavor 1 quart of fruit sorbet. You can buy flavor essences in large supermarkets and specialty shops and through catalogs.

FLAVOR TIPS ▼ **To boost the flavor of strawberries** • When sweetening 1 or 2 pints of strawberries, reserve the best ones whole or halved, then mash the remaining ones with sugar to taste, and add ¼ to ½ teaspoon wild strawberry essence (and ½ teaspoon vanilla extract, if desired).

To flavor vanilla pastry cream, pudding, or mousse • For some reason, apricot flavor essence greatly enhances vanilla creams and custards. Add ¼ to ½ teaspoon to every 2 to 3 cups after removing the food from the heat.

To mix or match flavor essences • Dozens of flavor essences are available: strawberry, raspberry, peach, pineapple, pistachio, chocolate, caramel, and coffee, to name just a few. They always work well when matching, say, fresh pineapple with pineapple essence, but you can experiment

f

FOUNDATIONS OF FLAVOR

There is more to flavor than what your taste-buds tell you. What we call flavor is a complex combination of aroma, taste, and texture. To enjoy the fullest flavor of food, all three of these sensations work in harmony. Here's a little Q&A to answer some of the more interesting questions about flavor.

How many flavors are there? Old scientific studies say that there are but four basic flavors: sweet, sour, salty, and bitter. These are the basic flavors that our tastebuds most easily recognize. In fact, these four flavors are so basic that they can be identified without the assistance of aroma. And the foods we enjoy most are a combination of several or all of these basic four flavors. But studies have found that at least four more categories of flavor sensation must be added to the list:

Pungent: Spicy-hot ingredients such as chile peppers and black peppercorns enrage and excite the tastebuds. They are neither sweet, sour, salty, nor bitter. They are pungent.

Astringent: Tannin, found in chocolate, tea, unripe fruit, and spinach, causes a contraction of tissues within the mouth. This flavor is best described as astringent.

Cooling: Menthol, found in mint, has a cooling, refreshing effect in the mouth, and a certain numbing sensation. This flavor is not captured by any of the basic four categories.

Umami: Named by the Japanese, *umami* could also be described as flavor enhancing. This category includes mushrooms and monosodium glutamate, or MSG, ingredients which tend to deepen the savory flavor of foods.

What are tastebuds? These are tiny receptors—about 10,000 in all—at the nerve endings in our tongues. Even with thousands of tastebuds, only 10 percent of any flavor is tasted by tastebuds. We taste 90 percent of flavor because of aroma. Our sense of smell is much more efficient than our tastebuds. That's why food doesn't taste so good when you have a cold.

Why do some flavors linger longer than others? The flavors of any food will last longer when fat is present. Food with a creamy consistency often tastes "better" because its fat content helps prolong the release of the food's flavor. In this sense, fat is a flavor carrier. Ice cream tastes so good because the butterfat in it coats the mouth and prolongs the release of flavors.

Does the temperature of food affect flavor? Yes. The melting point of certain foods such as chocolate, butter, and gelatin pleasantly prolongs the release of flavor. This is why some foods taste richer than others. Many foods, such as cheese, are best at room temperature. Others, such as baked goods, are better warm.

Why do some foods taste better than others? When foods contain a wide range of aromas, flavors, and textures in balance, more senses are excited and the food tends to taste better than any simpler flavor. Of course, taste is also very personal, and often, our emotions and taste memories come into play. One person might think that a can of tomato soup is the best flavor imaginable, while another might find it totally unpalatable.

Can you add too much flavor? Yes. Balance is crucial. Big flavors are very popular, but more is not necessarily better. Two or more unusual flavors combined can actually cancel out one another, resulting in an unpleasant taste.

and add caramel along with the pineapple essence to create a flavoring similar to brown sugar–pineapple upside-down cake. Or use coffee essence and chocolate essence to make a mocha flavor.

To add extra nuttiness to cookies • Add pistachio, almond, walnut, or hazelnut essence to cookies containing nuts.

To add extra flavor to fruit cocktail or fruit salads • Add 1 to 3 fruit flavor essences, such as ¼ teaspoon each of passion fruit, peach, and raspberry, per 4 cups of your favorite fruit concoction.

To flavor buttercreams • When adding 1 teaspoon vanilla extract to buttercream, also add ¼ to ½ teaspoon flavor essence.

To flavor lemonade • Add ¼ to ½ teaspoon of complementary flavor essence when making 4 to 5 cups lemonade. For example, make raspberry lemonade, strawberry lemonade, or grape lemonade.

Flaxseed

One of the oldest sources of textile fiber, flax has long been used to make linen. And its seed oil, known as linseed oil, is a key component in paints and varnishes. Whole flaxseed is also highly nutritious, containing protein, soluble fiber, and heart-healthy omega-3 fatty acids, as well as lignans, which have powerful antioxidant and cancer-fighting properties.

BASICS ▼ **To choose** • If you're using whole flaxseed for its nutritional benefit, buy the cracked or milled forms, which readily give up the nutrients inside. The whole seed has a very hard shell, which the body cannot digest to get to the nutrients inside. You can also buy whole flaxseed and grind it in a coffee grinder at home. Ground flaxseed can be added to muffins, breads,

and other baked goods. Or sprinkle on hot cooked cereals as you would wheat germ.

To store • Flaxseed has a high fat content, which makes it go rancid easily. For the longest storage, keep flaxseed in the refrigerator or freezer for up to 6 months.

To use whole • Flaxseeds can be added whole to bread doughs, quick breads, muffins, cookies, or pancake mixes for extra crunch.

To toast • Spread flaxseeds in a pan or skillet in a single layer. Bake at 350°F or toast over medium heat until fragrant, 3 to 5 minutes, shaking the pan occasionally.

To soften • Soak flaxseeds in water overnight to soften. Add softened flaxseeds to baked goods or to cereals. You can also puree softened flaxseeds to use in shakes or soups.

To use in place of eggs in baking • Combine 1 tablespoon milled or ground flaxseed with 3 tablespoons water. Let stand a few minutes to thicken. Use to replace 1 egg in baked goods. Note that ground flaxseed has the binding but not the leavening properties of eggs; baked goods made with ground flaxseed instead of eggs may not be as light in texture.

FRIED RICE WITH FLAX In a skillet or wok, toast ¼ **cup flaxseeds** over medium-low heat until fragrant, 2 minutes. Remove from the pan and set aside. In the same pan over medium heat, sauté ½ **chopped onion** and ½ **cup chopped red bell pepper** in **2 teaspoons olive oil**, 4 minutes. Stir in **3 cups cooked rice**, ½ **cup cooked shredded chicken**, and **4 sliced scallions.** Cook 2 minutes. Stir in ¼ **cup bottled stir-fry sauce** and reserved toasted flaxseeds. Cook until heated through, 2 minutes more. *Makes 4 servings.*

Flour *see also* Baking; Breads, Quick; Breads, Yeast

Though the term refers to the ground meal of various edible grains, flour is most commonly made from wheat. There are several styles of wheat flour, which vary mainly in the nature of the gluten-forming proteins in each particular style. When water is mixed with flour, these proteins join to make strong elastic sheets of gluten. High-protein flour makes for dense, sturdy breads and pasta. Low-protein flour makes tender cakes, quick breads, and pastries.

BASICS ▼ **To store all-purpose, pastry, or bread flour** • Transfer the flour to airtight containers and store at room temperature for up to 6 months. If the temperature rises above 75°F, transfer the flour to the refrigerator or freezer. Bugs and mold are more likely to infest flour at warm temperatures.

To store whole wheat and other whole grain flours • Whole grain flours contain more of the natural oils found in the germ and bran. Since these oils can turn rancid quickly, wrap whole grain flours airtight and refrigerate for up to 6 months or freeze for up to 1 year (double-wrap if

WHOLE GRAIN AND ALTERNATIVE FLOURS

Ground from a wide range of grains, grasses, and starches, whole grain and alternative flours cover a broad spectrum of tastes and textures.

Amaranth Flour: High in protein, this flour has an assertive, nutty taste and blends well with other grains such as rye and whole wheat flours. Use it in quick breads, particularly pancakes, waffles, and muffins.

Barley Flour: Low-protein barley flour has an earthy, sweet flavor and a slightly chewy texture. Use it with regular or whole wheat flour to make scones, bread, muffins, and pancakes. For more even baking, reduce the oven temperature by 25°F.

Buckwheat Flour: Also known as kasha, buckwheat is not technically a grain but the seed of a plant in the rhubarb family. When ground, buckwheat makes a low-protein flour that makes delightfully tender baked goods. Light buckwheat flour is cream-colored and has a subtler flavor than dark buckwheat flour, which has a stronger, almost bitter taste and a

purple-gray hue. Pair buckwheat flour with fruits such as prunes, apples, sour cherries, and pumpkin to make breads and muffins.

Chestnut Flour: Ground from dried chestnuts, chestnut flour is best during the chestnut season of late fall and winter. The flavor of the flour will vary depending on how the nuts have been prepared. Sometimes, they are roasted over an outdoor fire, lending a distinctive smoky flavor. Chestnut flour makes wonderful muffins, dumplings, pancakes, and pizza dough, but because it has no gluten, it must be used in combination with all-purpose flour.

Millet Flour: High-protein millet flour has a mild, slightly nutty taste that pairs well with cornmeal and with other grains such as oats, rye, and rice.

Oat Flour: Although rich in protein, oat flour will not rise with yeast, and because it has no gluten, it must be combined with all-purpose flour for baking. The sweet, earthy taste of oats freezing). Bring to room temperature before using.

To tell whether whole grain flour is rancid • Smell it. Rancid flour is immediately recognizable by its unpleasant odor.

To measure • If a recipe calls for "1 cup sifted flour," sift the flour first, and then measure. If the recipe says "1 cup flour, sifted," that means you should measure 1 cup and then sift. If the recipe uses weight instead of volume, it doesn't matter what you do first; ¼ pound of flour will weigh the same amount whether it's aerated by sifting or not. If the recipe doesn't specify sifting, stir the flour with a spoon, then spoon it into a measuring cup. Level off the cup with the edge of a knife or another straight edge. Avoid scooping flour directly into a cup, which compacts the flour so that you might end up with too much. Keep a straight edge readily on hand by storing a chopstick or a tongue depressor (clean, please) in with your flour.

To substitute all-purpose flour for cake flour • For each cup of all-purpose flour used, remove 2 tablespoons and replace it with 2 tablespoons cornstarch. Sift before using.

goes well with other grains such as rye, millet, and whole wheat.

Potato Flour: When dried and ground, starchy potatoes make a delicious flour that's often used in breads. Potato flour is quite dense and cannot be used interchangeably with potato starch or instant mashed potato flakes.

Quinoa Flour: Mild-tasting quinoa flour is quite high in protein and makes wonderful quick breads. Combine it with cornmeal, spelt, oats, or barley.

Rice Flour: For quick breads, either the delicate white variety or the denser brown rice flour. Combine with oats, graham, or spelt to make biscuits, quick breads, and cakes. Rice flour is not recommended for use in yeast breads.

Rye Flour: Whole grain rye is ground to make light, medium, and dark flours. The very coarsest rye flour is what we know as pumpernickel. You can make quick breads from rye, but add white flour to prevent them from turning out coarse-grained and flat.

Soy Flour: When used in combination with other flours, soy flour gives baked goods a golden crust and delicate flavor. High in both fat and protein, soy flour also works as a preservative by slowing rancidity and adding moisture. Look for stone-ground soy flour at a health food store. It has better flavor and is more nutritious than the highly refined, defatted flour. Because soy flour makes a crust that browns quickly, reduce the oven temperature by 25°F when baking with it.

Teff Flour: There are three main types of teff: ivory-colored light teff, the darker brown version labeled "dark," and red teff, usually found only in ethnic markets. Brown teff flour has a rich, molasses-like flavor that goes well with spicy gingerbread and makes distinctive waffles, pancakes, and quick breads.

Triticale Flour: High in protein but low in gluten, this hybrid of rye and wheat is a popular ingredient in whole grain breads. Combine it with wheat flour for the best texture.

f

WHICH FLOUR WHEN?

The texture of baked goods changes dramatically depending upon the type of flour used. To choose the right flour, check the protein content. For yeast bread, choose flour with 12 to 14 grams of protein per cup; for quick breads and pastry, choose 9 to 11 grams of protein per cup.

Flour Type	% Protein	Best Uses
Cake	5–8	Cakes, particularly those high in sugar
Pastry	8–9	Biscuits, cookies, pie crusts, pastries
Whole wheat pastry	9–10	Quick breads and muffins
All-purpose	9–12	Quick breads, yeast breads, cakes, cookies, and most everyday baking
Bread	12–13	Pizza crusts, yeast breads, and bread machine breads
Whole wheat	14	Use in combination with other flours to make hearty, hearth-style breads

f

To substitute cake flour for all-purpose flour • Use 1 cup plus 2 tablespoons cake flour for each cup of all-purpose flour.

To substitute all-purpose flour for self-rising flour • Replace each cup of self-rising flour called for with 1 scant cup all-purpose flour mixed with 1½ teaspoons baking powder and 1 teaspoon salt.

To substitute flour for cornstarch as a thickener • Use 2 tablespoons flour for each tablespoon cornstarch.

PROBLEM SOLVERS ▼ **To get consistent results with baked goods** • Use the same brand of flour every time. Brands vary in protein content, which means that your favorite cookie recipe can turn out tender one time, tough another, cakey a third time, and thinner a fourth time.

To sift flour without a sifter • Place flour in a mesh strainer and gently tap the edges of the strainer over a bowl or sheet of parchment. This is also a good technique for lightly dusting a work space or a cake pan with flour.

To easily measure out flour • Store in a wide-mouthed container.

To remove lumps of flour in a sauce • Beat vigorously with a whisk. If that doesn't work, try pressing the sauce through a wire sieve.

To get rid of the taste of raw flour in a thickened sauce or gravy • Be patient and keep cooking until the flavor cooks out.

To avoid bugs in your flour • Place a couple of bay leaves in your flour and store it in a dry, cool cupboard. If you don't use much flour, or if you have particular problems with bugs in your flour, double-wrap it and store in the freezer.

HEALTHY HINTS ▼ **To replace all-purpose flour with whole wheat flour** • Replace up to 50 percent of the white flour in recipes with whole wheat flour. Or try white whole wheat flour, made from white wheat berries. It is lighter in color and flavor and slightly sweeter than regular whole wheat flour.

To get tender results when replacing all-purpose flour with whole wheat flour • Fold batters very gently, particularly when mixing quick bread batters. It's especially important to avoid overmixing because whole wheat flour contains additional gluten, which will make baked goods tough if the batter is overmixed. For even more tender results, use whole wheat pastry flour. Made from soft wheat berries with less gluten content, whole wheat pastry flour is a perfect substitute for white flour when making desserts and quick breads. The end results will yield a softer, lighter texture, as well as a milder wheat flavor, than that of regular whole wheat.

Flowers, Edible

Though they may seem like a surprise ingredient to some, fresh flowers have a range of delightful flavors from spicy to sweet. They can be used in a variety of dishes, or use them as edible garnishes.

EDIBLE FLOWERS AND THEIR USES

Here are some of the more popular edible types. Be sure to eat only the blossom of the flower and not the rest of the plant. Serve on top or mix into the dish as desired.

Flower	Flavor	Best Uses
Begonia	Sweet and lemony	Fruit salads, desserts
Borage	Cucumber-like	Salads
Calendula	Slightly tangy	Salads, soups, dips, spreads, egg dishes
Chive blossoms	Mildly oniony	Salads, soups
Daisy	Mild	Salads
Dandelion	Mild	Soups
Daylily	Ranges from sweet to tart	Salads
Dianthus	Similar to clove or nutmeg	Salads
Hollyhock	Mild	Salads, main dishes
Lavender	Sweet	Fruit salads, desserts
Marigold	Citrusy	Salads, soups, main dishes
Nasturtium	Watercress-like	Salads, egg dishes
Pansy	Mild, like lettuce	Salads, main dishes
Rose	Highly aromatic	Beverages, desserts
Squash blossoms	Slightly sweet	Salads, egg dishes
Viola (Johnny jump-up)	Mild	Salads, desserts
Violet	Sweet	Fruit salads, desserts

f

BASICS ▼ **To choose** • Make sure that the flowers you use are indeed edible. Some flowers are poisonous, and others can cause allergic reactions. It's also important that the flowers are grown without pesticides. Your safest bet: Buy fresh flowers from a food store, or grow edible varieties at home without pesticides. Generally, flower shops are not good sources because the flowers are usually treated with pesticides.

To store • Flowers are best eaten the same day they are picked. To store for brief periods, rinse fresh flowers thoroughly but gently under a slow steam of cool water. Drain, place between layers of paper towels, and refrigerate until ready to use.

Food Processors *see also*

Chopping; Mincing; Puree

Introduced to home kitchens in the 1970s, food processors have become one of the most important kitchen tools for quicker cooking. They can be used to chop, slice, shred, grind, blend, and puree a variety of foods. They can also knead bread, cut butter into flour for baking, and grate large quantities of cheese.

BASICS ▼ **To choose** • Keep in mind that food processors and blenders perform many of the same tasks, but a food processor is better for blending solid mixtures, such as doughs, crumbs, and bases for savory mousses. A blender is better suited to liquids, such as soups, beverages, and sauces. If you are in the market for a food processor, look for one that has a mini bowl that fits into the larger bowl, so that you can process small jobs as well.

To evenly chop • Pulse the machine on and off.

To make dough • Use the plastic dough blade for yeast doughs. Use the steel knife for other doughs, such as pasta, pastry, and cookies. A food processor is not appropriate for most cakes because the batter requires aeration.

FOOD PROCESSOR SHRIMP MOUSSE
In a food processor, puree **12 ounces very cold, peeled and cleaned shrimp** with **2 egg whites** and **a pinch of nutmeg.** With the processor running continuously, slowly add **2 cups very cold heavy cream** until mixture is the consistency of softly beaten cream. Divide mixture among 6 greased ramekins or custard cups (5 ounces each). Place the filled ramekins in a baking dish. Pour enough boiling water into the baking dish to come halfway up the sides of the ramekins. Cover with greased parchment and bake at 350°F until mousse is set, about 25 minutes. Remove the ramekins from the water bath and invert each onto a plate. Blot liquid from plates. For a simple sauce, heat ½ **cup tomato puree (canned or fresh), 2 tablespoons extra-virgin olive oil, 1 tablespoon red wine vinegar, ¼ teaspoon salt,** and ⅛ **teaspoon ground black pepper** to a simmer. *Makes 6 servings.*

PROBLEM SOLVERS ▼ **To puree soup without spills** • Use a slotted spoon to transfer only the solids to the processor. Add enough liquid to cover (work in batches if necessary). Puree, then stir the puree back into the soup.

To make cleanup easier • Spray the inside of the work bowl and the blade or shredding disk with cooking spray before using. This helps prevent sticky foods such as dried fruit from adhering to the blade. When the bowl is dirty, put a small amount of warm water and some dishwashing soap in the processor and blend briefly. In most cases, you can then just rinse and dry.

To soak a food processor bowl to the top • Stick a champagne cork in the center shaft so that water cannot leak out.

Food Safety *see also* Thermometers

Perhaps the most important foundation of cooking, food safety helps ensure great-tasting food, a clean environment, and avoidance of illness. See "Five Rules of Food Safety."

FIVE RULES OF FOOD SAFETY

Most foodborne illness is caused by mishandling of food. Here are five steps to ensure that your food is safe to eat.

Shop smart. In the store, buy perishable items last, and avoid buying items that you won't use before the expiration date. Don't buy cans or glass jars with dents, cracks or bulging lids. At home, follow this cardinal rule: When in doubt, throw it out.

Keep foods chilled. Set your refrigerator to no higher than 40°F and your freezer to 0°F. As soon as you return home from shopping, refrigerate or freeze perishables. If you won't use meat, poultry, or fish within a few days, freeze it. When refrigerating raw meats, poultry, or fish, leave them in the store's packaging (when possible) and place in a shallow pan so that the food's juices are contained. When defrosting and marinating, do so in the refrigerator rather than on countertops. For more even cooking, remove marinated foods from the fridge during the last 20 minutes to bring to room temperature.

Clean often. Wash your hands with hot, soapy water before and after handling food, and especially after using the restroom, changing diapers, and playing with pets. Use hot, soapy water on all dishes, utensils, and work surfaces as well. Soak cutting boards in a mild chlorine bleach solution (¼ teaspoon bleach to 2 cups water) and replace cutting boards with deep cuts, which could harbor bacteria. Kitchen towels should be washed in the hot cycle of your washing machine, and sponges should be washed in hot water or put in the dishwasher daily to kill bacteria.

Avoid cross-contamination. Keep raw meat, poultry, seafood, and eggs away from ready-to-eat foods. When prepping food, cut vegetables and salad ingredients first, then raw meats and poultry. After preparing raw meat, wash all cutting boards, utensils, and work surfaces with hot, soapy water. Be careful to avoid placing cooked food on a plate that previously held raw meat, poultry, eggs, or seafood (unless the plate has been cleaned). When soaking up meat and poultry juices, use disposable towels instead of sponges. Discard all unused marinades or, if using, bring to a boil first to kill bacteria.

Use a thermometer. To be certain that food has cooked to a safe temperature, use an instant-read thermometer and check the Doneness Tests and Temperatures chart on page 572. Avoid eating uncooked meat, poultry, seafood, and eggs. When reheating leftovers, make sure that they reach a temperature of at least 165°F.

f

Freezing

Few methods of preserving food are as easy as freezing. But while cold temperatures slow the deterioration of foods, they do not stop the process entirely. Freezing can also damage the cells of many foods.

BASICS ▼

To set your freezer to the proper temperature • The ideal temperature is about 0°F. At this temperature, foods freeze quickly. Freezers that are too warm (between 25° and 31°F) take too long to freeze food, causing large ice crystals to form on the food and give frozen food a poor texture.

To prepare food for freezing • Cool hot food to room temperature (at least) before freezing. Cold food freezes faster, and putting hot food into your freezer can thaw adjacent foods and raise your freezer's temperature.

To freeze food faster • Set food on the lowest shelf in the freezer, where the temperature is lowest and the food will freeze more quickly than it will on a higher shelf, where the temperature is likely to be slightly warmer. Leave some room around the food for cold air to circulate. Once food is frozen solid, it can be moved to another shelf. Also, avoid overfilling your freezer. Keeping it too full can increase the temperature.

To organize your freezer • Designate sections of the freezer for categories of food. Aside from ice cubes and ice cream, the big four are (1) proteins, (2) vegetables and fruits, (3) baked goods, and (4) prepared foods. If you have room, it's also helpful to keep one section empty for quickly chilling or freezing foods.

To conserve freezer space • Store food in plastic freezer bags rather than in rigid plastic containers. Use zipper-lock bags designed for freezing. Other plastic bags are gas permeable, allowing oxygen into the bag, which will cause the food to deteriorate more rapidly. Plastic freezer bags save space and help preserve quality by allowing only a minimum of oxygen to touch the food. Label the bag with the contents and the date. When possible, use the chart on the opposite page to jot down the "expiration date." Place the food in the bag, close it to within ½", insert a straw into the opening, and suck out as much of the air from the bag as you can. Now, with the dexterity of a sleight-of-hand artist, slip out the straw and close the bag without letting any air back in. When freezing raw meats, press out excess with your hands instead of using a straw.

To make your freezer easier to clean • Line the floor of the freezer with foil, being careful not to cover the fan vent, which would cause the freezer to overheat.

To prevent freezer burn • Store food in zipper-lock plastic bags designed specifically for freezer use. Or store it in nonpermeable plastic wrap or in plastic containers. Freezer burn happens when the moisture on the surface of food evaporates. It also helps to squeeze out as much air as possible from the bag, plastic wrap, or container before sealing.

To know whether or not frozen food has deteriorated • The color of food should not have changed dramatically. If it has, the food has probably been frozen too long. If the surface of the food looks dry and is covered with pale gray spots, it likely has freezer burn. Frost on food indicates that food was frozen too slowly or that it has partially thawed and refrozen.

To keep vegetables from turning brown in the freezer • Blanch vegetables before freezing.

To freeze meat • Remove meats from their packaging and wrap tightly in good-quality freezer paper. Heavy-duty plastic bags work well too, but be careful not to let any bones puncture the plastic. A moistureproof wrap (not the flimsy plastic on packaged meats) will protect food from the drying effects of the freezer and help prevent freezer burn.

To easily cut thin slices of raw meat • Partially freeze the meat or poultry. Use a sharp serrated knife to slice or "saw" off wafer-thin slices. These are ideal for stir-fries. The meat can then be marinated, and it will thaw quickly.

To freeze individual pieces of food • Cookies, unbaked cookie dough, chicken pieces, meatballs, berries, or individual pastries are best placed on a rimmed baking sheet and frozen uncovered until firm. Then, transfer to zipper-lock freezer bags and store. This keeps the individual pieces from sticking together as they freeze, making it easier to use a portion without defrosting the entire bag.

To use empty freezer space • On the off chance that you have an extra freezer or empty freezer space, here's what to put there. Flour, especially whole grain flour, is a good choice because it goes rancid quickly at room temperature. (If storing flour for longer than a few weeks, put it in tightly closed plastic bags before freezing.) Dried herbs are another good choice; you can extend their shelf life indefinitely by keeping them in the freezer. Keep a small amount in your spice rack for immediate use and store the rest frozen in zipper-lock plastic bags. Nuts are another freezer contender. Like anything containing oil, they will become rancid in time, and freshness can be prolonged by freezing. To use

f

SHELF LIFE OF FROZEN FOODS

Here's how long you can expect common foods to last in the freezer. Use this guide to write the "expiration date" on foods before freezing them.

Food	Shelf Life	Food	Shelf Life
Beef and lamb (steaks, roasts)	1 year	Duck (whole)	6 months
Breads	2–3 months	Duck (parts)	3 months
Butter	2 months	Fish, lean white	6 months
Cakes	6 months	Fish, oily	2 months
Chicken and turkey (whole)	1 year	Fruit	1 year
Chicken and turkey (parts)	6 months	Ground meat	3 months
Cream, heavy	1 month	Pies, unbaked fruit	6 months
Dough, cookie	1 month	Pies, baked chiffon	1 month
Dough, pie	3 months	Pork (chops, roasts)	4–8 months
Dough, yeast	3 months		

frozen nuts in baking, bring them to room temperature first by warming in a 250°F oven for a few minutes.

To safely thaw frozen food • Allow frozen foods to thaw in the refrigerator rather than on a countertop.

To quickly thaw frozen food • If the food has not been frozen in a zipper-lock plastic bag, transfer it to one, and put the bag into a large bowl of cool water.

To defrost meats • The greatest lie ever perpetrated by cookbook authors is "defrost overnight in the refrigerator." Almost nothing defrosts overnight in a refrigerator. A frozen chicken would be better used for bowling than dinner after 12 hours in a fridge. A turkey might defrost over the week in the refrigerator, but "overnight"? No way. Defrosting frozen meats in the refrigerator takes at least 24 hours and more often 48.

FLAVOR TIP ▼ **To make instant sorbet** • Freeze a can of fruit packed in heavy syrup until solid. Open the can, dig out the frozen contents, chop into chunks, and puree in a food processor until smooth. Voilà, sorbet! You can add flavoring if you want. A little vanilla or almond extract is great with peaches. Try lime juice for pears, and a little fresh ginger with litchis.

French Fries *see also* Potatoes

Known as *pommes frites* in France, french fries get their name from a special cutting technique called frenching, in which potatoes or other foods are cut into long sticks or strips.

FLAVOR TIP ▼ **To get the best flavor and texture** • Soak the cut potatoes in cold water and pat dry before cooking. Also, fry them twice: once to soften them and next at a higher temperature to brown them.

BEST FRENCH FRIES Peel and cut **1½ pounds starchy russet potatoes** into ¼"- to ⅜"-thick sticks. Soak in cold water 20 or 30 minutes. Drain and pat dry. Bring 1" of **vegetable oil** to 330°F in a large, heavy skillet or deep fryer. Drop in the potatoes and fry until soft, 3 to 5 minutes. Remove to paper towels (at this point, the potatoes can be held for several hours). Bring oil to 365°F, then drop the potatoes in again until brown and crisp, 3 to 4 minutes. Cook in batches without crowding, if necessary. Drain on paper towels and sprinkle with ½ **teaspoon salt** while still hot. *Makes 4 servings.*

CRUNCHY BATTERED FRIES In a bowl, stir together **1 cup all-purpose flour, 2 teaspoons *each* ground red pepper and ground cumin, 1 teaspoon *each* dried oregano, dried thyme, and salt,** and ½ **teaspoon ground black pepper.** Whisk in **1½ cups cold water** to make a smooth batter. Chill 1 to 24 hours. Follow the recipe for **Best French Fries** (above), frying potatoes only once, at 330°F. Cool to room temperature. Whisk the batter, then dip cooled potatoes to coat. Fry at 365°F until brown and crisp, 3 to 4 minutes. For something different, serve with **bottled blue cheese dressing** or **Thousand Island dressing** instead of ketchup. *Makes 4 servings.*

HEALTHY OVEN FRIES Peel and cut **1½ pounds Yukon gold or baking potatoes** into ¼"-thick sticks. Toss in a large bowl with **1 tablespoon olive oil,** ½ **teaspoon salt,** and ¼ **teaspoon paprika.** Place in a single layer on 2 baking

sheets coated with cooking spray. Bake at 450°F until evenly browned, about 40 minutes total, turning every 10 minutes. Serve immediately. You can substitute sweet potatoes or carrots for potatoes.
Makes 4 servings.

Frosting *see also* Cakes

Whether simply spread over the top or piped into elaborate decorations, frostings are the final touch that make even the most ordinary cake worthy of a celebration.

BASICS **To frost a cake** • Make sure that the cake has cooled completely before applying the frosting. If the cake is too warm, the frosting may melt.

To remove crumbs from a cake before frosting • Brush it clean with a pastry brush.

To give frostings a smooth finish • Use a 6" scraper from a hardware store. It's smaller than a spatula and easier to handle. Hold the scraper perpendicular to the side of the cake and pull it gently across the frosting. It's the perfect tool for making sharp corners on square cakes.

To drizzle icing over cake, quick breads, or cookies • Use a spoon, dipping it back into the icing as needed.

BROWNED BUTTER FROSTING Melt **1 stick (½ cup) butter** in a small skillet over medium heat. Cook until butter turns a deep brown color. Pour into a deep medium-size bowl and chill until set. Then, return butter to room temperature. Add **2 tablespoons white vegetable shortening**. Beat with an electric mixer until fluffy, about 30 seconds. Sift **3 cups confectioners' sugar** and beat in ½ cup at a time. As frosting stiffens, begin beating in **2 tablespoons milk**, ½ teaspoon at a time, alternately with the remaining sifted sugar. Beat in **1 tea-**

THE RIGHT AMOUNT OF FROSTING

You never want to run out of frosting when decorating a cake. It's always better to have too much than too little.

Cake Size	Frosting Needed
8" or 9" two-layer round cake, top and sides only	1½–2½ cups
8" or 9" two-layer round cake; top, sides, and filling	2½–3½ cups
8" or 9" three-layer round cake; top, sides, and filling	4 cups
8" square cake, top only	¾–1 cup
8" square cake, 2" tall, top and sides	1½–2¾ cups
8" × 12" sheet cake, top only	1½–2 cups
9" × 13" sheet cake, top only	1½–2 cups
2"–3" round cupcake	2 Tbsp

spoon vanilla extract. If necessary, beat in a few more drops of milk, until frosting is a good spreading consistency. Apply while fresh, then chill to set. *Makes about 2 cups.*

PROBLEM SOLVERS ▼

To stiffen egg white frosting • Transfer the frosting to a double boiler and beat it over simmering water.

To stiffen cooked buttercream frosting • Refrigerate it until stiffened. Or beat in a little more butter.

To thin a frosting that's too thick to spread easily • Beat in a few drops of milk or boiling water.

To save frosting that has become granular from sugar • Add a squirt of lemon.

To avoid lumps when sweetening with confectioners' sugar • Press sugar through a sieve before using.

To spread frosting that is hardening or getting gooey • Heat the spatula in hot water or briefly over a burner between passes.

To frost a cake without mess • Cut a circle the size of the cake out of a piece of corrugated cardboard and use this to hold the cake when frosting. Transfer to a plate when complete. Cover the cardboard cake round with plastic wrap so that it can be reused. To catch drips, place the cake (with a cardboard base cake round) on top of a cooling rack with a piece of waxed paper or parchment paper underneath. If you do not have a cardboard round, arrange narrow strips of waxed paper or parchment paper around the rim of a cake platter, tucking them slightly underneath the cake, to catch the excess. Once the cake is frosted, pull the papers out, and the serving plate will still be clean.

To keep a cake stable while frosting • For "glue" put a dab of icing in the

MAKING A PAPER PIPING CONE

Small cones of parchment or waxed paper are easy to make and ideal for piping soft icings or melted chocolate onto cakes and cookies.

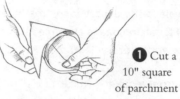

❶ Cut a 10" square of parchment or waxed paper in half diagonally to make 2 triangles. Pull the long sides of one triangle around to its midpoint to make a cone. Hold the cone tight while wrapping the second triangle around.

❷ Tuck the points into the cone to secure them. Use a small spatula to fill the bag with icing or melted chocolate. Be careful not to fill the bag more than halfway full.

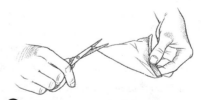

❸ Fold the open end of the cone over several times to close the cone. Cut a tiny bit off of the end to make a round tip. To make a tip for piping icing leaves or petals, cut a small triangle out of the tip.

middle of a flat plate, cardboard cake round, or turntable before setting the cake on top.

To keep layers from sliding • After frosting the bottom layer, add the top layer and insert a skewer through the center of both layers to secure.

To prevent fillings from leaching into frosting • Do not spread the filling to the very edges of the cake. Also, spread ½" of extra frosting in the gap between the two layers on the sides of the cake.

To center an inscription on a cake • Use a toothpick to outline the inscription first. If it fits and looks centered, follow up with piping. If it doesn't, smooth over and try again.

To fix a mistake when writing on a cake • Use the rounded end of a butter knife to lift it off.

To fix frosting that has cake crumbs mixed into it • Cover the frosting with a layer of ground nuts, crushed cookies, toasted coconut, candies, or any other complementary camouflage.

TIME SAVERS ▼

To quickly frost cupcakes • Dip them in frosting rather than frosting with a spatula.

To make a disposable decorating bag • Fill a zipper-lock plastic bag with frosting and snip a corner. Or make a parchment paper piping cone (see the illustrations on the opposite page).

FIVE EASY LOW-FAT FROSTINGS

Each of these frostings makes enough to frost and fill an 8" or 9" two-layer round cake.

Marshmallow Creme Frosting: Fold 1¼ **cups whipped cream** into 1¼ **cups marshmallow creme.** Use immediately.

Cream Cheese Frosting: Whip **6 ounces** *each* **low-fat and fat-free cream cheese** with an electric mixer until creamy. Blend in ⅓ **cup sugar** and **2 teaspoons lemon juice** until creamy. Fold in 1½ **cups fat-free nondairy whipped topping.** Use immediately.

Pudding Frosting: Whisk together **1 box (4-serving size) instant pudding mix** (any flavor) and **1 cup 2% milk** until thickened. Fold into **2 cups fat-free nondairy whipped topping.** Use immediately.

Yogurt Frosting: Drain 1½ **cups low-fat vanilla yogurt** in a colander lined with cheesecloth or a large coffee filter for 30 minutes, to make ¾ cup. Fold into 2½ **cups fat-free nondairy whipped topping** along with ½ **teaspoon vanilla extract.** Use immediately.

Banana Frosting: Melt **1 tablespoon butter** in a small skillet over medium heat. Continue cooking until butter is deep amber. Pour into a bowl and chill until set. Return to room temperature. Meanwhile, mash **1 banana** with **1 tablespoon fresh lemon juice.** Beat in browned butter, **1 teaspoon vanilla extract,** and **3 cups confectioners' sugar.** For the filling and garnish, arrange **3 to 4 sliced bananas** on cake, brushed with **1 tablespoon lemon juice.**

EASY CHOCOLATE SOUR CREAM FROSTING Melt **6 ounces semisweet chocolate chips** in a bowl set in a microwave oven on high power, 45 seconds, stopping to stir every 15 seconds. Stir until smooth. Mix in ½ **cup sour cream** until smooth. *Makes about 1½ cups.*

Fruit, Dried

With their dense texture and concentrated flavor, dried fruits have an altogether different character from their fresh counterparts. Enjoy them as a snack, or add them to baked goods and fruit compotes.

BASICS
▼

To choose • Look for plump fruits with a bright, even color. Read labels and avoid any that contain unnecessary additives.

To store • Transfer to a tightly covered container and refrigerate or store in a dark, dry place.

To eliminate sugar crystals on the surface • Dip the fruit in boiling water and dry thoroughly.

To plump • Soak in warm water, wine, or even tea for 10 to 15 minutes. Raisins and dried currants benefit from plumping before being added to baked goods. Avoid soaking dried fruit any longer than necessary. Oversoaking dried fruits robs them of flavor.

To poach • Transfer the fruit and its soaking liquid to a saucepan, cover it, and simmer until softened. Wait until the fruit is tender before adding sugar, which can slow the absorption of water.

To chop • Use kitchen scissors instead of a knife. Dip the scissors in flour if the fruit is sticky. If using a knife, coat the blade with cooking spray to prevent sticking, or dip it into flour. Also, for easier chopping, freeze dried fruit for 30 to 45 minutes.

To replace fresh fruit • Use 1 pound reconstituted dried fruit for every 4 pounds fresh.

To separate sticky pieces • Roll the pieces in your hands with a small amount of flour.

TIME SAVER
▼

To speed-soak • Place the fruit in a 2-cup measuring cup, cover with water, cover with plastic, and microwave on high power for 2 minutes. Let it rest 3 minutes.

BAKED STUFFED APPLES Mix together ¼ cup *each* **chopped pitted dates and golden raisins; 1 slice raisin bread, diced; 2 tablespoons orange juice;** and ¼ **teaspoon ground cinnamon.** Core **4 apples** (Rome Beauty is best) and stuff with fruit mixture. Place in an 8" × 8" baking dish with ¾ **cup apple juice** and **2 tablespoons honey.** Bake at 375°F until tender, 40 minutes. *Makes 4 servings.*

HEALTHY HINT
▼

To avoid sulfites • Commercially dried fruits often contain sulfites. These sulfur-based preservatives are used to prevent or reduce discoloration in some fruits and vegetables, such as dried apples and potatoes. Some people are sensitive to sulfites and could have an allergic reaction or asthma attack. As an alternative, look for freeze-dried fruits. Also, check in health food stores for fruits dried without sulfites. Although they are not as colorful, they contain just as much flavor and are nearly as nutritious.

Fruit, Fresh *see also specific types*

Whether it's one of spring's first strawberries, a juicy summer peach, an apple on an autumn day, or a grapefruit on a winter morning, there are few pleasures that compare with enjoying fresh fruit at the peak of

its season. And when baked, fried, frozen, or stewed, fruits make wonderful desserts.

BASICS

To choose • Look for locally grown fruit harvested at the peak of its growing season. In general, fruit is most flavorful and nutritious when allowed to reach its peak before picking. It also costs less when it hasn't traveled far. Make sure to choose plump, healthy-looking fruits that have not been coated with wax or sprayed with preservatives. Also, smell the fruit: Fragrance is a primary indicator of flavor.

To store • Ripe fruit should be refrigerated until ready to eat. If fruit has not quite reached its peak, leave it at room temperature, where it will continue to ripen. Check the fruit for signs of spoiling while storing it. Just a little bit of mold can infect a whole basket of berries or spread through a bag of peaches. Discard any fruit that shows signs of spoilage.

To freeze • You can freeze fruit at peak season, when the flavor is optimum, and use it in the dead of winter for pies, tarts, and crisps. Place it in single layers on waxed paper–lined trays, freeze until solid, then place in double-wrapped freezer bags and freeze for up to 5 months.

To ripen fruit picked before its peak • Seal it in a brown paper bag and leave it at room temperature until the fruit has ripened. If you have an apple or banana handy, add it to the bag. They emit ethylene gas, which helps speed the ripening process.

PROBLEM SOLVERS

To use tropical fruit with gelatin • Mangoes, pineapples, and kiwifruit all have an enzyme that breaks down the protein in gelatin and keeps it from setting. To avoid this problem, use the cooked or canned versions of these fruits when combining them with gelatin.

To use over-the-hill fruit • Make fruit puree, which has endless uses. Peel, core, and trim any bruised spots from the fruit. For each cup of fruit, add 2 tablespoons sugar and 1 teaspoon lemon juice and puree in a blender or food processor. To make a quick fruit sauce, place the puree in a saucepan, cover it, and cook over low heat for 10 minutes. Add a little water or liqueur if the mixture gets dry. Use over ice cream or cakes. You can also make fruit pops by pouring fruit puree into frozen-pop molds or 4-ounce paper cups, partially freezing it, then inserting a wooden craft stick and freezing until solid. Or, make fruit parfaits by mixing together ¾ cup low-fat plain yogurt, ¼ cup low-fat sour cream, and 2 tablespoons honey. Layer yogurt and fruit puree in 4 parfait glasses. Chill and serve.

FRUIT BREAD Preheat oven to 350°F. In a saucepan over medium heat, melt **1 stick (½ cup)** butter. Remove from heat and mix in **1 cup sugar, ½ teaspoon ground cinnamon** or **ginger, 1 teaspoon vanilla extract, 1½ cups fruit puree, ¼ cup sour cream, 2 eggs, 1 teaspoon baking soda,** and **½ teaspoon baking powder** until smooth. Mix in **2 cups flour** and **⅔ cup nut pieces** until well-blended. Spoon into a greased nonstick loaf pan and bake until a tester comes out clean, about 30 minutes. *Makes 10 slices.*

Chef's Tip: Keep canned fruit nectars on hand to use instead of fruit juice. They are a bit sweeter but generally have more flavor. To compensate for the extra sweetness, reduce the sugar in the recipe. Or add a tart juice such as lemon or lime, or tamarind nectar, which is available frozen in Latin American and Indian grocery stores.

f

MIX–AND–MATCH FRUIT DESSERTS

Cobbler, crisp, crumble, crunch, brown betty, and grunt are among America's simplest and best-loved desserts. All are essentially sweetened baked fruit with a crumbly or biscuitlike topping. Here are four easy steps to creating 36 possible flavor combinations. Just pick a fruit filling, match it with any of the toppings, and bake as directed. Each recipe makes 4 to 6 servings.

1. Pick a fruit.

Apricot-Raspberry: 4 cups thickly sliced pitted apricots (about 1½ pounds whole apricots) and 1 pint fresh raspberries

Plum: 6 cups thickly sliced pitted fresh plums (about 2½ pounds whole plums)

Apple-Pear: 3 cups *each* peeled, cored, and sliced Granny Smith apples and Bosc pears (1 pound whole apples and 1½ pounds whole pears)

Mixed Berry: 1 pint *each* fresh raspberries, blueberries, and blackberries

Strawberry-Rhubarb: 4 cups ½"-long rhubarb pieces (about 1¼ pounds) and 1 pint hulled and quartered fresh strawberries

Mango-Raspberry: 4 cups pitted, peeled, and cubed mangoes (about 3 medium mangoes) and 1 pint fresh raspberries

2. Toss fruit with ½ cup sugar, 1 tablespoon lemon juice, and 2 tablespoons flour. Spread in a greased 2-quart baking dish.

3. Choose a topping (at right).

4. Bake at 400°F until the top is golden brown and bubbly, 30 to 40 minutes. Serve warm with ice cream or heavy cream.

Crumble

1¼ **cups all-purpose flour**

½ **cup rolled oats**

⅓ **cup packed brown sugar**

¾ **teaspoon ground cinnamon**

¼ **teaspoon salt**

6 **tablespoons cold, unsalted butter, cut into small pieces**

In a food processor, combine the flour, oats, brown sugar, cinnamon, and salt. Add the butter and pulse just until the mixture is the texture of coarse crumbs. Sprinkle the topping over the fruit in the baking dish.

Crunch

1 **stick (½ cup) unsalted butter, cut into pieces**

1 **cup packed brown sugar**

¾ **cup flour**

⅓ **cup chopped pecans or walnuts**

½ **teaspoon ground cinnamon**

¼ **teaspoon freshly grated nutmeg**

¼ **teaspoon salt**

Melt the butter in a saucepan over low heat or in a microwaveable bowl on medium power for 2 minutes. Stir in the sugar, flour, nuts, cinnamon, nutmeg, and salt. Sprinkle the topping over the fruit in the baking dish.

Cobbler

1 cup all-purpose flour

4 tablespoons sugar, divided

1 teaspoon baking powder

½ teaspoon baking soda

¼ teaspoon salt

½ stick (¼ cup) cold unsalted butter, cut into small pieces

⅔ cup buttermilk

In a food processor, combine the flour, 3 tablespoons of the sugar, the baking powder, baking soda, and salt. Add the butter and pulse just until the mixture resembles coarse crumbs. Add the buttermilk and pulse just until the mixture comes together. Spoon the dough over the fruit in the baking dish and sprinkle the top with the remaining 1 tablespoon sugar.

Crisp

¾ cup packed dark brown sugar

½ cup rolled oats

½ cup all-purpose flour

1½ teaspoons ground cinnamon

½ teaspoon salt

1 stick (½ cup) cold unsalted butter, cut into pieces

In a food processor, combine the brown sugar, oats, flour, cinnamon, and salt. Add the butter and pulse until the mixture resembles coarse crumbs. Sprinkle the topping over the fruit in the baking dish.

Brown Betty

3 tablespoons unsalted butter

¾ cup graham cracker crumbs

¾ cup packed dark brown sugar

½ teaspoon ground cinnamon

½ teaspoon ground nutmeg

¼ teaspoon salt

Melt the butter in a saucepan over low heat or in a microwaveable bowl on medium power for 2 minutes. Stir in the graham cracker crumbs, brown sugar, cinnamon, nutmeg, and salt. Sprinkle the topping over the fruit in the baking dish.

Grunt

5 tablespoons unsalted butter, cut into pieces

2 cups flour

3 tablespoons sugar

2 teaspoons baking powder

¾ teaspoon salt

¾ cup milk

Melt the butter in a saucepan over low heat or in a microwaveable bowl on medium power for 2 minutes. In a bowl, combine the flour, sugar, baking powder, and salt. Stir in the melted butter and the milk until all ingredients are moistened. Spoon the batter over the fruit in the baking dish.

Frying *see also* Fats and Oils

Cooking food by completely immersing it in hot fat is a technique used all around the world. Deep-fat frying produces wonderfully crisp, flavorful foods and is perfect for preparing foods that don't have a dense or fibrous structure, such as fish, shellfish, and vegetables. While there is no arguing that fried foods can taste greasy, if you actually measure the oil after frying, you will find that you typically lose no more than a few tablespoons of fat for about a pint of oil used.

BASICS ▼

To choose a frying oil • Look for an oil with a high smoke point such as peanut, soybean, or safflower oil. Safflower tends to have the lightest taste.

To choose a frying pan or pot • Choose a pot that's larger than the burner you'll be cooking on, and never fill it more than half-full of oil. Oil catches fire easily, and a large pot helps avoids spills. Make sure that you have at least 3" between the surface of the oil and the top of the pot. If oil should drip or spill, turn off the heat and clean the spill before proceeding.

To keep the oil at proper frying temperature • Use a candy thermometer. This tool makes frying a cinch. Add the food the instant that the oil reaches the correct temperature (usually, 365° to 375°F), and maintain that temperature throughout the frying. Also, bring the oil back to the proper temperature before adding more batches of food. If you fry often, invest in an electric deep fryer and follow the manufacturer's directions; this is a foolproof way to maintain temperature control. Or try this trick if you have neither a candy thermometer nor an electric fryer: Throw a cube of bread into the oil. If it browns all over in less than a minute's time, your oil has gotten too hot.

To ensure even cooking • Avoid crowding the pot. The oil should bubble up freely around each piece, and the pieces should never touch each other while they're frying. Crowding the pot may cause the temperature of the oil to drop too low. Also, be sure to remove food in the exact order it was added.

To drain fried foods • Drain well by holding each piece over the pot as you remove it, letting any oil drip back into the pot. Then, set the fried food on a cooling rack set over a baking sheet that is lined with paper towels. As fried foods drain, keep them warm by putting them, the draining rack, and the baking sheet in a 200°F oven while you continue frying.

To handle oil that has begun to smoke • Discard it and start over. Smoke indicates burned oil, which will give fried foods an unpleasant flavor.

To discard used oil • Allow hot oil to cool before moving the pot and disposing of the oil.

To hold batter-dipped ingredients before frying • Set on a cooling rack placed on top of a rimmed baking sheet. Clean the rack and pan so that they can be used again to drain fried foods.

To recycle fat after deep-frying • Cool it, then clarify it by straining it through a paper coffee filter. Store in an airtight container in the refrigerator. Empty peanut cans or coffee cans are good containers. Frying fat can be recycled 2 or 3 times before it becomes unusable.

PROBLEM SOLVERS ▼

To deep-fry at high altitudes • In general, reduce the oil temperature by 25°F.

To avoid burning your hands • Use a pair of tongs to place foods into hot fat.

To avoid splatters • Invest in an inexpensive splatter screen, available in most stores' cookware sections, or cover the food with a large mesh sieve. Make sure that the food does not have water on it before adding it to the hot fat. It also helps to gently submerge and remove the food individually with a long-handled skimmer.

To douse a fat fire in a pan • Place a lid over it. Baking soda will also put out a fat fire.

To avoid a fishy flavor • When frying a variety of foods that include seafood, fry the fish or seafood last. Otherwise, once the oil has absorbed the fish aroma, it will flavor the other foods that are cooked in it.

To prevent oil from blackening when deep-frying • Add a wedge of carrot, which will act as a magnet for black flecks that can accumulate when deep-frying.

LEMON BATTER FOR FRYING In a bowl, stir together **1 cup all-purpose flour, ½ cup cornstarch,** and **¾ teaspoon salt.** While whisking constantly, add **1¼ cups cold water** and **⅓ cup lemon juice.** Cover and chill 1 hour. Whisk before using. Excellent for frying seafood and vegetables. *Makes about 2 cups.*

HEALTHY HINT ▼

To avoid deep-fried foods • Oven-fry them instead. The technique of frying food in hot fat can be simulated by using a hot oven and coating the surface of the food with a film of fat. Coat the food with batter, if using. Then, coat the food generously with cooking spray. Place on a rimmed baking sheet and bake at 475°F until brown and crisp. Oven-frying makes delicious french fries and breaded chicken.

f

G

Garlic

A relative of onion, garlic has an assertive flavor that is an essential ingredient in many of the world's great cuisines, including those of France, China, Mexico, Italy, and Southeast Asia. Keep in mind that heating garlic mellows its flavor, while chopping it intensifies the taste. Whole bulbs of roasted garlic have the mildest flavor, and raw, minced garlic has the most intense garlic taste. Also, oversize bulbs of elephant garlic have a very timid flavor that is likely to disappoint true garlic fans.

BASICS ▼ **To choose** • Look for firm bulbs that are heavy for their size and show no signs of mold or sprouting.

To store • Keep garlic in a cool, dark place with plenty of ventilation. Avoid refrigerating garlic, which promotes rot.

To loosen cloves from the bulb • Set the bulb upside down on your work surface and press down hard on the root with the palm of your hand. The cloves will break free. You can also microwave 1 head of garlic for 1 minute on high power, turning halfway through cooking. Let stand until cool enough to handle. The skins will slip right off. Use immediately, or simmer leftover garlic in oil to cover for 5 minutes. Store in the refrigerator for up to 1 week.

To peel • Place the flat side of a large chef's knife or Asian cleaver over the garlic and smack it assertively, but not too hard, with the heel of your hand or your fist. The jolt will crack the peel, making it easy to remove. Pound more forcefully, and you will separate the peel and crush the clove at the same time, which will give you a head start on chopping or mincing. You can also lay a garlic clove on the counter and roll it back and forth with your palm. This loosens the skin, making it easier to peel. Or, drop the cloves into a pot of boiling water for 45 seconds. Drain and cool briefly, then pinch the cloves, and the peel will pop right off. This blanching works well when you have pasta water boiling anyway.

Fascinating Fact: In Gary, Indiana, it is illegal to ride public transportation or enter a movie house or theater within 4 hours of eating garlic.

To chop • For best results, use a large chef's knife instead of a tiny paring knife.

Turn the clove up on its ridge, then cut lengthwise into thin slices. Turn the clove on its flat side and slice lengthwise again to make short sticks. Now, turn the clove and cut crosswise to mince. The garlic may spread across the board as you chop. Use your knife to scrape it back to the pile and continue chopping with a back-and-forth, rocking motion until the garlic is chopped very fine.

To mash to a paste • Use a garlic press. Or cover the cloves with parchment and mash with a meat pounder. You can also smash garlic cloves with a heavy object, then sprinkle with a little salt. Mash with the flat side of a heavy knife.

PROBLEM SOLVERS ▼

To prevent sticking when mincing • Sprinkle the garlic with salt, using about ⅛ teaspoon for 3 cloves. The salt will help absorb the liquid in garlic, making it less sticky. Adjust the salt in your recipe as necessary.

To avoid burning when sautéing • Chop it fine. Large pieces of garlic are more likely to burn than small ones. Also, avoid adding garlic to hot oil. Add the garlic and oil to the pan at the same time. Then, proceed to heat.

To remove garlic odors on hands • Rub your fingers over a stainless steel spoon under running water. Any stainless steel surface will work. This trick also works with onions, leeks, and other onionlike vegetables in the allium family. You can also rub your hands with lemon juice and salt (provided you have no cuts on your hands). Or, keep a bowl of coffee grounds near the sink. Dip your hands in to get rid of garlic odors.

To remove garlic odors from a cutting board • Scrub with a paste of baking soda and water.

To remedy garlic breath • Chew on fresh parsley leaves, on chlorophyll tablets, or on fennel seeds. Or drink some lemon juice (tempered with a little honey, if desired). You can also eat some lemon or lime sherbet.

Fascinating Fact: The city of Chicago is probably named after garlic. "Chicago" is an Algonquian name probably meaning "garlic place," referring to the garlic or wild onions originally growing in the meadows by Lake Michigan. The name was first applied to the river, then to the town that was built by it in the early 19th century.

TIME SAVERS ▼

To save chopping time • Use a garlic press. Don't bother peeling the garlic. Just place the unpeeled clove in the chamber of the press, close it with gentle pressure, and scrape off the emerging garlic paste with a knife.

To unclog the holes of a garlic press without a cleaning attachment • Use a toothpick. Or scrub out stubborn shards of garlic with a toothbrush.

To make ready-to-use garlic cloves • Cover peeled cloves with olive oil and store in a closed container in the refrigerator for up to 2 weeks. The oil will keep air away from the garlic, and when the garlic is used up, you will be left with garlic-infused oil that is wonderful on salads, whipped into mashed potatoes, drizzled over pasta, or blotted by bread.

FLAVOR TIPS ▼

To tame the bite of raw garlic • Sauté it briefly in a little oil, just to soften but not color. This is a good technique before making recipes that usually begin with raw garlic, such as pesto or baba ghanoush. You can also drop unpeeled garlic cloves in boiling water for 1 minute. The peels will slip off easily and the garlic flavor will have mellowed. Or you can toast unpeeled cloves in a dry skillet over medium-high heat for 5 minutes, shaking the pan occasionally. Peel and use as desired.

g

ROASTED GARLIC

Roasting garlic is simple, involving nothing more than a splash of olive oil or other liquid and an hour in a hot oven.

To roast a head of garlic: Don't worry about owning one of those clay garlic roasters. Any baking dish or even foil will do. Cut ½" from the top of 1 or several heads of garlic, trimming just enough to expose the tips of the garlic cloves. Remove any loose papery skin. Place the whole head in an 8" baking dish and drizzle generously with olive oil (alternatively, add water or chicken broth to come about ½" up the sides of the garlic). Cover tightly with foil and bake at 325°F until tender when pierced, about 1 hour.

To quick-roast a head of garlic: Trim the head of garlic as described above. Pour ⅛" of milk in a microwaveable dish. Place the garlic, cut side down, in the milk and cover. Microwave on medium power until it just begins to tenderize, 7 minutes. Uncover. Turn the garlic upright, drizzle with ½ teaspoon olive oil, and roast in a 375°F oven until completely tender, about 20 minutes.

To roast individual cloves of garlic: Toast in a dry skillet over medium heat, shaking the pan occasionally, until browned all over, about 12 to 15 minutes total. Or, wrap the cloves in a single layer in aluminum foil, crimping well to seal. Place in a small, ovenproof pan with ½" of water. Bake at 325°F until tender, about 1 hour.

To use roasted garlic: Serve roasted garlic heads whole with sliced crusty bread and squeeze the cloves onto the bread, spreading with a knife. Or, squeeze the garlic into a bowl or a mini food processor and mash to a paste.

To use roasted garlic paste: Add to sauces, soups, vegetable purees, rice and grain dishes, dressings, dips, and spreads. Spread under the skin of poultry, or brush on the cooked surfaces of grilled meats or fish for added flavor.

Roasted Garlic Alfredo Pasta: In a medium saucepan over medium heat, heat **1 cup fat-free evaporated milk** with **½ cup half-and-half** until bubbles just start to form around the rim of the pan. Stir in **1 cup grated Parmesan cheese** until smooth. Remove from heat and stir in **8 mashed roasted garlic cloves, 2 chopped scallions,** and **¼ teaspoon ground black pepper.** Toss with **12 ounces cooked pasta.** Sprinkle with **¼ cup Parmesan cheese** and serve. *Makes 4 servings.*

Roasted Garlic Falafel: In a food processor, combine **2 cans (15 ounces each) rinsed and drained chickpeas, 3 sliced scallions, ½ cup chopped fresh parsley, 1 egg white, 6 roasted garlic cloves, 1 teaspoon ground cumin,** and **⅛ teaspoon ground red pepper** until texture resembles coarse meal. Refrigerate 30 minutes. Shape into patties about 2" around and ½" thick. Heat **1 teaspoon olive oil** in a large nonstick skillet over medium heat. Add patties and cook until golden, 3 minutes per side. Serve with **whole wheat pitas, lettuce,** and **tomatoes.** *Makes 4 servings.*

Roasted Garlic Dressing: In a medium bowl, mash **6 roasted garlic cloves.** Stir in **⅓ cup** *each* **reduced-fat mayonnaise and low-fat plain yogurt, 2 tablespoons** *each* **Dijon mustard and chopped fresh parsley, 1 chopped scallion,** and **1 tablespoon white wine vinegar.** Great for slaws and salads. *Makes about 1¼ cups.*

To flavor mashed potatoes • When making a pot of mashed potatoes, add 1 to 3 whole, peeled garlic cloves to the cooking water with the potatoes. After draining, mash as usual, garlic cloves included. The cooked garlic will add a mellow garlic flavor.

HEALTHY HINTS ▼ **To help lower cholesterol** • Research indicates that eating ½ to 1 clove of garlic a day may reduce blood cholesterol levels by about 9 percent. Garlic is also believed to be beneficial in the prevention and treatment of cancer.

To reap the full health benefits of garlic • Although fresh is best, use garlic in cooked or powdered forms as well, since each has its own important healing compounds. When cooking with fresh garlic, chopping it finely will increase the surface area and release the full benefits of the healthful compounds within. Also, cook fresh garlic only briefly, or add it during the last few minutes of cooking, as overcooking can destroy some of its delicate compounds.

Garnishes

"The eyes are the first to feast" is an old saying that contains more than a grain of truth. Garnishes can be as simple as a sprig of parsley or as elaborate as exotically carved vegetables and ice sculptures. (See page 208 for four easy and inviting garnishes.)

BASICS ▼ **To garnish food** • Make sure that the garnish complements the dish. For example, if a chicken dish is seasoned with basil, tuck a few leaves of fresh basil under the chicken as a garnish. Or use lemon twists on seafood. Always garnish a plate just before serving. Garnishes that sit on a plate for too long, even if refrigerated, are likely to fade and look less than fresh by the time they get to the table.

To make a simple citrus twist • Cut a thin slice from a lemon, lime, or orange. Cut the slice from the center to one edge. Twist and stretch to form an S shape.

Gelatin

Many classic desserts, including Bavarian creams, mousses, and sweet soufflés, depend on gelatin to give them their characteristic light-as-air body. Gelatin is most commonly available in powdered form, but sheet gelatin, often used in professional kitchens, is sometimes found in specialty shops. Though the two types produce identical results, sheet gelatin requires a longer soaking period.

BASICS ▼ **To store** • Wrap airtight and keep in a cool, dry place. It will last indefinitely.

To use powdered gelatin • Sprinkle the gelatin over a little bit of cold liquid in a small bowl or saucepan and let soak 5 minutes. The ratio is about ¼ cup liquid for each ¼-ounce package of gelatin. Once the gelatin has softened, melt it by stirring it into a warm mixture (such as a custard) or by warming the liquid directly on the stove over low heat. Avoid letting the mixture boil. Too much heat will destroy gelatin's gel-ability. Once the gelatin has melted, incorporate it into the other ingredients as directed in your recipe.

To incorporate a flavored gelatin mixture into whipped cream or egg whites for a mousse or soufflé • Chill the gelatin mixture and custard or base mixture over a bowl of ice water until it feels cool and thickens slightly. Then, fold in the cream or egg whites. If the gelatin hasn't set enough, it will be too liquid to blend easily with the whipped ingredients.

g

EASY GARNISHES

A few eye-catching decorations can give any meal or buffet a professional touch. To keep fresh vegetable garnishes crisp and bright, put them in ice water in the refrigerator until you're ready to use them.

Tomato Roses

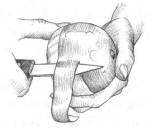

1 Using a sharp paring knife, peel the skin from a tomato in 1 continuous strip.

2 Roll into a spiral to create a rosebud. Finish with a leaf of fresh basil.

Apricot Roses

1 Sprinkle a work surface with sugar. Place 7 small dried apricots on the surface and sprinkle them with sugar. Using a rolling pin, roll each apricot out to a thin petal shape. Using your hands, gently roll 1 apricot into a cylinder, gradually pinching an end into a cone shape.

2 Arrange remaining apricots around the pinched end of the cylinder, slightly overlapping and fanning the last few petals outward. Secure the base with toothpicks.

If it has set too much, it will be too firm to fold in evenly.

To soften a gelatin mixture that has set too firmly before other ingredients are added • Gently warm the gelatin mixture until softened.

To set gelatin-based desserts • Refrigerate until set, about 6 hours. Avoid freezing gelatin-based desserts. Frozen gelatin will separate when thawed.

To serve gelatin-based desserts • Serve within 36 hours of chilling. Gelatin-

Scallion Flowers

1 Cut off the root end and excess greens from a scallion so that you end up with a piece that's about 4" long. Make slits on both ends, reaching about 1½" up, leaving about ½" in the middle that's uncut.

2 Place in a pan or bowl of ice water until the petals curl, about 2 hours.

Chile Flowers

1 Cut off the tip of a jalapeño, serrano, or other elongated chile pepper. Cut long petals that widen toward the stem end, stopping about ½" from the base. (Wear plastic gloves when handling.)

2 Rinse the pepper under running water and remove the seeds. Place in a bowl of ice water until the petals curl.

g

based desserts will toughen or lose some of their shape if kept for too long.

To ensure that gelatin-based desserts set • Avoid combining gelatin with any of the following ingredients, which contain an enzyme that destroys protein molecules, preventing gelatin from setting: mango, pineapple, papaya, kiwi, figs, honeydew, melon, and fresh ginger. To avoid this problem, use the cooked or canned versions of these foods when combining them with gelatin. Highly acidic ingredients can also prevent gelatin from setting. When using acidic ingredients, such as citrus, you may want to add an extra package of gelatin to ensure that the dessert sets.

Fascinating Fact: Gelatin is not commonly made from beef bones or cartilage, as it was years ago. Commercial gelatin is usually a by-product of pig skin.

PROBLEM SOLVERS ▼ **To prevent gelatin desserts from setting too quickly** • Add gelatin to the base mixture (such as a fruit puree) while the gelatin is still warm. Gelatin tends to set rapidly as it cools. If both the gelatin and the base are cold, the gelatin will set as soon as it comes in contact with the base and can form strings.

To prevent sticking for easy unmolding • Lightly coat a gelatin mold with cooking spray. If gelatin is already stuck in the mold, run a knife tip around its edge. Then, submerge the mold three-fourths of the way in a bowl of hot water for 30 seconds. If this does not loosen the gelatin enough, place the mold back in the hot water for another 30 seconds.

To prevent fruit from sinking to the bottom of the mold • Add the fruit after the mixture has set enough to suspend it.

To center a mold of gelatin on a platter • Dampen the platter with cold water so that the gelatin can be moved into position.

TIME SAVER ▼ **To set gelatin quickly** • Dissolve 1 envelope (¼ ounce) powdered gelatin in ¼ cup boiling liquid. When completely dissolved, add 1¾ cups ice water or other iced liquid, and stir until the mixture starts to thicken. Remove any remaining ice and refrigerate until fully set, about 30 minutes. Other quick-setting methods are to spread the gelatin in a metal baking pan, or

set the bowl or mold in a bowl of ice water. You can also start chilling in the freezer. Transfer the mold to the refrigerator after 20 minutes, though; allowing gelatin to freeze solid will cause it to weep when it defrosts.

FLAVOR TIP ▼ **To add extra flavor to gelatin desserts** • Dissolve the gelatin in a liquid other than water, such as coffee, wine, or fruit juice. Choose a liquid that complements the flavor of your dessert.

Ginger

This tropical rhizome (an underground stem) is one of the essential flavors of Asian cuisine. Its pleasantly pungent flavor comes from naturally occurring chemical irritants that also create a warm sensation on the tongue.

BASICS ▼ **To choose fresh** • Choose the hardest, smoothest pieces you can find. The longer ginger sits around, the more wrinkled it gets. Avoid any pieces that show signs of mold. To test for freshness, break off one of the knobs. If the ginger is fresh, it will break with a clean snap.

To store fresh • Keep it at room temperature for up to a week, or wrap it in a paper towel, seal it in a plastic bag, and refrigerate for 2 to 3 weeks. Or, keep unpeeled ginger in a pot or container of horticultural sand. Cover with well-pierced foil to provide ventilation, and store in a cool, dark place.

To freeze • Place whole, unpeeled knobs of ginger in a zipper-lock freezer bag for up to 3 months. Slice or break off what you need and return the rest to the freezer. Freezing ruptures its cells and changes its texture, but the flavor remains intact. Avoid freezing fresh ginger after it is peeled and chopped.

To store in liquid • Peel pieces or slices of ginger, place them in a glass jar, and fill with dry sherry or vodka. Secure the lid and refrigerate for 4 to 6 weeks. The sherry (or vodka) and ginger will exchange flavors during storage. You can use ginger-kissed sherry in stir-fry sauces or marinades.

To juice • When you want the pure essence of ginger without the fibers, make ginger juice. A tablespoon or two is great in sauces or marinades for chicken breast strips or shrimp. The easiest method is to keep a chunk of ginger in the freezer. When you're ready to use it, thaw it, then press out the juices with a garlic press. You can also peel fresh ginger, cut it into chunks, and shred it on a cheese grater or puree it in a food processor. Then, wrap the shredded or pureed ginger in a piece of cheesecloth and squeeze out the juice.

To use ground ginger • Avoid using ground ginger to replace fresh ginger. It's made from the same rhizome as fresh ginger, but it has a very different flavor. Ground ginger works best in gingerbread, pumpkin pie, and other baked goods, as well as in curries with other Indian spices.

To use candied ginger • Crystallized, or candied, ginger is usually made from slices of fresh ginger that have been softened in a sugar syrup and coated with crystallized sugar. Store it in a jar with a tight-fitting lid. Chop or snip with scissors and add freely to cookie doughs, muffins, scones, or ice cream. Crystallized ginger also makes an elegant addition to glazes for roasted poultry or braised root vegetables.

To use Japanese pickled pink ginger • When tender young spring and fall ginger is sliced paper-thin and pickled, it turns a lovely pink color. Eat pickled ginger with sushi and sashimi, or add to relishlike condiments, marinades, and mayonnaise.

PROBLEM SOLVERS ▼ **To avoid problems with using ginger and gelatin** • Heat ginger before adding it to a gelatin mixture. Ginger contains an enzyme that prevents gelatin from setting properly. Heat destroys the enzyme. The microwave oven makes this a quick fix: Heat the ginger on medium power until heated through, 20 seconds.

To chop candied ginger without sticking • Chop in a mini food processor with a bit of granulated sugar (if the recipe you're making includes sugar, use some of the sugar to chop the ginger, then add the sugar to the recipe). Or, if chopping small amounts with a knife, spray the knife blade with cooking spray or dip the blade into flour. You can also use scissors. Or, for convenience, you may want to keep prechopped crystallized ginger on hand in a tightly sealed jar at room temperature.

TIME SAVERS ▼ **To quickly peel** • Scrape the skin with the side of a teaspoon, following the curves and bumps of the root. You can also use a vegetable peeler, but it tends to take a bit of flesh with it. The flesh just beneath the skin layer is often the most flavorful.

To avoid peeling • If you are slicing ginger to flavor a marinade or tea, or if it will be grated, there is no need to peel it.

To quickly chop or mince • For large amounts, cut into ½" chunks. Place in a mini food processor and mince in 2- to 3-second pulses to desired fineness. For small amounts, cut into small chunks and place in a good-quality garlic press. Press over a small bowl or directly into the food. This will yield mostly ginger juice, so scrape off the garlic press to get the flesh as well.

To avoid chopping or mincing • Use preminced or prechopped ginger, a widely available product. If you frequently use ginger and garlic together, look for ginger-garlic paste in Asian markets.

g

To grate • Grating ginger is much easier and faster than mincing it. Simply peel away the skin from one of the knobs, hold the entire unpeeled root with your free hand, and grate the peeled section on a cheese grater or rasp. If you're frustrated by the tiny fibers of fresh ginger that can clog graters and rasps, look for a special ginger grater at an Asian market. Made from strips of bamboo or a solid porcelain plate, ginger graters have small teeth that crush the flesh of the ginger but leave the hairs attached to the stub of ungrated ginger.

FLAVOR TIPS ▼

To flavor beverages • Add sliced or grated ginger to lemonade, fruit juices, or your favorite iced tea.

To add flavor to gingerbread • Add finely chopped, candied ginger to the batter. Use in addition to any ground ginger called for in the recipe.

To flavor roasts and cooked meats • Cut crystallized ginger into slivers. Make tiny incisions in roasts or large pieces of pork, beef, turkey, or chicken and insert ginger slivers. The ginger will dissolve during the cooking and disperse its flavor into the meat or poultry.

GINGER SYRUP In a small saucepan, combine **1 cup** *each* **sugar and water** and **about ⅓ cup sliced, unpeeled ginger.** Bring to a boil over medium heat. Reduce heat to low and simmer 5 minutes. Cool to room temperature and discard ginger. Store in a tightly sealed jar in the refrigerator. Add to seltzer or club soda to make ginger ale. *Makes about 1 cup.*

GINGER-LIME CHICKEN SKEWERS Toss together **1 pound cubed boneless, skinless chicken breasts; 2 table-** spoons chopped fresh cilantro; 1 ta- blespoon *each* white balsamic vinegar and grated fresh ginger; and 1 tea- spoon *each* sesame oil and grated lime peel.** Let marinate, refrigerated, 1 hour. Preheat the grill or broiler. Thread chicken on skewers and grill or broil until chicken is no longer pink and juices run clear, 3 to 5 minutes per side. Serve with your favorite bottled or homemade dipping sauce. *Makes 4 servings.*

HEALTHY HINTS ▼

To combat motion sickness • Stir ¼ teaspoon fresh or ground ginger into water or juice and drink 20 minutes before needed. Repeat every few hours if necessary. You can also drink flat ginger ale or suck on a piece of candied ginger.

To settle an upset stomach • Make ginger tea by adding 1 cup boiling water to 3 or 4 slices fresh ginger. Let steep 3 minutes, and sip as needed.

To get maximum health benefits • Grating or juicing ginger releases more of its potent juices than slicing or chopping.

Goose *see also* Doneness Tests and Temperatures (page 572)

Though it is entirely dark meat, rich, moist goose is not the least bit gamy tasting. The bird is quite fatty, though, releasing a quart or more of fat into the pan as it cooks. One consolation: The fat is concentrated in the skin, while the meat itself is quite lean.

BASICS ▼

To choose • There is a great deal of skin, fat, and bones in proportion to meat on these birds, so always buy the largest goose you can find.

To prepare for roasting • Run your fingers between the fat and the meat before cooking. Also, prick the skin all over with a sharp-tined fork. This helps excess fat melt better and drain away during cooking.

To roast • Cook the bird in a 375°F oven for 45 minutes. Then, increase the temperature to 400°F and continue cooking until the juices run clear and the thigh meat registers 175° to 180°F on an instant-read thermometer (for a whole goose) or the center is still slightly pink (for a breast), about 12 to 15 minutes per pound. Put a little water in the bottom of the roasting pan. This helps draw the fat out of the bird and creates steam, which keeps the skin from browning too quickly.

Grains *see also* Flour *and specific types*

The fruits of grasses, grains are among the most nutritious of foods. All grains have 3 basic parts: the germ or seed, the endosperm, and the bran. Many grains are processed to remove both the germ and bran, leaving only the endosperm. Whole grains have all their parts intact and offer more nutrients than processed ones.

BASICS **To choose** • Freshness is an important consideration when buying grains. Whole grains, which have a higher fat content and a greater tendency to turn rancid, are more perishable than refined grains. Shop where there is a large turnover of grains and buy them in small quantities.

To store • Store grains in tightly covered jars either at room temperature or in the refrigerator or freezer. Grains with a high oil content, such as wheat germ, should always be refrigerated.

To cook fluffy grains • Use a wide pan, such as a Dutch oven or a deep skillet. (See "Cooking Times for Grains" on page 214.)

To reheat cooked grains • Heat in a covered saucepan with a thin layer of water.

FLAVOR TIP **To boost flavor** • Before cooking grains, toast them in a skillet over medium heat, just until fragrant. You can also cook grains in a flavorful stock or in canned broth instead of in water.

Grapefruit

A cross between a sweet orange and a pomelo, grapefruit most likely originated in Barbados in the 1700s. Grapefruit is the largest citrus fruit commonly available and comes in two basic varieties: white-fleshed or pigmented. For the best flavor, buy grapefruit with seeds. The seeded varieties are also easier to separate into segments.

BASICS **To make supremes** • When segments of citrus fruit are separated from the membranes holding them together, they are often called supremes. Slice off the top (stem end) just below the pith, then do the same at the bottom. Cut off the zest and white pith in strips all around the fruit, keeping the knife just below the pith. Hold the skinless grapefruit in one hand and use a paring knife to cut directly next to the membrane on both sides to remove each segment or supreme. With practice, you can run the knife down one side of the segment, then underneath and up the other side in one swift movement. When all the segments have been removed, squeeze out the juice from the accordion-like membranes left in your hand.

To easily remove the white pith • Drop the whole grapefruit in a pot of boiling water, remove the pot from the heat, and let stand 3 minutes. Remove the fruit and let cool. Then, peel it; the white pith will easily come off the fruit.

To release maximum juice • Pierce the skin in several places with the tines of

g

COOKING TIMES FOR GRAINS

Most grains are incredibly easy to cook. For those listed below, measure the water into a saucepan and bring to a boil (unless otherwise indicated). Add ¼ teaspoon salt and/or 1 tablespoon butter or oil if you like. Then, stir in the grain and return to a boil. Reduce the heat to medium-low, cover, and simmer until tender. If necessary, drain off any excess liquid.

Grain	Amount of Grain (cups)	Water (cups)	Cooking Directions	Yield (cups)
Barley, pearl	¾	3	Simmer 45 min	3
Barley, quick-cooking	1¼	2	Simmer 10–12 min	3
Barley, whole (with hull)	¾	4	Soak overnight in the 4 c water; do not drain; bring to a boil, reduce heat, cover, and simmer 55 min	3
Buckwheat groats (kasha)	⅔	1½	Add to cold water; bring to a boil; cover and simmer 10–12 min	2
Bulgur	1	2	Add to cold water; bring to a boil; cover and simmer 12–15 min	3
Cornmeal	1	2¾	Combine cornmeal and 1 c cold water; add to the 2¾ c boiling water; cover and simmer 10 min	3½
Farina, quick-cooking	¾	3½	Simmer 2–3 min; stir constantly	3
Hominy grits, quick-cooking	¾	3	Simmer 5 min	3
Millet	¾	2	Simmer 15–20 min; let stand, covered, 5 min	3

a fork. Microwave for 20 seconds on high power. Let stand 2 minutes before using.

FLAVOR TIP ▼ **To avoid tart grapefruit** • If the tartness of grapefruit deters you from eating it, reach for the sweeter hybrids, such as pomelos, oroblancos, or melogolds.

HEALTHY HINTS ▼ **To benefit from the lycopene in grapefruit** • Select the red or pink varieties, which are a good source of lycopene, an antioxidant that has been shown to reduce the risk of prostate cancer and heart disease.

To receive maximum nutritional benefits • Peel the fruit and eat it in sections like an orange to get more pectin and fiber. Also try to make use of the peel (also a valuable source of pectin) by grating it and adding to baked goods.

Grapes

There are thousands of varieties of grapes. Some are grown for snacking, others for making wine, and there are also special varieties for raisins, grape juice, and jelly.

Grain	Amount of Grain (cups)	Water (cups)	Cooking Directions	Yield (cups)
Oats, rolled, quick-cooking	1½	3	Simmer 1 min; let stand, covered, 3 min	3
Oats, rolled, regular	1⅔	3	Simmer 5–7 min; let stand, covered, 3 min	3
Oats, steel-cut	1	2½	Simmer 20–25 min	2½
Quinoa	¾	1½	Rinse thoroughly; simmer 12–15 min	2¾
Rice, brown	1	2¼	Simmer 35–45 min; let stand, covered, 5 min	3
Rice, white	1	2	Simmer 15 min; let stand, covered, 5 min	3
Rye berries	¾	2½	Soak overnight in the 2½ c water; do not drain; bring to a boil, reduce heat, cover, and simmer 30 min	2
Wheat, cracked	⅔	1½	Add to cold water; bring to a boil, cover, and simmer 12–15 min; let stand, covered, 5 min	2
Wheat berries	¾	2½	Soak overnight in the 2½ c water; do not drain; bring to a boil, reduce heat, cover, and simmer 30 min	2
Wild rice	1	2	Simmer 45–55 min	2⅔

g

BASICS **To choose** • When shopping for table grapes, look for full, plump clusters with no bruises or soft spots. Check the stem; it should be green and very pliable.

To store • Refrigerate in a loosely closed plastic bag. Many varieties of grapes have a white powder coating known as bloom, which helps keep grapes moist. Avoid washing off the bloom until just before serving or using.

To freeze • Lay individual grapes in a single layer on a baking sheet and freeze until solid. Then, transfer to plastic bags or an airtight container in the freezer. The high sugar content in grapes keeps them from freezing solid. They'll last as long as a month in the freezer, and they make a cool treat on a hot summer day. Frozen grapes can also be used as flavorful ice cubes in drinks, punches, or sangrias.

To serve grapes • For the most pronounced flavor, bring to room temperature before serving.

To cook with grapes • Use red grapes, which maintain their shape better when heated.

Fascinating Fact: The word *grape* comes from the name of the tool used long ago to "grapple" this fruit from the vines.

FLAVOR TIP ▼ **To add a burst of flavor** • Add a handful of seedless green or red grapes to salads, to couscous, or to stir-fries made with chicken, pork, or seafood.

HEALTHY HINT ▼ **To get nutritional benefits from grape juice** • Drink 12 ounces a day and choose dark grape juice, since the flavonoids are in the skin. Drink 100 percent grape juice rather than grape drink, which is a watered-down, sweetened beverage containing very little actual grape juice.

Gratin

Any baked or broiled dish topped with a mix of cheese or bread crumbs and butter is known as a gratin. Potatoes are one of the most popular ingredients for a gratin, but many vegetables take well to being prepared this way. Baked pastas, such as macaroni and cheese, and grains, such as polenta and rice, also make wonderful gratins.

BASICS ▼ **To bake** • Use a shallow, ovenproof pan that will give you the most surface area, which allows for a high proportion of crisp topping.

To choose vegetables for a gratin • Consider the starch content of the vegetable, as well as its ability to absorb or render liquid. Starchy vegetables such as potatoes work well because they absorb some of the cooking liquid and thicken it at the same time. When using vegetables that don't absorb much liquid, such as leeks, artichokes, and onions, cook them briefly before adding to the gratin, and add more liquid along with them.

To serve • Let gratins rest for 15 minutes before serving. This will give them time to absorb any liquid left in the dish.

FLAVOR TIP ▼ **To add color, flavor, and aroma** • A good sprinkling of grated Parmesan cheese over any gratin will greatly improve it. Paprika makes a nice touch too.

ROASTED GARLIC, POTATO, AND LEEK GRATIN In a large saucepan over medium heat, combine **2 cups milk** (any kind), **1 bay leaf, ⅛ teaspoon grated nutmeg,** and **1¼ teaspoons salt.** Bring to a simmer. Add **2 pounds peeled and sliced russet or Idaho potatoes, ½ sliced leek,** and **1 tablespoon roasted garlic paste.** Bring to a gentle simmer and cook until potatoes are just tender, 10 to 14 minutes. Using a slotted spoon, transfer potatoes to a shallow 1½-quart baking dish. Remove and discard bay leaf. Stir **2 tablespoons sour cream** (reduced-fat or regular) and **2 teaspoons Dijon mustard** into milk mixture. Pour over potatoes and bake at 425°F, 10 minutes. Sprinkle on ½ **cup grated Gruyère** or **Swiss cheese** and bake until cheese browns, another 15 minutes. *Makes 4 servings.*

Gravy *see also* Fat Skimming; Sauces

Surely one of the best loved of all sauces, gravy is made from the juices left in the pan after roasting meat, chicken, or fish. It may be thickened with flour or cornstarch or simply skimmed of fat and seasoned.

BASICS ▼ **To choose the right pan** • When planning to make gravy, use a roasting pan that encourages sticking. The browned bits stuck to the bottom of the pan add intense flavor to the sauce. Avoid nonstick pans.

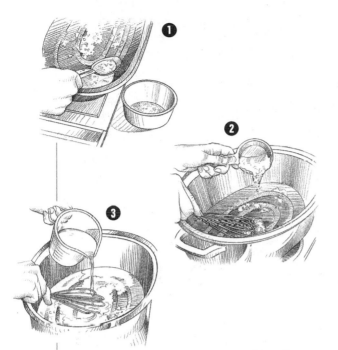

To make in the roasting pan • Transfer the roasted meat from the pan to a serving platter. Traditionally, the pan is tipped so that all the fat and drippings collect in the corner; then, all but 1 to 2 tablespoons of the fat is spooned out and discarded, while the browned bits in the bottom of the pan are retained ❶. Alternatively, pour all the pan juices into a large measuring cup, then spoon off some of the fat from the surface and return it to the pan. Pour off and discard the remaining fat, and reserve the juices.

Place the pan over medium heat and whisk a little flour into the fat, scraping the brown bits on the bottom of the pan as you whisk ❷. Cook until a smooth paste forms and the flour begins to smell toasty, 1 to 2 minutes.

Whisk in the reserved pan juices and/or other hot liquids, such as stock or canned broth, or cider, beer, wine, or other spirits ❸. Simmer the gravy until it has thickened and no longer tastes floury, about 10 minutes. Strain the gravy, season with salt, pepper, and/or herbs, and keep warm until ready to serve.

To make out of the roasting pan • Some cooks find it awkward to make gravy the traditional way in a roasting pan with a wide surface area. Alternatively: Start the gravy while the roast is cooking. In a heavy saucepan, melt 1 tablespoon butter. Add 1 tablespoon flour and stir over medium heat until the flour starts to brown, 5 minutes. Add 2 cups broth (chicken or beef, depending on desired flavor), and simmer 10 minutes. Season with ¼ teaspoon salt and ⅛ teaspoon ground black pepper. When the roast is done, remove it from the roasting pan to a cutting board. Skim the fat from the surface of the drippings and add another ½ cup broth (or wine) to the drippings in the roasting pan. Stir all of the brown bits from the bottom of the pan into the liquid and pour it all into the sauce you have made. Heat to a simmer and stir to mix.

To skim fat from pan drippings • Pour them into a fat separator. The fat will rise to the surface and the drippings can be poured out from the bottom spout. Or, for small amounts of fat, sop them up with a piece of soft, absorbent bread or strips of paper towel. Or instead, place a few ice cubes in a slotted spoon and drag it across the surface. The ice will act as a magnet, attracting the fat. Then, throw the ice cubes away. If you are using a baster, avoid trying to extract the thin layer of fat on top. Instead, position the baster tip at the bottom of the pan and extract the drippings, leaving the fat in the pan. Use the drippings to flavor gravy or sauce.

To stir gravy in the roasting pan • Use a flat-edged wooden spatula or a flat wire whisk. The flat shape allows you to reach into the corners of the pan and stir every last bit of goodness into your gravy.

g

To darken • Cook the skimmed drippings in the pan over medium-low heat for 2 to 3 minutes before adding liquid. You can also add browning liquid (available in most grocery stores). Or, roast some carrots, onions, and celery in the pan in which the meat is roasting. Add the vegetables 1 hour before the meat is scheduled to be done. Remove and serve the vegetables. They will leave behind rich, brown, crusty bits in the pan that will boost the color and flavor of gravy made from pan drippings.

To thicken • First, try cooking it down over medium heat to evaporate excess liquid. Or, if you don't want to reduce the volume, thicken the gravy with cornstarch, flour, or arrowroot. Use 1½ tablespoons flour for each cup of liquid (see the chart at right). If you're using cornstarch or arrowroot, dissolve 2 teaspoons cornstarch or arrowroot in 1 tablespoon cold water (and 2 tablespoons dry white wine, if desired). Stir into 1 cup of hot broth at the end of cooking time, and cook until thickened, 30 seconds to 1 minute, stirring constantly. Then, cook 1 minute more. These proportions will make about 1 cup of medium-thick gravy.

To minimize lumps when thickening • Dissolve the thickener in a small amount of cold water before adding to the gravy.

To remove lumps • Beat vigorously with a whisk. Or pour the gravy through a mesh sieve, pressing out the lumps. You can also dip an immersion blender into the gravy to make it smooth, or run the gravy through a food processor. Another trick? Use instantized flour, such as Wondra, that has been formulated not to lump.

To boost flavor • Use good broth or stock. If you are using stock, boil it over medium-high heat until reduced by half to intensify its flavor. Add a big pinch of fresh

GREAT GRAVY

Use this chart to determine the amount of flour, fat, and liquid you'll need to make perfect gravy every time.

Servings	Liquid (cups)	Fat (Tbsp)	Flour (Tbsp)
6	2	2	3
8	2⅔	2½	4
10	3⅓	3⅓	5
12	4	4	6
14	4⅔	4½	7
16	5½	5	7½

herbs and use dry sherry, cognac, port, or wine in place of some or all of the broth. Or add 2 teaspoons of bottled seasoning such as Worcestershire sauce or soy sauce per cup of gravy.

To make creamy gravy • Add about ¼ cup heavy cream after the gravy thickens. Cook and stir 2 minutes longer.

SIMPLE BROTH FOR CHICKEN OR TURKEY GRAVY Place the **giblets** and **neck** in a medium saucepan and add water to cover. Add **1 halved onion, 1 small bunch parsley,** and **1 bay leaf** to the pot. Simmer gently over medium heat at least 1½ hours. Strain, then use as the broth for making gravy. *Makes about 2 cups.*

MUSHROOM GRAVY Warm **1 tablespoon butter** or **oil** in a medium saucepan over medium heat. Add about 1½ **ounces finely chopped mushrooms** and **1 finely chopped onion.** Sauté until tender, 10 minutes, stirring often. In a small bowl, combine **2 tablespoons cornstarch** and ¼ **cup broth from 1 can (14½ ounces) reduced-sodium beef broth** or **chicken broth.** Stir until smooth. Add to mushrooms along with **2 tablespoons chopped fresh parsley, 1 tablespoon dry sherry,** and **remaining broth.** Heat to boiling, stirring constantly. Reduce heat to low and cook 1 minute, stirring occasionally. *Makes 2 cups.*

Greens, Cooking *see also*

Salads

Hearty, leafy greens, such as chard and beet tops, make savory additions to soups and stews and delicious side dishes on their own.

BASICS **To choose** • Look for cooking greens during the cool months of fall, winter, and early spring. They don't tolerate heat well and can become bitter in the summer months. Choose fresh bunches of greens that are vibrant and brightly colored.

To store • Cover fresh greens with a perforated plastic bag and store in the refrigerator. Clean just before using.

To wash • Cut and discard the hard ends from the stems. Slice the stems into ¼" to ½" pieces and cut the leaves into 1" to 2" pieces. Toss together in a large bowl and cover with cold water. Swoosh the greens in the water vigorously to rid them of sand and dirt. Lift the greens from the water, leaving the dirt in the bottom of the bowl. Do not pour into a colander or a strainer to drain, which will throw the dirt back onto the leaves.

To cook tender greens • Greens such as spinach, beets, dandelion, and watercress have tender leaves that don't require much cooking. Trim and wash 1 to 1½ pounds of tender greens, leaving them slightly wet. Heat 1 tablespoon olive oil in a large heavy skillet. Add the wet greens along with a big pinch of salt, a small pinch of red-pepper flakes, and 1 minced garlic clove. Cover and cook until tender, anywhere from 1 minute for baby spinach to 7 minutes for turnip greens. Avoid cooking tender greens longer than 7 minutes because they will lose their bright green color. Remove the cover and boil off any remaining liquid.

To cook tough greens • Fibrous greens such as kale, collards, mustard, and broccoli rabe require slightly longer cooking to soften their leaves and tame any aggressive flavors. Simmer these greens in a few cups of water or other flavored liquid in a covered pan until soft, about 5 to 25 minutes, depending upon the toughness of the green.

FLAVOR TIP **To flavor cooked tender greens** • Add sesame oil and sesame seeds for an Asian flavor. Or add lemon zest for an Italian flavor.

COLLARD GREENS IN SMOKY BROTH Simmer **2 smoked ham hocks** in a big pot of water, about 3 hours. Strain and chill until fat rises to surface. Discard hocks. Skim off and discard fat. Trim, wash, and chop **2 big bunches (about 2 pounds) collard greens.** Cook chopped collards in 4 cups of the broth until very tender, about 1 hour. (Freeze any leftover broth to use for soups.) Add ⅛ **teaspoon ground red pepper** for a flavor kick. *Makes 4 to 6 servings.*

HEALTHY HINTS **To get maximum nutrients** • Cut the tougher greens such as kale and Swiss chard greens into strips and cook them in boiling water. This will allow them to cook quickly to a tender state, preserving the maximum amount of nutrients.

To make low-fat Southern-style greens • Replace the traditional ham hocks with an equal amount of smoked turkey wings.

Grilling *see also* Barbecue
and specific foods

Preparing food outdoors over a live flame is one of the oldest and most enjoyable methods of cooking. And for good reasons: flavor and convenience! A hot fire caramelizes the natural sugars in foods, coaxing out incredible flavors. And charcoal or hardwood lends a wonderful smoky taste. Plus, there are no pans to clean up. Technically, *grilling* is defined as cooking relatively tender foods quickly over high heat, while *barbecue* refers to fairly tough meats cooked slowly over low heat. But in the real world, the term *grilling* is used to describe just about anything cooked on a grill.

BASICS **To choose a grill** • There many styles of grills ranging from tabletop hibachis to expensive, elaborately designed models that will take over your backyard. They're all essentially fire containers, so choosing among them is a matter of deciding what appeals most to you, to your pocketbook, and to your backyard. Consider the options. First, consider getting a cover for your grill. It will give you more control over the fire and allow you to do some low-heat barbecuing as well as high-heat grilling. Second, keep in mind that a large grilling surface can be helpful. It not only lets you prepare more food at once but also allows you to move food from hotter to cooler parts of the grill, a great help when your dinner starts looking charred before it has cooked through. Finally, consider your fuel options. Charcoal takes longer to light and is more finicky when it comes to heat control, but it imparts incredibly smoky flavors. Propane is ultra-convenient, minus the smoky flavor. You can also get a gas/charcoal grill, which gives you both flavor and convenience.

To control the temperature of a charcoal fire • To make the fire hotter, open all the grill vents, push the coals together, and tap the coals to loosen the insulating cover of ash. To make it cooler, partially close the vents or spread the coals apart.

To season a grill to keep foods from sticking • Heat the grill rack over a hot fire. Wearing mitts, remove from the fire and coat with cooking spray, or rub oil in with a kitchen towel. Place the rack back over the fire.

To clean a grill • On a charcoal grill, just let the fire burn as hot as possible. On a gas grill, close the cover, if the grill has one. If it doesn't, cover the rack with heavy-duty aluminum foil, shiny side down. Then, crank up the heat to high and cook the empty grill until any debris clinging to the rack carbonizes. Scrape off the remaining stubborn particles with a wire brush or a crumpled piece of foil.

PROBLEM SOLVERS **To avoid lifting and tilting a full bag of charcoal** • Carve a scoop out of a gallon-size plastic milk container.

To minimize the wait when coals are too hot • Use tongs to spread them out. Or partially close the grill vents to limit the amount of oxygen going to the fire.

To prevent foods from sticking to the grill rack • Make sure that the rack is good and hot before adding foods, and

CHARCOAL GRILLING 101

The charcoal grill is undoubtedly the most unruly medium for cooking a meal, but there's nothing like it once you've learned how to tame the flame.

Test the fire's heat level. The first challenge is knowing how hot the fire is. Here's a simple test: See how long you can hold your hand 5" above the cooking surface. One second means you've got a searing-hot fire. Two seconds equals medium-hot. Three to 4 seconds is a medium fire. Five seconds equals medium-low. After 6 seconds, you've got a low fire on your hands.

Add food at the right time. Use the fire's heat level to determine when to place foods on the grill. For example, to get a nice, dark sear on a steak, you want a hot fire. Similarly, you want a hot fire for a pork tenderloin, which is best when brown and crusty on the outside while light pink and tender inside. To cook firm, thick cuts of fish, such as tuna or salmon steaks, wait until the coals are medium-hot. Many firm vegetables also do well with a medium-hot fire, such as eggplant, zucchini, summer squash, and asparagus. A medium fire is best for chicken breasts in order to crisp the skin without burning it and to cook the meat through evenly. For delicate fish fillets, use a medium-low fire.

Make a two-level fire. Like a stove-top burner, a grill would ideally have adjustable heat. When grilling over charcoal, the answer is to build a two-level fire. When the coals are hot, use a grill poker to make two piles of coals, one lower pile and one higher pile. These are your two levels of heat to work with: medium-low and high. For example, if you like your steak well-done, it's best to sear it over the high fire first, then move it to the medium-low fire so that it can cook through to well-done without charring to a black, crusty slab. Similarly, with pizza, you can crisp and toast the crust over a hot fire, but finish cooking it with the toppings over low heat. Two levels of heat also allow you to simultaneously cook a variety of foods that might need different levels of heat. When grilling something dense, such as a pork loin, pile the coals on just one side of the grill, then cook the roast on the opposite side, where there is no flame. This form of indirect grilling helps dense roasts cook slowly and evenly.

g

clean the rack after each use to remove charred bits. You can also lightly brush oil onto foods that tend to stick. If you're grilling foods that have a sweet, sticky glaze or that have been marinated in a fat-free marinade, coat the grill rack with cooking spray. (Preheat the rack over the fire, then remove from the heat and coat with spray. Return the rack to the fire.) High-heat cooking sprays, designed especially for use with hotter cooking methods such as grilling, are now available in cookware stores and large supermarkets.

To prevent delicate foods from falling through the rack • Have an extra grill rack on hand and place it so that its bars are perpendicular to the rack beneath it. Or, if you do not have an extra grill rack, use a cooling rack. You can also make a grill topper with a double thickness of heavy-duty aluminum foil. Perforate the foil all over using a large fork. Or use a vegetable grill tray, available in cookware stores and large supermarkets.

To ensure uniform cooking when grilling vegetables in a wire basket • Cut the vegetables into equal-size pieces. Or, if you are using a mix of vegetables, grill the ones that take longer to cook before mixing in the faster-cooking ones.

To avoid piercing meat and losing the natural juices • Use tongs when handling meat. In fact, a pair of spring-loaded tongs is the most valuable tool you can have for all kinds of grilling tasks.

To prevent a kettle grill from rusting • Always clean out any remaining ashes before storing your grill away for the winter. Ashes attract moisture, promoting rust. Also, be sure to close the vents so that critters can't nest inside for the winter.

To improvise a grill cover • Buy an inexpensive tarp or rain poncho.

To check the gas level on a propane tank • Pour a cup of boiling water down the side of the tank. Where there is propane, condensation will form and the tank will be cool to the touch.

To best preserve charcoal • Store it in a dry place. If storing it outdoors, keep it in a sealed trash can or other weatherproof container with a tight-fitting lid.

To avoid getting smoke in your eyes • Lift a grill lid away from your face. Also make sure that you are not standing downwind from a breeze.

To grill without a grill • Use a ridged iron skillet (grill pan). Season the pan as you would any cast-iron cookware (see page 138). Coat the seasoned grill pan with oil. Heat the skillet over high heat until very hot. Add the food and grill as you would over charcoal.

TIME SAVERS ▼ **To light charcoal quickly** • Use a chimney starter. These tall, metal canisters with handles are inexpensive and available in cookware stores. Place the chimney starter in the center of your grilling pit. Put a piece of crumpled newspaper in the bottom and fill the rest of the chimney with charcoal. Light the newspaper. The upward draft created by the chimney will make the charcoal grill-ready within 7 to 8 minutes. Just pick up the chimney and spread the charcoal into an even layer. You can add more charcoal at this point if necessary.

To improvise a chimney starter • Cut both ends off a large, empty coffee can. When the coals are ready, grasp the lip of the hot can with pliers and lift it to free the hot coals.

To light charcoal quickly with newspaper • If you do not have a chimney starter, place sheets of newspaper on the grate of your grill pit and cover with a tall pyramid of coals, layering newspaper twice through the pyramid. Light the layers of newspaper and wait until the coals are red-hot, about 20 to 30 minutes, before spreading them out.

To grill faster • Give grilled foods a head start in a microwave oven. This is especially helpful with tough or fibrous foods that require long grilling times, such as chicken, ribs, and potatoes. See specific food entries for detailed tips. Also, leave at least 1" of space between the pieces of food on the grill. Or, when grilling ingredients on a skewer, leave about ¼" between pieces. When grilling foods such as chicken or ribs, which require thorough cooking, brown the food on all sides over a medium-hot fire, then adjust the heat to medium-low and cover with a disposable aluminum pan or a sheet of foil to speed up the cooking. You can also baste meats with room-temperature or warm sauce. Avoid basting with cold sauce, which will slow down the grilling.

To slash or butterfly thick meats for fast grilling • Slashing or butterflying speeds grilling and ensures even cooking of thick pieces of meat, poultry, or fish, such as turkey breast, leg of lamb, or whole salmon. To butterfly a turkey breast or leg of lamb, remove the meat from the bone (any butcher will do this for you). Make a deep cut into, but not through, the thickest part of the meat, then open it up like a book. If the thickest part is now 2" thick or less, it is ready to grill. If it is thicker, repeat the slash-and-open method until the thickest section is 2" or less. To slash a whole fish for grilling, make diagonal cuts about 2" apart through the thickest part of the fillet on both sides of the fish, cutting all the way to, but not through, the bone. Season and rub with oil, then grill.

FLAVOR TIP ▼ **To add the smoky flavor of herbs** • Sprinkle leftover herb stems on hot coals right before grilling. Save the stems from other uses by tossing them in a bag and freezing until needed.

HEALTHY HINTS ▼ **To reduce fat in marinades for grilled foods** • Replace most of the oil with mild fruit or vegetable juices, canned broth, or plain yogurt. Leave in 1 tablespoon oil to help prevent sticking on the grill.

To keep lean meats moist • Avoid overcooking. If you have a covered grill, use the cover during part or all of the grilling to help keep the food moist. If your grill does not have a cover, improvise

g

ADDING FLAVOR WITH SMOKE

To boost flavors in grilled or smoked foods, cook with hardwood chips or dried grapevines. For the smokiest flavor, soak wood or vines in water for 30 minutes and make a foil tent over the food to hold in more smoke. If you want a subtler flavor, toss them on the fire without soaking. For meat that will grill longer than 15 minutes, start grilling the meat first, then add the chips during the last 15 minutes of grilling. For shish kebab, seafood, and other short-cooking foods, toss the chips onto the fire before starting to cook.

Wood Type	Flavor	Best Uses
Alder	Clean, mild, sweet	Salmon, scallops, chicken
Apple/Peach	Subtle, tangy	Veal, pork, fish, vegetables
Cherry	Sweet, subtle cherry flavor	Duck, poultry, game birds
Grapevine	Winey, slightly sweet	Lamb, fish, vegetables
Hickory	Slightly spicy, rich smoke	Pork, beef, ribs, turkey
Mesquite	Earthy, tangy, honey-sweet	Pork, beef, lamb
Oak	Robust, clean flavor	Beef, pork, poultry, vegetables
Pecan	Sweet, delicate, mildly nutty	Poultry, fish, vegetables

by using a large, disposable foil roasting pan inverted over the food.

To avoid charring meats • When meat drippings fall directly onto hot coals, they create cancer-causing compounds that are carried back to the food via the smoke. There are several precautions you should take to avoid this potential health hazard. Trim all visible fat on meats and keep the oil in marinades to a minimum. Also, precook large pieces of meat in a microwave oven to reduce their grilling time over coals. Avoid flare-ups on the grill; be ready with a spray bottle of water to put out any flames. And avoid using a lot of mesquite briquettes, which burn hotter than other woods and could cause charring. If charring occurs, trim off the blackened areas before eating the food.

g Grinders

If you appreciate fresh-tasting coffee and spices, keep a grinder in your kitchen. Most models are fairly inexpensive. Cooks who enjoy making their own sausage may also want to invest in a meat grinder.

BASICS ▼ **To choose the right grinder for coffee or spices** • The small, inexpensive propeller grinders are the most popular type of grinder for both spices and coffee. Though they are fine for spices, propeller grinders are not particularly efficient for grinding coffee. Propeller grinders tend to produce grains of uneven size, which can slow the passage of water through coffee in a filter and cause a bitter, sour taste in the finished brew. Serious coffee aficionados may want to purchase one of the more expensive and more precise burr grinders.

To keep the flavor of coffee and freshly ground spices pure • Buy two grinders and use one for spices and one for coffee. Or clean your grinder before switching the contents to be ground.

To clean a spice grinder • Sweep it out with a pastry brush reserved just for that purpose.

To clean a burr-type coffee grinder • Run some raw rice through it.

To use a meat grinder • Cut the food to a size and shape that allows it to drop easily through the feed tube. Use the tamper only to free foods that stick to the mouth of the feed tube, not to force food down the feed tube. Be sure to chill the meat grinder before using. This is an important sanitary precaution and it will produce the best texture in ground meat.

Grits

Old-fashioned stone-ground grits (or hominy grits) are as American as can be. They are very popular in the South and are often served for breakfast, either sweetened like hot cereal or cooked with savory flavorings such as cheese and beer. Many cooks make creamy grits by cooking them in milk and cream until tender.

BASICS ▼ **To boil** • As a general rule for boiling grits, use 5 parts water to 1 part grits.

OLD-FASHIONED CREAMY GRITS Place **1 cup old-fashioned grits** (not quick-cooking) in a small bowl and cover with cold water. Soak overnight, then drain. In a medium nonstick saucepan, bring **2 cups water** to a boil. Stir in the grits and return to a boil. Reduce heat to low and simmer until thick, 3 to 5 minutes, stirring frequently. Add **2 cups chicken broth** and return to a boil over high heat.

Reduce heat to low and simmer until very thick, 1 hour, stirring frequently. Add ½ **cup half-and-half** and simmer, partly covered, 30 minutes. Add ¼ **cup heavy cream.** Cook and stir about 15 minutes longer. If mixture becomes too thick, add ¼ **cup water** or **broth.** Serve hot, topped with **a pat of butter.** *Makes 4 servings.*

CASSEROLE OF CHEESE GRITS Preheat oven to 350°F. Lightly grease a shallow 12" × 8" casserole. In a saucepan, combine **2 cups chicken broth, ½ cup beer, 1 small minced garlic clove,** and ¼ **teaspoon salt.** Bring to a boil. Remove from heat and gradually whisk in ½ **cup old-fashioned grits** (not quick-cooking). Stirring constantly, return to a boil. Reduce heat to low and cook until very thick and tender, about 20 minutes, stirring frequently. Remove from heat and stir in **1 cup grated sharp Cheddar cheese** and ¼ **cup grated Parmesan cheese.** In a large bowl, whisk **3 large eggs** with **1 teaspoon Worcestershire sauce** and ⅛ **teaspoon** *each* **ground red pepper and ground black pepper.** Stir in the hot grits. Turn into the casserole dish and sprinkle with ¼ **cup** *each* **grated Cheddar and Parmesan.** Bake in the top of the oven until lightly browned, 20 to 25 minutes. Serve hot. *Makes 4 servings.*

Guacamole *see also* Avocados

No dip could be simpler than mashed avocados mixed with a little lime juice and seasonings.

PROBLEM SOLVER ▼ **To prevent browning** • Always add a bit of lime juice. The acid will help keep the color bright. You can also press a sheet of plastic wrap directly onto the surface,

smoothing out any air bubbles (oyxgen causes avocados to darken). Store at room temperature for no more than 1 hour. Guacamole is best served soon after it is made. If, despite your efforts, browning does occur, simply scrape off the browned part before serving.

AUTHENTIC MEXICAN GUACAMOLE Cut **1 garlic clove** in half crosswise. Score the cut side and rub onto the insides of a Mexican molcajete, a large mortar, or a sturdy bowl. Discard garlic. Add **1 finely chopped fresh jalapeño chile pepper** (seeded if less heat is desired), **2 to 3 tablespoons chopped fresh cilantro, 1 sliced scallion,** and ½ **teaspoon salt.** Pound with a pestle or a flat-bottomed spice jar until juices are released. Add **1 peeled and pitted ripe Haas avocado** and **2 teaspoons lemon** or **lime juice.** Mash slightly with a fork, but leave avocado in chunks. If desired, fold in **1 or 2 seeded and chopped plum tomatoes.** *Makes about 1 cup.*

1-MINUTE GUACAMOLE Peel and pit **1 ripe avocado.** Mash coarsely in a bowl with the back of a fork or a wire pastry cutter. Mix in the **juice of ½ lime, 1 to 2 teaspoons hot-pepper sauce, 1 tablespoon olive oil,** and ¼ **teaspoon salt.** *Makes about 1 cup.*

HEALTHY HINT ▼ **To reduce fat in guacamole** • Replace up to one-fourth of the avocado with an equal amount of pureed fresh tomatillos or well-drained canned tomatillos. Or, replace up to half of the avocado with an equal amount of pureed white beans or pureed green peas (use canned or frozen cooked peas).

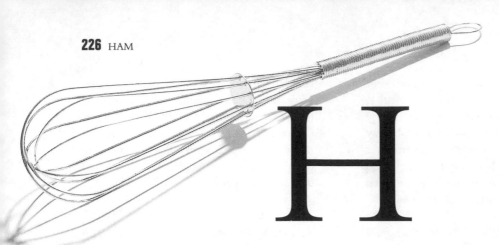

H

Ham *see also* Pork; Prosciutto; Doneness Tests and Temperatures (page 572)

Broadly defined as the hind leg of a pig, hams are cured, smoked, or sometimes both to preserve the meat and add flavor to it.

BASICS ▼ **To choose** • The National Pork Producers Council grades hams according to the ratio of water to protein. The more protein, the better the ham. If you find a ham simply labeled "ham," it has at least 20 percent protein. "Ham with natural juices" must have at least 18 percent protein, and those labeled "water added" have 17 percent or less. Stick with bone-in hams for the best flavor and texture. Partially boned hams are easier to carve than bone-in hams, but they have a funny, football–like shape. Boneless hams must be reshaped to fill in the space where the bone used to be, and their texture suffers in the process. Avoid hams labeled "ham and water product." You're paying more for a lot of added water, which makes the texture mushy and the flavor diluted. (See "Types of Ham" on the opposite page.)

To get the most meat from a bone-in half-ham • Purchase the shank half. It is easier to carve and contains less fat and gristle. If the package does not indicate which half it is, look for one with a tapered end; that will be the shank half. The butt half is more rounded in shape.

To cook a bone-in ham • Put the ham in a roasting pan and cover loosely with foil. Bake at 275°F for about 25 minutes per pound. Let the ham rest for at least 20 minutes before carving.

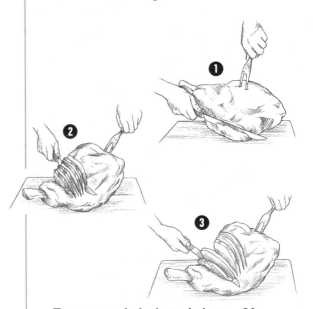

To carve a whole, bone-in ham • Use a carving fork to steady the ham. With a long, flexible knife, cut a few slices from the thin side of the ham ❶. Turn the ham onto the cut surface so that it lies flat. Cut out a small wedge of meat at the shank

TYPES OF HAM

Ham generally refers to the hind legs of a pig. Hams can be whole, with or without skin (rind), partially boned, or boned, rolled, and tied into a neat, round shape. Ham from the front leg (shoulder) is called picnic ham or butt. Hams are available from other cuts of pork as well, such as loin. Ham hocks, or the lower trimmed portions of each ham, are cured and smoked like whole hams. Why so many varieties? Simply because there are hundreds of variations on curing and smoking techniques. Just remember that there are but two basic ways of curing: wet curing and dry curing.

Wet-Cured Ham: Most hams available in stores are wet-cured. This type of ham is created by submerging the ham in a salty brine solution or injecting the brine into the ham. Often, sugar and seasonings are added and sometimes, nitrates are added to improve color and help preserve the meat. In general, wet-cured hams are milder and less salty than dry-cured hams. They are also moister and have a finer texture. Most of these hams are fully cooked, but some are partially cooked, so pay close attention to labels and cooking instructions. Wet-cured hams have not been fully preserved and require refrigeration.

Dry-Cured Ham: In this broad category, the ham is rubbed all over with salt and then left to cure. Country hams, prosciutto, and Serrano hams are all dry-cured and have not yet been cooked; the salt acts as a preservative and helps ward off bacteria. Dry-cured hams often contain sugar and other seasonings to balance the saltiness and contribute flavor. These hams are always salty and the flavor is concentrated, while the texture is coarser and drier than in wet-cured hams.

Smoked Ham: All of the most popular American hams have been smoked. Hickory-smoked ham has always been an American favorite, but you can also buy hams that have been smoked over pecan, apple wood, maple, cherry, oak, and other hardwoods. Some of the lesser-quality smoked hams are not smoked at all but bathed in vaporized smoke flavoring. You can buy whole, half, or pieces of smoked ham. Most of these will be labeled "fully cooked" or "ready to eat."

Baked Glazed, Smoked Ham: Slice off the rind from **1 whole bone-in smoked ham,** leaving ½" layer of fat. (Some smoked hams are sold with the rind already removed.) Score the fatty layer in a diagonal 1" grid, cutting through fat, just down to the meat. Then, stud with about **30 whole cloves,** sticking 1 clove in the center of each diamond on the grid. Place on a rack in a shallow roasting pan lined with aluminum foil. Roast at 325°F until heated through to the bone, about 10 minutes per pound. Let rest 20 minutes. Increase oven temperature to 425°F. Spoon about **1 cup apricot jam** over ham (or **¾ cup brown sugar** and **½ cup Dijon mustard**). Bake until lightly browned, and glazed, about 15 minutes. Let rest 20 to 30 minutes before carving.

Country Ham: The hogs used to make country hams are usually raised on corn and then fed an expensive diet that can include acorns, peaches, and peanuts, which affects the flavor of the ham. All country hams are dry-cured, and most are smoked and uncooked. They are extremely salty and have

h

(continued)

TYPES OF HAM (cont.)

been preserved. To reduce saltiness, country hams must be soaked for at least 24 hours in cool water, changing the water three or four times. Older hams, which are even saltier, should soak for up to 48 hours. After soaking, country hams are usually simmered in a big pot of water for 3 to 4 hours (for a 15- to 20-pound country ham). The ham is allowed to cool in the water for about 2 hours. It can then be sliced and eaten, or baked and glazed.

Baked, Glazed Country Ham: Soak and simmer **1 whole bone-in country ham** as described above. When cool, transfer to a board and cut off the rind, leaving just ½" layer of fat. Score the fatty layer in a diagonal 1" grid, cutting through fat, just down to the meat. Stud with about **30 whole cloves,** sticking 1 clove in the center of each diamond on the grid. Pat **1 cup packed brown sugar** all over the ham (or use ½ **cup bread crumbs** and ½ **cup brown sugar**). Place on a rack in a shallow roasting pan lined with aluminum foil. Roast at 350°F until heated through and glazed, about 45 minutes. Makes 16 to 20 servings. (For 8 to 10 servings, buy a half-ham and halve all the ingredients.)

Spiral-Cut Ham: These fully cooked, wet-cured, smoked hams have been ingeniously sliced using a special spiral slicing machine that cuts the ham in a continuous motion from top to bottom. The result is a ham that retains its full shape, though the slices can be simply removed. Simply heat them through in a 325°F oven.

Supermarket and Deli Ham: These fully cooked hams are usually brine-injected and quickly wet-cured. They may be briefly smoked too, lending just a subtle smoke flavor. Deli ham is usually sold boneless or semi-boneless, but look for it on the bone for the best flavor.

Canned Ham: Ready-to-eat, canned hams are always wet-cured but not always smoked. They require refrigeration and can be stored at 40°F or colder for up to a year. Canned hams are boneless, skinless, and often made up of several hams so that pieces will fill the can. In general, bake at 325°F for about 20 minutes per pound, or until the internal temperature reaches 130° to 140°F on an instant-read thermometer.

Prosciutto: Generally, these salty hams have been dry-cured and aged but not smoked or cooked. The curing process kills any harmful bacteria, so they can be eaten without cooking. This type of ham has also been pressed, so the texture is firm, making it easy to cut wafer-thin slices.

Serrano and Iberico: Spain produces two of the world's greatest cured hams. Serrano is the most popular, but Iberico is considered the very best. Serrano ham is made from Spanish white pigs, while Iberico ham comes from the wild, dark Iberico pig, which is allowed to forage for wild acorns and herbs. Use these Spanish hams as you would use prosciutto.

Tasso: This Cajun specialty is cured, heavily spiced, and smoked. Pieces of ham are usually taken from the shoulder; thus, tasso is sold in chunks rather than in whole hams. It is most often chopped and used as a seasoning in gumbo, jambalaya, stuffings, and other Louisiana regional specialties.

h

end. Then, make even, vertical slices along the ham, cutting right down to the bone ❷. Using a sawing action, cut beneath the slices right along the bone to release the slices from the bone ❸.

PROBLEM SOLVERS ▼

To prevent saltiness • Soak the ham for several hours in a pot of cold water before heating.

To prevent from drying out • Bake the ham in a foil wrap with the cut side down in the roasting pan.

To use a leftover ham bone • Add it to the pot when making soup, such as split pea soup. Or wrap it well and freeze until needed.

TIME SAVER ▼

To cook ham faster • Cut the ham into steaks, which heat through much more quickly than a whole ham. Cut ½"-thick slices across the broad face of the whole ham. Heat an iron skillet over high heat for 3 minutes. Coat with cooking spray and brown the steaks on both sides. You can also broil or grill the ham steak 4" from a medium-hot fire until the ham browns lightly on both sides, about 4 minutes per side.

QUICK HONEY-HOISIN GLAZED HAM STEAKS Mix together ¼ **cup** *each* **honey and hoisin sauce,** ½ **teaspoon hot-pepper sauce, 1 teaspoon cider vinegar,** and ¼ **teaspoon garlic powder. Brush four** ½"-**thick ham steaks (6 ounces each)** with the glaze and broil 4 minutes per side, turning the steaks often and basting with sauce at each turn. *Makes 4 servings.*

FLAVOR TIPS ▼

To use as a flavoring • Just a little smoked ham, chopped into bits, adds great flavor to home-fried or scalloped potatoes, rice casseroles, fried rice, and paella.

HAM AND RICOTTA CHEESE FILLING Stir together **1 container (15 ounces) ricotta cheese;** ¼ **cup** *each* **finely chopped smoked ham, grated Parmesan cheese, and chopped fresh parsley;** ¼ **teaspoon salt;** and ⅛ **teaspoon ground black pepper.** Use to fill stuffed shells, manicotti, or ravioli. *Makes about 2 cups.*

BOW-TIE PASTA WITH HAM AND CREAM In a skillet, sauté **1 finely chopped onion** in **1 tablespoon butter** until softened, 3 to 5 minutes. Add **1 large minced garlic clove** and ½ **teaspoon dried oregano.** Cook 1 minute. Add **1 cup chopped smoked ham (6 ounces)** and **1 cup heavy cream** (or half heavy cream and half light cream). Bring to a boil and simmer until slightly thickened, about 5 minutes. Add **1 cup frozen and thawed peas** and ⅛ **teaspoon grated nutmeg.** Cook 3 minutes. Boil ½ **pound bow-tie pasta** until tender but firm. Drain and add to sauce. Toss for a minute over high heat. Add ⅓ **cup grated Parmesan cheese,** toss, and serve hot, with **extra grated Parmesan cheese** and **ground black pepper.** *Makes 4 modest servings.*

Hazelnuts *see also* Nuts

Also known as filberts, hazelnuts have a distinctively sweet, nutty flavor. The nickname "filbert" comes from the feast day of Saint Philibert (August 22), the day on which filberts are said to be ready for picking from the hedgerows where they grow in England.

BASICS ▼

To roast and peel • Place hazelnuts on a baking sheet and toast at 350°F until golden beneath the skin, about 12 min-

h

utes, shaking the pan once or twice. While the nuts are still hot, place them on a clean towel or cloth and rub to remove the skin (it's okay if some bits of skin remain). Another way to remove the skins is to boil the nuts before you toast them. Combine 3 cups water and 3 tablespoons baking soda in a saucepan over medium-high heat. Add the hazelnuts and boil 3 minutes. Drain in a sieve and rinse under cold water. The water will end up a murky mess, but the skins will vanish. Pat the skinned nuts dry, then toast them at 350°F until golden, 10 to 12 minutes.

h

HAZELNUT TEA BALLS Soften **2 sticks (1 cup) unsalted butter** to room temperature. Roast, peel, and finely chop **3 ounces hazelnuts** to make ¾ cup. Preheat oven to 375°F. Meanwhile, sift **1 box (1 pound) confectioners' sugar** into a 13" × 9" pan. In a large bowl, combine butter with ¾ cup of the confectioners' sugar. Beat 30 seconds with an electric mixer or a stiff whisk. Stir in **2¼ cups all-purpose flour, hazelnuts, 1 teaspoon vanilla extract,** and **½ teaspoon salt.** Using about 2 teaspoons dough for each cookie, roll into balls and arrange 1" apart on an ungreased baking sheet. Bake until pale golden on the bottom, about 12 minutes. Use a spatula to transfer cookies to the pan of sugar and roll around to coat. Let cool to room temperature in the sugar. Roll around again to coat a second time with sugar. *Makes about 3 dozen.*

Herbs *see also* Spices *and specific herbs*
Need flavor? Add herbs. They are the simplest way to boost the character of a dish. Use them in baked goods, too.

BASICS **To choose fresh herbs** • Look for herbs with a vibrant color and aroma. Black spots, off odors, and yellow leaves indicate old, tired herbs that are losing much of their flavor. Farmers' markets carry field-grown herbs, which have a stronger aroma than the greenhouse herbs usually sold in grocery stores.

To wash fresh herbs • Put the herbs in a large bowl of cool water and swish them about with your hands to loosen any bits of grit. Lift the herbs out of the water, leaving the grit in the bottom of the bowl. If the herbs are very gritty, repeat the process. Then, spin them dry in a salad spinner or blot dry by rolling up in a kitchen towel.

To store tender fresh herbs • Tender fresh herbs include parsley, cilantro, basil, dill, and tarragon. Remove any rubber bands or fasteners from the herbs, then trim the stems. (If the herbs still have the roots attached, skip the trimming step.) Put the unwashed herbs, stem side down, in a tall container with enough water to cover the stems. Cover loosely with a plastic bag, then store on the top shelf of the refrigerator (the warmest part) for up to 5 days. The exception here is basil: Store it loosely covered in a container of water at room temperature to protect its delicate leaves from the cold, which could cause them to turn brown.

To store hardy fresh herbs • These include thyme, rosemary, and sage. Wrap the stem ends in a damp paper towel, put the herbs in a plastic bag, and refrigerate, unsealed, for up to 2 weeks.

To freeze fresh herbs • When herbs are in season or you simply have some left over, pluck the leaves from the stem and plunge them into boiling water just until wilted, about 5 seconds. Drain, pat dry, and chop. For every ¼ cup chopped herbs, drizzle with 2 teaspoons olive oil and toss well. Line a plate with plastic wrap and dot with teaspoon-size mounds of the oiled herbs. Freeze until the mounds are solid. Peel from the plastic and place in a zipper-lock freezer bag for up to 6 months. If you are cooking with the herb, there is no need to defrost before using. You can also chop fresh herbs and place a tablespoon in each compartment of an ice cube tray. Add water or oil to cover, and freeze solid. Then, remove and freeze in zipper-lock freezer bags for up to 6 months. To thaw, place them in a strainer under cold water until the ice melts. Use immediately.

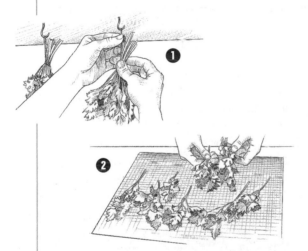

To dry fresh herbs • Tie hardy herbs, such as thyme and rosemary, together in a bouquet. Then hang it upside down in a dry, well-ventilated area until crumbly, 3 to 6 days ❶. If the herb has seeds you'd like to catch for future plantings, tie a bag around the stems so that the seeds fall into the bag as the herb dries.

To dry tender herbs, such as basil and parsley, spread them on a mesh screen and leave in a dry, well-ventilated area until crumbly. Store in airtight containers ❷.

To coarsely chop fresh herbs • Stuff the leaves into a glass, insert the pointed end of scissors into the herbs, and snip, rotating the scissors 90 degrees with each snip. Or just tear the leaves into pieces with your fingertips.

To shred fresh herbs • Stack the leaves no higher than ¼". Roll the stack lengthwise into a cigar. Cut crosswise into paper-thin slices, also known as chiffonade.

To mince fresh herbs • Use a large, tapered chef's knife, and quickly chop back and forth across the herbs, using the point of the knife as a pivot. Or tear the herbs coarsely and chop them in the work bowl of a mini food processor.

To get powdery-light chopped parsley for garnish • Place finely chopped parsley in a towel and twist the towel to ring out every bit of moisture. Parsley can stain, so use a dark-colored towel.

To choose dried herbs • The flavors of hardy herbs such as rosemary, thyme, and sage are well-preserved by drying. But don't waste your money on dried basil, parsley, or cilantro. The delicate flavors of these tender herbs fade when commercially dried. If possible, smell dried herbs before buying them. The best-tasting dried herbs will have a powerful aroma. If they don't, pass them by.

To store dried herbs • Keep them tightly sealed, away from heat and light. Next to the stove in clear containers is the worst place. For easy access, store opaque bottles of dried herbs in alphabetical order in a closed cabinet. To keep track of freshness, write an "expiration date" on the bottles. They usually lose most of their flavor within a year of opening the bottle.

To substitute dried for fresh • Generally, use about one-third as much dried as fresh. But avoid adding more than a teaspoon or two of any dried herb to a dish, unless you are cooking in large quantities. Excessive amounts of dried herbs can easily overpower the other flavors in the food.

To perk up limp herbs • Snip ¼" off the stem ends and place, stem end down, in a glass of ice water for 30 minutes.

To use limp or leftover herbs • Mince them and freeze as directed in "To freeze fresh herbs" on page 230.

To preserve the unique color of purple basil • Serve fresh only. When cooked, the pigments in purple basil revert disappointingly to ordinary green.

Fascinating Fact: Rosemary extract is a patented natural food additive used to retain the flavor and color of processed foods. The antioxidants in rosemary prevent oils from going rancid and plant pigments from deteriorating.

To quickly remove leaves from hardy fresh herbs • For thyme, rosemary, and oregano, pluck off the tender top leaves, then pinch the top of the stem and run your fingers down the length of the stem to strip off the rest of the leaves.

To quickly dry fresh herbs • Place fresh herb leaves in a single layer between

MAKING A BOUQUET GARNI

This small bundle of assorted herbs tied together, sometimes in cheesecloth, is often called for in slowly cooked dishes. Usually, it includes parsley, thyme, and a bay leaf. Sometimes, leek or celery is added, even a ribbon of orange zest in the south of France. A bouquet garni can be made with fresh or dried herbs. A bouquet garni is perfect for a pot roast, but there is no reason to make one for the stockpot or for other dishes that will be strained.

When using fresh herbs, tie the herbs together with string.

When using dried herbs, wrap them in a double layer of cheesecloth or a coffee filter and tie it into a bundle. Leave a long end of string attached and tie it to the pot handle so that the bouquet garni will be easy to remove later. Just make sure that the string isn't long enough to reach the heating element.

paper towels. Microwave on medium power for 2 to 4 minutes, or until almost dry. Set on a rack and let sit overnight until herbs are crumbly. Place in a tightly sealed container and store in a cool, dark place. Use as you would store-bought dried herbs.

FLAVOR TIPS ▼

To get the best flavor from fresh herbs • Add tender herbs such as basil, parsley, cilantro, and dill toward the end of cooking time. Or sprinkle on top of the finished dish. Cooking these tender herbs rapidly diffuses their flavor. Add strong-flavored hardy herbs such as thyme, marjoram, or rosemary earlier in the cooking process so that they have time to mellow. Added at the end, these hardy herbs may be too overpowering.

To get more flavor from dried herbs • Just before using, rub dried herbs between your fingers to release their flavor-carrying essential oils. Also, add dried herbs at the beginning of cooking time so that they have a chance to heat up and release more flavor.

To make herbes de Provence • This popular dried herb mixture hails from the Provence region of France. To make it at home, combine dried thyme, savory, and fennel or anise. Include rosemary, sage, bay leaf, and lavender, if desired. Use herbes de Provence to flavor meats (especially lamb), poultry, and omelettes.

FINES HERBES Mix together **1 tablespoon** *each* **dried tarragon, dried marjoram, dried thyme, dried rosemary, dried mint, and dried parsley flakes.** Use to season fish or vegetables. *Makes 6 tablespoons.*

SOUP SEASONING Mix together **1 tablespoon** *each* **dried thyme, dried parsley flakes, dried basil, dried mar-** joram, ground celery seeds, and dried dillweed, and **1½ teaspoons** *each* **dried rubbed sage and dried rosemary.** *Makes 7 tablespoons.*

HERBAL SALT Mix together **2 tablespoons onion salt, 1 tablespoon** *each* **garlic salt and dried parsley flakes, 1 teaspoon** *each* **dried basil and dried marjoram,** and **½ teaspoon** *each* **ground black pepper, dried dillweed, and dried thyme.** *Makes about ⅓ cup.*

BEEF SEASONING Mix together **1 tablespoon** *each* **dried parsley flakes, garlic powder, onion powder, and ground black pepper.** *Makes ¼ cup.*

PORK SEASONING Mix together **2 tablespoons** *each* **dried rubbed sage and dried parsley flakes, 2 teaspoons** *each* **dried thyme and dried rosemary,** and **1 teaspoon garlic salt.** *Makes 6 tablespoons.*

POULTRY SEASONING Combine **1 tablespoon** *each* **dried marjoram, dried basil, dried dillweed, and dried parsley flakes** and **1 teaspoon** *each* **dried thyme and store-bought dried lemon peel.** *Makes about ¼ cup.*

LAMB SEASONING Mix together **1 tablespoon** *each* **dried parsley, dried rosemary, and dried thyme.** *Makes 3 tablespoons.*

FISH SEASONING Mix together **1 tablespoon** *each* **dried tarragon, dried basil, dried dillweed, dried marjoram, and dried parsley flakes.** *Makes about ⅓ cup.*

ITALIAN HERB SEASONING Combine **2 tablespoons** *each* **dried oregano and dried basil,** and **2 teaspoons dried thyme.** *Makes about ¼ cup.*

High-Altitude Cooking

Cooking at high altitudes can be a challenge, especially if you're baking. Because the air is thinner and drier, breads and cakes dry out more quickly. And because liquids boil at a lower temperature, cooking times can vary dramatically.

BASICS **To choose eggs** • Use extra-large eggs, which offer additional moisture.

To store flour • Keep in an airtight container to prevent moisture loss.

To cook • In general, foods require a higher temperature, a longer cooking time, and more water at higher elevations than they do at sea level.

To simmer pasta or beans • Use a pressure cooker, which will raise the temperature at which the water boils so that these foods will cook properly.

To deep-fry • Reduce the temperature of the fat by 3°F for each 1,000 feet above sea level, and slightly increase the frying time.

To bake • In general, you'll need to use more liquid, less leavener, and a higher oven temperature in order for batters and doughs to set before the gases overexpand. For all altitudes of 3,000 feet above sea level or more, increase the oven temperature by 25°F and slightly reduce the baking time. For baked goods leavened with baking powder or baking soda, make the following adjustments according to the altitude at which you are baking:

WATER BOILING POINTS

At sea level, water boils at 212°F. But at higher altitudes, water boils at lower temperatures because there is less air pressure. Boiled foods also take longer to cook at higher altitudes, so allow extra time if you're above sea level.

Altitude	Boiling Point
Sea level	212°F (100°C)
2,000 ft	208°F (98°C)
5,000 ft	203°F (95°C)
7,500 ft	198°F (92°C)
10,000 ft	194°F (90°C)

At 3,000 feet, reduce the amount of sugar by ½ to 1 tablespoon per cup, reduce leavening by ⅛ teaspoon per teaspoon, and increase the liquid by 1 to 2 tablespoons per cup. At 5,000 feet, reduce the amount of sugar by ½ to 2 tablespoons per cup, reduce leavening by ⅛ to ¼ teaspoon per teaspoon, and increase the liquid by 2 to 4 tablespoons per cup. At 7,000 feet, reduce the amount of sugar by 1 to 3 tablespoons per cup, reduce leavening by ¼ teaspoon per teaspoon, and increase the liquid by 3 to 4 tablespoons per cup.

To beat egg whites • Beat no further than to soft peaks.

To make successful cakes and quick breads • Let cake and quick bread batters stand for 15 minutes before baking to allow some of the leavening gases to release. Also, fill pans only halfway to allow room for greater rise.

To rise bread dough • Avoid letting bread dough rise beyond doubling in bulk. Punch down and allow a second rise, then punch down again to develop texture and flavor.

To reduce the rate at which a bread dough will rise • Reduce the amount of yeast by 20 percent. You can also place the dough in the refrigerator to retard the rising rate.

Honey

A thick, luscious sweetener, honey is the product of bees, made from the nectar they collect as they travel among various flowers.

BASICS ▼ **To choose** • The flavor and color of honey is determined by the type of blossom from which the nectar is collected. Generally, the darker the color, the stronger the flavor. Commercial honey producers usually blend different varieties of honeys for a consistent color and flavor. Wildflower honeys are not blended but are made from the nectar of several different flowers. Single-blossom honeys are made when beekeepers position their hives so that the bees collect nectar from just a single variety of flower. These honeys tend to have the most pronounced flavors.

To store • Store honey in an airtight container at room temperature. When stored at too cold a temperature, honey may crystallize.

To substitute honey for sugar • For general cooking, substitute 1 cup honey for 1¼ cups sugar and reduce the liquid in the recipe by ¼ cup. For baking, use the same ratios, but replace no more than half the amount of sugar in the recipe. Also,

add ⅛ teaspoon baking soda to the dry ingredients if the recipe has no baking soda, baking powder, or other acid (such as citrus, yogurt, or sour cream). Reduce the oven temperature by 25°F to prevent over-browning. For jams, jellies, or candies, use the same ratios as for general cooking, but slightly increase the cooking temperature to allow the extra liquid to evaporate.

To easily remove baked goods made with honey from pans • Allow an additional 5 to 10 minutes of cooling time before removing.

HONEY-PEAR BUTTER Puree **4 large, peeled and cored pears** in a blender or food processor. Place in a large, deep saucepan with **¾ cup honey, 1 teaspoon ground cinnamon, ½ teaspoon ground ginger, ¼ teaspoon ground cloves,** and **1 tablespoon lemon juice.** Bring to a simmer and cook until reduced to 2 cups, about 1¼ hours, stirring occasionally (stir frequently during the last 20 minutes of cooking). Place in jars or containers and refrigerate for 2 months or freeze up to 8 months. Use on toast, muffins, waffles, and other quick breads. *Makes 2 cups.*

HONEY-GLAZED CARROTS Peel **4 to 6 medium carrots** (1 pound) and cut crosswise on an angle into ½" slices. Combine in a saucepan with **2 ribbons (1" × 3" each) orange zest, ½ cup orange juice, 3 tablespoons honey, 1 tablespoon** *each* **butter and chopped crystallized ginger,** and **½ teaspoon salt.** Add **½ cup water.** Bring to a boil. Cover and simmer 4 minutes. Uncover, increase heat to medium-high, and cook, tossing or stirring, until most of liquid has evaporated

h

and carrots are glazed. Add **a pinch of ground black pepper** and serve hot. *Makes 4 servings.*

Fascinating Fact: Bees were first domesticated in artificial hives in 2500 B.C. by the ancient Egyptians.

To prevent honey from crystallizing • Store in a dark, dry place at room temperature.

To liquefy crystallized honey • Put the container in a pot of hot water until the crystals dissolve. Or microwave the honey container on medium power for 5 seconds if cloudy or 10 seconds if crystallized solid. Make sure that the container doesn't have any metal parts, and loosen or remove the top to allow steam to escape.

To prevent honey from sticking to a measuring cup or spoon • Coat the utensil with cooking spray or dip it in oil before measuring. Likewise, to avoid sticky lids on honey jars, wipe the lid and rim of the jar clean with a hot, damp cloth. Then, spray some cooking spray on both the lid threads and the jar rim.

Fascinating Fact: To make a pound of honey, worker bees must forage nectar from millions of flowers. To communicate the location of nectar sources, the bees perform several different and distinct dances.

Horseradish

With its nubby brown skin, this fleshy white root belongs to the mustard family. It can grow up to 15" in length. It has virtually no aroma until you scratch its skin; then, it will emit a sharp, penetrating aroma, similar to mustard oil, causing your eyes to water.

Horseradish enrages the tastebuds and nostrils with its highly volatile oils and hot, pungent flavor. It also clears the sinuses. It's a favorite for seasoning beef, smoked fish, and strong-flavored vegetables.

To choose • Look for clean, unbroken roots with firm (but not dry) flesh. When fresh horseradish is unavailable, use prepared horseradish, which has been grated and preserved in vinegar. Some makers of bottled prepared horseradish pack it with grated beet, which colors it purple-red and gives it a sweet flavor.

To store • Keep fresh horseradish tightly wrapped in a plastic bag and refrigerate for up to 3 weeks or freeze for up to 6 months. Or grate it and freeze it immediately by lining a plate with plastic wrap and dotting it with teaspoon-size mounds of horseradish. Freeze until the mounds are solid, then peel them from the plastic and place them in a zipper-lock freezer bag for up to 6 months. Return to room temperature before using. Use bottled prepared horseradish within 1 month of opening it; after that, it turns bitter.

To use fresh • Peel the root and remove the fibrous core before grating. Use or freeze grated horseradish immediately, as its flavor tends to fade quickly.

CREAMY HORSERADISH SAUCE Peel and grate **1 medium knob fresh horseradish** to make ¼ cup grated. Place in a bowl and stir in **½ cup *each* sour cream and plain yogurt, 1 tablespoon lemon juice** or **distilled white vinegar, ½ teaspoon salt,** and **⅛ teaspoon ground black pepper.** Serve with roasted meats, poultry, or seafood. *Makes 1¼ cups.*

Hummus

A great party dish, this rich and earthy Middle Eastern dip is made from mashed chickpeas, sesame paste (also called tahini), olive oil, and other seasonings, such as garlic.

FLAVOR TIP ▼ **To serve hummus attractively** • Spread the hummus on a large serving platter. Using the back of a spoon, make a series of decorative swirls, radiating from the center outward. Drizzle with 2 tablespoons good-quality green olive oil. Sprinkle with 1 chopped tomato and ½ cup small, whole black olives. If desired, decorate edges with flat parsley leaves. Serve with hot pita triangles.

HIGH-FLAVOR HUMMUS In a food processor or with a potato masher in a medium bowl, puree **2 cans (16 ounces each) rinsed and drained chickpeas.** In a small skillet over low heat, cook **2 large minced garlic cloves** in **3 tablespoons olive oil** with **1 teaspoon ground cumin** until garlic is just soft and cumin is fragrant, about 1 minute. Turn out over chickpeas. Add ⅔ **cup well-stirred tahini, ¼ cup lemon juice, 1 tablespoon toasted sesame oil,** and **1 teaspoon salt.** Process or mix until smooth. Add ⅔ **cup water** or **chickpea canning liquid** and blend briefly. If too thick, add water, 1 tablespoon at a time. Cover and chill. Great with hot pita triangles. *Makes about 4 cups.*

h

I

Ice Cream *see also* Sherbet; Sorbet

A frozen blend of cream, sweetener, and sometimes eggs, ice cream is one of the world's best-loved desserts. There are many excellent premium ice creams in markets, but few can compare to the fresh flavor and texture of homemade ice cream.

BASICS **To choose commercial ice cream** • Hold 2 same-size containers of different ice cream brands in your hands. Take home the heaviest container, which will have the least amount of air. Premium ice cream contains more milk fat and has less air pumped into it, while "regular" ice cream can be composed of as much as half air. Also, if the container is sticky, leave it at the store. The ice cream has very likely thawed and been refrozen. And make sure to read the label: If the ice cream is labeled simply "vanilla ice cream," it has been made with all natural ingredients. Those labeled "vanilla-flavored ice cream" include artificial flavoring. If it reads "artificial vanilla ice cream," more than half of its flavoring comes from artificial ingredients.

To store • Wrap the carton of ice cream in an airtight plastic bag to prevent it from absorbing freezer odors.

To use a hand-cranked ice cream freezer • Begin cranking slowly at first, and increase the speed once the ice cream begins to thicken.

PROBLEM SOLVERS **To prevent ice crystals** • Create an airtight seal over the ice cream with waxed paper or plastic wrap.

To soften when rock-hard • Microwave the unopened container on low power for 20 seconds for 1 pint, 45 seconds for 1 quart, or 1 minute for ½ gallon.

To scoop hard ice cream • Dip the spoon or ice cream scoop in a bowl of hot water between scoops.

To prevent drips in an ice cream cone • Stuff a miniature marshmallow in the bottom of a sugar cone.

TIME SAVER **To save time when serving to guests** • Make scoops of ice cream in advance, storing them on a prechilled rimmed baking sheet in the freezer. Cover them tightly with plastic wrap. This trick can save you from disaster when hosting a birthday party full of hungry kids.

FLAVOR TIPS **To enhance the flavor of homemade ice cream** • Add a little bit of salt to the custard base.

To make smooth homemade ice cream • Heat any milk or half-and-half in the recipe to 175°F. (If you are using heavy cream, which has less protein, you do not

THREE PROCESSOR ICE CREAMS

Using a food processor, some frozen fruit, and a little bit of milk, cream, or yogurt, you can make a nearly instant version of homemade ice cream. If you don't have superfine sugar, process granulated sugar in a food processor until very fine. Each recipe makes about 4 servings.

Strawberry Ice Cream: In a liquid measure, combine ¼ cup *each* milk and half-and-half, 2 tablespoons strawberry liqueur (optional), and 1 teaspoon vanilla extract. Place **1 pint frozen unsweetened strawberries (one 16-ounce package)** and ½ cup superfine sugar in a food processor. Pulse until finely chopped. With the machine running, add cream mixture and process until smooth, scraping down the bowl as needed. Serve or freeze.

Pineapple Sherbet: Cube ½ **fresh pineapple** to make 2 cups. Freeze cubes in a single layer on plastic-lined baking sheets. In a liquid measure, combine ½ **cup milk; 2 tablespoons melon liqueur, such as Midori (optional);** and 1 teaspoon vanilla extract. Place frozen pineapple and ½ cup superfine sugar in a food processor. Pulse until finely chopped. With the machine running, add milk mixture and process until smooth, scraping down the bowl as needed. Serve or freeze.

Peach Frozen Yogurt: In a glass measure, combine ½ **cup peach or plain yogurt, 2 tablespoons peach schnapps (optional),** and 1 teaspoon vanilla extract. Set aside. Place **2 cups frozen unsweetened peach slices (one 16-ounce package)** and ½ **cup superfine sugar** in a food processor. Pulse until finely chopped. With the machine running, add yogurt mixture and process until smooth, scraping down the bowl as needed. Serve immediately or freeze. If frozen, let stand in the refrigerator 20 minutes before using.

---

need to heat it.) To control the temperature of the ice cream freezer, use a mixture of 1½ tablespoons table salt and 6 pounds ice cubes. It also helps to chill the base for 4 to 12 hours before freezing.

CHERRY-ALMOND ICE CREAM WITH CHOCOLATE CHUNKS Rinse **1 pound firm, ripe Bing cherries.** Pull off stems, cut in half, and pit cherries. Combine in a large bowl with ¾ **cup sugar, 3 tablespoons amaretto liqueur, 2 teaspoons vanilla extract,** and ½ **teaspoon almond extract.** Cover and let sit overnight in the refrigerator. Stir in **2 cups light cream** and **1 cup heavy cream.** Freeze in an ice cream freezer according to manufacturer's directions. Add **4 ounces coarsely chopped semisweet chocolate,** transfer to a freezer container, and freeze. *Makes about 1½ quarts.*

Immersion Blender

This handheld tool makes easy work of pureeing soups, sauces, dips, and smoothies. It has a long, narrow stem with rotary blades at the end so you can immerse it right into the pot, bowl, or glass.

To choose • Pick a blender with a powerful motor; it will be the most versatile. Weight matters too, so hold the blender in your hand and make sure that it is lightweight enough to hold comfortably. Check to see that the on/off and speed controls are easy to use. The stem is another consideration: A removable metal stem will last longer than a plastic stem and makes cleaning much easier because you can transfer the dirty part to the sink or dishwasher without the electrical components. Cordless models also offer great convenience. Finally, don't be overly impressed by attachments. Only buy them if you know that you will use them.

To clean • Make sure that the blender is unplugged before washing. Wipe the stem with a damp cloth and wash the blade under hot running water. Or, if you have a removable stem, wash it under running water or in the dishwasher.

Instant Coffee *see also* Coffee

Although instant coffee isn't very good for drinking, it's great for adding flavor to desserts. In general, dissolve 1 to 2 teaspoons granules in 1 to 2 tablespoons boiling water before using.

To boost flavor in chocolate batters • Dissolve 1 to 2 teaspoons instant coffee granules in 1 to 2 tablespoons boiling water (or other warm liquid in the recipe) and stir in with the liquid ingredients. Reduce the total amount of liquid if necessary.

COFFEE SAUCE In a saucepan, heat **1½ cups milk** over medium heat until it almost simmers. Remove from heat and stir in **1 tablespoon instant coffee granules** and **2 tablespoons coffee liqueur, such as Kahlúa or Tía Maria.** Cover and set aside. In a metal bowl or the top of a double boiler, whisk **4 egg yolks** with **¼ cup sugar.** Gradually whisk in hot milk mixture. Place bowl over a pan of barely simmering water and stir until sauce thickens, about 15 minutes. Do not let sauce simmer. Cool to room temperature. In another bowl, whisk ¼ **cup heavy cream** until soft mounds form. Stir into cool sauce. Chill before using. Excellent on ice cream or chocolate desserts. *Makes about 2 cups.*

COFFEE CRÈME BRÛLÉE Preheat oven to 325°F. Warm **2½ cups heavy cream** until almost simmering. Remove from heat and stir in **2½ tablespoons instant coffee granules.** In a large bowl, whisk **4 egg yolks** with ⅔ **cup sugar.** Very gently whisk in half of hot cream (avoid forming bubbles). Gently stir in remaining hot cream. Arrange six ¾-cup ramekins or custard cups in a large, shallow roasting pan. Divide cream mixture among ramekins. Add about 1" of hot tap water to the roasting pan. Cover loosely with foil and bake until set, about 1 hour (centers can be slightly soft; they will set further upon cooling). Let cool to room temperature, then chill at least 3 hours or up to 2 days. When ready to serve, preheat broiler. Press **6 tablespoons brown sugar** through a sieve and sprinkle 1 tablespoon over each ramekin. Broil as close to heat as possible until sugar caramelizes, 30 to 60 seconds. Serve. *Makes 6 servings.*

Jam *see also* Jelly

Made from fruit, sugar, and sometimes pectin cooked to a thick paste, jams are best loved on toast and pastries. They also make great fillings for cookies and cakes and are simple to make at home.

BASICS ▼ **To choose fruit for homemade jam** • Look for the ripest fruits in the market. If you spot less-than-perfect fruits that won't do for eating out of hand, pick them up for jam.

To make homemade jam • Wash and peel fruit, removing any pith, damaged bits of flesh, stalks, or pits. Put the fruit in a wide, shallow pan, crushing the bottom layer to provide moisture as the fruit cooks. Simmer, uncovered, until soft. Add the sugar (use about 1 cup sugar for every 3 to 4 cups fruit) and stir until the sugar dissolves. Continue cooking and stirring until the mixture comes to a boil. Reduce heat to medium-low and cook until the mixture thickens, about 10 to 20 minutes, depending upon amounts of fruit and sugar used.

To test jams for doneness • Put a small drop of jam on a plate. If it stays put when you tip the plate, the jam is done.

To store homemade jam • Pour the hot jam into hot, scalded preserving jars, leaving ⅛" headspace. Wipe the rims clean, attach the lids, and tightly screw on the caps. Invert jars for 10 seconds. Cool on a rack. Store in the refrigerator.

EASY RASPBERRY-PEACH JAM Canning is not necessary with this recipe. In a small saucepan, combine **2 cups peeled, coarsely chopped peaches (fresh or frozen and thawed); 1 cup fresh raspberries (or individually quick-frozen raspberries); ⅓ cup sugar;** and **2 tablespoons brandy.** Bring to a boil. Cook over medium heat until thick, about 15 minutes, stirring often. Let cool to room temperature. Stir in **2 teaspoons vanilla extract.** Cover and refrigerate up to 10 days. Best at room temperature. *Makes about 2½ cups.*

JAM-FILLED JELLY ROLL Preheat oven to 375°F. Bring **4 large eggs** to room temperature. Lightly grease a 15" × 10" × 1" rimmed baking sheet. Line with waxed paper or parchment. In a large bowl, beat eggs with ¼ **teaspoon salt** until thick and light. Gradually beat in ⅔ **cup sugar** and beat until stiff and thick. Have ready ¾ **cup sifted plain cake flour.** Sift flour again with **1 teaspoon baking powder.** Sift again over egg mixture and quickly but carefully fold together with a spatula. Turn into the prepared pan and spread evenly.

j

Bake until center springs back when lightly touched and edges begin to pull away from pan, about 10 minutes. Run a knife around edges. Invert onto a clean towel dusted with confectioners' sugar. Peel off the paper and trim away crisp edges all around. Staring at one narrow end, roll up cake, towel and all, and let cool in rolled position. Gently unroll cake and remove the towel. Spread with **1 cup seedless raspberry** or **blackberry jam.** Roll up again and place, seam side down, on a serving plate. Cover and let stand 1 hour. Sift **1 tablespoon confectioners' sugar** over top and cut on an angle into slices. *Makes 10 to 12 servings.*

Jelly *see also* Jam

Clarity is the sign of a well-made jelly. By extracting the juice from fruit, straining it, and cooking it with sugar, home cooks can make clear, flavor-rich jellies that hold their shape but are not stiff or gummy.

BASICS ▼ **To choose fruit** • For best results, use high-pectin fruits, such as apples, plums, and cranberries.

To make jelly from low-pectin fruits • When making jelly from cherries, pears, peaches, or figs, combine them with a high-pectin fruit to help the jelly set up. Or add commercial pectin.

To make homemade jelly • Wash the fruit well and remove any pith, damaged bits of flesh, stalks, or pits. Put the fruit in a wide, shallow pan, crushing the bottom layer to provide moisture as the fruit cooks. Fruits that tend to be less juicy, such as apples and pears, will require additional water. Add enough that you can see the water through the top layer of fruit but never so much that the fruit floats. Cook over low heat until the fruit is quite soft and has begun to lose its color. Wet a jelly bag with cold water, then strain the juice through the bag. Measure the strained juice and transfer it to a large, shallow, stainless steel pan. Simmer the juice, uncovered, for about 5 minutes, skimming any foam. Add the sugar (use about 1 cup sugar for every 1 cup juice) and stir until the sugar dissolves. Cook until the jelly is firm enough to hold its shape, 10 to 30 minutes, depending on the type of fruit and amount of sugar used.

To make the most flavorful jelly • Use as little water as possible.

To keep a jelly bag from absorbing too much of the fruit juice • Wet the bag and wring it out before straining the fruit juice.

To make a sparkling-clear jelly • Avoid squeezing the jelly bag while the juice is straining.

To help jelly set properly • Add liquid fruit pectin along with the sugar.

To test the jell point of jelly • Put a small amount of jelly on a spoon and let it drip back into the pan from the side of the spoon. At first, the jelly will drip from the spoon in 2 large drops along the edge of the spoon. Continue testing until the 2 drops come together to form a single drop in the center of the spoon. This is known as sheeting and indicates that the jelly should be removed from the heat.

To store homemade jelly • Pour the hot jelly into hot, scalded preserving jars, leaving ⅛" headspace. Wipe the rims clean, attach the lids, and tightly screw on the caps. Process in a boiling-water canner 5 minutes. Cool on a rack. Processing in a boiling-water canner enables you to store homemade jelly at room temperature rather than in the refrigerator.

FLAVOR TIP ▼ **To use as a glaze** • In a small saucepan over low heat, melt ½ cup jelly (currant, apple, or raspberry is good). Brush over a fresh fruit tart and chill so that jelly sets.

Or brush over a baked ham every 8 to 10 minutes during the last 30 minutes of baking to glaze the ham.

Jerk

Like American-style barbecue, Jamaican jerk barbecue refers to a seasoning and a cooking technique, as well as to a type of food. Jerk barbecue was originally made with wild boar, then pork, and now, chicken is traditional. The meat is marinated in a paste of spices, herbs, and fiery Scotch bonnet chile peppers and then cooked slowly over an open fire of green wood, preferably allspice wood (known as pimento in Jamaica).

BASICS **To use homemade jerk seasoning** • Let the paste sit at room temperature for a few hours before using. If it is too stiff to spread, stir in a little oil, rum, molasses, and/or lime juice just before using. Rub the paste over the meat and marinate in the refrigerator for at least 4 hours or as long as overnight before cooking.

To store homemade jerk seasoning • Refrigerate the paste in a tightly sealed container for up to 3 weeks.

DRY JERK SEASONING Chop 30 scallions, a 5" piece peeled fresh ginger, ¼ cup peeled garlic cloves (about 6 whole), 6 bay leaves, and 4 seeded and chopped Scotch bonnet peppers. Continue chopping finely to make a paste (or use a food processor). Put in a bowl and stir in 2 tablespoons *each* ground nutmeg, ground cinnamon, ground black pepper, and ground coriander; 1 tablespoon *each* ground allspice and salt; and 1 cup fresh thyme leaves. Mix well. *Makes about 4 cups.*

Jerusalem Artichoke

These tasty tubers have crisp, sweet flesh with a flavor similar to globe artichokes. Jerusalem artichokes are not from the Middle East, nor are they botanical relatives of artichokes. They are the root of a perennial sunflower, which is why they are also called sunchokes.

BASICS **To choose** • Though available year-round, Jerusalem artichokes are at their best in fall and winter. Look for ones that are firm and smooth without too many hard-to-clean knobs protruding from them. Avoid any that are green or beginning to sprout.

To store • Wrap Jerusalem artichokes in plastic and refrigerate for up to 1 week.

To prepare • Scrub Jerusalem artichokes well to remove loose skin. Don't worry if you don't get every last bit. Small pieces of the pale, papery peel will not be noticeable in a finished dish.

PROBLEM SOLVER **To prevent browning** • Toss cut surfaces with lemon juice. Or dip into acidulated water (¼ cup lemon juice mixed with 4 cups water).

FLAVOR TIP **To use** • Shred or slice raw chokes for salads or crudités, or cook them in stir-fries or soups. Or boil or steam Jerusalem artichokes and then toss them with melted butter, lemon juice, salt, and pepper for a hot side dish. You can also serve baked whole Jerusalem artichokes as you would baked potatoes, or mash them right along with potatoes for a side dish.

JERUSALEM ARTICHOKE SOUP Toss 1½ pounds scrubbed and sliced Jerusalem artichoke with the juice of ½ lemon. Sauté in ½ stick (¼ cup) melted butter with 1 chopped onion, 1 peeled

j

and chopped parsnip, and ¼ teaspoon *each* salt and ground black pepper in a covered pot until soft, about 20 minutes, stirring occasionally. Add **3 cups chicken stock** or **canned broth** and simmer 20 minutes more. Puree soup and reheat. Stir in ¾ **cup buttermilk** over low heat. Do not reboil. *Makes 4 servings.*

Jicama

Strip away the thin, brown skin of this scruffy-looking tuber (pronounced "HEE-ka-mah"), and you'll be delighted by its refreshingly crunchy, juicy flesh.

BASICS ▼ **To choose** • Look for firm, unblemished tubers with smooth skin. Scratch the skin with a fingernail; it should be quite thin, and the flesh beneath it should be juicy. Thick-skinned jicamas with dry flesh will likely be fibrous and starchy and not much good for eating raw, but they can be used in stir-fries and other cooked dishes.

To store • Refrigerate jicama unwrapped for up to 3 weeks. Once it has been cut, wrap in plastic wrap and use within 1 week.

To peel • Cut off the two ends with a knife. Starting at either end, scrape the skin with the side of a teaspoon from end to end, following the curve and bumps of the jicama. The thin, papery peel will strip away with very little pressure.

FLAVOR TIPS ▼ **To use in place of crackers** • Cut disks of jicama for a tasty cracker substitute. They won't discolor or lose their crunch.

To use in stir-fries • Peeled and cut strips of jicama stay crunchy in stir-fries and take well to flavorful sauces. They also make a great substitute for water chestnuts.

To make a classic Mexican snack • Chill a medium jicama. Peel it and cut in half lengthwise. Cut crosswise into slices about ¼" thick. Squeeze fresh lime juice over the slices and sprinkle with salt and pure hot chile powder.

To add crunch to chicken salad • Stir ½ cup or more of peeled and chopped jicama into your favorite chicken salad.

JICAMA-ORANGE SALSA In a bowl, combine **2 small peeled and chopped jicamas, halved supremes of 3 oranges (orange segments with the protective membrane removed), ½ cup orange juice, 3 to 4 tablespoons lime juice, ¾ teaspoon salt,** and **⅛ to ¼ teaspoon ground red pepper.** Stir in **1 chopped medium tomato.** Serve with corn tortilla chips or spoon over grilled fish or chicken. *Makes about 4 cups.*

Julienne *see also* Slicing

Long, narrow rectangular slices of food are known as julienne. Cut about ⅛" thick, or roughly the size of a matchstick, julienne slices expose a large surface area of the food for quick cooking, as in a stir-fry. Julienne slices also make an attractive garnish for salads.

BASICS ▼ **To cut julienne strips** • Peel the ingredient if necessary and cut a thin strip from one side so  that it can lie flat on the work surface. Cut the ingredient crosswise into pieces 2" long. Cut each piece lengthwise into thin, vertical slabs. Stack the slabs and cut them lengthwise again into thin strips.

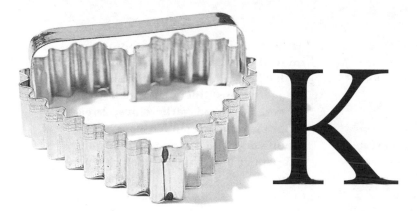

K

Kabobs *see also* Grilling

The ancient Turks, Greeks, and Romans made kabobs, but it's likely that cavemen or any primitive peoples who had some bits of meat and twigs did as well. They are a great way to grill meat, fish, or vegetables, all held together and quick to cook.

BASICS ▼ **To choose fish for kabobs** • Use firm-fleshed fish, such as salmon, tuna, or mako shark. It will hold its shape better than flaky fish such as cod or halibut. Seafood such as shrimp and scallops also work well.

To cook evenly • For foolproof kabobs, put each type of food on a separate skewer.

To cook mixed-food kabobs • Put quick-cooking and long-cooking items on separate skewers. For instance, vegetables, poultry, and seafood can be mixed on one skewer, while longer-cooking meats should go on a separate skewer. When mixing foods on one skewer, cut the faster-cooking foods, such as fruits, into larger chunks than the slower-cooking foods, such as zucchini or onions, so that they will all be done at the same time.

To cook thoroughly • Leave about ¼" between pieces (especially meats) to ensure thorough cooking.

To add firm vegetables to kabobs • Blanch or steam potatoes, carrots, cauliflower, and broccoli until almost tender before threading onto skewers.

To use bamboo or wooden skewers • Soak the skewers in water for 30 minutes before using to keep them from catching fire on the grill.

To use rosemary skewers • The thick, woody stems of large rosemary plants make wonderful skewers for kabobs. They're decorative and flavor food with rosemary's intoxicating scent. They work best with soft foods, such as tofu, zucchini, and other vegetables. For more flavor, keep the leaves on, poke a hole through the food with a metal skewer, then insert the whole rosemary branch, woody end first. This method works well with firm foods such as beef and pork.

PROBLEM SOLVERS ▼ **To prevent food from slipping on skewers** • Use 2 skewers for each kabob. Hold the skewers ¼" apart and thread food onto both 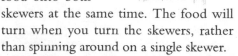 skewers at the same time. The food will turn when you turn the skewers, rather than spinning around on a single skewer.

To prevent food from sticking to skewers • First coat skewers (metal or soaked wooden ones) with cooking spray.

To avoid last-minute prep • Thread food onto skewers first, then marinate in a shallow dish or directly in a zipper-lock plastic bag.

FLAVOR
TIPS
▼ **To flavor kabobs** • Cut California bay leaves in half and thread the pieces between each chunk of food (especially good with chicken, swordfish, and tuna). Grill or broil as usual and discard the leaves as you eat.

To make moist chicken kabobs • Use boneless, skinless chicken thighs, cut into cubes or strips. They will remain moister than chicken breasts when grilled.

To make very tender beef kabobs • Use filet mignon. It's a bit more expensive, but the results are fabulous. No marinating is necessary for tenderness, but you can marinate for flavor. Use any simple vinaigrette or simply ½ cup red wine plus 1 tablespoon dried herbs. After cutting the beef into 1" cubes, marinate 2 to 24 hours in the fridge.

BANANA-COCONUT SHRIMP KABOBS Puree or mash ¼ **large banana** with **2 tablespoons lime juice, 1 tablespoon olive oil, ½ teaspoon ground turmeric,** and ¼ **teaspoon** *each* **salt and hot-pepper sauce.** Toss with **1 pound large, shelled, deveined shrimp** and marinate 1 hour in the refrigerator. Preheat the grill or broiler. Meanwhile, in a bowl, combine ⅓ cup *each* **cracker crumbs and toasted grated coconut.** Dip shrimp in crumb mixture and thread on skewers. Grill over a medium-hot fire or broil until shrimp is opaque, 4 to 6 minutes, turning halfway through cooking. Serve with lime wedges. *Makes 4 servings.*

INDIAN GROUND MEAT KABOBS (SEEKH KABAB) Preheat the grill. In a bowl, mix **1 pound lean ground lamb** or beef, **1 finely chopped onion** or **6 minced scallions,** ¼ **cup** *each* **chopped fresh cilantro and chopped fresh mint, 2 tablespoons finely chopped fresh ginger, 1 minced garlic clove, 2 teaspoons ground coriander seeds,** ¾ **teaspoon salt,** and ¼ **teaspoon** *each* **ground red pepper and ground black pepper.** Mix well, then form into sausage shapes 3" to 4" long and 1" thick. Carefully push each sausage lengthwise down through a separate skewer and squeeze slightly onto the skewer to make compact. Brush or spray lightly with oil and grill over a medium-hot fire until meat is no longer pink, 8 to 10 minutes, turning once or twice. *Makes 4 servings.*

Kasha

When buckwheat kernels have been hulled, roasted, and cracked, they are called kasha, or buckwheat groats. Although usually lumped in with grains, buckwheat is actually the seed of a plant related to rhubarb. It has a strong nutty flavor and bold earthy quality. Kasha is very popular in Eastern Europe and Russia for making kasha varnishkes (kasha with noodles). Buckwheat flour is also used to make blini and Japanese soba noodles.

FLAVOR
TIP
▼ **To add flavor and texture to salads** • Cook Basic Kasha (below). Add to pasta salads, green salads, or Caesar salad.

BASIC KASHA In a bowl, stir together **1 cup kasha** and **1 egg.** Let stand 3 minutes. Heat a skillet or saucepan over medium heat. Add kasha mixture to the dry pan and stir until dry but not browned, about 3 minutes. Add **2 cups chicken broth, beef broth,** or **water; 2 tablespoons butter;** ¾ **teaspoon salt;** and ⅛

k

teaspoon ground black pepper. Cover and simmer until liquid is absorbed and grains are tender, about 15 minutes. Fluff with a fork and serve hot. *Makes 4 servings.*

KASHA VARNISHKES Cook **Basic Kasha** (opposite page). Meanwhile, heat **3 tablespoons rendered chicken fat, butter,** or **vegetable oil** in a separate large skillet. Add **1 large, finely chopped onion** and sauté until golden, 5 to 8 minutes. Boil ½ **pound bow-tie pasta** or **wide noodles** until tender, about 8 minutes. Drain. Add noodles and

kasha to onion mixture and toss. Add ½ **teaspoon salt.** If dry, splash in a little water or broth. Sprinkle with **1 tablespoon chopped fresh parsley.** For **Mushroom Kasha Varnishkes,** sauté ½ **pound sliced mushrooms** along with onions. **Add** ⅓ **cup chopped toasted almonds** or **pecans** along with noodles. *Makes 4 servings.*

Ketchup

The British learned to make ketchup condiments from the Chinese (who called it *ke-tsiap***), but it was Mr. Heinz who borrowed the idea**

KETCHUP CUISINE

Most regular ketchup users have yet to see its culinary potential outside of garnishing burgers and fries. Here are 3 recipes to broaden that horizon.

Bubby Heinz's Brisket: Rub **2 to 3 pounds beef brisket** with ½ **teaspoon salt** and ¼ **teaspoon ground black pepper.** In a large skillet or Dutch oven, heat **1 tablespoon oil** until hot. Add brisket and brown on both sides. Remove. Add **2 large chopped onions** and stir until browned. Add 2½ **cups** *each* **ketchup and water.** Heat to a simmer over medium heat. Add brisket, cover, and simmer until meat is fork-tender, about 2 hours. Skim fat from gravy. Slice brisket and serve with gravy. *Makes 6 to 8 servings.*

Red Bacon Dressing: In a deep skillet, sauté **1 finely chopped onion** and **1 large minced garlic clove** in the **rendered fat of 3 cooked bacon slices (about 1 tablespoon).** Add ½ **cup apple cider vinegar, 2 tablespoons**

sugar, **1 tablespoon ketchup,** ¼ **teaspoon salt,** and ⅛ **teaspoon ground black pepper.** Use hot, tossed with **1 head of strong-tasting greens such as escarole, chicory** or **curly endive,** broken into bite-size pieces. Crumble the bacon into the salad if you've cooked it just for this purpose. *Makes 4 servings.*

Thai Fried Noodles: Soak ¾ **pound rice vermicelli** in hot water, 15 minutes. Drain. Stir-fry **3 minced garlic cloves** and ½ **teaspoon red-pepper flakes** in **3 tablespoons oil** over medium-high heat, 10 seconds. Add **1 tablespoon sugar, 3 tablespoons fish sauce,** and **2 tablespoons ketchup.** Stir until sugar dissolves. Add drained noodles and **2 beaten eggs** and stir-fry 1 minute. Add ¾ **cup bean sprouts** and stir-fry another minute. Turn onto a plate and garnish with ¼ **cup raw bean sprouts, 2 tablespoons** *each* **chopped peanuts and chopped fresh cilantro, 2 sliced scallions,** and **1 sliced lime.** *Makes 4 servings.*

k

from Great Britain, adding tomato to please American tastebuds. Before that, ketchup was a runnier concoction, often made from mushrooms or walnuts.

BASICS ▼ **To store** • Unopened bottles of ketchup will keep indefinitely if stored in a cool, dark place. Once opened, ketchup will keep indefinitely in the refrigerator.

To loosen ketchup that won't pour • Hold the bottle on its side, so that air can get around the ketchup in the bottle, and shake the ketchup loose. If that fails, stick a table knife into it while holding the bottle on its side. Rotate the knife until the ketchup starts to pour.

QUICK AND EASY KETCHUP In a large nonstick saucepan, combine **3 cans (6 ounces each) tomato paste,** ½ **cup packed light brown sugar,** 1½ **teaspoons** *each* **salt and celery salt,** ½ **teaspoon** *each* **ground red pepper and ground cinnamon,** and ¼ **teaspoon** *each* **ground cloves and ground black pepper.** Gradually stir in 1½ **cups hot water,** ⅔ **cup apple cider vinegar,** and **1 tablespoon Worcestershire sauce.** Bring to a boil over medium heat. Reduce heat to low and simmer until thick and rich, 15 to 20 minutes, stirring often. If mixture splatters, cover with a splatter screen. Pour into clean jars or bottles with tight lids and store in the refrigerator. *Makes about 3 cups.*

Kitchen Flow *see also* Mise en Place

The single most important element determining the speed and ease of cooking happens long before you chop a carrot or preheat an oven. It is the basic layout of your kitchen.

BASICS ▼ **To set up an efficient kitchen layout** • Whether you're starting from scratch or working with an existing layout, arrange your kitchen for a smooth flow of work from storage areas to preparation areas to cooking areas to cleaning areas. Start with a plan on paper. Draw walls, doors, and windows to scale on a piece of graph paper. Make paper or cardboard cutouts to scale of all appliances. Use the cutouts to determine the best arrangement of work areas in your space. Depending on room size and shape, choose a U-shape, L-shape, or open galley layout.

To form a work triangle • Whatever shape you settle on, try to link the refrigerator, sink, and stove in a triangle, which minimizes walking and eliminates the need to cross one work area to get to another. If possible, keep the total distance between storage, cooking, and cleaning areas to no more than 23 feet. When planning a work triangle, consider how people will walk through the kitchen. Avoid planning a walking path that crosses through the triangle, especially the space between the stove and sink.

To choose locations of counters • Link all work areas with counters, if possible. Once you have found the best placement for major appliances, connect them with a system of level and continuous counters to make cleanup easy and to ensure that you have work surfaces and resting surfaces where you need them. Alternatively, you can plan for separate work stations. If linked counters aren't possible, plan a center island or place a freestanding roll cart where you'll need it most. Leave room to chop and prepare ingredients near the stove or sink.

To choose countertop materials • Choose materials for the counters that fit

COOKING IN A CRAMPED KITCHEN

If you have a small kitchen and limited counter space, you can still cook *and* cook to entertain.

Minimize. Kitchens are natural breeding grounds for gadget overgrowth. Keep only what you use, and give away the rest. Less clutter, less frustration. Stow away rarely used items that you just can't part with, be they pasta makers or ice crushers. For easy recall, keep a list of these items and their locations on the back of a cupboard door or in a utility drawer.

Choose compact appliances. Small appliances keep your precious counter space open. Instead of a gargantuan standing mixer, consider a handheld mixer. Go for an immersion blender rather than a conventional blender. Choose a handheld citrus reamer over an electric juicer. And a reliable chef's knife can often take the place of a food processor. Or choose a mini processor.

Keep cookbooks in bookcases. If counter space is tight, why cram in a favorite cookbook? Instead, photocopy favorite recipes, then tape them up on a wall near your work space. Or use a fork for a recipe card holder. If you love working directly from cookbooks, consider buying a cookbook holder, which will prop it up and hold open the page, taking up less counter space.

Think vertical. If you don't have shelving in your kitchen, put some up. Inexpensive units are widely available and easy to install. Use a cutlery magnet strip to keep knives at hand but up on the wall rather than in a block on precious counter space. Consider placing a Peg-Board on your wall to hang utensils, strainers, stainless steel bowls, even pans. Or use baskets or wall-mounted magazine racks.

Clean as you go. This is a cardinal rule of cooking, even when space is abundant. Keep a large bowl of sudsy water in your sink (or fill the whole sink) and place dirty utensils, bowls, and dishes there as soon as you're done with them. Position a trash can or bucket by your side so that any waste can be immediately removed.

Stack instead of spreading. When making batches of baked goods such as cookies, stack baking sheets or cooling racks, propping the racks on tin cans. Stack bowls too, whether they contain finger foods or the evening's side dishes. Place a plate in between each bowl and a thin towel on top of the plate if the surface seems slippery.

Create surfaces. Expand your counter space by sleuthing out hidden horizontal surfaces. Any unused tables nearby? Use them to set out food, equipment, or utensils. Place items on the top of your refrigerator. Any unused burners on the stove? They make a great place to warm plates or hold platters. If you aren't using the oven, take advantage of the racks inside for extra storage (you might want to tape over the heat controls so that no one accidentally turns on the oven). You can also pull out a cabinet drawer and set a tray on top of it to hold foods or utensils. Straddle a cooling rack or baking sheet over half of the sink for added space. You can even open up a sturdy ironing board and cover it with a long cloth for a buffet table.

k

their use. Stone or ceramic tile near the stove or oven gives you a place to rest hot pots and pans; a cutting board near a sink speeds cleanup after chopping.

To plan lighting • A combination of focused light and diffused light works best to illuminate specific work areas and to provide pleasant ambient lighting for the rest of the room. Place focused lights, such as under-cabinet lights, directly over work areas. Or choose small, flexible spotlights so that you can direct the light to where it's needed most. Place overhead lighting in the center of the room and over dining areas.

To organize items in your kitchen • Easy access is the key to kitchen efficiency. Place items where you'll need them most: near the stove, cutting surface, or preparation area.

To store pots and utensils • Hang pots on racks or hooks near the stove, or keep them in heavy-duty drawers beneath or next to the stove. Keep knives near cutting surfaces in a knife block, on a magnetic strip on the wall, or sheathed and stowed in nearby drawers. Store often-used utensils next to appropriate work areas. Place metal spatulas, slotted spoons, and stirring spoons upright in a crock or jar near the stove. Whisks, scrapers, and mixing spoons go in another crock near the prep area to keep them from getting splattered with grease.

To keep work areas tidy • Nothing slows you down more than slicing or dicing at awkward angles to avoid piles of food. Instead, keep bowls near the cutting area to transfer prepped food. Also, have a scrap bowl on hand to readily dispose of waste such as vegetable trimmings. It also helps to stow small appliances; you can use corners or deep counters to keep them out of the way.

To have salt at the ready • Keep a small bowl or low-sided container of salt near your stove. If your prep area is far from the stove, have another salt bowl there as well. These let you readily dip into the salt with a measuring spoon instead of trying to pour the salt from a container (always a guaranteed spill). Bowls let you pinch up some salt and sprinkle it too, which gives you a much better feel for how heavily you are salting than if you use a salt shaker. Bowls also minimize clumping, whereas a salt shaker used over a hot stove usually absorbs steam and gets annoyingly clogged. Kosher salt works best near the stove because its bigger grains are easier to pinch up. Near the prep area, stick with table salt, to ensure proper measuring for baked goods.

To keep oil from going rancid • Store oils close to the stove, but not too close. Oils are used most at the stove but will spoil faster if kept too close to the heat. The ideal spot is between your stove and prep area. That way the oils can be easily accessed from both areas and kept safe from heat. Use dark containers or closed cabinets to keep the oils out of the light, which also speeds spoilage.

Kiwifruit

Kiwi is an ideal fruit to pack: juicy, not bulky, and nutritious. In fact, kiwi is often regarded as one of the most nutritious fruits, followed by papaya, mango, and orange. Two kiwis contain more potassium than a banana, as much fiber as a grapefruit, and twice as much vitamin C as an orange.

BASICS ▼ **To peel** • Cut a slice from both ends of the kiwi and remove the peel in strips running from end to end, using a small knife or vegetable peeler. Or, after cutting off the ends, hold the kiwi in your hand and insert a dinnerware tablespoon into one end of the kiwi, right next to the skin. Rotate the spoon around the fruit just under the skin. The fruit will pop right out of its skin.

TIME SAVERS ▼ **To ripen faster** • Place kiwi in a brown bag with an apple or a banana. Seal and let stand at room temperature overnight. Ethylene gas emitted by apples and bananas helps other fruits ripen more quickly.

To quickly slice • Use an egg slicer.

KIWI-ENDIVE SALAD Slice **2 Belgian endive heads** on the diagonal and place on 4 plates (or use about **5 ounces clean spinach**). In a bowl, toss **3 peeled, quartered, and chopped kiwifruit**; **½ peeled, seeded, and chopped papaya**; **3 quartered and sliced plum tomatoes**; and **⅓ cup vinaigrette, such as Citrus Vinaigrette (page 422)**. Spoon over endive. *Makes 4 servings.*

Knives *see also* Chopping

Almost any good cook will tell you that a good-quality knife is the single most important tool in the kitchen.

BASICS ▼ **To choose** • There's no reason to buy a lot of knives. Just be sure to stock 3 top-quality ones: a chef's knife (for chopping, slicing, and dicing), a paring knife (for, um . . . paring), and a serrated knife (for bread and tomatoes). The chef's knife is most important. Men are usually comfortable with an 8" or 10" chef's knife; many women prefer a 6" knife for its lighter weight. Hold the knife in your hand. It should feel comfortable and be easy to grip. The knife that feels good in your hand is the right knife for you.

To get a sturdy blade • Look for knives that are fully forged or full-tang, meaning that they are made from a single piece of metal that is beaten, ground into shape, and extends from the blade to the back of the handle, where it is usually riveted into place. Avoid stamped knives, cut from sheet metal, because they are not as strong. Also, make sure that the blade is made of high-carbon stainless steel, which keeps its edge longer and won't stain or discolor food.

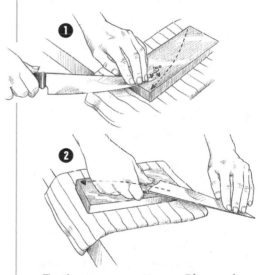

To sharpen on a stone • Place a clean whetstone on a damp towel to prevent slipping. Position the stone and towel near the edge of a sturdy surface. Lubricate the stone with water or mineral oil to help reduce friction, which could eventually harm the blade. Position the wide end of the knife blade against the upper corner of the stone and tilt the blade up at an angle of about 15 degrees. Move the blade toward you in an arc over the stone, beginning with the wide end and ending with the tip, so that the entire length of the blade gets sharpened ❶. It will feel like you are shaving slices off the top of the stone. Repeat 10 to 15 times, keeping an even pressure.

k

Turn the knife over and repeat with the opposite side of the blade, making an equal number of strokes and keeping an equal amount of pressure ❷, page 251. Always sharpen the blade in the same direction to ensure that the edge remains even and properly aligned.

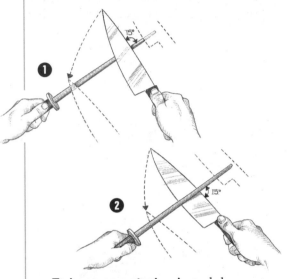

To hone on a steel • A steel does not sharpen a knife, but it hones or aligns the blade between sharpenings to keep its cutting edge razor-sharp. Find a spot where you have plenty of room to work safely. Grip the steel safely behind the guard with your thumb and forefinger.

Hold the wide end of the blade against the tip of the steel at an angle of about 15 degrees. Draw the blade of the knife down along the steel, curving slightly so that the entire edge touches the steel. Keep the pressure even ❶.

Reverse the knife, holding the other side of the blade against the other side of the steel. Draw the blade down in the same direction as before, curving slightly as you go ❷. Use a light touch, stroking evenly and consistently. The knife should make a slight ringing sound as you work.

A heavy grinding sound means that you're applying too much pressure. Do five sweeps on each side of the blade. If the blade requires more than five strokes per side, it should be sharpened on a stone.

To clean • Wash knives in hot, soapy water but never in the dishwasher, which could ruin the blade and the handle (especially if the handle is wooden). Also, avoid dropping knives into a sink full of water, where they can be dulled by other utensils or metal pots and could injure anyone reaching into the sink. Be sure to dry knives thoroughly between cutting tasks and before you store them.

To save storage space • A knife block works well but takes up counter space. To save space, install a cutlery magnetic strip on the wall.

To protect knife blades for storage • If storing knives in a drawer, stick the sharp point of each knife into an old wine cork. The cork helps protect the knife tip and helps prevent the blades from knocking into each other. Alternatively, you can make a homemade sheath from an old cardboard box. Using scissors, cut off a rectangular piece of corrugated cardboard that's just large enough to fit over the knife blade. Starting at a short end of the rectangular piece, use the scissors to snip through the center of the corrugation, creating a pocket for the blade. Stop just short of the other end, so that the blade will not poke through. Insert the knife blade into the sheath. Store flat in a drawer.

To help preserve a knife blade • Always cut on wood or plastic. Avoid glass, metal, and stone, which can ruin the blade.

TIME SAVER ▼ **To sharpen knives quickly** • Use an electric knife sharpener. These items are available from most kitchen stores and cooking catalogs. They are somewhat expensive but save loads of time.

Lamb *see also* Doneness Tests and Temperatures (page 572)

Known for its tenderness and delicate, yet rich flavor, lamb is the meat of sheep that are less than 1 year old. Mutton is lamb that is more than 2 years old.

BASICS ▼ **To choose** • Look for bright, moist lamb that is not sticky or slimy. The fat on the surface should be white and waxy-looking. Depending on the age of the animal, the color of the flesh should range from pink to pale red.

To store • For the freshest flavor, cook lamb on the same day that you buy it. Whole cuts keep best and may be refrigerated for up to 4 days. Ground lamb has a greater area of exposed surfaces and is more susceptible to contamination, so refrigerate it for no more than 2 days.

To freeze • Carefully wrap and freeze whole cuts for up to 9 months and ground lamb for up to 4 months.

To cook firmer cuts • Moist-heat cooking methods such as braising, poaching, or stewing help tenderize firmer cuts of lamb, such as shank, breast, shoulder, neck slices, and riblets.

To cook tender cuts • Dry-heat methods such as broiling or grilling work well with tender cuts such as shoulder chops, rib chops, sirloin, butterflied whole leg, leg steaks, and cubed kabobs.

To roast • Roasting works best for rolled and tied boneless leg and shoulder roasts, or for bone-in leg of lamb.

FLAVOR TIP ▼ **To make "lamburgers"** • Substitute lean ground lamb pound for pound when making hamburgers. Top each burger with a few mint leaves.

ORANGE-MINT MARINADE FOR LAMB Combine **3 tablespoons** *each* **bottled steak sauce and orange juice, 2 tablespoons chopped fresh mint,** and **1 tablespoon white wine vinegar.** Use to marinate **1 pound sirloin or leg steaks,** then grill or broil. *Makes about ½ cup.*

ROASTED LAMB WITH HERBES DE PROVENCE Rub **3 tablespoons herbes de Provence (page 233)** into **1 bone-in lamb leg roast (about 5 pounds).** Arrange **2 pounds sliced golden potatoes** on the bottom of a roasting pan. Place lamb on potatoes and roast at 325°F until a thermometer inserted into the center registers 145°F (medium-rare), about 2 hours. Let stand 10 minutes before slicing. *Makes 10 to 12 servings.*

1

BRAISED LAMB SHANKS Trim fat from **4 small, meaty lamb shanks (4 pounds total).** In a large, deep Dutch oven, sauté 2 lamb shanks in **1 tablespoon vegetable oil** until well-browned all over, 6 minutes. Repeat with other 2 shanks. Transfer to a large bowl. To the pan, add **2 finely chopped onions, 2 finely chopped celery ribs,** and **2 finely chopped carrots.** Sauté until lightly browned. Add **1 can (28 ounces) crushed tomatoes, 1 cup dry red wine, 1 tablespoon chopped fresh rosemary (or 1 teaspoon dried), 1 cinnamon stick (3"),** and **2 teaspoons sugar.** Return shanks to pot. Cover and braise gently over low heat until fork-tender, about 2 hours, turning once or twice. Blot off fat from surface with a paper towel. Add **½ teaspoon salt** and **¼ teaspoon ground black pepper.** Serve hot with pasta, rice, or couscous. Sprinkle with fresh parsley to garnish. *Makes 6 to 8 servings.*

GRILLED LAMB WITH CILANTRO AND CUMIN In a food processor, combine **1 quartered onion, 2 tablespoons** *each* **olive oil and fresh cilantro, 1 teaspoon ground cumin,** and **¼ teaspoon** *each* **salt and ground black pepper.** Use mixture to coat **4 to 6 double-rib lamb chops** or **8 to 12 single-rib chops.** Cover and marinate, refrigerated, 2 hours or overnight. Preheat the grill. Brush off marinade and grill over a medium-hot fire until juices run clear and center registers 145°F (medium-rare) on an instant-read thermometer, about 5 minutes per side for double-rib chops and 3 minutes per side for single-rib chops. *Makes 4 to 6 servings.*

1

Lasagna *see also* Pasta

Thin sheets of noodles are probably one of the earliest forms of pasta. In this popular baked dish, lasagna noodles are boiled and layered with various cheeses and, usually, tomato, meat, or white sauce.

TIME SAVER ▼ **To save time** • Use no-boil lasagna noodles. Be sure to cover the noodles completely with sauce or cheese so that they absorb enough moisture to become tender.

FLAVOR TIP ▼ **To add flavor** • When layering your favorite lasagna, add dabs of pesto interspersed with dabs of ricotta cheese. Or, add 20 fresh basil leaves, torn in pieces. See also recipe on opposite page.

Leeks

One of the sweeter members of the onion family, leeks look like overgrown scallions.

BASICS ▼ **To choose** • Available year-round, leeks tend to be best from the fall until the spring, when their cores begin to turn tough. Look for those with bright, crisp leaves, and buy the smallest ones in the market, which tend to be sweeter.

To store • Put leeks in a perforated plastic bag and refrigerate up to 1 week.

To wash • Leeks often hide a great deal of grit in their many tight leaf layers. The easiest way to wash them is to slice or chop them first, then place the pieces in a large bowl. Fill the bowl with cool water. Swish the leeks about with your hands to loosen any dirt, which will settle at the bottom of the bowl. Lift out the cleaned leek pieces with a slotted spoon or small strainer. Avoid pouring the leeks and water from the bowl through a strainer or

Cheese and Sausage Lasagna

The sauce for this dish can be made ahead of time and refrigerated or even frozen until you're ready to make the lasagna. You can also assemble the entire dish ahead of time and freeze it until you're ready to bake it. Just transfer the frozen lasagna directly from the freezer to the oven and add 15 minutes to the cooking time.

2	**tablespoons olive oil**
1	**pound sweet Italian sausage, casings removed**
2	**onions, finely chopped**
2	**small carrots, finely chopped**
⅓	**cup finely chopped fresh parsley**
4	**garlic cloves, minced**
2	**cans (28 ounces each) whole tomatoes, drained**
1½	**teaspoons salt**
½	**teaspoon ground black pepper**
12	**lasagna noodles**
1	**container (15 ounces) ricotta cheese, divided**
12	**ounces thinly sliced or shredded fresh mozzarella cheese, divided**
¼	**cup grated Parmesan cheese**

1. Warm the oil in a large skillet over medium heat. Add the sausage and cook until no longer pink, 5 minutes, stirring. Add the onions and carrots and cook until the onions begin to soften, 5 minutes, stirring. Add the parsley and garlic. Cook 1 minute longer. Stir in the tomatoes, crushing them with the back of a spoon. Add the salt and pepper. Simmer until thick, 20 minutes.

2. Preheat the oven to 375°F. Lightly oil a 13" × 9" baking dish.

3. Meanwhile, cook the lasagna according to package directions. Spread a thin layer of the tomato sauce in the bottom of the prepared baking dish. Top with a layer of noodles. Spread with one-third of the ricotta and one-quarter of the mozzarella. Top with one-third of the sausage and 1 cup of the tomato sauce. Add another layer of noodles. Continue layering until all the ingredients are used, ending with a layer of tomato sauce sprinkled with the final layer of the mozzarella and all of the Parmesan.

4. Bake until the top is brown and bubbly, 45 minutes. Let stand at least 15 minutes before serving.

Makes 10 servings

colander, which could cause the dirt to fall back onto the cleaned leeks.

To slice • Trim off the root and the dark green leaves at the top of the leek, leaving about 1" of the pale green part attached to the white. Cut the leek in half lengthwise, and then cut crosswise into thin slices.

Leftovers

Leftovers are an opportunity. Because most of the cooking is already done, time is cut to a minimum. Check out the ideas below. For more ideas, see Beef (page 31), Chicken (page 103), and Turkey (page 520).

Lemongrass

The stalk of the lemongrass plant has a floral, lemon-lime flavor that is one of the hallmarks of many Vietnamese, Malaysian, Thai, and other Southeast Asian dishes. Each stalk looks like a stiff, fibrous scallion and can be used raw or cooked in marinades, salads, curries, and soups.

BASICS
▼
To choose • Look for lemongrass stalks that are firm and pale to medium green, with pink-tinged white bulbs at the base. Any that are dry and yellow are past their prime and have lost most of their flavor and fragrance.

HOW TO LEVERAGE LEFTOVERS

Inside every leftover is another meal waiting to happen.

From leftover pot roast, Mexican Beef Tostadas: Finely chop **6 to 8 slices leftover pot roast.** In a medium skillet over high heat, sauté **1 small chopped onion** in **2 teaspoons olive oil** until lightly browned, about 4 minutes. Add the meat, **2 minced garlic cloves,** and **2 teaspoons chili powder.** Stir 2 minutes. Stir in **2 tablespoons ketchup.** Warm **8 corn** or **flour tortillas** in a microwave oven on high power, 1 minute. Serve 2 tortillas per person, each topped with ¼ **cup warmed refried beans,** a layer of the meat mixture, ¼ **cup shredded lettuce, 1 tablespoon shredded Cheddar cheese, 1 avocado slice,** and **1 tablespoon salsa.** *Makes 4 servings.*

From leftover roast turkey or chicken, Mole Poblano: In a saucepan, sauté **2 chopped onions** in **2 tablespoons oil** until tender. Add **4 minced garlic cloves, 2 teaspoons ground cumin, 1 teaspoon** *each* dried oregano and dried thyme, ½ **teaspoon ground cinnamon,** ¼ **cup canned crushed** tomatoes, and **2 tablespoons cornmeal.** Stir to mix. Add **2½ cups chicken broth,** ¼ **teaspoon salt,** and ⅛ **teaspoon ground black pepper.** Heat to boiling. Add **1 drained can (11 ounces) corn kernels** and **1½ pounds leftover roasted turkey or chicken meat,** cut into chunks. Simmer 10 minutes. Stir in ½ **ounce finely chopped semisweet chocolate** and **2 tablespoons chopped fresh cilantro.** *Makes 6 to 8 servings.*

From leftover poached or baked fish, Fettuccine with Fish, Capers, and Tomato: Boil **12 ounces dried fettuccine** according to package directions. While pasta cooks, sauté **1 finely chopped onion** in **2 tablespoons olive oil** until tender, 2 minutes. Add **1 minced garlic clove, 1 tablespoon chopped fresh dill leaves, 1 drained can (15 ounces) diced tomatoes, 1 tablespoon tomato paste,** and **2 tablespoons capers.** Heat to boiling. Add the **juice of ½ lemon, 1 cup leftover flaked poached salmon** (or other fish), ¼ **teaspoon salt,** and ⅛ **teaspoon ground black pepper.** Drain pasta and toss with sauce. *Makes 4 servings.*

1

To store • Wrap lemongrass in plastic wrap and refrigerate for up to 2 weeks. Or, for longer storage, peel off the tough outer leaves, wrap tightly in plastic wrap, seal in a zipper-lock freezer bag, and freeze for up to 3 months.

FLAVOR TIPS ▼ **To use in broths, soups, and stews** • Peel off and discard the tough outer leaves until you reach the scallion-like bulb. Pound it with a mallet to soften the fibers and release flavors. Add to hot liquids near the beginning of cooking time, and simmer. Remove before serving.

To use in marinades, salads, and stir-fries • Peel off and discard the tough outer leaves until you reach the scallion-like bulb. Slice the bulbs into thin rounds, then finely chop and add as a flavoring.

Lemons *see also* Citrus Fruits; Zest

Prized for their sweet, acidic juice and flavorful zest, lemons have a wide range of uses in the kitchen. They're essential for rounding out the flavors of many sauces and are the primary flavoring in a host of desserts. A bit of fresh lemon juice is often all that is needed to enliven a dull-tasting dish, especially chicken and seafood.

BASICS ▼ **To choose** • Look for lemons with smooth, brightly colored rinds and no tinges of green. The best are firm, plump, and heavy for their size.

To store • Refrigerate for 2 to 3 weeks.

To freeze • Both grated lemon zest and fresh-squeezed juice can be frozen. Pour the juice into ice cube trays and freeze. When they are solid, transfer the cubes to zipper-lock freezer bags and freeze for up to 6 months. Freeze grated zest in freezer bags for up to 6 months.

To remove zest • Be sure to remove the zest before squeezing the juice, or it will be a nearly impossible task. Also, to avoid a bitter taste, make sure that you remove only the outer yellow layer, or zest, and not the inner white pith. Special zesting tools do the job best. Or you can rub a lemon back and forth over the small, nubby side of a grater to make zest. Once you have removed the zest from a lemon, the remaining whole fruit can be refrigerated for up to 1 week. One medium lemon yields 2 to 3 teaspoons of zest.

Fascinating Fact: The states of California and Arizona produce approximately 95 percent of the U.S. lemon crop.

To squeeze juice • An inexpensive, handheld citrus reamer is excellent for juicing lemons. Just cut the lemon in half and firmly twist the reamer into each half. If you don't have a reamer, use a fork, twisting the tines into each lemon half. An average medium lemon yields 2 to 4 tablespoons of juice.

To squeeze maximum juice • Bring lemons to room temperature and roll under your palm to soften the fruit and get the juices flowing. Or, pierce 1 lemon with a fork and microwave it on medium power for 10 to 20 seconds.

To catch seeds when juicing • Place a mesh sieve over the bowl or dish into which you are squeezing the juice. Use a rubber spatula to press out any extra juice that has settled in the strainer. Or, squeeze the lemon over the tines of a fork, which will catch any seeds. You can also wrap a piece of cheesecloth over each lemon half

1

Sweet–Tart Lemon Cake Bars

Two of our most basic flavors, sweet and tart, blend in perfect harmony in these cakey, crumbly bars. The vanilla and walnuts in the frosting contribute additional layers of flavor.

Bars

1½	**cups all-purpose flour**
½	**teaspoon baking soda**
3	**large eggs, separated**
¼	**teaspoon salt**
1	**cup sifted confectioners' sugar**
1	**stick (½ cup) butter, softened**
¾	**cup granulated sugar**
1½	**teaspoons grated lemon zest**
⅓	**cup lemon juice, divided**

Vanilla–Walnut Frosting

2	**tablespoons butter, softened**
1⅓	**cups sifted confectioners' sugar**
1	**tablespoon milk**
1½	**teaspoons vanilla extract**
½	**cup finely chopped walnuts**

1. *To make the bars:* Preheat the oven to 350°F. Grease and flour a 13" × 9" baking pan.

2. In a medium bowl, combine the flour and baking soda.

3. In a large bowl, using an electric mixer on medium speed, beat the egg whites and salt until soft peaks begin to form. Gradually beat in the confectioners' sugar and beat until almost stiff.

4. In another large bowl, beat the butter until smooth. Gradually beat in the granulated sugar. Beat in the egg yolks, one at a time. Add the lemon zest and one-third of the flour mixture. Beat just until blended. Beat in half of the lemon juice. Beat in another one-third of the flour mixture and the remaining lemon juice. Beat in the remaining flour mixture just until blended. Stir in a large spoonful of the egg whites. Quickly fold in the remaining egg whites. Spread evenly into the prepared baking pan. Bake until a wooden pick inserted in the center comes out clean, 30 to 35 minutes. Cool in the pan on a rack until just warm, 15 minutes.

5. *To make the frosting:* In a medium bowl, with an electric mixer on medium speed, beat the butter 10 seconds. Beat in the confectioners' sugar. Add the milk and vanilla extract. Beat until smooth.

6. Spread frosting evenly over the slightly warm cake. Sprinkle with the walnuts. Allow to cool before cutting.

Makes 24 bars (½ cup frosting)

1

before juicing. If any seeds fall into the juice, remove them with a fork.

To extract just a few drops of juice • Pierce the lemon with a toothpick or the tip of a paring knife. Squeeze out some juice through the hole. Refrigerate the leftover lemon in a zipper-lock plastic bag and use within a few days.

LEMONADE Squeeze **4 to 6 lemons** to make 1 cup juice. In a pitcher, combine ¾ **cup sugar** and **1 cup hot tap water.** Stir until sugar is completely dissolved. Let cool. Add the lemon juice and **3 additional cups cold water.** If desired, add **5 or 6 thin lemon slices.** Chill. Serve over ice cubes. Add more water, sugar, or lemon juice to taste. Also try with lime juice. *Makes 4 servings.*

PROBLEM SOLVERS ▼ **To keep low-acidity foods from darkening** • Foods such as bananas, peaches, and avocados darken quickly when exposed to air. To delay this oxidation, rub any cut surfaces with lemon juice.

To cut the acidity of lemon juice • Add a pinch of salt or baking soda.

HEALTHY HINT ▼ **To soothe a sore throat or congested head** • Put 1 or 2 thin slices of lemon in a teacup or mug. If desired, add 1 slice fresh ginger, pricked all over to release the juice. Add boiling water to fill. Sweeten to taste and sip like tea.

Lentils

One of the oldest cultivated crops in the world, high-protein lentils are small, thin-skinned, and fast-cooking, requiring no soaking. They are delicious, economical, and extremely versatile.

BASICS ▼ **To choose** • All lentils have an earthy, almost nutty flavor. Brown lentils, sometimes called green, are the most common type and are greenish-brown in color. Small French green lentils are smaller and darker green, and they cook up firmer than brown lentils. They hold their shape well and have excellent flavor. Red lentils are slightly smaller and more orange than red. They are popular for making Indian dals (lentil dishes) and turn bright yellow during cooking. Yellow lentils also fall into the red lentil category; they cook fast and fall apart during cooking, making them ideal for dal. A final color, black lentils, also called beluga lentils, are very tiny and harder to come by.

To sort and rinse • Lentils are sometimes dusty and may have tiny pebbles mixed among them. To sort the bad from the good, spread the lentils out in a single layer on a baking sheet and pick out the stones and any shriveled or discolored beans. Then, dump the beans into a large bowl of water and swish around. Discard any beans that float to the top. Transfer to a sieve and rinse the beans under running water, then transfer to a pan for cooking.

To cook • There is no need to soak lentils. Simply mix ½ pound lentils (1⅛ cups) with 3 cups water and heat to boiling. Reduce the heat to low and simmer until lentils are soft, about 15 to 25 minutes. Add garlic, onions, herbs, or spices to the water to season the lentils, but avoid adding salt or acidic ingredients such as tomatoes until the lentils are fully cooked. Adding these ingredients too early prevents the lentils from softening, thereby increasing cooking time. If using lentils for salad, drain them. If making a soup, keep the cooking liquid. One cup dried lentils makes about 3 cups cooked.

EASY LENTIL SALAD Sauté **1 large chopped onion** in **2 tablespoons olive oil** until tender. Add **1 minced garlic clove, 2 bay leaves, ¼ teaspoon red-pepper flakes,** and **3 cups (1⅓ pounds) sorted and rinsed brown lentils.** Add **2 quarts water** and simmer until lentils are tender, about 30 minutes. Drain, remove bay leaves, and mix in **2 tablespoons extra-virgin olive oil** and **3 tablespoons lemon juice.** Cool. Toss with **½ cup bottled garlic salad dressing, ¼ cup chopped fresh parsley, ¼ teaspoon salt,** and **⅛ teaspoon ground black pepper.** Chill. Serve garnished with **1 tomato** cut in wedges and **12 oil-cured black olives.**

Makes about 8 servings.

LENTIL SOUP WITH BACON Cut **4 to 6 slices bacon** into small pieces. Cook in a large soup pot over medium heat until cooked through, crisp, and browned. Tilt pan and spoon off all but 1 tablespoon of the fat. Add **1 large chopped onion, 3 peeled and chopped carrots, 2 sliced celery ribs,** and **1 large minced garlic clove.** Cook over medium-low heat until softened, 5 to 8 minutes. Add **6 cups chicken stock** or **canned broth** and **2 cups water.** Bring to a boil over medium-high heat. Add **2¼ cups (1 pound) sorted and rinsed lentils** and **1 teaspoon dried basil, oregano,** or **thyme.** Reduce heat to medium-low and simmer until tender, about 30 minutes. Add **1 cup diced canned tomatoes with juice** and **1 teaspoon salt.** Simmer 15 minutes longer. If too thick, add broth to thin.

Makes 8 servings.

Lettuce *see also* Salads

Sweet, juicy lettuce leaves are the base for a wide range of refreshing salads.

BASICS **To choose** • The best heads of lettuce are dense and heavy for their size with unblemished leaves. Avoid limp heads with brown spots or hollow centers.

To store • First, soak the lettuce in cold water to help the leaves absorb as much moisture as possible. Then, spin off all the moisture left on the surface of the leaves in a salad spinner. Layer the lettuce leaves between paper towels to absorb any remaining water, and transfer the leaves to a zipper-lock plastic bag. Squeeze the air out of the bag and refrigerate for up to several weeks.

To core non-headed leaf lettuce • Snap the leaves off individually from the core, starting at the outermost leaves and working your way inward.

To remove the rib from a leaf of lettuce • Fold the leaf in half lengthwise, down the center of the rib. Slice or pull the leaf along the edge of the rib and lift the rib out.

To shred • Remove the ribs and stack the leaves 3 or 4 high. Starting at a long side, roll into a tight cylinder like a cigar. Slice the cigar crosswise. The slices will unravel into fine shreds.

Lima Beans *see also* Beans, Dried

In general, lima beans cook fast and require no soaking. Sometimes, however, dried limas have been sitting on the shelf so long that they never become tender. If you know that your lima beans are more than 1 year old, soak them to be safe.

TIME SAVER ▼ **To shell fresh lima beans quickly** • Cut a thin strip from the inner edge of the pod with scissors. The beans will fall out as the pod opens.

FLAVOR TIP ▼ **To avoid tough limas** • Hold off on adding acidic ingredients, such as tomatoes, vinegar, or wine, until after the lima beans have cooked through. Acids react with the starch in beans and prevent them from swelling.

LIMA BEANS WITH TOMATOES AND HAM In a large soup pot, combine **1 pound (2⅔ cups) sorted and rinsed large dried lima beans** and **5 cups cold water.** Bring to a boil over medium heat. Reduce heat to low and simmer, partly covered, until beans are plump and almost tender and most of the water has been absorbed. In a skillet, sauté **1½ cups chopped ham, 1 large chopped onion, 1 large minced garlic clove,** and **1½ teaspoons dried basil** in **1 tablespoon olive oil** until onion is soft, about 5 minutes, adding **2 tablespoons water** halfway through. Add to lima beans along with **1 can (28 ounces) whole tomatoes with juice.** Break up tomatoes with a spoon and stir in **1 cup chicken broth** and **½ teaspoon salt.** Simmer about 15 minutes to blend flavors.
Makes 4 to 6 servings.

Limes *see also* Citrus Fruits; Lemons; Zest

The two most popular types of limes on the market are Tahiti limes and Mexican limes. Of the two, Tahiti limes (or Persian limes) are the most common. They never have seeds, so there is no need to take precautions for catching seeds when juicing them. Mexican limes, called limones in Mexico and Key limes in the United States, are becoming increasingly more available. Limes are more aromatic and slightly more acidic than lemons, but they can often be used interchangeably.

BASICS ▼ **To choose** • Look for plump limes with smooth, brightly colored rinds.

To store • Limes will keep at room temperature for about a week or in the refrigerator for up to 3 weeks.

To freeze • Both grated lime zest and fresh-squeezed juice can be frozen. Pour the juice into ice cube trays and freeze. When the cubes are solid, transfer them to zipper-lock freezer bags and freeze for up to 6 months. You can also freeze grated zest in freezer bags up to 6 months.

To remove zest • Make sure to remove the zest before squeezing the juice, or it will be a nearly impossible task. Special zesting tools are perfect for the job. Or you can rub the lime back and forth over the small, nubby side of a grater to make zest. Whole limes with the zest removed can be refrigerated for up to 5 days. A medium lime will give 1 to 2 teaspoons of zest.

To squeeze maximum juice • Bring limes to room temperature and roll under your palm to soften the fruit and get the juices flowing. Or, pierce 1 lime with a fork and microwave it on medium power for 10 to 20 seconds. An inexpensive, handheld citrus reamer is excellent for squeezing out juice. Cut the lime in half and firmly twist the reamer into each half. Or use a fork, twisting the tines into each lime half. A medium lime will give 1 to 2 tablespoons juice.

To extract just a few drops of juice • Pierce the lime with the tip of a paring knife. Squeeze out some juice through the hole. Refrigerate the leftover lime in a zipper-lock plastic bag and use within a few days.

FLAVOR TIP ▼ **To make a margarita meringue pie •** Substitute lime juice for the lemon juice in your favorite lemon meringue pie recipe, and replace 2 tablespoons of the water with 1 tablespoon *each* white (clear) tequila and Cointreau.

LIME SORBET In a medium saucepan over medium heat, combine **1 cup *each* sugar and water.** Bring to a bare simmer. Remove from heat and stir to dissolve sugar. Combine with **1 cup cold water** and let cool. Combine with **1⅓ cups lime juice** and **2 teaspoons grated lime zest.** Freeze in an ice cream maker, following the manufacturer's directions. *Makes about 4 cups.*

Liver *see also* Doneness Tests and Temperatures (page 572)

One of the most nutritious organ meats, liver is best when it comes from a young animal. Calf's liver tends to have a more tender texture and better flavor than beef liver.

BASICS ▼ **To choose •** Fresh liver has vivid color and a moist, but not shiny, surface. It should have a clean, fresh scent too. The more-tender calf's liver is pale pink-brown in color. Beef liver is reddish brown. Other popular animal livers include lamb, pork, chicken, turkey, and goose.

To store • Wrap it in waxed paper and refrigerate up to 1 day.

FLAVOR TIP ▼ **To ensure tender cooked liver •** Avoid overcooking. Thinly sliced (about ¼" thick) calf's liver should be cooked over medium-high heat, just until pink in the center, about 2 minutes per side.

LIVER, BACON, AND CAPERS In a large skillet, cook **3 strips bacon, cut into ¼" squares,** until crisp and cooked through. Add **1 finely sliced medium onion** and sauté until lightly browned. Remove with a slotted spoon and reserve. Thinly slice ¾ **pound calf's liver** and season with ½ **teaspoon salt** and ¼ **teaspoon ground black pepper** all over. Add to the pan and cook over medium-high heat just until meat is pink in the center, about 2 minutes per side. Transfer to a plate. Return onion and bacon to the pan. Deglaze with **2 tablespoons capers and their liquid.** Pour over liver. *Makes 4 servings.*

Lobster *see also* Doneness Tests and Temperatures (page 572)

When buying live lobster, don't worry about its mottled greenish-brown appearance. The deep red pigment in the shell, known as astaxanthin, will shine through as color-binding proteins break down during cooking.

BASICS ▼ **To choose live lobster •** Look for live, active lobsters in seawater. Their tails should curl under when picked up. If stored on ice, they may be sluggish, but the tails should still curl under. Bacteria form quickly in dead lobsters, so make sure that lobsters are alive before you buy and cook them. One whole lobster (1 to 1½ pounds) yields about ¼ pound of meat, enough for 1 serving.

1

HOW TO CRACK COOKED LOBSTER

Here's how to get into the nooks and crannies to get the most lobster meat. Make sure to wear a bib (or a napkin tucked into a shirt collar) to avoid getting splattered with juices. Or, if biblike attire is unsuitable for the occasion, hold a cloth napkin over the lobster when you crack it open.

❶ Placed the cooked lobster on its back and twist off the claws. Using a nutcracker, crack each claw to expose the meat.

❷ With your hands, crack the lobster in half crosswise to separate the tail piece from the body.

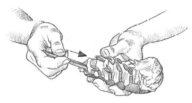

❸ Bend the flippers back to break them off the tail. Insert a fork where the flippers were broken off and push out the tail meat.

❹ Separate the back shell from the body. This section contains the tomalley (liver) and, in females, the coral-colored roe, which many consider a delicacy.

❺ Open the body by cracking apart the sides. There is good meat in here.

❻ The meat from the small claws can be sucked out like sipping through a straw.

1

To choose frozen tails • If buying frozen lobster tails, check that there are no signs of frost or dry-looking portions of meat.

To store • Live lobsters should be cooked as soon as possible. If necessary, they can be wrapped in a wet cloth and refrigerated on a bed of ice for 1 day.

To prepare for cooking • Some cooks find it more humane to kill a lobster before cooking it. To kill it instantly, insert a large knife between its eyes.

BOILED LOBSTER Bring a large pot of salted water to a boil. Plunge in **one lobster** at a time, cover, and return to a boil. Cook 8 minutes for the first pound, then an additional 3 to 4 minutes per pound after that (a total of 10 to 12 minutes for an average 1½-pound lobster). Meat should be just firm and opaque. Avoid overcooking. Remove and let sit 5 minutes before serving. Serve with **2 lemon wedges** and **2 tablespoons melted butter.** *Makes 1 serving.*

GRILLED LOBSTER Preheat the grill. Just before cooking, split a **2- to 2½-pound live lobster** in half lengthwise. To do so, insert a large knife between the eyes, then cut down straight through the antennae. Turn the lobster around and continue cutting from the first cut, splitting in half lengthwise down through the tail (use kitchen shears if necessary). Remove the head sac. Use the butt end of the knife handle, or a meat pounder, to slightly fracture the shell surrounding the claws and legs so that heat can more readily penetrate through the shell. Brush the meat lightly with **olive oil** and grill each half, meat side up, 5 minutes over a medium-hot fire. Sprinkle meat with ¼ **teaspoon salt** and ¼ **teaspoon ground black pepper.** Turn over and grill just until meat is opaque, 3 to 5 minutes more. Serve with **2 lemon wedges** and **2 tablespoons melted butter.** *Makes 1 to 2 servings.*

PROBLEM SOLVERS ▼

To keep a lobster tail from curling as it cooks • Assuming that the lobster has been killed before cooking, insert a metal or bamboo skewer along one side of the tail. If the lobster is alive, strap a heat-safe chopstick to its tail and up to its torso.

To save face when you've overcooked lobster • Pull together a quick cream sauce. It won't make the lobster any less tough, but it will help divert guests' attention from all that chew. Alternatively, if you have the time and do not have a room full of guests anticipating the joys of eating lobster from the shell, remove the meat, shred it finely, and serve it in a salad, sandwich, or pasta dish. If combining it with cooked foods, add at the last minute to avoid further cooking.

1

M

Macadamia Nuts *see also* Nuts

Although native to Australia, where it also goes by the names Queensland nut and Australian hazel, the macadamia nut is practically synonymous with Hawaii.

BASICS ▼ **To store** • Macadamia nuts are among the richest nuts in the world. They turn rancid quickly, so store them in a tightly closed jar in a cool place and use as soon as possible. Always taste one first.

To chop easily • Place a clean kitchen towel between the nuts and the cutting board so that the nuts won't bounce off the board while chopping.

FLAVOR TIPS ▼ **To add crunch to rice pilaf** • Add about ½ cup chopped macadamia nuts when making your favorite rice pilaf.

To use salted macadamia nuts for sweets • Place them in a strainer and rinse under running water to wash off the salt. Place them in a dry skillet and shake the pan over low heat until dry.

MACADAMIA NUT BLONDIES Preheat oven to 350°F. Grease an 8" × 8" pan. Line the pan with foil, and grease the foil. In a large bowl, beat **1 stick (½ cup) softened butter** 15 seconds. Add **1 cup packed light brown sugar, 1 large egg,** and **2 teaspoons vanilla extract.** Beat until thick and light, 1 minute. Stir together **1 cup all-purpose flour, ½ teaspoon baking powder, ¼ teaspoon baking soda,** and **⅛ teaspoon salt.** Stir flour mixture into butter mixture just to blend. Stir in **1 cup coarsely chopped, unsalted macadamia nuts.** Turn into the prepared pan and bake until a tester inserted in center comes out moist, 30 minutes. Cool in the pan on a rack. Loosen edges and pull out by the foil. Cut into 16 squares. *Makes 16 bars.*

Macaroni and Cheese

see also Pasta

First made in the 19th century, macaroni and cheese originally consisted of boiled noodles that were layered in a buttered baking dish and topped with grated American, Cheddar, or Swiss cheese. The dish was then baked until the cheese melted. Today, most macaroni and cheese recipes call for the cheese sauce to be made separately.

FLAVOR TIPS ▼ **To boost flavor** • Use various cheeses such as Monterey Jack or provolone. Try adding either ¼ teaspoon ground red

m

Classic Macaroni and Cheese

To make this dish a day ahead, prepare it up to the point where it goes into the oven. Instead of baking it, cover it tightly with plastic wrap and refrigerate. When ready to bake, put the macaroni into the hot oven and add 10 minutes to the baking time. To make 1 cup fresh bread crumbs, tear 4 pieces of fresh bread and process into crumbs in a blender or food processor.

5	tablespoons butter, divided
3	tablespoons flour
2	cups milk
3	cups (12 ounces) grated sharp Cheddar cheese
1½	teaspoons Dijon mustard
1	teaspoon salt, divided
¼	teaspoon ground black pepper
	Pinch of ground red pepper
2¼	cups (12 ounces) elbow macaroni
1	cup fresh bread crumbs

1. Preheat the oven to 350° F. Grease a 1½-quart baking dish.

2. Melt 3 tablespoons of the butter in a medium saucepan over medium heat. Add the flour and cook 1 minute, stirring. Whisk in the milk and bring to a boil. Reduce the heat to medium-low and simmer 5 minutes, stirring occasionally. Remove from the heat. Whisk in the cheese, the mustard, ¾ teaspoon of the salt, and the ground black pepper and ground red pepper.

3. Meanwhile, cook the macaroni according to package directions, until just slightly underdone. Drain and combine with the cheese sauce. Transfer to the prepared baking dish.

4. In the same saucepan, melt the remaining 2 tablespoons butter. Place the bread crumbs in a medium bowl. Drizzle with the butter and the remaining ¼ teaspoon salt. Toss to mix. Sprinkle the bread crumbs over the macaroni. Bake until the bread crumbs begin to brown and the sauce is bubbling, 30 minutes.

Makes 4 to 6 servings

Macaroni and Three Cheeses: Instead of all Cheddar cheese, use 1 cup shredded sharp Cheddar cheese, 1 cup shredded fontina cheese, and 1 cup grated Parmesan cheese.

Southwestern Macaroni and Cheese: Use a 2-quart baking dish instead of a 1½-quart baking dish. Instead of all Cheddar cheese, use 2 cups shredded sharp Cheddar cheese and 1 cup shredded hot-pepper Monterey Jack cheese. Drain 1 can (15 ounces) Mexican-style diced tomatoes and fold into the cheese sauce along with the macaroni.

m

pepper or 2 tablespoons chopped pickled jalapeño or fresh jalapeño chile peppers. When baking macaroni and cheese, use crushed crackers or potato chips for the topping.

Mandarin Oranges *see also*

Oranges

Quite a number of varieties fall under the heading of *mandarin orange:* tangerines, clementines, zipper-skin oranges, and kid-glove oranges, to name a few. They all have a peel that is easily pulled off and are highly aromatic with a tropical perfume.

FLAVOR TIP ▼ **To use in place of oranges** • Whenever a recipe calls for oranges and you want a more complex citrus flavor, use mandarin oranges instead. Use mandarin orange juice for drinks and sauces; segments for salads or salsas; and zest for baking.

TANGERINE PUDDING CAKE In early America, this dessert was called sponge pudding. Preheat oven to 350°F. Lightly grease an 8" × 8" baking dish or shallow 2-quart casserole. Separate **3 large eggs.** Put whites in a deep bowl and add ⅛ **teaspoon salt.** Beat until soft peaks form. In a large bowl, combine ⅔ **cup sugar** and ¼ **cup all-purpose flour.** Whisk in **1 cup milk,** egg yolks, **3 tablespoons melted butter,** ¼ **cup** *each* **tangerine juice and lemon juice,** and **1 teaspoon grated tangerine zest.** Add about one-fourth of this mixture to egg whites and quickly stir together. Pour back into remaining three-fourths tangerine mixture and fold together. Pour batter into the prepared pan. Place in a roasting pan that is larger than the baking

dish you are using. Pour very hot tap water into the roasting pan to come halfway up the sides of the baking dish. Bake until top is golden brown, about 40 minutes. Remove from water bath and cool slightly. The dessert will separate into a cakelike layer on top and a delicate custard layer on the bottom. Serve warm, with chocolate ice cream if desired. *Makes 4 to 6 servings.*

Mangoes *see also* Fruit, Fresh

Though considered exotic by many, mangoes are a staple in the equatorial regions of the world. They have been cultivated in India since 2000 B.C. Mangoes comes in all shapes and sizes, from oblong and pear-shaped to long and skinny. Some weigh 4 ounces; some weigh 4 pounds. Skin color ranges from greenish yellow to red-blushed, while the flesh can vary from lemon yellow to brilliant reddish orange.

BASICS ▼ **To choose** • Press the stem end, hold it close to your nose, and take a whiff. Fresh mangoes will have a sweet, resinous scent. No scent means no flavor. If the fruit smells sour or alcoholic, it has begun to ferment and has passed its prime. You may detect the astringent odor of kerosene, which mangoes actually contain. Also, cradle the mango in the palm of your hand. It should feel firm, and the skin should be tight around the flesh. If the skin is loose or wrinkled, the fruit is old.

To store • Keep mangoes at room temperature, where they will continue to ripen and become increasingly aromatic. Only refrigerate fully ripe mangoes, and use them within a few days. Mangoes prefer tropical climes and don't take well to the cold.

m

To seed • Stand the mango upright on a cutting board and slice through the flesh on one of the flatter sides, curving around the seed. Repeat on the other side to make 2 disklike portions of fruit plus a third center section with the seed.

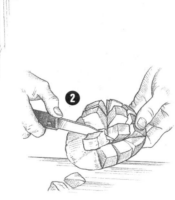

To dice or chop • After cutting the flesh off the seed, place 1 mango half, skin side down, on a countertop or in a doubled-up kitchen towel in the palm of one hand. Score the flesh all the way down to the skin in a checkerboard pattern. Be careful not to slit the outer skin ❶.

Gently push up the skin side in the center to expose the cubes of flesh. Cut away the flesh from the peel ❷. For the center section of the mango, cut the flesh away from the seed, then slice off the skin.

To slice • After cutting the flesh off the seed, follow the directions for dicing (above), but only make lengthwise cuts

(omit the crosswise cuts, which make the checkerboard pattern). Push up the skin side in the center to expose the flesh, then cut each strip of flesh from the peel. Slice each strip into thin slices.

TIME SAVER ▼ **To save pureeing time** • Purchase frozen mango puree, available in Latino markets and some large supermarkets.

MANGO SALSA In a bowl, stir together **¼ cup chopped sweet onion** or **red onion** and **¼ cup** *each* **orange juice, lime juice,** or **lemon juice and chopped fresh cilantro.** Add **1 seeded and diced mango** and **1 finely chopped small red bell pepper.** Add **1 finely chopped fresh jalapeño chile pepper (remove seeds for less heat)** and **1 minced garlic clove.** Excellent with seafood, pork, and chicken. *Makes about 3 cups.*

MANGO-PINEAPPLE SORBET Blend **1 large diced mango** with **1 can (8 ounces) crushed pineapple, ⅓ cup coconut milk,** and **1 tablespoon dark rum** until smooth. Freeze in an ice cream maker according to manufacturer's directions. Or freeze in a metal pan until ice crystals form, then stir with a fork to break up the crystals, and continue freezing and breaking up the crystals until mixture is nearly solid. *Makes 4 servings.*

Maple Syrup

Sweet, rich-tasting, pure maple syrup is made from the boiled and reduced sap of the sugar maple tree, which thrives in the cold climates of the northeastern United States and Canada. Excellent over pancakes and waffles, maple syrup also makes a delicious

glaze for pork, poultry, and vegetables, and can be used to flavor frostings, puddings, cakes, and pies.

BASICS **To choose** • Maple syrup is graded according to its color and flavor: the darker the color, the stronger the flavor. The lightest syrup is Grade A amber, called "fancy" in Vermont. It has the most delicate flavor of any maple syrup and is the most expensive. These are followed by slightly darker and stronger-flavored Grade A medium amber and Grade A dark amber. Syrups graded B and C have the darkest color and most assertive flavor; they are often used for baking and cooking. When buying maple syrup, look for the word *pure* on the label. If it's not there, you're probably buying corn syrup with maple flavoring.

To store • Once opened, maple syrup should be kept in the refrigerator, where it will keep for up to 1 year.

Fascinating Fact: Because maple tree sap (also called maple water) is about 98 percent water and just 2 percent sugar, about 40 gallons of water must be boiled off to make 1 gallon of maple syrup.

PROBLEM SOLVERS **To liquefy crystallized maple syrup** • Gently heat the bottle of syrup in a pan of hot water over low heat until the crystals dissolve. If the container is plastic, transfer to a glass jar or heatproof bowl before heating in hot water. You can also heat the container in a microwave oven on medium power for 10 to 15 seconds.

To salvage moldy maple syrup • If your syrup develops a thin layer of mold on the surface, it is harmless. Simply remove it, or strain it out with a fine-mesh sieve. Then, bring the strained syrup to a boil. Store in a clean jar or bottle.

To stop drips on a syrup pitcher • Dab the inside of the spout with butter, or rub it with a piece of waxed paper.

To loosen a stuck cap from a syrup bottle • Run it under very hot water.

To keep syrup bottles from getting sticky • Wipe them clean with a towel soaked in hot water after each use.

FLAVOR TIP **To get the best flavor** • When chilled, maple syrup becomes thicker and the flavor is milder. For more flavor, bring the syrup to room temperature before using; it will be thinner in texture but deeper in flavor. Better yet, warm it over low heat in a saucepan or in a microwave oven.

EASY BLUEBERRY SYRUP Place ½ cup **maple syrup** in a heatproof container and add ½ cup *each* **blueberries and chopped bananas**, ½ teaspoon **grated orange peel**, and **a pinch of cinnamon**. Microwave on high power until warmed, 15 to 30 seconds. *Makes 1 cup.*

MAPLE GLAZE FOR ROAST POULTRY OR PORK Mix ½ cup **pure maple syrup**, 1 tablespoon **Worcestershire sauce**, and 1 tablespoon **oil**. Brush onto roasting meat during the last 30 minutes of roasting. *Makes about ⅔ cup.*

MAPLE-WALNUT ICE CREAM In a large bowl, combine **2 cups heavy cream, 1 cup half-and-half**, and **1 tablespoon vanilla extract**. Whisk in ¾ cup **pure maple syrup** (preferably Grade B dark amber). Taste for sweetness and add more syrup if desired. Freeze in an ice cream freezer according to manufacturer's directions. Add **1 cup chopped walnuts** and mix in to distribute. Pack into a freezer container and freeze. For a special treat, serve the ice cream on Belgian waffles with a generous drizzle of maple syrup and a sprinkling of walnuts. *Makes about 5 cups.*

Margarine *see also* Butter; Fats and Oils

Used as a butter substitute, stick margarine is made from vegetable oil that has been hydrogenated to transform it from a liquid oil into a solid fat.

BASICS **To choose** • Read margarine labels carefully so that you know just what you're buying. Regular margarines are 80 percent fat and 20 percent water, flavoring, coloring, and other additives. Butter-margarine blends offer more butter flavor and are usually 40 percent butter and 60 percent margarine. Reduced- and low-fat margarines are mostly water and cannot be used for baking.

To store • Refrigerate margarine for up to 2 months and freeze for no more than 6 months.

HEALTHY HINT **To reduce fat intake** • Buy tub margarine instead of stick margarine. Tub margarine contains less than half the amount of trans fatty acids (a harmful type of fat) that stick margarine does. And some tub margarines have no trans fatty acids. Generally, tub-style margarines are not suitable for baking because of their high water content.

Marinades

Typically blends of an acid (such as vinegar), plus oil, salt, and seasonings, marinades are a terrific way to boost the flavor of meats and fish. The acid and salt tenderize tough fibers, while the oil acts as a flavor carrier.

BASICS **To marinate successfully** • Use a nonreactive container, such as one made of glass, ceramic, or even plastic. Avoid aluminum containers because the acid in your marinade will react with this metal and begin to corrode it, causing off flavors in the food. Also, always refrigerate foods while they marinate, and keep in mind that the larger the food, the longer its marinating time will be. If using the marinade for basting, avoid cross-contamination by setting aside a small amount of marinade before adding any raw meat, poultry, or fish to it. If you forget to do this, be sure to boil any used marinade for at least 5 minutes to kill harmful bacteria. Then, the leftover marinade can be used for basting. Or, you can boil it down to use as a sauce.

To help marinades penetrate more deeply • Prick the food with a skewer before adding to the marinade.

To tenderize tough meats • Marinades are best at delivering flavor. Avoid relying on them to make meat tender. Instead, choose naturally tender meats. That said, some marinade ingredients have a tenderizing effect that can be beneficial for tough cuts of meat. Yogurt, papaya, pineapple, and kiwifruit are natural meat tenderizers because of the enzymes that they contain. Add ¼ cup plain yogurt, fresh or canned papaya juice, pineapple juice, or pureed kiwifruit to the marinade for every 1 pound of meat being marinated. Marinate in the refrigerator at least 3 hours to allow the enzymes in the marinade to start to break down the meat fibers. Or include buttermilk or sour cream in the marinade to help tenderize the meat.

PROBLEM SOLVERS **To avoid mushy marinated foods** • Limit the amount of time that foods soak in the marinade. In general, foods with open-textured flesh, such as fish and seafood, need less than 45 minutes of soaking.

Chicken breasts break down after about 1 hour (skinless breasts even faster), but thighs and wings can stand up to marinade for up to 2 hours. Foods with firmer flesh, such as beef and lamb, can spend several hours in a marinade without becoming mushy. Also, ingredients such as yogurt, papaya, pineapple, and kiwifruit tenderize by enzymatic action. If your marinade includes any of these, marinate fish, seafood, and chicken for no more than 30 minutes, and marinate sturdier meats such as beef and lamb for no more than 24 hours.

To avoid tough marinated foods • Go easy on the acid in the marinade, which can toughen the proteins in food. Tender meats such as chicken breasts will toughen fairly quickly in an overly acidic marinade. For beef, pork, or chicken, use no more than an equal part of acid to oil to make about ½ cup marinade per pound of meat.

To avoid tough seafood • Use a marinade with little or no acidic ingredients (lemon juice, vinegar, and wine are common acidic ingredients). The acid virtually "cooks" the raw seafood. If acid is used, add no more than 2 tablespoons per ¼ cup oil in the marinade. One exception here is the Latin American dish known as seviche, in which raw fish is soaked in an acidic marinade, usually including lime juice. The acid in the marinade makes the fish firm in texture and opaque in color as if it has been cooked. But this dish is never actually heated, so absolute freshness of the fish is crucial. To marinate fish or seafood without using acid, use a nonacidic liquid such as an herb-infused oil, or use a spice rub instead. You can always add an acid for flavor once the fish is cooked.

TIME SAVERS ▼ **To save prep time** • Use bottled salad dressing, the most convenient and basic marinade available. Choose a dressing that complements the flavor and tenderness of the food to be marinated. Mild, rich dressings such as ranch work well with delicate foods such as fish, seafood, or chicken. You can also use a light vinaigrette for chicken. Higher-acidity dressings made with lots of vinegar are better for tougher meats such as beef. Alternatively, you can use yogurt or buttermilk as a base for dressings. These naturally balanced marinades need only some seasoning added.

To save marinating time • Keep in mind that marinades are used both for imparting flavor and for tenderizing, but imparting flavor doesn't take very long. For instance, delicate fish fillets or boneless chicken breasts do not need tenderizing, so the only reason to marinate them is for flavor, which can be accomplished in 30 minutes or less. Even with denser meats, such as beef or pork, full flavoring takes less than an hour or two, especially with thin cuts, such as steaks and chops. Extended marinating (over 12 hours) is necessary only for very large roasts or very tough game meats.

To save cleanup time • Mix up the marinade in a zipper-lock plastic bag, then marinate right in the bag by adding the food, squeezing out air, and sealing. Shake the bag to coat the food completely, then refrigerate, turning occasionally. Marinating in a bag works great for cookouts where you bring your own food because you can simply throw the bag away.

FLAVOR TIP ▼ **To add flavor through marinating** • You can add large amounts of highly flavored ingredients to marinades because only some of it will penetrate and flavor the meat. For example, you can add ¼ to ½ cup of chopped fresh herbs or just as much fresh grated ginger to about 1 cup of

m

liquid. Don't be afraid to get creative, either: Fruits and fruit juices make wonderful marinade ingredients. Use lime juice, tangerine juice, pineapple juice, passion fruit juice, or tomato juice for the liquid in your marinade. Also add flavor with sour cherries, balsamic vinegar, or sliced carambola.

GARLIC AND MINT YOGURT MARINADE Combine **1 cup plain yogurt, ¼ cup extra-virgin olive oil, ½ teaspoon hot-pepper sauce, 4 minced garlic cloves, 2 tablespoons lemon juice, 2½ tablespoons dried mint leaves, ½ teaspoon salt,** and **¼ teaspoon ground black pepper.** Use with 3 to 4 pounds chicken, fish, shellfish, lamb, veal, or turkey. *Makes about 1½ cups.*

RANCHERO MARINADE In a blender, combine **1 quartered small onion, 2 sliced large garlic cloves, 1 to 2 sliced fresh jalapeño chile peppers (leave the seeds in for more heat), ¼ cup chopped fresh cilantro, 1 teaspoon ground cumin, 3 tablespoons lime juice, 2 tablespoons sugar,** and **¼ cup Mexican beer,** such as Tecate, Negro Modello, or Dos Equis. Puree, then add **¾ cup more beer** and blend until mixed. Use to marinate chicken pieces, whole shrimp, or beef or pork cubes for kabobs. *Makes about 1½ cups.*

SATAY MARINADE FOR PORK OR BEEF In a bowl, combine **1 tablespoon curry powder, ⅓ cup unsweetened coconut milk, 2 tablespoons lime juice, 1 tablespoon brown sugar, ½ teaspoon salt,** and **¼ teaspoon ground red pepper.** Cut about **1½ pounds pork loin** or **beef sirloin** into pieces about 3" long, ½" wide, and ¼" thick. Add to marinade and marinate in the refrigerator 1½ hours. When ready to cook, preheat the grill. Thread meat onto presoaked bamboo skewers, brush with oil, and grill over a hot fire until no longer pink. *Makes 6 servings.*

Marshmallows

Whether they're floating in a cup of hot chocolate or roasting over an open fire, the soothing taste of marshmallows is something you never outgrow.

PROBLEM SOLVERS ▼ **To keep marshmallows from drying out •** Freeze them in a zipper-lock plastic bag. Frozen marshmallows are also easier to cut than those at room temperature.

To soften hardened marshmallows • Place them in a tightly sealed plastic bag with a couple of slices of white bread and let stand for a few days.

HEALTHY HINT ▼ **To buy vegetarian marshmallows •** Marshmallows are made with gelatin, an animal by-product avoided by many vegetarians. Health food stores carry marshmallows made with non-animal gelatin.

Mayonnaise *see also* Emulsions; Sauces

A simple emulsion of oil, egg yolks, and lemon juice or vinegar, mayonnaise is one of the classic French sauces.

BASICS ▼ **To make •** For each egg yolk, use 1 tablespoon lemon juice, ½ teaspoon salt, and ½ cup oil. Using a whisk or food processor,

m

beat together the egg yolks, lemon juice, and salt. While whisking constantly, or with the food processor running, blend in the oil drop by drop at first, then in a thin steady stream until blended and thick.

To make very thick • Whisk lemon juice into the egg yolks and freeze for at least 8 hours before making the mayonnaise. Thaw in the refrigerator, then bring to room temperature before using. Freezing thickens the yolks, helping to make a thicker mayonnaise. You can also add salt to the egg yolks.

To ensure that mayonnaise forms an emulsion • Have all the ingredients at room temperature, and include a powdered ingredient, such as ground red pepper or powdered mustard. Also, be sure to begin by adding the oil one drop at a time, then in a thin, steady stream.

To make mayonnaise that won't separate • Use a refined vegetable oil, such as corn, canola, olive, or peanut oil. Unrefined oils, such as extra-virgin olive oil, tend to separate after a day or two.

PROBLEM SOLVER ▼ **To fix a homemade mayonnaise that breaks** • Beat together a couple of egg yolks and some commercially prepared mayonnaise. Slowly beat this mixture into your broken mayonnaise.

FLAVOR TIP ▼ **To freshen up commercial mayonnaise** • For each ¼ cup mayonnaise, whisk in 1 teaspoon *each* lemon juice and fruity green olive oil.

CHIPOTLE MAYONNAISE In a measuring cup, combine **¼ cup mayonnaise** and **1 teaspoon finely chopped canned chipotle chile peppers in adobo.** Taste and add 1 to 2 teaspoons more chipotle, if desired. *Makes about ¼ cup.*

LEMON-BASIL MAYONNAISE In a cup, combine **¼ cup mayonnaise, 1 teaspoon lemon juice,** and **2 tablespoons chopped fresh basil.** *Makes about ⅓ cup.*

HEALTHY HINT ▼ **To avoid risk of salmonella** • Since mayonnaise contains raw eggs, a potential salmonella risk, you may want to use commercially prepared mayonnaise, which has been treated to kill harmful bacteria.

MAYONNAISE SUBSTITUTE In a small saucepan, whisk together **1 tablespoon cornstarch, 1¼ teaspoons dry mustard, 1 teaspoon honey,** and **½ teaspoon salt.** Gradually whisk in **¾ cup buttermilk,** then whisk in **1 egg.** Cook over medium heat, whisking constantly until mixture thickens and begins to bubble. Whisk in **2 tablespoons lemon juice** and **1 tablespoon olive oil.** Cover with plastic touching the surface and refrigerate until cold. Refrigerate for up to 5 days. *Makes about 1 cup.*

Measuring *see also* Scoops

While measuring ingredients may seem simple, the wording of some recipes can be confusing and the best technique for measuring ingredients may not always be clear.

BASICS ▼

To measure liquids • Always measure liquids by volume, expressed in teaspoons, tablespoons, cups, pints, quarts, and gallons.

m

The number of fluid ounces of volume is the same as the number of ounces in weight. Place a clear glass or plastic spouted measuring cup on a flat surface and bend down so that you're at eye level with it. (Holding the measuring cup up tends to make the liquid slosh around.) Pour in the liquid until it rises to the appropriate mark. For spoon measurements, hold the measuring spoon flat and pour in the liquid until it just reaches the top. Use liquid measuring cups for thick liquids such as honey and molasses too.

To measure viscous, sticky liquids • To accurately measure honey, molasses, corn syrup, maple syrup, or jelly, lightly oil the measuring cup or spoon first. Or, if the recipe calls for oil, measure the oil first in the same measure. Then, every drop will slide right out.

To measure dry ingredients • Use a metal or plastic dry cup, or graduated measuring spoons. Rather than dipping the cup or spoon into the ingredient, which compacts its volume, spoon the dry ingredient (such as flour, sugar, cornmeal, or baking powder) into the cup or measuring spoon until it's overflowing. Then, level off the ingredient with the flat side of a knife or a spatula. If the dry ingredient seems packed down in its container, fluff it gently with a spoon before measuring. Ingredients such as rice and nuts can be leveled off with your fingers instead.

To measure brown sugar • Gently or firmly pack the sugar into a dry measure according to the recipe directions. Then, level it with a straight edge. Brown sugar should hold its shape when emptied from the cup or spoon.

For absolute accuracy with dry ingredients • If the recipe lists both weights and volumes, go with the weights and weigh the ingredients on a kitchen scale. Dry ingredients have a different weight-to-volume ratio than liquid ingredients. For instance, 1 cup of flour may weigh as little as 4 ounces or as much as 6 ounces, depending on how much flour is compacted into the cup.

To properly interpret recipe measurements • In an ingredient listing, any instruction that follows the comma should be done after measuring. For example, if a recipe calls for "1 cup sifted flour," sift the flour before measuring. If it says "1 cup flour, sifted," measure the flour first and then sift it. If the recipe uses weight instead of volume, it doesn't matter when you sift. Six ounces of flour will always weigh 6 ounces whether it's sifted or not; only the volume will change.

To easily measure sticky solid ingredients • Use the displacement method. That is, if you need ½ cup peanut butter, fill a 2-cup liquid measure with 1 cup water. Add enough peanut butter to the water for the liquid level to rise to 1½ cups. Pour off the water before using.

To accurately measure both wet and dry ingredients • Keep 2 sets of measuring cups and spoons: one for dry ingredients (such as baking powder) and another for wet ingredients (such as vanilla extract). This saves time washing and drying as you assemble your ingredients. If you have only one set of measuring cups and spoons, measure dry ingredients first. Once a measuring vessel is wet, dry ingredients placed in it will stick to the cup or spoon, making it useless for accurate measurement.

To accurately divide doughs or batters into equal parts • Use a scale to measure the total weight and then, accordingly, the divided weight. For instance, to divide a dough into thirds, measure the dough's total weight, divide by 3, and divide the dough into 3 parts with equal weight.

Chef's Tip: A 1-cup dry measuring cup has the exact same volume as a 1-cup liquid measuring cup. It's the nature of the contents—the fluidity (and spill-ability) of liquid ingredients, and the challenge of leveling off dry ingredients—that makes the two different types of measuring cups useful and necessary kitchen tools.

PROBLEM SOLVERS ▼ **To avoid losing track of what you've measured** • Place unmeasured ingredients to the left of your work space and move to the right as they are measured. It also helps to count out loud while measuring.

To keep track of the number of eggs you've cracked • Move the exact number of eggs you need to one side of the egg carton and proceed to crack. Or, if the carton is full when you start, it's easy enough to keep track by the number of emptied cups.

To avoid spilling ingredients into a mixing bowl • Never measure over the mixing bowl. Measure over a piece of paper towel, parchment, or waxed paper, so that you can pour any spills back into the ingredient box or container.

To measure salt without spilling all over the counter • This always seems to happen with those metal spouts. To catch spilled salt, hold a larger measuring spoon under the spoon into which you are mea-

suring. Any overflow will cascade into the larger spoon. Or, if you tend to measure a lot of salt, store it in a lidded container or salt box so that the pouring dilemma is eliminated. All you have to do is dip in with a spoon.

TIME SAVERS ▼ **To save prep time** • Eyeball your measurements. Except in baking, where the structure of the finished product is dependent on an exact ratio of ingredients, precise measurement is not always essential in most recipes. Experienced cooks learn to approximate small measurements, such as teaspoons and tablespoons, by eyeballing them, a practice that is worth learning because it can greatly speed up the assemblage of ingredients. To learn to eyeball measurements, measure a teaspoon of salt or sugar and pour it into your hand. Observe it and try to remember its shape and mass, feel how much it weighs, and notice what area it takes up in your palm. Now, try pouring that much salt directly into your hand from a container. Test your accuracy by pouring the contents of your hand back into a measuring teaspoon.

To save time measuring flour and sugar • Keep a ½-cup measure in the bin. That way, you'll always have an easily multipliable measure ready. For measurements of less than ½ cup, use spoon measures.

Meat *see also* Beef; Lamb; Pork; Veal; Doneness Tests and Temperatures (page 572)

The USDA defines meat as the muscle of cattle, sheep, goats, and pigs.

BASICS ▼ **To choose** • Remember that meat is muscle. How that muscle has been used determines the taste and tenderness of the cut. Little-used muscles, such as the tenderloin, will be tender, with a fine grain and a relatively mild flavor. Cuts taken from a stronger, more-exercised muscle, such as the shoulder or leg, will be tougher and more flavorful. In addition, look for meats labeled "organic." While the USDA does not recognize the term, many states have standards that must be met in order for meat to be labeled organic. These meats are raised on organic farms without steroids, antibiotics, pesticides, or synthetic hormones, and must be processed in ways that have the least harmful effect on the environment.

To store • Unless you plan to cook meat the day that you buy it, remove the meat from its packaging, wrap it loosely in waxed paper, and store it in the coldest part of the refrigerator. Ground beef treated this way should be used within 2 days; all other cuts of beef will keep for 3 to 4 days. Frozen ground beef is best if used in 3 to 4 months. Use others cuts of frozen beef in 6 to 12 months.

To freeze individual hamburgers, steaks, or chops • Freeze with sheets of freezer paper or parchment paper between them. It will make it much easier to separate them for thawing.

To make raw meat easier to slice thinly or grind • Freeze it for 30 to 45 minutes to firm it up before slicing or grinding. For grinding, start with stew or cubed meat, then freeze the cubes.

To prepare • Match your cooking method to the cut. Tougher cuts of meat benefit from braising, stewing, and other slow-cooking, moist-heat methods. More-tender cuts require a quick-cooking, dry-heat method such as sautéing, grilling, or roasting to bring out their flavor while preserving their juices.

To tenderize meat by pounding it • Spray the interior of a large zipper-lock plastic bag, 2 sheets of plastic wrap, or 2 sheets of waxed paper lightly with cooking spray. Place the meat to be pounded between the sprayed surfaces and pound with a gentle slapping motion using a meat mallet or the bottom of a heavy pan. The pounding will break down the meat's connective tissue, and the spray will keep the surface of the meat lubricated so that it will move and stretch as it thins, rather than getting crushed. Keep in mind that pounded meats are thinner and will cook more quickly.

To tenderize meat using a marinade • Soak the meat in a mildly acidic marinade.

PROBLEM SOLVER ▼ **To avoid fat fires when cooking fatty cuts of meat** • Trim excess fat before cooking. Trimming also helps reduce fire flare-ups when grilling meats. When broiling, scatter pieces of bread in the pan under the broiler rack. They'll help soak up excess fat.

TIME SAVERS ▼ **To save prep time** • Have your butcher trim your meat the way you want to use it. Butchers do not charge extra for trimming fat, cutting pockets into chops, separating racks of ribs, cutting stew meat, grinding meat, and many other basic preparation tasks.

To cook meat faster • Remove it from the refrigerator at least 1 hour before roasting, 30 minutes before grilling, or 10 minutes before sautéing. Room-temperature meat cooks faster than cold meat.

FLAVOR TIPS ▼ **To get the most flavorful, juicy meat** • Buy cuts that are still on the bone. The process of cutting out the bones severs the muscle fibers and allows flavorful juices to escape.

m

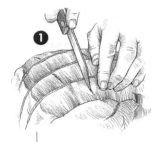

To infuse meat with flavor • When relatively large pieces of meat are pierced and highly flavored ingredients such as garlic, herbs, ginger, bacon, or chorizo (see page 121) are inserted, the flavors penetrate during roasting or braising.

Make shallow slits (no more than 1" deep) in the meat, 3" to 5" apart, all around the surface ❶.

Insert slivers of garlic, ginger, or bacon, or small amounts of chopped herbs or ground chorizo deep into each of the slits ❷. The flavor will permeate, infusing the meat as it cooks.

HEALTHY HINT ▼ **To reduce fat** • Choose the leanest cuts. For beef, choose tenderloin, top loin, sirloin, top round, eye of round, tip, or flank steak. For lamb, choose whole leg, loin chop, blade chops, fore shank, or sirloin roast. For pork, choose tenderloin, sirloin, or lean boneless ham. For veal, use any cut except commercially ground. Or buy game meats, if you can. Generally, they are much less fatty than commercially produced beef, pork, veal, or lamb.

VENISON CHOPS WITH ORANGE AND BOURBON In the refrigerator, marinate **8 venison chops** (each ¾" thick) in a mixture of **3 tablespoons bourbon,** ⅓ **cup** orange juice, **2 crushed garlic cloves,** and **2 fresh rosemary sprigs,** 1 to 6 hours. Remove from marinade and cook on a preheated grill or in a grill pan over medium heat until centers register 145°F on an instant-read thermometer, 4 to 6 minutes. *Makes 4 servings.*

ROLLED ELK STEAK Flatten a **1½-pound elk steak** to ¼" thickness. Combine **2 chopped shallots, 2 ounces chopped Canadian bacon,** ¾ **cup fresh bread crumbs,** ½ **teaspoon dried marjoram,** and ¼ **teaspoon** *each* **ground allspice, salt, and ground black pepper.** Sprinkle over meat, roll up lengthwise, and tie at 2" intervals. Sauté in a deep, nonstick skillet over medium heat in 2 teaspoons olive oil until browned, about 8 minutes, turning often. Add ½ **cup white wine,** cover, and simmer gently until meat is fork-tender, about 1 hour. Turn the meat occasionally and add a few tablespoons of water if liquid evaporates too quickly. Cut into 4 to 6 slices. *Makes 4 to 6 servings.*

Meatballs *see also* Beef; Meat; Meat Loaf

Versatile and easy to improvise, meatballs are made from a seasoned mixture of ground meat, often including beef, veal, pork, lamb, or a combination. They can be cooked by practically any method: grilling, braising, poaching, or baking.

BASICS ▼ **To shape meatballs** • Wet your hands with cold water to keep the meat from sticking. Pinch off a small amount of the seasoned meat mixture and roll it gently into a ball between your hands.

m

To form evenly sized meatballs • Form the meat mixture into a cylinder with a diameter equal to the desired diameter of the meatballs. Cut the cylinder crosswise into equal-size pieces and roll each piece into a ball.

To make tender, light-textured meatballs • Handle the meat as little as possible. Overhandling makes for tough meatballs.

To give stewed meatballs a crisp, browned crust • Sauté the meatballs until evenly browned before adding to the sauce. Or, broil the meatballs, turning frequently to brown completely.

To help fried meatballs brown without sticking or crumbling • Dredge the meatballs with flour before frying.

To prepare meatballs ahead of time • Put uncooked meatballs on a baking sheet and freeze them uncovered. Once frozen, transfer to a zipper-lock plastic bag. Defrost just the number of meatballs that you need in the refrigerator before cooking. Or freeze cooked meatballs: After cooking, cool them to room temperature, then freeze and store in the same way.

Meat Loaf *see also* Beef; Meat; Meatballs

Except for its shape, meat loaf is similar to meatballs in every way. It's usually a blend of ground meat, eggs, bread crumbs, onions, and seasonings.

BASICS **To make tender, moist, and juicy** • Use a blend of beef, pork, and veal. Using ground beef alone makes a dry, bland meat loaf. This mixture is often available in supermarkets, sold as meat loaf mixture. Make sure the beef isn't too lean; it should be at least 15 percent fat. Also, mix the ingredients with your hands until just combined. Avoid overhandling.

To make meat loaf with a greater portion of browned crust • Shape the meat directly on a parchment-lined, rimmed baking sheet rather than patting it into a loaf pan.

TIME SAVER **To cook faster** • Skip the loaf pan and form meat loaf on a parchment-lined roasting pan, making the loaf as long and narrow as possible, which allows heat to penetrate into the center of the loaf faster.

FLAVOR TIPS **To add flavor** • Replace the tomato sauce in your favorite meat loaf recipe with bottled barbecue sauce, both in the meat mixture and for topping.

To add flavor and moisture • Wrap strips of bacon around the shaped loaf before baking.

To seal in flavor and moisture • Use a clay pot casserole. Soak an unglazed clay casserole in water for 10 minutes, then add the meat loaf. Cover and place in a cold oven, then follow the baking time instructions that come with your pot.

To add hard-cooked eggs through the center • Hard-cook 6 eggs, then cool them and remove the shells. Shape half of the meat mixture into a loaf shape. Arrange eggs lengthwise on the meat from end to end, with each egg touching the other. Top with remaining meat mixture and shape into a loaf. Bake as usual.

To make miniature muffin-cup meat loaves • Lightly grease 2 standard 12-cup muffin pans and fill each muffin cup with meat loaf mixture. Top with crushed tomatoes or ketchup and bake at 350°F until center registers 160°F on an instant-read thermometer and meat is no longer pink, 20 to 30 minutes.

m

EASY TURKEY MEAT LOAF In a large bowl, combine **1½ cups crumbled dry bread stuffing mix, 1 cup bottled ranch dressing, ½ cup milk, 1 egg, ½ teaspoon salt,** and **¼ teaspoon ground black pepper.** Add **2 pounds ground turkey** and mix with your hands until well-blended. Form into a loaf on a rimmed baking sheet, in a 6-cup casserole, or in a 9" × 5" loaf pan. Bake at 375°F until center registers 165°F on an instant-read thermometer and meat is no longer pink, about 1 hour. *Makes 6 servings.*

CLASSIC MEAT LOAF In a bowl, combine **1 finely chopped onion, 2 eggs, ½ cup ketchup, 1 tablespoon Worcestershire sauce, 2 teaspoons spicy brown mustard, ½ teaspoon salt,** and **¼ teaspoon ground black pepper.** With your hands, mix in **2 pounds ground meat** blended together for meat loaf (2 parts beef, 1 part veal, 1 part pork). Soak **2 slices crustless bread** in **½ cup milk** and crumble into the meat mixture. Form mixture into a rough loaf and bake on a rimmed baking sheet, in a 6-cup casserole, or in a 9" × 5" loaf pan. Bake at 375°F until center registers 160°F on an instant-read thermometer and meat is no longer pink, about 1 hour. *Makes 6 to 8 servings.*

HEALTHY HINT **To reduce fat** • Place meat loaf on a rack over a roasting pan to drain excess fat. Or, replace half of the ground beef in your recipe with ground turkey or chicken.

Melons *see also* Cantaloupe; Watermelon

While many American markets carry only the big three (cantaloupe, honeydew, and water-melon), there are countless other varieties of melons and a huge range of sizes, colors, and flavors. Try Crenshaw for a spicy-sweet flavor. Or serve football-shaped Santa Claus melon around the holidays.

BASICS **To choose** • You'll find the best melons during the summer season, when long days and warm nights provide the ideal conditions for these fruits to ripen. (An exception is Santa Claus melon, with a peak season in December.) Look for melons that are hard, with no soft spots. Also, weigh a few of the same size and choose the heaviest one. You can slap the melon with your palm too: You should hear a hollow ring, not a dull thud. If the seeds rattle when the melon is shaken or slapped, it is probably overripe. Other signs of quality include a paler bottom, which means that the melon was ripened on the vine, not picked immaturely and ripened in shipping. If the melon still has a bit of stem attached, look for a sweet-smelling ooze at that spot. If you are choosing a thin-skinned melon such as a cantaloupe, there should be a sweet fragrance coming from the scar at its base.

To store ripe whole or cut melons • Seal the melon in a zipper-lock plastic bag and refrigerate until ready to eat. Ripe melons are best if eaten within 2 days of purchase.

To prepare melon halves • For food safety, always wash melons with hot, soapy water before slicing. Cutting through the rind of a melon can draw bacteria from the surface of the rind into the flesh. Once you've washed it, cut the melon in half through the stem end and scoop out the seeds and any pulp or strings.

To cut melon halves into smaller pieces • Slice each half into wedges and cut off the rind. You can then cut these wedges into smaller chunks if you like.

To cut melon rings • Cut the rind off the entire melon, then cut the melon crosswise into ½"-thick slices. Scoop out any seeds and pulp before serving.

Fascinating Fact:

In Japan, where space is at a premium, growers have devised a method to grow square melons. In the fields, the melons are placed in boxes. As they grow, they develop flat bottoms and sides, making them perfect for stacking and packing.

TIME SAVER ▼ **To quickly peel and seed** • Cut a thin slice from either end of the melon. Place the melon on one of its flat, cut ends and use a sharp, thin-bladed knife to slice off the peel in strips running from top to bottom, rotating the melon until all of the peel has been removed. Cut the peeled melon in half and scoop out the seeds with a spoon. This works for most melon varieties except watermelon.

MELON-PINEAPPLE SOUP In a food processor or blender, puree **4 cups cubed and seeded (4 pounds whole) honeydew; 1 small trimmed, cored, and cubed pineapple (2 cups cubes); 1 tablespoon lime juice; 2 tablespoons honey** or **brown sugar; ⅓ cup** *each* **plain low-fat yogurt and reduced-fat sour cream;** and **a pinch of allspice.** Chill. Serve in bowls, garnished with chopped strawberries and mint leaves. *Makes 4 servings.*

MELON-SCALLOP SALAD In a large bowl, toss together **2 cups chopped (2 pounds whole) melon, 4 chopped plum tomatoes, ½ cubed cucumber,** **3 sliced scallions,** and **1 tablespoon chopped fresh mint.** Toss with ⅓ **cup Citrus Vinaigrette** (page 422) and spoon onto 4 lettuce-lined plates. Top with ¾ **pound cooked scallops.** *Makes 4 servings.*

HEALTHY HINT ▼ **To get the maximum nutrients** • Avoid buying cut melons. Once they are cut and the flesh is exposed to light, the nutrients begin to break down. Also, for a more nutritional melon, choose honeydew over watermelon. Honeydews have more than 3 times as much folate and twice as much potassium as watermelons. For maximum folate, store melons, cut or whole, in a cool place, as folate is easily destroyed by heat.

Meringue *see also* Egg Whites

Made from a combination of egg whites and sugar, meringue is used to top pies and other desserts, such as puddings and baked Alaska. It's also folded into batters to lighten them and used as a frosting for cakes. Meringue can be a dessert in its own right, as when it is poached in dollops to make floating "islands"; or it can be baked crisp to make meringue shells or meringue cookies.

BASICS ▼ **To make a soft meringue** • Use 2 tablespoons sugar per egg white. Beat the whites until soft peaks form, then add the sugar a few tablespoons at a time until the whites hold a peak with the beater is lifted. Soft meringue is the most common type of meringue; it is used on top of lemon meringue pies, other custard pies, and puddings.

To make a hard meringue • Use ¼ cup of sugar per egg white and beat as for soft meringue. Spoon or pipe the meringue onto baking sheets and dry in a low-temperature oven (200°F). Use hard meringues to make meringue shells, which

m

can be filled with custard, ice cream, or fruit, and to make the French meringue cakes known as dacquoises. Store hard meringues in a tightly sealed container for up to 4 days.

To make a Swiss meringue • Use 1 cup of sugar for each egg white. Beat the egg whites in a metal bowl, preferably copper, so that the heat is transferred evenly. Begin by beating the egg whites and sugar until they are well-mixed. Set the bowl over a pan of simmering water and continue beating the egg whites until they hold stiff peaks. Remove the bowl from the heat and continue beating until the egg whites are cool. Swiss meringues work best with tart fruits such as limes; the extra sugar in the meringue balances the tartness of the fruit.

ITALIAN MERINGUE Also known as boiled icing, this type of meringue is traditionally made by beating hot sugar syrup into beaten egg whites. This version combines all of the ingredients in one bowl to save time. It should be made over a saucepan of simmering water so that the egg whites reach a temperature of at least 160°F to kill any harmful bacteria. In a metal bowl, combine **3 room-temperature egg whites, 1 cup + 2 tablespoons sugar, 3 tablespoons cold water,** and **¼ teaspoon cream of tartar.** Place over a saucepan of gently simmering water and beat with an electric mixer on low speed, 4 to 5 minutes. Increase speed to high and beat until very thick, about 4 minutes more. Remove bowl from saucepan and beat off the heat until light and fluffy, another 4 minutes. Italian meringue is often folded into mascarpone cheese to make the Italian dessert tiramisu. *Makes about 4 cups.*

EASY OVERNIGHT HARD MERINGUE Preheat oven to 200°F. Sift together **1 cup confectioners' sugar** and ½ **cup granulated sugar.** Beat **4 room-temperature egg whites** with an electric mixer until frothy. Add ¼ **teaspoon cream of tartar (or ½ teaspoon lemon juice)** and ¼ cup of the sugar mixture. Beat on high until soft peaks form. Add the remaining sugar, ¼ cup at a time, until meringue is firm and glossy. Pipe or spread into desired shapes on baking sheets lined with parchment paper. Bake 1 hour. Turn off oven and go to bed. When you awake, you will have perfectly dry meringues. Peel them from the paper backing and store in a tightly closed container for up to 3 weeks. If the weather is very humid, freeze them. *Makes 2 large cake layers or 4 large meringue "cups" for filling.*

SOFT MERINGUE In a medium bowl with an electric mixer, beat **3 room-temperature egg whites** with ¼ **teaspoon cream of tartar** and **a pinch of salt** until very soft peaks form. Beat in ⅔ **cup superfine sugar,** 1 tablespoon at a time, at high speed until stiff peaks form, 7 to 10 minutes. (If you don't have superfine sugar, grind granulated sugar in a food processor until very fine.) Beat in ½ **teaspoon vanilla extract.** Bake as directed in your recipe. *Makes about 4 cups.*

MERINGUE SHELLS Follow the recipe for **Soft Meringue** above. Spoon meringue in ⅓-cup mounds onto parchment- or foil-lined baking sheets. Using a spoon, make a hollow in center of each mound to create a bowl. Bake at 275°F until golden and set in center, 35 to 45 minutes. Fill with sorbet, melon balls, or fruit salad. *Makes about 12.*

m

COCOA MERINGUE COOKIES Follow the recipe for **Soft Meringue** (page 281). When complete, stir in **2 tablespoons sifted unsweetened cocoa powder** and **½ teaspoon ground cinnamon.** Pipe or drop onto parchment- or foil-lined baking sheets in 2" rounds. Dust with additional cocoa powder, if desired, and bake at 200°F, 2 hours. Cool and peel from sheets. *Makes about 40.*

PROBLEM SOLVERS ▼

To avoid a deflated meringue foam • Add sugar gradually, about 1 tablespoon at a time, after the beaten egg whites have begun to form soft peaks. Also, use it immediately after making. Whipped egg whites can begin to collapse soon after beating.

To ensure that sugar has dissolved in a meringue • Rub a bit of the beaten meringue between your thumb and finger. It should feel smooth. If it feels grainy, continue beating until the sugar is dissolved.

To prevent soft meringue from shrinking, beading, and weeping • Dissolve 1 tablespoon cornstarch with ⅓ cup water over medium-low heat until it forms a thick gel. Cool slightly, then beat the cornstarch mixture, 1 tablespoon at a time, into egg whites that have been beaten to soft peaks. It also helps to cook the meringue for the correct amount of time. Undercooking and overcooking can cause weeping. To prevent beading or sweating on top, it's best to go with high heat (about 425°F) for a short period of time (about 5 minutes). To prevent shrinking, spread the meringue so that it touches the edges of the dish (or the crust, for a pie) all the way around.

To avoid puddling beneath a soft meringue topping • Make sure that the mixture it is being placed atop is piping hot, so that the beaten egg whites cook through quickly and do not break down.

To make perfectly rounded free-form meringue shells • Trace circles of the desired shell size onto a sheet of parchment paper. Pour the meringue inside the circle's border and spread with the back of a soup spoon to round out and make a hollow in the center.

To prevent hard meringues from sticking to the baking sheet • Make sure to use parchment paper.

MERINGUE MADE EASY

A few simple steps help ensure perfect meringue every time.

- Separate the eggs one at a time, placing each white in a small cup to check for yolks. Just a hint of yolk will not allow the whites to whip properly.

- Let egg whites come to room temperature before whipping; you will get a greater whipped volume with slightly warm egg whites.

- Be certain that the bowl and beaters are clean and grease-free.

- Use a glass or metal bowl (copper is best) for maximum volume.

- Beat egg whites and cream of tartar to soft peaks before adding the sugar.

- Add the sugar gradually, about 2 tablespoons at a time, to ensure a fluffy meringue.

- Make meringue on a dry day. Any moisture in the air will be absorbed by the meringue, turning it sticky.

m

To avoid a soft and gooey hard meringue • Do not make on humid or rainy days or in a steamy kitchen.

To redry hard meringues that have become soft • Place in a 200°F oven for 30 minutes or up to several hours.

To help meringue shells retain crispness • Let cool for at least 5 to 10 minutes before filling. Also, wait to fill the shells until just before serving.

To mask the dark color of an overcooked meringue • Sift powdered sugar on top, or cover it with chocolate syrup or fruit syrup.

To make a clean slice into meringue • Run the knife blade under hot water beforehand and, if necessary, between slices.

Microwave Cooking

Microwave ovens emit short, high-frequency electromagnetic waves to make food vibrate at a spectacularly rapid rate, causing the food to heat up quickly. For accurate timing, it's essential to know the wattage and size of your oven, as timing varies according to these details. If you are unsure of how long to heat a food, lean toward caution. You can always continue to heat the food if it is not quite done.

BASICS **To cook successfully in a microwave**
▼ **oven** • Follow recipe directions exactly. The size and shape of the dish will affect the timing, as will the amount of food. By doubling the ingredients, you may need to double the cooking time. Also check the recommended oven wattage. Timing will need to be adjusted if you are using an oven with low wattage (less than 700 watts).

To convert recipes for low-wattage ovens • Most recipes are developed for a 700-watt microwave oven. If you have a 600-watt oven, add 10 seconds for each minute called for in the recipe. If you have a 500-watt oven, add 20 seconds for each minute called for in the recipe.

To choose cooking vessels and equipment • Ceramic, glass, or plastic containers are best. Make sure that any plastic containers are made specifically for microwave oven use; if not, they may melt. Also, use dishes that contain no traces of metal, including the trim and handles. If using plastic wrap or paper towels, be sure that they are clearly labeled as safe to use in a microwave oven. Avoid using the following containers in a microwave oven: polystyrene (such as foam coffee cups and take-out dishes); glass bottles; cans; metal pots (or anything metal, for that matter); wooden bowls; mugs or ceramic ware with glued-on handles; and plastic storage containers that are not specifically intended for microwave use.

To seal a plastic microwave cooking bag • Tear a thin strip of plastic wrap to make a tie. Dental floss also works. Avoid twist ties that contain metal wires.

To defrost food • Place the food in its wrapper on a microwaveable plate. If your microwave oven has a preprogrammed defrost cycle, use it. If not, defrost on medium power. Microwave in 5- to 8-minute intervals, turning the food between intervals, until the food is defrosted but still cold. When defrosting frozen blocks of smaller pieces, such as chicken parts, break them apart into individual pieces as soon as possible during the defrosting cycle to speed thawing.

To bring hard cheese to room temperature • Microwave on medium power for 20 seconds.

To liquefy cloudy oil or crystallized honey • Microwave on medium power for 10 to 30 seconds, depending upon the amount.

To toast whole spices • Ingredients with a naturally high oil content, such as spices and nuts, can be toasted effortlessly in a microwave oven. Spread ¼ to ½ cup whole spices or 1 cup nuts on a microwaveable plate and cook on high power, uncovered, until fragrant, 3 to 5 minutes.

To cook frozen vegetables • Unwrap 1 box (10 ounces) of any frozen vegetable and place on a microwaveable plate. Microwave on high power 4 to 5 minutes, rotating the box once.

To sweat vegetables • Recipes for sauces, soups, and stews often begin by sweating vegetables. This slow, gentle form of sautéing is used to release the flavor of vegetables without browning them. To speed sweating in a microwave oven, toss 1 quart vegetables with 2 tablespoons oil, ½ teaspoon salt, and ¼ teaspoon ground black pepper in a 2-quart microwaveable bowl or baking dish. Cook, uncovered, on high power until vegetables are tender, 4 to 6 minutes.

To steam fish fillets • Microwave ovens excel at steaming delicate foods such as fish and vegetables. Place 4-ounce, ½"-thick fish fillets on a microwaveable plate in a single layer. Season as desired and cover with microwaveable plastic wrap. Microwave on high power until fish is opaque (for salmon) or flakes easily when gently pressed (for all other fish), 1 to 2 minutes for 1 fillet, 2 to 3 minutes for 2 or 3 fillets, or 4 to 5 minutes for 4 fillets.

To steam fish steaks • Place 8-ounce, ¾"-thick fish steaks on a microwaveable plate in a single layer. Season as desired and cover with microwaveable plastic wrap. Microwave on high power until fish is just opaque, 3 minutes (for 1 steak), 4 to 5 minutes (for 2 or 3 steaks), or 7 to 8 minutes (for 4 steaks).

To precook potatoes for baking • Roasting, baking, and grilling techniques cannot be duplicated in a microwave oven. But a microwave oven can be very effective for precooking foods so that they will roast, bake, or grill faster. Preheat your regular oven to 425°F. Wash 4 large baking potatoes, prick with a fork, and microwave on high power 9 minutes. Then, bake in a conventional oven until skin is crisp and interior is soft and fluffy, 15 to 20 minutes.

To precook chicken parts or pork ribs for grilling • Toss 4 pounds meat in a microwaveable baking dish with 1 cup barbecue sauce. Microwave, uncovered, on high power 15 minutes, turning once. Preheat the grill. Grill the meat over a medium-hot fire, basting with more sauce, until the meat is browned and registers 160°F (for pork) or 170°F in the thickest portion (for chicken) on an instant-read thermometer, 5 to 8 minutes.

To easily caramelize sugar • Although caramelizing sugar in a microwave oven is no faster than doing it on the stove top, it does take less hands-on attention. Place 1 cup sugar mixed with ⅓ cup water in a 4-cup glass measure. Cover with a double thickness of plastic wrap and microwave on high power until deeply caramel-colored and completely fluid, about 9 minutes. Pierce the plastic to release steam, and use the caramel immediately as needed. Makes about 1¼ cups.

PROBLEM SOLVERS ▼ **To avoid boil-overs** • Heat soups or sauces in a container that's at least twice the food's volume. For instance, heat 1 cup soup in at least a 2-cup container.

To avoid blowouts • Prick foods that have casings, such as sausages or whole potatoes, before heating in a microwave

m

oven. Never microwave an egg in its shell unless you have an egg cooker specifically designed for microwave ovens.

To avoid a blowout when melting butter • Cut into tablespoon-size pieces, cover the container loosely with plastic wrap, and use medium power.

To prevent plastic wrap from collapsing onto food • Some studies report that molecules migrate from plastic wrap to food when it is allowed to touch the food during microwaving. To avoid any problems, make sure that the plastic does not touch the surface of the food, and remove the container as soon as it is done. Immediately poke a hole in the plastic to release any steam; otherwise, as the steam cools, the plastic will deflate onto the surface of the food.

To avoid steam burns • When uncovering a microwave dish, lift the lid or plastic wrap on the side away from you.

TIME SAVERS ▼ **To speed cleanup** • If your microwave oven doesn't have a removable glass liner, line the bottom of the oven with a sheet of waxed paper before using.

To microwave foods faster • Covering dishes tightly will trap steam for better heat penetration. Use glass dish covers, microwaveable plastic, or waxed paper, and try to keep plastic wrap an inch or more above the food. It also helps to use room-temperature foods because they cook faster

than cold foods. To warm foods to room temperature safely, take them directly from the refrigerator to the microwave oven, and microwave on medium power in 1-minute intervals until the surface loses its chill.

To eliminate cold spots • Use a carousel, which will also speed cooking. Low-cost carousels or turntables are widely available; just make sure that the size fits the interior of your microwave oven. If you don't have one of these devices, turn the food twice during cooking. If you use your microwave oven often, it also helps to become familiar with how it distributes heat. Line the oven bottom with waxed paper, then cover the paper with pancake batter and cook on high power, stopping every 30 seconds to watch how and where the batter is and is not cooking. Use the hot spots and cold spots as a guide when arranging food in your microwave oven.

To arrange foods for the most efficient cooking • Arrange them in a circular or spoke pattern. Also, since microwave ovens cook hotter on the edges than in the center, arrange foods with the thicker or tougher portions toward the edges. Place the thickest ends of chicken breasts and drumsticks outward. For stalk vegetables such as broccoli, arrange them in a circular spoke pattern with the tougher stems pointing outward and the tender heads inward.

To cook cut-up foods thoroughly • Use small, uniform-size pieces whenever possible. A microwave oven's short waves penetrate only about 1" into foods.

To cook soups, stews, and casseroles thoroughly • Stop periodically to stir and redistribute the food.

m

Milk *see also* Buttermilk; Cream; Dry Milk; Evaporated Milk; Soy Milk; Sweetened Condensed Milk

Cow's milk is not only one of the most popular beverages in the United States but also an important ingredient in many recipes.

BASICS

To choose • Always check the sell-by date stamped on the carton, and buy the freshest milk available. Also, in some areas, organic milk is available and often of higher quality. Look for "certified organic" on the label. Organic milk is usually produced on organic farms without steroids, antibiotics, pesticides, or synthetic hormones, and must be processed in ways that have the least harmful effect on the environment. Be sure to check the fat content on the label and choose the one that's right for you and your family. Whole milk contains about 3½ percent milk fat, or about 10 grams of fat per cup. Two percent milk has had 98 percent of the fat removed; it has about 5 grams of fat per cup. One percent is 99 percent fat-free, with about 3 grams of fat per cup. Fat-free milk has less than 1 percent milk fat and less than ½ gram of fat per cup.

To store • Milk is highly perishable and should be stored in the refrigerator. It should be fine to drink for 1 week after the sell-by date. Keep milk in a tightly sealed container: It absorbs odors easily and can easily take on the flavor of last night's leftovers.

To scald • Milk was originally scalded to kill bacteria. Today's pasteurized milk needs no scalding, unless you are simply heating it to help melt fats such as butter or to dissolve ingredients such as sugar. For this purpose, milk can be heated. In a saucepan over medium heat or in a microwaveable container on medium-high power, heat milk until tiny bubbles begin to form around the edge, 4 to 5 minutes for 1 cup in a saucepan or 2 to 3 minutes for 1 cup in a microwave oven.

To replace • To replace 1 cup whole milk, use 1 cup fat-free milk mixed with 2 tablespoons melted unsalted butter. Or use ½ cup evaporated milk mixed with ½ cup water. You can also use ¼ cup powdered whole milk mixed with 14 tablespoons water. Or, to replace 1 cup fat-free milk, use ⅓ cup powdered fat-free milk mixed with ¾ cup water. To replace 1 cup sour milk, place 1 tablespoon lemon juice or white vinegar in a 1-cup measure. Add enough milk to equal 1 cup. Let stand 5 minutes to thicken.

PROBLEM SOLVERS

To avoid running out • Always stock dry milk in your pantry for emergencies. If all you have is evaporated milk, it can work too. Reconstitute with equal parts water.

To keep milk from scorching • Before you heat milk on the stove top, rinse out the pan with cold water. This helps prevent the milk from scorching and sticking to the pan. Also, avoid boiling the milk. Heat it over medium-high heat just until tiny bubbles form around the edge. A nonstick saucepan is ideal.

To keep a skin from forming when heating • Keep the pan covered, or whisk the milk vigorously until a foamy surface is created.

HEALTHY HINTS

To reduce fat • Choose 2%, 1%, or fat-free milk. Use fat-free milk when you're consuming lots of milk on a regular basis, such as in coffee, drinking by the glass, and with cereal. Also use it in stronger-flavored dishes, such as cheese sauces and flavored puddings, and in baked goods. Use 1% milk when you need a little more body and flavor, such as in strong coffee and in rice puddings, cream pies, white sauces, and thickened milk-based soups or chowders.

m

Finally, choose 2% milk when the dish really relies on the flavor of milk as a main ingredient and there is little other fat in the recipe. Examples include plain puddings, flans, custard sauces, and béchamel sauce.

To get the most calcium • Choose lower-fat milk. It is the most calcium-dense. Both fat-free and 1% milk have 10 more milligrams of calcium than whole milk. Also, use fat-free evaporated milk whenever possible. Cup for cup, fat-free evaporated milk has more than twice the amount of calcium of regular fat-free milk. Use it in baking, sauces, casseroles, and hot and cold beverages, as well as on cereal.

Mincing *see also* Chopping; Food Processors

An essential preparation technique, mincing means cutting food into very small pieces, usually less than ⅛". This cut is often used for garlic, shallots, and fresh herbs. It vastly increases the cooking area, helping foods release all their flavors.

BASICS ▼

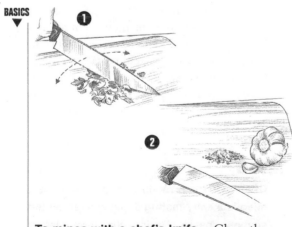

To mince with a chef's knife • Chop the food into very small pieces, gather them into a pile, then center the knife blade over the pile. Lift the blade so that it rests on its point. Cut down with the knife, quickly chopping from side to side over the food, pivoting on the knife point ❶. If necessary, place your hand over the top of the tapered end of the knife to steady it.

Continue rocking the knife over the food until it is very finely chopped and all the pieces are about the same size ❷.

To help prevent sticking • Sprinkle the food with a little salt.

To mince in a mini food processor • Fill the well of the chopper half-full with the ingredient. Mince in 1- to 2-second pulses until the desired fineness is reached.

Mirepoix

When sautéed in a bit of fat, the combination of chopped onions, celery, and carrots becomes the aromatic base known as mirepoix, the classic French foundation of flavor for an enormous range of sauces, braises, soups, and stews.

BASICS ▼ **To make classic mirepoix** • Use twice as many onions as carrots and celery.

To prepare vegetables for quick-cooking sauces • Cut the vegetables into a very fine dice. The small pieces will release their flavor more quickly during the short cooking time.

To prepare for long-cooking soups and braises • Cut the vegetables into medium-size pieces. With the longer cooking, they'll have plenty of time to release all their flavors.

To get maximum flavor • Sweat the vegetables over low heat in a covered pan rather than sautéing them. Sautéing over high heat seals flavor in the vegetables. Slowly sweating the vegetables releases their flavor into the pan, where it's transferred to the cooking liquid and infused into the other ingredients as they cook.

m

Mirin

A must in Japanese cooking, this sweet rice wine is used for flavoring and glazing foods. It has a pale golden color and imparts mild sweetness and a slightly fermented flavor dimension to foods. It plays an important part in teriyaki sauces and glazes.

BASICS ▼ **To replace** • Simmer ⅔ cup sake or dry sherry mixed with ⅓ cup sugar about 5 minutes. It won't be identical, but it will be very good.

TERIYAKI SAUCE WITH MIRIN Combine ⅓ **cup** *each* **sake, mirin, and tamari** and **1 tablespoon sugar.**
Makes about ⅔ cup.

Mise en Place *see also* Kitchen Flow; Timing

This French cooking term should be a part of every home cook's vocabulary—not to impress, but because it holds the secret to the most fundamental cooking tip of all: "everything in its place." By following the principles of *mise en place* as you progress through a recipe, you will become a quicker, more efficient, and cleaner cook.

BASICS ▼ **To read a recipe** • Read through the entire recipe first. Rough out the sequence of steps to help determine your timing, a critical factor when coordinating several dishes to be served at the same time.

To gather ingredients • Assemble all the ingredients in front of you before you start cooking. Nothing frazzles a cook more than having to look for an ingredient in the middle of cooking, especially if you find that you're fresh out.

To prepare ingredients and equipment • Measure and prepare all ingredients and equipment ahead of time. This means doing any washing, trimming, chopping, slicing, sifting, melting, toasting, or chilling called for in the recipe. Also, grease any baking pans if necessary or prepare any other equipment as required. Whenever possible, combine ingredients during this prep stage. Look through the recipe and combine ingredients that will be going into the pot at the same time. Everything you need should be measured, prepped, and ready to go before you actually start cooking. This is especially helpful when stir-frying or sautéing because the actual cooking time is very short.

To organize ingredients • Have small plates and bowls on hand to hold chopped ingredients. Disposable paper cups and bowls are perfect for this task. If you are using them for dry ingredients, they can be wiped out and used again.

To save prep time • Accomplish like tasks together. Assemble all of your produce first. Then, wash it, dry it, and chop it at the same time, rather than preparing the carrots, then the celery, then the beans. This will simplify your movement around the kitchen and keep all your activity in one place at a time, saving total prep time.

To save cleanup time • Clean as you go. A tidy work space goes a long way toward helping you cook more efficiently.

Miso

Often used for seasoning soups and sauces, miso is a salty-tasting Japanese fermented soybean paste. During the fermentation process, a dark liquid rises to the top. Known as tamari, this dark liquid is a strong-tasting form of soy sauce.

m

BASICS **To choose** • Miso is ordinarily sold in vacuum-sealed pouches or tubs. There are darker, stronger, and chunkier misos, and dozens of variations in between. Experiment and find the ones that you like best. When choosing and using, keep in mind that the darker the color, the stronger, saltier, richer, and more robust the flavor will be. There are four basic varieties of miso, each with a different color and flavor. *Aka* (red miso) is dark reddish-brown in color and has the most intense, salty flavor. *Shinshu* or *chu* (yellow miso) is golden or deep yellow in color with a mild, subtly tart flavor that is somewhat salty tasting. *Shiro* (white miso) has a gold color, a fine texture, and a mild, mellow, slightly sweet, less salty taste. *Hatcho* (dark brown miso) has a rich, mellow flavor.

To store • After opening, seal tightly (in a separate jar with a tight-fitting lid, if necessary) and refrigerate for up to 2 years. Miso keeps well due to a very high sodium content.

To use • When using miso in heated mixtures, dissolve it first in a small amount of the hot liquid in a separate bowl (using 2 parts liquid to 1 part miso), then stir back into the entire mixture.

FLAVOR TIP **To use in place of anchovies** • Due to its salty flavor, miso makes a fair substitute for anchovies in a pinch. Use roughly equal amounts.

ORANGE-MISO DRESSING In a blender or food processor, combine **1½ grated carrots; ⅓ cup fresh orange juice; 2 tablespoons *each* red** or **yellow miso, mayonnaise, and rice vinegar; 1 tablespoon ginger juice** (fresh ginger pressed in a garlic press); **1 teaspoon *each* toasted sesame oil and sugar;** and **½ teaspoon grated orange zest.** Blend to puree. Use immediately or cover and refrigerate for up to 2 weeks. Excellent on spinach salad. *Makes about 1⅓ cups.*

MISO SOUP Make **4 cups dashi** (basic Japanese fish stock), starting with instant dashi if desired. In a bowl, dissolve **¼ cup red miso** in ¼ cup of the hot stock, stirring with a fork until smooth. Slowly add mixture back into the soup pot or saucepan containing dashi. Add **1 pound cake tofu (drained and cut into ½" cubes)** and **4 to 6 fresh shiitake mushroom caps (or white mushrooms, sliced thin).** Heat through, but do not boil. *Makes 4 servings.*

HEALTHY HINT **To maintain maximum health benefits** • Add miso at the end of the cooking process to preserve its beneficial enzymes. Heat gently, but do not boil.

Molasses

A by-product of processing white sugar, molasses is what remains when sugar is separated from the juice of the sugar cane. The sugar is extracted in three stages, and each stage produces a different grade of molasses: light, dark, or blackstrap.

BASICS **To choose** • Generally, unsulphured molasses has a cleaner, sweeter flavor. For table syrup, use molasses labeled "light" or "mild." This type is light-bodied with a sweet, mild taste. Serve it over pancakes, waffles, and hot biscuits. For baking, use dark molasses, which is thicker-bodied with a fuller, less sweet flavor than mild molasses. In a pinch, light and dark molasses can be used interchangeably, but the

m

light molasses will have a less robust flavor. The last type of molasses, blackstrap, is bitter and barely sweet. It is best used in recipes that specifically call for it.

To store • Keep molasses tightly sealed and away from heat and light. It will last about 2 years.

To measure easily and accurately • Coat the measuring cup or spoon with cooking spray before measuring. Every last drop of molasses will pour right out.

To use in baking • Include baking soda in the dry ingredients to counteract the acidity of the molasses. Also, if you increase the amount of molasses specified in the recipe, reduce the oven temperature by 25°F to avoid overbrowning.

Mortar and Pestle

A mortar is a sturdy bowl, and a pestle is a club-shaped tool with a rounded bottom. The pestle is used to pound ingredients in the mortar, reducing them to a thick paste. A mortar and pestle is the ideal tool for making authentic rustic-style pesto.

BASICS ▼ **To choose** • If you plan on owning only one mortar and pestle, buy a large one with a mortar that's at least 5" across and 3" deep. The larger size offers more versatility for making sauces. Also, pay attention to the pestle: It should be heavy, to reduce the effort needed to pound ingredients properly. It should also be comfortable (hold it in your hand to test that it fits well) and should have a wide base for good leverage and coverage.

To use • When you are crushing several ingredients, pound the hardest ingredients first, followed by the softer ingredients. For instance, crush nuts first, and then add herbs and cheese and pound to blend.

To make mashing easier • Add a bit of salt. It will help draw moisture from the ingredients, making them easier to mash.

PROBLEM SOLVER ▼ **To substitute for** • Use an electric propeller-blade coffee grinder, which works well for finely grinding seeds and spices. But first, clean out the coffee grinds and odors by partially filling the grinder with uncooked rice and ½ teaspoon baking soda. Grind this mixture until pulverized, then use a pastry brush or clean toothbrush to remove particles. If you don't have a coffee grinder, you can make a homemade mortar and pestle, using a wooden bowl as the mortar and a round, fist-size rock wrapped in plastic wrap as the pestle. When pulverizing something strong-flavored, such as cumin seeds or garlic, double-line the bowl with plastic wrap so that the bowl does not absorb the odors.

Muffins *see also* Breads, Quick

Popular morning quick breads, muffins are easy to make and lend themselves to countless variations.

BASICS ▼ **To make easily** • Combine the dry ingredients with a whisk. Whisking helps distribute the ingredients evenly and aerate the flour so that it will blend easily with the wet ingredients. Whisk together the wet ingredients to blend them thoroughly. Then, add wet to dry and stir just enough to moisten the dry ingredients. Spoon the batter into prepared muffin pans and bake as directed. Cool the pans on a rack for a few minutes before removing the muffins. Serve warm or let cool completely.

To ensure light-textured muffins • Mix the dry and wet ingredients with a

m

rubber spatula just enough to moisten the dry ingredients. Avoid making a smooth batter; it should have some lumps. Overmixing makes for tough muffins.

To grease muffin pans • Use cooking spray. Hold the pan up on its side and spray each cup around its walls and across its bottom. Avoid using too much oil, or it will form a puddle in the bottom of the cup. Coat the top of the pan too, so that any oversize muffin tops don't stick.

To make muffins with evenly rounded tops • Fill standard-size muffin cups no more than two-thirds full. If using larger or jumbo muffin cups, fill each cup three-quarters full.

To evenly portion muffin batter into pans • Use an ice cream scoop. A #8 scoop (4 ounces) will fill a standard muffin cup two-thirds full.

To keep muffin pans from warping • Fill empty cups with water before baking.

To freeze baked muffins • Let cool completely, transfer to zipper-lock freezer bags, and freeze.

To reheat frozen muffins • Put frozen muffins on a baking sheet and warm in a 350°F oven until warmed through, 10 to 15 minutes.

To use stale muffins • Crumble stale muffins and lightly toast them in a 350°F oven for about 15 minutes. Use the toasted crumbs to top desserts such as crisps, cobblers, betties, buckles, and crumb cakes.

To save cleanup time • Line muffin pans with paper muffin cups. No greasing necessary.

To make ahead • Prepare the batter the night before. Scoop prepared batter into prepared pans and cover the whole pan with plastic wrap. Refrigerate overnight. In the morning, remove prepared pans from the refrigerator and preheat the oven to 350°F. Bake until the muffins are puffed and browned and a tester inserted into the center of one of the center muffins comes out with just a crumb clinging to it. Cool in the pan 5 minutes before removing and serving.

To make jam-topped muffins • Place 1 teaspoon jam on top of the batter in each muffin cup before baking.

To make upside-down muffins • Spoon 1½ teaspoons jam or cranberry sauce in the bottom of each well-coated muffin cup, top with batter, and bake as directed. Run a knife around the sides, and invert hot muffins onto a rack.

To boost nutrients • Add fruit, dried or fresh, for additional vitamins and cancer-fighting phytochemicals. For more fiber and vitamins, use whole wheat pastry flour in place of half of the all-purpose flour in the recipe. Or replace one-fourth of the flour with oat flour or soy flour. Try using soy milk in place of the liquid in the recipe.

To create moistness in reduced-fat muffins • Use moist add-ins such as chopped fresh fruits or chopped dried fruits that have been rehydrated; add in about ½ cup per 12-muffin batch. You can also add fruit purees, such as applesauce, substituting ½ cup for ¼ cup of the liquid in the recipe. If using chopped frozen dry-pack fruits, bake an additional 3 to 5 minutes.

To create tenderness in reduced-fat muffins • Use low-fat or fat-free dairy products such as sour cream, yogurt, or buttermilk. These products will contribute tenderness as well as help retain the muffin's moisture. Replace half of the

m

Basic Tender Muffins

When combining the wet and dry ingredients for muffins (or any quick bread), mix as minimally as possible. Lumps are desirable. Even some spots of unmoistened flour are okay. To get "more-tender" or "most-tender" muffins, use the ingredients listed in the basic recipe below, but follow the special mixing instructions included farther down. See the flavor variations, too, which can be used with either the basic, more-tender, or most-tender muffins.

1 **stick (½ cup) butter**

2½ **cups all-purpose flour**

¾ **cup sugar**

2 **teaspoons baking powder**

½ **teaspoon baking soda**

½ **teaspoon salt**

2 **large eggs**

1 **cup buttermilk**

1. Adjust the oven rack to the lower-middle position. Preheat the oven to 400°F. Grease a 12-cup muffin pan. (Use a standard-size muffin pan with 2½"-diameter cups.)

2. In a small saucepan, melt the butter over medium-low heat.

3. In a large bowl, combine the flour, sugar, baking powder, baking soda, and salt.

4. In a small bowl, whisk together the eggs, buttermilk, and melted butter. Add to the flour mixture. Stir just enough to lightly blend.

5. Divide the batter evenly into the prepared muffin cups (the cups will be full). Bake until

liquid in the recipe with sour cream, yogurt, or buttermilk. Or replace one-third of the liquid in the recipe with cream cheese; blend the remaining liquid with the cream cheese until smooth.

Mushrooms, Dried

Dried mushrooms have intense flavor. Mushrooms are mostly water, so when all of the moisture evaporates, the flavor becomes highly concentrated.

BASICS ▼ **To choose** • Look for large pieces with a uniform, dark color, since darker dried mushrooms usually have more flavor. Avoid dried mushrooms with tiny holes in the flesh, which may indicate that bugs have been living there. If possible, smell dried mushrooms before you buy them: They should have a deep, rich aroma.

To choose among varieties • The variety of dried mushroom you choose will, of course, depend on the dish, but here are three ideas to get you started. If you are golden brown, 20 to 25 minutes. Cool in the pan on a rack 3 minutes before removing the muffins.

Makes 12

More-Tender Muffins: Instead of melting the butter, cut cold or frozen butter into ¼" cubes and place in a medium bowl. (You could also shred the frozen butter on a box grater.) Add a generous cup of the flour mixture. Using a fork or pastry blender, cut the butter into the flour just until moistened; do not overmix. (If the butter pieces no longer feel cold, place the bowl in the freezer for 10 minutes to chill.) Add the butter-and-flour mixture back into the large bowl with the flour mixture. Gently stir to combine. Proceed with the recipe.

Most-Tender Muffins: In a small bowl, combine the flour, baking powder, baking soda, and salt. Instead of melting the butter, soften it, then cut it into tablespoon-size pieces. Combine the softened butter with the sugar in a large bowl. Using an electric mixer on medium speed, beat the butter and sugar until fluffy and light, 2 minutes. Thoroughly beat in the eggs, one at a time. Beat in half of the flour mixture. Add ⅓ cup of the buttermilk. Alternate, adding the remaining flour mixture and buttermilk in two more additions. Beat until the batter is fully blended. Proceed with the recipe.

Blueberry-Orange Muffins: Add 1 tablespoon orange zest, ½ teaspoon ground cinnamon, and a pinch of ground nutmeg to the flour mixture. Once the batter is mixed, blend in 1½ cups blueberries.

Candled Ginger Muffins with Golden Raisins and Pecans: Add ¼ teaspoon ground ginger and an additional 2 tablespoons sugar to the flour mixture. Once the batter is mixed, blend in ¼ cup finely chopped crystallized ginger, ½ cup golden raisins, and ½ cup chopped pecans.

Chocolate Chip Muffins: Once the batter is mixed, stir in ¾ cup chocolate chips.

making a cream sauce or a veal or poultry dish, consider dried morels. These darlings of the dried mushroom world have wonderful earthy flavor and meaty texture. For Chinese dishes, consider dried shiitakes, also called black Chinese mushrooms. They have tough stems that should be cut off and discarded after soaking (or you can add them to stock for flavor). For polenta, risotto, and other Italian dishes, try dried porcini mushrooms. Their rich, earthy taste marries well with most Italian flavors.

To store • Keep dried mushrooms in the freezer, where they will be safe from insect infestation. Use within 1 year.

To prepare • Soak each ½ ounce of dried mushrooms in ½ cup hot tap water for 30 minutes. Pluck out the reconstituted mushrooms with a slotted spoon, leaving the liquid in the bowl. Squeeze the mushrooms with your fingers to release as much of the liquid as possible back into the bowl. The mushrooms will have given up much of their flavor to the soaking

(continued on page 298)

A DOZEN DELICIOUS MUSHROOMS

While some mushrooms have mysterious-sounding names, many are named for what they look like, such as hen-of-the-woods, pom pom, oyster, and black trumpet. Here's a guide to the more exotic varieties that are now more available.

Beech *(Hypsyzygus tessulatus):* Also called clam shell or hon-shimeji. This mushroom variety has the most sensational and sensual texture imaginable. Beech mushrooms are bouncy, resilient, almost crunchy, and very juicy. With a mild mushroom flavor and nutty undertone, beech mushrooms largely take on other flavors during cooking. A quick sauté in olive oil or butter or a quick grilling (brushed lightly with oil) shows them off best. They also stand up well in soups, stews, stir-fries, and salads. The flavor of beech mushrooms can be enhanced with a smidgen of minced garlic, a pinch of fresh herbs, and a splash of wine or sherry. And they are terrific alongside mashed potatoes, soft polenta, and other foods with a creamy consistency.

Chanterelle *(Cantharellus cibarius):* Also called girolle or Pfifferling. While many "wild" mushrooms are now cultivated, chanterelles defy cultivation. They will be expensive when you come across them because they are hand-picked by experts in the wild. Chanterelles are easily recognized by their delicate orange or apricot color and trumpet shape. Black trumpets *(Craterellus fallax)* are a similar, related variety. The texture of chanterelles should be firm yet spongy and the flavor mild and just a bit woodsy. Some have a subtle apricot nuance. They are especially delicious with cream sauces, chicken, and pasta.

Cremini *(Agaricus bisporus):* Also called crimini or brown mushrooms. Some years ago, the brown color of these wonderful mushrooms was bred out of the variety, resulting in the very common white button mushrooms. It was only after cooks sought out brown mushrooms with more flavor that cremini became popular again. Cremini mushrooms have a flavor similar to white mushrooms, except deeper, a bit bolder and more mushroomy. It's an earthy yet sophisticated flavor that greatly enhances the flavors of other foods. Cremini can be sliced or chopped and sautéed, then used in stuffings and soups. They are also perfect for stuffed mushroom caps.

Enoki *(Flammulina velutipes,* formerly *Collybia velutipes):* Also called enokitake, enokidake, and golden mushrooms. These waifs of the mushroom world are easily identi-

m

fied by their long, skinny stems and tiny caps, which are the size of pencil erasers. They grow in clusters and are sold in vacuum-packed pouches to extend their shelf life. Trim off about 1" from the stems at the bottom, where the fused stems begin to separate. The taste of these mushrooms is fairly bland, but the texture of the caps is firm and bouncy. Because they are so exotically beautiful, enoki are often added to salads and open-faced sandwiches, dropped into a stir-fry or hot soup at the last moment, or used as a garnish. They are best when eaten raw or just slightly cooked.

Hen-of-the-Woods (Grifola frondosa): Also called maitake, sheep's head, and dancing butterfly mushrooms. When you come across hen-of-the-woods, you will see a cluster of ruffled-looking caps and stems attached at a base. These clumps can be enormous, sometimes growing several feet wide. Both the stems and caps can be eaten, but many people prefer the stem over the cap because the stem has a firmer texture. The whole clump is generally firm in texture compared with other mushrooms, yet tender and a bit crumbly, with a nutty, woodsy flavor and a hint of garlic. Pull apart the cluster to make smaller portions. Hen-of-the-woods stands up well to simmering and braising. Great with chicken or veal in cream sauce or with beef stroganoff.

Morel (Morchella angusticeps or Morchella elata): *Elegant* and *expensive* are words that come to mind at the mention of morels. Perhaps the most easily recognized mushroom, morels have an unusual shape: a rounded, hollow elongated cone with a honeycomb-like, spongy cap and a hollow stem. They have a rich flavor that suggests nuts or spice. Morels take especially well to creamy sauces, flavoring and soaking up the sauce in a delicious way. Wonderful with elegant seafoods, poultry, and veal, morels also make a great addition to vegetable dishes. Dried morels are quite good and some of them are lightly smoked during the drying process, boosting their flavor even more.

Oyster (Pleurotus): Also called pleurotte. A rainbow of color will greet you in the oyster mushroom section of food markets: They grow in hues ranging from silver, cream, white, and buff, to golden, yellow, pale blue, lavender, pink, gray, and black. Cream is the most common color, and don't worry about trying every color variety. Most of the color fades during cooking,

m

(continued)

A DOZEN DELICIOUS MUSHROOMS (cont.)

and the flavors of each variety are similar. Oyster mushrooms have a delicate earthy flavor, not bold at all, and will taste best when cooked simply and quickly. A very short sauté in butter or olive oil until just wilted and a light sprinkle of salt and pepper are all that is needed. They can also be quickly grilled or broiled, then dressed with a vinaigrette. Or try them scattered over seafood. Delicate oyster mushrooms begin to decay quickly, so buy them fresh and dry, and use them as soon as you can.

Porcini (Boletus edulis): Also called Bolete, King Bolete, porcino, cèpe, or Steinpilze. Large and precious, perhaps the greatest of all mushrooms, porcini defy cultivation. Great celebrations follow porcini seasons throughout Europe. The caps can grow up to a foot across! The stems can be quite bulbous but are delicious and should not be discarded. Although some wild porcini come to market from the West Coast, most are imported. They are very expensive, both fresh and dried. But the reward is a deep, meaty, woodsy flavor and tender, beefy texture. The caps, or even whole fresh porcini cut into thick slices, are ideal for grilling. Just brush with olive oil and sprinkle with salt and pepper. Simple is best when it comes to cooking these treasures of the forest. Dried porcini are also sensational. They have such a deep, robust taste that ½ ounce or less is enough to flavor an entire pot of pasta sauce.

Portobello (Agaricus bisporus): Also called portabella. When cremini mushrooms are left to grow larger, they turn into portobellos. Cultivation of portobellos has flourished in recent years and their price is coming down as supply increases. In a way, they are an inexpensive substitute for porcini mushrooms. They have a deep, meaty flavor and texture. The stems are tough and woody, often removed and added to soups and stock for flavor, but you can also slice and sauté them. The large caps are the real draw in portobellos. They are wonderful for grilling or broiling whole. They can also become "burgers" or a mushroom "pizza" crust when topped with tomato and cheese, then baked. When thinly sliced, the caps make a pretty arrangement over traditional pizza. If using in light sauces, scrape out the dark gills from the undersides of the caps to avoid darkening the sauce.

Shiitake (Lentinus edodes): Also called black mushrooms, Chinese black mushrooms, black forest mushrooms, and golden oak mushrooms. Here we have one of the most successfully cultivated mushrooms. The dark, almost pointy caps range from just 1" to a very large 8"

in diameter. The color of the caps is usually dark brown, almost black, but sometimes you will find them with a variegated or crackled beige appearance. The wonderful woodsy aroma and flavor of shiitake intensifies when the mushroom is dried. Fresh shiitake should be firm and dry. The stems are always tough and should be removed before using. Shiitake can be grilled or broiled and they can star in simple stir-fries. Incidentally, shiitake mushrooms were used as models for the dancing and singing mushrooms in the movie *Fantasia*.

Truffles (*Tuber* spp.): Looks aren't everything. At first sight, a truffle looks like a lumpy, warty, rough, and irregularly shaped mass. But the flavor is smooth as velvet. Truffles are highly prized fungi that grow underground, most abundantly beneath certain oak and hickory trees in France and Italy. They are extremely expensive because it takes keen pigs and dogs to sniff out their spontaneous subterranean locations in the fall and winter. The average truffle is the size of a walnut, but they can grow up to 6" across. Many varieties exist, but black and white are the most important. Black truffles (nicknamed black diamonds) come from the Périgord region of France. The color is actually a dark brown or grayish purple-black. They have an incredibly earthy aroma and rich, subtle flavor with nutty undertones. Slight cooking brings out the best flavor. White truffles are more fragrant and pungent, tan or light brown in color, and grow abundantly in the Piedmont region of Italy. Their musky, earthy

aroma and flavor includes nuances of garlic and aged cheese, with an occasional peppery bite. White truffles are almost always added raw to Italian dishes, frequently shaved into wafers over pasta, risotto, and cheese sauces. When purchasing truffles, go by aroma. To store them, bury the truffles in rice grains and refrigerate up to 10 days. Use the truffle-flavored rice too. For an economical way to enjoy the flavor of truffles, buy truffle oil, store it in the refrigerator, and use within 1 year. Truffle oil is wonderful drizzled over bread, salads, pasta, risotto, polenta, seafood, or vegetables. Canned truffles are also available, but they have much less flavor than fresh and shrink to half their size, creating a denser consistency and darker color.

Wood Ear (*Auricularia polytricha, A. auricula*): Also called tree ears and cloud ears. These slippery, black-brown, wafer thin, petal-like mushrooms were once available only dried (they easily reconstitute and look similar to the fresh variety, which is becoming more available). They have very little flavor and are used mostly for their slightly crunchy texture. You can easily recognize wood ears in Chinese dishes such as hot and sour soup and moo shu pork. Fresh wood ears need only a brief rinsing and blanching. Dried wood ears will keep well for several years. When buying the dried version, choose the tiniest ones that you can find; they blow up to 4 to 5 times their size after soaking, and the huge ones will be very chewy.

m

liquid, but you can chop them and add them to the recipe for texture. Strain the soaking liquid through wet cheesecloth or a damp coffee filter to remove any grit. The liquid will be highly flavored, especially when rehydrating porcini mushrooms. Whenever possible, add this mushroom "liquor" to the recipe, replacing other liquids in the recipe if necessary. Freeze any leftover soaking liquid to flavor sauces, stews, braises, and risottos.

To retain more flavor in dried mushrooms when soaking • Rehydrate them in cold water instead of hot. It will take longer, but more flavor will remain in the mushroom. This rehydrating technique is especially useful if you are using only the mushrooms, and not the soaking liquid, in a recipe.

To make mushroom powder • Another way to use dried mushrooms without soaking them is to grind them into a powder that can be added to a recipe as a seasoning. (No worries about grit this way, either; any grit in the mushrooms will be ground so finely that it will be unnoticeable.) Dried mushroom powder can be sprinkled into a sauce, a stew, or a soup. It will swiftly season a breading for fried chicken as well as the gravy that is served with it. Dried mushroom powder can be added to salad dressing or pasta dough or sprinkled into simmering rice. To make it, coarsely chop a few dried mushrooms, place them in the well of a mini food processor or other small-size food processor, and process in pulses until finely chopped (you can also use a clean propeller-blade coffee grinder). Then, process continuously until the mushrooms turn into powder. Store in a tightly closed container indefinitely.

To dry fresh mushrooms • Choose unblemished, very fresh mushrooms (wild or domestic) and slice about ¼" thick. Place on a rack and set in a convection oven set to 100°F or a conventional oven set to "warm" or 120°F. Warm until the mushrooms are dry, about 8 hours.

TIME SAVERS ▼ **To save soaking time** • Use boiling water instead of hot tap water. Soaked in boiling water, most dried mushrooms will rehydrate in 10 to 15 minutes. When you use boiling water, more flavor will be released into the soaking liquid, so be sure to add the soaking liquid to the recipe, if possible.

To soak ahead of time • Soak dried mushrooms in cold water, then store them in a covered jar in the refrigerator for up to 2 weeks.

FLAVOR TIPS ▼ **To boost the flavor of fresh mushrooms** • When sautéing fresh white or brown mushrooms, add rehydrated porcini mushrooms and their strained soaking liquid just after the fresh mushrooms begin to brown.

To flavor spaghetti sauce • Add ½ ounce soaked and softened porcini mushrooms to 8 cups of your favorite spaghetti sauce and simmer as usual. Even better when ½ to 1 pound sliced sautéed mushrooms are added as well.

Mushrooms, Fresh

Mushrooms do double duty as both a seasoning and a vegetable in their own right. In fact, white button mushrooms contain *umami,* a natural flavor enhancer that boosts the flavor of any food that the mushrooms are cooked with. For more on umami, see page 184.

BASICS ▼ **To choose** • Look for mushrooms that are firm and slightly moist, with no signs of decay. They should be heavy for their size and smell like the woods. To ensure freshness, check the gills on the underside of the mushroom. If they're tightly closed, the mushroom is young, mild-tasting, and will last longer; if they're open, the mushroom is more mature and will have a more concentrated flavor but will not last long once you get it home. Use older mushrooms soon after purchase. If you can, choose so-called "wild" mushrooms, most of which are now cultivated. Though they're more expensive than other varieties, shiitakes, creminis, chanterelles, and other wild mushrooms have more intense, interesting flavors, and a little bit tends to go a long way.

Chef's Tip: Only mushroom experts should pick or use fresh mushrooms in the wild. Identifying mushrooms in the wild can be very tricky, and some varieties are poisonous.

To store • Keep mushrooms cool and dry. Refrigerate them in a basket or an open paper bag and avoid cleaning them until you're ready to use them. They should stay fresh for 4 to 5 days.

To clean • Trim the stems but avoid washing the mushrooms because they absorb water like a sponge. Instead, wipe them clean with a damp cloth or scrape them gently with a paring knife. If bits of dirt cling stubbornly to the mushrooms, go ahead and rinse them off, but cook them soon after washing, as the water promotes decay.

To prepare • Some varieties of fresh mushrooms (such as enoki) can be eaten raw. But most mushrooms need to be thoroughly cooked, particularly wild ones, which contain proteins that can be difficult to digest.

To cook for maximum flavor • Cook mushrooms in a small amount of fat over low heat. Be sure to cook them long enough that all their flavor is released.

Then, continue cooking until the liquid has evaporated. Their texture should be slightly crisp, not slippery.

To grill white mushroom caps • Thread 2 parallel skewers through the diameter of the caps. This way, they will cook evenly on both sides and will not fall through the grill rack.

To season • Use a light hand with acidic ingredients such as lemon juice, vinegar, and wine. They tend to diminish the flavor of the mushrooms.

STUFFED MUSHROOMS Twist and pull off stems from **18 medium-large white** or **brown cremini mushrooms.** Place caps, gill side up, in a 12" × 8" shallow baking dish. Finely chop stems. Sauté **1 finely chopped small onion** and ⅓ **cup finely chopped smoked ham** in **1 teaspoon olive oil** to soften onion, about 3 minutes. Add **1 small minced garlic clove,** ½ **teaspoon dried oregano,** ¼ **teaspoon salt,** and ⅛ **teaspoon ground black pepper.** Cook 30 seconds. Add chopped mushroom stems and cook 2 minutes. Pour in **3 tablespoons dry white wine** and cook until it evaporates. Turn out into a bowl and add **3 tablespoons** *each* **plain dry bread crumbs, chopped fresh parsley, and grated Parmesan cheese.** Brush edges of mushroom caps with olive oil and fill them with the stuffing, mounding slightly. Sprinkle tops with about **1½ tablespoons additional grated Parmesan cheese.** If making ahead, cover with plastic and refrigerate several hours. Bake in the top of a 375°F oven until lightly browned, 8 to 10 minutes. *Makes 18.*

PROBLEM SOLVERS ▼ **To make paper-thin slices** • Place mushrooms on a baking sheet in the freezer for 5 minutes to firm. Then, slice thinly with

m

Ol' Mushroom Soup

Here's a tip from the Mushroom Council: A closed veil (the thin membrane under the mushroom cap) indicates a delicate flavor. An open veil means a richer flavor. The veils open as the mushrooms age, which means that you might actually want to buy older mushrooms for more flavor. Many markets sell such unsightly produce at a fraction of the regular price. It's a great buy, and there are gallons of good soup in a bushel of marked-down mushrooms.

2   **tablespoons butter**

1   **onion, finely chopped**

1   **garlic clove, minced**

1   **parsnip, peeled and chopped**

1   **celery rib, peeled and chopped**

½   **pound old mushrooms, sliced**

½   **pound old mushrooms, finely chopped**

2   **tablespoons all-purpose flour**

2   **cans (15 ounces each) chicken broth**

½   **teaspoon salt**

¼   **teaspoon ground white or black pepper**

2   **cups light cream**

2   **egg yolks**

⅓   **cup chopped fresh chives**

1. In a heavy soup pot, melt the butter over medium heat. Add the onion, garlic, parsnip, and celery. Cook until softened, 5 minutes. Add the sliced mushrooms. Cook until the mushrooms begin to release their liquid, 3 minutes. Add the finely chopped mushrooms. Cook 3 minutes longer. Add the flour and cook 2 minutes, stirring constantly. Add the broth and season with the salt and pepper. Simmer 20 minutes.

2. Add the cream and return to a simmer.

3. In a medium bowl, beat the egg yolks with 1 cup of the soup. Add back to the soup pot and stir until lightly thickened. Do not allow the soup to boil after the yolks have been added. Garnish with the chives.

Makes 8 servings

a vegetable peeler. Or use a handheld garlic slicer, which is like a small-size mandoline (a hand-operated slicing machine).

To salvage mushrooms that have begun to shrivel • Use a paring knife to lob off the wrinkled top portion of the rounded cap, then peel around the cap edges to remove the shriveled sides.

To use leftover mushroom stems • Don't throw them out! Chop them finely by hand or in a food processor, then sauté them in butter until their liquid evaporates. Freeze the mixture to have instant mushroom flavor on hand. Toss them into rice, or toss with chopped fresh herbs and minced garlic to use as a stuffing for chicken, omelettes, or ravioli.

To use leftover cooked mushrooms • Make mushroom paste. Grind leftover cooked mushrooms in a food processor or blender, adding enough broth to form a loose paste. Freeze in ice cube trays. When the cubes are frozen, pop them out and store in a zipper-lock freezer bag. Use the cubes to add mushroom flavor to pan sauces, soups, gravies, stuffings, cooked grains, or pasta sauces.

To avoid the dark stain of portobello mushrooms • Scrape the dark gills from the underside of each mushroom cap before cooking. The gills tend to bleed a dark juice that stains other foods that are cooked with portobello mushrooms.

To evenly cook mushrooms with thick, firm stems • Slit the stem in half three-fourths of the way up to the cap. That way, the heat can penetrate through the stems at the same rate as the more tender caps.

To brown white button mushrooms • Drain off the juices partway through cooking and set aside in a bowl to add to the recipe later for flavoring.

To avoid dark, off-colored cooked mushrooms • Do not cook them in an aluminum pan.

To salvage dry, overcooked mushrooms • Simmer them in some stock or canned broth, water, wine, or cream for a few minutes. Or just eat them as is—their flavor will be wonderfully concentrated.

To help white mushrooms retain their color • Wipe them with a paper towel moistened with fresh lemon juice, spritz them with lemon water from a spray bottle, or lightly coat them with a vinaigrette, if appropriate. This trick works well when you want fresh white mushrooms to retain their color in a salad.

To avoid watery stuffed mushrooms • Roast the mushroom caps for about 20 minutes, turning them halfway through cooking. Then, stuff them and cook further to heat through the filling. This precooking allows the moisture in the mushrooms to release and evaporate; it also browns the mushrooms nicely for optimum flavor.

To fit the maximum amount of stuffing into a mushroom cap • Using a melon baller, scrape some of the flesh from the underside of the cap. Chop the excess flesh and add it to the stuffing mixture.

TIME SAVERS ▼ To quickly clean a large amount of mushrooms • Place the mushrooms in a large bowl. Spray with cold water, loosening as much dirt as possible until the bowl is half-filled with water. Vigorously swish the mushrooms back and forth for no more than 30 seconds, until most of the dirt loosens from the mushrooms and falls to the bottom of the bowl. Quickly lift out the mushrooms with your hands and transfer them to paper towels to absorb any excess moisture. Slice and use immediately.

To make perfect sliced mushrooms in a jiffy • Trim the stems and slice the mushrooms one at a time in an egg slicer.

Mussels *see also* Doneness Tests and Temperatures (page 572)

A bivalve mollusk (like clams, oysters, and scallops), mussels come in many different species. The two most common varieties are blue-black mussels, found along the Atlantic, Pacific, and Mediterranean coasts, and the less-common New Zealand green mussels, imported from New Zealand. The two varieties have a similar flavor, but the green ones are a bit larger and more expensive.

m

BASICS ▼ **To choose** • When buying live mussels, tap the shells. They should snap shut, indicating that the mussel is alive. (Avoid mussels with broken shells.) Note that smaller mussels are usually more tender than larger ones.

To choose between wild and farm-raised • This is somewhat of a trade-off between taste and texture. Some people prefer the flavor of wild mussels, but the cleaner farm-raised ones are easier on the teeth because they usually contain less grit.

To store • Place live mussels in a single layer on a tray and cover with a damp cloth. Refrigerate for up to 2 days. Discard any dead mussels before using (they will feel lighter than the others).

To scrub and debeard • Using a stiff brush, scrub the mussels under cool running water. Yank off the mossy-looking "beard" from each mussel. Rinse again.

To rid mussels of sand • Soak them in cool, salted water for 1 hour (⅓ cup salt per gallon of water).

To steam • Although you can pry open mussels with a paring knife or an oyster knife, it is easiest to steam them open. Place the mussels in a large pan and add about ½ cup water. Cover and steam over high heat until they open, about 3 minutes. Usually, the ones that do not open are either dead or filled with mud. But sometimes they are just stubborn, so it is worth trying to pry open and check the unopened ones before discarding.

MUSSELS MARNIÈRE In a large sauté pan or Dutch oven, sauté **8 finely chopped large shallots** or **1 finely chopped onion** in **3 tablespoons olive oil** or **butter** until soft, 3 to 5 minutes. Add **3 to 4 dozen scrubbed and debearded mussels, 1 teaspoon dried thyme,** and **2 cups dry white wine.** Cover and bring to a boil. Steam until mussels open, about 3 minutes. Toss with **3 tablespoons chopped fresh parsley** and serve hot. If desired, remove all of the mussels, discard half the shells, strain the broth through cheesecloth or a coffee filter to remove any grit, then pour the broth back over mussels; stir in **1 to 2 tablespoons butter** and serve with crusty French bread for sopping. *Makes about 4 servings.*

Mustard

When young, the green leaves of the mustard plant can be cooked and eaten like turnip greens. When the plant blooms, its luminous flowers produce flavor-rich mustard seeds, which are used whole as a spice, ground to a powder to make dry mustard, and made into prepared mustard, the base for countless sauces and an essential condiment for hamburgers and hot dogs. Another form of mustard, mustard oil, is also used in Indian cooking. There are three species of mustard, which produce seeds in four different colors: *Brassica nigra* (black), *Brassica juncea* (brown), and *Brassica alba* or *hirta* (white and yellow).

BASICS ▼ **To choose mustard seeds** • Brown mustard seeds are highly aromatic; they make a good all-purpose choice. White mustard seeds are actually pale yellow, and they are slightly larger than brown. Though they have little aroma, white mustard seeds are spicy-hot. Black mustard seeds are the most potent of all. Because they are difficult to harvest, black mustard seeds are not grown commercially. Mustard seeds are not always labeled "brown" or "white," but you'll know the difference if you taste them. Brown mustard seeds go straight to your sinuses, while white seeds are tasted more on the tip of the tongue.

To use mustard seeds • Crush them with the side of a knife or in a mortar and pestle. The seeds are flavorless until they're broken open or toasted to release their essential oils. Add mustard seeds to marinades and use them to flavor curries and chutneys.

To store mustard seeds • Keep mustard seeds in a tightly closed container, where they will keep for up to 1 year.

To choose dry mustard • Milled from both brown and yellow mustard seeds, dry mustard is sometimes labeled "mustard flour" or "mustard powder."

To store dry mustard • Keep dry mustard in a tightly closed container and store it away from heat and light. Its flavor will begin to fade within a few months of purchase, so buy dry mustard in small quantities.

To make prepared mustard from dry mustard • Stir the powder into a cold liquid such as water, wine, or vinegar. Add herbs and other seasonings if you like.

PROBLEM SOLVERS ▼ **To prevent a bitter, off taste in homemade prepared mustard** • Avoid mixing dry mustard with hot liquids; the volatile oils in mustard are heat-sensitive. The mustard will take on a bitter flavor until, over time, the taste fades completely.

To tame homemade prepared mustard that's too hot • Stir in a bit of cream and brown sugar.

FLAVOR TIPS ▼ **To improve the flavor of homemade prepared mustard** • Let it cure in the refrigerator for a week or two before using. Also, vary the flavor by stirring any of the following into ¼ cup homemade prepared mustard: 1 tablespoon maple syrup or honey; 2 teaspoons coarsely chopped capers; or ½ teaspoon grated orange, lemon, or grapefruit zest.

To flavor grilled cheese sandwiches • Very lightly spread a little mustard on the bread before assembling and grilling the sandwich. Especially good with Muenster cheese and sliced tomato.

HOT CHINESE MUSTARD In a cup, combine **2 tablespoons Colman's dry mustard** and **1 tablespoon very hot tap water** or **boiling water.** Stir in **1 teaspoon rice vinegar** and **¼ teaspoon salt.** Let stand 10 minutes to develop flavors. *Makes about 3 tablespoons.*

MUSTARD BAKED CHICKEN Pull the skin from about **3½ pounds chicken parts.** Combine them in a large bowl with **⅔ cup Dijon mustard** to coat completely. Cover and marinate at room temperature 30 minutes. Lightly grease a shallow 13" × 9" baking pan or casserole. In a large, shallow bowl, combine **3 cups coarse fresh bread crumbs, 1 tablespoon paprika, ¾ teaspoon crumbled dried tarragon,** and **½ teaspoon** *each* **salt and ground black pepper.** In a medium, shallow bowl, whisk **2 large eggs** with **1 tablespoon water.** Melt **3 tablespoons butter,** remove from heat, and stir in **3 tablespoons lemon juice.** Set lemon butter aside. One at a time, remove chicken pieces from their bowl, making sure that each is coated with mustard. Dip each piece into egg to coat, then roll in crumbs and arrange in the prepared pan. When all are coated, drizzle **lemon butter** over top and bake at 375°F until tops are golden, juices run clear, and thickest portion registers 170°F on an instant-read thermometer, 50 to 60 minutes. Let stand 10 minutes before serving. *Makes 4 to 6 servings.*

m

n

Nectarines

Essentially a smooth-skinned peach, nectarines are the queen of stone fruits with a pronounced peachy, almondy flavor. (Stone fruits are those with pits, such as peaches, plums, apricots, and cherries.) The skin color of a nectarine can be white, yellow, orange, red, or a combination. Flesh colors range from the more common golden to silvery white, a particularly succulent variety.

BASICS **To choose** • The best nectarines come to market in July and August, but they are available from May through September. Look for brightly colored skin and a fragrant aroma. Avoid bruised or blemished nectarines; the fruit should give slightly to gentle pressure.

To store • Refrigerate ripe nectarines up to 5 days.

TIME SAVERS **To speed ripening** • Place underripe nectarines in a paper bag with an apple that has been pierced in several places. Set at room temperature for several hours or up to several days until ripe. Check at least once a day, because ripening can accelerate quickly.

To use in place of peaches • Nectarines never need peeling. Save yourself some time and substitute nectarines in any recipe calling for peaches.

Nonstick Pans *see also*

Cookware

Nonstick coatings are made of polytetrafluoroethylene, a lot of syllables for what is essentially a miraculous plastic, also said to be the most slippery substance in the world.

PROBLEM SOLVERS **To avoid scratching a pan's nonstick surface during use** • Always use plastic or wood utensils, never metal.

To avoid scratching nonstick pans in storage • Place a cloth or a piece of paper towel between the nonstick cooking surface and any other pans or cookware that might be placed on top of the pan.

To outwit cooking oil's tendency to bead up in a nonstick pan • Brush or spray the food you're cooking with oil instead of spraying the pan. Coating the food also helps prevent an oily buildup on the pan, which can eventually turn a nonstick pan into one that sticks. Burned oil can destroy the coating too.

Noodles, Asian

Wheat, rice flour, buckwheat, and mung bean starch are all used to make different types of Asian noodles. These noodles are used throughout Asia to make an enormous variety of soups and stir-fries. Shop for these noodles in Asian markets or in the international aisle of your supermarket.

BASICS ▼ **To choose dried rice noodles** • There are two main types of rice noodles: rice sticks and rice vermicelli. The thin, flat rice sticks are called *jantaboon* in Thailand and *banh pho* in Vietnam. Add rice sticks to soups and use them to make pad thai and other stir-fried dishes. Thin spaghetti can be substituted for rice sticks. The very thin and delicate rice vermicelli are known as *bun* in Vietnam and *sen mee* in Thailand. They are often sold in nests. Use them in salads, soups, and stir-fries. Rice papers (sheets of rice noodle) are used to make spring rolls or summer rolls. When rice papers are quickly softened in hot water, filled, and rolled, they are called summer rolls. When fried after filling and rolling, they are known as spring rolls.

To prepare dried rice noodles to use in soups, salads, and stir-fries • Soak them in cold water for 30 minutes and then boil about 5 minutes for rice sticks and about 2 minutes for rice vermicelli.

To deep-fry rice vermicelli • Drop the dry noodles directly into a deep pot of hot oil. Remove with a pair of tongs as soon as the noodles are puffed and crisp. Use as a nest for serving stir-fried vegetables and meat.

To choose fresh rice noodles • One-pound sheets of rice noodles, called *sha he fen*, can often be found in the refrigerated section of Chinese markets.

To prepare fresh rice noodles • Cut the noodle to the desired width and add directly to soups and stir-fries toward the end of cooking time.

To choose Chinese wheat noodles • Look for dried versions in supermarkets and Chinese markets in 1-pound packages of either long, straight noodles or swirled

nests. Imported noodles are sometimes labeled "imitation noodles," but are in fact the real thing. The mislabeling is done intentionally to conform to confusing FDA packaging regulations. Some imported noodles may be flavored with shrimp or fish roe. If you can't find dried Chinese wheat noodles, angel hair pasta can be substituted. Fresh Chinese wheat noodles are also sold in a range of sizes. Thick, oval strands are known as Shanghai noodles, and flat, wide noodles are called chow fun. Chinese egg noodles are usually labeled "mein." Spaghetti-shaped ones are called regular mein, and fettuccine-like noodles are known as wide mein. A similarly shaped pasta such as spaghetti or linguine can be substituted in a pinch. Fresh sheets of Chinese wheat noodles made with egg are used for egg rolls and wontons. Fresh sheets of lasagna can be substituted.

To prepare dried Chinese wheat noodles • Cook them in a large pot of boiling water until very tender. Avoid going by times on package directions, which tend to be inaccurate. Use these noodles in soups and stir-fries.

To choose mung bean–flour noodles • Also known as cellophane noodles or bean threads, these clear noodles are usually quite thin. Rice vermicelli can be substituted.

To prepare mung bean–flour noodles • Soak in hot water for about 20 minutes and then add directly to soups, braises, and stir-fries.

To deep-fry mung bean–flour noodles • Drop the dry noodles into a deep pot of hot oil. Remove with a pair of tongs as soon as the noodles are puffed and crisp. Use as a nest for serving stir-fried vegetables and meat.

To choose Japanese wheat noodles • There are three main types of Japanese wheat noodles. The buckwheat ones,

Soba Noodles with Peanut Sauce

This lightened peanut sauce has less fat and more cancer-fighting isoflavones than most. Some of the peanut butter is replaced with silky-smooth tofu.

½ **pound buckwheat noodles (soba) or whole wheat spaghetti**

1 **red bell pepper, cut into thin strips**

2 **garlic cloves, unpeeled**

½ **cup (2 ounces) drained and crumbled firm silken tofu**

⅓ **cup natural peanut butter**

¼ **cup water**

2 **tablespoons soy sauce**

4 **teaspoons honey**

1 **tablespoon rice wine vinegar**

2 **teaspoons grated fresh ginger**

1½ **teaspoons toasted sesame oil**

Pinch of ground red pepper

3 **scallions, cut into thin, 2"-long slivers**

¼ **cup chopped fresh cilantro, divided**

3 **tablespoons chopped peanuts**

1. Bring a large pot of lightly salted water to a boil. Add the noodles and stir gently until boil returns. Immediately add 1 cup cold water and stir again until boil returns. Add another cup cold water and stir again until boil returns. Then, boil until tender yet firm to the bite, 3 to 4 minutes longer. Add the bell pepper to the cooking water during the last 2 minutes of cooking. Drain the noodles and bell pepper and rinse with cold water. Drain well and chill.

2. Meanwhile, place the garlic in a small, microwaveable dish. Add enough water to just cover the garlic. Cover with plastic wrap and microwave on high power, 40 seconds. Discard the water.

3. When cool enough to handle, squeeze the garlic into a blender or mini food processor. Add the tofu, peanut butter, water, soy sauce, honey, vinegar, ginger, sesame oil, and ground red pepper. Process until smooth, 2 minutes. Scrape into a large bowl.

4. Add the noodles, scallions, and half of the cilantro. Toss to mix. Place on a serving dish. Garnish with remaining cilantro and the peanuts.

Makes 4 servings

known as soba, are made with both wheat flour and buckwheat flour. They are sold both fresh and dried and served both hot and cold with a dipping sauce or in a broth. Whole wheat vermicelli can be substituted for soba noodles. *Udon* are also wheat noodles. They come both round and flat and are sometimes found fresh in Japanese markets, but are more often available dried. These are typically served in broth. *Somen* are delicate wheat noodles sold dried in a variety of colors. Green somen are colored with tea, egg yolks are used in the yellow version, and pink somen get their color from red shiso oil (red shiso is an herbaceous plant).

To prepare Japanese noodles • Add the noodles to a large pot of lightly salted boiling water. As soon as the water returns to a boil, add 1 cup cold water to the pot and cook until the noodles are tender but still a bit chewy. Drain and rinse the noodles briefly under cold water.

Nuts *see also* Chestnuts; Hazelnuts; Macadamia Nuts; Peanuts; Pecans; Walnuts

Whenever possible, buy nuts in the shell instead of shelled nuts. They taste better, stay fresher longer, and are less expensive.

BASICS **To choose nuts in the shell** • Look for whole, clean shells with no holes or cracks. Pick up the shell and shake it: If the nuts rattle freely, they're likely old and dry.

To choose shelled nuts • Look for plump, unbroken nutmeats. Discolored and shriveled nuts are past their prime. If possible, taste nuts before you buy them. You can spot a rancid nut by its oily feel and unpleasant, bitter flavor.

To store • All nuts, shelled or unshelled, require cool, dry storage. Shelled nuts should be tightly wrapped and refrigerated for up to 4 weeks or frozen for a few months, unless they are in a vacuum-packed can (then, store them at room temperature). Nuts in the shell can be refrigerated for several months. In general, unsalted nuts stay fresh longer than salted nuts.

To shell • Use a hinged nutcracker and a nut pick, if necessary, to coax out reluctant bits of nut. You can also remove stubborn nutmeats by dropping the cracked nut into a bowl of water: The nutmeat should sink toward the bottom, while the shells float to the top. To crack hard-shelled nuts such as Brazil nuts, freeze them for a few hours before shelling.

To blanch • Blanching, or removing the skin from shelled nuts, is done either when the appearance of the dark skin would be unattractive or when the slightly bitter flavor of the nut skin is unwanted. To blanch nuts, plunge the shelled nuts into boiling water for 1 minute (or pour the boiling water over the nuts and let stand a few minutes). Drain and transfer to a clean towel, wrapping the towel around the nuts, then rub gently and the skins will slip right off. If you are blanching hazelnuts, which tend to have more stubborn skins, add 1 tablespoon baking soda for every cup of water that you use for blanching. You can also remove the skins from shelled hazelnuts, walnuts, peanuts, and pistachios by toasting.

To toast • Toasting nuts intensifies their flavor and makes them slightly lighter, which means that they are less likely to sink to the bottom of a batter. Because toasted nuts turn rancid more quickly than raw ones, be sure to use them within a few days of toasting.

To toast in oil • Coat a skillet with 1 teaspoon oil. Add 1 cup nutmeats and stir to coat. Place over medium-high heat and stir until fragrant, about 2 minutes. The nuts may show no signs of browning yet. Turn off the heat and continue stirring until they darken by a shade or two, about 2 minutes more. Remove from the pan and cool. This method works well when other foods will be sautéed in the nut-flavored oil.

To dry-toast on the stove top • Place a single layer of nutmeats in a dry skillet

n

and cook, shaking the pan often, over medium-low heat until the nuts are fragrant and slightly browned, 2 to 3 minutes. Remove from the heat and stir until the nuts cool slightly and emit a pronounced toasted aroma. Use this method in warmer months, when you don't want to heat up the kitchen by turning on the oven.

To dry-toast in an oven • Spread the nuts on a baking sheet and toast in a 300°F oven just until fragrant, 5 to 15 minutes depending on the size of the nuts. Consider this method when the nuts will be used for baking.

To quick-toast in a microwave oven • Spread 1 cup nutmeats on a microwaveable plate and cook on high power, uncovered, until the nuts are lightly browned, 4 to 5 minutes. Because of their high oil content, pine nuts and coconut will toast a little faster, 3 to 4 minutes. This method won't brown the surface of the nuts but works well when time is of the essence.

To chop or grind nuts • A knife works well for chopping, but the nuts tend to fly around on the cutting board. To prevent a mess, place a clean kitchen towel between the nuts and the cutting board. Or place the nuts in a zipper-lock plastic bag and crush with a rolling pin or heavy pan. You can also place a small amount (½ to 1 cup) of nuts in a food processor or blender, and pulse until they are chopped. Make sure that both the work bowl and the blade are dry, and process the nuts in small batches, using short pulses. Nuts can swiftly turn to paste in a food processor. If you're using ground nuts in a recipe that contains sugar, grind the nuts with the sugar. The sugar will absorb the oil from the nuts and keep them from turning into a paste.

To use salted nuts when unsalted are called for • Drop the salted nuts into a pot of boiling water for 2 minutes. Drain and dry on a baking sheet in a 250°F oven.

SWEET HOT-PEPPER PECANS In a large skillet over medium-low heat, toast **2 cups pecan halves** in **1 tablespoon vegetable oil,** 2 minutes. Add **½ cup sugar** and cook until sugar caramelizes. Turn out onto a rimmed baking sheet and sprinkle with **1 teaspoon** *each* **salt and ground red pepper** and ¼ **teaspoon ground cinnamon.** Store in a tightly closed tin for a day or two. *Makes 2 cups.*

TIME SAVERS ▼

To easily chop frozen nuts • Nuts are best stored in the freezer, especially those with a high oil content, but they are hard to chop right out of the freezer. Warm the nuts first by placing them in a microwaveable dish and heating on high power for 2 minutes. Chop as desired.

To quickly grind a small amount of nuts • Use an inexpensive cylinder-style, hand-cranked cheese grater.

Fascinating Fact: Cashews are never sold in the shell because the oil that surrounds the shell is a skin irritant and can cause blisters. Cashews are actually in the same family as poison ivy.

HEALTHY HINTS ▼

To reduce amounts in baking • Replace some of the nuts with chopped dried fruits, Grape-Nuts cereal, or granola.

To boost nut flavor in baking • Replace 1 to 2 tablespoons of the fat in the recipe with an equal amount of flavorful nut oil, such as hazelnut or walnut oil.

Oats

A cereal grass, oats were first brought to the United States in 1602, when they were planted on an island off the coast of Massachusetts by a sea captain. This whole grain is highly nutritious in all of its many forms.

BASICS ▼ **To choose** • The type of oats you choose depends on how you plan to use them. Old-fashioned oats, which have been steamed, rolled into flakes, and dried, make a popular hot cereal but also add instant crunch to crumb toppings and supply whole-grain nutrition to a soup or stew. Quick-cooking oats, which are cut into small pieces and then steamed and flattened like old-fashioned oats, can be used in baking in place of old-fashioned oats. Steel-cut oats (Irish oats) are cut into small pieces but not rolled; they look like tiny, irregularly shaped grains and take a bit longer to soften than old-fashioned rolled oats. Instant oats are cut into tiny pieces, precooked, and then dried, so you can just add hot water to reconstitute them. Avoid using these in baking; their very fine texture can make baked goods turn out gummy. Oat flour is a whole-grain flour made by grinding the grain to a powder. It must be combined with gluten-containing flour when used in

yeast breads because it lacks gluten. Oat bran is the fiber-rich outer coating of the oat kernel; it makes an easy and healthful add-in to cereals, quick breads, and yogurt. When substituting it for flour in baking, replace only about one-quarter to one-third of the total amount of flour with oat bran, since it can impart a slightly bitter taste when used in large amounts. Like oat flour, oat bran lacks gluten, so it is not suitable to use in large quantities for bread doughs. But it makes a great addition to ground meat mixtures such as meatballs, meat loaf, chilies, and casseroles. Add about ½ cup oat bran for each pound of ground meat.

To store • Oats will keep in a sealed container in a cool, dry place for up to 6 months. Store oat bran in the refrigerator for up to 3 months.

To make oat flour • Grind old-fashioned or quick-cooking oats in a food processor or blender until they reach the texture of fine meal. Use in baked goods, substituting up to one-third of regular flour with oat flour.

TIME SAVER ▼ **To reduce the cooking time of steel-cut oats** • Combine the oats and water in a saucepan (use 1 part oats to 4 parts water). Cover and let stand overnight. Then, bring to a simmer and cook until tender.

FLAVOR TIP ▼ **To boost flavor** • Toast oats by spreading them in an even layer on a baking sheet. Bake at 350°F until fragrant, 6 to 8 minutes. Cool and store or use immediately in baked goods, granolas, or cereal.

OAT SCONES Preheat oven to 425°F. In a medium bowl, combine **1 cup rolled oats, ¾ cup** *each* **flour and whole wheat pastry flour, ¼ cup brown sugar, 1 tablespoon baking powder, ½ teaspoon** *each* **baking soda and salt, and ½ cup dried currants** or **chopped raisins.** Make a well in the center and pour in **2 tablespoons** *each* **melted butter and vegetable oil, 1 beaten egg,** and **½ cup buttermilk.** Stir to-

Chewy Oatmeal Cookies

These cookies beg for a glass of milk. They're tender and chewy, with a dark sweetness from the molasses and brown sugar.

½ **stick (¼ cup) butter**

¾ **cup 1% milk**

3 **cups old-fashioned rolled oats**

⅔ **cup granulated sugar**

⅔ **cup packed brown sugar**

¼ **cup canola oil**

2 **tablespoons molasses**

1 **egg**

1 **cup raisins (optional)**

¾ **cup all-purpose flour**

½ **cup whole wheat flour**

1 **teaspoon ground cinnamon**

¾ **teaspoon salt**

½ **teaspoon baking soda**

1. Preheat the oven to 350°F. Grease 2 baking sheets.

2. Melt the butter in a small saucepan over medium heat. Cook until fragrant and golden brown, 3 minutes. Scrape into a large bowl. In the same pan, cook the milk just until small bubbles form. Remove from the heat. Add the milk and oats to the bowl. Stir to mix and set aside to cool.

3. Add the granulated sugar, brown sugar, oil, and molasses to the oat mixture. Stir vigorously until blended. Stir in the egg and raisins, if using.

4. In a medium bowl, combine the all-purpose flour, whole wheat flour, cinnamon, salt, and baking soda. Add to the oat mixture, stirring just until combined. Drop level tablespoons of the batter onto the prepared baking sheets, leaving 2" between cookies.

5. Bake until lightly crisped around the edges, 10 to 12 minutes. Cool on racks and store airtight in a cool place.

Makes 4 dozen

gether until moistened. Turn out onto a floured surface, knead gently into a ball, and pat to an 8" circle. Cut into 8 wedges and place on a baking sheet. Bake until firm to the touch and a pick inserted comes out clean, about 12 minutes. Cool on a rack and serve warm. *Makes 8.*

LEMON CHICKEN SOUP WITH OAT-MEAL In a saucepan over medium heat, brown **½ pound chopped boneless, skinless chicken meat** in **1 tablespoon oil** until no longer pink. Add **2 peeled and sliced carrots, 2 peeled and sliced celery ribs,** and **1 chopped onion.** Sauté until vegetables are tender, 3 to 4 minutes. Add **1 tablespoon finely chopped lemon zest, 3 minced garlic cloves, 1 teaspoon ground coriander,** and **a pinch** *each* **ground ginger and red-pepper flakes.** Stir, and add **1 quart chicken broth** and the **juice of 1 lemon.** Season with **½ teaspoon salt** and **¼ teaspoon ground black pepper.** Simmer 5 minutes. Stir in **⅓ cup old-fashioned oatmeal.** Simmer until oatmeal is tender but not mushy, 10 minutes. Stir in **¼ cup chopped fresh parsley.** Serve immediately. *Makes 6 to 8 servings.*

Octopus *see also* Doneness Tests and Temperatures (page 572)

Most octopus is sold cleaned and frozen. If it hasn't been cleaned, ask your fishmonger to clean it for you. Generally, octopus will weigh about 3 pounds.

FLAVOR TIPS ▼ **To tenderize** • All around the world, cooks have their own techniques for tenderizing the octopus's rubbery flesh: It is thrown against rocks with great force

many times; it is hooked from the head and tentacles and lowered very slowly into boiling water, then lifted out, cooled, and lowered in the boiling water twice more; some cooks insist on floating a cork in the cooking water; others rub the octopus with grated radish. Of these, the most reliable technique for home cooks is triple-dipping. But you can achieve a similar tenderness by simply braising the octopus for an extended time or by cooking it very quickly on a grill. Both long, low-heat simmering and short, high-heat, dry-heat cooking make for tender octopus.

BRAISED OCTOPUS Place a cleaned **3-pound octopus** in a saucepan or small Dutch oven. Add **2 cups dry white wine** and enough **cold water** to almost cover. Add **1 sliced small onion, 2 smashed garlic cloves,** and **15 whole cloves.** Bring to a boil over medium heat. Simmer gently over low heat, partly covered, until tender, about 1½ hours. Jab the octopus with a long fork or knife to pierce. Let cool in the braising liquid, then remove. The broth may be strained and used for Italian seafood risottos or other seafood dishes, or as a braising liquid. The octopus itself can now be cut up and used to make salad or brushed with olive oil and grilled. *Makes 8 servings.*

OCTOPUS SALAD Follow the recipe for **Braised Octopus** above. Cut cooled octopus into 1" pieces. In a large bowl, whisk **3 tablespoons lemon** or **lime juice** with **½ teaspoon salt** and **⅛ teaspoon ground black pepper.** Whisk in **⅓ cup olive oil.** Add the octopus; **1 chopped tomato; ½ cup sliced, pimiento-stuffed green olives; 2**

O

sliced large scallions; ¼ chopped onion (sweet if available); ¼ cup *each* chopped fresh cilantro and parsley; and **2 tablespoons small capers.** Toss and chill. If desired, poach ½ pound shrimp and/or sliced squid to make a seafood salad. *Makes 8 servings.*

Odors

When all goes well in the kitchen, the air is perfumed with pleasant aromas. When it doesn't, you have odors instead. See "Odor Eaters" (opposite page) to find out how to get rid of them.

Okra

African slaves brought okra with them to the American South, where the vegetable is still popular. The green, ridged pods contain seeds and tend to become slippery or gelatinous when cooked. This texture makes okra a key ingredient in gumbo and other stews.

BASICS ▼ **To choose** • The best okra comes to us fresh during the summer growing season. Look for okra pods that are heavy for their size. The pods should be plump, moist, and brightly colored, with their stems intact and no blemishes, bruises, or browning. For the best texture and flavor, choose pods that are no bigger than your little finger. Large pods tend to be fibrous.

To store • Keep fresh okra in a paper bag on one of the upper shelves of your refrigerator for no more than a day or two. Okra does not keep well and is damaged by temperatures of less than 45°F.

To prepare • Tiny pods of okra need only to be rinsed and trimmed of their stems. For larger pods, trim off the caps, but take care not to expose the seeds. If the pods are particularly fuzzy, remove the

fuzz by rubbing them in a towel before you wash and trim them.

To steam • Arrange small, whole, trimmed okra on a steamer rack. Cover and steam over simmering water just until tender, 3 to 5 minutes.

To fry • Cut trimmed okra into ½"-thick slices. Toss in a bowl with yellow cornmeal (about ½ cup for 1 pound okra) until well-coated. Heat 1" vegetable oil to 365°F and fry okra in small batches until crisp and golden, about 3 minutes. Remove with a slotted spoon and drain on absorbent paper. Sprinkle lightly with salt and serve hot.

To grill • Pierce 2 parallel skewers through the long sides of about 6 small, whole, trimmed okra. (If using bamboo skewers, soak them in water for 30 minutes before using). Brush generously with olive oil and grill over medium heat until lightly charred, turning several times. Sprinkle lightly with salt.

Olive Oil *see also* Fats and Oils

All olive oils are graded according their acidity. Choosing among them is largely a matter of taste.

BASICS ▼ **To choose** • The best way to judge an olive oil is by tasting it. Color is not a sign of flavor. But the label may be of some help. The best olive oils are "cold-pressed," meaning that no solvents were used in the extraction process. They have the lowest acidity.

Extra-virgin olive oils are made from the first pressing of olives and contain only 1 percent acid or less. They are very rich in flavor, ranging in color from bright gold to deep green. Extra-virgin oil costs a bit more, so many cooks reserve it for uncooked dishes or for drizzling in at the end

ODOR EATERS

Often, the first thing to inspire our tastebuds is not what we see or what we taste, it is what we smell. But food does not always deliver mouth-watering aroma. Think fish, garlic, or anything charred. Whatever the offender, odors can permeate your hands, your equipment, your kitchen, and your entire home. Here's how to minimize and eliminate odors.

Yourself: Cooking is a hands-on task, so your hands absorb the odor of whatever you are working with. A little soap and hot water will remedy this most of the time. For more stubborn odors, rub your hands with vinegar or lemon juice (make sure that you have no cuts on your hands or they will sting). Then, wash with soap and hot water. Repeat if necessary. To remove garlic odors from your hands or fingers, rub them in the bowl of a stainless steel spoon (or any other stainless steel utensil) under running water. Follow by washing your hands with soap.

Your Equipment: When working with strong-smelling foods, use glass or stainless steel bowls. Avoid using plastic, which is more porous and, thus, more absorbent. To get rid of odors in plastic containers, ball up a piece of newspaper and seal it inside the container for a few days. When it comes to pots and pans, submerge them in hot, soapy water as soon as they are cool enough to go into the sink. Immediate soaking helps prevent odors, particularly strong ones, such as fish odors, from becoming embedded in the pan. If the odor is still present after washing, scrub with a paste of baking soda and water. As with pans, countertops and cutting boards should be cleaned immediately; but if time passes, these surfaces also respond well to lemon juice or a paste of baking soda and water.

The Dreaded Fridge: If your refrigerator smells, the first step is to identify the source of the odor and throw it out. To help prevent future odors, clean out the fridge at least once a week. You can also use the old trick of storing an open box of baking soda in the fridge. Change the box every 4 months to maintain effectiveness. Here are a few other odor eaters that work well in the refrigerator: coffee grounds, charcoal, or a cotton ball soaked with vanilla extract. Take your pick.

Lingering throughout a Room: When a kitchen or an entire home picks up an insistent odor, open a window or turn on the exhaust fan to freshen the air. Then, you can either absorb the odors or cover them up. To absorb them, set out a baking sheet scattered with baking soda (the more surface area the baking soda has, the more odor it can absorb). To replace the foul odors with pleasant aromas, bake an apple or a few orange peels. Or bake a pie plate sprinkled with cinnamon. Burn a scented candle. Or toast coffee beans in a small, dry skillet over medium heat.

The Drain: Often, it happens that whatever stinks up your kitchen ends up down the drain. Then, it's the sink that stinks. If you have a garbage disposal, throw a lemon in it. If not, pour 1 cup baking soda and 1 cup salt down the drain; follow it up with 1 to 2 quarts of boiling water to flush out the smells. To clean the sink basin itself, dampen a paper towel with bleach and thoroughly wipe it out.

O

O

of cooking time, so that its flavor is readily enjoyed. Avoid frying with extra-virgin olive oil because its flavor breaks down at high temperatures.

Virgin olive oil has a slightly higher acidity, 1 percent to 3 percent, and is not quite as delicate as extra-virgin. It's a good oil for sautéing.

Fine olive oil is a blend of virgin and extra-virgin oils.

Pure olive oil (or simply "olive oil") is extracted with the aid of chemical solvents and refined. It is almost the lowest-quality olive oil available.

Pumace olive oil is the lowest-quality olive oil on the market. After multiple pressings of olives, and after chemical solvents have been added to extract even more oil, the dregs are heated to extract the very last drips of oil. Even at a low price, it's hard to find a reason to buy this low-quality oil.

Light olive oil has the same amount of fat as other olive oils. The name refers not to its fat content, but rather to its light color and extremely mild flavor, a result of being highly refined. The fine filtration process used to make this oil raises the oil's smoke point, so it's a good choice for frying. It can also be used for baking when you don't want a noticeable olive flavor.

To store • If you use olive oil on a regular basis, keep it in a cool, dark place for up to 6 months. For longer storage, refrigerate it for up to 1 year. Olive will partially solidify at cold temperatures; simply bring it to room temperature before using.

FLAVOR TIPS ▼ **To use in sweets** • It may sound strange at first, but cookies, pastries, and cakes made with olive oil can be sensational. After all, the olive is a fruit.

To use solidified olive oil • Olive oil solidifies in the refrigerator, which can be

seen as a drawback or an opportunity. Solidified olive oil makes a flavorful, cholesterol-free spread that is also low in saturated fat. Use solidified olive oil like butter. You can even stir in garlic, herbs, or other seasonings for flavor.

Olives *see also* Tapenade

Regardless of its stage of ripeness, an olive picked right from the tree is so acrid that it is inedible. Curing raw olives in oil, water, brine, salt, or lye leaches out the glucoside that makes them taste so foul and transforms these bitter fruits into incredible little nuggets of flavor.

BASICS ▼ **To choose** • Olive nomenclature can be confusing. Most are named for their area of origin, such as niçoise and Liguria. Others, such as Picholine and Salona, are named for the variety of olive, while olives such as Greek and Sicilian style are marketed according to the method by which they were cured. Olives are also distinguished by color, but keep in mind that green olives are simply less ripe than black olives. Green olives tend to be sharper and more pungent, whereas black ones taste richer. (One exception is canned black olives from California, which were developed to be bland-tasting yet firm enough to slice. They work best in California-Mexican cooking or in other dishes where they don't interfere with the flavors in the food.) Choosing olives is largely a matter of personal taste. It's best to shop where you can sample before you buy. Then, take home the ones you like best. When possible, buy olives packed in brine.

To store • Although olives submerged in brine can be safely stored at room temperature, they will last longer in the refrigerator. For the best flavor, bring olives to room temperature before using. If mold develops on the surface of your olives, simply scrape it off and discard it. The mold is harmless.

To remove pits • Hit the olives hard with the flat side of a chef's knife to break the flesh; then, cut the meat from the pit. You can also press firmly on the olive with your thumb, then use your thumb tip to scoop out the pit. Or, for a large amount of olives, you can roll over the olives several times with a heavy rolling pin to loosen the pits, and then separate the pit from the meat. Or, for the ultimate in convenience, insert the olive into a special press called an olive pitter.

TIME SAVER ▼ **To save prep time** • Buy pitted olives. Good-quality, pitted kalamata or niçoise olives are now widely available. They are slightly more expensive, but when you calculate the weight of the pits into the cost, the price differential is not so great.

MARINATED OLIVES In a large bowl, combine about **1 pound olives, such as ¼ pound each tiny niçoise olives, large kalamata olives, green Sicilian olives, and large Chilean Alfonso olives.** Add ⅔ **cup olive oil, ⅓ cup red wine vinegar, 2 ribbons of orange zest (1" × 3" each), 1½ tablespoons dried oregano, 2 crushed garlic cloves, 3 bay leaves, 1 teaspoon *each* dried thyme and dried rosemary,** and ½ **teaspoon ground black pepper.** Marinate at room temperature 1 day, then cover and store in the refrigerator. The olives will be delicious right away and will continue to develop flavor for a couple of weeks. Remove bay leaves before serving. Serve at room temperature. *Makes 1 pound.*

Omelettes *see also* Eggs

One of the world's most popular egg dishes, omelettes are designed to cook quickly. However, the Guinness World Record of 427 plain omelettes cooked in 30 minutes by a single cook might be a bit faster than necessary.

PROBLEM SOLVERS ▼ **To avoid overbrowning** • Have all filling ingredients prepped before cooking the eggs. Also, turn the heat down to low before adding the fillings.

To prevent toughness • Bring the eggs to room temperature before adding them to the pan. Cold eggs take longer to cook through. Also, make sure that the pan is well-heated before adding the eggs.

To avoid an unwieldy omelette • Make individual omelettes using just 2 or 3 eggs per omelette. Larger omelettes are difficult to handle.

To avoid sticking • Use a nonstick or well-seasoned cast-iron pan with sloped sides, so that you can easily slide out the finished omelette. Also, use unsalted butter on the pan; salted butter tends to promote sticking. And hold off on adding sticky fillings such as cheese or bulky fillings such as chopped ham until the eggs have begun to set.

To facilitate flipping • As the eggs cook, push the eggs that have set toward the center of the pan, allowing the uncooked egg mixture to flow toward the edges. This puts the bulk of the omelette's weight in the middle, making the sides lighter and easier to flip. Also, use a fork or a heatproof rubber spatula to push the eggs as they cook. Avoid using a whisk, which makes a clumpier omelette.

To prevent tearing • Fold the omelette into thirds rather than in half. Also, cut filling ingredients into small

O

FILLED AND FOLDED OMELETTES

Usually reserved for breakfast or brunch, omelettes can satisfy at any time.

Basic Omelette: In a bowl, whisk **2 or 3 large eggs** with **2 or 3 tablespoons water, wine, milk, cream,** or **broth**. Add **¼ teaspoon salt** and **a pinch of ground black pepper**. Place an 8" nonstick skillet over medium heat and add 2 teaspoons butter or vegetable oil. When hot, pour in egg mixture. Let cook for a few seconds. As the eggs cook, push cooked portions toward the center with a pancake turner, allowing uncooked eggs to flow toward edges. Repeat as necessary, tilting the pan. When eggs are just about set, spoon the filling over half of the omelette and fold in half to enclose the filling. (Or spoon filling down center and fold the omelette into thirds over the filling.) Slide out onto a warm plate. Makes 1.

Mushroom Omelette: Melt **1 teaspoon butter** in a nonstick skillet over medium-high heat. Add **1 ounce mushroom slices** of your choice and quickly sauté to soften, 30 seconds. Add **1 tablespoon white wine, 2 teaspoons chopped fresh parsley,** and **a pinch** *each* **salt and ground black pepper**. Cook 30 seconds. Scatter over omelette, fold, and serve.

Ranchero Omelette: Cut **2 slices bacon** into small pieces. Cook in a skillet until crisp and cooked through. Pour out all but 1 teaspoon of the fat. Add **½ finely chopped onion** and **½ peeled, seeded, and chopped fresh jalapeño chile pepper (leave in the seeds for more heat)**. Sauté to soften, 3 minutes. Add **½ chopped tomato** and cook 1 minute. Remove from heat and stir in **2 tablespoons chopped fresh cilantro** and **a pinch** *each* **salt and ground black pepper**. Arrange over omelette and sprinkle with **1 tablespoon crumbled** *queso Cotija*, **farmer cheese,** or **Monterey Jack cheese**. Fold and serve with a corn tortilla.

Smoked Salmon and Cream Cheese Omelette: Cut **1½ ounces cold-smoked salmon** (Nova Scotia or Scottish) into slivers and toss with **½ teaspoon lemon juice, a pinch of ground black pepper,** and **1½ teaspoons sliced fresh chives** or **small scallion greens**. Cut **1 ounce room-temperature cream cheese** into bits and scatter over omelette. Arrange salmon mixture on top, fold, and serve.

Spinach-Dill Omelette: Melt **1 teaspoon butter** in a small saucepan. Add **1 tablespoon finely chopped onion** or **1 finely chopped large shallot** and cook to soften, 2 minutes. Add **3 cups coarsely chopped spinach, 2 teaspoons chopped fresh dill,** and **a pinch** *each* **grated nutmeg, salt,** and **ground black pepper**. Cook over medium-high heat until most of the liquid evaporates. Stir in **2 tablespoons sour cream** and **½ teaspoon lemon juice (optional)**. Arrange over omelette, fold, and serve.

pieces, so that they are less apt to tear through the cooked egg.

To improvise when an omelette is stuck to the pan • Make a frittata instead.

Cook the eggs until they are almost set. Sprinkle with toppings, cover, and cook until eggs are cooked through. Cut into wedges to serve.

To rescue an omelette that tears during folding • Camouflage tears with finely chopped fresh parsley, leftover fillings, or salsa. Or, cover the omelette with shredded cheese and place it briefly under the broiler to melt.

To salvage an omelette that has completely fallen apart • Chop it up and serve it as a version of scrambled eggs, or tuck it between slices of toast or a baguette and serve it as an egg sandwich.

FLAVOR TIP ▼ **To boost flavor** • Mix mayonnaise into the eggs (use 1 to 2 tablespoons mayonnaise for every 2 to 3 eggs). Beat vigorously until the mayonnaise is thoroughly incorporated.

Onions *see also* Scallions; Shallots

Few vegetables are quite as versatile or as essential to the cook's larder as onions. They can be used raw in salads and on sandwiches, cooked on their own as a side dish, and combined with a host of other ingredients in countless soups, stews, braises, sautés, and stir-fries.

BASICS ▼ **To choose** • Look for onions that are firm and crisp, without soft spots or signs of mold. There are two basic types: fresh onions (or sweet onions) and storage onions.

To choose fresh onions • These onions come into season in early April, and most are named after the regions where they're grown: Vidalia (from Georgia), Maui (from Hawaii), Walla Walla (from Washington), and Nu-Mex or Texas 1015 Super Sweets (from Texas) are some of the more popular varieties. Prized for their sweetness, fresh onions have a high water content and are not at all hot.

They are also low in sulfur, which makes them less likely to bring tears to your eyes when you are chopping. Cipollini are fabulous Italian onions with a flattened, squat shape that makes them easy to recognize. They are usually mild and sweet, perfect for roasting.

To choose storage onions • This type of onion is picked at the peak of the summer harvest and dry-cured to help prevent decay. Yellow onions are the most popular, but Spanish onions, red onions, white onions, and even shallots are considered storage onions. These onions tend to be quite firm, with less water and a stronger, more pungent flavor than fresh, sweet onions. To help choose among storage onions, keep in mind that Spanish onions are nothing more than large yellow onions. Red or purple onions (sometimes called Bermuda onions, though not from Bermuda) are among the sweetest and hottest in the category. And white onions are the mildest and juiciest with less sweetness. Small white onions, about 1" in diameter, are also called boiling onions or creaming onions. Tiny white onions are known as pearl onions.

To store fresh onions • Fresh onions have a very short shelf life. Keep them in the refrigerator and use within 1 week. To extend their shelf life, store them so that they are not touching one another.

To store storage onions • Keep storage onions in a cool, dry, dark place with good ventilation. For the longest storage, empty the bag and store the onions in a single layer. Also, keep onions away from potatoes. The potatoes give off moisture, which causes onions to rot.

To use fresh onions • The sweet, crisp flesh of these onions is best enjoyed raw; cut them into rings for salads and sandwiches. The high sugar content in

O

HOW TO PEEL AND DICE AN ONION

When an ingredient is used as often as the onion, it helps to know the easiest way to chop it up. Here's a fast method for dicing.

1 With a sharp knife, cut through the stem end, stopping just before you cut through the last layers of papery skin. Use the knife to peel back the skin.

2 Place the onion on end and cut it down the middle lengthwise.

3 Set one onion half, cut side down, on a cutting board. Make several parallel horizontal cuts almost to the root end. Don't cut all the way through, or the pieces will fall apart and scatter.

4 Make several parallel vertical cuts, going all the way through the onion layers but, again, not cutting through the root end.

5 Finally, cut across the grain to make pieces of the desired size.

fresh onions also means that they caramelize well; however, if you cook them, be sure to do so slowly over low heat to avoid burning.

To use storage onions • Heat enhances the sugar in these onions and makes them less pungent. Cook storage onions slowly with a little fat for robust flavor.

To enjoy all onions at their best • Slice onions just before you use them. Cut onions oxidize quickly when exposed to air, which gives them a bitter flavor. Or, rinse cut onions in water and store them in an airtight glass jar filled with ice water. Stored this way, onions will keep their fresh onion flavor for 3 to 4 hours.

To roast • One of the easiest side dishes possible is a roasted onion. You don't even peel them. Simply bake whole onions at 400°F until tender when pierced with a fork or knife, about 1 hour. Cut in half lengthwise and serve in their jackets, topped with butter, salt, and ground black pepper. Excellent when paired with a steak-and-potatoes menu.

To grill • Peel large onions and cut them in half or into ½"-thick slices. Poke small, soaked bamboo skewers through the halves or slices in two directions to prevent onions from falling apart. Brush or spray generously with oil and sprinkle lightly with salt and ground black pepper. Grill over a medium-hot fire until softened and browned, about 5 minutes per side (for slices) or 8 minutes per side (for halves).

FRENCH ONION SOUP In a large soup pot or saucepan, heat **2 tablespoons olive oil** and **1 tablespoon butter** over medium-low heat. **Cut 4 large onions (½ pound each)** in half lengthwise and thinly slice crosswise. Add to pan and sauté until softened and lightly colored, 20 minutes. Add **1 minced garlic clove, 2 teaspoons sugar,** and ½ **teaspoon dried thyme.** Increase heat to medium-high and cook until caramel-brown, 20 to 30 minutes, stirring often. Stir in **1½ tablespoons flour.** Add ¾ **cup dry red wine** and stir to deglaze the pan bottom. Stir in **1½ tablespoons tomato paste** and ¼ **cup brandy.** Add **6 cups beef broth** or **stock, 2 bay leaves,** and **1 teaspoon lemon juice.** Simmer 15 minutes to blend flavors, then remove and discard bay leaves. Add **a pinch of salt.** Toast **12 thick slices French bread,** such as baguette. Place one slice of toast in 6 individual onion soup bowls, and place bowls on a baking sheet to easily move to oven. Top each toast with a ¼"-thick slice **Gruyère or Swiss cheese.** Ladle in the soup. Place a second slice of toast on top of each serving and top each with ¼ **cup shredded Gruyère or Swiss cheese.** Bake in the top of a 450°F oven until cheese melts and browns, 10 minutes. Serve hot. *Makes 6 servings.*

CARAMELIZED ONION PIZZA In a large nonstick skillet, heat **2 teaspoons olive oil** over medium-low heat. Add **4 sliced onions, ¼ teaspoon salt,** and **a pinch of ground black pepper.** Cook until tender and lightly browned, about 20 minutes. Stir in **1 tablespoon balsamic vinegar,** remove from heat, and cool. Divide **1 pound prepared pizza dough** into fourths, shaping each into a 6" round. Place on baking sheets that have been sprinkled with **cornmeal.** Sprinkle each pizza with **3 tablespoons shredded mozzarella cheese** and arrange one-fourth of onions on top of each. Top each with **2 tablespoons chopped, oil-cured**

black olives and sprinkle with **1 table-spoon chopped fresh parsley.** Bake at 500°F until bottoms are crispy and golden, 10 to 15 minutes. *Makes 4 servings.*

To minimize or prevent tears when chopping • Sulfuric compounds in onion cells are released into the air when an onion is chopped. As the compounds come into contact with the fluid in your eyes, they create a mild form of sulfuric acid, which irritates the eyes and causes them to release tears. There are several ways to avoid the problem. You can freeze the onion for 20 minutes before you cut it, since a cold onion won't release its irritating sulfuric compounds as readily as a warm one. You can also leave the root end of the onion intact while you chop; the sulfuric compounds are concentrated there. It also helps to chop near an open window, a fan, or an overhead stove vent (turned on). If you wear contact lenses, you're fortunately less apt to be induced to tears, but if you don't, you can wear protective eye goggles (such as those for skiing or woodworking) if you're not overly fashion conscious. When slicing or chopping large amounts, use a food processor, which gets the job done fast and with fewer tears.

To remove the green sprout in the center • Simply slice the onion in half lengthwise and pluck out the sprout, which is harmless.

To tame the taste of a too-hot onion • Soak the cut onion in ice water for 15 to 45 minutes (depending on how large and how hot it is), changing the water twice. Pat dry before using. To speed up this process, add vinegar to the ice water (2 tablespoons vinegar for every 4 cups water). This way, you only need to soak the onion for 5 to 30 minutes.

To jump-start onions that are slow to caramelize • Sprinkle them with brown sugar.

To salvage scorching onions • Remove those that are not burnt and discard the rest. If all of the onions are burnt, start over again with new onions, since burnt ones taste unpleasantly acrid. If starting over is out of the question, you can sprinkle the scorched onions with a little bit of sugar to help disguise the off taste.

To remedy red onions that have turned gray-blue upon cooking • Add a splash of something acidic, such as lemon juice or vinegar.

To prevent pearl onions from falling apart while cooking • Cut an X into the root end with the tip of a paring knife.

To remove onion odors from a cutting board • Scrub it with a paste of baking soda and water.

To remove odors on hands • Rub your fingertips on the bowl of a stainless steel spoon under warm, running water. This trick also works with garlic, leeks, and other onionlike vegetables in the allium family. Any stainless steel utensil will do the job.

To disguise cooking odors from onions • In a saucepan, combine 6 cups water, 1 cup vinegar, and 1 teaspoon ground cloves. Bring to a boil and simmer 5 minutes.

To remedy "onion breath" • Eat a sprig or two of parsley. Or rinse your mouth with equal parts water and lemon juice.

Household Hint: Onions have the ability to neutralize paint fumes. If you've just painted a room and want to get rid of the fumes, cut an onion in half and set it, cut side up, on a plate in the room. In the morning, the paint smell will be gone.

TIME SAVERS ▼ **To quickly peel pearl onions** • Drop them into boiling water, boil 1 minute, then transfer with a slotted spoon to a bowl of ice water. When the onions are cool, pinch the root end of each onion and the onion will slip from its peel. You can also microwave pearl onions on high power in a covered dish in about ¼" of water for 3 minutes, then transfer them to ice water. Again, the skins will pinch right off when cool. If a recipe calls for a lot of pearl onions, save yourself the trouble and buy peeled pearl onions from the freezer section of your supermarket.

To save chopping time • Use a few large onions rather than many small ones. Coarsely chop them, then finish chopping in a food processor instead of by hand.

To save cooking time • Sautéed, grilled, or roasted onion can be kept for a month or more in the freezer. Spread out the cooked onion on a rimmed baking sheet in a single layer and freeze until solid. Separate any clumps, and transfer the onion to a zipper-lock freezer bag. Another easy way to save time, since onions and garlic are often sautéed together, is to sauté more of them than you need and freeze the leftovers. They're an instant start to sautés, soups, sauces, and stews.

HEALTHY HINT ▼ **To get the most nutrients** • Choose yellow or red storage onions. These onions contain higher amounts of flavonoids, the powerful antioxidants that help protect the body from disease.

Oranges *see also* Citrus Fruits; Mandarin Oranges; Zest

Native to southern China and southeast Asia, oranges have been cultivated for approximately 4,000 years.

BASICS ▼ **To choose** • There are three main categories of oranges: sweet oranges, mandarin oranges, and sour oranges. Sweet oranges are usually large, sweet, and juicy, with firm skins. They include navel oranges (popular for eating out of hand because most are seedless), Valencia oranges (extremely juicy, and popular for juicing), and blood oranges (prized for their red flesh). Mandarin oranges, such as tangerines, clementines, tangelos, and honey oranges, all have thin, loose skins. Mandarins range in flavor from sweet to slightly tart, and many make excellent eating oranges. Sour, or bitter, oranges are usually used to make marmalade and liqueurs such as Grand Marnier and curaçao. The most famous bitter orange is Seville. Bergamot is another important bitter orange, lending its characteristic flavor to Earl Grey tea. Regardless of which type you choose, pick oranges that feel heavy for their size and have no signs of mold or soft spots. Don't go by color. Fully ripe, sweet, juicy oranges may have green shading, and some oranges are dyed with food coloring.

To store • Keep in a cool, dry place for a few days or refrigerate for up to 2 weeks.

To zest and juice • Use a citrus zester, a grater, or a vegetable peeler. Avoid taking the bitter white pith beneath the outer orange zest. Be sure to zest oranges before juicing them; it's nearly impossible to remove the zest once they've been juiced.

To make orange "supremes" • Orange segments that are free of their protective outer membrane are often called supremes. Slice off about ½" from the top (stem end) and bottom of a large, firm navel orange, removing the zest and white pith as you cut. Stand the orange on end and cut downward all around, cutting just

O

beneath the white pith, to remove the entire rind in strips. Stand the rindless orange on end (or in your hand) and remove one orange segment at a time by running the knife close to the membrane, releasing each segment. Squeeze the remaining accordion-like membrane over the supremes to extract any juice.

ORANGE-NUT COFFEE CAKE Preheat oven to 375°F. Grease an 8" × 8" baking pan. In a small bowl, combine ½ **cup chopped walnuts** or **pecans,** ¼ **cup** *each* **all-purpose flour and sugar, 2 teaspoons grated orange zest,** and **1 teaspoon ground cinnamon.** Add **2 tablespoons thinly sliced butter** and work in with your fingertips until crumbly. Set aside. Melt another ½ **stick (¼ cup) butter** in a small pan over low heat. Let cool slightly. In a large bowl, stir together another **1 cup all-purpose flour,** another ¼ **cup sugar, 1 teaspoon baking powder,** another **1 tablespoon grated orange zest,** and **a pinch of salt.** Make a well in the center and add ½ **cup orange juice, 1 large egg, 1 teaspoon vanilla extract,** and the melted butter. Stir just to combine ingredients into a batter. Pour into the prepared pan. Crumble nut mixture over batter and bake until a toothpick inserted in center pulls out clean, about 30 minutes. Cool in the pan on a rack 15 minutes.
Makes 6 to 8 servings.

Organic Foods

As it applies to food, the term *organic* generally means that the food has been grown without chemicals or other incidental additives such as pesticides, using ecologically friendly farming techniques such as crop rotation and composting, and that it has been produced with minimal processing.

BASICS ▼ **To choose** • While federal standards for organic foods are still being debated, any foods that are labeled "organic" according to the standards of the California Organic Foods Act have met the toughest measures to date, and you can be assured of the purity of their origins. When you're selecting organic produce, don't reject it because it is misshapen, unevenly colored, or slightly blemished. Because they are raised without the aid of pesticides, or-

---

TOP ORGANIC FOODS

The Environmental Working Group, a nonprofit environmental research organization based in Washington, D.C., found that the following foods have the most or least amount of pesticide residue.

Most Pesticide	Least Pesticide
1. Strawberries	1. Avocados
2. Bell peppers	2. Corn
3. Spinach	3. Onions
4. Cherries	4. Sweet potatoes
5. Peaches	5. Cauliflower
6. Cantaloupe (Mexican)	6. Brussels sprouts
7. Celery	7. Grapes
8. Apples	8. Bananas
9. Apricots	9. Plums
10. Green beans	10. Green onions
11. Grapes (Chilean)	11. Watermelon
12. Cucumbers	12. Broccoli

ganic fruits and vegetables may not always look perfect, but their flavor is usually quite good.

Ovens *see also* Convection Oven; Microwave Cooking; Stoves

Standard equipment in most kitchens, ovens are used for baking, roasting, braising, and broiling. Ovens that include stove-top burners are known as ranges.

BASICS ▼ **To check for accuracy** • Use an oven thermometer. Oven temperatures can be off by as much as 50°F, so don't rely solely on the numbers painted on the temperature knobs. For example, if the knob says 400°F and the thermometer says 450°F, your oven runs 50°F hot. Adjust recipes accordingly by subtracting 50°F from the temperature specified in the recipe.

To deal with hot spots • Most ovens heat unevenly. For even baking, try rotating baking pans from top to bottom and front to back at least once during baking time.

To clean • Scrub with a paste of baking soda and water.

TIME SAVER ▼ **To speed cleanup** • Line the oven floor with foil (avoid covering any vents). When the foil is dirty, toss it in the trash.

FLAVOR TIP ▼ **To brown meat in the oven** • Some meats are obvious choices for browning in the oven, such as a chicken or a roast, but you can also brown meats such as meatballs or chunks of beef for stew. Simply brush the meat with oil, butter, or other fat, place it in a shallow pan, and roast it in the top of a preheated 450°F oven until browned.

Oysters

Whether enjoyed raw on the half-shell or in a creamy bowl of stew, no food so perfectly captures the sweet, salty taste of the sea as an oyster. In spite of the long list of names you may be presented with at an oyster bar, there are just four species of oysters: Atlantic or Eastern oysters, European flat oysters, Pacific or Japanese oysters, and tiny Olympias. What makes one oyster different from another depends on where it is grown.

BASICS ▼ **To choose** • Forget what you may have heard about not eating oysters in any month that doesn't have an *r* in it. The truth is that oysters are safe to eat all year round; they just aren't as good in the summer months, when the waters warm up. This is when the oysters spawn, and their normally firm flesh turns milky and soft. Winter is a better time to eat oysters because that's when the waters are coldest and the oyster's flavor is best. When you're at the store, note how the oysters are displayed. They should be kept flat on a bed of ice or in a refrigerator. If they're all jumbled together in a bag, their juices will run out. Also, make sure that the oyster shells are tightly closed. If the shell is open, even a crack, the oyster meat will dry out. If you will be serving raw oysters on the half-shell, they will always taste best if shucked just before serving. When the oysters are to be cooked, it's generally okay to buy shucked, vacuum-packed oysters. All shucked oysters should be plump and uniform in size, smell sweetly of the sea, and have clear liquid (often called liquor).

To eat oysters safely • Stick with cold-water oysters. Those from the North Atlantic and Pacific Coasts are the safest bet. Gulf Coast oysters carry the toxic organism *Vibrio vulnificus,* a naturally occur-

O

ring marine bacterium that has resulted in outbreaks of illness. Also, never eat an oyster that isn't icy cold. Harmful bacteria lie relatively dormant when it's cold, but once the temperature warms up, they can cause trouble. Keep in mind, too, that alcohol can lower your resistance to harmful bacteria. It's best not to consume too much alcohol if you plan on eating raw oysters. A final caution: If you are pregnant or your immune system is compromised, avoid oysters altogether.

To store • Once you get live oysters home, arrange them flat on a baking sheet or a plate, cover them with a damp cloth, and store them in the refrigerator. Depending on when they were harvested, live oysters will keep for about 1 week in the refrigerator, but they will taste best when consumed as soon as possible. Shucked oysters can be covered in their liquor and refrigerated up to 2 days or frozen up to 3 months. Avoid soaking oysters in water, however, which dilutes their flavor.

To shuck • Use an oyster knife, which is short and sturdy, with a pointed tip for boring into the shell hinge to pop it open. You can also use the pointed tip of a can or bottle opener to pop the shell, then use a dull knife to cut the oyster meat from the shell. Avoid using a sharp kitchen knife, which could cause serious injury. Before you begin, cover your hand with a thick, folded dish towel, a pot holder, or a specially designed oyster glove to protect yourself from a slip of the knife and the rough edges of the shell. (See the illustrations for shucking clams on page 123.)

To make oysters easier to shuck • Place the raw oysters in the freezer for about 15 to 20 minutes, which will weaken the oysters and cause them to release their grips on their shells slightly. Of course, oysters are not quite as fresh when using this method.

To speed up shucking for cooking • If the oysters are to be cooked, simplify shucking by placing them, deepest shell down, directly on a gas burner. Turn on the heat to medium for 3 to 5 seconds. The heated oysters should easily pry open. Or arrange 6 to 8 oysters around the rim of a plate, hinged side facing outward. Microwave on high power just until the shells begin to open, 30 seconds.

To cook shucked oysters • Oysters take literally seconds to cook. Heat a non-stick skillet until very hot. Add the oysters and stir until they plump, 30 to 45 seconds, depending on the number of oysters in the pan. Immediately remove from the pan with a slotted spoon. Use the liquid in the pan to create a sauce. Be careful to avoid overcooking oysters, which causes them to become tough.

POACHED OYSTERS IN LEMON-BUTTER SAUCE Brush **8 slices French bread** with **3 tablespoons olive oil** and rub with **1 split garlic clove.** Toast and place 2 slices on each of 4 plates. In a skillet, heat **¼ cup white wine, 2 tablespoons white wine vinegar,** and **1 finely chopped shallot** to a simmer. **Add 2 dozen shucked oysters** and simmer until oysters are plump and their edges just start to curl, 30 seconds. Using a slotted spoon, transfer oysters to the toasts and keep warm. Turn heat to medium-high and cook until liquid reduces to 3 tablespoons. Reduce heat to low and add **1 tablespoon lemon juice** and **6 tablespoons unsalted butter.** Pour over oysters. *Makes 4 servings.*

FRIED OYSTERS Shuck **2 dozen oysters.** Place ⅓ **cup flour** in a shallow dish or pie pan. In another shallow dish or pie pan, combine **2 large eggs** and **2 tablespoons cream** or **water.** Place **2 cups Japanese panko crumbs** or **plain dry bread crumbs** in a third shallow dish (you can also use fresh bread crumbs, cracker crumbs, or half flour and half coarse cornmeal). Heat ½" of **vegetable oil (or butter, or half butter and half olive oil, or half vegetable oil and half lard or bacon fat)** in a skillet or wok over medium heat. Working with two oysters at a time, roll in flour to lightly coat, dip into egg mixture, and dredge in crumbs to coat. Place in hot oil. Coat more oysters, but avoid crowding in the pan. Fry 1 to 1½ minutes. Then, turn and fry until deep golden, 1 minute longer. Drain on paper towels. Sprinkle very lightly with **salt** and serve hot with **lemon wedges** or **tartar sauce.** For an elegant presentation, save the deepest halves of oyster shells; after draining, place 1 fried oyster in each half-shell. To vary the flavor, drain the shucked oysters first, then marinate in 1 to 2 tablespoons lemon juice or fresh ginger juice for 30 minutes before breading and frying.

Makes about 4 servings.

p

Paella

In Spain, paella is nothing short of a national passion. Many of the ingredients can vary: Some cooks include sausage, while others use chicken, seafood, and/or a wide range of vegetables. But the heart and soul of true paella is medium-grain Spanish rice.

BASICS **To choose the rice** • Look for the Spanish variety known as bomba. If you can't find it, substitute another medium-grain rice. Italian Arborio rice works fine in paella, but avoid using a long-grain rice.

To choose a pan • If possible, use a paella pan, which is wide and shallow with sloping sides. The shape of the pan helps to ensure that the rice cooks in a thin layer by maximizing the amount of rice touching the bottom of the pan. A good paella pan is made of very thin, heat-conductive metal, usually plain or enameled steel. If you don't have a paella pan, substitute a large skillet. Avoid using cast-iron pans, which retain too much heat, and nonstick pans, which don't allow the rice to caramelize on the bottom of the pan.

To ensure evenly cooked rice • Cover the paella pan with foil for the last 2 minutes of cooking.

To test for doneness • Break apart a grain. You should see a pinpoint-size white dot in the center, meaning that the rice is cooked through but still slightly firm to the bite.

To ensure a caramelized crust of rice • Increase the heat at the end of the cooking time and pay close attention to the sound of the rice as it cooks. It should crackle a bit and smell toasty but not burnt. After a minute or two, poke a spoon under the foil and feel for a bumpy resistance on the bottom of the pan. This crust is called the socarrat and is the sign of a well-made paella.

To round out flavors after cooking • Cover the pan with a towel and let it rest off the heat for 5 to 10 minutes.

To serve in the traditional style • Let your guests eat paella directly from the pan, starting at the outside edge and working toward the center.

FLAVOR TIP **To boost flavor in seafood paella** • Replace 1 cup of the chicken broth with 1 cup bottled clam juice.

Pancakes *see also* Crepes; Waffles

Traditional American pancakes are light and fluffy, the perfect medium for soaking up pure maple syrup. **Technically a quick bread, pancakes are leavened with baking soda, baking powder, or sometimes a combination of both.**

BASICS ▼ **To mix** • Start by combining the dry ingredients, whisking them together to make sure that they are evenly blended and free of any lumps. Stir together the wet ingredients in another bowl and, when ready to make the pancakes, gently combine the wet and dry ingredients with a rubber spatula or a wooden spoon.

To ensure that pancakes are light and tender • Take care not to overmix the batter. It's better for the batter to contain a few lumps than to overbeat it and end up with tough pancakes.

To choose the right pan • A flat, heavy griddle is ideal for cooking pancakes. If you don't have one, use a large, heavy skillet instead. Nonstick pans also work well.

To determine whether the pan is at the right temperature • Flick a drop of water into the preheated pan. If it bounces when it hits the griddle, the pan is ready. If it bounces out of the griddle, it is too hot. If it does not bounce at all, the pan needs further preheating.

To make even-size pancakes • Mix the batter in a large liquid measuring cup. Pour the same amount of batter for each pancake.

To make creative shapes • Use a bulb baster (a turkey baster) to form pancakes. You can take advantage of the flexibility of the baster to get creative with shapes. It also allows you to dispense just the right amount each time.

To make a test pancake • Always make a test pancake first to judge the consistency of the batter and the temperature of the griddle. Preheat the griddle or pan over medium heat. Lightly oil the hot pan.

Pour about ⅓ cup batter in the center. Leave the pancake undisturbed until bubbles appear and then burst. When the edges of the pancake look dry, slide a thin spatula or pancake turner under the pancake and flip it over in the same place where it had been. Judge the color: If it is too brown, lower the heat slightly for the next batch. Also, if the pancake is too thick, add a splash of milk to the batter.

To keep cooked pancakes hot • Transfer to a cooling rack set over a baking sheet and keep in a 200°F oven.

To store leftover pancakes • Layer cooked pancakes between sheets of waxed paper. Transfer to zipper-lock freezer bags and freeze for up to 1 month.

To reheat frozen pancakes • Brush the frozen pancakes lightly with melted butter (if desired), and lay them in a single layer on a cooling rack set over a baking sheet. Heat in a 350°F oven until warmed through, about 10 minutes.

PROBLEM SOLVERS ▼ **To minimize spreading** • Make sure that the griddle is good and hot. If the pan is hot and the pancakes are still spreading, you may need to thicken the batter. Make a paste with a few tablespoons of flour and a few tablespoons of water. Blend in with the remaining batter to thicken.

To lighten pancake batter that is producing dense, heavy pancakes • Thin it with additional liquid. If the pancakes are still leaden, it is possible that your leavener is inactive. Try adding more baking soda and/or powder (depending on the recipe) from freshly opened containers, adding ½ teaspoon at a time. If neither of these options helps, next time, try lowering the protein in your flour by replacing ¼ cup all-purpose flour with ¼ cup cornstarch for every cup of all-purpose flour used.

p

p

Pancakes/Waffles

Beaten egg whites are the secret to this batter. It makes both light, fluffy pancakes and crisp, airy waffles. A bit of whole wheat flour adds fiber and texture.

1½	**cups all-purpose flour**
½	**cup whole wheat pastry flour**
1	**tablespoon sugar**
2	**teaspoons baking powder**
¾	**teaspoon salt**
2	**eggs, separated**
2	**cups milk**
⅓	**cup butter, melted and cooled**

1. In a large bowl, whisk together the all-purpose flour, whole wheat pastry flour, sugar, baking powder, and salt. In a medium bowl, beat the egg yolks into the milk. Stir in the butter. In a small bowl, beat the egg whites until stiff peaks form.

2. Stir the milk mixture into the flour mixture. Gently fold in the egg whites.

3. Grease and preheat a large nonstick skillet or preheat a waffle iron to medium heat. Pour ⅓ cup to ½ cup of the batter into the skillet or waffle iron. For pancakes, cook until golden brown, 3 minutes per side, turning once. For waffles, cook until the waffle stops steaming and is golden brown, 4 to 5 minutes. Repeat to use all of the batter.

Makes twelve to sixteen 4" pancakes or about 12 waffles

Banana-Pecan Pancakes/Waffles: Gently fold ½ cup sliced bananas (tossed with lemon juice) and ½ cup toasted chopped pecans in with the egg whites.

Berry Pancakes/Waffles: Gently fold ½ cup fresh or frozen berries in with the egg whites.

Chocolate Chip Pancakes/Waffles: Gently fold ½ cup chocolate chips in with the egg whites.

To keep pancakes from cooling too quickly on the plate • Serve on warmed plates with warmed syrup. Heat the plates and syrup in a microwave oven on medium power until warmed, 30 seconds to 1 minute.

TIME SAVERS ▼ **To save prep time** • Combine the dry ingredients and prep the wet ingredients in separate bowls the night before. Come morning, just mix the two together.

To save cleanup time • Mix the batter in a zipper-lock plastic bag. Refrigerate until ready to cook, and then snip off a bottom corner and dispense the amount of batter you need, as you would use a pastry bag. This trick works for cake batters and other batters, too.

HOMEMADE BUTTERMILK PANCAKE MIX Mix together **3 cups all-purpose flour, ¼ cup sugar, 1 tablespoon baking powder, 1 teaspoon baking soda,** and **a pinch of salt.** Store in a tightly sealed container at room temperature for up to 3 weeks. When it comes time to make the pancakes, combine the entire container of mix with **3 eggs, 3 cups buttermilk, 1 teaspoon vanilla extract,** and **3 tablespoons melted butter.** Ladle ⅓-cup portions of batter on a hot, greased griddle over medium-high heat and cook until pancake surfaces are bubbly all over. Flip and cook on the other side until centers feel springy. *Makes about 1 pound of pancake mix, or 18 large pancakes.*

Pancetta *see also* Bacon

The exact same cut of streaky pork belly that's used to make bacon is also used for pancetta. The difference is that while bacon is smoke-cured, pancetta is cured with salt and a lot of pepper and has a subtler flavor. It also has a different appearance because the pork belly is rolled so that each slice is a spiral design. Pancetta, or Italian bacon, is most often used as a flavoring for braises and stews.

BASICS **To choose** • Look for pancetta with pale red meat that is streaked with creamy-colored fat. The meat shouldn't look greasy.

To store • Keep pancetta tightly wrapped in the refrigerator for up to 3 weeks, or freeze for up to 6 weeks.

To prepare • Chop pancetta and cook it in a skillet over medium heat until much of its fat is rendered. Use it as a seasoning base for cooking other foods.

FLAVOR TIPS **To start a sauce** • Whether you are making a Bolognese sauce for pasta or a quick sauce for cauliflower or any other vegetable, start by chopping a few slices of pancetta and sautéing them in the pan before adding minced garlic, onion, or other ingredients. Often, a mixture of finely chopped carrot, celery, and onion, called battuto, is sautéed in the pancetta fat.

To flavor and baste a chicken • Place a couple of thin slices of pancetta over the breast meat of a chicken. Tie it with cotton string to hold it in place, and roast as usual.

Panko

The sooner you discover panko, the happier you will be. Panko are special Japanese bread crumbs that are shaped more like slivers or crystals than rounded bread crumbs. The crumbs are designed so that tiny points stick out in all directions. Not only do they maximize crispness but they also taste lighter and less dense (see Fried Oysters, page 325).

BASICS **To use** • Look for panko in Asian food markets or buy them from specialty food catalogs. Use them as you would use any other bread crumbs.

TONKATSU (BREADED PORK CUTLETS) Cut eight ¼"-thick slices from a **boneless pork loin (1½ pounds).** Score any fat on the edges to prevent curling. Set up 3 shallow dishes or pie pans: In one, place **¼ cup flour;** in another, whisk **1 large egg** with **1 tablespoon water;** in the third, place about **1¼ cups panko.** In a large skillet, heat **¼" of vegetable oil**

p

over medium–high heat. Dip one slice of pork in flour to lightly coat. Dip into egg mixture, then into panko to coat evenly. Place in the hot oil. Lower heat slightly. Coat more cutlets and fry without crowding the pan, until crisp and golden. Turn and cook until just a trace of pale pink juice runs from the center of a cutlet when pierced with a knife, 2 minutes longer. Drain on paper towels. Cut into strips and arrange on a plate. Serve with commercially bottled tonkatsu sauce, lemon wedges, or hot Chinese mustard.
Makes 4 to 6 servings.

Papayas

Pear-shaped papayas thrive in the tropics. Their smooth, yellow flesh is sweet and soft, with a delicate floral flavor. Most markets sell the relatively small (½- to 1-pound) yellow-green papayas that flourish in Hawaii. Other varieties are grown in Mexico, the Caribbean, and Florida, to a whopping 15 to 20 pounds.

BASICS ▼ **To choose** • Available year-round, papayas are most plentiful in the spring and fall. Look for small fruits that yield to gentle pressure. Papayas with spotty coloring usually have more flavor.

To store • Keep unripe papayas at room temperature. Once they are fully ripened, store them in the refrigerator and eat within a day or two.

To prepare • Cut the fruit in half lengthwise and scoop out the seeds. Scoop the flesh out with a spoon or peel off the skin with a vegetable peeler.

PROBLEM SOLVER ▼ **To use with gelatin** • Heat the papaya before adding it to the gelatin. Uncooked papaya contains an enzyme that prevents gelatin from setting properly (the enzyme is destroyed upon cooking).

TIME SAVER ▼ **To speed ripening** • Put the papaya in a paper bag with a banana for a day or two. Or score the papaya lengthwise in quarters, cutting through the skin but not into the flesh. Set the fruit, narrow end down, in a glass and let it sit for a few days.

FLAVOR TIPS ▼ **To use in savory dishes** • Papaya is delicious in both sweet and savory dishes. Try it chopped in stir-fries with poultry, pork, or seafood, or stuff papayas and bake them.

To use in marinades • Papaya contains an enzyme that tenderizes meat; it is often included in commercial tenderizers. To get the tenderizing benefits in a home-made marinade, puree the papaya finely and add it to the marinade or rub it over the surface of the meat.

GREEN PAPAYA SALAD Using a vegetable peeler, remove the skin from **1 small (12-ounce), firm, green papaya.** Cut it in half and remove seeds. Grate papaya through the large holes of a grater. Peel **1 cucumber,** then cut in half lengthwise and spoon out the seeds. Grate cucumber as you did papaya. Peel **1 large carrot** and grate it, too. In a large bowl, combine ¼ **cup lime juice, 1 tablespoon sugar, 1 large minced garlic clove, 3 tablespoons cilantro leaves, ½ teaspoon salt,** and ⅛ **teaspoon** *each* **ground black pepper and ground red pepper.** Add grated vegetables and papaya. Toss to mix. If necessary, add a pinch more salt. Cover and chill for 1 hour. Great with chicken and shrimp.
Makes 4 servings.

Parchment Paper

A sulfuric acid bath makes parchment paper strong enough to stand up to both heat and water. The smooth, hard surface of the paper is impermeable, so it doesn't soak up grease or moisture. Most brands of parchment are coated with silicone, which means that they're nonstick as well as nonporous.

BASICS ▼ **To make cleaning baking sheets easier** • Line them with sheets of parchment instead of greasing them. Food won't stick, and you won't have any greasy pans to wash.

p

FOUR DISHES IN THE BAG

Cooking food *en papillote* (in parchment or foil) makes an easy, elegant presentation. For each of the recipes below, follow the wrapping illustrations on page 332. Each recipe makes 4 servings.

Salmon with Orange and Tomato: Divide **4 skinned salmon fillets** (4 to 5 ounces each), skin side down, among 4 sheets of parchment or foil. In a small saucepan, combine ½ cup *each* orange juice and white wine, ¼ chopped onion, 2 minced garlic cloves, and 1 tablespoon finely grated orange zest. Bring to a boil over medium-high heat and cook until liquid is reduced to ¼ cup. Spoon 1 tablespoon over each portion of salmon. Top each with **2 tablespoons chopped tomato, a pinch *each* salt and ground black pepper, 1 teaspoon extra-virgin olive oil,** and **1 basil leaf.** Wrap and seal tightly. Bake at 375°F until packages are fully puffed and fish is opaque, 10 to 12 minutes. Slit open, remove contents (if desired), and serve.

Chicken with Roasted Peppers: Pound **4 boneless, skinless chicken breast halves** (¼ pound each) to ¼" thickness. Divide among 4 sheets of parchment or foil. Drizzle each with **1 teaspoon *each* walnut oil and lemon juice, ¼ teaspoon salt, ⅛ teaspoon** *each* minced garlic, ground coriander, and ground cumin, and a pinch of ground red pepper. Top each with ¼ roasted red bell pepper, cut into strips, and 1 tablespoon chopped fresh cilantro. Wrap and seal tightly. Bake at 375°F until packages are fully puffed, thickest part registers 160°F on an instant-read thermometer, and juices run clear, 15 to 18 minutes. Slit open, remove contents (if desired), and serve.

Ginger-Soy Shrimp: Place **1 pound shelled and deveined large shrimp** on a large sheet of parchment or foil. Top with a mixture of ¼ **teaspoon minced garlic, 1 teaspoon chopped fresh ginger, 1 tablespoon** *each* **toasted sesame oil, honey, and soy sauce,** and ¼ **cup dry sherry.** Wrap and seal tightly. Bake at 375°F until liquid in package is bubbling and shrimp are opaque, 10 minutes. Slit open and serve shrimp with the sauce in the package.

Bananas with Lime and Rum: Divide **4 peeled and split bananas** among 4 sheets of parchment or foil. Drizzle with a mixture of **1 tablespoon honey, ¼ cup rum,** and the **grated zest and juice of 1 lime.** Wrap and seal tightly. Bake at 375°F until packages are fully puffed, 10 to 12 minutes. Slit open and serve.

p

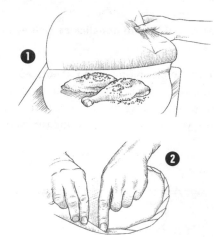

To cook *en papillote* • The French name for steaming food in a paper package comes from the word for butterfly, *papillon,* which refers to the traditional heart shape of the paper before it is folded and sealed around the food. Although parchment paper is the classic wrapper, foil can be used instead. This cooking method is perfect for delicate foods such as fish, chicken, or vegetables because it gently steams the food, locking in moisture and flavor. Another bonus: Food can be wrapped en papillote and stored in the refrigerator several hours before it is cooked, making it convenient for entertaining.

Cut a piece of parchment or foil that is twice as long as it is wide. Coat with cooking spray or brush with melted butter. Place the food on one half of the paper or foil. Add herbs or seasonings and fold the wrapper over to cover the food ❶.

Make a series of small double folds all the way around the edge of the paper. Overlap each fold to seal the package tightly ❷. Bake according to the timing and temperature that you would use if the food were not wrapped. As it bakes, the papillote will puff with steam (if well-sealed) and brown lightly. When done, let diners open the packets at the table by making a slit in the puffed top with a sharp knife.

Parsnips

A member of the parsley family, parsnips are a white root vegetable with a pleasantly sweet flavor. They are often boiled and mashed like potatoes or in combination with them.

BASICS ▼

To choose • Look for parsnips that are 8" to 10" in length, and avoid those that look limp or spotted. When left to grow, parsnips can reach up to 20" in length. These larger roots have a stronger flavor and more fibrous texture with a woody center. To use larger parsnips, cut out the fibrous centers before using.

To store • Place them in a perforated bag and refrigerate up to 2 weeks. The longer you keep parsnips, the sweeter they will get. Trim off any green growth at the top of the root before using.

To use in soups and stews • Parsnips turn mushy when overcooked, so add them to soups, stews, or vegetable sautés during the last 10 minutes of cooking.

HEALTHY HINT ▼

To retain the maximum nutrients • Peel parsnips after cooking them. Almost 50 percent of the nutrients in parsnips are water-soluble, meaning that they will leach out during cooking. Also, the majority of the flavor in parsnips is found just beneath the skin, so you don't want that to leach out either. Steam parsnips whole or in large chunks until tender, then scrape or peel away the skin. Like carrots, well-scrubbed fresh parsnips may not need peeling.

PARSNIP PATTIES Steam **1 pound trimmed parsnips** and **2 carrots** in a steamer basket over simmering water until tender, 10 minutes. When cool enough to handle, scrape off and discard skins. Place in a bowl and mash. Stir in ½ **teaspoon** *each* **ground ginger and salt** and ⅛ **teaspoon** *each* **ground allspice and ground white pepper.** Using floured hands, shape into 1¼" balls and flatten into patties. Heat **2 teaspoons olive oil** in a nonstick skillet over medium heat. Add patties and cook until golden brown, 3 to 4 minutes per side. *Makes 12 to 14.*

Pasta *see also* Couscous; Lasagna; Macaroni and Cheese; Noodles, Asian

One of the world's most versatile and popular foods, pasta is simple to make and pleases almost everyone. The major difference between fresh and dried pasta is that fresh pasta contains egg and most dried pasta does not. Dried egg noodles are a notable exception.

BASICS ▼ **To choose dried pasta** • Look for pastas made from durum wheat. Many of the best brands are imported from Italy.

To choose ready-made fresh pasta • Do a trial tasting of several different ones to find one that you like. When choosing fresh filled pastas, look closely at the dough. It should be sheer enough to see the filling inside.

To measure out a single portion of pasta • For each portion, use approximately ½ cup dried pasta or measure ½" diameter of dried strand pasta such as spaghetti (about the size of a dime). This will yield approximately 1 cup cooked pasta.

To choose a pasta machine • Go for a roller-type machine. Extruder-type pasta machines tend to make poor-quality pasta. When buying a roller-type machine, look for one that is sturdy and well-built. Check that the narrowest setting will produce a very thin sheet of pasta. If you make pasta often, consider buying a machine with extra-wide rollers. These are more expensive but well worth the investment because they save you time.

To clean a roller-type pasta machine • Crank the machine backward while simultaneously wiping the rollers clean with a pastry brush. It's best to do so immediately after rolling out fresh pasta. Otherwise, scraps of dough may dry and clog the machine.

To roll homemade pasta with a roller-type pasta machine • Lightly dust the machine's rollers and the area around the machine with flour. Set the rollers at the widest setting and pinch off about one-quarter of the dough, keeping the rest well-wrapped so that it doesn't dry out. Flatten the dough into a disk and put one end into the space between the two rollers. Turn the crank handle with one hand while holding the palm of your other hand under the dough as it emerges from the rollers, guiding it away from the machine with your hand. Pass the dough through the rollers 5 or 6 more times, folding the dough into thirds each time before you put it back between the rollers. Set the rollers at the next narrowest setting and pass the dough through 3 more times, folding it in half each time. Continue rolling and resetting the machine; pass the dough through 3 times at each successively narrower setting. If the dough becomes too thin to handle, cut it into more manageable lengths. When the dough has reached the desired thinness, cut it into shapes with a knife or with the cutting attachments on your pasta machine.

To keep fresh pasta dough soft and supple • Work quickly as you stretch and

p

roll it. The dough will start to dry out the longer it is exposed to air, and it will become difficult to work with. Overly dry dough will make pasta that cooks unevenly.

To imbed whole flat parsley leaves in homemade pasta • When rolling sheets of homemade pasta, as the sheets near the desired thinness, arrange flat parsley leaves on one sheet and top with a second sheet of pasta. Carefully hold the sheets together as you put both through the pasta roller again, which will embed the leaves within the pasta. Because of the pasta's thinness, you will see the whole parsley leaves. This makes a beautiful addition to soup. Just cut the pasta into squares, boil until tender, and float in a simple broth.

To dry fresh-cut homemade pasta • Separate the strands or pieces and hang them over a dowel or a broom handle until they are no longer moist. Dust the pasta lightly with semolina flour to keep it from sticking together, wrap it in coils, and set it on racks until completely dry.

To store fresh homemade pasta • You can store thoroughly dried, fresh pasta in a tightly sealed container at room temperature for several days.

To cook • Whether fresh or dried, pasta should be cooked in a large pot of rapidly boiling salted water. Bring the water to a boil, then add about 1 teaspoon salt per quart of water. Add the pasta, or place it in a pasta insert and submerge it in the water (avoid cooking more than 2 pounds of pasta at a time; it will cook unevenly). Stir once. Cover the pot and return to a boil. Uncover and boil the pasta until tender. Remove from the heat. Drain, but leave a little water clinging to the surface of the pasta to help the sauce flow.

To prepare pasta for casseroles or soups • Reduce the cooking time by

about one-third. The pasta will finish cooking while baking or simmering in the dish.

To test for doneness • Frequently taste-test the pasta before it is scheduled to be done. Start timing as soon as the water returns to a boil. Begin testing fresh pasta and very thin shapes after about 30 seconds and dried pasta after about 7 minutes. Lift a piece of the pasta out of the boiling water using tongs or a long-handled fork. Let cool slightly, then bite into it. It should be tender but slightly resistant. Drain pasta immediately once it's done. Pasta continues to cook from residual heat and can easily overcook.

To serve • Never rinse pasta unless it will be baked or used in a salad. The starch on the surface of the pasta will help the sauce cling to the pasta. For best results, warm the serving dishes. Also, pasta will stay warm longer when served in shallow bowls rather than on flat plates.

To substitute one for another • Many pastas are interchangeable, within reason. You can certainly substitute one long, thin pasta for another or one macaroni shape for another. You can also substitute rice noodles or lo mein for angel hair or spaghetti and use wonton skins or egg roll wrappers to make ravioli or tortellini.

To use wonton skins or egg roll skins for ravioli • Generally, egg roll skins are better than wontons because some wonton skins are too thin. In a cup, combine 1 egg yolk and 1 tablespoon water, to use as "glue." Place a thick wonton skin or one 3" square cut from an egg roll skin in front of you. Add about 1½ teaspoons filling in the center. Brush two edges with the egg yolk mixture and fold them over, squeezing out air as you form a triangle. Pinch the edges together to seal and arrange ravioli on a tray or baking sheet dusted with cornstarch or flour. Repeat with the remaining filling. To make larger, square ravioli, place one skin in front of you, add 2 teaspoons filling, brush egg glue around all four edges, then top with a second skin.

To cook ravioli made from wonton skins • Boil gently, uncovered, just until tender but firm to the bite, 3 to 5 minutes. Scoop out with a slotted spoon and toss with butter or olive oil, and continue cooking any remaining ravioli.

PROBLEM SOLVERS ▼ **To prevent pasta from sticking** • Perhaps the most common mistake in making pasta is not using enough water. Keep in mind that about a quart of water will be lost during the cooking process due to absorption and evaporation. Use about 4 quarts for every pound of pasta and stir occasionally. When the pasta is finished, toss it with sauce in the pan or a warmed serving bowl as soon as possible after draining. Pasta will begin to stick as soon as it cools; keeping it warm will help keep the pieces separate. As for the sauce itself, always prepare it before cooking the pasta so that the pasta never has to sit (and turn sticky and gluey) while the sauce finishes cooking. If the pasta finishes cooking before the sauce is ready, toss the warm pasta with a small amount of olive oil and keep it warm while the sauce finishes cooking.

To unstick pasta • Submerge it in hot water and separate.

To prevent lasagna noodles from clinging during assembly • Rinse them with cold water after draining to remove surface starch.

PAIRING PASTA WITH SAUCE

Matching pastas to sauces is pretty simple. Strand pastas, such as spaghetti and linguine, work better with smooth sauces. Shaped pastas, such as penne or bow-ties, work best with chunky sauces. Tiny pastas work best in soups and salads. Here's a bit more detail.

Basic Pasta Shapes	Specific Pasta Names	Best Sauces
STRAND PASTA		
Long and thin	Angel hair, thin spaghetti, vermicelli, capellini	Oil-based sauces and light, thin broth
Long and wide	Fettuccine, spaghetti, linguine, pappardelle, perciatelli	Light cream sauces, Alfredo sauce, and light tomato sauces
SHAPED PASTA		
Short and chunky	Rigatoni, shells, ziti, cut fusilli, penne, farfalle	Chunky sauces, meat sauces, primaveras, pasta casseroles, pasta salads
Tiny	Ditalini, orzo, alphabets, tubetti, pastina, small shells	Soups, stews, salads

p

To prevent boil-overs • Before the pasta pot gets hot, rub a thin layer of oil around the interior lip of the pot. If the pot isn't too heavy and a boil-over is imminent, simply remove the pot from the heat and transfer it to another burner. If the pot is too heavy, you can blow over the water's surface to keep it at bay while you lower the heat on the stove. You can also plunge a wooden spoon into the water, which helps control foaming.

To salvage overdone pasta • Skip the step of tossing the pasta with the sauce. In this situation, it's best to just spoon it on top. A rinse in tepid water will also help minimize the stickiness of overdone pasta. If the pasta is a real failure, just cook up a second batch of dried. Pasta is easy and cheap enough. Save the overcooked pasta to use in another dish, such as an omelette or Low-Fat Pasta Frittata (page 338).

To strain ravioli without tearing • Scoop them out of the water individually with a slotted spoon or a flat, mesh skimmer. If some of them tear, serve the torn ones under the intact ones, and it's likely that no one will notice. If a number of them tear, cover them up with sauce, crumbled bacon or a mixture of toasted bread crumbs, garlic, and herbs.

Fascinating Fact: Ravioli got its name in Genoa, Italy, from the word *rabioli,* which means "rubbish." Ravioli was so named because it is considered an excellent vehicle for filling with leftovers.

TIME SAVERS ▼ **To cook pasta ahead of time** • Cook the pasta until just slightly underdone. Cool the cooked pasta in a bowl of ice water. As soon as it reaches room temperature, drain it and toss it with oil to prevent sticking.

Refrigerate it in a zipper-lock plastic bag. To reheat, plunge the pasta into a large pot of boiling water. Stir until pieces of pasta separate, about 20 seconds, and drain. Toss with sauce.

To save draining time • Use a large pot equipped with a perforated insert.

To save boiling time • Add salt to the pasta water after it comes to a boil. Salted water takes longer to come to a boil than unsalted water.

To save cooking time • Use fresh pasta, which cooks in a few seconds (for thin pasta such as angel hair) to just 3 minutes (for large stuffed ravioli or tortellini). You can also save on cooking and cleanup time by cooking vegetables in the same pot with pasta. Trim and chop the vegetables and add them to the boiling pasta so that they are done cooking at the same time as the pasta. Add potatoes right along with the pasta; broccoli florets 3 minutes before the noodles are to be ready; asparagus 2 minutes before; and delicate leaves, such as spinach, just before the pasta is drained. Drain the vegetables right along with the pasta.

QUICK ARTICHOKE PASTA SAUCE Chop **1 jar (6 ounces) marinated artichoke hearts.** Toss artichokes, their marinade, and **1 cup crumbled feta cheese** with ¾ **pound pasta** for an ultra-simple and succulent sauce. *Makes 4 servings.*

FLAVOR TIP ▼ **To create exciting textures** • Use more than one shape in a single dish. Many short, shaped pastas can be easily mixed, such as penne, rotini, and gemelli. Or mix strands and shapes. Half orecchiette and half thin spaghetti or vermicelli makes a nice combination.

p

FRESH EGG PASTA Place **3 cups all-purpose flour** in a large bowl, or mound the flour on a large surface. Make a well in the center. Beat **4 large eggs** with **1 tablespoon water** and add to the well. Begin stirring eggs and water with a fork in a circular motion, gradually drawing in some of the flour from around the edge as you stir. Continue to incorporate flour until dough forms a stiff, rough mass that is neither dry nor wet. (You may need a little more flour if the weather is wet and humid, or less if the weather is dry.) Knead the dough until silky-smooth and very elastic, working in a bit of extra flour if dough becomes too sticky. Kneading is the key to tender, resilient pasta, so don't shortcut this step. Wrap dough in plastic wrap and let rest at least 30 minutes, preferably 1 hour. Roll and cut into desired shapes or refrigerate up to 2 days. To make **Fresh Whole Wheat Pasta,** replace 1 cup of the all-purpose flour with whole wheat flour. For **Fresh Tomato Pasta,** add 3 to 4 tablespoons tomato paste along with eggs. For **Fresh Spinach Pasta,** omit the water. Instead, in a saucepan, cook 8 to 10 ounces cleaned fresh spinach until wilted. Drain and let cool. Squeeze out as much liquid as possible, then chop with a knife as finely as possible. Add to well along with eggs. *Makes 1 to 1¼ pounds.*

FETTUCCINE ALFREDO Follow the recipe for **Fresh Egg Pasta** (above), roll dough, and cut into fettuccine (or buy 1 to 1¼ pounds prepared fresh fettuccine). Heat a large pot of water to boiling. Add **1 tablespoon salt** and the fettuccine. Stir and return to a boil. Cook until firm-tender, 1 to 2 minutes. Meanwhile, melt **½ stick (¼ cup) butter** in a large skillet. Drain pasta, saving ¼ cup of cooking water. Add pasta to the skillet along with **1 cup heavy cream.** Bring to a boil, then remove from heat. Add **1 cup grated Parmesan cheese, another ½ teaspoon salt,** and **¼ teaspoon ground black pepper.** Toss to mix. If dry, add some of the cooking water. Serve hot with grated Parmesan cheese. *Makes 4 to 6 servings.*

1950s-STYLE MACARONI AND BEEF In a large pot of boiling salted water, cook **½ pound large or medium elbow macaroni** until tender but firm to the bite, 7 to 9 minutes. Meanwhile, in a large skillet, sauté **1 large chopped onion** in **1½ tablespoons olive oil** to soften, 3 to 5 minutes. Push to one side of the pan and crumble in **8 to 12 ounces lean ground beef,** ½ teaspoon *each* **dried basil and dried oregano,** and **1 minced garlic clove (optional).** Cook, stirring, until beef is no longer pink. Add **1 can (28 ounces) whole tomatoes,** with juice, breaking up tomatoes with a spoon. Add **1 teaspoon salt** and ¼ **teaspoon ground black pepper.** Bring to a boil. Drain pasta, add to sauce, and bring to a boil. Serve hot. *Makes 4 to 6 servings.*

SHELL PASTA WITH LENTILS Bring a large pot of unsalted water to a boil. Add **1½ cups (about 11 ounces) red lentils,** reduce heat to medium, and simmer 10 minutes. Add **2 teaspoons salt** and **1 pound small shell pasta.** Cook until pasta and lentils are tender, about 10 minutes. Drain and toss with ¼ **cup extra-virgin olive oil,** ⅓ **cup** *each* **chopped fresh parsley**

p

and grated Parmesan cheese, 1 minced garlic clove, and a pinch of red-pepper flakes. *Makes 4 to 6 servings.*

LOW-FAT PASTA FRITTATA Instead of throwing out leftover pasta, use it to make a frittata. In a medium, nonstick, oven-proof skillet, sauté 4 sliced scallions in 2 teaspoons olive oil, 2 minutes. Remove from heat and stir in 2 cups leftover cooked pasta and ¾ cup jarred sliced roasted red pepper. In a large bowl, whisk together 4 eggs, 4 egg whites, ⅓ cup low-fat ricotta cheese, 1 tea-

spoon chopped fresh rosemary, ½ teaspoon salt, and ¼ teaspoon ground black pepper. Return the skillet to low heat, stir in egg mixture, cover, and cook until eggs are almost set, 8 minutes. Place under a preheated broiler (5" from heat) and cook until top is set, 2 to 4 minutes. Top with ¼ cup grated Cheddar cheese (optional). *Makes 4 servings.*

HEALTHY HINTS ▼

To increase fiber • Look for whole wheat pasta. Although both regular and whole wheat pasta are high in complex carbohydrates, whole wheat pasta contains 3 times the fiber of regular pasta (1 cup of whole

---

FOUR HEALTHFUL PASTA SAUCES

Use any of these sauces with ½ pound of dried pasta. Each makes 4 modest servings; enough for a first course or side dish.

Clam Sauce: In a nonstick skillet, sauté 2 chopped garlic cloves in 1½ teaspoons olive oil, 2 minutes. Stir in 1 can (10 ounces) baby clams, with juice, and ¼ cup white wine. Simmer 2 minutes. Remove from heat and stir in ¼ cup chopped fresh parsley. Toss with hot pasta. Top with ¼ cup skillet-toasted bread crumbs.

Lemon-Caper Cream Sauce: In a non-stick skillet over medium heat, combine ½ cup half-and-half, 3 tablespoons vodka, 2 teaspoons grated lemon zest, and ⅛ teaspoon ground white or black pepper. Cook until hot. Toss with 2 tablespoons capers and hot pasta.

Chicken and Asparagus Sauce: In a nonstick skillet, sauté 1 chopped garlic clove and 1 teaspoon chopped fresh rosemary in 2 teaspoons olive oil, 15 seconds.

Add ½ pound thinly sliced boneless skinless chicken breasts and cook, stirring, until no longer pink and juices run clear, 3 minutes. Add ½ pound trimmed and diagonally sliced asparagus, ½ cup chicken broth, and 2 tablespoons chopped fresh parsley. Increase heat to high and boil until liquid reduces slightly, 4 minutes, stirring occasionally. Stir in ⅓ cup reduced-fat sour cream. Toss with hot pasta.

Roasted Pepper, Arugula, and Goat Cheese Sauce: In a skillet, sauté ¼ cup chopped shallots, ⅛ teaspoon red-pepper flakes, and 2 chopped garlic cloves in 2 teaspoons olive oil, 2 minutes. Stir in 1 drained jar (7 ounces) sliced roasted red peppers and simmer 5 minutes. Stir in 2 cups coarsely chopped arugula leaves and ½ teaspoon dried basil. Cook 2 minutes. Toss with hot pasta and sprinkle ⅓ cup crumbled goat cheese over top.

wheat pasta has 6 grams of fiber). To get used to the slightly nutty taste of whole wheat pasta, try mixing whole wheat pasta with equal amounts of regular and/or spinach pasta. Gradually increase the amount of whole wheat pasta.

To avoid wheat pasta • If you are allergic to wheat, look for Italian pastas made from corn or artichoke. You can also find wheat-free pasta made from kamut grain; whole grain and white spelt; rice (examples include rice vermicelli and rice sticks); rye; quinoa; and wild rice; as well as bean thread noodles and 100 percent buckwheat soba noodles. Look for the Asian pastas in the international section of your grocery store. Others can be found in most health food stores.

Pastry Bags

Cone-shaped canvas pastry bags fitted with metal tubes are the most efficient tools for decorating cakes and shaping wet batters for cookies and pastries.

BASICS ▼ **To choose** • Buy a pastry bag that's larger than what you think you need. A 10" to 12" bag is a good all-purpose size.

To choose the right decorating tip • For writing, stringwork, or simple figures, use a plain tip. To make ridged borders and rosettes, use a star tip. For ribbed leaves, use a notched leaf tip. To make curved petals for flowers, use a rose petal tip. And to make flowers with a single squeeze of the bag, use a drop leaf tip.

To insert a decorating tip • Fold down the top of the bag around its edges and push the decorating tip into the small opening at the base of the bag. Half of the tip should protrude from the opening.

To fill • Twist the bag just above the tip and stuff the twisted part of the bag into the tip to form a plug. This will keep any frosting or batter from leaking out while you fill the bag. With one hand, hold the bag loosely about halfway up; with your other hand, fold back the top of the bag to make a large cuff that rests on the hand that is holding the bag. Or nestle the bag in a 1-quart measuring cup or container and cuff it over the rim. Using a spatula, scoop the batter or frosting into the bag until half-full. Scrape the spatula against the cuff to remove any excess. Unfold the cuff and twist the bag above the piping mixture to close the top. Untwist the tip end of the bag to allow the piping mixture to pass through.

To eliminate air bubbles • Before you begin piping, hold the bag over a bowl and twist the top of the bag to force the piping mixture all the way to the tip. Squeeze until a few inches of the mixture pushes through the end of the bag.

To use • Guide the bag with your dominant hand while squeezing the top of the bag gently with your other hand. Begin squeezing just before you start to move the bag, and stop squeezing the moment before you stop moving the bag.

TIME SAVER ▼ **To improvise a pastry bag** • Fill a heavy-duty zipper-lock plastic bag no more than two-thirds full. Twist the top closed, forcing the piping mixture into one of the corners. Snip off the tip of the corner with scissors. Cut off as little as possible; you can always make the piping hole bigger. Proceed to pipe. You can also make a piping cone from parchment paper (see page 196).

Pastry Cream

A gently cooked custard thickened with flour, pastry cream is used to fill fruit tarts, cream puffs, éclairs, napoleons, and cakes.

p

To keep pastry cream from curdling • Cook the cream over low heat and stir constantly as the cream cooks.

To keep a skin from forming on pastry cream • Press a sheet of plastic wrap directly against the surface of the cream.

SATIN-SMOOTH PASTRY CREAM In a mixing bowl, combine **4 egg yolks** (or 6 yolks for a richer cream) and **½ cup sugar.** Using a whisk or electric mixer, beat until mixture is light-colored and falls from the whisk or beaters in a thick ribbon. Sift **¼ cup flour** and beat it into yolk mixture along with **a pinch of salt.** In a saucepan, combine **2 cups milk** and **1 split vanilla bean (or add vanilla extract later).** Bring to a boil over medium heat. Remove vanilla bean (or stir in 1 teaspoon vanilla extract, if using). Slowly pour hot milk into egg mixture, whisking or beating constantly. Pour through a strainer into a saucepan to remove lumps. Cook over low heat until cream is thick and clings to the back of the spoon, stirring constantly. Transfer to a bowl and let cool, stirring occasionally. Press a sheet of plastic wrap directly onto surface of cream and chill at least 1 hour before using.
Makes about 2 ½ cups.

Pâté

An elegant version of meat loaf, pâté (pronounced "pah-TAY") is made from seasoned ground meat and can be smooth-textured or pleasingly coarse. In addition to ground meat, pâté often contains liver, cream, cognac, eggs, and spices. Some pâtés are embedded with strips of meat, vegetables, or truffles through the center so that a beautiful design is revealed when they are sliced.

Though most often purchased, pâté is an easy dish to fix at home and doesn't require special equipment or exotic ingredients.

To safely test the seasoning of home-made pâté • Fry a small patty of the raw meat mixture and let it cool before tasting. Adjust the seasoning if necessary.

To choose a dish • There's no need to invest in an expensive terrine dish. Use any heavy dish that conducts heat slowly, such as one made from ceramic, earthenware, enamel, or glass. Avoid using a metal pan, which will conduct too much heat.

To keep pâté tender and moist as it bakes • Cover the pâté tightly with foil and bake it in a water bath.

To create a compact shape and firm texture • Weight the baked pâté with a heavy can or a foil-wrapped brick. Secure the weight with rubber bands or masking tape and refrigerate for at least 24 hours.

To remove any congealed juices from the surface • Rinse the pâté quickly under running water and pat dry with paper towels.

To slice easily • Cut the pâté while it is still cold from the refrigerator.

To best enjoy the flavor • Let the slices come to room temperature for at least 30 minutes before serving.

EASY CHICKEN LIVER PÂTÉ Chop **5 slices smoked bacon** into pieces and cook in a skillet over medium heat until crisp. Tilt the pan and spoon off all but 1 tablespoon of fat. Add **1 finely chopped onion** and **1 minced garlic clove.** Sauté to soften, 3 minutes. Add **1 pound halved chicken livers** and cook until well-browned and no longer pink in center. Standing back and averting your face, add ¼ **cup cognac** or other brandy. Touch with a match to ignite (flambé). Shake the pan gently until the flames subside. Add ⅓ **cup heavy cream, 1 teaspoon salt,** and ¼ **teaspoon** *each* **ground black pepper, ground nutmeg, and dried thyme.** Bring to a boil, then reduce heat to medium and simmer 2 to 3 minutes to thicken slightly. Remove from heat and let cool to room temperature. Transfer to a food processor and add **2 hard-cooked eggs.** Blend to a puree. Add ½ **stick (¼ cup) softened butter** and pulse to blend. Pack into a crock or bowl. Cover and chill at least 3 hours. Serve with toast, crackers, or crostini. *Makes about 3½ cups.*

Peaches

When the peach industry devised a machine to brush the fuzz from the peach's surface, sales of peaches rose nearly 50 percent.

BASICS **To choose** • There are two broad categories of peaches: clingstone and freestone. As the names suggest, clingstone peaches have flesh that clings to the pits, while the flesh of freestone peaches pulls freely from the pits. In general, clingstone are the earliest varieties, followed by freestone at the height of summer. Little white peaches are generally sweeter and juicier than yellow peaches. Whichever variety you choose, look for well-colored fruit with no green spots. The flesh should yield slightly when lightly pressed and should have a fragrant peach aroma.

To store • Keep them in a fruit bowl at room temperature. Once ripe, peaches can be stored in the refrigerator to extend freshness. But be gentle; peaches bruise very easily.

To peel • Due to their tough, fuzzy skins, peaches are usually peeled before cooking. Drop up to 6 peaches into a large pot of boiling water for about 30 seconds. Remove 1 peach with a slotted spoon and push on the peel to see if it is loose. If it isn't, return it to the pot for another 15 seconds. Cool the peaches under running water, then slip off the skins with your fingers or peel them with a paring knife. If you have very soft peaches, you can peel them the easy way: Partially freeze them to firm slightly, then run under hot tap water. The skins will slip right off.

To pit • Slice around the peach, perpendicular to its crease line. Twist the two halves apart. Then, dislodge the pit out of the half that held on to it.

To slice soft peaches • Freeze them partially—just enough to firm them up for mush-free slicing. This will take about 20 minutes.

PROBLEM SOLVER ▼ **To prevent cut peaches from discoloring** • Dip them into acidulated water (1 tablespoon citrus juice per cup of water) or spritz with citrus juice.

TIME SAVER ▼ **To speed ripening** • Place peaches in a loosely closed paper bag at room temperature for 1 to 3 days. Check them often, at least twice a day, as ripening peaches can move from rock-hard to rotten while your back is turned. As the peach ripens, its acid content reduces, making it sweeter. At the same time, juice develops within the fruit, causing it to soften and ripen.

GRILLED PEACHES Divide **4 pitted and sliced peaches** among four 8" pieces of foil. Top each with ¼ **of a vanilla bean (or ¼ teaspoon vanilla extract), 1 teaspoon chopped crystallized ginger,** and **1 teaspoon** *each* **unsalted butter, honey, and orange liqueur (such as Grand Marnier).** Wrap the foil around its contents, sealing tightly. Grill over a medium-hot fire 5 minutes. Serve over ice cream. *Makes 4 servings.*

p

SHORTCUT PEACH MELBA Toss **4 pitted peach halves** in **1 tablespoon sugar, ½ teaspoon vanilla extract,** and **2 teaspoons brandy.** Set aside 5 minutes. Mash **½ pint raspberries** with **1 teaspoon honey** and **1 tablespoon raspberry liqueur (framboise)** until saucy. Divide peach halves among 4 dessert plates. Next to peaches, place scoops of **vanilla ice cream,** glazed with some of the macerating liquid. Spoon the raspberry sauce in a wide band overlapping both the peach half and the ice cream. *Makes 4 servings.*

Peanut Butter

Originally promoted as a health food, peanut butter is a blend of peanuts, oil, and, usually, salt.

BASICS **To choose** • There are two basic types: smooth and chunky (which contains bits of peanuts). Peanut butters labeled "natural" contain only peanuts and oil.

To store • Keep standard peanut butters at room temperature up to 6 months. Store natural peanut butters in the refrigerator up to 6 months.

OLD-FASHIONED PEANUT BUTTER COOKIES Preheat oven to 350°F. In a medium bowl, stir together **1½ cups all-purpose flour, 2 tablespoons corn-** starch, and **1 teaspoon baking soda.** In a large bowl, beat **1 stick (½ cup) softened butter,** 10 seconds. Beat in **½ cup granulated sugar** and **⅓ cup light brown sugar.** Add **1 large egg, 2 teaspoons vanilla extract,** and **¼ teaspoon salt.** Beat until thick and light, about 1 minute. Beat in **¾ cup chunky or smooth peanut butter.** Stir in flour mixture. Using 1½ tablespoons dough for each cookie, roll into balls and arrange on baking sheets, leaving 2" to 3" between each. Dip a fork into sugar and press on top of each cookie in two directions to flatten and make a crosshatch design. Bake until golden brown around edges, about 12 minutes. Transfer to a rack and cool. *Makes about 40.*

Fascinating Fact: Americans eat 700 million pounds of peanut butter every year, enough to coat the floor of the Grand Canyon.

Peanuts *see also* Nuts

We call them nuts and treat them like nuts, but peanuts are not nuts at all. They're legumes. Also called groundnuts, earthnuts, and goobers, peanuts seem as American as baseball. The most amazing thing happens when peanuts grow: They start out on a stem where a flower grew, but after the flower dies, the stem bends over, and as the peanut develops, it mysteriously buries itself in the earth. Mature peanuts are then dug up.

BASICS **To choose** • The two most common varieties of peanuts are small, round Spanish peanuts (often seen in peanut mixes) and larger, oval-shaped Virginia peanuts (often sold in the shell). When buying in-the-shell peanuts, look for clean shells with no breakage. Shake the peanuts and buy those that make no sound. If they rattle, the peanuts are old and beginning to dry out.

To store • Unshelled and vacuum-packed shelled peanuts can be kept at room temperature for a few weeks, but it's best to refrigerate them. Tightly wrap un-shelled peanuts and keep in the refrigerator up to 6 months. Once they are opened, refrigerate vacuum-packed, shelled peanuts in the jar up to 3 months.

EASY MICROWAVE PEANUT BRITTLE
Lightly grease a rimmed baking sheet. In a 2-quart microwaveable glass measure, combine **1 cup sugar, ½ cup light corn syrup,** and **¼ cup water.** Microwave on high power 4 minutes, stirring after 2 minutes. Add **1 cup raw or roasted peanuts** and **2 tablespoons butter.** Microwave on high power until light golden, 3½ to 4 minutes. Carefully and quickly stir in **1 teaspoon vanilla extract** and **½ teaspoon baking soda.** Pour out onto the prepared pan. Let cool for a minute, then pull and stretch using 2 forks or cold, buttered fingers to make it thinner. Immediately loosen from pan and turn out onto waxed paper. Let cool. Break into pieces and store in an airtight tin.
Makes 4 to 5 cups pieces.

Fascinating Fact: Peanut oil is one of the ingredients in nitroglycerin, an explosive liquid used to make dynamite.

Pears

With over 5,000 varieties, pears are enjoyed in everything from pies and tarts to salads and sauces. They are often best when simply prepared or eaten out of hand.

BASICS ▼ **To choose** • Though they're available year-round, pears reach their peak of flavor in the fall. They're best when picked unripe, then left to ripen at room temperature until the flesh gives slightly when pressed. Smell a pear before you buy it; the best have a sweet, fruity fragrance. Pears for snacking should be slightly soft at the stem end when ripe. Baking pears should be firm but not hard.

To ripen • Wrap pears separately in newspaper and set them in a cardboard box or paper bag (avoid plastic bags). Store in a cool, dark place until the pear yields slightly to the touch at the neck end. To speed ripening, you can add an apple or banana to the bag.

To core • Cut pears in half lengthwise and scoop out the cores with a melon baller or grapefruit spoon. Remove the gritty flesh around the core as well.

To cook • Always remove the skin, as it will toughen and darken in color during cooking. To prevent discoloration, immediately toss cut pears with lemon juice.

FLAVOR TIPS ▼ **To grill pears** • Peel a firm-ripe pear. Cut in half lengthwise and scoop out the core with a melon baller. Brush generously with melted butter and grill over a medium-hot fire until tender, 5 to 10 minutes, turning and basting with butter several times. If desired, drizzle with maple syrup and serve with vanilla ice cream.

To use leftover syrup from poached pears • Make granita. Strain the poaching syrup and add a big splash of orange juice and a small splash of lemon juice. Taste and add sugar if necessary (dissolve sugar in boiling water, then stir into liquid). Pour into a freezer tray or shallow bowl and partially freeze, stirring when ice crystals begin to form. Continue freezing and stirring until granular.

p

PEARS POACHED IN WHITE WINE In a small saucepan, combine ¾ **cup water** and ⅓ **cup** *each* **sugar and sweet white wine (such as Sauternes or sweet Riesling), 1 cinnamon stick (3" long), 1 ribbon of orange peel (1" × 3"), ½ split vanilla bean or 1 tablespoon vanilla extract,** and **4 whole cloves.** Bring to a boil over medium heat. Reduce heat to medium-low and simmer 5 to 10 minutes. Add **4 peeled, halved lengthwise, and cored Bosc or Bartlett pears** (or poach the pears whole by peeling them and then digging out the core from the bottom with a melon baller). Simmer until tender, 10 to 15 minutes. Serve drizzled with some of the poaching syrup and a scoop of vanilla ice cream, if desired. *Makes 4 servings.*

CHOCOLATE-PEAR CAKE Preheat oven to 350°F. Grease and flour a 9" springform pan. Combine **1 cup cake flour, 3 tablespoons unsweetened cocoa powder,** and ½ **teaspoon baking powder.** Peel and core **3 ripe Bartlett pears.** Cut each lengthwise into eighths. In a large bowl using an electric mixer, beat ⅔ **cup sugar** and ⅓ **cup softened butter** until smooth. Beat in **2 eggs** until fluffy, 2 minutes. On lowest speed, mix in flour mixture just until combined. Spread 1½ cups batter in prepared pan and arrange pear slices on top, slightly overlapping. Dollop remaining batter on top and spread (it will not cover fruit completely). Bake until a pick inserted comes out clean, 30 to 35 minutes. Cool on a rack and dust with confectioners' sugar. Unmold and serve. *Makes 10 servings.*

Peas, Dried

Also known as field peas, these yellow or green peas are grown specifically for drying and are usually split along their natural seam, giving them the name split peas.

BASICS ▼ To store • Keep in a sealed container in a cool, dry place for up to 1 year. Or freeze for several years.

To sort and rinse • Pick through whole dried peas or split peas before using them, to discard any discolored or shriveled peas or small pebbles.

To soak whole dried peas • Place them in a bowl and cover generously with cold water, then soak overnight. There is no need to soak split peas.

PROBLEM SOLVER ▼ To prevent toughness • Hold off on adding salt (or salty ingredients, such as some hams) until dried peas have been cooked to tenderness. Salt will inhibit peas from becoming tender during cooking.

TIME SAVER ▼ To quick-soak whole dried peas • Cover with water and heat to boiling. Boil 1 minute. Cover, remove from heat, and soak 1 hour. Drain and cover with fresh water before cooking further.

Peas, Edible Pod

There are two main categories of fresh green peas: those that have edible pods (such as snow peas and sugar snap peas), and shelling peas (garden peas). Snow peas have flat pods and sugar snaps have fat pods, but both are sweet and tender enough to be eaten in their entirety. All edible pod peas can be eaten after just a quick rinse under cool water or a brief heating.

Foggy Day Split Pea Soup

The best way to make split pea soup is to simmer a meaty, smoked ham bone in advance. Simmering extracts the smoky meat juices from the bones, resulting in a robust stock. If you chill the stock and remove the fat after it solidifies, you have a practically fat-free pea soup with all the smoked flavor of the ham. This soup has chunks of potato and carrot, but you can leave them out if you prefer.

1 **small, meaty, smoked ham bone or smoked ham hock (about 1 pound)**

12 **whole cloves**

1 **pound (2¼ cups) dried green split peas, rinsed and picked over**

2 **bay leaves**

1 **teaspoon dried thyme, crumbled**

1 **large all-purpose or boiling potato, peeled and cut into small cubes**

2 **carrots, peeled and cut into small cubes**

¼ **cup dry sherry or white wine**

Chopped reserved ham (from stock)

1 **teaspoon salt**

⅛ **teaspoon ground black pepper**

1. Place the ham bone or ham hock in a large soup pot or Dutch oven. Add cold water to cover generously. Add the cloves. Simmer, partly covered, until the joint falls apart and the meat is very tender, 3 to 4 hours. Place a colander over a large bowl and strain the broth. When the ham is cool enough to handle, remove the meat from the bones. Discard the fat and bones. Cover and chill the meat. Cool the stock to room temperature, then chill overnight. When the stock is well-chilled, remove and discard the fat from the top.

2. Place the peas in a 4-quart soup pot over medium heat. Cover with 4 cups cold water. Add the bay leaves and thyme. Bring to a boil, stirring often so that the peas do not clump together. Skim any foam from the top and discard. Simmer, partly covered, 15 minutes.

3. Add the stock. Bring to a boil. Simmer 15 minutes, stirring occasionally. Add the potato, carrots, and sherry or wine. Simmer until the vegetables are tender and the peas fall apart, 20 to 30 minutes, stirring occasionally. Add the ham, salt, and pepper. Simmer 5 minutes. Remove and discard the bay leaves before serving.

Makes about 10 cups

p

To choose snow peas • The pods should be crisp and bright green with just the suggestion of peas forming beneath the surface. Bend a pod in half. If it doesn't snap, the pods are old and rubbery.

To choose sugar snap peas • The best sugar snaps will look just like good shelling peas: vibrant, crisp, and moist.

To store edible pod peas • The sugar in peas quickly converts to starch once the vegetable leaves the vine. Rush pod peas home from the market and refrigerate them in a perforated plastic bag until you're ready to eat them, but don't expect their flavor to last beyond a day or so.

To prepare edible pod peas • Unless you've stumbled upon a stringless variety, your peas will need to have their strings removed. Simply break off the stem and pull it down the length of the pod; any string should come right with it (there may be just one string or a string on each side). If you're planning on serving them cool or at room temperature, you can string the peas after you cook them. Some cooks swear that this makes them even sweeter.

To cook snow peas • Pull off the stems and strings from whole snow peas. To boil them, drop them into salted boiling water, cook until tender yet crunchy (about 30 seconds), then drain. If serving them cold, rinse them under cold water to stop the cooking. You can also steam snow peas: Place the trimmed peas in a steamer basket over boiling water, cover, and cook until tender yet crunchy, 30 seconds to 1 minute. Or stir-fry them over medium-high heat in a small amount of oil until tender yet crunchy, 30 seconds to 1 minute. If you are adding snow peas to already-cooking dishes, add them at the last minute and cook until they turn bright green, about 30 seconds.

To cook sugar snap peas • Snap off the stem ends, then pull off the strings from whole sugar snap peas. Drop the peas into a large pot of salted boiling water and cook for 1 to 2 minutes. Drain. To serve them hot, toss with melted butter, salt, and pepper. To serve cold, rinse under cold water. Sugar snaps are also delicious raw.

STIR-FRIED BEEF WITH SNOW PEAS Cut **1 pound lean, trimmed flank steak** across the grain into slices 2" to 3" long and ⅛" thick. In a bowl, combine meat with **2 tablespoons dark soy sauce (tamari), 1 tablespoon** *each* **dry sherry and cornstarch,** and **1 teaspoon sugar.** Marinate in the refrigerator 30 minutes. Trim stems and pull strings from **½ pound snow peas.** Heat a wok or skillet over high heat. Add **2½ tablespoons peanut oil** or **vegetable oil, 3 thin slices fresh ginger,** and **1 small minced garlic clove;** stir-fry 10 seconds. Stir beef mixture, add all at once to the wok or skillet; stir-fry until meat is no longer pink, 1½ to 2 minutes. Add snow peas and **½ cup sliced water chestnuts;** stir-fry 15 seconds. Add **¼ cup chicken broth;** stir-fry until peas are crisp-tender. Stir in **½ teaspoon toasted sesame oil,** if desired. *Makes 4 servings.*

Peas, Shelling

Also known as English peas or garden peas, these are the familiar green peas found in countless dishes. They must be shucked from their tough pods before they are eaten. If you've never tried freshly shucked green peas, you're in for a revelation.

BASICS **To choose** • Pea season runs from early spring to the first weeks of summer. You'll find the best peas inside bright green, moist-looking, medium-size pods. The peas inside the biggest pods are likely to be too starchy, while the peas inside very tiny pods will not have developed full flavor. Always open a couple of pea pods at the market and sample them before buying. If the peas in your market are not fresh, frozen peas may be a better choice. Frozen peas are picked, shelled, quickly cooked and frozen for maximum flavor. Frozen petite peas are reliably tender.

To store • Because the sugar in any type of peas quickly converts to starch after picking, it's best to eat them the day that they are picked. Or, refrigerate unshelled peas for no more than 2 days.

To shell • Wait to shell peas until just before you are ready to cook them. Break the stem from each pod and pull it down to remove the string that runs along the seam. (See the illustration on the opposite page.) Press on the seam with your fingertip and the pod will pop open. One pound of peas in the pod equals 1 cup shelled.

To substitute frozen peas • In general, substitute 1 package (10 ounces) frozen peas for 1½ pounds fresh shelling peas in the pod.

To cook • In a large pot of salted boiling water, cook 2 cups shelled, fresh peas just until tender, 30 seconds to 1 minute. Drain, return to the pot, and add about 2 tablespoons butter and ¼ teaspoon *each* salt and ground black pepper. Serve hot.

To cook frozen • Skip the instructions on the box. Frozen peas have already been cooked; they only need to be cooked very briefly. A minute or so in a small amount of hot water will do the trick. Also, there is no need to thaw frozen peas before adding them to a recipe. A few minutes' contact with hot ingredients will warm them through. If adding them to a cold salad, thaw in hot water for a few minutes before tossing with other ingredients.

VENETIAN RICE AND PEAS In a large saucepan, sauté ½ **chopped onion** and ½ **cup chopped smoked ham (3 ounces)** in **1 tablespoon butter,** 3 minutes. Add **1½ cups shelled fresh peas** and **1 cup short-grain rice (such as Arborio).** Sauté 2 minutes. Add **3 cups chicken stock** or **broth** and ½ **cup dry white wine.** Cover and simmer over low heat until rice and peas are tender, about 20 minutes, stirring occasionally. Stir in ½ **cup grated Parmesan cheese, 3 tablespoons chopped fresh parsley,** and ⅛ **teaspoon ground black pepper.** Serve hot. *Makes 4 servings.*

Pecans *see also* Nuts

In the American South, where pecans flourish, just about everyone has at least one pecan tree (and plenty of very happy squirrels). Pecans have a higher fat content than any other nut (70 percent), giving them a distinguished and complex flavor. Their high fat content also makes them more perishable than most nuts.

BASICS **To choose** • Unshelled pecans reach peak season in the fall. Look for clean, uncracked shells. Shake the pecans. If they rattle, they are old.

To store • Keep unshelled pecans tightly wrapped in a cool, dry place up to 6 months. Store shelled pecans in a sealed container in the refrigerator up to 3 months, or freeze up to 6 months.

p

To shell • Crack from end to end with a nutcracker. To make shelling easier, you can place the unshelled nuts in a saucepan with water to cover. Bring to a boil, then remove from heat, cover, and let cool 15 minutes. Pat the nuts dry before cracking.

To toast • Scatter ½ pound pecan halves on a baking sheet and bake at 325°F until fragrant and lightly browned, 5 to 10 minutes, tossing occasionally. Finely chopped pecans will take half the time, and toasting a full pound of nuts will take almost twice as long.

FLAVOR TIPS

To add flavor and crunch to stuffing • Stir about 1 cup chopped toasted pecans into 6 to 8 cups of your favorite poultry stuffing.

To add excitement to chicken salad • Add about ½ cup chopped toasted pecans to every 2 to 3 cups chicken salad.

To flavor green salads • Add a handful of chopped toasted pecans. In the dressing, use a nut oil, such as walnut, and perhaps raspberry vinegar.

SPICED PECAN PIE Make 1 recipe **Flaky Tart or Pie Shell** (page 403) for a single-crust 9" pie. On a lightly floured surface, roll chilled pastry to an 11" round. Loosely drape into a 9" pie pan and press to conform to pan without stretching dough. Fold overhanging pastry under to make a raised edge. Press all around edges with the tines of a fork. Preheat oven to 325°F. In a saucepan, combine ¾ **cup** *each* **packed dark brown sugar and dark** or **light corn syrup, ½ stick (¼ cup) butter, 1½ teaspoons ground cinnamon, ¼ teaspoon ground cloves,** and **⅛ teaspoon salt.** Stir over medium heat just until butter melts. Remove from heat and whisk in **4 large eggs,** one at a time. Stir in **1¼ cups chopped pecans.** Pour into pie shell. Arrange about **1 cup pecan halves** in concentric circles on top, starting around outer edge and working toward center. Set on a baking sheet and bake until puffed in the center and browned around the edges, 50 to 60 minutes. Cool on a rack. Serve warm or at room temperature. *Makes 8 servings.*

Peppercorns *see also* Spices

The world's most popular spice, pepper comes in shades of black, white, and green. Regardless of their color, all peppercorns come from the same plant and are harvested while still green, then processed to yield the differences in color and flavor. Pink peppercorns aren't really peppercorns at all, but the berry of an unrelated tree.

BASICS

To choose • No matter what color of peppercorn you're shopping for, always buy the largest peppercorns available. They have had the advantage of extra growing and ripening time, which gives them a fuller flavor. Also, buy whole peppercorns rather than preground pepper. The dusty, dull taste of preground pepper can't come close to the rich, full flavor of pepper that's ground fresh just moments before it is used.

To choose black peppercorns • The very best black peppercorns come from India's Malabar Coast and have a bold, fruity fragrance with none of the sharpness found in lesser-quality peppercorns. Look for the top grade of Malabar peppercorns, labeled Tellicherry, in gourmet shops and mail-order catalogs.

PEPPERONI **349**

To choose white peppercorns • Top-quality white peppercorns are produced in Borneo and Sumatra. The most desirable ones have a creamy white color.

To choose green peppercorns • Traditionally packed in a salty brine, green peppercorns are slightly milder than black or white ones. Dried green peppercorns have only recently become available and are so fragile that they can be crushed with your fingers.

To store • Keep peppercorns in a tightly sealed container in a cool, dark place. They'll stay fresh this way for up to 1 year.

To coarsely crack pepper • If your pepper mill doesn't adjust to make coarse cracked pepper (or if you don't have a pepper mill), place peppercorns in a small, zipper-lock plastic bag. Seal the bag and whack with a heavy skillet or crack with a rolling pin.

Fascinating Fact: Peppercorns were once more valuable than gold.

FLAVOR TIP **For a subtle pepper flavor** • Use whole peppercorns. Many stocks and braised dishes call for whole peppercorns because cracked or ground pepper would over-pepper the dish. Adding whole peppercorns lends just a nuance of pepper.

PEPPERED STEAK Scatter **1 tablespoon coarsely ground black pepper** over a sheet of waxed paper. Cut **1 to 1½ pounds beef tenderloin** into ¾"-thick slices. Press beef into pepper to coat both sides. Heat **1 tablespoon vegetable oil** in a large skillet over high heat. Add steaks and brown well, turning once, about 8 minutes. Transfer to a warm plate and cover with foil. In a bowl, whisk together **¼ cup heavy cream, 1 tablespoon flour,** and **¾ cup beef broth.** Spoon off any fat from the skillet or blot the fat with a paper towel. Avert your face from the pan and carefully pour in **¼ cup brandy** or **cognac** (but do not ignite the alcohol). Deglaze the pan, scraping up any browned bits. Add cream mixture and stir over medium heat until sauce simmers and thickens. Pour over steaks and sprinkle with **2 tablespoons chopped fresh parsley.** *Makes 4 to 6 servings.*

Pepperoni

Made from a well-seasoned mixture of pork and beef, pepperoni is air-dried and ready to eat. Keep a stick in your refrigerator and you will never be at a loss for adding sparks of flavor to pizza, pasta, breads, and salads.

BASICS **To store** • Long links of pepperoni keep well in the refrigerator for several months. After slicing, shelf life diminishes.

FLAVOR TIPS **To better disperse the flavor of pepperoni** • Big slices of pepperoni can sometimes overpower a pizza or salad. To disperse the flavor, cut thin slices of pepperoni, then stack them about 5 pieces high. Cut into julienne strips about ⅛" wide. Scatter over a pizza, pasta, or salads when assembling.

To make pepperoni bread • When making a loaf of bread, knead in ½ cup julienned pepperoni before shaping and rising. Glaze the top with an egg wash after the final rise and sprinkle with another 1 to 2 tablespoons julienned pepperoni. Bake as usual.

p

MEAT LOVERS' FRENCH BREAD PIZZA In a large skillet, sauté ½ **pound lean ground beef** in **1 tablespoon olive oil,** 2 minutes. Add **4 large sliced mushrooms; 1 large minced garlic clove;** ½ **teaspoon** *each* **dried oregano, dried basil,** and **salt;** and ¼ **teaspoon ground black pepper.** Cook until mushrooms are soft and meat is no longer pink, 2 to 3 minutes. Stir in ½ **cup** *each* **julienned pepperoni** and **tomato spaghetti sauce** or **pizza sauce.** Split **a loaf of French** or **Italian bread** (16" long) and place on a baking sheet. Using your fingers, pull out some of the soft bread from the centers to make the halves slightly concave. Spread about another ¼ **cup spaghetti sauce** or **pizza sauce** over each half. Shred ½ **pound mozzarella cheese** to make 2 cups. Sprinkle **1 cup shredded mozzarella cheese** over meat filling and quickly toss. Divide the mixture among bread shells and top each with ½ **cup shredded mozzarella** and **1 tablespoon grated Parmesan cheese.** Bake at 400°F until hot and lightly browned, about 12 minutes. Cut into slices on the diagonal and serve hot. *Makes 4 servings.*

Peppers, Sweet *see also* Chile Peppers, Dried; Chile Peppers, Fresh

As summer comes to an end, sweet peppers come into season, and markets fill with an amazing variety of these glossy, brilliantly hued fruits. The most popular sweet peppers are bell peppers, named for their shape. All bells are green (or purple-green) when immature; they turn yellow, orange, or red upon ripening. **Other sweet peppers include red pimientos (often sold in jars), long and tapered Cubanelles (frying peppers), and long, yellow banana peppers.**

BASICS To choose • Look for firm-fleshed peppers with no soft spots or wrinkles. Also, color indicates ripeness, so look for peppers with a deep, even tone. Green and purple bell peppers are immature, which is why they are less sweet than red and yellow bells. Purple bell peppers will turn green when cooked, but they add great color when sliced raw for salads.

To store • To keep peppers longer than a day or two, refrigerate them in a perforated plastic bag. Otherwise, they'll be fine kept at room temperature.

To easily stem and seed • Slice about ⅛" from the tip of the pepper. Set the pepper upright on its flattened tip and slice downward from stem to tip, following the shape of the fruit and slicing the sides off of the core. Trim any strips of white membrane from the interior of the pepper. Discard the core with its stem, seeds, and veins. This method works for chile peppers as well.

To freeze • When red and yellow bell peppers are most plentiful and least expensive, buy extra and freeze them. Place stemmed, seeded pepper pieces on trays and freeze until solid. Store frozen in zipper-lock freezer bags for up to 6 months and use as needed. Since the texture will be a bit softer, use frozen peppers in cooked sauces, casseroles, soups, and stews rather than in raw dishes such as salad.

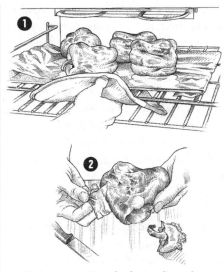

To roast • Cook them directly over a flame until bubbly and blackened all over, turning occasionally with a pair of tongs. Or spread them on a baking sheet covered with aluminum foil and roast under a broiler.

Position the sheet so that the peppers are about 3" below the heat source. Broil, turning the peppers often, until the skin is charred black all over and is bubbling loose from the flesh ❶.

When the peppers are cool enough to handle, pull out the stem and the core with its seeds. Peel off the skin with your fingers or the edge of a knife ❷.

You can also roast peppers after cutting them so that they lie flat. This saves you the trouble of turning the pepper to roast all sides. Remove the core and seeds, slice down one side of the pepper, and lay it out flat, skin side up, on a baking sheet. Roast it under a broiler until charred on top. When it is cool enough to handle, remove and discard the skin.

To easily remove skins from freshly roasted peppers • Rub them off with a sheet of paper towel.

PROBLEM SOLVERS ▼ **To scrape out the white membranes to make whole stuffed peppers** • Remove them with a melon baller.

To help prevent stuffed peppers from collapsing when baking • Place them in small ovenproof bowls, ramekins, or muffin-pan cups.

Chef's Tip: If you have difficulty digesting green peppers, try the sweeter and more mature red, yellow, or orange bell peppers.

FLAVOR TIP ▼ **To flavor meat loaf** • Add about 1 cup roasted, peeled, and chopped red bell pepper (⅔ of a whole pepper) when making your favorite meat loaf.

SIMPLE RED PEPPER SAUCE In a small saucepan, combine **2 large stemmed, seeded, and chopped red bell peppers; 2 tablespoons chopped onion; ½ minced garlic clove;** and **1 tablespoon** *each* **toasted sesame oil and lemon juice.** Bring to a boil, cover, and simmer until pepper is soft. Puree until smooth. *Makes ¾ cup.*

SAUSAGE AND PEPPER HEROES Cut **2 large bell peppers** into ½"-wide strips (use different colors of peppers if desired). In a large skillet, sauté **2 sliced onions,** separated into rings, in **3 tablespoons olive oil** until soft, about 5 minutes. Add pepper strips, **2 minced garlic cloves,** and ½ **teaspoon salt.** Cover and cook over low heat until soft, about 25 minutes. Meanwhile, in another large skillet, combine **6 Italian sausages (4 to 5 ounces each; sweet, hot, or both, as desired),** pricked all over with a fork, and ¼ **cup water.** Cook over medium heat, turning often, until water evaporates and sausages begin to sizzle. Continue cooking until sausages are browned outside and no longer pink inside, about 15 minutes. Add to peppers and onions. Serve on **6 split hero rolls.** *Makes 6 sandwiches.*

PASTA WITH SAUSAGE AND PEPPERS
Follow the recipe for **Sausage and Pepper Heroes** (page 351). Omit hero rolls. After cooking sausages, cool them slightly, then cut into slices and add to peppers and onions along with **1 can (16 ounces) diced tomatoes.** Simmer 10 minutes. In a large pot of salted boiling water, cook **12 ounces penne** until tender yet firm to the bite, 7 to 9 minutes. Drain and toss with sauce. *Makes 6 servings.*

Persimmon

A luscious, red-orange tree fruit, persimmons are native to China. There are two main types: the more common, acorn-shaped Hachiya persimmon, which is unpalatably tannic and bitter unless it is very ripe and soft, and the squat, tomato-like Fuyu persimmon, which isn't at all bitter and remains firm when ripe.

BASICS ▼ **To choose Hachiya persimmons •** Look for deep-orange fruits with no trace of yellow. If you plan on eating them right away, look for very soft fruits that are almost translucent. If only hard Hachiyas are available, take them home and ripen them for a few days before eating.

To choose Fuyu persimmons • Look for plump fruits with a brilliant orange color. Fuyus should be firm, yet give gently when pressed in your palm.

To store • Keep persimmons at room temperature and eat within a few days. Or freeze very ripe Hachiya persimmons: Cut off the pointed tip of the persimmon first, and wrap the fruit tightly in plastic wrap. It will keep in the freezer for up to 3 months. It's best not to freeze unripened Hachiyas. Freezing will soften the fruit but will not alter its bitter, tannic flavor.

To ripen • Put the fruit in a paper bag with a banana or an apple and leave it at room temperature until the fruit is quite soft, 3 to 4 days.

To enjoy Hachiya persimmons • Eat the soft, ripe fruit with a spoon or puree it and use as a base for puddings, cookies, and cakes. You can also slice the fruit in half, wrap it in plastic, and freeze the halves for at least 4 hours. Then, dig out the fruit with a spoon, like sherbet.

To enjoy Fuyu persimmons • Slice the fruit like an apple and eat it as a snack or use it in salads.

Pesto

The seductive blend of fresh basil, olive oil, pine nuts, garlic, and grated cheese known as pesto is a burst of instant flavor. Use it as a sauce for pasta, a dressing for salads, a stir-in for soups, or a simple spread. While pesto can be made in a food processor or blender, traditionalists insist that for the best texture and flavor, pesto can be made only with a mortar and pestle.

BASICS ▼ **To choose the best basil •** Look for either Genovese basil, with large, toothed leaves, or Piccolo Fino Verde, which has small, finely formed leaves. Either one of these two Italian varieties will make a richly flavored, authentic-tasting pesto.

To use pesto as a pasta sauce • Use a combination of butter and olive oil in the paste. The addition of butter helps the sauce adhere to the pasta.

To store • Press a sheet of plastic wrap directly onto the surface of the pesto and refrigerate for several days, to help keep the surface from darkening. Or, to freeze, make the pesto without adding cheese or butter, and freeze for up to 3 months. Thaw and stir in the cheese and butter just before using.

FLAVOR TIP ▼ **To flavor stuffed pasta fillings** • Stir pesto into ricotta cheese when making a filling for ravioli, tortellini, or manicotti.

BASIL PESTO In a food processor, combine **2 cups packed basil leaves, 2 minced garlic cloves** (sauté the garlic if you prefer the taste of cooked garlic), **⅓ cup extra-virgin olive oil, ¼ cup pine nuts, ¼ teaspoon salt,** and **⅛ teaspoon ground black pepper.** Process to a fine puree. Transfer to a bowl and stir in **½ cup grated Parmesan cheese, ¼ cup grated Romano cheese,** and **1 tablespoon softened butter.**

Makes 1 cup pesto (enough for 1 pound pasta).

WHITE BEAN PESTO DIP Follow the recipe for **Basil Pesto** (above). Add **1 rinsed and drained can (15 ounces) white beans** and process until smooth. Serve with crackers or crudités.

Makes about 2½ cups.

HEALTHY HINT ▼ **To reduce fat** • Use broth in place of half of the oil. You can also replace up to half of the Parmesan cheese with a small amount of light miso.

LOW-FAT PESTO In a food processor, combine **2 slices toasted white bread (crusts removed), 1 cup packed basil leaves, 3 tablespoons toasted walnuts,** and **1 garlic clove.** Process until very finely chopped. Add **3 tablespoons grated Parmesan cheese** and **2 tablespoons** *each* **olive oil and chicken broth.** Pulse just until combined.

Makes about ¾ cup.

Phyllo

Translated from Greek, *phyllo* means "leaf," the perfect name for these tissue-thin sheets of dough. Phyllo dough can be rolled and folded into an enormous variety of shapes and used to make both sweet and savory pastries such as Spanakopita (page 478) and baklava.

BASICS ▼ **To choose** • If you live near a Greek bakery that makes fresh phyllo dough, buy it there. The flavor and texture of fresh phyllo beats frozen supermarket versions by a mile. If you are buying frozen phyllo, keep in mind that a 1-pound box contains 20 to 25 sheets of pastry. The average size of a full sheet is 18" × 14", but the size may vary according to the brand used. You can also buy frozen phyllo shells that are ready for filling.

To thaw • Frozen phyllo thaws best in its original wrapper overnight in the refrigerator. Let stand unopened at room temperature for 2 hours before using. (If thawed completely at room temperature, phyllo sheets may stick together.)

To keep the dough pliable as you work • Remove the dough from its packaging at the last possible moment, when you have all your ingredients and equip-

p

ment ready before you. Then, unroll the sheets of pastry on a dry work surface away from direct sunlight or any source of heat. Work with one sheet of dough at a time, keeping the rest covered with a sheet of plastic wrap or a damp cotton towel. Lightly brush each sheet with melted butter; spots of unmoistened dough are okay. If your phyllo sheets are especially delicate, you can use a spray bottle to spritz them with melted butter or oil instead of brushing on the butter.

To avoid frustration • Thin, fragile sheets of phyllo sometimes tear. But it is good to know that the dough is very forgiving. Simply layer an extra scrap over a tear wherever needed and the pastry will bake up beautifully.

To properly prepare fillings for phyllo pastries • Make sure that the fillings are not too runny; chill them before adding them to the phyllo to firm them up. Overly moist fillings will make the pastry soggy.

To store unbaked phyllo pastries • Cover the prepared pastries with plastic wrap and refrigerate for up to 1 day. Well-wrapped phyllo pastries can also be frozen for up to 1 month before baking.

To bake frozen phyllo pastries • Put the pastries directly into a preheated oven. Avoid thawing them before baking or the pastries will become soggy.

CHICKEN AND GOAT CHEESE PAS-TRIES Preheat oven to 400°F. In a large skillet, sauté **1 finely chopped onion** in **1 tablespoon olive oil** to soften, 3 to 5 minutes. Add **2 minced garlic cloves** and **1 teaspoon dried tarragon.** Cook 1 minute. Crumble in **1 pound ground chicken.** Sprinkle with **1 teaspoon salt** and **¼ teaspoon ground black pepper.**

Cook, stirring, until meat is no longer pink. Stir in **2 tablespoons flour** and cook 1 minute. Add **⅓ cup white wine** and cook until thickened, 2 to 3 minutes. Remove from heat and let cool. Stir in **1 tablespoon lemon juice, 4 large sliced scallions,** and **6 ounces crumbled mild goat cheese**. Set aside. Cut a **1-pound stack of thawed phyllo sheets** lengthwise into 4 strips. Stack strips onto a sheet of plastic wrap and keep them covered while you work. In a small saucepan, melt **1 stick (½ cup) butter** with **¼ cup olive oil.** Brush one strip of phyllo with dabs of butter mixture, leaving some spots unbuttered. Top with a second strip and dab with butter mixture. Spoon about 2 teaspoons reserved meat filling at a short end of strip, and fold up one corner to begin forming a triangle. Continue folding it, flag-style, to enclose filling in a triangle. Lightly brush top with butter mixture and place on a baking sheet. Repeat with remaining phyllo and filling. In a small bowl, mix **2 egg yolks** with **1 tablespoon water.** Brush over pastries. Sprinkle **2 tablespoons sesame seeds** over pastries. Bake until golden brown, 10 to 12 minutes. Serve hot. Filled, unbaked pastries may be frozen and baked later. To bake frozen pastries, add 5 to 10 minutes to baking time. *Makes 60 pastries.*

TIME SAVERS ▼ **To save prep time** • Use a wide brush for faster coverage when coating phyllo sheets with butter or oil. Also, moisten the brush with water first, shaking off the excess, so that the butter isn't absorbed into the bristles. This makes for easier cleanup, and it saves precious butter or oil for coating the pastry. Alternatively, you can use a spray bottle to quickly and evenly coat the pastry with melted butter or olive oil. Another option is to use shredded phyllo, called knafa, which is available in some Middle Eastern groceries. It has the light crispness of phyllo but requires much less work. To prepare knafa, thaw the dough according to package directions and place it in a large, metal baking dish that is stove-top safe. For each pound of knafa, pour 1 cup clarified butter over the dough and place it over very low heat. Mix it with your hands until all of the dough shreds are coated with butter and the whole thing is soft and slightly moist. Use in place of phyllo for pastries. You can't roll knafa as you can phyllo, but it makes an excellent top and bottom crust.

To substitute wonton skins for phyllo when making tartlet shells • Phyllo is sometimes used to make crispy tartlet shells. Wonton skins make an easy stand-in; prepare the same way as phyllo. Brush each wonton skin with butter and stack them in a custard cup or muffin pan cup, staggering the skins so that the points do not sit directly over one another.

RICOTTA PASTRIES WITH KNAFA
Knafa is an easy-to-use form of phyllo dough available in Middle Eastern markets. Preheat oven to 325°F. Place **1 pound knafa,** thawed according to package directions, in a large, metal baking dish that is stove-top safe. Pour **1 cup clarified butter** over dough and place over very low heat. Mix with your hands until dough shreds are evenly coated with butter. Place half the buttered dough in a greased 11" × 7" baking dish. Combine **1 pound ricotta cheese, 1 tablespoon grated orange zest (optional), and 1 teaspoon vanilla extract.** Spread over dough in the dish. Top with remaining dough. Bake until golden brown, 30 minutes. Meanwhile, combine **1 cup *each***

sugar and water and heat to boiling. Stir in **2 tablespoons orange juice.** When pastry is done, pour this syrup evenly over the surface while it is still hot. Scatter ¼ **cup chopped pistachios** over top. Serve warm. *Makes 8 servings.*

HEALTHY HINTS ▼ **To reduce butter or oil for brushing** • Combine 1 tablespoon beaten egg white and 2 tablespoons melted butter or olive oil. Use sparingly, as sheets of phyllo don't need to be completely moistened. You can also use a misting of cooking spray instead of butter. Or, for savory dishes, sprinkle a light coating of dried bread crumbs, cracker crumbs, or cookie crumbs between layers of pastry sheets to help keep them separate and flaky. For sweet dishes, sprinkle granulated or brown sugar between layers of pastry sheets to help keep them separated.

To use in place of pastry • Phyllo makes a good low-fat substitute for the traditional puff pastry in *tarte Tartin,* the classic French upside-down apple pie. You can also use phyllo as a low-fat alternative to pastry for both turnovers and apple dumplings.

Pickles

When preserved in vinegar or brine, almost any produce will make crisp, delicious pickles to serve on sandwiches or as a snack. Cucumbers are by far the most popular vegetables for pickling, but there are many others, including beets, cauliflower, onions, watermelon rind, and okra.

BASICS ▼ **To choose produce** • Look for fresh, firm produce. Avoid using produce that has been coated with wax; the vinegar won't be able to penetrate the wax barrier.

p

To make crisper pickles • Refrigerate vegetables before pickling. Cold produce makes crisp pickles.

To choose vinegar • Make sure that your vinegar is at least 4 percent to 6 percent acetic acid (most commercial vinegars are; check the label). Also, use a mild-tasting vinegar that won't interfere with the flavor of the pickles. Distilled white vinegar, white wine vinegar, and cider vinegar are all great for making pickles.

To keep pickling brine clear • Season the pickles with pickling salt, kosher salt, sea salt, or any other salt that doesn't include additives. Avoid standard table salt, which contains additives and will turn a brine cloudy. Also, use only whole spices to season your pickles. Chopped or crushed spices will make the brine cloudy.

To safely process pickles • Use sterilized jars, lids, tongs, and other canning equipment. Scald the equipment in gently boiling water, then pour the pickles into the hot, scalded jars, leaving ¼" headspace. Wipe the rims clean, attach the lids, and tightly screw on the caps. Invert the jars for 10 seconds. Place the filled jars back in boiling water to inactivate any spoilage enzymes that may ruin your pickles. The USDA recommends processing at least 10 minutes for pint-size jars and 20 minutes for quart-size jars. Also, let processed jars of pickles cool undisturbed for at least 12 minutes. Avoid touching the bands on the jars after they have been processed, as any tightening can break the seal.

To test the seal on a processed jar of pickles • Gently remove the screw bands and lift the jar by its lid. If the lid pops off, the seal is not firm. Refrigerate the pickles and eat them within 2 weeks.

To develop full flavor • Let sealed, processed jars of pickles sit for at least 6 weeks before eating.

TIME SAVER ▼ **To save canning time** • Make refrigerator pickles. When you make small batches of pickles that will be stored in the refrigerator and used quickly, there is no need to sterilize jars or use special equipment.

FLAVOR TIPS ▼ **To add spark to salads** • Add equal parts finely chopped sweet pickles and dill pickles to salads such as potato, tuna, chicken, salmon and seafood. Start with ¼ cup of each per 4 cups salad.

To serve with pâté • Tiny, sour French cornichons (made with gherkins) complement pâté in a most delightful way.

REFRIGERATOR DILL PICKLES Rinse and lightly scrub **10 Kirby cucumbers or pickling cucumbers** (about 2 pounds). In a large glass bowl, dissolve ½ **cup coarse kosher salt** (avoid using table salt) in **5 cups cold water.** Submerge whole cucumbers completely in the brine and weight down with a stainless steel can or heavy pot. Let stand at room temperature 48 hours, checking occasionally to make sure that cucumbers are submerged. Drain and rinse. In a stainless steel saucepan, combine **1 cup water, 1 tablespoon** *each* **kosher salt and whole coriander seeds, 2 bay leaves,** and ½ **teaspoon hot-pepper flakes.** Bring to a boil. Remove from heat and let cool. In a large glass bowl, combine **1¾ cups cold water, 1 cup apple cider vinegar, 2 sliced garlic cloves, ⅓ cup fresh dill sprigs,** and **1½ teaspoons dill seeds.** Stir in cooled brine mixture. Put cucumbers and brine in a tall glass jar or ceramic crock, weighting down as before, if necessary, to keep cucumbers submerged. Refrigerate at least 1 to 2 days before serving. Eat within a week or two. *Makes 10.*

Picnics

Picnic food should be fun and easy rather than fussy. Choose picnic foods that are equally good hot or cold; that way, you don't need to worry about maintaining temperatures between the kitchen and the picnic site.

BASICS **To bring enough food** • Picnics tend to make people hungry, so always bring extra food. Perhaps it's the great outdoors. Or maybe it's just a craving for the kind of food so often included in a picnic, such as sandwiches, potato chips, lemonade, wine, champagne, pâté, old-fashioned home-made baked beans, potato or macaroni salad, coleslaw, pickles, deviled eggs, baked ham, watermelon, and fruit pie or strawberry shortcake.

To ensure food safety • Commercially bottled mayonnaise has fairly high acidity, which greatly slows down growth of harmful bacteria. So, when planning a picnic menu with mayonnaise-dressed foods, be sure to use jarred mayonnaise rather than homemade. Also, always store cold foods in a cooler packed with ice or ice packs. Avoid leaving cold food unchilled for more than an hour. If it's possible, bring two coolers: one for items that will be frequently retrieved (such as beverages) and one for protein foods such as meat, eggs, sandwiches, and salads. This way, the protein foods will remain as cold as possible. Pack watermelon and other fruit with the beverages. To pack raw meat that will be grilled, seal it in zipper-lock plastic bags and then seal again in a second zipper-lock bag to protect against any leakage. Store meat in a cooler, close to ice packs, and keep it cold.

To pack deviled eggs • Put two deviled egg halves together, face to face, and wrap in plastic. Or, bring the egg white halves unfilled and bring the deviled yolk mixture in a zipper-lock plastic bag. At the picnic, snip a corner from the bag and squeeze the filling into the whites.

PICNIC MACARONI SALAD In a large pot of salted boiling water, cook ½ **pound elbow macaroni** until tender, about 8 minutes. Drain and rinse under cold water, shaking colander to remove excess water. Turn out into a large bowl and toss with **2 tablespoons olive oil.** Hard-cook **4 large eggs.** Set aside 1 for garnish; chop the others and add to macaroni. Add **4 finely chopped small bell peppers (2 red and 2 green), 2 finely chopped celery ribs, 1 finely chopped carrot, 4 large thinly sliced scallions,** and ¼ **cup chopped fresh parsley.** Drain **1 can (6 ounces) pitted black olives** and save 3 for garnish. Slice the other olives and add to salad. In a bowl, mix ¾ **cup mayonnaise, 1 tablespoon** *each* **cider vinegar and brown mustard,** and ½ **teaspoon** *each* **dried basil, dried oregano, dried tarragon, salt, and ground black pepper.** Pour over salad and toss to mix. Cover and refrigerate 1 hour. Mound on a platter if desired. Slice the reserved egg and use as garnish along with the reserved whole black olives and a sprig of parsley. Dust with paprika and serve cool.
Makes 6 servings.

TOMATO AND TARRAGON TART Preheat oven to 375°F. Grate **6 tablespoons Parmesan cheese.** Cut **6 ounces goat cheese** into ¼"-thick slices and **3 large beefsteak tomatoes** into 6 slices each. Pluck **2 tablespoons fresh tarragon leaves** from their stems. Sprinkle bottom of a baked **Flaky Tart or Pie Shell** (page

403) or prepared pie crust with half the Parmesan. Top with half the goat cheese, then half the tarragon leaves, then half the tomatoes, forming layers. Layer with the remaining Parmesan, then the remaining tarragon, then the remaining tomatoes. Top with the remaining goat cheese. Bake 35 minutes. To serve warm, wrap in several layers of heavy-duty foil and serve within 2 hours. Or serve chilled.

Makes 6 servings.

TIME SAVER ▼ **To cut corners** • Make a few items at home and buy the others from a store. Homemade fried chicken tastes great at a picnic, but there are quite a few fast-food restaurants that sell very good fried chicken.

Pie Crusts *see also* Pies

The ingredient list is simple enough: flour, fat, salt, and water. It's the handling of those ingredients that can make a pie crust tough and chewy or tender, flaky, and rich with flavor. Don't be confused by terminology here. Pie pastry, pie dough, pie crust, and pie shell are all the same thing. *Pastry* refers to the uncooked pie dough. When it is formed and baked, it is called a pie crust (or shell).

BASICS ▼ **To make a nicely browned pie crust** • Choose either a medium-heavy aluminum pan with sloping sides and a dull finish or a heatproof glass pie pan. Both will absorb heat and distribute it quickly, helping to set the crust. Avoid highly polished metal pans, which deflect rather than absorb heat. These pans bake more slowly and can interfere with the setting of the crust.

To roll pie pastry easily • Roll the dough between 2 lightly floured sheets of waxed paper, parchment paper, or plastic wrap. The paper or plastic helps prevent adding too much flour, which can make for a tough pie crust. The paper also lets you move the dough more easily to the pie pan with less chance of tearing it. Remove the top sheet before moving the pastry.

To transfer rolled pastry to a pie pan • Gently fold the circle into fourths. Center the 90-degree corner of the folded pastry in the pie pan. Unfold the pastry and gently fit it into the pan bottom to press out air bubbles without stretching the dough. You can also loosely roll the dough around the rolling pin, then slowly unfurl the dough over the pie pan, centering the dough as much as possible. Lift the dough gently by one edge to encourage it to conform to the bottom edge of the pan. Once the dough is lining the pan snugly, press across the bottom to make sure that there are no air bubbles trapped under the surface.

To prevent shrinking during baking • Avoid stretching or pulling the pastry as you lay it in the pie pan. Pie pastry has a memory; if you stretch it to fit into a pan, it will shrink back to its original size and shape during baking.

To trim pastry overhang • Trim the perimeter of the pastry to extend no more than 1" over the edge of the pan. Fold this overhang under to make a thick pastry rim around the edge of the pan. If making a single-crust pie, crimp the edge before filling or storing. If making a double-crust pie, fill and roll out the top crust in the same way as the bottom, positioning it over the filling. Crimp the top and bottom crusts around their edges to seal.

To make a free-form pie crust • Line a pie pan with pastry, but do not trim or tuck under the edge. Fill the crust with fruit filling and flip the overhang of pastry over onto the filling. It will form an uneven circle that leaves the fruit in the center exposed. Dot the top with 2 table-

HOW TO MAKE A TENDER, FLAKY PIE CRUST

The key to tenderness and flakiness is keeping everything cold, particularly the butter, shortening, or other fats. Cold fat makes steam in the oven, which puffs the layers apart and makes a flaky pastry. If the fat warms up during handling, it will melt and be absorbed by the flour, creating a tough, chewy pie crust.

- Chill all your equipment in the refrigerator for 30 minutes before using: mixing bowl or food processor bowl and blade, pastry cutter, rolling pin, and pastry board. Avoid working in a hot room or near a hot oven.

- Use cold butter and minimize handling. Use a metal bench scraper or sharp knife to quickly cut a stick of butter into ¼" cubes. After chopping the butter, chill it for 20 minutes before cutting it into the flour.

- If you have warm hands, chill them under cold running water or in a bowl of ice water. Dry thoroughly before making the pastry.

- If it's taking too long to cut the butter into the flour (especially by hand), refrigerate the mixture for 20 minutes.

- Mix the dough quickly in a food processor instead of by hand. You're less likely to over-work the dough, warm it, or add water, all of which can make a tough and chewy crust.

- If you don't have a food processor, use a pastry cutter. This inexpensive kitchen tool works much more efficiently than the last-resort option of using the tines of a fork or 2 table knives. If you prefer to use your fingertips, you'll need to keep them cold and work quickly.

- While cutting the butter into the flour, constantly keep the butter covered with flour to help avoid mashing the butter. The goal is a coarse mixture in which the flour-coated butter pieces are about the size of small peas. Avoid cutting in the butter too finely.

- As you add water or other liquid to gather the dough into a ball, work quickly and with a gentle hand. Handle the dough as little as possible—just enough for it to come together. Little gobs of butter in the formed dough are a good sign.

- Overhandling dough develops excess gluten, a network of protein strands that makes tough pie dough. To help prevent gluten development, add a bit of lemon juice as you gather the dough into a ball.

- Press the ball of pastry into a flattened disk and chill for 20 minutes. Then, let it soften until it can be gently squeezed (10 minutes or so at room temperature) before rolling it out. This keeps the fat cold and makes the pastry easier to roll.

- Roll out the pastry on a marble slab, if possible. Marble is always at least 10 degrees cooler than its surroundings.

- Avoid overworking dough. Flour the work surface just enough to avoid sticking.

- Roll dough from the center outward rather than back and forth. Turn the dough (or pastry board) clockwise a little each time you roll. Ease up slightly on the rolling pin as you near the edge of the dough to prevent flattening the edges.

- If the dough feels difficult to roll out, let it rest in the refrigerator for 20 minutes.

- After placing the pastry in the pie pan, chill it for 20 minutes before filling and baking.

spoons butter and sprinkle with ¼ cup light brown sugar. Bake at 375°F for 50 to 55 minutes. The effect is simple and rustic.

To prevent excessive bubbling during baking • When prebaking (or "blind-baking") a pie shell, prick the pastry once or twice with a fork before baking to allow any air trapped beneath to come up through the air holes. (Avoid overpricking, though. The trapping of air between layers within the pastry helps make a pie crust tender and flaky.) Also, be sure to bake the pastry on a baking sheet rather than directly on the oven rack.

To create a glossy finish • Brush the pie, but not the fluting (which would brown too much), with an egg wash. For the egg wash, mix together 1 egg yolk and 1 teaspoon water; this will make enough to glaze 3 pies. You can also sprinkle the glaze with granulated sugar or coarse granulated sugar.

To create a fluted edge • Place the thumb of one hand flat against the inside edge of the pie crust. Then, press the dough around your thumb, using the thumb and index finger of your other hand.

To make a rickrack fluted edge • First, make a fluted edge (above), then press each "flute" into a point with your thumb and forefinger.

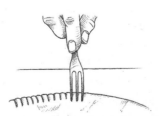

To create a fork-edged rim • Use the tines of a fork to make a decorative pattern around the edge of the crust.

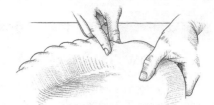

To create a rope edge • Grip the pie rim firmly between your thumb and index finger, pressing toward the side of the pan with your thumb. Continue pressing as you rotate the pan with your other hand.

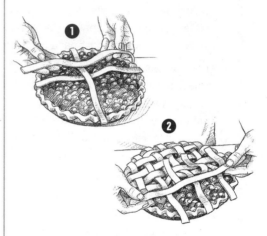

To create a lattice crust • Make enough pastry for a 2-crust pie and roll the top crust into a 12"-long rectangle. Cut 12 to 14 strips, each about ½" wide, with a knife, a pizza cutter, or a pastry wheel with a crinkled edge. Criss-cross the 2 longest strips over the center of the pie. Then, cover the top strip with another long strip in the opposite direction ❶.

Fold back every other strip and lay the cross strips in place. Then, return the folded-back strips to their original position ❷. When all the strips are in place, attach the ends of the strips to the edge of the pastry in the pan by moistening with water and pinching together to seal. Create a decorative edge as desired.

PROBLEM SOLVERS ▼ **To prevent the crust of a fruit pie from sticking to the pan** • Grease and flour the pan before lining it with the pastry.

To prevent overbrowning the edge • Cover the edge with a sheet of foil. Or, for pies that will cook for a long time, use a tart pan with a removable bottom. It has very little edge, which will help keep the crust from overbrowning.

To make an even crumb crust • Push crumbs loosely into place with your fingers, then press down and around edges with another same-size pie pan.

Fascinating Fact: The old saying "you have pastry hands" refers to someone with cold hands, which are excellent for making tender, flaky pastry.

TIME SAVERS ▼ **To always have pastry ready** • Prepare batches of pastry and freeze them. Separate the pastry into disks that are 7" in diameter and ½" in thickness (each large enough to make 1 crust, about 12 ounces). Wrap individually in plastic and freeze until firm. Pack in a plastic zipper-lock freezer bag for up to 2 months. You can also buy refrigerated or frozen pastry at your market, but pastry made from scratch by practiced hands will always produce a better result than store-bought doughs.

To save assembly time • Metal pie pans can be lined with pastry and frozen weeks before you're planning to serve them, or they can be prebaked before freezing for instant pie shells just waiting to be filled. To freeze a pie shell, baked or unbaked, wrap the shell in its pan as tightly as possible with plastic. Make the plastic conform to the surface of the crust rather than stretch over the top (use a pie pan of the same size to help the plastic conform to the crust). Freeze until solid. Once solid, pie crusts of similar size can be stacked together and stored in a 2-gallon freezer bag. Avoid freezing crusts in glass or ceramic pie pans. Not only are these pans quite heavy and bulky, but they are also not easily transferred from freezer to oven.

To save time when making crumb crusts • In a food processor, crumb large batches of graham crackers or other cookies for pie crusts. Pack in single-size amounts (usually about 1½ cups for a 9" pie crust) in zipper-lock plastic bags and refrigerate for 2 months or freeze for up to 8 months.

FLAVOR TIPS ▼ **To add flavor** • Boost the flavor of a sweet or savory pie crust with your favorite spices (ground allspice, cinnamon, or ginger), seeds (anise, caraway, or cumin), and/or oils (lemon, basil, or chili). For crumb crusts, experiment with different ingredients for making the crumbs, using them individually or in combination. Try chocolate or vanilla wafers, flavored teddy bear graham crackers, granola cereals, Cheerios, shredded wheat cereals, barley nugget cereal, amaretti cookies, biscotti, wheat crackers, and pretzels.

To flavor with bacon • Fry 6 to 8 slices bacon until crisp, browned, and cooked through. Drain. Crumble or chop and add to the pastry along with the water. Chill and roll as usual for savory pies such as pot pies.

COOKIE CRUMB CRUST Preheat oven to 350°F. Grease the inside bottom (but not the sides) of a 9" metal pie pan. Crush about **30 vanilla or chocolate wafer cookies or graham crackers or gingersnaps** to make 1½ cups fine crumbs. Place in a large bowl and mix with **3 tablespoons packed brown sugar** and **1**

All-Purpose Pie Pastry

This recipe makes one 9" pie crust. If you are making a 2-crust pie, avoid doubling the recipe. You are more likely to overwork the dough that way. Instead, make one crust, and as that chills in the refrigerator, make the second. To make the crust without a food processor, use a bowl and a pastry blender (or 2 knives) to cut in the butter and shortening, then stir in the water and lemon juice with a spoon. To bake a 2-crust pie, follow the baking instructions of the pie recipe you are using. If you are making the crust for a savory dish, such as a quiche, omit the sugar. If using the prebaked pie shell for a filling that is prone to turning the shell soggy, brush with an egg white immediately after removing the prebaked shell from the oven. This will create a moisture-resistant barrier.

1¼ **cups all-purpose flour**

1 **tablespoon sugar**

½ **teaspoon salt**

6 **tablespoons butter, chilled and cut into ¼" pieces**

2 **tablespoons shortening, chilled and cut into teaspoon-size pieces**

3½–4½ **tablespoons ice water**

1 **teaspoon lemon juice**

1. In the bowl of a food processor, combine the flour, sugar, and salt. Pulse to blend. Add the butter and pulse with six 1-second pulses, until the butter pieces are coarsely broken up and coated with flour. Add the shortening and pulse with five 1-second pulses, until the butter pieces resemble small peas.

2. Add 3½ tablespoons of the water and the lemon juice. Pulse 3 times. Add more water

teaspoon ground cinnamon (optional). While stirring, drizzle in **3 tablespoons melted butter** until crumbs are evenly coated. Turn out into the pie pan. Using your fingers, evenly distribute crumbs over the bottom and up the sides without pressing. Then, press the bottom into an even thickness with your fingers or a same-size pan placed over top. Bake on a baking sheet until lightly browned, 8 to 10 minutes. Cool on a rack. Fill as desired. Great for cooked or uncooked pudding fillings, Bavarian cream, mousse, and ice cream. *Makes one 9" crust.*

COOKIE DOUGH CRUST Any cookie dough can be used as a pastry crust. In a large bowl, beat **1 stick (½ cup) butter, 1 egg yolk, 6 tablespoons sugar,** and **½ teaspoon vanilla extract.** Stir in **1 cup all-purpose flour.** Break off pieces of dough and press into a pie plate starting at the center and working across the if necessary, 1 teaspoon at a time, and pulse 1 or 2 times, until the dough just adheres when pinched between your fingers.

3. Turn the mixture out into a medium bowl and gather the dough into a ball. Press into a disk shape, about 1" thick. Wrap in plastic wrap and chill in the refrigerator at least 30 minutes or up to 24 hours.

4. Remove the dough from the refrigerator and let stand at room temperature 10 minutes to soften. Spread a 16" piece of plastic wrap or parchment paper on a work surface. Lightly coat with flour. Place the dough on top, lightly dust with flour, and cover with another sheet of plastic wrap or parchment. Roll the dough from the center out into a 12" circle. If the dough sticks to the plastic, carefully unpeel and lightly coat the plastic with more flour.

5. Remove the top sheet and slide your hands underneath the bottom sheet. Carefully invert over the pie pan, centering the dough as much as possible. Lift the dough gently

by one edge to encourage it to conform to the bottom of the pan. Gently press across the bottom to make sure that there are no air bubbles trapped under the surface. Trim any extra dough so that there is only ½" of overhang. Tuck the dough edge under so that it hangs about ¼" beyond the pan edge. Crimp the edges as desired. Lightly cover with plastic wrap and refrigerate at least 1 hour.

6. *To prebake:* Adjust the oven rack to the middle position. Preheat the oven to 400°F. Line the pie crust with foil or parchment paper, fitting it in snugly along the curve of the crust (use another pan of the same size for a very snug fit). Drop dried beans onto the foil, distributing them evenly and fitting them snugly along the curve of the crust. Bake 18 minutes. Carefully remove the beans and foil. Cook until light golden brown, 12 to 15 minutes longer. If the crust begins to bubble, prick with a sharp knife to deflate. Transfer to a rack to cool.

Makes one 9" crust

---

bottom and up the sides. If crumb mixture sticks to your fingers, press it into place with the bottom of a small glass. Bake as directed in your pie recipe.

Makes one 9" crust.

HEALTHY HINTS ▼ **To boost nutrients in pie crusts** • Replace up to 40 percent of the all-purpose flour with oat flour, which also creates more tenderness when you are reducing fat in the crust. Or, replace up to 50 percent of the flour with whole wheat pastry flour, or up to 25 percent of the flour with cornmeal or wheat germ. Alternatively, you can use pastry flour or cake flour to replace the all-purpose flour. These soft wheat flours have less gluten, providing more tender results in reduced-fat crusts.

To reduce fat in pie crusts • Replace up to one-fourth of the butter with Neufchâtel or reduced-fat cream cheese. You can also add sugar to the dough for tenderness, using 1 tablespoon sugar per cup of flour. Adding a little baking powder

p

will give the crust a lighter, flaky texture. Use ½ teaspoon baking powder for 1¼ to 1½ cups of flour. Or replace some of the all-purpose flour with cornstarch for more-tender results. For each cup of flour, replace 2 tablespoons of the flour with an equal amount of cornstarch.

To reduce fat in crumb crusts • Substitute 1 tablespoon beaten egg white for 2 tablespoons of the butter in a crumb crust.

OATMEAL PIE CRUST In a food processor, grind ½ **cup quick-cooking oats** until ground into fine flour, 1 to 2 minutes. Add ¾ **cup flour, 1 teaspoon sugar, ¼ teaspoon baking powder, ¼ teaspoon salt,** and ½ **stick (¼ cup) chilled butter,** cut into 16 pieces. Process until mixture resembles coarse meal. Add **2 tablespoons cold water** and pulse just until mixture forms small clumps, adding more water if needed. Scrape onto plastic wrap, gather into a ball, and press into a compact disk. Wrap airtight and chill at least 1 hour. Preheat oven to 400°F. Roll out dough between sheets of plastic wrap to a 13" circle. Carefully fit into a 9" pie plate, decoratively crimping edges. Prick bottom of crust with a fork and bake until golden, 12 minutes. Cool completely on a rack. *Makes one 9" crust.*

LOW-FAT TWO-CRUST PASTRY Melt **2 tablespoons butter** in a small skillet and cook until fragrant and browned, about 2 minutes. Stir in ½ **cup canola oil** and **1 cup flour** until blended. Transfer to a small bowl and freeze 30 minutes. In a large bowl, combine another **1½ cups flour, 2 tablespoons sugar,** and **1 teaspoon salt.** Add chilled flour mixture, cutting in with pastry blender until mix-

ture has the texture of coarse meal. Sprinkle on **4 to 6 tablespoons ice water,** gently stirring just until dough holds together. Divide in half and scrape onto 2 separate sheets of plastic wrap. Gather each mound of dough into a ball, press into a flattened disk, wrap tightly, and chill 30 minutes. Preheat oven to 400°F. Roll out dough between sheets of plastic wrap to a 13" circle. Carefully fit into 9" pie plate, decoratively crimping edges. Prick bottom of crust with a fork and bake until golden, 8 to 10 minutes. Cool completely on a rack. *Makes two 9" crusts.*

Pies *see also* Meringue; Pie Crusts

In the most basic terms, a pie is simply a filling paired with a crust. It may be sweet or savory, offered as dessert or a main course, and have 2 crusts or just 1. The combinations are endless.

BASIS **To bake a fruit pie with a dome-topped crust** • Add extra fruit to the filling and pile it high in the center of the pie. The crust will rise high rather than lie flat.

To store fruit pies • Cover with plastic wrap and store at room temperature for 3 days.

To freeze a cornstarch-thickened fruit pie • Freeze the filled pie shell before baking. Otherwise, the baked filling will thin out upon thawing.

Fascinating Fact: In early America, pie was eaten three times a day. Pie was always popular for breakfast. It was largely replaced during the last part of the 20th century with toaster tarts and other breakfast confections.

To store custard pies • Cover with plastic wrap and refrigerate for no more than 3 days.

No-Gap Two-Crust Apple Pie

There's nothing more disappointing than cutting into your mile-high apple pie to find a big gap between the filling and the crust. This sometimes happens when the top crust cooks firm, then the filling reduces as it cooks, falling below the level of the already-set top crust. The solution, from food scientist Shirley Corriher, is to cook the filling separately. For apples, try Gala, Golden Delicious, or another somewhat yellow variety.

All-Purpose Pie Pastry for a 2-crust pie (page 362)

2 **tablespoons butter**

10 **apples, peeled and cut into chunks**

1 **lemon**

¼ **cup cornstarch**

⅓ **cup water or apple juice**

¾ **cup granulated sugar**

2 **tablespoons packed brown sugar**

1 **teaspoon ground cinnamon**

¼ **teaspoon grated nutmeg**

½ **cup chopped toasted walnuts**

1 **egg**

1 **tablespoon water**

1. Preheat the oven to 425°F. Melt the butter in a deep, wide skillet. Add the apples and cook 2 minutes. Grate the zest from the lemon into the pan. Cut the lemon in half and squeeze the juice into the pan.

2. In a small bowl, dissolve the cornstarch in the water or apple juice. Stir the sugar, brown sugar, cinnamon, nutmeg, and cornstarch mixture into the pan. Cook, stirring, over medium heat until the apples soften and the liquid thickens, 5 minutes. Add the walnuts and cook 1 minute.

3. Spoon the apple mixture into the prepared bottom pie pastry. Spoon any thickened liquid over the filling. Cover with the remaining pastry and crimp the edges.

4. In a small bowl, whisk together the egg and water. Brush over the top crust. Sprinkle with 1 teaspoon sugar, if desired.

5. Bake 15 minutes. Reduce the oven temperature to 350°F. Bake until the filling is bubbly and the crust is browned, another 15 to 20 minutes.

Makes 8 servings

To store meringue-topped pies • Cover the pie with plastic wrap that has been lightly coated with vegetable oil, and refrigerate for no more than 3 days.

LATTICE-TOP PEACH PIE Prepare **All-Purpose Pie Pastry** (page 362) for a 2-crust pie. Preheat oven to 425°F. Peel and

Banana Cream Pie

This recipe is a winner. The reduced-fat crust retains a flaky texture by using a combination of butter, Neufchâtel cheese, and yogurt. The filling is a simple custard, using low-fat milk and fat-free half-and-half.

Reduced-Fat Pie Crust

- 1 **cup all-purpose flour**
- 2 **tablespoons confectioners' sugar**
- ½ **teaspoon salt**
- ½ **stick (¼ cup) butter**
- 2 **tablespoons Neufchâtel or reduced-fat cream cheese**
- ⅓ **cup plain yogurt (or milk with ¼ teaspoon vinegar)**

Filling

- ½ **cup granulated sugar**
- ¼ **cup cornstarch**
- 1 **egg**
- ⅛ **teaspoon salt**
- 1⅓ **cups 1% milk**
- ⅔ **cup fat-free half-and-half**
- 1 **teaspoon vanilla extract**
- 3 **bananas, halved lengthwise and sliced**

  Pinch of ground cinnamon

1. *To make the crust:* Coat a 9" pie plate with cooking spray.

2. In a medium bowl, combine the flour, confectioners' sugar, and salt. Cut in the butter and Neufchâtel or cream cheese with a pastry blender until the mixture resembles coarse meal. Stir in the yogurt just until moistened. On a work surface, flatten into a disk. Wrap airtight in plastic wrap and chill at least 1 hour.

3. Preheat the oven to 400°F. Roll the dough out between floured sheets of waxed

slice **3 pounds (6 to 8 large) ripe freestone peaches** (avoid using very hard peaches). Or use 2 packages (20 ounces each) frozen and thawed peach slices. You should have about 5 cups peach slices. Place peaches in a large bowl and toss with **2 tablespoons lemon juice.** In a small bowl, stir together ¾ **cup sugar, 2 tablespoons** *each* **flour and cornstarch,** ½ **teaspoon** *each* **ground cinnamon and**

grated nutmeg, and ¼ teaspoon salt. Toss with peach slices. Add **2 tablespoons butter,** cut in bits, and toss again. Turn into unbaked 9" pastry shell. Weave a lattice top directly over the filling. Glaze with a mixture of **1 egg** and **1 tablespoon water.** Sprinkle with another **1 tablespoon sugar.** Bake on a foiled-lined baking sheet until light golden brown, 20 to 25 minutes. Reduce oven temperature paper to a 13" circle. Fit it into the prepared pie plate. Crimp the edges decoratively and prick the bottom of the crust with a fork to prevent air bubbles from forming under the crust. Line the inside of the crust with heavy foil. Bake 10 minutes. Remove the foil and bake until golden, 8 to 10 minutes longer.

4. *To make the filling:* In a medium saucepan, whisk together the sugar and cornstarch. Add the egg and salt and whisk until blended. Whisk in the milk. Bring to boil over medium heat, whisking constantly. As the mixture begins to thicken, whisk until smooth, 30 seconds.

5. Remove from the heat. Gradually whisk in the half-and-half and vanilla extract. Place the bananas in the pie crust in an even layer. Pour the filling evenly over the bananas. Cover with plastic wrap touching the surface. Chill to set fully, 8 hours or overnight. Sprinkle with the cinnamon just before serving.

Makes 8 servings

Crust Variations

Reduced-Fat Nut Crust: Add 2 tablespoons finely ground nuts such as hazelnuts or pecans to the dough along with the flour.

Reduced-Fat Cheese Crust: If making the crust alone for a savory filling, omit the confectioners' sugar. Add 2 tablespoons grated Parmesan cheese to the dough along with the flour.

Reduced-Fat Herb Crust: If making the crust alone for a savory filling, omit the confectioners' sugar. Add 1 tablespoon finely chopped fresh herbs such as parsley, chives, or thyme to the dough along with the flour.

Filling Variations

Chocolate-Banana Cream Pie: Whisk in 3 tablespoons sifted unsweetened cocoa powder and ½ teaspoon instant coffee or espresso powder with the sugar.

Coconut-Banana Cream Pie: Add ½ teaspoon coconut extract along with the vanilla extract. Top the pie with ½ cup toasted coconut.

to 350°F and bake until filling is bubbly and crust is golden, 20 to 25 minutes longer. Cool on a rack. Serve warm or at room temperature. *Makes 8 servings.*

PROBLEM SOLVERS ▼ **To prevent custard fillings from spilling •** Put the unfilled pie shell on a rack in the oven, then pour in the filling.

To prevent an air pocket in a 2-crust fruit pie • Cook the filling (fruit and other ingredients) in a saucepan until the fruit is softened. Drain, if necessary, and pat the cooked filling down in the bottom of the pie shell before covering with the top crust. Bake as usual.

To prevent a fruit-pie filling from spilling over • Place a large piece or two of uncooked ziti or penne in the pie's center. The bubbling juices will rise inside the pasta tunnels instead of spilling out. If the pie has a lattice top, place a handful of ziti or penne throughout the pie, between the lattice's weave.

To avoid pie juices burning on the oven bottom • Place a baking sheet lined with aluminum foil or parchment on the rack underneath the pie to catch any spills.

To make clean pie slices • Wipe the knife down after each slice. This is particularly important with cream pies.

To fix a pie that does not have enough filling • Fold the edges down a notch and crimp so that it looks like you intended to make a shallow pie. (You might want to call it a tart.)

To rescue a baked pie that looks cooked from the outside but is undercooked inside • Loosely wrap it in foil and return it to the oven to cook through.

TIME SAVER ▼ To save prep time on fruit pies • Cook the fruit filling ahead and freeze it. Then, thaw, pour into pie shell, and bake.

MAKE-AHEAD FRUIT PIE FILLING Trim about **3 pounds fruit** of their peels, stems, leaves, and seeds. Cut into ½"-wide wedges or chunks and place in a large skillet. Add **2 tablespoons butter, ½ cup sugar, 1 teaspoon lemon juice,** and **½ teaspoon ground cinnamon** or other flavorings. Cook over medium heat until fruit starts to soften and release its juices, about 4 minutes. Add more sugar, if necessary. Do not overcook. Cool the filling. Mix in **2 tablespoons cornstarch.** Spoon into a zipper-lock plastic bag and refrigerate up to 2 weeks or freeze up to 4 months. Thaw and pour into a 9" pie shell. Bake at 375°F until fruit is bubbly and crust is lightly browned, 25 to 35 minutes. *Makes enough filling for one 9" pie.*

FROZEN-FRUIT PIE FILLING Thaw **3 pounds frozen fruit** (any variety or combination) in a microwave oven in the fruit's storage bag on the defrost cycle in 3-minute cycles, until the fruit is softened. Or submerge the bag of frozen fruit in tepid tap water 10 to 20 minutes, changing the water as it gets too cold. Drain liquid from the bag and toss fruit with **⅓ cup flour, ⅓ to ½ cup sugar** (depending on sweetness of fruit), and **a pinch of salt.** Transfer to a prepared pie shell. Top with a crust or a crumb topping. Bake at 375°F until fruit is bubbly and crust is lightly browned, 25 to 35 minutes. *Makes enough filling for one 9" pie.*

SUPER-FAST CHIFFON BUTTERMILK PUMPKIN PIE Preheat oven to 375°F. Mix **1½ cups canned pumpkin** with **1 teaspoon ground cinnamon, ½ teaspoon ground ginger, 1 cup packed light brown sugar, 3 large egg yolks,** and **⅔ cups buttermilk.** Beat **3 egg whites** and **¼ teaspoon salt** until soft peaks form when beaters are lifted from the bowl. Fold into pumpkin mixture. Pour into unbaked **All-Purpose Pie Pastry** (page 362) and bake until custard is set, 1 hour. Cool. *Makes 8 servings.*

HEALTHY HINTS ▼ To reduce fat in cream pie fillings • Replace milk or cream with a combination of fat-free milk and reduced-fat cream cheese for a velvety texture and rich flavor. You can also replace up to one-fourth of the milk with fat-free half-and-half. Whisk in the half-and-half off the heat after the pudding has cooked.

To reduce fat in cream-topped pies • Instead of topping with whipped cream, use Marshmallow Creme (page 197) on unbaked or already-baked pies.

Pilaf

The pilaf method for cooking grains calls for the grain to be lightly sautéed in hot fat and then simmered in a hot liquid until the liquid is absorbed. Coming from Turkey, Greece, Persia, and other Middle Eastern countries, pilaf is usually made with sautéed rice, vegetables, and broth. Sometimes meat, pasta, or nuts are added.

BASICS ▼ **To bring out the nutty flavor of grains** • Begin making your pilaf by toasting the grains in a dry pan over medium heat until the grains are fragrant and well-browned. Remove the toasted grains from the pan and set aside until needed.

To add flavor • Sauté onions or shallots in hot fat until they are well-browned. The caramelized onions provide a rich foundation of flavor to the pilaf.

To keep grains from sticking • Stir the toasted grains into the sautéed vegetables and toss to coat the grains with the hot fat.

To test for doneness • The grains should be tender but still a bit chewy; the cooking liquid should be absorbed. If the grains are done but some liquid remains in the pan, just pour off the remaining liquid. If all the liquid has been absorbed but the grains are not quite done, add ½ cup hot water, cover the pan, and continue cooking until the grains are tender.

ALMOND RICE PILAF In a medium saucepan, cook ½ **cup slivered almonds** in **2 teaspoons vegetable oil** until golden, 3 to 4 minutes, stirring often. Turn out and set aside. Add another **2 teaspoons oil** to the pan along with **1**

chopped onion and **1 small chopped carrot.** Sauté to soften, about 3 minutes. Stir in **1½ cups long-grain white rice** and cook until lightly toasted, 4 to 5 minutes, stirring often. Add ½ **cup water** and cook until it is absorbed, about 2 minutes. Add **2 cups chicken stock** or **vegetable broth** and ½ **teaspoon salt** (unless broth is salty). Bring to a boil. Remove from heat and stir in **1 tablespoon butter, 1 teaspoon toasted sesame oil,** and ⅓ **cup chopped fresh parsley.** Turn into a greased 8" × 8" pan or a shallow 2-quart casserole. Cover tightly with greased aluminum foil and bake at 350°F until rice is tender and liquid is absorbed, about 20 minutes. Let stand 10 to 15 minutes before uncovering. *Makes 4 servings.*

Pineapples

A favorite tropical fruit, pineapple is formed by the fusion of about 100 separate flowers recognizable as "eyes" on its thorny hide and yellow flesh.

BASICS ▼ **To choose** • Smell the fruit. A ripe pineapple emits a sweet, fruity fragrance. Also, look for plump fruits with crisp, green leaves. Avoid pineapples with rinds that look shriveled, soft, or dry. And keep in mind that larger fruits have a greater proportion of edible flesh.

To store ripe pineapple • Put the pineapple in a perforated zipper-lock plastic bag and refrigerate for up to 3 days.

To store underripe pineapple • Keep at room temperature, away from heat and strong light, for up to 5 days.

To store cut pineapple • Refrigerate cut pieces of pineapple in an airtight container up to 3 days.

p

To trim fresh pineapple • Cut off the spiky top about 1" below the leaves, and cut about ½" from the base so it can stand upright. Place the fruit upright on its cut bottom end. The eyes of a pineapple follow a spiral pattern running from top to bottom, counterclockwise. To remove the rind and spiky eyes at once, cut off the rind in vertical strips from top to bottom, following the slightly spiraling rows of eyes and the contour of the fruit. Cut about ⅛" to ¼" deep. Trim away any remaining eyes with the tip of a vegetable peeler.

To create sunburst slices • Trim as described above. Then, cut diagonal V-shaped grooves along the spiraling rows of eyes. Cut crosswise into ¾"-thick slices, which will resemble sunbursts.

To cut rings • Cut a peeled, uncored pineapple into rounds and use a small, round cookie cutter or the tip of a paring knife to cut out the core from each slice.

To cut wedges or chunks • Cut the peeled fruit lengthwise into quarters and remove the woody core by slicing along the length of each piece just under the core. Then, slice the cored fruit into wedges or chunks.

To slow-roast a whole pineapple • Cut most of the green, leafy top from a just-ripe pineapple, leaving 1" intact. Do not cut into the pineapple flesh or juice will run out. Place the fruit on its side in a shallow roasting pan and roast at 325°F until very tender, about 1 hour. Turn off the heat and leave it in the oven for 1 hour longer. Slice off the top and bottom and then quarter the pineapple lengthwise. Slice off the pointed core from each piece. Slice the flesh from the rind, then slice it crosswise and return the slices to the rind for a nice presentation. Or serve slices with vanilla ice cream.

To use pineapple with gelatin • Pineapple contains an enzyme called bromelain that prevents gelatin from jelling. To destroy the enzyme, heat the pineapple or juice before adding to gelatin.

To use pineapple as a meat tenderizer • The bromelain in pineapple also helps tenderize meats because it breaks down protein. When making a marinade for tough cuts of meat such as flank steak, add pineapple juice. Or layer thin slices of pineapple between steaks and refrigerate for 1 hour before grilling. If using this trick with poultry and seafood, marinate for no more than 30 minutes, to prevent the meat from becoming mushy.

PINEAPPLE AND MACADAMIA NUT UPSIDE-DOWN CAKE Preheat oven to 350°F. In a small saucepan over low heat, melt **6 tablespoons butter.** Remove and set aside 2 tablespoons for batter. To the remaining butter in the saucepan, add ⅓ **cup packed dark brown sugar, ¼ cup dark or light corn syrup,** and **2 teaspoons water.** Simmer briefly to dissolve sugar. Pour into a greased 9" pie plate or 8" × 8" pan. Arrange **20 glacé or maraschino** cherries around edges. Drain **1 can (8 ounces) crushed pineapple** and combine with **¾ cup chopped unsalted macadamia nuts** (if nuts are salted, rinse before chopping). Sprinkle in the pan. In a small bowl, stir together **1 cup all-purpose flour, 1 teaspoon baking powder,** and **⅛ teaspoon salt.** In a large bowl, beat **2 large eggs** until foamy, about 30 seconds. Gradually beat in **⅔ cup granulated sugar** and the reserved 2 tablespoons butter. Add flour mixture and beat briefly just to blend. Beat in **½ cup milk** and **2 teaspoons vanilla extract.** Pour batter over pineapple. Bake in the lower third of the oven until a toothpick inserted in center comes out clean, about 35 minutes. Run a knife around edge to loosen cake. Cool in the pan on a rack 10 minutes. Invert a plate over cake and unmold. Quickly replace any nuts or cherries that have fallen off. Serve warm or at room temperature. *Makes 9 servings.*

HEALTHY HINTS ▼

To optimize your vitamin C intake • Look for the "gold" variety of pineapple. Loaded with 4 times the vitamin C of regular pineapple, this variety is exceptionally sweet, with golden-colored flesh.

To soothe a sore throat or a head cold • Pour canned pineapple juice into a saucepan and bring to a boil. Sip hot from a teacup, and you will soon feel better.

Pizza

A simple savory tart, pizza is typically made from a yeast dough topped with any number of toppings, including vegetables, cheeses, and meats. Pizza actually originated in Greece, where flatbread would be made with a rim around it to hold food as a sort of edible plate. That's one delicious way to avoid washing dishes.

BASICS ▼

To make pliable pizza dough • Knead the dough for at least 5 minutes longer than you would a yeast dough for bread.

To make a thin, crisp crust • Refrigerate the risen dough for several hours. Roll the dough about ¼" thick while it is still cold and bake it immediately in a hot oven before the dough has a chance to warm up and begin to rise again.

To create a thick, chewy crust • Stretch the dough about ½" thick and let it rise slightly before baking.

To shape pizza dough with a rolling pin • On a lightly floured surface, roll the dough into a circle by rolling just to but not over the edge of the dough.

To shape pizza dough with your hands • Hold a flattened disk of dough vertically, turning it like a wheel and letting gravity stretch the dough.

To transfer pizza dough to a hot oven • Use a flat wooden paddle known as a baker's peel, or use a thin, rimless baking sheet. You can also assemble the pizza on a sheet of aluminum foil or parchment set on the back side of a baking sheet. Then, just slide the foil (or paper) from the pan onto a preheated baking sheet to bake.

To keep pizza dough from sticking to a baker's peel or baking sheet • Dust the peel or baking sheet generously with cornmeal before laying down the dough.

To create an exceptionally crisp crust • Bake the dough directly on unglazed quarry tiles or a baking stone preheated in a very hot oven.

To make gooey cheese crisper on homemade pizza • Turn on the broiler during the last few minutes of cooking.

PROBLEM SOLVERS ▼

To avoid a soggy crust • Bake the pizza dough shells without any sauce or toppings for 5 minutes. Press down any major

p

EASY HOMEMADE PIZZA

You can use a prebaked pizza shell for any of the recipes below. But if you've never had homemade pizza dough, you're in for a treat. Each recipe makes one 10" × 14" rectangular pizza or two 12" round pizzas.

Basic Pizza Dough: In a small bowl, combine ¼ **cup warm tap water** (105° to 115°F) and **1 teaspoon sugar.** Sprinkle **1 teaspoon active dry yeast** over top and stir to moisten. Cover loosely and let proof until foamy, about 5 minutes. In a food processor fitted with a dough blade, combine **2 cups bread flour** or **all-purpose flour** with **1 tablespoon olive oil** and ½ **teaspoon salt.** Pulse to blend. Add the proofed yeast and ½ **cup barely warm water** (not as warm as proofing temperature). Process to make a soft dough, and continue processing 1 minute to knead. Lightly dust your hands with flour and remove dough. Knead by hand 1 minute longer. Place in a bowl coated with olive oil. Turn once to oil top. Cover loosely with plastic wrap and place in a larger bowl half-filled with warm water. Let rise until doubled in size, 1 to 1½ hours. Do not punch down. Lightly flour a work surface. Gently turn dough out onto

surface without totally deflating. Quickly push and stretch dough with your hands into a 10" × 14" rectangle. Generously sprinkle a large wooden pizza peel or rimless baking sheet with coarse cornmeal. Place dough on it with one end close to the edge. Cover loosely with plastic and let rise 30 minutes. Meanwhile, preheat a pizza stone or baking sheet on the lowest oven shelf at 475°F for 30 minutes. Uncover pizza dough and top with your favorite toppings. Place the pizza peel or baking sheet holding the dough at the back edge of the preheated pizza stone or baking sheet. Give it a short, sharp jerk (or two) to loosen the pizza onto the stone or baking sheet. Bake until lightly browned and bubbly, 8 to 10 minutes. Makes one large (10" × 14") pizza.

Pepperoni Pizza: Spread partially risen dough with about ¾ **cup canned crushed tomatoes** (for slightly thicker sauce, stir in 1 tablespoon tomato paste). Scatter **2 cups shredded mozzarella cheese** on top. Add ¾ **cup whole, quartered,** or **julienned slices pepperoni.** Sprinkle with ½ **teaspoon dried oregano.** Bake as directed above.

bubbles with the back of a wooden spoon, then add toppings. You can also sauté moisture-laden topping ingredients, such as spinach or mushrooms, to cook off some of the water. (With spinach, you might also want to squeeze it dry between some paper towels.) It also helps to sprinkle a light layer of cheese over the crust before saucing, or brush the dough with oil before adding toppings. Finally, add toppings just before putting the pizza

in the oven. If the toppings sit on the unbaked dough for long, they'll be absorbed into it and the crust will be soggy.

To rescue pizza with a burning crust • Wrap foil around the crust, or cover it with a good sprinkling of grated cheese to protect and camouflage. If the bottom of the crust is burning, place the pizza on a higher rack in the oven. If just one side of the pizza is burning, rotate it: Your oven might be heating unevenly. If the outer

Sausage and Mushroom Pizza: Slit the casing of **1 or 2 Italian sausages** (4 to 5 ounces each) and crumble meat into a skillet over medium heat. Sauté until no longer pink. Drain off fat and wipe out the skillet. Sauté **6 thinly sliced mushrooms** in **1 tablespoon butter** or **olive oil** to soften, about 2 minutes. Spread partially risen dough with about **¾ cup canned crushed tomatoes** (for slightly thicker sauce, stir in 1 tablespoon tomato paste). Scatter **1 cup shredded mozzarella cheese** on top. Add sausage, mushrooms, **½ teaspoon dried oregano, ¼ teaspoon salt**, and **⅛ teaspoon ground black pepper**. Top with another **1 cup shredded mozzarella** and bake as directed on the opposite page.

Fresh Tomato Pizza: Thinly slice **2 large tomatoes** and arrange slices over partially risen dough. Sprinkle with **2 tablespoons chopped fresh basil** and **1 cup finely crumbled feta cheese** or **½ cup grated Parmesan cheese**. Top with **½ teaspoon cracked black pepper**. Bake as directed on the opposite page.

Roasted Red Pepper Pizza: Roast and peel **2 large red bell peppers** (or use jarred). Spread partially risen pizza dough with about **¾ cup canned crushed tomatoes** (for thicker sauce, stir in 1 tablespoon tomato paste). Cut peppers into strips and arrange all over pizza. Top with **2 cups shredded mozzarella cheese** or **½ pound sliced mild provolone** and sprinkle with **½ teaspoon dried oregano, ¼ teaspoon salt**, and **⅛ teaspoon ground black pepper**. Bake as directed on the opposite page.

Caramelized Onion and Black Olive Pizza: Combine **1 tablespoon** *each* **butter and olive oil** in a large skillet over medium heat. Add **2 large chopped onions** and sauté until onions are well-browned, about 25 minutes, stirring often. (If onions seem dry at any point, add 1 to 2 tablespoons water to moisten and prevent scorching.) Let cool. Scatter onion mixture over partially risen dough along with **15 large pitted and chopped kalamata olives**. Sprinkle with **1 tablespoon chopped fresh rosemary** (or 1 teaspoon dried and crumbled) and **¼ teaspoon** *each* **salt and ground black pepper**. Drizzle with another **2 tablespoons olive oil**. Bake as directed on the opposite page.

---

edge of the crust is miserably burnt, just cut it off and serve it crustless. It's unlikely that anyone will turn away a pizza for lack of a crust.

To avoid compressing the dough of a deep-dish pizza • Prebake the untopped crust until slightly risen and faintly browned, 10 to 15 minutes. Add toppings and continue baking.

To cut pizza without a pizza cutter • Use a pair of kitchen scissors.

TIME SAVER ▼ **To make a quick crust** • If you're in a hurry, skip the homemade pizza dough and opt for one of these speedy alternatives: refrigerated fresh or frozen pizza dough or bread dough, prebaked pizza shells, focaccia or flatbread, flour tortillas, whole wheat pitas, halved sandwich–size English muffins, or halved bagels.

Fascinating Fact: On average, Americans eat 18 acres of pizza every day.

p

To enrich mozzarella cheese • Coarsely grate or shred ½ pound mozzarella cheese. Toss it with 1½ tablespoons olive oil and ¼ teaspoon ground black pepper. Let it marinate while you prepare the pizza.

To make your own frozen pizza • Frozen pizzas from the supermarket are generally lacking in flavor and texture. To easily make your own frozen pizza, order a plain or topped pizza from your favorite pizza parlor. Add toppings, if desired. Cut into individual slices, wrap individually in foil, and freeze the slices. When you want pizza, pop the frozen slices into an oven or toaster oven.

To increase the fiber in pizza dough • Replace up to 50 percent of the all-purpose flour with whole wheat flour. Whole wheat flour adds fiber as well as a nutty flavor to the crust.

To prevent the top of pizzas from drying out • When making pizzas with little cheese on top, spray with a mist of olive oil and bake as directed.

Plantains

Though they belong to the banana family, plantains are much starchier and must be cooked. Sliced fried plantain slices, called tostones, accompany many Latin American and Caribbean dishes.

To choose • As plantains ripen, the fruit becomes sweeter and the skin color changes from green to yellow to half-black and finally to black. The stage of ripeness indicates how the plantain should be prepared. Any plantain that isn't squishy soft, moldy, cracked, or dried and hard is good to eat. Occasionally, you will come across a plantain that does not soften, no matter how dark it gets. It should be discarded.

To prepare green plantains • Green plantains are hard and starchy and not sweet at all. Treat them like potatoes and fry, roast, or boil them for a comparable length of time. Try adding chunks of green plantain to soups and stews and braising them with meat.

To prepare yellow plantains • Prepare yellow plantains just like green ones; they will taste slightly sweeter and have a smoother texture. Yellow plantains are delicious mashed and combined with other sweet vegetables such as winter squash.

To prepare black plantains • Treat black plantains as you would ripe bananas. They tend to hold their shape better than common bananas, so they can be cooked longer, which develops their complexity and allows the fruit to absorb more flavor.

To store • Keep them at room temperature until ready to use. After plantains ripen to black, they can be refrigerated to prolong life.

To peel • Plantains have thicker, tougher skins than bananas. If using a yellow or half-black plantain that will be sliced, cut it crosswise through the skin in 3" to 4" lengths. Score the skin lengthwise and remove it. To remove the skin from a green plantain, cut off the ends and make 3 or 4 lengthwise slits in the skin, cutting just to the fruit. Place it in a bowl of warm water to cover, and let it soak until the skin is softened, about 10 minutes. Run your thumb under the slits to ease the skin off the fruit.

TOSTONES (PLANTAIN CHIPS) Cut **1 yellow** or **half-black plantain** crosswise in 3" or 4" lengths. Score the skin lengthwise and remove it. Cut plantains, on an angle if desired, into ½"-thick slices. Soak slices in **salted water (1 tablespoon salt** per **2 cups water**) 30 to 60 minutes. Drain and pat dry. Heat **2 to 3 tablespoons vegetable oil** in a large skillet over medium heat. Sauté slices until tender and golden brown, 3 to 4 minutes per side. Arrange slices on a board and cover with a sheet of waxed paper. Using a mallet, pound slices to about ⅛" thickness. These can be made ahead and reheated in a dry, nonstick skillet (or in the oven). Great with roast pork, chicken, or ham. *Makes about 12 chips.*

Plums

There are dozens of plums to choose from, and they come in just about every color of the rainbow: yellow, orange, red, purple, blue, green, and black. Large plums can be the size of a tennis ball, while small ones can look like oversize playing marbles. Plums have a luscious texture and flavor, both sweet and tart, that makes them great for eating out of hand and for cooking in cobblers, crisps, tarts, puddings, pies, sauces, ice cream, and even savory dishes such as stir-fries and barbecued rib sauces.

BASICS To choose • The best plums will have ripened on the tree, where most of the natural sweetness and flavor develop. Look for richly colored fruit that gives slightly to gentle pressure. Avoid those with soft spots, cracks, or discoloration. If you see a gray film on the skin, don't worry; it's a natural product of the fruit.

To ripen • Place them in a paper bag for 1 to 2 days. To speed ripening, add an apple to the bag.

To store ripe plums • Refrigerate in a zipper-lock plastic bag up to 5 days.

To prepare • When halved around the center, plum pits are easily removed. Don't bother peeling plums; it's not necessary.

FLAVOR TIP To add excitement to fruit cocktails • Add slices of plum. For terrific texture and color, add one each of two or three colors.

PLUM-PECAN UPSIDE-DOWN CAKE Preheat oven to 325°F. Melt **5 tablespoons butter** in a 9" to 10" cast-iron skillet (or in a small saucepan, if you will bake the cake in a cake pan). Remove and set aside 2 tablespoons of the melted butter. To the pan with the remaining butter, add ⅓ **cup packed light brown sugar** and **2 teaspoons water.** Boil mixture until melted and foamy, 2 to 3 minutes. If using a 9" cake pan instead of a skillet, grease the pan, then pour mixture into it. Cut **8 red plums** (about 1 pound) in half and pry out pits. Cut each half into 4 wedges and arrange wedges close together in the skillet or cake pan, in two concentric circles, beginning around the edge. Sprinkle **1 cup chopped pecans** or **walnuts** around the edge and in the center of the pan. In a medium bowl or on a sheet of waxed paper, stir together **1 cup all-purpose flour, 1 teaspoon baking powder,** and ¼ teaspoon *each* grated **nutmeg and ground cinnamon.** Separate **3 large eggs,** placing whites in a large bowl and setting yolks aside in a cup. Add **a pinch of salt** to whites and beat until soft mounds form. Gradually beat in ⅔ **cup granulated sugar** and beat until stiff peaks form when beaters are lifted. Beat in reserved yolks, ⅓ **cup milk,** and **1 teaspoon vanilla extract.** Add the flour mixture and the reserved 2 tablespoons butter. Beat just to blend and pour over plums in the prepared pan. Spread evenly and bake until deep golden brown and a toothpick inserted in center comes out clean, 40 to 45 minutes. Let rest in the pan 5 minutes, then run a knife around edges to loosen cake. Invert a serving plate over cake and turn over to unmold. Replace any plums or nuts that have fallen off. Let cool. Serve warm or at room temperature. *Makes 8 servings.*

p Poaching

This moist-heat cooking method is best for preparing delicate foods such as fish, shellfish, chicken, eggs, and fruit. Keeping the cooking liquid just below a simmer is the key to gentle, even poaching.

BASICS ▼ **To poach foods perfectly** • The cooking liquid should hover between 160° and 170°F. The surface of the water should show some movement and look like it's just about to bubble, without ever reaching a simmer. Keep the food completely submerged in the poaching liquid, but don't cover the pot, which will increase the cooking temperature.

PROBLEM SOLVERS ▼ **To keep poached foods submerged in the cooking liquid** • Press a sheet of parchment paper directly onto the surface of the cooking liquid.

To help lift delicate ingredients, such as fish, from poaching liquid without damage • Wrap the food in a length of cheesecloth long enough to allow some overhang at each end. When the food is finished poaching, use the overhang as handles to lift it from the poaching liquid.

TIME SAVER ▼ **To speed up poaching time** • Smaller pieces poach faster than large ones. In many cases, you can just pour boiling water over the food. To poach medium-size shrimp, quartered scallops, ¼"-thick slices of fish, or paper-thin strips of boneless, skinless chicken breast, heat the poaching liquid to boiling. Pour it over the thin or sliced food. Stir once, cover tightly, and set aside for 1 to 2 minutes. Remove poached ingredients with a slotted spoon.

SEASONED POACHING BROTHS

Use these poaching liquids to flavor beef, pork, chicken, and fish. After poaching, the liquid can be strained, frozen, and reused. Or you can reduce the liquid to make a sauce or use it as a stock. Each recipe makes about 8 cups poaching liquid.

Wine Broth: In a large saucepan or skillet, simmer **6 cups water, 3 cups white wine, 2 teaspoons salt,** and **2** *each* **chopped onions, carrots, and celery ribs** for 20 minutes. Strain and use to poach fish or shellfish.

Orange Spice Broth: In a large saucepan or skillet, simmer **3 cups** *each* **water and orange juice, 2 cups white wine, 1 large sliced leek, 4 star anise,** and **6 allspice berries** for 15 minutes. Strain and use to poach chicken or pork.

Rosemary and Red Wine Broth: In a large saucepan or skillet, simmer **3 cups** *each* red wine and water, 2 cups vegetable cocktail juice, 1 chopped red onion, 2 rosemary sprigs, and ½ teaspoon peppercorns for 15 minutes. Strain and use to poach beef.

Polenta

The Italian word for cornmeal, *polenta* **also refers to a dish made by cooking cornmeal in boiling water until it forms a soft mass. Polenta is served either soft or cooled and cut into slices, which are then baked, grilled, or fried. It's interesting that polenta is considered Italian: After all, Italy got corn and cornmeal from the Americas, and polenta is really no different from American "mush." But it turns out that Italians had a long history of making polenta from other grains, such as barley, but simply preferred to make it with cornmeal once they "discovered" the American grain.**

BASICS **To choose cornmeal** • Polenta may be made from white or yellow cornmeal, though yellow is more common. Choose a coarse-grained cornmeal for polenta with a more robust texture. Fine-grained cornmeal will make polenta with a smoother, creamier texture.

To tell when polenta is done • When the polenta forms a mass that pulls cleanly away from the sides of the pot, remove it from the heat.

To serve soft polenta • Pour the cooked polenta into a bowl moistened with cold water. Let stand for about 10 minutes, then unmold the polenta onto a platter and serve hot.

To make firm polenta for grilling or frying • Spread the cooked polenta onto a baking sheet and let it cool until firm.

To store firm polenta • Cover with plastic wrap and refrigerate for up to 3 days before using.

To cut firm polenta into squares • Use a pizza cutter or a knife dipped in hot water.

To bake • Arrange ½"-thick slices of firm polenta in a single layer on an oiled baking sheet. Bake at 350°F until heated through.

To grill • Cut squares of firm polenta about ¼" thick. Brush the squares with olive oil and grill over a medium-hot fire until browned on both sides.

To fry • Slice squares of firm polenta about ¼" thick and cut them into narrow strips. Fry in hot oil until crusty and golden brown. Drain well and serve hot.

To sauce and broil • Slice firm polenta into squares or rounds ½" thick and sauté in butter or olive oil to lightly brown. Top with tomato sauce and Parmesan cheese, then run under the broiler or bake in the top of a hot oven. Hot, soft polenta can also be spooned into a gratin dish, then topped with sauce and cheese and baked until golden.

To make polenta "lasagna" • Cut firm polenta into slices about ½" thick and use them to replace lasagna noodles in your favorite lasagna recipe.

To clean the polenta pot • Don't bother to scrub the dried polenta from the

p

sides of the pot. Instead, fill it with cold water and let it stand overnight. In the morning, the dried polenta will easily pull away from the pot.

POLENTA Place **1 cup coarse yellow** or **white cornmeal** with **4 cups cold water** and **2 teaspoons salt** in a medium saucepan. Whisk vigorously. Bring to a boil over high heat. Reduce heat to low and boil gently until very thick, 30 to 40 minutes, stirring almost constantly. If desired, stir in ¾ **cup grated Parmesan cheese, 2 to 3 tablespoons butter** or **olive oil,** and **3 tablespoons chopped fresh herbs** (basil, parsley, thyme, rosemary). To serve soft polenta, pour into a bowl moistened with cold water. Let stand about 10 minutes, then unmold polenta onto a platter and serve hot. To serve firm polenta (to slice and fry, grill, or broil), spread the cooked polenta onto a baking sheet or into a loaf pan and let cool until firm. Cut into slabs or squares and cook as desired. *Makes 6 servings (¾ cup each).*

PROBLEM SOLVERS ▼ **To avoid lumps** • Classic Italian recipes instruct you to very slowly sprinkle the cornmeal into boiling water as you stir constantly. This assures that the grains are separate and constantly moving. An easier way to avoid lumps is to add the cornmeal all at once to the cold water in the saucepan, whisk vigorously, then bring it to a boil.

To rescue polenta that has burned on the bottom • Transfer it to a new pan without scraping the burned bottom. Continue to cook, adjusting the heat if necessary and taking care to stir frequently.

To fix lumpy polenta • Remove it from the heat and smooth it out by whisking vigorously by hand or using an immersion blender.

TIME SAVERS ▼ **To save prep time** • Buy prepared polenta in the refrigerated section of your supermarket. Just cut slices and brown, broil, or grill them.

To quickly cool and set • Spread it in an even layer across a baking sheet. Once polenta is set, use biscuit cutters or tuna cans (cleaned and lids removed) to cut out polenta rounds.

MICROWAVED SOFT POLENTA Combine **4 cups water, 1 teaspoon salt,** and **1 cup yellow** or **white cornmeal** in an 8-cup glass measure or bowl. Stir well. Microwave at full power 7 minutes, uncovered. Stir. Cover with 2 layers of paper towel and microwave at full power, 7 minutes more. Add **2 tablespoons butter, ¼ cup freshly grated Parmesan cheese,** and **a few grindings of black pepper.** Stir. Serve immediately.
Makes 6 servings (¾ cup each).

MICROWAVED FIRM POLENTA Follow the recipe for **Microwaved Soft Polenta** (above) but increase cornmeal to 1½ cups. Pour finished polenta into a loaf pan and let stand until cool. Invert the pan to remove polenta, then cut into ½"-thick slices. Brown in olive oil or brush with olive oil and broil or grill.
Makes 6 servings (¾ cup each).

Pomegranates

When broken open, the leathery skin of a pomegranate reveals a shimmering sea of tiny seeds encased in a translucent ruby-red pulp. The sweet-sour seeds can be used as a garnish for salads and desserts, and they make a delicious snack on their own.

BASICS ▼ **To choose** • Look for large, heavy fruits with thin skins that feel as if they are about to burst open from all the seeds packed inside.

To store • Whole pomegranates keep in the refrigerator for as long as 3 months. The seeds can also be scraped out of the fruit, packed in an airtight container, and frozen for 3 months.

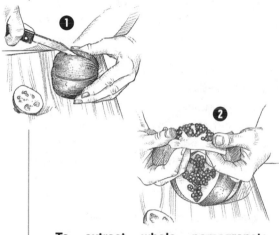

To extract whole pomegranate seeds • Cut a thin slice from the blossom end of the fruit, taking care not to pierce any of the seeds. Lightly score the skin of the fruit from stem to blossom end in four to six places, without cutting through to the seeds ❶.

Gently break the fruit apart along the scored lines, then bend back the rind of each piece to reveal the seeds. Gently free the seeds from the pithy membranes ❷. Pomegranate juice stains easily, so protect your clothing as you work.

To extract the juice • Cut the fruit in half around its equator. Cover the cut sides with 2 layers of dampened cheesecloth and tie them to hold in place. Squeeze the juice from each half through the cheesecloth into a bowl (as you would squeeze an orange). Or you can roll the pomegranate against a countertop to crush the seeds beneath the skin and release their juice (be careful not to burst the skin). With a sharp knife, cut around the stem, and remove the stem and the plug of flesh beneath it to create a hole. Invert the pomegranate over a bowl and gently squeeze the fruit, draining the juice through the hole. You can also remove the seeds and puree them in a blender. Then, strain the juice before using.

Popcorn *see also* Corn

These dry, hard kernels of corn actually contain 13.5 percent moisture. When heated, the moisture begins to expand and ultimately causes the tough outer layer of the corn kernel to rupture or pop.

BASICS ▼ **To store** • Unpopped popcorn will retain its moisture best when refrigerated or frozen in an airtight container. Leftover popped (unbuttered) popcorn can be kept in a zipper-lock plastic bag at room temperature for 2 weeks. If it has been buttered, refrigerate it. To reheat, spread the popcorn on a rimmed baking sheet and bake at 325°F for 5 to 10 minutes.

OLD-FASHIONED POPCORN Popping corn is so easily done from scratch, it's a wonder that it was ever streamlined into a convenience food. Heat **3 tablespoons corn oil** or **other vegetable oil** in a large, heavy pot with a tight-fitting lid over high heat until very hot. Add **3 kernels popping corn** and heat until the kernels pop. Add **1 cup popping corn.** Cover and shake gently over high heat until you hear the corn start to pop, about 30 seconds. As kernels pop, shake vigorously and crack the lid just enough to let steam vent. Keep shaking and venting until the popping subsides, about 2 minutes. Remove from heat. Turn out into a bowl and toss with seasonings, if desired. Serve hot. *Makes 6 servings.*

VANILLA POPCORN Follow the recipe for **Old-Fashioned Popcorn** (page 379). Add **1 split vanilla bean** along with the popping corn. When the corn is popped, remove vanilla bean and toss popped corn with **2 tablespoons melted butter, 1 tablespoon superfine sugar,** and **½ teaspoon salt.** Scrape the seeds from the vanilla bean and add to the popcorn. *Makes 6 servings.*

PROBLEM SOLVERS ▼ **To revive dry popcorn kernels** • Some popcorn can get too dry to pop. Bring it back to life by soaking it overnight in cold water. Drain and dry it thoroughly before using.

To avoid soggy popcorn • Remove the pan lid immediately after popping so that the steam does not condense on the lid and fall back into the pot of fresh-popped popcorn.

To minimize salt loss in the bottom of the popcorn bowl • Toss the popcorn in melted butter (or coat it with cooking spray) first. This creates a moist surface for the salt or other seasonings to cling to.

HEALTHY HINTS ▼ **To reduce fat** • Place popping corn kernels in a paper bag and mist them with cooking spray. Fold the bag over to seal and microwave on high power until the kernels are popped, 2 to 4 minutes.

To perk up low-fat microwave popcorn • Mist it with cooking spray (so that the spices adhere), then toss it with seasonings. Toss the seasoning mixes that follow with 8 cups popped corn (made from 1 cup kernels).

BARBECUE CHEESE POPCORN SEASONING Mix **¾ teaspoon chili powder, ½ teaspoon garlic salt,** and **⅓ cup grated Parmesan cheese.**

SPICED TRAIL POPCORN MIX Mix **1 tablespoon superfine sugar, ¾ teaspoon ground cinnamon,** and **⅛ teaspoon ground allspice.** Toss with **¾ cup raisins** and **⅓ cup peanuts** before tossing with popcorn.

Popovers

These muffinlike breads are leavened with eggs and steam to create a crisp, brown crust and a moist, airy interior. Serve them for breakfast with jam, as a side dish with sandwich spreads or a salad, or with the traditional roast beef dinner. Popovers are especially good when split in half and filled with poached or scrambled eggs. You don't have to have special pans to make popovers. Small ovenproof bowls, ramekins, or even muffin pans will do the trick.

PROBLEM SOLVERS ▼ **To avoid trouble with sticking** • Use well-greased pans.

To avoid trouble with lumps • Use instantized flour (such as Wondra).

To prevent collapsing • Do not open the oven door while popovers are baking. Also, after they have baked, it helps to prick the popovers with a toothpick or skewer to allow steam to escape. Return popovers to the oven, which should be turned off but still hot, to dry the interior for a few minutes.

To maximize puff • Bring the milk and eggs to room temperature before making the batter.

To salvage collapsed popovers • Slice them open and melt butter into the interior crevices and layers. No one will be able to resist them.

To save prep time • Mix popover batter in a blender and pour it directly from the pitcher into the popover cups.

To make ahead • Mix popover batter up to 24 hours in advance and refrigerate it. Remove it from the refrigerator 1 hour before baking to bring it to room temperature. Stir just before using.

EASY PARMESAN POPOVERS Preheat oven to 425°F. Using a whisk or electric mixer, beat together **2 room-temperature eggs, 1 cup room-temperature milk, 1 tablespoon melted butter** or **vegetable oil,** ¼ **teaspoon dried thyme,** and ½ **teaspoon** *each* **sugar and salt.** Gradually beat in **1 cup all-purpose flour,** 1 tablespoon at a time, until mixture is smooth. Divide among the well-greased cups of a 12-cup popover or muffin pan. Sprinkle ½ **cup grated Parmesan cheese** over batter, dividing among the cups. Bake 15 minutes. Do not open the oven door. Reduce temperature to 350°F without opening the oven door. Bake until puffed and golden brown, 15 minutes. *Makes 12.*

Pork *see also* Bacon; Ham; Meat; Prosciutto; Ribs; Doneness Tests and Temperatures (page 572)

One of the most versatile meats, pork is mild enough to take on a range of seasonings yet distinctive enough to stand on its own.

To choose • Look for moist meat that is firm to the touch. Cuts from the loin should be pale with a light tinge of pink, and the fat should be pure white, not yellow. Shoulder and leg cuts will be darker, with a slightly coarser texture. Avoid any pork that is dry, gray, red, or discolored.

To store • Whole cuts can be refrigerated for 2 to 4 days or frozen for 9 months. Refrigerate ground pork and use within 2 days or freeze for up to 3 months.

To prepare • The key to cooking pork is knowing which part of the animal a particular cut comes from. This will tell you how tender the cut is, which helps determine the best cooking method. Cuts from the front of the animal, particularly shoulder cuts, are tough and fibrous (but also quite flavorful) and are best suited to tenderizing cooking methods such as poaching and braising. Ham cuts that come from the rear of the animal are tender enough to roast or fry. The meat from the back of the pig receives the least amount of exercise and is quite tender. The loin and blade cuts are very tender, while the tenderloin (which runs alongside the loin) is the most tender cut. Loin and blade cuts are perfect for roasting or sautéing. When it comes to pork spareribs, grilling is the preferred method. Recipes often call for pork spareribs to be precooked before grilling. Precooking is not absolutely necessary but helps make the meat very tender. To precook, you can simmer the ribs in water for 1 hour or bake them at 300°F for 1½ to 2 hours before grilling. Another bonus: Precooking can be done a day in advance.

To perfectly grill pork chops • Grill them directly over a medium-hot fire, cover with the grill hood, and turn the chops halfway through cooking. When done, the meat will register 160°F on an instant-read thermometer and the juices will run clear. You can also poke the center of the chops with tongs; there

p

should be a slight give. Total cooking time depends on the thickness of the chop: Count on 8 minutes for ¾"-thick chops, 8 to 10 minutes for 1"-thick chops, and 12 to 16 minutes for 1½"-thick chops.

To perfectly grill pork roasts • Grill them over indirect heat. Bank medium-hot coals to one side of the grill (or light only one half of a gas grill) and place the roast on the grill rack on the other side, away from the heat. Place a foil drip pan filled with 2 cups of water beneath the roast to catch meat juices. Cover with the grill hood and grill until the internal temperature reaches 155°F on an instant-read thermometer and the juices run clear. Plan on about about 15 to 20 minutes total cooking time per pound of meat. Let the roast stand for 10 minutes before slicing.

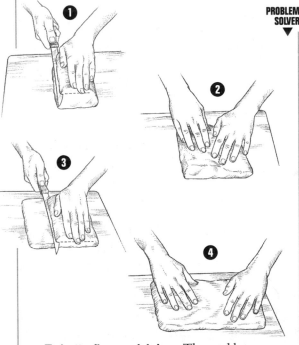

To butterfly a pork loin • The goal here is to make 2 cuts in the loin so that it unfolds like a three-sided brochure into a rectangle

that is ½" thick. Start with a center-cut pork loin about 1½" to 2" thick. Place the loin square on a cutting board. Hold your knife parallel to one long side of the loin and cut through the side, ½" down from the surface of the pork. Stop cutting ½" from the opposite edge ❶. Lay open the loin, folding back the ½"-thick slab and patting it flat with your palms and fingertips ❷.

Next, start slicing where you stopped the first cut, slicing in the opposite direction (or rotate the loin so you can cut in the same direction). Cut into the meat, slicing ½" down from the surface. Cut through the pork to the opposite edge, stopping ½" from the edge ❸.

Lay open the loin, folding back the ½"-thick slab and patting it flat. The entire loin should now be a ½"-thick rectangle that is ready for filling and rolling ❹.

PROBLEM SOLVER ▼

To prevent dryness • Avoid overcooking. Pork is bred to be very lean, so it's easy to overcook it, resulting in dry meat. Properly cooked pork is juicy and tender with a hint of pink in the center. The internal temperature should read 155°F for roasts or 160°F for chops, and the juices should run clear when the meat is pierced. Some older cookbooks recommend cooking pork to 175° to 180°F. Disregard those recommendations because they would overcook the meat, making it very dry. These higher temperatures were recommended before the modern commercial production of pork, which greatly reduces risk of trichinosis. Today's pork is perfectly safe to eat when cooked to an internal temperature of 155°F to 160°F.

FALL-APART TENDER PORK CHOPS
Heat **1 tablespoon vegetable oil** in a large skillet over medium-high heat.

FOUR WAYS TO FLAVOR PORK TENDERLOIN

Pork tenderloin is the filet mignon of the pork world. It's the most tender cut and is rather small, weighing in at 12 to 16 ounces. The marinades below are for whole tenderloins. Cooking options follow the recipes. To use any leftover marinade, boil it for 5 minutes and use it to make a sauce. Each recipe makes 6 servings.

Orange-Rosemary Pork Tenderloin: In a large zipper-lock plastic bag, combine the **grated zest from 1 orange, ½ cup orange juice, 2 tablespoons chopped fresh rosemary (or 2 teaspoons dried), 1 minced garlic clove,** and **½ teaspoon ground black pepper.** Add **2 whole tenderloins** and marinate in the refrigerator 1 to 6 hours, turning occasionally. For more flavor, cut ½"-deep slits in the pork and insert small rosemary sprigs before marinating. Cook as desired.

Chinese Black Bean Pork Tenderloin: In a large zipper-lock plastic bag, combine **¼ cup dry sherry** or **white wine, 2 tablespoons** *each* **soy sauce and chopped Chinese fermented black beans, 1 tablespoon grated fresh ginger, 1 minced garlic clove, 2 thinly sliced scallions (with green tops),** and **2 teaspoons sugar.** Add **2 whole pork tenderloins.** Marinate in the refrigerator 1 to 6 hours, turning the bag occasionally. Cook as desired.

Sage and Beer Pork Tenderloin: In a large zipper-lock plastic bag, combine **1 cup dark beer, 8 chopped fresh sage leaves (or 1½ teaspoons dried rubbed sage), 1 finely chopped small onion, 1 minced garlic clove,** and **½ teaspoon ground black pepper.** Add **2 whole pork tenderloins** and marinate in the refrigerator 1 to 6 hours, turning the bag occasionally. Cook as desired.

Barbecue Pork Tenderloin: In a large zipper-lock plastic bag, combine **½ cup dry white wine, ¼ cup** *each* **apple cider vinegar and bottled barbecue sauce, 1 finely chopped onion, 1 minced garlic clove, ½ teaspoon ground red pepper,** and **½ teaspoon ground black pepper.** Add **2 whole pork tenderloins** and marinate in the refrigerator 1 to 6 hours, turning the bag occasionally. Cook as desired.

Cooking Options: After marinating the tenderloin, remove it from the marinade. **To grill or broil:** Place the grill or broiler rack about 4" from the heat. Preheat the grill to medium, or preheat the broiler. Cook pork until center registers 155°F on an instant-read thermometer and juices run clear, about 10 to 15 minutes, turning occasionally. Let meat rest 10 minutes, then cut into ½"-thick slices. **To pan-grill or roast:** Heat 1½ tablespoons vegetable oil over medium-high heat. Add pork until browned all over, about 5 minutes, turning frequently. If pan-grilling, reduce heat to low, cover, and continue cooking until center registers 155°F on an instant-read thermometer and juices run clear, about 10 minutes, turning occasionally. Or, to roast, transfer browned meat to a roasting pan and bake at 300°F until center registers 155°F on an instant-read thermometer and juices run clear, about 15 minutes. Let meat stand 10 minutes before serving. To make a simple sauce, add any leftover marinade and some chicken broth to a skillet and boil 5 minutes, scraping up any browned bits. Serve with pork.

p

Stuffed Pork Roast

Boneless pork loin tends to be a fairly lean cut, which can translate to "dry and lacking in flavor." Yet it is an attractive cut that is simple to cook and can feed many. Butterflying the loin open, filling it, and then rolling it back up is an effective way to infuse flavor into the loin. For this recipe, choose your favorite filling: garlic-herb (given in the recipe), cranberry-orange, ginger-hoisin, or roasted red pepper (given as variations).

Filling

- 2 tablespoons chopped fresh parsley
- 1½ tablespoons chopped fresh thyme
- 1 tablespoon chopped fresh rosemary
- 3 minced garlic cloves
- 3 tablespoons olive oil
- 2 teaspoons Dijon mustard
- ¼ teaspoon salt
- ¼ teaspoon ground black pepper

Pork Loin

- 1 boneless center loin pork roast (about 2 pounds)

- ¾ teaspoon salt, divided
- ½ teaspoon ground black pepper, divided
- 1 tablespoon olive oil

1. *To make the filling:* In a small bowl, combine the parsley, thyme, rosemary, garlic, oil, mustard, salt, and pepper.

2. *To make the pork loin:* Preheat the oven to 350°F. Butterfly the pork loin (see the illustrations on page 382). Sprinkle the top side of the butterflied loin with half of the salt and pepper. Spread the filling evenly across the loin, leaving a ½" border along the edge where you made the first cut.

Add **6 thick (1" or thicker) pork loin chops** and brown all over in batches. Arrange in a 13" × 9" baking dish. Add **1 pound sliced white** or **brown mushrooms** to drippings in the skillet. Cook over medium-high heat without stirring, 3 to 4 minutes. Stir in **2 minced garlic cloves; 1 teaspoon *each* salt, dried oregano, and dried basil;** and **¼ teaspoon ground black pepper.**

Sprinkle **3 tablespoons flour** over mushrooms and stir to moisten. Pour in **1 cup dry white wine** and bring to a boil. Add **1 cup cream** and **½ cup chicken broth.** Simmer, stirring, to thicken. Pour over pork chops. Cover tightly with a double layer of foil. Bake at 325°F until pork chops are fork-tender, 2 to 2½ hours.

Makes 6 servings.

3. Beginning at the opposite edge, roll the loin up to wrap the filling. Using kitchen twine, tie the loin every 1½" to hold its shape.

4. Rub the roll with the oil and sprinkle with the remaining salt and pepper. Place in a small roasting pan and position on the center rack of the oven. Roast until the center registers 155°F on an instant-read thermometer and the juices run clear, 60 minutes. Let rest for 15 minutes before carving. To prevent slices from unrolling, skewer the roast every ¼" with wooden picks along the edge where the roll ends. Slice crosswise between the wooden picks and ties.

Makes 6 servings

Cranberry-Orange Stuffed Pork Roast: Omit the garlic-herb filling. Instead, in a small saucepan, bring ½ cup dried cranberries, ¼ cup sherry, and ¼ cup orange juice to a boil. Reduce the heat to low and simmer until the cranberries are plumped, 3 minutes. Strain the cranberries and set the liquid aside. In a food processor, combine the cranberries, 1 garlic clove, 8 walnuts, and 2 tablespoons olive oil. Puree into a coarse paste. Blend in ¼ teaspoon salt, ¼ teaspoon ground black pepper, and 1½ teaspoons orange peel. Spread and roll as directed. Use the reserved cranberry liquid to baste the roast halfway through cooking.

Ginger-Hoisin Stuffed Pork Roast: Omit the garlic-herb filling. Instead, in a small bowl, combine ¼ cup hoisin sauce, ½ teaspoon finely grated fresh ginger, 1½ tablespoons sesame oil, 4 large coarsely chopped scallions, ½ minced garlic clove, ¼ teaspoon salt, ¼ teaspoon ground black pepper, and ¼ cup roasted soybeans, coarsely ground (optional). Spread and roll as directed.

Roasted Red Pepper Stuffed Pork Roast: Omit the garlic-herb filling. Instead, in a small bowl, combine ½ cup finely chopped roasted red peppers, 1 minced garlic clove, 2 tablespoons extra-virgin olive oil, 2 tablespoons finely chopped fresh parsley, 1 teaspoon balsamic vinegar, 2 tablespoons pine nuts, coarsely ground (optional), ¼ teaspoon salt, and ¼ teaspoon ground black pepper. Spread and roll as directed.

CUBAN PORK ROAST In a mortar or small bowl, combine **6 minced garlic cloves, 2 teaspoons grated orange zest, 1 tablespoon** *each* **dried oregano and ground cumin,** and **1 teaspoon** *each* **salt and ground black pepper.** Mash to a paste with a pestle or sturdy fork. Rub all over **1 pork shoulder roast (5 pounds),** trimmed of excess fat. Chop **1 onion** and put half in a shallow baking dish. Add pork roast. Combine ¼ **cup** *each* **orange juice, lemon juice, lime juice, and dry sherry.** Pour over pork and top with remaining chopped onion. Cover and marinate in the refrigerator 24 hours, turning meat occasionally. Remove from marinade (setting aside marinade). Transfer to a shallow baking dish and roast at 325°F until internal temperature reaches 155°F

Pork and Apple Potpie with Sweet Potato Topping

Pork and apple makes a delicious alternative to chicken for pot pie.

1½ **teaspoons olive oil, divided**

3 **Granny Smith apples, peeled, cored, cut into ¾" chunks, and divided**

1 **pound lean cubed pork, cut into ¾" chunks**

1½ **teaspoons salt, divided**

¼ **teaspoon ground black pepper**

1 **large onion, chopped**

1 **green bell pepper, chopped**

1 **large celery rib, chopped**

½ **pound mushrooms, quartered**

1 **teaspoon dried thyme**

½ **teaspoon ground ginger**

¼ **teaspoon ground allspice**

1 **can (14 ounces) fat-free chicken broth**

2 **tablespoons flour**

2 **tablespoons water**

⅓ **cup low-fat sour cream**

2½ **pounds sweet potatoes, peeled and sliced ½" thick**

1. In large nonstick skillet or Dutch oven, heat ½ teaspoon of the oil over medium-high heat. Add two-thirds of the apple chunks and cook, stirring, until golden and just beginning to soften, 6 minutes. Remove to a large bowl and set aside.

2. Heat ½ teaspoon of the remaining oil in the same pan. Add the pork in a single layer and sprinkle with ¾ teaspoon of the salt and the black pepper. Cook, stirring, until browned, 6 minutes. Add the remaining ½ teaspoon oil and the onion, bell pepper, and celery. Cook until softened, 6 minutes. Add the mushrooms, thyme, ginger, allspice, and broth. Bring to a simmer, cover, and cook until the pork is no longer pink, 25 minutes.

3. In a cup, dissolve the flour in the water and add to the pan. Cook, uncovered, until thickened, 5 minutes. Remove from heat. Stir in the cooked apples and sour cream. Spoon into a 2-quart baking dish.

4. Meanwhile, preheat the oven to 425°F. Bring a large saucepan of water to a boil. Place the sweet potatoes and the remaining apple chunks in a steamer basket over the pot. Cook until fork-tender, 15 to 18 minutes. Drain, discarding the cooking liquid. Place the potato mixture in a large bowl. Add the remaining ¾ teaspoon salt. Mash until smooth. Spoon evenly over the apple mixture, leaving a ½" border. Bake until heated through, 15 to 20 minutes.

Makes 6 servings

and juices run clear, about 2½ hours, basting occasionally with marinade. Let stand 15 minutes before slicing.

Makes 10 to 12 servings.

Potatoes *see also* French Fries

Few foods can compete with the versatility of the potato. Whether baked, mashed, boiled, roasted, fried, or used in salads, soups, or stews, potatoes appeal to even the most ardent vegetable avoiders.

BASICS
▼

To choose • Potatoes should be firm and heavy for their size. Avoid any potatoes with a light green cast. The green color indicates the presence of solanine, a mildly toxic alkaloid that gives potatoes a bitter taste and may give you a bellyache. If you find any green spots in potatoes that you've already purchased, cut them out. Also keep an eye out for sprouts. They indicate that a potato is starting to grow, and they may also mean that the vegetable's texture has begun to turn spongy and soft.

To choose for baking, mashing, or frying • Look for a high-starch potato, such as a russet, Idaho, or Burbank. Low in moisture and high in starch, they bake up fluffy and make mashed potatoes that soak up plenty of milk and butter.

To choose for roasting or using in a gratin • Look for a medium-starch, all-purpose potato, such as white, blue, or purple, or one of the golden-fleshed potatoes such as Yellow Finn or Yukon gold. They're moister than high-starch potatoes and hold their shape well.

To choose for salads • Use a low-starch potato, such a red-skinned potato or a white California potato. Sometimes called waxy potatoes, these hold their shape better than other types of potatoes. However, many old-fashioned Southern recipes for smashed or mashed potato salad start with baking potatoes because you want them to fall apart, and the starchiness helps hold the dressing in such a salad.

To test for starch content • Slice the raw potato with a knife. If the knife is coated with a creamy white substance or the potato clings to the knife, it's a starchy potato. If not, it's a waxy potato. If it's somewhere in between, it's an all-purpose potato. You can also spot a good baking potato by placing it in a brine of 1 part salt to 11 parts water. Good baking potatoes will sink (because they're high in starch).

To store • Keep potatoes in a cool, dark place with good air circulation for no more than a few weeks. A hanging basket inside a pantry is a good spot. Avoid storing potatoes next to onions. They shorten each other's shelf life.

To bake • Choose potatoes that are roughly the same size, so that they'll cook evenly. Pierce them several times with the tines of a fork to allow moisture to escape. These steam holes will prevent a potato explosion and make a drier, lighter-tasting potato. Bake the potatoes at 400°F directly on an oven rack until tender inside and crisp outside, 50 to 60 minutes. Avoid wrapping them in aluminum foil, which steams them and makes for dense, gummy results. If you like a soft, pliable skin, rub the potato with a little bit of butter or olive oil before baking. For a crisp skin, bake it without any fat. While the potatoes are baking, turn them every 15 to 20 minutes to ensure that they cook evenly.

To bake several at once • Stand the potatoes on end in a 6-cup or 12-cup muffin pan. This makes them easier to move in and out of the oven and provides

ample air space around each potato to ensure even cooking.

**To test baked potatoes for done-
ness** • Wrap your hand in an oven mitt
or a kitchen towel and give the potatoes a
squeeze. When the potatoes give slightly
and feel soft, they're done.

**To serve baked
potatoes** • Cover the
baked potato with a
kitchen towel (or
wear an oven mitt)
and roll it gently on a
surface. While it is still hot,
slice a shallow X on the top,
then pinch each end, pressing inward to
force up the steamy flesh. Rolling and cutting the potato open while it is still hot allows the steam to release, creating a
fluffier, better-tasting potato.

To make perfect mashed potatoes •
Choose high-starch potatoes that are
roughly the same size so that they'll cook
evenly. Boil the potatoes with their skins
intact: They'll hold their shape better, absorb less water, and have a better flavor.
They'll also be easier to peel after they've
been cooked. Mash the potatoes with a
food mill, a potato masher, or even a
spoon, but avoid using a food processor,
which makes gluey mashed potatoes. Take
care not to overbeat. Also, to prevent
lumps in mashed potatoes, warm any milk
or cream before adding it.

To make perfect roasted potatoes •
Before roasting, boil small all-purpose or
low-starch potatoes with their skins intact
to give them a creamier texture. Then, cut
the boiled potatoes into even-size chunks.
Toss them with olive oil, salt, and ground
black pepper, and spread them, cut sides
down, on a baking sheet. Roast in a 425°F
oven, stirring occasionally, until the potatoes are crisp and golden.

Fascinating Fact: It's been said that in
late-16th-century France, potatoes were for-
bidden because they were believed to cause
leprosy. In Scotland, the Protestants thought
potatoes unfit to eat, as they weren't mentioned
in the Bible.

**PROBLEM
SOLVERS**
▼

**To keep raw cut potatoes from turning
brown** • Place them in a bowl of acidulated water (4 cups water and 4 tablespoons lemon juice or 2 teaspoons vinegar).
Remove the potatoes as soon as possible to
prevent excess water absorption, which
will dilute their flavor.

**To whiten cut potatoes that have
oxidized** • If you've cut potatoes and they
have started to turn brown, cook them in
milk at a bare simmer to whiten them.

**To keep potatoes white long after
cooking** • Add a few teaspoons of lemon
juice to the cooking water.

**To delay sprouting in stored pota-
toes** • Place an apple in the bag with the
potatoes.

**To keep potatoes from sticking to
your knife when slicing them** • Coat the
knife with cooking spray before and
during slicing.

**To test potatoes for doneness without
breaking up the flesh** • Use a cake tester
or a bamboo skewer.

To avoid soggy mashed potatoes • If
the mashed potatoes are done but the rest
of the meal isn't, place a kitchen towel beneath the lid covering the pot of mashed
potatoes. The towel absorbs condensation,
preventing it from falling back into the
potatoes.

**TIME
SAVERS**
▼

To boil faster • Peel and cube the potatoes first, dropping them into cold acidulated water as you work, to prevent
darkening. Drain and drop them into a
large pot of salted boiling water over high

heat and boil just until tender, about 5 minutes. Do not overcook.

To bake faster • Insert an aluminum nail lengthwise through the center of each potato. Look for aluminum potato nails in cookware stores, or use an aluminum nail from a hardware store. Scrub the dirt from the potato skin, insert the potato nail, and bake at 400°F directly on an oven rack until tender inside and crisp outside, about 35 minutes (15 to 20 minutes faster than without the nail). Remove the nail before serving. Do not use a nail in a microwave oven. Another option is to precook the potatoes in a microwave oven: Prick 4 large russet potatoes and place them in a microwave oven in a spoke pattern. Cook at full power, 9 minutes. Meanwhile, preheat your conventional oven to 425°F. Transfer the potatoes to the conventional oven and bake 20 minutes.

To use instant mashed potato flakes • Generally, potato flakes make second-rate mashed potatoes. But that doesn't keep them from being a useful cooking ingredient. Fried chicken breaded with mashed potato flakes comes out sweet and crispy; potato-breaded sautéed fish is spectacular; and vegetable soup thickened with instant mashed potatoes tastes homemade and hearty without being starchy.

FAST BUTTERMILK MASHED POTA-TOES Scrub **2 pounds baking potatoes** and chop into eighths. Cook in a large pot of salted boiling water until tender, about 12 to 18 minutes, depending on the size of the potatoes. Drain and run through the coarsest screen of a food mill, which will remove the peel. Beat **2 tablespoons butter, 1 cup buttermilk, ½ teaspoon salt,** and **¼ teaspoon ground black pepper (or more to taste)** into the pureed potato flesh. *Makes 4 servings.*

POTATO-BREADED CHICKEN OR FISH In a large, shallow dish, combine **1 cup buttermilk, 1 teaspoon** *each* **garlic powder and ground cumin,** and **1½ teaspoons** *each* **salt and ground black pepper.** Add **2 pounds white fish fillets** or **boneless chicken breasts** and soak 1 hour. Remove from buttermilk and dredge in **2 cups potato flakes.** Cook in **¼" of oil** heated to 375°F until fish flakes easily or until inside of thickest portion of chicken registers 160°F and juices run clear, about 4 minutes per side. *Makes 4 servings.*

FLAVOR TIPS ▼ **To boost flavor for mashed potatoes** • Steam the spuds instead of boiling them. That way, less potato flavor leaches out into the water.

To use potato cooking water • Leftover water from boiling cut potatoes is ideal to use in yeast bread baking. It adds leavening power to the yeast and produces a softer, moist texture in the bread.

To use potatoes as a crust • Use thinly sliced potatoes as a crust for savory casseroles, quiches, and meat pies. Grease a foil-lined baking sheet and lay out thinly sliced potatoes. Bake at 400°F just until tender. Grease a pie plate or baking dish and arrange the potatoes, slightly overlapping, to cover the surface of the pan. Fill and bake as directed in your recipe.

CRISPY PARMESAN POTATO SKINS Scrub **6 medium russet baking potatoes.** Pat dry and prick several times with a fork. Bake directly on center oven rack at 375°F until tender, 40 to 50 minutes. (Bake a day ahead, if desired.) Let cool to room temperature. Cut lengthwise into quarters. Spoon out soft centers, leaving enough

p

Cheddar Twice–Baked Potatoes

This is a great make-ahead dish that everyone gobbles up fast.

8	**russet baking potatoes**
1	**cup sour cream**
2	**tablespoons butter, softened**
1	**tablespoon cider vinegar**
¾	**teaspoon salt**
¼	**teaspoon ground black pepper**
1¼	**cups grated sharp Cheddar cheese, divided**
3	**small scallions, minced**
¾	**teaspoon paprika**

1. Preheat the oven to 400°F.

2. Prick each potato several times with a fork. Bake directly on the oven rack until tender when pierced, 50 to 60 minutes. Set aside until cool enough to handle.

3. Cut out a "lid" on each potato. Peel off and discard the skin from the lids. Put the potato flesh in a large bowl. Using a melon baller or spoon, scoop the flesh from the potatoes, leaving a ¼"-thick shell. Add the flesh to the bowl. Place the shells in a 13" × 9" baking dish.

4. Mash the potato flesh. Stir in the sour cream, butter, vinegar, salt, and pepper. Stir in 1 cup of the cheese and the scallions. Stuff into the shells. Sprinkle with the remaining ¼ cup cheese. Sprinkle lightly with paprika. Bake until golden brown, 40 to 45 minutes. Serve hot, or let cool and reheat.

Makes 8

---

potato to make ¼"-thick shells. (Refrigerate soft centers for another purpose, such as a casserole, soup, or salad.) Arrange potato skins close together on a baking sheet and brush with ½ **stick (¼ cup) melted butter** (or use any of the flavored butters on page 81). Sprinkle with ¼ **cup grated Parmesan cheese** and ½ **teaspoon** *each* **salt and ground black pepper.** Bake at 475°F in the top third of the oven until crisp and deep golden brown, about 25 minutes. Serve hot. If desired, add **2 tablespoons sour cream** to one end of each potato skin and sprinkle with ½ **teaspoon sliced fresh chives** or **chopped fresh parsley** and **a pinch of paprika.** Or add a dab of caviar. *Makes 6 servings.*

PARSLEYED NEW POTATOES Pour **6 to 8 cups chicken stock** or **reduced-sodium canned broth** into a large pot and bring to a boil. Add **2½ pounds small new boiling potatoes** (red-skinned or waxy type). Boil, partly covered, until firm-tender, about 12 minutes (do not overcook because potatoes will cook further). Remove with a slotted spoon, cover with foil, and reserve. Boil the stock or broth until reduced to ¾ or 1 cup. Add potatoes and **2 tablespoons butter.** Toss gently and simmer until potatoes are hot and tender, 5 to 10 minutes. Add **½ cup chopped fresh parsley, ½ teaspoon salt,** and **¼ teaspoon ground black pepper.** *Makes 4 servings.*

POTATOES IN CREAMY DILL SAUCE Boil **2 pounds small new potatoes (16 to 20)** in salted water to cover until tender, 15 minutes. Cool slightly and peel. Melt **2 tablespoons butter** in a saucepan over medium heat. Stir in **2 tablespoons flour** and cook 1 minute. Add **1 cup light cream** or **half-and-half, 2 to 3 tablespoons chopped fresh dill,** and **½ teaspoon salt.** Bring to a boil and stir until thickened and smooth. Add potatoes and toss. *Makes 4 servings.*

HEALTHY HINTS ▼ **To retain maximum nutrients during cooking** • Microwave, bake, or steam potatoes. Although boiling is one of the most popular methods of cooking potatoes, you can lose up to half of the potato's nutrients in the water. If you boil potatoes, save the vitamin-rich cooking liquid and use in soups, sauces, or bread doughs.

To reap the cancer-fighting abilities of potatoes • Eat the peels whenever possible. The peel of a potato contains anti-carcinogenic compounds that absorb carcinogens found in grilled or smoked foods.

HOMEMADE LOW-FAT POTATO CHIPS Scrub **1 baking potato.** Very thinly slice the potato using a Japanese mandoline (a hand-operated slicing machine), a vegetable peeler, or the thin slicing blade of a food processor. Arrange in a single layer on a baking sheet coated with cooking spray. Generously coat tops of potatoes with cooking spray. Bake at 400°F 30 minutes, turning slices halfway through cooking. Reduce oven temperature to 275°F and bake until crisp, 20 minutes more. *Makes 4 servings.*

Pot Roast *see also* Beef; Slow Cookers

One of America's ultimate comfort foods, pot roast is slowly braised beef that develops a rich, deep flavor and exceptional tenderness.

FLAVOR TIPS ▼ **To flavor pot roast** • Add a whole 3" cinnamon stick to the braising liquid.

To make a Cuban pot poast • Using a long, narrow sharp knife, make a hole lengthwise through the center of the roast. (If necessary, use a knife-sharpening steel or the handle of a wooden spoon to help make the hole all the way through the roast.) Force smoked Spanish chorizo links into the hole, pushing them so that they run all the way through. If desired, add 2 rows of chorizo. Brown the roast, then braise it gently with tomato sauce and beef or chicken broth until fork-tender. After cooking, let the pot roast rest 20 minutes. Then, slice it crosswise so that each slice is studded with chorizo.

BASIC POT ROAST Heat **1½ tablespoons vegetable oil** in a heavy Dutch oven over medium-high heat. Add **1 beef chuck (tied if boned), bottom round, rump roast,** or **brisket (3 to 4 pounds)** and brown on all sides, 12 to 15 minutes. Remove. Spoon off all but 2 tablespoons fat. Add **1 large chopped onion, 2 chopped celery ribs,** and **2 chopped carrots.** Sauté to lightly brown, about 5

p

p

minutes. Add **1 cup** *each* **dry red wine and beef broth, 2 bay leaves,** and **1 teaspoon dried thyme.** Bring to a boil. Add beef, reduce heat to low, cover tightly, and braise very gently until beef is tender when pierced with a fork, about 2 hours, turning beef every 30 minutes (thicker roasts may take an hour longer to cook). The key is to cook the beef until it is slicing-tender but not falling apart. Remove meat and transfer to a platter. Cover with foil to keep warm. Blot any fat from surface of drippings. Then, melt **2 tablespoons butter** in a saucepan. Stir in **2 tablespoons flour** and cook 1 minute over medium heat. Pour in defatted pan drippings, **another 1 cup beef broth,** and **another ¼ cup red wine.** Bring to a boil, stirring constantly, to thicken slightly. Add ¼ teaspoon *each* **salt and ground black pepper (or more to taste).** Serve with boiled potatoes, potato pancakes, or buttered noodles. *Makes 10 to 12 servings.*

ITALIAN POT ROAST WITH MUSH-ROOMS Follow the recipe for **Basic Pot Roast** (page 391). Before cooking beef, soak ½ **ounce dried porcini mushrooms** in ½ **cup hot water** until soft, 30 minutes. Make 20 to 30 little slits in beef with a paring knife. Cut **8 garlic cloves** into slivers and stuff slivers into slits in meat. Brown as directed. Omit the thyme and add **2 teaspoons oregano** and ½ **teaspoon rosemary.** After adding red wine and beef broth to braise the meat, remove mushrooms from soaking liquid, setting aside liquid. Chop mushrooms and add to the pan. Strain soaking liquid to remove grit, and pour liquid into the pan (or skip the straining and pour carefully, leaving grit behind). Approximately 30 minutes before beef is done, sauté **1½ to 2**

pounds fresh assorted mushrooms in **2 tablespoons olive oil** or **butter** until soft, 8 minutes. Add to pot roast and continue cooking. Serve with pasta or potatoes. *Makes 10 to 12 servings.*

JEWISH POT-ROASTED BRISKET OF BEEF Trim excess fat from a **first-cut** or **thin-cut beef brisket (4 pounds).** Pat dry and rub all over with **1 teaspoon** *each* **salt and ground black pepper.** Heat **1 tablespoon vegetable oil** in a Dutch oven over medium-high heat. Add beef and brown on both sides, about 15 minutes. Remove. Pour off all but 2 tablespoons fat and add **3 large coarsely chopped onions.** Sauté over medium heat to soften and lightly brown, 6 to 8 minutes. Stir in **1 tablespoon paprika** and **2 large minced garlic cloves.** Cook 1 minute longer. Pour in **2 cups beef broth** and bring to a boil over high heat. Return beef to the pan, reduce heat to low, cover tightly, and braise very gently until fork-tender but not falling apart, about 3 hours, turning beef once or twice. If necessary, add **another 1 cup beef broth** during cooking. Serve hot with potatoes or noodles. *Makes 10 to 12 servings.*

Poultry *see also* Chicken; Cornish Game Hens; Duck; Goose; Turkey; Doneness Tests and Temperatures (page 572)

Bone marrow pigment in poultry, especially in frozen poultry, sometimes leaches out as the meat cooks, creating a bright red area close to the bone. Not to fear: It is safe to eat as long as the chicken, turkey, or duck is cooked to the required temperature.

BASICS ▼ **To clean and refresh poultry** • You can clean out the cavity of poultry by squeezing fresh lemon or lime juice in the cavity and rubbing it with the cut side of the citrus. Rinse it before cooking. This will also remove any unpleasant "refrigerator" odor.

To evenly roast a whole bird • Place it on a V-shaped roasting rack with its breast side up. Once it starts to brown, turn it on its side. Once brown, turn it on its other side. Once the sides are brown, turn the bird so that the breast is facing down.

To guarantee a moist, juicy bird • Soak it in brine (see page 64) ahead of time.

To get a crisp, golden skin on roasted poultry • Brush frequently with melted butter while it is in the oven.

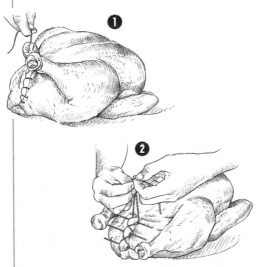

To truss • If you will be stuffing a chicken or turkey, here are three ways to keep the stuffing from spilling out. The traditional method: Using a large needle and cotton trussing thread or string, stitch the cavity closed. Loop one end around the legs to hold them close to the body. Pull the drumstick ends close together and tie them closed with cotton string or unflavored dental floss ❶. If you're in a hurry, you can skip the stitching step; instead, loop the string around the tail, then loop it around the legs, pulling taut to cover the cavity with the legs and tail. An alternative method: Pierce wooden skewers through the flaps of skin on each side of the cavity opening. Trim off any unnecessary length on the skewers, then weave cotton string or dental floss around the skewers like a shoelace to lace the bird shut. Tie it off at the top ❷.

PROBLEM SOLVERS ▼ **To disguise tough breast meat** • Slice it thinly, which will give the meat the appearance of being delicate.

To avoid burning the breading on poultry cutlets before the meat has cooked through • Pound the meat to about ¼" thickness first.

To prevent breaded poultry cutlets from getting soggy • Set them on a rack if they are not going directly into a preheated pan.

To save the day when you've overcooked a roasted bird • Serve it with gravy, barbecue sauce, a dipping sauce, chutney, or salsa. These moist accompaniments will work as a foil to the dryness.

Praline

This hard caramel candy is made from burnt sugar and almonds or hazelnuts and is different from the soft caramel candies with the same name. Praline can be eaten as candy or ground and mixed into mousses, ice creams, cakes and pastries.

BASICS ▼ **To store** • Keep praline in an airtight container at room temperature for several weeks, or freeze for up to 1 year.

To grind to a fine powder • Place broken pieces of praline in a food processor and pulse until finely ground.

p

PRALINE Combine **3 cups sugar** and **2 cups whole unblanched hazelnuts** or **almonds** in a heavy saucepan. Heat over low heat, stirring often, until the sugar melts. Continue cooking until sugar turns a deep, golden brown (about 310°F on a candy thermometer) and nuts begin to pop, a sign that they are toasted. Remove the pan from heat and carefully pour praline mixture onto a greased baking sheet. Spread mixture with a wooden spoon and let cool completely. Crack cooled praline into small pieces. *Makes about 4 cups.*

Pressure Cookers

Practically anything that is cooked in liquid can be cooked faster in a pressure cooker. For example, see the entries for Beef (page 31), Artichokes (page 11), and Risotto (page 413), and "Pressure Cooking Beans" on page 30. A special, airtight, locking lid makes a pressure cooker different from an ordinary pot. The lid forces pressure to build inside the pot as the liquid inside comes to a boil. The trapped steam causes the internal temperature to rise beyond what it would be capable of under normal pressure, decreasing cooking times by two-thirds or more. The increased pressure also softens the fibers in foods, which makes pressure cookers ideal for cooking tough cuts of meat. While early-model pressure cookers sometimes exploded under pressure and were considered dangerous by some cooks, current second-generation pressure cooker designs include safety features that make such explosions next to impossible.

BASICS
▼

To choose • Buy a pressure cooker that has a minimum 6-quart capacity. Since safety precautions demand that pressure cookers never be completely filled, anything smaller will be too limiting.

To use safely • Never fill the cooker to more than one-half to two-thirds of its capacity, depending on the design of the cooker and the type of food you're preparing. Most cookers have maximum-fill lines marked inside the pot.

To prepare conventional recipes in a pressure cooker • In general, pressure-cooked foods will cook in one-quarter to one-third of the time that it would take using a conventional cooking method. Reduce the amount of liquid by 20 to 40 percent to compensate for the lack of moisture evaporation in a pressure cooker. Also, look in the pressure cooker's instruction booklet for a similar recipe that will give you general cooking guidelines.

To cook in a pressure cooker • Once you've combined the ingredients inside the pot, seal it by locking on the lid. Set the pot over high heat to bring it up to pressure as quickly as possible. Once the desired pressure level is reached, reduce the heat to maintain the pressure without increasing it or letting it drop. Begin calculating the cooking time at the moment that the pot reaches high pressure. Once the timer goes off, reduce the pressure completely before removing the lid.

To speed the time it takes for the cooker to reach high pressure • Boil any liquid before adding it to the pot.

To prevent overcooking tender foods like chicken and vegetables • Quickly release pressure by holding the pressure valve down with a long-handled spoon until all of the pressure has been released. Then, move the cooker to the sink and let cold water run down one side of the cover. Tilt the pot slightly to keep the water running away from the pressure vents or regulator.

To release pressure naturally • Remove the pot from the heat and let the pressure drop of its own accord. Use this pressure-release technique for foods such as beans and potatoes, and for other foods that have a skin that you wish to keep intact. Also use it when cooking beef, which will toughen when pressure is released too quickly, and to preserve the creamy texture of puddings.

Prosciutto *see also* Ham

Pronounced "pro-SHOO-toh," this Italian ham is a seasoned, salt-cured, air-dried rear leg of pork. There are two kinds of prosciutto: *crudo,* **which is cured and aged but not cooked and can be eaten raw, and** *cotto,* **which receives a mild cure and is precooked by roasting or steaming, much like American boiled ham. The hams are cured only with salt and aged at least 10 months or up to 2 years. The result is a distinctive fragrance and subtle flavor that makes prosciutto one of the world's best-loved hams.**

BASICS **To choose** • The best prosciutto comes
▼ from Parma in the Emilia-Romagna region of Italy. The process for curing prosciutto there is dictated by law and is overseen by the Parma Ham Consortium. All consortium-approved hams have the five-pointed Parma crown seared into their sides. The ham should be covered with a thick layer of creamy, white fat that fades to rose color where it touches the meat. The meat itself should be a soft, rosy pink. Before buying any prosciutto, ask for a taste. It should have a sweet, earthy flavor with a slight saltiness in the background. Don't buy any ham that has even a slight rancid flavor, an indication that it has not been stored properly.

To store • Prosciutto's delicate flavor begins to fade as soon as it is sliced, so buy it the day you plan to serve it. Avoid stacking thin slices; instead, lay them side by side. Store well-wrapped slices in the refrigerator. Bring to room temperature about 1 hour before serving time. Avoid freezing prosciutto, which destroys its creamy texture and diminishes its flavor.

To serve • Prosciutto's delicate flavor is best appreciated when the ham is cut into paper-thin slices and served at room temperature. Fresh melon, figs, or other sweet, juicy fruits complement the salt in the ham.

To cook with prosciutto • If you are adding a bit of prosciutto to part of the seasoning base in a recipe, buy thick slices and chop it into coarse chunks before adding. You can also add thin-cut pieces to a warm sauce just before serving (to prevent the heat from drying out the ham).

PASTA SHELLS WITH RICOTTA AND PROSCIUTTO In a large pot of salted boiling water, cook ½ **pound medium pasta shells** or **orecchiette** until tender but firm to the bite, 6 to 8 minutes. Meanwhile, in a large skillet, combine **2 tablespoons olive oil, 1 minced or crushed garlic clove,** and ½ **teaspoon dried oregano.** Cook over low heat to soften but not color garlic, 4 minutes. Stir in **1 container (15 ounces) ricotta cheese** and heat until mixture begins to simmer. Add ¼ **cup dry white wine,** ¼ **teaspoon salt,** and ⅛ **teaspoon** *each* **grated nutmeg and ground black pepper.** When mixture returns to a simmer, add ¼ **pound thinly sliced and chopped prosciutto, 2 large sliced scallions,** and ¼ **cup chopped fresh parsley.** Remove from heat and cover to keep warm. Drain pasta, setting aside ¼ cup cooking water. Add to sauce along with ¼ **cup grated Parmesan cheese,** and toss. If mixture seems dry, add some reserved cooking water. Serve hot, topped with more chopped fresh parsley and more Parmesan cheese, if desired. *Makes 4 servings.*

p **Prunes** *see also* Fruit, Dried

Dried plums (prunes) can be used like almost any other dried fruit.

FLAVOR TIP ▼ **To flavor desserts** • Make prune compote. It keeps forever when refrigerated and adds flavor to countless desserts from chocolate cake to vanilla ice cream.

COMPOTE OF PRUNES AND BRANDY

In a saucepan over medium heat, combine **1 pound pitted prunes, the juices of 1 lemon and 1 orange, the julienned zests of ½ lemon and ½ orange, 1 stick cinnamon (3"), 2 whole cloves, ½ vanilla bean (or add extract later), 5 tablespoons honey,** and **½ cup water.** Simmer 5 minutes. Remove from heat and add **½ cup brandy** (and ½ teaspoon vanilla extract, if using). Cool and refrigerate. Serve as needed. *Makes 3 cups.*

HEALTHY HINT ▼ **To replace fat with prune puree in baked goods** • Prune puree is one of the best fat replacements, adding rich, sweet flavor and moisture to baked goods. Since prunes have a strong dried-fruit flavor, the puree is best used in recipes that have a base of chocolate or strong spices that will mask the prune flavor. Prune puree is easy to make at home, but you can also use jarred baby food prunes instead. One jar (4 ounces) equals ⅓ cup prune puree. Or use lekvar or prune butter, another commercially available substitute found in the jam,

baking, or ethnic section of the supermarket.

PRUNE PUREE In a blender or small food processor, combine ⅔ **cup (4 ounces or 12 whole) pitted prunes.** Add **3 tablespoons boiling water** and process until smooth. Store in the refrigerator up to 1 year. *Makes about ¾ cup.*

LOW-FAT CHOCOLATE BROWNIES

Preheat oven to 350°F. In a large bowl, stir together **1¼ cups sugar, ¾ cup unsweetened cocoa powder, 1 cup flour,** and **½ teaspoon baking powder.** Transfer to waxed paper. In the same bowl, beat **7 egg whites** until foamy. Stir in ⅔ **cup prune puree, ¼ cup low-fat sour cream,** and ¾ **cup chopped toasted walnuts.** Stir in dry ingredients until blended. Scrape into a 13" × 9" baking dish coated with cooking spray. Bake until a tester inserted in center comes out very moist, 25 to 30 minutes. Cool and cut into 2" squares. *Makes 24.*

LOW-FAT CHOCOLATE-PECAN FUDGE

In a large saucepan, combine **2½ cups sugar, ¾ cup fat-free evaporated milk,** and **2 tablespoons butter.** Bring to boil over medium heat, stirring constantly, and cook 5 minutes. Remove from heat and stir in **1 package (12 ounces) chocolate chips** until melted. Stir in **1 jar (7 ounces) marshmallow creme, ⅓ cup prune puree, ½ cup chopped toasted pecans,** and **2 teaspoons vanilla extract** until combined. Spread level in a 13" × 9" baking pan lined with waxed paper. Refrigerate until firm, and cut into 1" × 2" bars. *Makes about 52 pieces.*

Pudding

A simple custard made with sweetened, cooked milk and eggs, pudding has a creamy consistency that's supremely comforting. When made with rice or bread, it is known as rice pudding or bread pudding.

PROBLEM SOLVERS ▼

To intercept a pudding that is beginning to curdle • Immediately remove it from the heat and whisk vigorously to work out the clumps.

To get a smooth texture with a finished pudding • Press it through a fine-mesh sieve.

To rescue a pudding that has burned on the bottom • Transfer it to a new pan, leaving the burned bottom behind.

To crisp up a soggy crust on bread pudding • Sprinkle it with sugar and place it under a broiler to caramelize the sugar.

To rescue dry, overcooked bread pudding • Pour warm milk or cream over the pudding and warm it in the oven. You can also mask the dryness by serving with it ice cream, a generous dollop of whipped cream, a warm fruit sauce, or caramel sauce.

TIME SAVER ▼

To speed cooling • Transfer pudding from the hot saucepan into a bowl or other container. To cool it even faster, spread pudding in a rimmed baking sheet. The more exposed surface, the quicker it will cool.

DOWN-AND-DIRTY RICH CHOCOLATE MOUSSE Melt **3 ounces chopped semisweet chocolate.** Remove from heat and beat in **3 egg yolks** and **2 tablespoons liquor** (such as brandy). At first, the chocolate will bind up, but then it will become smooth again. In another bowl, beat **2 egg whites** until soft peaks form when the beaters are lifted. Fold into chocolate mix-

ture in two additions. Beat ¼ **cup heavy cream** to soft peaks and fold into chocolate. Pour into 4 wine glasses or goblets, cover with plastic wrap, and chill. Top with whipped cream, if desired. *Makes 4 servings.*

FLAVOR TIPS ▼

To flavor rice pudding • Simmer 6 to 8 whole cardamom pods in the milk before making your favorite rice pudding recipe. Remove the pods before serving. Also, choose a short-grain rice, which will create a creamier consistency.

To flavor bread pudding • Add thinly sliced Golden Delicious apples and dabs of apple butter to your favorite bread pudding. Bake as usual (in a hot water bath is best). You can also replace traditional bread with leftover quick breads such as pancakes, muffins, scones, or biscuits.

VANILLA PUDDING In a saucepan, whisk together ¾ **cup sugar** and **2 tablespoons** *each* **packed and leveled cornstarch and all-purpose flour** until well-blended. Make a well in the center. Add **1 large egg** and ½ **cup milk (any kind you like)** and whisk until smooth. Whisk in another **2½ cups milk.** Cook over medium heat, whisking or stirring constantly, until mixture is very hot. Reduce heat to low and whisk until thick and beginning to simmer. Cook 1 minute longer, whisking. Remove from heat and stir in **1 tablespoon butter** and **1½ teaspoons vanilla extract.** Pour into 6 dessert dishes or 1 large, shallow bowl. Let cool to room temperature. Chill and serve with whipped cream, if desired. *Makes 6 servings.*

CHOCOLATE PUDDING Follow the recipe for **Vanilla Pudding** (above). Stir in **1½ ounces (1½ squares) unsweet-**

P

ened chocolate** along with butter until melted. For even more flavor, stir in ½ teaspoon ground cinnamon with the sugar and ¼ teaspoon almond extract with the vanilla. You can also use ⅓ cup unsweetened cocoa powder instead of solid chocolate; stir it into sugar mixture before adding milk. *Makes 6 servings.*

BREAD PUDDING MUFFINS Preheat oven to 350°F. In a large bowl, combine **1½ cups milk (any kind), 2 egg whites, 2 whole eggs, ⅓ cup packed brown sugar, 2 tablespoons sour cream (regular or light), 2 teaspoons vanilla extract,** and **1 tablespoon canola** or **walnut oil.** Stir in **12 slices cinnamon-raisin bread (cut in ½" cubes)** and **½ cup golden raisins.** Let stand 5 minutes. Spoon into a greased 12-cup muffin pan. Bake until firm, 35 minutes. Serve with butter and maple syrup. *Makes 12.*

HEALTHY HINT ▼ **To reduce the fat in chocolate pudding •** Replace each ounce of solid chocolate with ¼ cup unsweetened cocoa powder. Also, use 1% milk instead of whole milk. To make a lighter topping, fold together ½ cup marshmallow creme and 3 tablespoons drained vanilla yogurt.

Puff Pastry

A wonderfully rich and flaky pastry, puff pastry is made by enclosing butter inside a sheet of pastry. Once the pastry is wrapped around the butter, the dough is rolled and folded several times to make many thin layers of butter and pastry. When it is baked, the pastry rises and separates into layers as the steam released from the butter lifts up the thin sheets of dough. Puff pastry makes incredibly luscious sweet and savory baked

goods, including tart shells and napoleons. Yeast is sometimes added to puff pastry to make the dough used for croissants.**

BASICS ▼ **To store •** Wrap well in plastic wrap and aluminum foil. Refrigerate for 3 days or freeze for up to 3 months.

PROBLEM SOLVERS ▼ **To prevent sticking when cutting shapes out of dough •** Dip the cookie cutter into flour.

    To avoid an uneven rise • Use a cookie cutter that has a relatively sharp edge. Cut straight down and lift straight up without twisting from side to side. If you are slicing pastry dough, use a pastry wheel or pizza cutter. If you are using a knife, it should be sharp. Press the blade through rather than dragging it through the dough. Also, make sure that any egg wash that you brush onto the cutouts does not drip down the sides.

TIME SAVER ▼ **To save prep time •** Stock commercially prepared, frozen puff pastry. It is widely available and is such a versatile product that it should be a staple in every home cook's freezer. Defrost the pastry in the refrigerator for 2 hours before using.

MINIATURE CREOLE CRAB TURNOVERS Sauté **1 minced scallion** in **2 teaspoons butter** until soft. Add **¼ pound cleaned lump crabmeat** and toss to mix. Add **2 tablespoons heavy cream** mixed with **½ teaspoon cornstarch** and **1 teaspoon hot-pepper sauce.** Simmer until lightly thickened. Season with **¼ teaspoon** *each* **salt and ground black pepper.** Let cool. *To assemble turnovers:* Cut **1 sheet frozen and thawed puff pastry** into a 4" × 4" grid, giving you sixteen 3" squares. Brush squares with **1 egg** beaten with **1 tablespoon milk.** Place a small mound of filling in the center of each square, and fold one corner over the filling to its opposite corner, forming a triangle. Press the open edges together and crimp with tines of a fork. Refrigerate several hours or freeze several weeks. Defrost before baking. Brush with more beaten egg and bake at 400°F until puffed and brown, 15 minutes. *Makes 16 pieces.*

CHICKEN WELLINGTON Rub **2 split, boneless, skinless chicken breasts** with **1 teaspoon salt** and ½ **teaspoon ground black pepper.** Heat **2 tablespoons olive oil** in a medium skillet. Add chicken and cook, turning, until browned all over and no longer pink inside. Cool. Cut a pocket in each chicken breast and insert ¼ **roasted red bell pepper** and **2 basil leaves** per pocket. Wrap **1 slice prosciutto** around each. Roll ¾ **pound frozen and thawed puff pastry** to ³⁄₁₆" thickness. Cut in quarters and wrap each chicken breast half in a section of pastry. Refrigerate 1 day or freeze several weeks. Defrost. Place, seam side down, on a dry rimmed baking sheet. Brush with **1 beaten egg.** Bake at 400°F, 10 minutes. Reduce oven temperature to 375°F and bake 10 minutes more. *Makes 4 servings.*

CHEESE STRAWS Roll **1 sheet (8 ounces) frozen and thawed puff pastry** to ³⁄₁₆" thickness. Brush on both sides with **1 beaten egg** mixed with **1 tablespoon milk.** Into both sides of pastry, press a mixture of **1 cup grated Parmesan cheese,** ½ **cup finely shredded Cheddar cheese,** and **1 teaspoon** *each* **ground red pepper and paprika.** Cut into strips that are ½" wide and 6" long. Twist each

strip 4 times and place on a dry rimmed baking sheet, pressing the ends down to hold the twists in place. Refrigerate up to several hours or freeze several weeks. Defrost and bake at 400°F, 15 minutes. *Makes 48.*

Pumpkin *see also* Squash, Winter

A type of gourd, pumpkins have a mildly sweet orange flesh and seeds, or *pepitas*, that taste wonderfully nutty when roasted. Prepare them any way you would prepare other winter squash.

BASICS **To choose** • The best cooking pumpkins are the small ones developed for pie making, called pie pumpkins or sugar pumpkins. There are also excellent large ones called cheese pumpkins; these have a bluish color on the rind. All cooking pumpkins have a distinct, sweet flavor and low moisture content. Avoid jack-o'-lantern pumpkins for cooking; they are generally too wet, fibrous, and flavorless. Take home vividly colored cooking pumpkins that feel heavy for their size. Avoid any with blemishes on the rind.

To store • Keep at room temperature up to 1 month or refrigerate up to 3 months.

To roast • Cut a pie pumpkin into quarters or sixths and scrape out fibers and seeds (reserve seeds for roasting, if desired). Arrange pumpkin pieces, skin side up, in a 13" × 9" baking pan. Add ¼" water and roast at 400°F until very tender when pierced, about 45 minutes. Scoop the soft flesh from the pieces and serve it in chunks with butter, salt, and ground black pepper, or puree it for pie.

TIME SAVER **To easily remove strings from fresh-cooked pumpkin** • Cook the pumpkin with the strings. Then, use an electric mixer to beat the cooked pumpkin. Any strings will attach to the beaters and can be easily removed by rinsing the beaters.

FLAVOR TIPS **To replace** • Use butternut squash. You can use it cup for cup in place of cooked pumpkin puree. It's great for pie.

To temper the flavor • If the taste of pumpkin is too strong for you, temper it by adding 1 tablespoon of an acidic ingredient, such as orange, or lemon juice, at the beginning of cooking time.

PUMPKIN SPICE BREAD Preheat oven to 350°F. In a large bowl, combine **2 cups flour, 1 tablespoon baking powder, 2 teaspoons pumpkin pie spice,** and ½ **teaspoon ground ginger.** Make a well in center and add **1 cup** *each* **packed brown sugar and canned pumpkin, 4 egg whites, ½ cup plain yogurt, ¼ cup applesauce,** and **2 tablespoons molasses.** Stir just until combined. Spoon into an 8" × 4" loaf pan coated with cooking spray. Bake until a tester inserted in center comes out clean, 1 hour. Cool 10 minutes on a rack, invert, and cool completely before slicing. *Makes 10 slices.*

Puree

Used to make soups, dips, and spreads, and to add body to sauces, purees are made by reducing solid foods to a paste. Purees may be savory or sweet. Vegetables such as potatoes, parsnips, or carrots can be pureed to make comforting side dishes. And fruit purees are often used as sauces and fillings for cookies, cakes, and tarts.

BASICS **To puree small quantities of food** • Use a mortar and pestle, the perfect tools for crushing small amounts of food with minimal effort.

To make chunky purees of vegetables or fruits • Use a wire masher.

To make the finest-textured purees • Add only a small amount of liquid.

To puree fruits and vegetables and eliminate any seeds or skins in the process • Use a food mill. The best ones have interchangeable plates to make fine to coarse purees.

To puree very liquid mixtures, such as soups • Use a food processor, blender, or handheld immersion blender.

To make perfectly smooth purees • Strain the puree through a sieve.

To store leftover purees • Refrigerate up to 4 days or freeze up to 1 month.

FLAVOR TIP **To use** • Vegetable purees make a unique and flavorful side dish, and when steamed, the vegetables retain their nutritional value. If serving more than one vegetable puree, place contrasting colors side by side, swirling the two together (such as spinach and butternut squash). You can also use a vegetable puree as a low-fat base for soups or sauces. Purees lend a velvety texture that allows you to eliminate or use less cream, milk, or other dairy products.

VEGETABLE PUREE Cut **1 pound peeled fresh vegetables** into 1" pieces, place them on a steamer rack, and steam until tender. (The time varies according to the vegetable; see page 569.) Puree with **2 teaspoons butter** and **2 tablespoons milk** (if needed) using a hand blender, food processor, or blender, until smooth. For very fibrous vegetables, use a food mill to screen out fibers. Season with ½ **teaspoon salt** and ¼ **teaspoon ground black pepper.** *Makes 4 servings.*

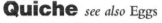

q

Quiche *see also* Eggs

This savory pie originated in the Alsace-Lorraine region of France. Quiche sounds fancy, but it's perfect for using up leftovers.

PROBLEM SOLVER ▼

To avoid a soggy crust • Prebake the pastry in advance. Also, sprinkle a light layer of grated cheese on top of the prebaked pastry while it is still hot, so that the cheese melts and creates a seal. Or brush the hot pastry with egg white for a similar effect. Parboil any watery vegetables and thoroughly drain before adding to the quiche mixture. For spinach, blanch it briefly in boiling water, then squeeze out excess liquid.

HEALTHY HINT ▼

To make in different containers • Use hollowed-out cooked vegetable shells, such as small peppers, zucchini, or potatoes, or raw, hollowed-out tomatoes to hold savory quiche custards.

Quick Cooking *see also* Mise en Place; Timing

Nothing slows down meal preparation like hunting down ingredients in every corner of your kitchen. Keep a well-organized, well-stocked pantry, and quick meals will always be at your fingertips. See also "Convenience Recipes" on page 131.

TIME SAVERS ▼

To choose the best cooking method • When you are in a rush, sautéing, frying, grilling, and pressure-cooking are faster methods than stewing, braising, and roasting. However, when you have plenty of time but you can't be in the kitchen to monitor the food, stewing, braising, baking, roasting, and slow-cooking require less attention than sautéing, frying, and grilling.

To choose the fastest equipment for the job • Use the right-size pan to help liquids boil faster and prevent areas of the pan from scorching before ingredients are done cooking. Also, you may want to invest in some gadgets and tools that make life easier, such as a garlic press and kitchen scissors. Consider buying a mini food processor. The mini versions do a better job with small batches of chopping (such as onions), and they're a lot easier to clean.

To speed prep time • Buy ready-cut fresh vegetables and greens, especially chopped onions, shredded carrots, baby spinach, and other ready-to-eat salad greens. Likewise, buy precut stew and stir-fry meat. Or purchase other quick-cooking cuts of meat and poultry, such as flank steak, boneless pork loin chops, lean ham, boneless skinless chicken and turkey breasts, turkey tenderloin, and

Quiche Lorraine

The original quiche Lorraine does not contain cheese or onions, just crisp bacon in a savory custard. But Gruyère cheese and sautéed onions add great flavor (see the variations below). After baking the pastry shell, brush it with egg white to keep the crust from getting soggy.

1 **prebaked Flaky Tart or Pie Shell (opposite page)**

1 **teaspoon Dijon mustard (optional)**

8 **slices bacon, cut into 1" pieces**

3 **large eggs**

1 **cup light cream, heavy cream, or half-and-half**

¼ **teaspoon salt**

⅛ **teaspoon ground black pepper**

Pinch of grated fresh nutmeg

Pinch of ground red pepper (optional)

1. Preheat the oven to 350°F. Lightly brush the tart shell with the mustard, if using.

2. Cook the bacon in a medium skillet over medium heat until golden brown and almost crisp, 5 minutes. Remove with a slotted spoon and drain on paper towels.

3. In a medium bowl, whisk together the eggs, cream, salt, black pepper, nutmeg, and red pepper, if using. Arrange the bacon in the tart shell. Pour in the custard mixture. Place on a baking sheet and bake until slightly puffy and a knife tip inserted near the center comes out clean, 30 to 40 minutes. Let cool 15 minutes before removing the outer ring of the pan.

Makes 8 servings

Classic Quiche Lorraine: Sauté ½ chopped onion in the bacon drippings until soft. Remove with a slotted spoon and drain on paper towels with the bacon. Arrange 1 cup shredded Gruyère or Swiss cheese over the tart shell. Top with bacon and onion. Pour in the custard mixture. Sprinkle with another 2 to 3 tablespoons shredded Gruyère.

Broccoli Quiche: Boil or microwave 1 cup small broccoli florets until tender, 2 to 3 minutes. Coarsely chop, if necessary, and arrange them in the tart shell. Sauté ½ chopped onion and 1 minced garlic clove in 1 tablespoon olive oil until soft, 3 to 4 minutes. Scatter over the broccoli. Sprinkle with ½ cup shredded Cheddar or Gruyère cheese. Pour in the custard mixture. Sprinkle with ½ teaspoon paprika.

Shrimp Quiche: Place 1 heaping cup shrimp in a saucepan. Add 1 cup cold water. Cook over medium heat until the water barely begins to simmer. Drain and rinse with cold water. Peel and devein the shrimp, if necessary, then arrange them in the tart shell. Top with ¾ cup shredded Gruyère cheese. Add 2 tablespoons dry white wine to the custard mixture. Pour it over the shrimp. Sprinkle with another ¼ cup cheese and ½ teaspoon paprika.

Flaky Tart or Pie Shell

The most tender, flaky pastry shells are made when everything is well-chilled and the dough is handled as little as possible. This shell is excellent for quiches.

1¼ **cups all-purpose flour**

¼ **teaspoon salt**

⅓ **cup solid white vegetable shortening, chilled and cut into small pieces**

1 **tablespoon butter, chilled**

¼ **cup ice water, divided**

1 **teaspoon white or cider vinegar**

1 **egg white, beaten (optional)**

1. In a large bowl, combine the flour and salt. Cut in the shortening and butter until the particles are as small as rice grains. Sprinkle half of the water and all of the vinegar over the flour mixture. Toss with a fork. Add the remaining water and toss with a fork. The dough should be just moist enough to hold together. Gently shape into a 5" disk. Cover with plastic wrap and chill 1 hour.

2. *To prebake:* Preheat the oven to 425°F. On a lightly floured surface, roll the pastry to a 12" round. Place a 9" or 9½" tart pan with a removable bottom on a baking sheet. Loosely drape the pastry in the pan. Push about ½" of the pastry down inside the shell. Trim off the overhanging pastry by running a rolling pin over the pan. Push the edges of the pastry up so that they extend about ¼" above the pan edge. Prick the bottom of the dough all over with a fork. If desired, crimp the top edge of the shell with a fork or a dull knife. Chill at least 15 minutes.

3. Line the shell with foil, pressing it to conform to the shape of the crust. Fill with pie weights, dried beans, or rice. Bake on the baking sheet, 18 to 20 minutes. Carefully remove the foil and weights. Bake until lightly browned, 6 to 8 minutes longer. Prick the shell with a fork if it bubbles. Cool on the baking sheet. Or, if using the shell with a filling that may make the shell soggy (such as quiche), glaze the shell with the egg white while still warm to create a moisture-resistant barrier.

Makes one 9" or 9½" shell

ground beef, chicken, and turkey. Most seafood is fairly quick-cooking. You can also round out quick meals with frozen vegetables.

To help food cook faster • Stir food constantly and consistently, which helps heat penetrate more evenly into the food and speeds up cooking. Also, allow ample room around foods so that heat can circulate. When cooking large quantities of an ingredient, remove individual pieces as they are done to equalize the cooking throughout the batch and allow unfinished pieces to cook faster.

Quinoa

Usually referred to and cooked like a grain, quinoa is actually the fruit of an herb. It resembles tiny, ivory-colored beads. Pronounced "KEEN-wah," this ideal staple food is hardy enough to grow in rocky mountain soil, produces its own natural insect repellent, cooks up twice as fast as rice, is high in protein, and has a wonderfully nutty taste.

BASICS **To store** • Keep in an airtight container in a cool, dry place for up to 1 year.

To rinse • Before cooking quinoa, rinse it in a sieve under cold, running water until the draining water turns from cloudy to clear. Shake out any excess water. Rinsing removes quinoa's saponin coating (a natural insect repellent), which has a bitter, soaplike taste.

To boil • Rinse ½ cup quinoa until the water runs clear. In a saucepan, bring 1 cup water to a boil. Stir in the rinsed quinoa, reduce the heat to medium-low, cover, and cook just until the grains are tender and the liquid is absorbed, 10 to 15 minutes. When cooked, each grain of quinoa will be translucent, revealing a curly white seed sprout. Makes 2 cups.

To use • Since quinoa's proportions are the same as rice, you can use it to replace rice in pilafs, baked casseroles, soups, and skillet dishes, decreasing the cooking time by 5 minutes. You can also cook quinoa with fruit juice and dried fruits to serve for breakfast, or use it to replace rice in your favorite rice pudding recipe.

To use for salads • Boil the quinoa as directed above. Use it to replace rice in your favorite rice salad. This will be especially delicious with a vinaigrette (particularly one made with lime juice) and even better with crunchy vegetables such as sliced radishes, diced carrots and celery, and sliced water chestnuts.

To use other forms • Use quinoa pasta as you would use any other pasta (look for it in large supermarkets and health food stores). Quinoa flour is also available. It has a high protein content and a mild taste, which makes it delicious in biscuits, waffles, and muffins. It can be combined with other whole grain flours such as cornmeal, spelt, oat, and barley.

QUINOA PILAF Rinse **1 cup quinoa** until water runs clear. Shake out excess water. In a medium saucepan, sauté **1 small chopped onion, 2 minced garlic cloves,** and **1 chopped carrot (optional)** in **1 tablespoon vegetable oil** until vegetables are soft, 5 minutes. Add rinsed quinoa and stir until grains are separate and golden, 4 to 5 minutes. Add **2 cups water** or **broth** and ½ **teaspoon salt.** Bring to a boil. Reduce heat to low, cover, and simmer until grains are tender, 10 to 15 minutes. If desired, stir in **1 tablespoon butter** and fluff grains with a fork. *Makes 4 cups.*

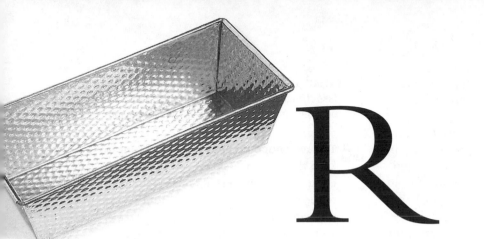

R

Radishes

These pungent roots are usually eaten raw in salads. The skin can be red, purple, black, or white. Asian radishes, or daikon, can run up to 18" in length.

BASICS **To choose** • Look for firm radishes with crisp, green leaves (if attached). Avoid any roots that feel soft when pressed. If buying daikon, avoid any that are wrinkled.

To use • Radishes are best in crisp, cold salads. But they can also be quickly sautéed or stir-fried. Shredded daikon are particularly good in stir-fries.

To store • Remove and discard any leaves, then store unwashed radishes in a zipper-lock plastic bag in the refrigerator up to 1 week. Wash radishes and trim the ends just before using.

To make radish flowers for garnish • Trim the ends. Cut a thin "petal" on the side of the radish from the tip down to, but not through, the root end, so that the petal is attached at the root end. Repeat cutting petals all the way around the radish (a medium radish will usually result in 4 such petals). Place the cut radishes in a bowl of ice water, cover, and refrigerate until the petals begin to curl away from the center, at least 1 hour.

To make radishes more crisp • Cover with ice water and refrigerate 2 to 3 hours.

Raisins

To make raisins, grapes are harvested by hand and arranged on rows of clean paper trays next to the vines, where they dry naturally in the sun for 2 to 3 weeks.

BASICS **To choose** • Raisins are usually made from Thompson seedless grapes. These are called seedless raisins and can be golden or dark purple-brown. Golden raisins are generally plumper and moister than dark raisins. There are also some exquisite seeded raisins such as Muscat and Malaga. If you are fortunate enough to find richly flavored Malaga raisins from Spain, which are dried by the bunch, enjoy the crunchy seeds rather than trying to seed them.

To store • Keep raisins tightly sealed at room temperature up to 4 months, or refrigerated or frozen up to 1 year.

PROBLEM SOLVERS **To replump dry raisins** • Pour boiling water over the raisins in a bowl and let soak 5 minutes. Or place them in a microwaveable dish and sprinkle with about 2 teaspoons water per cup of raisins. Cover with plastic wrap, prick the plastic in a few spots for ventilation, and microwave on high power 30 to 45 seconds. Let stand, covered, 1 to 2 minutes. You can also soak raisins in flavored liquids such as liquor, liqueur, or fruit juice overnight or longer. Use a liquid that complements the flavors in your recipe.

To unstick raisins that have clumped together • Run them under hot water in a sieve. Pat dry if necessary. Or microwave them on medium power for 40 to 60 seconds, checking every 10 seconds.

To chop sticky raisins • Coat your knife blade with nonstick cooking spray.

Fascinating Fact: A raisin dropped in a glass of fresh champagne will bounce up and down continually from the bottom of the glass to the top.

TIME SAVER ▼ **To save chopping time** • Freeze raisins to keep them from sticking to the knife and cutting board during chopping. Better yet, replace any chopped raisins in your recipe with an equal amount of dried currants, which taste and look like raisins but are much smaller and require no chopping.

GUIDELINES FOR ADJUSTING RECIPES

Recipes are typically designed as precise formulas. Yet sometimes, you may want to double or triple the recipe to increase its yield or halve it to decrease the yield.

The Ground Rules: Follow these basic guidelines when altering any recipe.

• When increasing the recipe, try to multiply by an even number.

• When decreasing the recipe, try to divide by an even number.

• Increase or decrease measurements proportionally. The one exception: salt and other seasonings, which you should hold back on increasing proportionally. You can always add more salt later if necessary.

• Look at the lowest common denominator. Some recipes don't divide in half neatly. For instance, you don't want to end up halving an egg.

• For clarity, rewrite the recipe with the changed amounts. Or, write the new amounts in the margin and follow them religiously.

• Timing can often change when altering a recipe, so it's more important to focus on visual cues and/or internal temperatures to determine doneness.

Doubling with Ease: Some foods double up with very few complications. For example, if you want to make an extra pound of pasta, simply increase the amount of cooking water. To make twice the standard amount of rice, double the water and use a wider, deeper pan.

Other recipes are a bit more tricky. The additional volume of food may mean that you'll need to add to the cooking time. For instance, you may want to double a cookie recipe and place 2 baking sheets in the oven when the recipe calls for 1 sheet. In this case, it's best to increase the total baking time slightly (and possibly reduce the oven temperature by 25°F for more delicate cookies). Also, place the sheets above and below on different oven racks, and rotate the sheets halfway through to ensure even baking.

To double a batch of food for sautéing, it's easy enough to use a larger sauté pan and increase the sautéing time slightly. But be careful

To get the maximum amount of iron from raisins • Raisins contain nonheme iron, which is a more difficult form of iron for the body to absorb. For maximum iron absorption, pair raisins with a food that's high in vitamin C, such as citrus, berries, cantaloupe, tomatoes, cabbage, or peppers.

Recipes *see also* Mise en Place; Timing

Recipes are like road maps. The first time you follow one, you need a little more time to get to the destination. Once you are familiar with the route, it is easier to go faster. Eventually, you may not even need the map.

To follow a recipe successfully • Read the recipe all the way through before starting to cook. Make sure that you have all of the necessary ingredients and equip-

not to use a pan so large that it heats unevenly on your burner. And if the amount of food will crowd the pan that you're using, sauté in batches instead. When doubling a recipe for a sauté, it's not necessary to add twice the amount of oil or butter to the pan at the start. Begin with the amount specified for 1 batch, and add more oil as needed.

The one caveat of doubling is this: Avoid doubling recipes for eggs in the same pan. When making scrambled eggs or omelettes, for example, too many eggs in one pan will take too long to cook and will turn rubbery. For the best results, cook the eggs in batches.

Reducing Amounts: Most recipes can be halved easily. Keep in mind that less food will cook in less time; you may need to reduce the total cooking time to avoid overcooking the smaller amount of food. For a sauté, there are fewer ingredients absorbing heat from the pan. Pull the food from the pan sooner, or cook it at a lower temperature or in a smaller pan to avoid overcooking. For cookies, make sure that the pan has no significant vacancies, or it may overheat and burn the cookie bottoms. For muffins

or cupcakes, if you aren't filling all of the cups in the muffin pan, add 1" or so of water to each empty cup to prevent the pan from overheating.

Baking by the Book: Altering baking-related recipes is decidedly more risky than altering any other recipe. Whenever possible, follow a baking recipe to the letter. Amounts of leavener, flour, sugar, liquid, and other ingredients are specifically calculated for balanced results in the crucible of the oven. Change the amounts, and the results can be drastically different. Cakes, for instance, are very temperamental. If you want to double the yield of a cake recipe, make 1 cake, then follow the recipe again to make another cake while the first one bakes in the oven. Or look for a cake recipe that is specifically written for a large cake. Likewise, with pie crusts for a 2-crust pie, it's best to make 1 crust according to the recipe, then make another one as the first crust chills to avoid overworking a large amount of pie dough (which results in tough, chewy pastry). Cookies, on the other hand, are generally more amenable to increasing or decreasing yields. That's yet another reason why cookies are so popular and versatile.

ment. Also, decide at the outset whether you want to make any substitutions. If you are preparing more than one recipe, an initial read-through of each allows you to make judgments about timing or about doing similar tasks at the same time. Reading recipes ahead also warns you about recipes within recipes, such as precooking an ingredient (roasting garlic, for instance) or preparing a sauce before the recipe can be completed. If you plan to multiply or divide the recipe, make sure to read the recipe all the way through first, so that you can make the necessary adjustments (see "Guidelines for Adjusting Recipes" on page 406). And the cardinal rule of following recipes: Don't try new recipes when you're in a hurry. Instead, rely on the tried-and-true.

TIME SAVER ▼ **To save time when preparing multiple recipes** • Combine similar tasks whenever possible. For instance, chop all of the vegetables together and coordinate items that could be baked together or boiled sequentially in the same pot.

Reduction *see also* Sauces

Any liquid cooked until reduced in volume can be referred to as a reduction. By reducing the volume of a cooking liquid, either rapidly over high heat or more slowly over low heat, you concentrate the flavors and thicken the consistency, making a quick, flavorful sauce. Often, reduction sauces are made by adding wine or broth to a pan that was used to sauté foods. Then, the browned bits from the bottom of the pan are scraped up and stirred into the cooking liquid so that they dissolve (called deglazing). When the browned bits dissolve and the liquid is reduced in volume, the flavor becomes tremendously rich.

BASICS ▼ **To make the most flavorful reductions** • Start with the best ingredients. The flavors of bad-tasting ingredients will only get worse when reduced and concentrated. Also, reduce liquids at a gentle boil, which causes some of the sauce to splash on the sides of the pan and caramelize. Stirring these caramelized bits back into the sauce creates additional flavor. And make sure to layer the reduction rather than adding liquids all at once. For example, first add wine to deglaze the pan and reduce the wine. Then, add some stock and reduce it. Finally, add some cream to the pan and reduce once more.

To create a smooth texture • Strain the reduced sauce before serving.

PROBLEM SOLVER ▼ **To prevent reduction sauces from becoming overly salty** • Add any salt after the liquid has reduced to the desired consistency. Also, avoid using canned broths, which are often too salty to be reduced and concentrated in flavor.

Rhubarb

Though technically a vegetable, rhubarb is treated like a fruit in the kitchen. Its long stalks or ribs range in color from cherry red to pale pink; it looks somewhat like celery that's blushing. Rhubarb is inedible raw and must be cooked, usually with a good dose of sugar to balance its tart flavor.

BASICS ▼ **To choose** • Field-grown rhubarb crops up in spring, with the bulk of it appearing in April and May. Hothouse-grown rhubarb is available year-round in many areas. Look for crisp, firm stalks without blemishes or cuts. Field-grown rhubarb has a bright red color and a more pronounced flavor than the pale pink hothouse-grown stalks. Any leaves attached to the stalks should be fresh-looking, not wilted or limp. Also, the thinnest and youngest rhubarb will be the most tender and require the least sugar.

To store • Refrigerate whole stalks in the crisper in perforated plastic bags for up to 3 days. Cut stalks can be stored in zipper-lock plastic bags up to 8 months.

To prepare • Rhubarb leaves are mildly toxic (they contain oxalic acid) and should always be discarded. If the stalks are fibrous, remove the strings with a vegetable peeler. Stalks that are more than 1½" wide should be cut in half.

HEALTHY HINT ▼ **To reduce amounts of sugar used with rhubarb** • Generally, the redder the stalk of rhubarb, the sweeter the flavor, requiring less sugar to be used when cooking. The smallest, thinnest stalks will also be the least tart and require the least sugar.

Ribs *see also* Beef; Pork

Barbecued ribs take time. Cook them too fast, and they become little more than charred sinew. To speed up the cooking of barbecued beef or pork ribs without causing them to toughen and burn, you can presteam them in a pressure cooker, braise them in an oven, or precook them in a microwave oven.

TIME SAVERS ▼ **To pressure-steam ribs before grilling** • Cook 5 pounds pork or beef ribs (cut into 3-rib or 4-rib sections) in 2 cups barbecue sauce in a pressure cooker until centers register 160°F on an instant-read thermometer (and juices run clear, for pork), 12 minutes. Release the steam and brown over a hot fire or under a broiler 4 to 5 minutes.

To braise before grilling • Brown the ribs in 1 tablespoon oil. Add 3 cups barbecue sauce, cover, and bake at 350°F until the meat is fork-tender, about 1 hour.

To precook in a microwave oven • Place 3 pounds pork or beef ribs (cut into 3-rib or 4-rib sections) in a microwaveable baking dish and cover with 1 cup barbecue sauce. Cover the dish and cook on high power 10 minutes. Turn the ribs over and microwave on high power until centers register 160°F on an instant-read thermometer (and juices run clear, for pork), 8 minutes more. Brown the ribs over a high fire or under a broiler 4 to 5 minutes.

GRILLED SPARERIBS WITH APRICOT GLAZE Cut **4 to 5 pounds meaty, trimmed pork spareribs** into 2-rib or 3-rib portions. Jab the tip of a paring knife several times between each rib so that marinade can penetrate. In a shallow dish or 2 large zipper-lock plastic bags, combine **½ cup grated fresh ginger; 1 small, finely chopped onion; 3 minced garlic cloves; ⅓ cup *each* soy sauce, dry sherry, and rice vinegar; ¼ cup sugar; and ¾ teaspoon ground black pepper**. Marinate in the refrigerator 8 hours or overnight, turning bags occasionally. Remove ribs and strain marinade, setting aside ⅓ cup. Bake ribs in a shallow pan at 300°F, 1½ to 2 hours, turning every 30 minutes. (Recipe can be made 2 days ahead up to this point.) Preheat a grill. In a small saucepan, combine **⅔ cup apricot preserves, 2 tablespoons brown mustard, 1 tablespoon toasted sesame oil, and ¼ teaspoon ground red pepper (or more to taste).** Simmer over low heat until slightly thickened, about 5 minutes. Grill ribs over a medium-hot fire 10 to 15 minutes, turning occasionally. Brush with glaze and continue cooking and brushing until meat is glazed and browned, juices run clear, and internal temperature registers 160°F on an instant-read thermometer, about 15 minutes longer. *Makes 4 to 6 servings.*

Rice *see also* Risotto; Wild Rice

The seed of a semiaquatic grass, rice is the primary food staple for more than two-thirds of the world's population. In China, the word for "rice" is actually a synonym for "food." In Japan, the word for "cooked rice" is synonymous with the word for "meal."

BASICS ▼ **To choose** • Rice is divided into three main categories based on the size of the seed: long-grain, medium-grain, and short-grain. The length of the grain determines texture and consistency. Long-grain rice is 4 to 5 times as long as it is wide; when cooked, it produces firm, fluffy grains that separate easily. Medium-grain rice cooks up into relatively moist, tender grains that tend to become stickier as the rice cools. Short-grain rice is almost round in shape and has a high starch content. It becomes moist, tender, and sticky when cooked. Sometimes called sweet, sticky, pearl, or glutinous rice (though it contains no gluten), short-grain rice is the preferred type for risotto, paella, sushi, and Asian desserts.

To store white rice • Keep in an airtight container and use within 1 year.

To store brown rice • Keep in an airtight container and use within 6 months. The oil in the bran remains intact on brown rice, making it more likely to become rancid than white rice.

To cook perfect white rice • Use 1½ to 2 cups water per cup of rice. (Use 2 cups water for long-grain rice, 1¾ cups for medium-grain rice, and 1½ cups for short-grain rice.) Bring the water to a boil in a saucepan. Add the rice, reduce the heat to low, cover, and simmer until the liquid is absorbed, about 12 minutes. Remove from the heat and immediately fluff with a fork to release steam. Serve it immediately. Or let the rice rest, covered, up to 30 minutes, and fluff it with a fork before serving.

To cook perfect brown rice • Use 2 to 2½ cups water per cup of rice. (Use 2½ cups water for long-grain rice, 2¼ cups for medium-grain rice, and 2 cups for short-grain rice.) Bring the water to a boil in a saucepan. Add the rice, reduce the heat to low, cover, and simmer until the liquid is absorbed, 35 to 45 minutes. Remove from the heat and immediately fluff with a fork to release steam. Serve immediately. Or let the rice rest, covered, up to 30 minutes, and fluff it with a fork before serving.

To ensure separate grains when cooking long-grain rice • Sauté the rice in a small amount of butter or oil before cooking. Add liquid and cook as directed. You can also use less water: For long-grain white rice, use 1¾ cups water per cup of rice. It also helps to rinse the rice before cooking to remove excess starch. Rinse the rice in a sieve under cool, running water until the draining water runs clear. All of these techniques are excellent for rice salads, where you want firm, separate grains.

To cook rice to a creamy consistency • Use medium or short-grain rice for its higher starch content. Arborio rice is an excellent choice.

To cook a large quantity of rice • Use a pot with a wide bottom (for example, a 10"-diameter Dutch oven for 4 or more cups of rice). Avoid using a tall, narrow pot because, if the rice is layered too deep, the bottom layer will turn to mush before the top layer cooks through. If you don't have a large pot with a wide bottom, use 2 saucepans.

To keep cooked rice warm • Place a double layer of paper towels under the lid so that steam will be absorbed by the towels and not condense, which would make the rice sticky.

To reheat rice • Place the rice in a saucepan or sauté pan and add 2 table-spoons of water per cup of cooked rice. Cover and cook over medium-low heat until heated through. Or, place the rice in a sieve over a pot of simmering water, and cover. You can also spread the rice in a mi-crowaveable dish, cover it with plastic wrap that has been punctured in a few spots (to vent steam), and warm it on high power, about 90 seconds per cup of rice. Or, if you are adding the rice to a soup, stir-fry, or other cooked dish, you can add frozen rice without defrosting. It will heat through in a few minutes.

Fascinating Fact: Arkansas is the lead-ing rice-producing state in America.

PROBLEM SOLVERS ▼ **To salvage bland or poor-quality rice** • Toast it over medium heat in a skillet until the rice begins to turn opaque, 5 minutes. Toasting intensifies the grain's flavor.

To brighten white rice • Sometimes white rice cooks up with a yellowish tint. For pure whiteness, add a squirt of lemon juice to the cooking water.

To make rice when you forget the water-to-rice ratio • Bring a large pot of water to a boil, and add the rice. Cook like pasta until the rice is tender. Drain in a sieve.

To prevent rice from boiling over as it cooks • Add 1 teaspoon oil or butter to the cooking water.

To prevent steam from escaping when your pan has a loose lid • Cover the pan with a layer or two of foil, then set the lid in place for a tighter seal.

To prevent sticky, clumpy rice • Avoid stirring, unless a recipe indicates to do so. Fluff cooked rice gently with a fork instead of stirring.

To finish cooking half-cooked rice when all the liquid has been absorbed • Add ¼ cup hot liquid per cup of rice, cover, and continue to cook, adding more liquid if necessary.

To cook rice when all your stove-top burners are occupied • Combine rice and boiling liquid in a baking dish or pan and cover tightly. Bake at 350°F, 25 to 30 minutes for long-grain white rice or 1 hour for brown rice. Baking rice works well when you have other dishes in the oven anyway. A rice cooker is another ex-cellent option.

To rescue mushy, overcooked rice • Add some extra bite by stirring in finely chopped, lightly sautéed carrots, onions, or other vegetables.

To remove excess moisture from cooked rice • Fluff it with a fork to help release steam. If that's not enough, remove the pan lid and set the pan over very low heat so that excess steam can cook off. Watch carefully so that the rice doesn't burn on the bottom. If there is a lot of water in the pan, strain the rice in a mesh sieve, then spread it on a foil-lined baking sheet. Bake at 250°F until the excess liquid evaporates, 10 minutes.

To rescue burned rice • If the rice is not fully cooked, your best option might be to start over again. If starting over is not an option, spoon the rice that is not scorched into a clean pan, add hot water, bring to a simmer, cover, and cook over low heat until tender. If the rice has picked up a scorched flavor, cover it with a slice of fresh bread and a pan lid. Let it sit long enough for the bread to absorb the burnt aroma, about 10 to 15 minutes.

To use leftover rice • Use it to make fried rice, enrich a soup or stew, or make a rice salad.

To restore fluffiness to leftover rice • Place 2 cups leftover rice in a serving dish with 2 tablespoons chicken broth. Cover and microwave on high power 2 to 3 minutes. Fluff the rice with a fork.

To avoid a crunchy texture in rice salads • Serve them at room temperature instead of chilled.

To clean a pan of burned or stuck-on rice • Let it soak in warm water for at least 30 minutes, then scrape it with a metal or plastic spatula. If necessary, heat the pan of water over low heat to help loosen the burned rice.

TIME SAVERS ▼ **To make a quick batch of rice** • Many cooks choose instant rice because it cooks in 5 minutes. But because this type of rice is precooked, it is nearly devoid of flavor and tends to turn out mushy. A better quick-cooking choice is basmati rice, which cooks in just 12 minutes and has a wonderful perfume, a nutty taste, and a firm texture. To cook it, rinse 1 cup basmati rice in several changes of cold water until the water runs clear. In a saucepan, bring 1¾ cups water and ½ teaspoon salt to a boil. Stir in the rinsed rice, cover tightly, and simmer over low heat until the water is absorbed, 12 minutes. Fluff the rice with a fork and mix in 2 tablespoons butter, if desired. Makes 4 servings.

To cook brown rice in half the time • Soak it for 4 hours or more. Drain, and proceed to cook it with fresh water. Water-to-rice ratios do not change.

FIVE WAYS TO SPICE UP RICE

There's no reason to settle for bland, boring rice. Two or three seasonings can turn it into something special. For each recipe below, combine the liquid and seasonings in a saucepan. Bring the mixture to a boil, then add 1 cup raw rice. Reduce the heat to low, cover, and simmer until the liquid is absorbed, about 12 minutes (for white rice) or 40 minutes (for brown rice). Remove the pan from the heat and let it rest, covered, about 10 minutes. Fluff the rice with a fork before serving. Each recipe makes 4 servings.

Recipe	Liquid	Seasonings
Coconut Rice	1½ cups water and ½ cup coconut milk	2 Tbsp chopped shredded coconut, 2 tsp honey, ½ tsp salt, and a pinch of allspice
Curried Rice	2 cups chicken broth	1 tsp curry powder and 3 Tbsp dried currants
Ginger-Soy Rice	2 cups water	2 tsp *each* soy sauce and grated fresh ginger, and 2 whole cloves
Lemon Rice	2 cups water	½ tsp salt, 2 strips lemon zest, and a pinch of nutmeg
Saffron Rice	2 cups vegetable broth	A pinch of saffron

QUICK SHRIMP FRIED RICE In a wok or large skillet, stir-fry ½ **finely chopped onion, 1 chopped celery rib,** and ½ **chopped red bell pepper** in **1 tablespoon oil.** When barely tender, push vegetables up the sides of the pan, add another **1 tablespoon oil** in the center, and stir-fry ¼ **pound chopped cleaned shrimp** for 30 seconds. Add **3 cups cooked leftover rice** and **1 cup frozen peas.** Stir-fry until the rice grains brown lightly. Add **1 beaten egg, 1 cup bean sprouts,** ½ **cup shredded spinach,** and **2 chopped scallions.** Stir-fry until heated through and eggs are cooked. *Makes 4 servings.*

FLAVOR TIPS ▼ To boost the nutty taste of rice • Toast the rice grains in a dry skillet or in a small amount of oil or fat, stirring until golden. Then, add the liquid.

To flavor rice pilaf • Add 1 cinnamon stick (3") along with the liquid. Cinnamon creates wonderful aromas, especially when the rice will accompany Indian or Mexican dishes.

SKILLET RICE AND SPAGHETTI In a skillet, sauté ½ **cup broken uncooked spaghetti** in **1 tablespoon oil** until browned, 1 minute. Add **3 cups leftover cooked rice, 2 cups chicken broth,** ½ **teaspoon salt,** and ¼ **teaspoon ground black pepper.** Cook until chicken broth is absorbed, about 10 minutes, stirring often. *Makes 4 servings.*

MEXICAN RICE Heat **2 teaspoons olive oil** in a large nonstick skillet over medium heat. Add **1 chopped onion, 1½ chopped red bell peppers,** and 1 **cup brown rice.** Cook and stir until rice is toasted, 5 minutes. Stir in **2 cups fat-free chicken broth;** ½ **cup tomato sauce; 1 can (4 ounces) diced green chile peppers, drained; 2 teaspoons chili powder; 1 teaspoon ground cumin; 1 chopped garlic clove;** and **2 chopped ancho chile peppers.** Bring to a boil. Reduce heat to low, cover, and simmer until rice is tender, 45 minutes. *Makes 4 servings.*

HEALTHY HINT ▼ To retain nutrients in enriched rice • Avoid rinsing enriched rice before cooking, which may flush out the added vitamins and minerals. Also, if there is extra water after cooking enriched rice, let the rice stand, covered, for 5 to 10 minutes to absorb the liquid. If there's still some left, reserve the leftover nutrient-dense cooking water to use in soups, stews, or sauces. Or use it in place of milk in baked goods.

Risotto

A magnificent, simmering stew of rice, broth, and seasonings, risotto is one of the great dishes of Northern Italy.

BASICS ▼ To make authentic risotto • Use an Italian short-grain rice, such as Arborio superfino or Carnaroli. These plump rices have a high starch content, which helps give risotto its characteristically creamy and chewy texture. Also, choose a heavy pan with a nonreactive lining. A thick bottom and sides help distribute heat evenly, and a stainless-steel, anodized aluminum, or enameled lining won't react with acidic ingredients such as tomatoes or wine. Finally, make sure to stir risotto frequently, about every few minutes. Constant stirring should not be necessary as long as you use a heavy pot that diffuses heat evenly.

r

To ensure a creamy texture • Never rinse the rice before cooking. Rinsing will wash away the starch necessary to create risotto's creamy texture.

To ensure that the rice absorbs liquid slowly without getting soggy • Heat butter or oil in the pan and stir in the raw rice over high heat until the rice begins to pop, 1 minute. This will toast the rice and help the grains maintain their shape.

To ensure that risotto cooks continuously • Always add hot broth to the risotto. It's easiest to keep a separate pot of simmering broth on hand. Also, add the broth in small batches of about ½ cup.

To test risotto for doneness • Take a bite. When the rice is done, it will be chewy and resilient. You can also spoon a little of the risotto into a bowl and shake it from side to side. The risotto should spread out very gently. If the rice stays in one place, it's too dry and needs a little more stock. If a puddle forms around the rice, it's too wet. Spoon off some of the liquid, or let the risotto stand for a few minutes to absorb the excess liquid.

PROBLEM SOLVERS ▼ **To avoid overcooking vegetables in risotto** • Add them toward the end of the cooking process, allotting just enough time for the vegetables to cook through.

To avoid burning risotto • Stir frequently, every few minutes. And never let the cooking rice completely lose moisture. When there is just a little liquid left in the pan, add more hot broth.

To rescue burned risotto • Transfer unscorched grains to another pot, add liquid, and continue to cook.

TIME SAVER ▼ **To save prep time** • Partially cook the risotto ahead of time. Or make risotto in a microwave oven or pressure cooker.

MAKE-AHEAD RISOTTO Sauté **½ finely chopped onion** in **1 tablespoon olive oil**. Add **1 cup Arborio rice** and toss with oil. Add **½ cup white wine**. Cook and stir until wine is absorbed. Add **3½ cups hot chicken broth**, ½ cup at a time, stirring frequently after each addition until the liquid is absorbed (as done for the wine), 25 to 35 minutes total. Cool to room temperature, cover tightly, and refrigerate up to 24 hours. To finish cooking, heat another **1½ cups chicken broth** to a boil in a saucepan. Add risotto and stir until creamy and heated through. Remove from heat and stir in **¼ cup grated Parmesan cheese** and **1 tablespoon butter**. *Makes 4 servings.*

MICROWAVE RISOTTO Pour **1 tablespoon extra-virgin olive oil** into a 10", deep-sided microwaveable baking dish. Microwave on high power 3 minutes. Add **1 chopped onion;** toss and microwave on high power 4 minutes. Stir in **1 cup Arborio rice;** microwave 2 minutes more. Add **1¾ cups chicken broth** and microwave on high power 8 minutes. Stir in another **1¾ cups chicken broth** and microwave on high power 8 minutes more. Let rest 3 minutes. Stir in **¼ cup grated Parmesan cheese** and **1 tablespoon butter**. *Makes 4 servings.*

FLAVOR TIP ▼ **To use leftover risotto** • Refrigerate it to use as a base for risotto pancakes.

LEMON-PARMESAN RISOTTO In a saucepan, combine **6 cups chicken broth** (preferably homemade) and **½ cup dry white wine**. Bring to a boil, reduce heat to low, and keep at a bare simmer while you cook. In a heavy 3- to 4-quart saucepan, heat **2 tablespoons olive oil** and **1 tablespoon butter** over medium heat. Add **1 pound Arborio rice** and stir until grains are chalky-looking, 3 minutes. Add about ½ cup broth, reduce heat to medium–low, and stir until liquid is absorbed. Continue ladling in ½ cup broth at a time, stirring after each addition until liquid is absorbed and rice is tender yet firm to the bite, 25 to 35 minutes total. Stir in another **1 tablespoon butter, 1 cup freshly grated Parmesan cheese, 1 teaspoon grated lemon zest, 3 tablespoons lemon juice,** and ½ **teaspoon ground black pepper.** Taste and add **a pinch of salt,** if needed. Serve immediately. Sprinkle with chopped fresh parsley, if desired.

Makes 6 servings.

LOW-FAT, LEMONY DATE RISOTTO
Similar to rice pudding, this sweet risotto is excellent with crisp cookies. In a medium saucepan, heat **1½ cups 1% milk** and **1 can (8 ounces) fat-free evaporated milk** to a bare simmer. In a large skillet, sauté **1 cup Arborio rice** in **2 tablespoons butter,** 2 minutes, stirring. Add half the hot milk mixture, along with the **grated zest of 1 lemon.** Cook until liquid is absorbed, stirring frequently. Stir in **3 tablespoons packed brown sugar** and ¼ teaspoon *each* **grated nutmeg and ground allspice.** Add remaining half of milk mixture and cook until liquid is almost absorbed, 15 minutes, stirring frequently. Stir in ¼ **cup chopped pitted dates** and cook until rice is just tender and liquid is absorbed, 5 minutes. Serve immediately. *Makes 4 servings.*

Roasting *see also specific foods and* Doneness Tests and Temperatures (page 572)

An essential cooking method, roasting cooks food by surrounding it with dry heat. Meat, fish, poultry, and vegetables are all excellent when roasted. The cooking is generally done at high temperatures, but some meats are first roasted at a high temperature to cook the surface and lock in juices, then the heat is reduced. Likewise, some recipes may specify roasting at a lower temperature for most of the cooking, then raising the heat at the end to create a browned surface.

r

BASICS
▼

To help roast evenly • Bring the food almost to room temperature before roasting. (If the food is refrigerated, remove it from the refrigerator about 1 hour before putting it in the oven.) It also helps to turn the food at least twice while it roasts. When roasting meats, place the roast on a rack above a drip pan to allow good air circulation all the way around the meat. If you don't have a rack, use a rimmed baking sheet, which has enough of a lip to catch juices but has sides short enough that air can circulate well around the roast. Or, prop the roast up on a bed of sliced potatoes and onions. If the roast is unevenly shaped, tie it with kitchen twine into a more uniform shape.

To keep meat moist while roasting • Place the meat fatty side up for the first half of the cooking time. This will allow the roast to baste itself.

To roast large, tender cuts of meat • Cuts such as ribs and tenderloin and premium-grade beef roasts are best suited to high-heat roasting. Rub oil onto any surfaces of the meat not covered with natural fat. Place the roast in a 500°F oven for 15 minutes to sear the meat, then reduce the temperature to 400°F until the meat is cooked through. (See Doneness Tests and Temperatures on page 572.) If your roast measures less than 5" in diameter, it can be roasted continuously at 500°F without burning. This method of beginning the roast at high heat, then reducing the heat after 15 minutes, helps create a nicely browned crust. You could also sear the meat in a pan before roasting.

To roast less-tender cuts of meat • Cuts such as rump, chuck, and sirloin tip tend to have little external fat or marbling. Be sure to rub them well with oil, and roast at 325°F until cooked through. (See Doneness Tests and Temperatures on page 572.)

To help poultry or fish brown during roasting • Coat it with oil before seasoning.

To time roasts perfectly • Remove the food about 5 to 10 minutes before it is fully cooked through. Roasted food will continue cooking for 5 to 10 minutes after it comes out of the oven. Also, consider the shape of the food being cooked. A plump 3-pound roast will take longer to reach the desired internal temperature than a 3-pound roast that is wide and thin. Likewise, a butterflied chicken will roast faster than a trussed bird.

To ensure that roasted meats are moist and juicy • Cover the roast with foil and let it rest at least 15 minutes before carving. This resting period allows natural juices to seep back into the center, which also makes carving easier because slices are less likely to fall apart.

To catch drips when carving a roast • Place the carving board over a towel to absorb drips. Even better, place it inside a rimmed baking sheet to catch the juices, and then pour the juices back over the carved meat.

To ensure that roasted vegetables cook at the same rate • Cut them into even-size pieces and keep them in a single layer in the pan. The vegetables will brown best on the surfaces that come in contact with the pan.

To create a denser texture in roasted soft-flesh vegetables • Tomatoes, eggplant, and other soft-flesh vegetables will become denser in texture if roasted at a lower temperature (375° to 400°F) for a longer time, rather than being roasted at a high temperature for a brief time.

To add garlic to roasted vegetables • The best method is to place unpeeled cloves of garlic in the oven as it preheats, for 5 to 8 minutes. Then, chop the garlic and add it to the vegetables at the end of roasting time. Preroasting the garlic this way takes off its bitter edge. You could also add raw chopped garlic to the vegetables 5 to 8 minutes before the end of roasting time so that the garlic cooks briefly. But avoid tossing raw minced garlic with vegetables that have just been roasted; the garlic will taste harsh and raw. Likewise, avoid adding garlic to raw vegetables and roasting it along with them, which results in vegetables speckled with burned bits of bitter garlic.

To test roasted vegetables for doneness • Insert a toothpick into the center of the largest one. If the vegetable is tender, the pick will pull out easily.

PROBLEM SOLVERS ▼ **To check a roast's doneness without opening the oven door** • Use a meat thermometer that is connected by wire to a base unit outside of the oven. These thermometers monitor the internal tem-

SLOW-ROASTED MEATS

The theory behind slow-roasting has the simplicity of genius: If the oven is set at the desired internal temperature of the meat, then the meat can never overcook because no part of it is subjected to a temperature above the optimum. The only possible danger is that bacteria can grow at temperatures below 140°F. But since all bacteria on a solid piece of meat are on its surface, an initial roasting at a high temperature eliminates that danger. Best of all, slow-roasting requires virtually no attention from the cook.

Slow-roasting works best with large roasts, particularly turkey. To convert a favorite roast for slow-roasting, plan on 3 times the amount of normal roasting time. Here's how it's done.

Preheat the oven to 450°F. Place the roast on a rack. Season the surface, but do not stuff. Roast for 1 hour to kill any bacteria on the surface of the roast. Reduce the oven temperature to the desired internal doneness temperature of the meat: 180°F for poultry, 160°F for beef cooked medium, and 155°F for pork. Roast until the meat reaches that temperature and the juices run clear, about 1 hour per pound for poultry, beef, veal, and lamb; about 1¼ hours per pound for pork. Let the roast stand for 10 minutes before slicing.

---

perature of meat and send off an alarm when the roast comes to the desired temperature. They often come with timers and can be found in most cookware stores.

To rescue meat that is drying out before it is finished cooking • Pour wine, broth, or water over the roast as needed. You might also need to lower the oven temperature.

To save face when you have overcooked a roast • Serve it with lots of gravy, brown sauce, or relish. Also, carve off any burnt surfaces.

To make the best of a tough roast • Slice it paper-thin across the grain. Serve it with a sauce, gravy, or relish.

To salvage a roast that's pale and undercooked • Continue cooking, and raise the heat 25°F if necessary.

To keep hungry guests pleased when a roast is out too rare • Make enough thin slices to give each person 1 serving, and place the slices under the broiler to cook them through. While everyone is enjoying that, put the remainder of the roast back in the oven until it is cooked to the desired doneness.

To avoid steam-cooking a roast • Baste it with just enough liquid (such as wine or broth) so that the liquid barely covers the bottom of the pan. Also, do not cover the roast with a foil tent.

TIME SAVERS ▼ **To roast meat more quickly** • Use high-heat roasting, which delivers exceptional flavor. The skin comes out cracklingly crisp and the meat succulently juicy. It's a particularly good method for cooking rare or medium-rare meat. High-heat roasting is not recommended for very large roasts, however, because they may need some time at a lower temperature to cook to the de-

r

VEGETABLE ROASTING TIMES

Almost any vegetable can be roasted, even greens. Winter squash takes on a wonderful flavor because the high heat enhances the vegetable's natural sugar. To roast any of the following vegetables, prepare them as necessary and roast on a lightly oiled, rimmed baking sheet in the lower third of a 450°F oven for the specified time. Toss any cut-up vegetables with 1 teaspoon olive or canola oil. The amounts are calculated for about 4 servings.

Vegetable	Amount	Preparation	Roasting Time
Acorn squash	1–2	Halve and seed; place, cut side up, on pan	50 min
Asparagus	1 lb	Trim	10–15 min
Beets	2 lb	Leave whole; scrub well	60–90 min; when cool enough to handle, slip off skins
Bell peppers	3	Cut into thin strips	12 min; stir halfway through cooking
Buttercup squash	1	Peel and cut into 1" chunks; cover with foil on pan	10–12 min
Carrots	1 lb	Cut into ½" sticks	18–20 min
Corn	4 whole ears	Soak in water 1 hour; place directly on oven rack	8–10 min
Eggplant	1 medium	Cut into ½"-thick slices; brush with 1 Tbsp oil	20 min; turn slices over halfway through cooking
Green beans	1 lb	Trim	12 min; stir halfway through cooking
Potatoes	2 lb	Cut into ½"-thick slices	30–35 min; turn halfway through cooking
Red onions	2	Leave unpeeled; halve; place, cut side down, on pan; cover with foil	25–30 min
Shallots	1 lb	Peel; leave whole	20 min; stir every 5 min
Sweet potatoes	2	Peel; cut into ¼"-thick slices; cover with foil	20 min; uncover and roast 10 min more
Tomatoes	2 lb	Use whole plum tomatoes	20–25 min; turn halfway through cooking
Zucchini	2 lb	Halve lengthwise and cut into 1½" chunks	20 min; stir halfway through cooking

sired doneness without scorching. Here's the basic method: Preheat the oven to 500°F. Place the roast in a roasting pan on a rack or on a bed of vegetables. Roast for about 35 minutes for a 3-pound chicken, 45 to 50 minutes for a 5-pound chicken, 45 minutes for a 9- to 10-pound beef sirloin, and about 20 to 25 minutes for a 5-pound tenderloin. See the Doneness Tests and Temperatures chart on page 572 for more information.

To quickly skim drippings from a roast • Insert a bulb baster into the drippings so that the tip is beneath the layer of fat floating on the surface. Use the baster to draw out the juices from beneath the fat.

To roast vegetables quickly • Chop them into small pieces, but no smaller than ½". Also, make sure that the vegetables are in a single layer.

To quickly roast sturdy vegetables • Potatoes, carrots, onions, celeriac, winter squash, turnips, and beets roast more quickly when cut into thin slices. Toss the slices with oil, salt, pepper, and herbs. Spread in an even layer on a rimmed baking sheet and roast in a 450°F oven until browned around the edges and soft in the middle, about 20 minutes.

FLAVOR TIP ▼ **To add flavor to roasts** • Use a bone-in roast. The bones add flavor to the meat and help the meat cook more quickly.

RUM-ROASTED PORK CHOPS Spread **3 peeled, cored, and thickly sliced tart apples** in an 11" × 7" baking pan. Sprinkle with ¾ **teaspoon dried thyme** and top with **4 boneless pork chops (each about ¾ " thick).** In a small dish, mix ½ **cup apple cider, 2 tablespoons** *each* **dark rum and brown sugar, 1 teaspoon ground ginger,** and ¼ **teaspoon ground allspice.** Pour over pork.

Roast at 400°F until center of a chop registers 160°F and juices run clear, about 30 minutes; turn chops halfway through cooking. *Makes 4 servings.*

SPICE-GLAZED ROASTED BANANAS Arrange **4 peeled and split-lengthwise bananas,** cut side up, in a small greased roasting pan. In a small dish, combine ½ **teaspoon ground cinnamon** and ¼ **teaspoon** *each* **ground allspice and ground ginger.** Sprinkle over bananas and drizzle with **2 tablespoons honey.** Roast at 350°F, 10 minutes. Baste with cooking juices, place under the broiler, and broil until golden brown, 2 minutes. Serve warm with ice cream, or as a side dish for pork, poultry, or game. *Makes 4 servings.*

Roux

A cornerstone of sauce making, roux is made by cooking flour and fat together until they form a paste. Roux is used primarily as a thickener, but it also adds complex flavor to whatever dish it's used in.

BASICS ▼ **To make** • Begin by heating the fat in a heavy saucepan. Butter is used most often, but roux can also be made with vegetable oil, lard, or duck fat. Once the fat has melted, add an equal amount of flour and stir until smooth. Cook the roux over medium-low heat, stirring constantly, until it has reached the desired color.

To make a roux for thickening but not for adding color or flavor • Cook the roux for only a few minutes without letting it color (known as a white roux).

To make a roux for thickening and adding a light color and flavor • Cook the roux until it turns golden blond in color. Use this type of roux to enrich cream-based soups and sauces.

To make a roux with a complex flavor but little thickening ability • Cook the roux until it turns dark brown. This is the most flavorful roux, but keep in mind that a roux loses its thickening power as it cooks. Dark roux is a traditional ingredient in Cajun gumbo (which gets extra thickening from cooked okra).

To add liquid • Warm the liquid slightly before whisking it in. This will help quicken the cooking time.

PROBLEM SOLVERS ▼

To prevent lumps • Make sure that any added liquid is not steaming hot. If it is, the sauce will thicken too quickly and become lumpy.

To eliminate any raw flour taste in a roux-thickened sauce • Cook the sauce at least 30 minutes before serving.

TIME SAVERS ▼

To cook a brown roux faster • Toast the flour first. Heat a small skillet over medium-high heat. Add 2 tablespoons flour to the hot, dry skillet and stir until the flour turns light brown (1 minute) or dark brown (2 minutes). Stir constantly to ensure that the flour doesn't burn. Remove the skillet from the heat and stir in 2 tablespoons butter or margarine until melted. Makes enough to thicken 2 cups liquid.

To save prep time • Whenever you make roux, make extra. Cooked roux can be kept in the refrigerator for several weeks. Use it by the tablespoon to thicken sauces, soups, or stews.

To skip cooking a roux • Mix together equal parts flour and water or broth. Or mash together equal parts flour and butter or margarine. Whisk either mixture into simmering liquid and cook at least 30 minutes to eliminate any flavor of uncooked flour.

Salad Dressings *see also* Fats

and Oils; Marinades; Mayonnaise; Sauces; Vinegar

A simple vinaigrette is all you need to dress a salad of greens. Made from a mixture of oil, vinegar, and seasonings, vinaigrettes are very easy to prepare and store indefinitely In the refrigerator. Aside from their classic use on salads, vinaigrettes also make great marinades and sauces.

BASICS ▼ **To make a simple vinaigrette** • In a small jar, such as an old mustard jar, combine salt and ground black pepper. Add vinegar, cover, and shake until the salt has dissolved. Add the oil, cover, and shake again until the ingredients are combined. The oil and vinegar will eventually separate, so shake the mixture just before using. A good ratio of ingredients is 3 parts oil to 1 part vinegar, with salt and pepper to taste.

To make a smooth vinaigrette • Using your favorite vinaigrette recipe, combine the ingredients in a jar with a tight-fitting lid and add 1 ice cube. Shake vigorously, then discard the ice cube.

To make an emulsified vinaigrette • Add a small amount of prepared or powdered mustard, paprika, or ground nuts. Any of these ingredients will help keep the oil and vinegar from separating.

To use salad dressing as a marinade • Marinate poultry or seafood in Italian or any garlic-and-herb dressing. Use a tomato-based dressing for pork or beef. Ranch dressings add richness to fish and white meat chicken. Mayonnaise-based dressings develop a tangy crust when used to marinate a grilled chicken breast or veal chop. You can also baste barbecued meats with salad dressing instead of using barbecue sauce.

To replace sour cream with yogurt in a vinaigrette • Slightly reduce the amount of vinegar in the dressing to balance out the yogurt's natural acidity.

To use the last of a jar of mustard or mayonnaise • For approximately every tablespoon of mayonnaise or mustard left in the jar, add ¼ cup each oil and wine vinegar or lemon juice, ½ minced garlic clove, and 1 teaspoon any seasoning (a combination of salt and dried Italian herb seasoning works well). Fasten the lid and shake to mix. Makes about ⅔ cup.

HONEY-MUSTARD DRESSING Whisk together **2 tablespoons spicy brown mustard, ¼ cup cider vinegar, 1 tablespoon *each* apple juice and honey, ½ cup vegetable oil, ¼ teaspoon salt,** and **⅛ teaspoon ground black pepper.** *Makes 1 cup.*

S

EASY RANCH DRESSING Whisk together ¼ **cup mayonnaise, 1 teaspoon cider vinegar, 3 tablespoons buttermilk, 1 teaspoon seasoned salt (or salt-free seasoning blend), ½ teaspoon onion powder, 2 minced garlic cloves,** and ¼ **teaspoon ground black pepper.**
Makes about ½ cup.

REAL RUSSIAN DRESSING Whisk together ¼ **cup** *each* **mayonnaise and sour cream, 2 tablespoons ketchup,** and **3 tablespoons lemon juice.** Fold in **2 tablespoons red** or **black caviar.** For Quick Russian Dressing, omit the caviar.
Makes about 1 cup.

ITALIAN TOMATO DRESSING Whisk together **3 tablespoons tomato puree, ½ minced garlic clove, 2 tablespoons red wine vinegar, ⅓ cup olive oil, 1 tablespoon chopped fresh herbs (basil works well), ½ teaspoon salt,** and ¼ **teaspoon ground black pepper.**
Makes about ¾ cup.

ORANGE-BASIL YOGURT DRESSING Whisk together **½ cup plain yogurt, the grated zest and juice of ½ orange, 1 minced garlic clove, ½ teaspoon** *each* **chopped fresh parsley and salt,** and ¼ **teaspoon** *each* **dried basil and ground black pepper.** *Makes about ¾ cup.*

FOUR QUICK VINAIGRETTES

Because vinaigrette is so simple, it is important to start with good-quality ingredients such as extra-virgin olive oil and high-quality wine vinegar. For each recipe below, follow the Basic Vinaigrette recipe, altering ingredients as necessary to make the flavor variations. Each recipes makes about ¾ cup.

Basic Vinaigrette: In a bowl or a jar with a tight-fitting lid, combine **½ minced garlic clove** or **1 small finely chopped shallot, 3 tablespoons red wine vinegar,** and **½ teaspoon** *each* Dijon mustard and salt. Whisk or shake until salt dissolves. Add about **½ cup extra-virgin olive oil,** drop by drop, to the bowl; as the ingredients begin to blend, add the oil in a steady trickle. If using a jar, add about ¼ teaspoon, shake vigorously, then add remaining oil and shake until blended. Add **½ teaspoon ground black pepper** to either the vinaigrette or the salad itself.

Creamy Vinaigrette: Replace red wine vinegar with ¼ **cup white wine vinegar** or **apple cider vinegar.** After adding oil, add ¼ **cup heavy cream** and **1 to 2 tablespoons chopped fresh herbs.**

Citrus Vinaigrette: Add **1 teaspoon grated lemon** and/or **lime zest** along with mustard. Replace vinegar with ¼ **cup fresh lemon** and/or **lime juice.**

Greek Vinaigrette: Replace red wine vinegar with lemon juice. Add ¼ **cup finely crumbled feta cheese** and **3 tablespoons** *each* **chopped fresh mint and chopped kalamata olives.**

EGGLESS CAESAR DRESSING Mix together **1 crushed garlic clove, 2 finely chopped anchovy fillets,** and **1 tablespoon Dijon mustard.** Add **1 tablespoon red wine vinegar, 1½ teaspoons lemon juice,** and **2 teaspoons Worcestershire sauce.** In a slow, steady stream, whisk in **½ cup olive oil.** Stir in **1 tablespoon grated Parmesan cheese** and **¼ teaspoon** *each* **salt and ground black pepper.** *Makes about ¾ cup.*

HOT-PEPPER PEANUT VINAIGRETTE Mix together **¼ minced garlic clove, 2 finely chopped scallions, ½ teaspoon hot-pepper sauce, 3 tablespoons rice wine vinegar, 1 teaspoon** *each* **soy sauce and finely chopped fresh ginger, a pinch** *each* **ground cumin and ground coriander,** and **2 tablespoons** *each* **peanut butter and vegetable oil.** *Makes about ⅔ cup.*

BALSAMIC VINAIGRETTE In a jar with a tight-fitting lid, combine **½ cup olive oil, ¼ cup balsamic vinegar, 1 tablespoon lemon juice, 1 minced garlic clove, a pinch of ground red pepper, ½ teaspoon salt,** and **¼ teaspoon ground black pepper.** Seal and shake until mixed. Shake each time you use it. *Makes ¾ cup.*

HEALTHY HINTS ▼ **To reduce saturated fat in creamy dressings** • Replace ½ cup of mayonnaise with half an avocado that has been pureed in a food processor or blender. This makes a delicious green dressing.

To replace oil in dressings • Substitute strong brewed tea for one-third of the oil in a standard vinaigrette. (The tea helps balance the acidity of the vinegar.) Or whisk in other liquids, such as broth, fruit juice, fruit nectars, fruit purees, vegetable juice, or vegetable purees. If using thin liquids such as fruit juice or broth, thicken the dressing with cornstarch, arrowroot, or gelatin so that it coats the greens better. To make a tomato-flavored vinaigrette with extra body, you can cut 1 fresh tomato in half and grate the halves on a hand grater into a bowl (the skins will be left behind). Use the fresh tomato pulp to replace about one-fourth of the oil. Another way to add body to a reduced-oil dressing is to puree it in a blender with ¼ cup well-cooked rice or a chunk of cooked potato.

BASIC LOW-FAT VINAIGRETTE In a small bowl or jar with a tight-fitting lid, combine **¼ cup chicken broth** or **apple juice, ¼ cup red wine vinegar, 2 tablespoons olive oil, 1 teaspoon Dijon mustard,** and **½ teaspoon** *each* **honey and salt.** Seal and shake until blended. *Makes about ⅔ cup.*

FRESH FRUIT DRESSING In a blender or food processor, combine **½ cup chopped fruit** (strawberries, ripe pears, peaches, or other fruit), **¼ cup lemon yogurt, 1 tablespoon lime juice,** and **1 teaspoon** *each* **honey and Dijon mustard.** Puree until smooth. Use to drizzle on fruit salads or green salads. *Makes about ¾ cup.*

RASPBERRY-MERLOT DRESSING In a blender or food processor, combine **5 tablespoons olive oil, ⅓ cup Merlot** or **fruity red wine, ½ pint fresh** or **frozen dry-packed raspberries, 1 sliced**

S

FIVE LOW-FAT CREAMY SALAD DRESSINGS

Rich, creamy salad dressings don't have to be sky-high in fat and calories. Try the basic recipe below or make the variations. Each makes about 1½ cups.

Basic Low-Fat Creamy Dressing: Whisk together ¾ cup low-fat mayonnaise, ½ cup fat-free sour cream, 2 tablespoons white wine vinegar, 1 teaspoon *each* Worcestershire sauce and Dijon mustard, and ¼ teaspoon ground black pepper.

Low-Fat Green Goddess Dressing: Stir in 3 tablespoons *each* chopped scallions and chopped fresh parsley, and ½ crushed garlic clove.

Low-Fat Russian Dressing: Add ⅓ cup bottled chili sauce, 2 tablespoons *each* chopped celery and pimiento, and another 1 teaspoon Worcestershire sauce.

Low-Fat Creamy Italian Dressing: Add 1 teaspoon jarred roasted garlic, ¼ teaspoon dried oregano, 1 chopped scallion, and ¼ cup chopped fresh basil.

Low-Fat Ranch Dressing: Replace the white wine vinegar with cider vinegar. Add ½ cup shredded carrots; 1 tablespoon chopped fresh parsley; ½ teaspoon *each* sugar, dried celery flakes, and celery seeds; and ¼ teaspoon onion powder.

---

shallot, 2 tablespoons *each* **low-fat sour cream and red wine vinegar, 2 teaspoons honey,** and ¼ **teaspoon** *each* **salt and ground black pepper.** Puree until smooth. *Makes about 1¼ cups.*

Salads *see also* Lettuce; Pasta; Potatoes; Rice

There are some basic guidelines, but there are few rules for making a salad. Just about any ingredient you can think of can go into one: Eggs, meat, beans, grains, fruit, fish, nuts, bread, and pasta are all fine salad ingredients. Some salads include cooked ingredients; others are made up entirely of raw vegetables. Many are served chilled, but some are best at room temperature.

BASICS **To make a green salad** • Buy the freshest greens you can find. Look at the greens closely and take a small taste if you can.

Pass by any that are wilted, overly bitter, limp, or browned. Remove the stems from small-leafed greens, such as watercress, arugula, or young spinach, but leave the leaves whole. Trim large-leaf greens, such as romaine or escarole, by tearing the leaves along the central rib. Make sure that all greens are completely dry. Excess water will prevent dressing from clinging to the leaves. Also, serve green salads immediately after dressing because the acid in the dressing will quickly wilt the leaves.

To dry a large amount of greens • Place them in a clean pillowcase and swing the case in wide circles, like a propeller, to fling off excess water (you may need to do this outside).

To make a pasta salad • After draining the pasta, toss it immediately with a tablespoon or two of olive oil to prevent the pasta from sticking as it cools. Tossing with oil is preferable to rinsing the pasta under cold water, which washes away much of the starch that helps the dressing cling to the pasta. Also, make sure that the pasta has cooled completely before combining it with any dressing. If the pasta is still warm, it will absorb too much of the dressing. It's best to cut any vegetables to about the same size as the pasta. This way, the salad will be easy to toss and to eat, and it will look better too.

PROBLEM SOLVERS ▼

To refresh wilting greens • Place them in ice water mixed with 2 tablespoons lemon juice and refrigerate 1 hour. Drain well, wrap in toweling, and keep them bagged in the refrigerator for at least 4 hours.

To prevent salad from becoming soggy • Wait to dress it until just before serving. Also, serve on chilled plates.

To save a salad with too much added dressing • Toss in additional greens and other ingredients.

To make perfect slices of hard-boiled eggs for garnishing a salad • Use an egg slicer or a wire cheese knife.

TIME SAVERS ▼

To save prep time • When chopping vegetables for salad, always cut extra and store them in zipper-lock plastic bags in the refrigerator. Next time you make a salad, they'll be ready to go. Whenever you can, buy precut vegetables, such as lettuce and lettuce mixes, shredded carrots, shredded or chopped cabbage, coleslaw mix, broccoli slaw, broccoli florets, celery sticks, cauliflower florets, and sliced mushrooms. You can also buy prewashed greens for salads, such as arugula, baby lettuces, baby spinach, and whole leaf spinach. Prewashed greens can be tossed into a salad as is; they usually need no trimming or washing, saving loads of prep time.

To skip blanching broccoli and cauliflower • Broccoli and cauliflower are often too fibrous and strong-tasting to add to salads raw. Many recipes call for them to be blanched first. Save yourself some time and use frozen and thawed vegetables instead. Or try bagged broccoli slaw from the supermarket. This form of shredded broccoli works well with any coleslaw dressing or tossed into salads.

To quickly add peas to a salad • Instead of simmering peas before adding to salad, use frozen peas and run them under cold water for 1 minute to thaw.

To quickly toss salad and dressing • Add the dressing right to the lettuce storage bag. Close the bag and shake until the leaves are coated.

To save cleanup time • Mix up salad dressing right in the salad bowl. Then, add the salad ingredients and toss.

To use leftover salads • Leftover meat, fish, pasta, and bean salads make great sandwich fillings. Split a pita pocket, stuff with the leftover salad, and garnish with fresh lettuce and chopped tomato.

EASY COLESLAW Toss **1 pound prechopped coleslaw mix** with **3 tablespoons bottled creamy coleslaw dressing, 3 tablespoons bottled Russian dressing, 2 large cored and coarsely grated Granny Smith apples,** and **1 bunch thinly sliced scallions.**
Makes 4 servings.

FAST SALMON AND WHITE BEAN SALAD Here's a wonderful way to use leftover salmon. In a large bowl, whisk **2 tablespoons olive oil** with **¼ cup wine vinegar, ½ teaspoon red-pepper flakes,** and **¼ teaspoon** *each* **salt and ground black pepper. Add 1½ cups** *each* **flaked cooked** or **canned salmon fillet and rinsed and drained canned white beans, 4 large thinly sliced scal-**

S

Salad Gazpacho

Never throw out leftover green salad. The vision of soggy lettuce, darkening mushrooms, and sodden croutons are cause for celebration, for they will provide you with everything you need for the best and easiest gazpacho ever.

2 **cups wilted dressed salad, tightly packed**

1 **small onion, chopped**

1 **large garlic clove, minced**

2–3 **cups vegetable cocktail juice**

2 **teaspoons hot-pepper sauce**

1 **cup seasoned croutons**

In a food processor or blender, combine the salad, onion, and garlic. Process until coarsely chopped. Transfer to a large bowl. Stir in 2 cups of the vegetable juice for a chunky gazpacho. For a soupier gazpacho, stir in an additional 1 cup vegetable juice. Add the hot-pepper sauce. Divide among 4 chilled bowls. Top with the croutons.

Makes about 4 cups

S

lions, **1 finely chopped small red onion, 2 tablespoons chopped fresh parsley,** and **1 minced garlic clove.** Toss to mix. Garnish with **12 chopped pitted kalamata olives.** *Makes 4 servings.*

EASY PESTO PASTA SALAD Mix **¼ cup jarred pesto sauce, 2 tablespoons extra-virgin olive oil, 1 drained can (6 ounces) flaked white water-packed tuna, 1 cup cooked shaped pasta such as rotelle, 1 seeded and chopped tomato,** and **the chopped white parts of 2 scallions.** *Makes 4 servings.*

FLAVOR TIPS ▼ **To spruce up purchased coleslaw** • Add a spoonful of orange marmalade and some toasted almonds.

To add bulk to a mix of mesclun greens • Add chopped red cabbage.

To boost flavor in green salads • Use a mix of flavorful greens such as chicory, endive, arugula, spinach, or radicchio. You can also add leaves or sprigs of fresh herbs, such as parsley, rosemary, thyme, cilantro, tarragon, basil, oregano, or chives.

To add instant color and panache • Toss in some edible flowers, such as nasturtium, violets, chive blossoms, or roses. See page 189 for more on edible flowers.

BROCCOLI SLAW Toss together **2 finely chopped Granny Smith apples, 1 finely chopped celery rib, 1 pound precut broccoli florets (or packaged shredded broccoli), ⅔ cup raisins, ¼ teaspoon ground ginger,** and **3 tablespoons** *each* **toasted walnut pieces, mayonnaise, and sour cream.** *Makes 4 servings.*

Chicken Salad Three Ways

What's your pleasure: Chinese, Italian, or Tex-Mex? Here's the Chinese chicken salad, redolent with the aromas of sesame oil, ginger, scallions, and soy sauce. Try the variations, too.

1½	**pounds boneless, skinless chicken breast halves**
1	**cup cold water**
2	**tablespoons rice vinegar**
2	**teaspoons Dijon mustard**
2	**teaspoons toasted sesame oil**
2	**teaspoons grated fresh ginger**
1	**teaspoon soy sauce**
½	**teaspoon salt**
¼	**teaspoon ground black pepper**
3	**tablespoons peanut oil or vegetable oil**
3	**scallions, chopped**

1. Place the chicken and water in a medium saucepan. Bring to a simmer over medium-high heat. Reduce the heat to medium-low and cook gently until a thermometer inserted in the thickest portion registers 160°F and the juices run clear, 15 to 20 minutes, turning occasionally. Remove the pan and set it aside until cool enough to handle. Do not pour out the broth.

2. Boil the broth over high heat until reduced to ¼ cup, 6 to 8 minutes. Cut the chicken into ¾" cubes. Place in a serving bowl and toss with the reduced broth.

3. In a medium bowl, whisk together the vinegar, mustard, sesame oil, ginger, soy sauce, salt, and pepper. Gradually whisk in the peanut or vegetable oil. Pour this dressing over the chicken. Add the scallions and toss.

Makes 4 to 6 servings

Italian Chicken Salad: Substitute olive oil for the peanut oil and lemon juice for the vinegar. Omit the sesame oil (or replace it with extra olive oil). Substitute 1 minced garlic clove for the ginger. Omit the soy sauce and add ½ teaspoon dried oregano. Roast, peel, and chop 1 large red bell pepper and add along with ¼ cup shredded fresh basil. Serve on salad plates or use it to stuff peeled, seeded, and hollowed beefsteak tomatoes.

Tex-Mex Chicken Salad: Substitute corn oil or olive oil for the peanut oil. Substitute lime juice for the vinegar. Omit the sesame oil. Substitute 1 minced garlic clove for the ginger. Omit the soy sauce and add ½ teaspoon ground cumin and ½ teaspoon dried oregano. Add 1 cup corn kernels, 1 to 2 teaspoons finely chopped fresh or pickled jalapeño chile peppers and ¼ cup fresh cilantro leaves.

S

Shrimp and Pasta Shell Salad

The saltiness of brine-cured olives is tempered by the sweetness of roasted red bell peppers in this summery salad. Half of the shrimp are ground, adding considerable flavor and texture. This tastes best after chilling an hour or two.

- **1 pound medium shrimp, peeled and deveined**
- **8 ounces medium pasta shells**
- **2 tablespoons olive oil**
- **½ cup chopped pitted black olives, such as kalamata, divided**
- **½ cup chopped roasted red bell pepper or jarred pimientos**
- **2 scallions, sliced**
- **¼ cup chopped fresh parsley**
- **¼ cup mayonnaise**
- **2 tablespoons lemon juice**
- **1 tablespoon small capers**
- **¾ teaspoon salt**
- **¼ teaspoon ground black pepper**

1. Place the shrimp in a large saucepan over medium heat. Cover with 2 cups cold water. Bring to a bare simmer. (Do not boil.) Cook until opaque, 2 to 3 minutes. Drain and rinse under cold water.

2. Meanwhile, cook the pasta according to package directions. Drain and rinse with cold water. Place the pasta in a serving bowl. Add the oil. Toss to coat.

3. In a food processor, combine half the shrimp and half the olives. Pulse to grind. Pour this mixture over the pasta. Cut the remaining shrimp in half. Add to the pasta along with the remaining olives, the red pepper or pimientos, and the scallions and parsley. Add the mayonnaise, lemon juice, capers, salt, and black pepper. Toss to coat. Cover and chill for 1 to 2 hours before serving.

Makes about 6 cups

WATERCRESS AND FENNEL SALAD Arrange **1 bunch trimmed watercress** on a serving plate. Thinly slice **2 bulbs fresh fennel,** reserving some of the green fronds for garnish. Place over watercress. Remove sections from **1 grapefruit** and arrange on salad. In a small bowl, whisk together **2 tablespoons** *each* **olive oil, balsamic vinegar, and grapefruit juice; ¼ teaspoon salt;** and **6 drops red hot-pepper sauce.** Drizzle over salad, garnish with fennel greens, and serve. *Makes 4 servings.*

ASIAN CUCUMBER SALAD In a large bowl, whisk together **1 tablespoon** *each* **rice wine vinegar and soy sauce, 2 teaspoons grated fresh ginger, 1 teaspoon sesame oil,** and **1 chopped shallot.** Stir in **1½ halved and thinly**

SALADS FROM THE PANTRY

There are at least a week's worth of entrée and side salads lurking in your kitchen. Frozen vegetables, canned beans, dried pasta, brown rice, pickles, artichoke hearts, peppers, salsa, tuna, and salad dressings are all waiting patiently to become dinner. Here are three throw-together salads to spark your imagination. Each makes 4 servings.

Succotash Salad: Whisk together ⅓ cup vegetable oil, ¼ cup cider vinegar, 3 tablespoons honey, 2 teaspoons brown mustard, ½ teaspoon salt, and ¼ teaspoon ground black pepper. Add 2 cups *each* canned corn kernels, frozen and thawed lima beans, and chopped ham, and ¼ cup finely chopped sweet pickles. Toss to mix.

Chickpea, Tomato, and Onion Salad: Toss together 2 cups canned chickpeas, ⅓ chopped red onion, 1 chopped tomato, 3 tablespoons *each* lemon juice and extra-virgin olive oil, ⅛ teaspoon red-pepper flakes, 2 tablespoons finely chopped fresh parsley, ½ teaspoon salt, and ¼ teaspoon ground black pepper. Chill.

Rice and Bean Salad: Toss 2 cups leftover rice with 2 cups canned black beans, 2 finely chopped jarred roasted red bell peppers, ½ minced garlic clove, ¼ cup *each* olive oil and red wine vinegar, the juice of 1 lime, 1 tablespoon chopped fresh parsley, ¼ teaspoon salt, and ⅛ teaspoon ground black pepper.

sliced cucumbers and 2 tablespoons chopped fresh cilantro. Let stand at least 30 minutes. Serve chilled. *Makes 4 servings.*

Chef's Tip: Caesar Cardini invented the Caesar Salad at Caesar's Restaurant in Tijuana, Mexico, during the 1920s. At that time, he used just the small inner leaves of romaine hearts, leaving them whole so that they could be picked up and eaten. Try this method the next time you make a Caesar salad.

HEALTHY HINT ▼ **To get more nutrients in salad greens •** Choose the darker-colored greens, which are generally more nutritious than their paler counterparts.

CURRIED CARROT SLAW In a large bowl, combine 3 tablespoons *each* low-fat mayonnaise and low-fat sour cream, 1 tablespoon cider vinegar, 2 teaspoons honey, ½ teaspoon curry powder, and ⅛ teaspoon ground ginger. Stir in 6 shredded carrots, ½ cup chopped fresh mint, ½ teaspoon salt, and ¼ teaspoon ground black pepper. *Makes 4 servings.*

Salmon *see also* Fish; Doneness Tests and Temperatures (page 572)

We have made great progress in farm-raising salmon. However, farmed salmon will never taste the same as wild salmon, which have deeper, more complex flavors.

BASICS ▼ **To choose •** Most varieties of salmon come from the Pacific coast of North America and range in color from pale pink to bright red. Chinook (or king) salmon is

S

Glazed Salmon with Warm Lentil, Apple, and Pecan Salad

Salmon is loaded with heart-healthy omega-3 fatty acids. Here's a delicious way to eat well and stay healthy.

Salmon

- **1 tablespoon soy sauce**
- **1 tablespoon honey**
- **1 teaspoon grated fresh ginger**
- **4 salmon fillets (1" thick), about 1½ pounds**
- **1 can (14½ ounces) vegetable or chicken broth**
- **¾ cup water**
- **3 scallions, chopped**

- **1 cup (7 ounces) green or brown lentils, picked over and rinsed**
- **2 carrots, quartered lengthwise and thinly sliced**
- **2 teaspoons chopped fresh rosemary**
- **¼ teaspoon salt**

Dressing

- **2 tablespoons lemon juice**
- **1 tablespoon honey**
- **2 teaspoons olive oil**

considered the best for its rich, soft flesh, which can be pink or red. Coho (or silver) salmon, a more firm-textured variety, tends to have red-orange flesh. Sockeye (or red) salmon has firm, deep red flesh.

To remove bones from a fillet • Even a so-called boned salmon fillet can be rid-

dled with tiny "pin" bones. These are easily and best removed before marinating or cooking. Lay the fillet flat, skin side down, and run your hand over the salmon in two directions until you locate any bones. Pull them out one at a time using a pair of clean tweezers or needle-nose pliers.

PROBLEM SOLVER ▼ **To transform a salmon fillet into the likeness of a salmon steak** • Cut the fillet crosswise, taking care not to cut through the skin. Fold the halves away from each other so that the skin sides are back-to-back. To keep the halves in place when cooking and especially when flipping, run a skewer through them.

1   **teaspoon mild hot-pepper sauce, such as Frank's**

1   **teaspoon white wine vinegar**

1   **teaspoon reduced-sodium soy sauce**

1   **Gala apple, cored and cut into ½" pieces**

½   **cup toasted pecans, chopped and divided**

3   **scallions, sliced**

1. *To make the salmon:* In an 11" × 7" baking dish, combine the soy sauce, honey, and ginger. Add the fish and toss with the soy sauce mixture to glaze. Arrange the fish, flesh side down, in the glaze. Set aside in the refrigerator to marinate. Preheat the oven to 375°F.

2. In a medium saucepan, bring the broth, water, and scallions to a simmer. Stir in the lentils. Cover and simmer 25 minutes. Stir in the carrots, rosemary, and salt. Simmer until the lentils are tender, 10 minutes longer. Drain and place in a bowl to cool.

3. Meanwhile, turn the fish, flesh side up, in the baking dish. Bake until opaque, 12 to 16 minutes.

4. *To make the dressing:* In a small bowl, whisk together the lemon juice, honey, oil, hot-pepper sauce, vinegar, and soy sauce until blended. Add the apple and toss to coat. Just before serving, toss in the lentil mixture and ¼ cup of the pecans.

5. Spoon the salad onto a serving platter. Top with the fish and sprinkle with the remaining ¼ cup pecans and the scallions.

Makes 4 servings

TIME SAVERS ▼

To save prep time • Whenever you cook salmon, make extra. Leftovers chill well for a day or two and can be quickly tossed into pasta or salads.

To add to potato or pasta salad • Break leftover cooked, boned, and skinned salmon into chunks and gently fold it into your favorite potato or pasta salad. A little bit of fresh dill and lemon juice will enhance the flavors beautifully.

FAST SALMON SOUP Cut ½ **pound cooked boneless, skinless salmon fillet** into ¼"-thick slices. Set aside. In a saucepan, stir together **4 cups chicken broth, 1 small minced garlic clove,** and **1 teaspoon grated fresh ginger.** Bring to a boil. Remove from heat and immediately stir in reserved salmon and **4 thinly sliced scallions.** Cover and let rest 1 minute. *Makes 4 servings.*

FLAVOR TIPS ▼

To accompany salmon • Just about any flavored mayonnaise (see page 273) or vinaigrette (see page 423) will be welcome with cooked salmon. Also try sorrel: It has a sour flavor that blends well with salmon's slightly sweet taste.

NORWEGIAN SAUCE FOR SALMON Peel and seed **2 cucumbers.** Coarsely grate into a bowl. Toss with **2 table-**

THREE MARINADES FOR SALMON

Use any of these marinades to flavor 1½ pounds salmon steaks or fillets. Marinate in the refrigerator for 1 hour, then remove the fish from the marinade. Either bake at 425°F for 10 to 15 minutes or grill over a medium-hot fire for 4 to 5 minutes per side. Salmon steaks are done when they are just barely opaque; fillets are done when opaque.

Herb-Mustard Marinade: Mix together **2** minced garlic cloves, **¼ cup** *each* chopped fresh dill and olive oil, **3** tablespoons Dijon mustard, **2** tablespoons white wine vinegar, **½** teaspoon salt, and **¼** teaspoon ground black pepper.

Provençal Marinade: Mix together **3** minced garlic cloves, **2** mashed anchovies, **1** teaspoon ground fennel seeds, a pinch of red-pepper flakes, **½** cup *each* white wine and crushed tomatoes, **¼** cup extra-virgin olive oil, the juice and grated zest of **½** orange, **½** teaspoon salt, and **¼** teaspoon ground black pepper.

Asian-Style Marinade: Mix together **¼** cup *each* soy sauce, rice vinegar, honey, and water; **1½** tablespoons grated fresh ginger; **1** tablespoon *each* peanut oil and dry sherry; **1** teaspoon sesame oil; **½** teaspoon ground ginger; and **¼** teaspoon bottled chili paste.

S

spoons cider vinegar and **1 teaspoon salt.** Turn out into a sieve and let drain 30 minutes. Press out excess liquid and return to the bowl. Add **½ small grated onion, ½ cup sour cream, 1 tablespoon lemon juice, 3 tablespoons chopped fresh dill,** and **⅛ teaspoon ground black pepper.** Serve with poached salmon (hot or cold). *Makes about 2½ cups.*

MISO SALMON IN A BAG Place a regular-size foil oven bag in a shallow baking pan (oven bags are available in most grocery stores). Lightly coat the inside of the bag with cooking spray. Combine **2½ cups (12 ounces) diagonally sliced fresh asparagus, 2 teaspoons** *each* **grated fresh ginger and toasted sesame oil,** and **½ teaspoon salt.** Add to the bag. Top with **two 1"-thick pieces salmon fillet (6 to 8 ounces**

each). In a bowl, mix **3 tablespoons sake, 1½ tablespoons miso, 1½ teaspoons** *each* **sugar and lemon juice, 2 sliced scallions,** and another **1 teaspoon grated fresh ginger.** Spoon over salmon. Fold in the edges of the bag to seal it, and bake at 450°F until fish is opaque, 18 to 20 minutes. Garnish with **1 teaspoon toasted sesame seeds,** and serve hot. *Makes 4 servings.*

Salsa

Highly seasoned salsas characterize much of the Mexican food that is served in America. The word itself simply means "sauce," and while traditional versions are based on tomatoes (or tomatillos in *salsa verde*), many American cooks have expanded salsas to include ingredients such as fresh fruits, corn, and beans.

BASICS
▼

To choose • There are three general categories of salsa. One is thin, sharp-tasting, vinegar-laced hot-pepper sauce, which is freely splashed onto tacos, empanadas, and scrambled eggs. Another is the relishlike *pico de gallo* or *salsa cruda,* chunky with tomatoes, chile peppers, and onions, which is used primarily with tortilla chips. (Fruit, corn, and bean salsas also fall into this category.) Finally, there are cooked salsas such as *salsa verde* and enchilada sauce, which are spooned liberally over tacos, tamales, and enchiladas.

To make the best-tasting fresh tomato salsa • Use vine-ripened tomatoes in season. If tomatoes are not in season, rely on plum tomatoes. They tend to have more flavor and denser flesh than other out-of-season tomatoes.

To make salsa with a traditional rustic texture • Chop the ingredients by hand. The finer the ingredients are chopped, the better the flavors will blend.

To get the best flavor and texture • Let salsa stand at room temperature an hour or two before serving. The flavors are best when they've had a chance to meld.

PROBLEM SOLVERS
▼

To avoid watery salsa • Seed the tomatoes before chopping them.

To avoid a mushy texture • Don't let fresh salsas stand at room temperature for more than 3 to 4 hours. The acidic ingredients will soften the salsa and ruin its fresh textures.

FLAVOR TIPS
▼

To freshen up bottled salsa • Add about ¼ cup chopped fresh cilantro and 1 teaspoon lime juice or lemon juice to 1 bottle (16 ounces) salsa.

To use as a topping • Salsa makes a no-fuss sauce for topping grilled chicken, turkey, pork, fish, or baked potatoes.

To season rice with salsa • Stir 1 cup salsa into 2 cups cooked rice.

FRESH TOMATO SALSA In a bowl, combine **4 large seeded and chopped summer tomatoes; ⅔ finely chopped sweet onion** (or 4 finely chopped scallions); **⅓ cup finely chopped fresh cilantro; 1 to 2 seeded and finely chopped fresh jalapeño chile peppers (leave the seeds in for more heat); 2 teaspoons lime juice;** and **1 teaspoon salt.** Toss, let sit 1 hour at room temperature, and serve. Great spooned over soft tacos or for scooping up with corn chips. *Makes about 3¼ cups.*

FRAGRANT CORN SALSA Combine the kernels cut from **2 ears cooked corn (or 2½ cups canned corn), ½ finely chopped red bell pepper, 1 tablespoon chopped fresh cilantro, 1 teaspoon** *each* **finely chopped jalapeño chile pepper and ground cumin, ½ teaspoon salt,** and **¼ teaspoon ground black pepper.** *Makes 2½ cups.*

BASIC GREEN SALSA Remove and discard papery husks from **8 large tomatillos** and place tomatillos in a saucepan. Cover with water and heat to boiling. Reduce heat to medium-low and simmer until tender, 5 minutes. Remove tomatillos with a slotted spoon and mash with a fork. Set the cooking liquid aside. Stir **⅓ chopped onion, 1 minced garlic clove, ½ teaspoon salt,** and **⅛ teaspoon red-pepper flakes (or more to taste)** into the tomatillos. Add enough of the reserved cooking liquid to make the mixture saucy. *Makes about 2¼ cups.*

S

SALSA RANCHERA Chop **3 slices meaty smoked bacon** and brown in a skillet until crisp and cooked through. Drain on paper towels. Spoon off all but 2 teaspoons fat. Add **1 chopped onion** and **1 to 2 seeded and finely chopped jalapeño chile peppers (leave the seeds in for more heat).** Cook over medium heat until soft, about 3 minutes. Add **2 pounds (4 large) peeled, seeded, and chopped tomatoes (or one drained and chopped 28-ounce can tomatoes); ½ pound roasted, peeled, and chopped poblano chile peppers** (wear plastic gloves when handling; or use 1 drained and chopped 4-ounce can mild green chile peppers); **1 teaspoon salt;** and **¼ teaspoon ground black pepper.** Simmer until slightly reduced and flavors blend, 15 to 20 minutes. Remove from heat and stir in cooked bacon and **3 tablespoons chopped fresh cilantro.** Use to top fried eggs served on softened corn tortillas and sprinkled with grated *queso Cotija,* farmer cheese, or Parmesan cheese.

Makes about 2 cups.

FENNEL-ORANGE SALSA Combine **1 trimmed and finely chopped fennel bulb, 1 small chopped scallion, 4 sectioned and chopped seedless oranges, 1 tablespoon chopped fresh basil, 2 teaspoons lemon juice, ¼ teaspoon** *each* **salt and ground black pepper, a pinch** *each* **red-pepper flakes** and **sugar,** and **1 peeled, pitted, and chopped avocado.** *Makes 3 cups.*

Salt

Salt is known to have more than 14,000 uses. Its use in cooking makes up less than 4 percent of the total salt produced each year.

PROBLEM SOLVERS ▼

To fill a salt shaker without spilling • Use a plastic funnel. Or make a cone with a piece of paper.

To prevent salt from clumping and clogging shakers • Add ½ teaspoon raw rice grains to the shaker to absorb moisture. If you keep your salt in a tub or crock, tie the rice in cheesecloth or a coffee filter and add it to the salt like a bouquet garni. Change the rice once a year. Or you can stir 1 tablespoon cornstarch into a 1-pound container of salt.

To prevent oversalting foods • Store salt in a small bowl or tub and use your fingers to sprinkle it over foods. This gives you more control and a better sense of how much salt you are using. Also, season foods near the end of cooking time. Many foods contain natural amounts of sodium that are concentrated during the cooking process. Be conservative. You can always add more salt; it's harder to take it back.

To fix an oversalted dish • If the dish has a bit of liquid in it, drop in a few peeled potato slices for the last 10 minutes of cooking. The potato will absorb some of the excess salt. Discard the potato before serving. You could also add more of everything except salt, perhaps doubling the recipe to balance the salt. Or try balancing the recipe by stirring in 1 teaspoon each sugar and white vinegar; cook 3 minutes, and taste for balance. Add more sugar and vinegar if needed. Or, if the dish is raw, you can rinse it with water to remove excess salt. To remove the saltiness of brined olives or feta cheese, soak them in cold water for several hours or overnight, changing the soaking water once.

Fascinating Fact: Salt can be traced back to 6500 B.C., when it was mined in Salzburg, Austria (translated as "salt town"). It has long been believed that the Devil hated salt and that throwing it in his face would banish the

PASS THE SALT: BUT WHICH ONE?

Salt is more than a flavor jump-start. It is one of the four basic flavors and an essential nutrient that our bodies rightfully crave. Often incorrectly referred to as sodium, salt consists of 40 percent sodium and 60 percent chloride. While all salts originate from the sea, a number of the major North American salt mines are nowhere near a presently existing ocean. Salt is concentrated in underground deposits in unexpected places such as Kansas, Ohio, and Michigan, which were at one point covered by the ocean.

As a general rule, use coarse salt crystals in cooking water or to sprinkle onto or into foods for seasoning. Fine-grained salts are preferred for most baking because they measure and dissolve evenly. Here's a guide to common forms of salt available today.

Table Salt: One of the most widely used salts, table salt goes through a refining process that removes traces of other naturally occurring minerals. Chemical additives such as sodium silicoaluminate, calcium phosphate, or magnesium carbonate are sometimes blended in to prevent clumping. Table salt and iodized salt are preferred in baking for their fine-grained texture and accuracy of measure.

Iodized Salt: A form of table salt, iodized salt is fortified with iodine that was lost during processing. Iodized salt was the first "functional food," fortified in the early 1920s in response to a Midwest-focused epidemic of goiter (hyperthyroidism) that was caused by iodine deficiencies.

Kosher Salt: This inexpensive coarse salt is evaporated from a brine, usually under specific conditions approved by the Orthodox Jewish faith. It contains no additives or added iodine. Kosher salt is popular among chefs because its coarse texture makes it easy to pinch up between your fingers and sprinkle onto foods. Measure for measure, 1 teaspoon of kosher salt contains less salt than the same amount of table or iodized salt.

Sea Salt: Available in both fine and coarse grains, sea salt has become increasingly available in markets but at a higher cost than table or kosher salt. Sea salt is made from evaporated sea water. Some salt farmers evaporate the water in enclosed bays along the shoreline, then rake up the salt by hand. This type of salt tends to include several naturally present trace minerals, such as iodine, magnesium, and potassium, which give sea salt a fresher, lighter flavor than standard table salt. Expensive varieties, such as *sel gris, Esprit du Sel,* and *Fleur de Sel* from France are usually gray in color and slightly moist. These are best used where their tremendous flavor and presence is pronounced, such as on a boiled potato or a slice of tomato. You can also get pink, brown, and black sea salts from India.

Rock Salt: Sold in large crystals, rock salt has a grayish hue because it is unrefined. Rock salt makes a great bed for serving oysters and clams. Or combine it with ice to make ice cream in hand-cranked ice cream makers.

S

HERBAL SALT SUBSTITUTES

Instead of using salt, try these herb mixes to boost the flavor of meats, poultry, fish, vegetables, pastas, and casseroles. Each makes about ¼ cup. Store them in your spice cabinet.

Mixed Herb Blend: Combine **2** tablespoons dried parsley, **1** tablespoon dried tarragon, and **2** teaspoons *each* dried oregano and celery flakes.

Lemon-Pepper Blend: Combine **1** tablespoon *each* store-bought dried lemon peel and garlic powder, **2** teaspoons dried oregano, and **½** teaspoon ground white pepper.

Italian Blend: Combine **1** tablespoon *each* dried basil and marjoram, **2** teaspoons *each* garlic powder and dried oregano, **1** teaspoon crushed dried rosemary, and **¼** teaspoon *each* dried thyme and ground red pepper.

creature. (The Devil, of course, could be found over your left shoulder.) Some cultures sprinkled salt on the thresholds and in corners of new homes to ward off the evil one, and Catholics once put salt on a baby's tongue as part of their baptism services.

Sandwiches

Set just about anything on any type of bread and you've made a sandwich. But credit for "inventing" the sandwich goes to the Fourth Earl of Sandwich (1718–1792). It is said that he couldn't bear to leave the gambling table, so he brought his meals right to the table between slices of bread. It caught on. Today, sandwiches are one of the world's most popular forms of food.

PROBLEM SOLVERS ▼

To make an easy-to-eat sandwich • Make sure that all the ingredients are securely enclosed by 2 slices of bread, wrapped in a tortilla, or stuffed into a pita. If the sandwich is made of many small ingredients, spread the bread with a thick dressing such as mayonnaise or mustard to help "glue" the ingredients together.

To prevent a soggy sandwich • Toast the bread.

To prevent sandwiches from getting crushed • Pack them in sturdy sandwich-size plastic containers. Or wrap in plastic and pack on top of other foods.

TIME SAVERS ▼

To make sandwiches ahead • Spread bread with butter or cream cheese to keep wet ingredients from making the bread soggy. Also, pack high-moisture ingredients, such as tomato, lettuce, and cucumber, separately. Add them to the sandwich just before eating. To keep moist sandwich spreads such as tuna or chicken salad from touching the bread until just before eating, place a sheet of plastic wrap between the filling and the bread on both sides. Just before eating, remove each slice of bread and peel off the plastic.

To freeze sandwiches • Wrap them in individual sandwich bags or plastic wrap, then wrap them again in bundles of no more than 3 or 4 in a freezer bag or foil marked with the contents and date. Freeze up to 2 weeks. Avoid freezing sandwiches that include mayonnaise, cheese, or fresh vegetables because these ingredients may separate during thawing.

To use frozen sandwiches for lunch • Remove individual sandwiches from the freezer in the morning. Do not refrigerate. They will thaw by lunchtime.

To use leftovers in sandwiches • Leftover cooked meats, fish, or grains make quick sandwich fillings. Grains such as rice work particularly well in wrap sandwiches, using pita as the bread.

FLAVOR TIP ▼ **To flavor a chicken salad sandwich** • Add 2 tablespoons finely chopped cored apple and 2 chopped toasted walnuts to ¾ cup chicken salad.

PROSCIUTTO AND MOZZARELLA ON FOCACCIA Split **1 large slice focaccia** horizontally through the side. Lightly toast cut sides under broiler. Drizzle with **2 teaspoons extra-virgin olive oil** and **1 teaspoon balsamic vinegar**. Add **2 to 3 slices** *each* **prosciutto and fresh mozzarella**, **3 whole basil leaves**, and **a pinch** *each* **salt and ground black pepper**. Assemble sandwich. *Makes 1.*

CUBAN SANDWICH Split **1 hero** or **French roll (7" long)** and top each half with **1 tablespoon mayonnaise** and **2 slices Monterey Jack** or **Muenster cheese**. Add **6 thin slices dill pickle** and **2 thin slices** *each* **smoked ham and roasted pork**. Assemble sandwich, pressing down to compact. Melt **1 teaspoon butter** on a hot griddle. Add sandwich and weight down with a cast-iron skillet or foil-wrapped brick. Cook until cheese melts and bread is deep golden, 3 to 4 minutes per side, adding another **1 teaspoon butter** when cooking second side. Cut on a diagonal and serve hot. *Makes 1.*

BEYOND GRILLED CHEESE

These easy griddle sandwiches were inspired by the classic American favorite. To cook each sandwich, spread the outsides of the bread with 2 teaspoons soft butter and cook on a preheated griddle until the cheese melts and the bread is toasted golden, 3 to 4 minutes per side. Cut each sandwich on the diagonal and serve it hot. Each recipe makes 1 sandwich.

Griddled Chicken-Cheese Sandwich: Spread **2 slices white** or **whole wheat bread** with **2 teaspoons mayonnaise** and **1 teaspoon mustard**. Top with **1 slice cheese per piece of bread** (Cheddar, Swiss, provolone, mozzarella, or American). Add **2 thin slices deli roast chicken breast** and **2 thin slices tomato**. Sprinkle with **a pinch** *each* **salt and ground black pepper**. Assemble sandwich.

Griddled Fontina and Mushroom Sandwich: Sauté **2 large sliced cremini** or **white mushrooms** in **1 teaspoon butter** until soft and light brown, 3 minutes. Arrange **3 to 4 thin slices fontina cheese** over **2 large slices country-style bread** such as sourdough. Add mushrooms and sprinkle with **a pinch** *each* **salt, ground black pepper, and dried oregano**. Assemble sandwich.

Griddled Artichoke-Mozzarella Sandwich: Arrange **3 to 4 thin slices mozzarella cheese** over **2 large slices country-style bread** such as sourdough. Add **2 drained and thinly sliced marinated artichoke hearts** and **a pinch of ground black pepper**. Assemble sandwich.

WALNUT BUTTER AND FIG SAND-WICH In a mini food processor or mortar, combine **1¼ cups walnut pieces, ¼ teaspoon brown sugar,** and **a pinch of salt.** Puree or pound with a pestle until smooth and thick. Spread **1 slice whole wheat bread** with **3 table-spoons of the walnut butter** (refrigerate remaining walnut butter for another use). Top with **2 sliced dried figs.** Spread **2 teaspoons raspberry preserves** over **another slice whole wheat bread.** As-semble sandwich. *Makes 1.*

Sardines

Small and soft-boned, sardines are usually air-dried, coated with seasonings, then canned in oil or flavored sauces.

FLAVOR TIP ▼ **To get the best flavor** • Norwegian bris-ling sardines are considered the best for their mild flavor and delicate texture. When fully mature, they measure 3" to 4" long. They are harvested in the summer months.

SARDINE SPREAD In a mini food processor, combine **1 drained can (3¼ ounces) oil-packed sardines, 4 ounces Neufchâtel cheese, 2 tablespoons chopped fresh parsley, 1 tablespoon** *each* **capers and lemon juice,** and **½ teaspoon paprika.** Process until smooth. Use as a spread for crackers or dip for cru-dités. *Makes about ⅔ cup.*

Sauces *see also* Reduction; Sauces, Dessert; *and specific types*

In the most basic terms, a sauce is any fla-vorful liquid used to accompany food. It can be as simple as melted butter or as complex as a Mexican *mole* **made of chile peppers, onions, chocolate, stock, and dozens of other ingredients. Sauces are important for adding moisture to dry foods and enhancing the taste of bland foods.**

BASICS ▼ **To thicken** • Keep cooking to further re-duce the liquid in a sauce, which will also concentrate the flavors. Or add a thick-ener, such as flour, cornstarch, arrowroot, rice, or mashed potato flakes. When thick-ening a sauce with flour, cornstarch, or ar-rowroot, first blend the thickener with a little bit of cold water or broth to create a paste. Then, whisk the paste into the sauce. The initial blending process helps prevent lumps.

To thicken a sauce that contains eggs • Add some of the hot sauce to the eggs in a separate cup, stirring to blend. Then, stir the egg mixture into the sauce. The initial blending helps prevent cur-dling. Always cook egg-based sauces over very low heat.

To thin • Whisk in more liquid until the sauce has reached the desired consis-tency.

To achieve a smooth, satiny finish • Whisk in cold unsalted butter, a little bit at a time, over low heat. Use 1 tablespoon butter for every ½ cup liquid. The butter should incorporate smoothly into the sauce without melting into an oily puddle. Avoid letting the sauce boil after you have added the butter.

To keep delicate sauces warm • Place the saucepan in a cast-iron skillet set over a low flame, which will help to buffer the heat.

To reheat • Always reheat sauces slowly over low heat to reduce the risk of curdling, seizing, or breaking (you'll know a broken sauce when you see the fat separating from the rest of the ingredients).

To deepen the color of brown sauce • Add a drop of Kitchen Bouquet or Gravy-Master, commercially available products made from caramelized sugar. Avoid using too much, as these products are very potent. You can also add instant coffee granules or unsweetened cocoa powder. For each 2 cups sauce, mix 1 teaspoon instant coffee or unsweetened cocoa with 1 tablespoon of the sauce in a separate cup. Whisk back into the simmering sauce.

Chef's Tip: Chefs often refer to the "mother sauces." These 5 sauces are the foundation for hundreds of classic sauces. The 5 mother sauces are béchamel (basic white sauce), velouté (stock-based light sauce), espagnole (stock-based brown sauce), emulsions (such as mayonnaise and hollandaise), and vinaigrettes (oil-and-vinegar combinations).

BASIC WHITE SAUCE Melt **2 tablespoons butter** in a saucepan over medium heat. Add ¼ **cup all-purpose flour** and stir 1 minute to cook out raw flour taste. Gradually whisk in **1 cup milk,** whisking constantly to prevent lumps. Add **1 teaspoon salt,** ⅛ **teaspoon ground black pepper,** and ⅛ **teaspoon grated nutmeg (optional).** Add another **1 cup milk** and whisk constantly until thick and simmering. Cook until very thick and smooth, 2 to 3 minutes. *Makes about 2 cups.*

CHEDDAR CHEESE SAUCE Follow the recipe for **Basic White Sauce** (above). After it has cooked and thickened, stir in **1½ cups (6 ounces) shredded sharp or extra-sharp Cheddar cheese,** 1 tea-spoon paprika, **1 teaspoon Dijon mustard (optional),** and ⅛ **teaspoon ground red pepper.** *Makes about 3½ cups.*

CLASSIC HOLLANDAISE SAUCE In a small saucepan over very low heat, whisk together **3 egg yolks,** ¼ **cup water,** and **2 tablespoons lemon juice.** Cook, whisking constantly, until bubbles form at edges. Gradually whisk in **1 stick (½ cup) cold unsalted butter** cut into 8 pieces, one piece at a time, until sauce thickens. Whisk in ¼ **teaspoon salt** and ⅛ **teaspoon *each* paprika and white or black pepper (optional).** Use immediately, or cover and chill. *Makes about 1 cup.*

PROBLEM SOLVERS ▼ **To prevent off flavors with wine-based pan sauces** • Avoid using cast-iron or aluminum pans.

To cook out the raw flour taste of sauce thickened with flour • Continue to cook, perhaps 30 minutes or more. Eventually, the raw taste will disappear.

To prevent curdling in a hot sauce made with yogurt or sour cream • Bring the yogurt or sour cream to room temperature first. Also, heat the sauce very gently, and do not boil.

To rescue a sauce that has begun to curdle • Immediately remove it from the heat and whisk vigorously.

To salvage a sauce that has begun to burn • Transfer the sauce to another pan, taking care not to scrape the contents of the burned bottom.

To avoid oversalting • Wait to add salt until the sauce has been reduced to the desired thickness. Otherwise, you risk concentrating the salt flavor. If using canned broth, use a low-sodium product.

To salvage an oversalted sauce • Dilute it with more liquid. Or add a few

S

Chunky Beef Sauce for Pasta

To fully develop the complex flavors of this sauce, the herbs are added at two stages during the long simmering. Browning the beef also contributes tremendous flavor. The broth reduces considerably, adding another layer of intensity. This chunky sauce is especially good with pappardelle (wide noodles) but is equally at home with fettuccine or wide egg noodles.

¼ **cup olive oil, divided**

2 **pounds lean beef chuck, cut into ¾" cubes and divided**

2 **onions, chopped**

2 **large garlic cloves, minced**

1½ **teaspoons dried thyme, divided**

1½ **teaspoons dried oregano, divided**

1 **can (28 ounces) whole tomatoes**

3 **tablespoons tomato paste**

4 **cups beef stock or canned broth**

1½ **cups dry red wine, divided**

½ **teaspoon salt**

1. Heat 1 tablespoon of the oil in a large saucepan or Dutch oven over medium-high heat. Add half of the beef cubes and cook until very brown, 5 minutes, without stirring. Turn the pieces and cook until brown, 2 to 3 minutes. Remove to a plate. Add 1 tablespoon of the remaining oil to the pan. Brown the remaining beef as done for the first batch. Remove to the plate.

2. Heat the remaining 2 tablespoons oil in the same pan over medium heat. Add the onions and cook until soft and lightly colored, 5 minutes, stirring occasionally. Add the garlic, 1 teaspoon of the thyme, and 1 teaspoon of the oregano. Cook 2 minutes.

3. Place a sieve over a bowl and drain the tomatoes, setting the juice aside. Cut the tomatoes in half crosswise and squeeze out the seeds into the sieve. Chop the tomatoes and add to the pan along with the reserved juice. Discard the seeds. Add the tomato paste, the stock or broth, 1¼ cups of the wine, and the salt. Return the beef to the pan and bring to a simmer. Reduce the heat to low and simmer gently, partly covered, until the beef is fork-tender, 2 hours.

4. Add the remaining ¼ cup wine, ½ teaspoon thyme, and ½ teaspoon oregano. Add about ½ cup water if the liquid reduces too much. Simmer until the beef is very tender but not falling apart, 15 to 30 minutes longer.

Makes about 8 cups
(enough for 2 pounds pasta)

slices of raw potato, which will absorb excess salt. Cook the sauce as long as possible without reducing it to nothing, then discard the potato. You can also add a pinch of sugar to balance the salt.

To remove lumps • Press the sauce through a fine wire-mesh sieve. Or puree it using a handheld immersion blender or a conventional blender.

To blot excess fat from the top of a sauce • Tilt the pan and skim the fat off with a spoon. Or place an ice cube or two in a slotted spoon and briefly drag it through the surface of the sauce. The ice will act like a magnet for the fat. Discard the ice cubes before they melt.

To prevent hollandaise sauce from curdling • Cook it over very gentle heat, preferably in a double boiler, and serve it immediately.

To keep hollandaise sauce warm • Set the bowl of sauce in a larger bowl filled halfway with hot water. Or, keep it in an insulated soup container. Preheat a small, insulated container by pouring hot water into it and letting it sit 5 minutes. Pour out the water and pour in the sauce.

To save broken hollandaise sauce • As you are making hollandaise, if the butter begins to separate and the egg breaks into curds, immediately remove the sauce from the heat. Add an ice cube to the sauce to stop further cooking, and beat the sauce vigorously with a whisk. Remove the ice cube as the sauce pulls back together. Continue whisking. If that doesn't do the trick, whisk together 1 egg yolk and a pinch of dry mustard in a separate pan. Gradually whisk in the curdled sauce to restore the emulsion. Serve immediately.

TIME SAVER ▼ **To save prep time** • Save pan drippings and cooking liquids from vegetables and meats to use in sauces. These liquids can be frozen in zipper-lock freezer bags or in

---

QUICK UNCOOKED SAUCES

Some of the easiest and best-tasting sauces need no cooking at all. Think salsa, pesto, and vinaigrette. Each of the quick sauces below makes enough for 4 servings.

Cold Sage Sauce: Combine **1 cup mayonnaise, the juice of ½ orange, 1 tablespoon finely chopped fresh sage,** and **1 teaspoon balsamic vinegar.** Serve with poached or grilled seafood, or roast pork or veal.

Tarragon-Raspberry Sauce: In a bowl, mash **¼ cup fresh** or **unsweetened frozen and thawed raspberries.** Whisk in **¼ cup raspberry vinegar, ½ cup walnut oil, 1 ta-** blespoon chopped fresh tarragon, **½ teaspoon salt,** and **a pinch of ground red pepper.** Toss with **another ¼ cup fresh** or **unsweetened frozen raspberries.** Serve with grilled meats, poached fish, roasted chicken, or sautéed liver.

Mint-Pesto Yogurt Sauce: In a food processor, finely chop **1 garlic clove, 2 tablespoons toasted almonds,** and **2 cups fresh mint leaves.** Add **¼ cup extra-virgin olive oil, ⅓ cup plain yogurt,** and **1 tablespoon lemon juice.** Process until combined. Serve with fish, seafood, chicken, or lamb.

ice cube trays. You can also freeze any left-over sauce in ice cube trays. When the cubes are solid, pop them out and store them in zipper-lock freezer bags. To use them, add them to a warm pan and heat until liquefied. Another trick: Puree left-over vegetables, soups, or stews and use as a base for sauces.

S

EASY MUSHROOM SAUCE In a skillet, cook **1 cup beef broth** until reduced to ¼ cup. Add **2 cups pureed canned cream of mushroom soup.** *Makes 2¼ cups.*

EASY HOLLANDAISE SAUCE Cut **1 stick (½ cup) unsalted butter** into tablespoon-size pieces and place in a microwaveable container. Cover with plastic wrap and melt on medium power, about 2 minutes. In a blender, combine **3 egg yolks, 2 tablespoons lemon juice, ¼ teaspoon salt,** and **⅛ teaspoon** *each* **dry mustard and paprika (optional).** Blend briefly. With the blender running, slowly pour in melted butter until sauce thickens. Serve or keep warm in a small, preheated insulated soup container (fill the container with hot water and let sit 5 minutes, then pour out water and add sauce). *Makes about 1 cup.*

EASY BARBECUE SAUCE Stir together **1 can (15 ounces) crushed tomatoes with puree, ¼ cup brown sugar, 3 tablespoons cider vinegar, 1 teaspoon Worcestershire sauce, ½ teaspoon dried oregano, ½ teaspoon salt,** and **¼ teaspoon ground black pepper.** Bring to a boil. Remove from heat and stir in **3 tablespoons prepared mustard.** *Makes about 1½ cups.*

FLAVOR TIPS ▼ **To extract flavors from vegetables, giblets, or herbs** • Chop them very finely before adding them to the sauce.

To flavor savory sauces • Instead of using the traditional grated nutmeg to flavor white sauces and cheese sauces, add a pinch of ground cardamom.

To boost flavor in white or red clam sauce • When making either sauce from canned clams, add 1 bottle (8 ounces) clam juice to deepen the flavor.

To doctor up store-bought barbecue sauce • Stir 1 tablespoon prepared mustard into 1 cup bottled barbecue sauce; taste and add more if desired. Other flavor options: 1 minced garlic clove, ¼ cup beer, 2 tablespoons maple syrup, 1 tablespoon chopped fresh oregano, ⅛ teaspoon hot-pepper sauce, or ¼ teaspoon Worcestershire sauce.

HOMEMADE STEAK SAUCE Melt ½ stick (¼ cup) butter. Whisk in **2 tablespoons Worcestershire sauce** and **1 tablespoon** *each* **brown mustard and tomato paste.** *Makes ½ cup.*

CLASSIC COCKTAIL SAUCE FOR SHRIMP In a bowl, combine **½ cup bottled chili sauce; 2 tablespoons** *each* **tomato paste, lemon** or **lime juice, and dry white wine; 1 tablespoon drained prepared horseradish; ½ teaspoon Worcestershire sauce; ¼ teaspoon hot-pepper sauce;** and **a pinch of salt.** Serve with **1½ to 2 pounds peeled and deveined medium or large poached shrimp.** *Makes about 1 cup.*

WASABI DIPPING SAUCE Combine **2 tablespoons soy sauce** and **1 teaspoon** *each* **wasabi paste and rice vinegar.** Use as a dip for seafood. *Makes about 3 tablespoons.*

TARTAR SAUCE Combine ½ **cup mayonnaise,** ¼ **cup** *each* **finely chopped sweet pickle (or relish) and finely chopped pimiento-stuffed green olives, 2 tablespoons finely chopped dill pickle, 1 tablespoon** *each* **Dijon**

mustard and lemon juice, and 1 teaspoon hot-pepper sauce. Cover and chill. *Makes about 1¼ cups.*

BLUE CHEESE SAUCE Rub a bowl with the cut sides of **1 garlic clove (optional).** Discard garlic. In the bowl, combine **1 cup crumbled blue cheese,** ½ **cup** *each* **sour cream and plain yogurt, 2 table-**

First-Aid Pan Sauce for Meats

When cooking steak, chicken breasts, or pork chops on the stove top, it can seem as if all it takes is a fleeting glance away, and the meat transforms from being slightly undercooked to being dry, tough, and overdone. Here's a quick rescue. Of course, you can use a pan sauce with perfectly cooked meat as well.

1 **cup liquid (see options below), divided**

1 **tablespoon finely chopped fresh herbs (see options below)**

2 **teaspoons butter (optional)**

⅛ **teaspoon salt**

⅛ **teaspoon ground black pepper**

1. Transfer cooked meat from the pan to a large plate. Remove all but 1 tablespoon of the fat from the pan.

2. Add ½ cup of the liquid to the pan. Set it over medium heat. Cook 2 to 3 minutes, scraping the pan bottom to loosen any browned bits. Increase the heat to high. Add the remaining ½ cup liquid, the herbs, and any juices from the meat. Boil 2

minutes to reduce. Add the butter (if using). Stir until the butter is melted and the sauce is blended. Remove from the heat. Add the salt and pepper (or more to taste).

Makes about ½ cup

Liquid and Herb Options

For chicken: Use all chicken broth. Or use ⅔ cup broth and ⅓ cup white wine. Recommended herbs: parsley or thyme.

For pork: Use all chicken broth. Or use ⅔ cup broth and ⅓ cup port wine. Recommended herbs: parsley or sage.

For beef or lamb: Use all chicken broth. Or use ⅔ cup broth and ⅓ cup red wine. Recommended herbs: parsley or rosemary.

S

spoons mayonnaise, **1 tablespoon dry white wine, ¼ teaspoon salt,** and **a pinch of ground black pepper.** Excellent with french fries or Buffalo wings. *Makes about 2 cups.*

S

GINGER-LIME PAN SAUCE Use this sauce to top sautéed shrimp, scallops, chicken, or pork. Remove sautéed seafood or meat from the pan. Add **¼ cup oyster sauce, the juice of 1 large lime, 1 minced garlic clove, 1 teaspoon grated fresh ginger, ⅓ cup dry sherry,** and **½ cup chicken stock** or **canned broth** to the pan. Boil 3 minutes over medium heat. Swirl in **1 teaspoon toasted sesame oil.** Serve over the seafood, chicken, or meat. *Makes about 1¼ cups.*

POMEGRANATE PAN SAUCE Use this sauce to top sautéed steaks. Remove steak from the pan. Add **2 tablespoons chopped onion** to the pan and sauté 1 minute. Add **1 cup red wine** and boil 2 minutes. Add **1 cup pomegranate juice** and boil 1 minute. Reduce heat to low and swirl in **2 tablespoons unsalted butter.** Serve over the steak. *Makes about 2¼ cups.*

CREAMY DIJON PAN SAUCE Use this sauce to top sautéed chicken or pork. Remove chicken or pork from the pan. Add **2 tablespoons** *each* **chopped shallot** and **butter** to the pan and cook until tender. Remove from heat and stir in **⅔ cup sour cream** and **¼ cup Dijon mustard.** Stir until mixture is hot. Do not boil. Serve over the chicken or pork. *Makes about 1¼ cups.*

HEALTHY HINT ▼ **To create a more healthful tomato sauce •** Add finely grated carrot (about 1 small carrot per 4 cups sauce). Grated

Roasted Red Pepper Cream Sauce

Crab cakes are a natural fit for this sauce. Try it on grilled fish too.

1 **cup roasted red peppers**

1 **teaspoon sherry or red wine vinegar**

½ **teaspoon sugar**

1 **small roasted garlic clove or ¼ teaspoon roasted garlic paste**

¼ **teaspoon salt**

⅛ **teaspoon ground red pepper**

2 **tablespoons Neufchâtel cheese**

In a food processor, puree the roasted peppers, vinegar, sugar, garlic, salt, and ground red pepper until very smooth, 2 minutes. Add the Neufchâtel and process until blended. Chill in an airtight container for up to 2 days.

Makes about 1 cup

LOW-FAT CREAMY SAUCES

Try these mix-ins for three easy, cool, and creamy sauces. Use them on cooked beef, pork, or chicken, in sandwiches, or with pasta. Each makes about 1⅓ cups.

Rémoulade: Stir together ½ cup *each* low-fat mayonnaise and low-fat sour cream, ⅓ finely chopped red bell pepper, 2 tablespoons white wine vinegar, 1 tablespoon *each* bottled chili sauce and bottled horseradish, 1 teaspoon *each* chopped fresh parsley and scallions, and ¼ teaspoon dried tarragon.

Horseradish-Pepper Sauce: Combine ½ cup *each* low-fat mayonnaise and low-fat sour cream, 2 tablespoons chopped fresh parsley, 4 teaspoons bottled horseradish, 1 tablespoon *each* lemon juice and Dijon mustard, ¼ teaspoon ground black pepper, and 3 drops hot-pepper sauce.

Chipotle-Chive Sauce: Combine ½ cup *each* low-fat mayonnaise and low-fat sour cream, 1 seeded and finely chopped chipotle chile packed in adobo (leave the seeds in for more heat), 2 tablespoons chopped fresh chives, 2 teaspoons ketchup, and ¼ teaspoon honey.

S

carrots add body to the sauce, and their sweetness tempers the acidity of tomatoes. When carrots are finely grated, most people can hardly tell that they are there.

LOW-FAT BASIC WHITE SAUCE In a small saucepan over medium heat, bring ¾ **cup 1% milk** to a simmer. Dissolve **1 tablespoon cornstarch** in another ¼ **cup 1% milk.** Whisk into the saucepan and simmer 2 minutes. Stir in ¼ **teaspoon salt** and ⅛ **teaspoon ground black pepper.** *Makes 1 cup.*

LOW-FAT CHEDDAR CHEESE SAUCE Follow the recipe for **Low-Fat Basic White Sauce** (above). Remove from heat and stir in ½ **cup finely shredded reduced-fat Cheddar cheese** and **a pinch of ground red pepper.** Stir until blended. *Makes about 1½ cups.*

Sauces, Dessert *see also*
Sauces

Usually made with chocolate, cream, or fruit, dessert sauces are an easy way to turn sweet endings into something special.

BASICS **To decorate with dessert sauces** • For a dramatic visual effect, spoon the sauce over the bottom of a plate and place the dessert on top.

To create a ring of hearts, fill a small squirt bottle with whisked yogurt or a sauce that contrasts in color with the one that you are using. Squirt small dots from the bottle in a circle about 1" in from the edge. Using a toothpick, pull through  the center of each dot to form a heart shape. Place the dessert in the center of the sauce.

To safely reheat chocolate or caramel sauces • Warm them in a double boiler or in a metal pan set over simmering water.

CHOCOLATE SAUCE In a medium saucepan, whisk together **1 cup packed brown sugar, ⅔ cup unsweetened cocoa powder, 1 teaspoon instant coffee granules,** and **1½ cups milk, cream,** or **half-and-half** (depending upon desired richness). Bring to a gentle simmer, whisking frequently, and cook 4 minutes. Remove from heat and stir in **3 ounces chopped semisweet chocolate (or chips)** until smooth. Stir in **1 teaspoon vanilla extract** and **a pinch of ground cinnamon.** Serve warm.
Makes about 3 cups.

MINT CHOCOLATE SAUCE Follow the recipe for **Chocolate Sauce** (above). Stir in **1 tablespoon mint liqueur** (such as crème de menthe) with the vanilla.
Makes about 3 cups.

CRÈME ANGLAISE In a saucepan, combine **2 cups milk, cream,** or **half-and-half** (depending upon desired richness); **⅓ cup sugar;** and **½ split vanilla bean (or add vanilla extract later).** Cook over low heat just until small bubbles begin to appear around edges. Remove from heat. In a bowl, whisk **4 to 6 egg yolks** (depending upon desired richness). Gradually whisk in the hot milk. Return to the pan and stir over low heat until mixture is just thick enough to coat a spoon, 170° to 175°F. Do not simmer or boil. As soon as sauce thickens, turn out into a clean bowl and set in a bowl of ice water (to help prevent curdling). Cool completely. Scrape seeds from vanilla bean and add to sauce (or stir in 1 teaspoon vanilla extract).
Makes about 2 cups.

HEALTHY HINT ▼ **To reduce fat in creamy dessert sauces** • Use reduced-fat sour cream or fat-free yogurt. Or use flavored yogurt cheese (see page 554) as a topping.

THREE SIMPLE FRUIT SAUCES

These light-textured sauces are perfect for topping angel food cakes, waffles, or fresh fruit. Each recipe makes about 2 cups.

Mixed Berry Sauce: In a saucepan, combine **1½ cups** *each* **frozen drypack raspberries and blueberries, ⅓ cup sugar,** and **¼ cup water.** Bring to a simmer over medium heat. Mix **1 tablespoon lemon juice** and **¾ teaspoon cornstarch.** Stir into berry mixture until thickened, 2 minutes.

Orange Sauce: In a saucepan over medium heat, boil **3 cups orange juice** until reduced to 1½ cups, about 20 minutes. Stir in **½ cup orange marmalade** and **¼ cup packed brown sugar.** Return to a simmer. Mix **1 tablespoon** *each* **cornstarch and lemon juice** or **water.** Stir into simmering mixture until thickened, 2 minutes.

Fresh Mango Sauce: In a blender or food processor, combine **1 large peeled, pitted, and chopped mango; 3 tablespoons brown sugar;** and **1 tablespoon lime juice.** Puree until smooth. For a smoother sauce, press through a sieve.

LOW-FAT CRÈME ANGLAISE In a saucepan, combine ⅓ **cup sugar, 1 tablespoon cornstarch,** and ⅛ **teaspoon salt.** Whisk in 1½ **cups 1% milk.** Cook over medium heat, stirring constantly and scraping bottom of pan, until thickened and boiling. Remove from heat. Whisk together ½ **cup fat-free half-and-half** and **1 egg.** Whisk into hot milk mixture. Warm over low heat 1 minute. Do not boil. Stir in **2 teaspoons vanilla extract.** Scrape into a container and cover with plastic touching the surface to prevent a skin from forming. Refrigerate up to 4 days, and serve chilled. *Makes about 2 cups.*

LEMON CURD In a stainless steel saucepan, combine **2 egg whites, 1 egg, ½ cup sugar, 3 tablespoons honey, ⅔ cup lemon juice,** and **1 tablespoon grated lemon zest.** Whisk until smooth. Cook over low heat until thickened, 6 minutes, whisking constantly. Do not boil. Remove from heat and whisk in **2 tablespoons butter.** Use warm as a sauce, or pour into pastry shells and chill. *Makes about 1⅔ cups.*

Sausage

Made from ground meats and seasonings, sausages come in a wide range of styles. They may be fresh, cooked, cured, or dried, and made from almost any kind of meat, including lamb, game, poultry, or fish. Vegetables and grains can also be made into sausages. Rice sausages are favored in China, while potato sausages are enjoyed in Finland.

BASICS **To store fresh sausages** • Refrigerate and eat them within 2 days. Or freeze fresh sausages for up to 2 months.

To store precooked sausages • Some common precooked sausages include hot dogs, bologna, and kielbasa. Refrigerate these and eat them within 3 to 5 days. Or freeze them up to 2 months.

To store partially dried sausages • Spanish chorizo and summer sausage are two examples of partially dried sausages. Refrigerate partially dried sausages and use them within 2 to 3 weeks.

To store fully cured sausages • Hard salami and pepperoni are two types of fully cured sausages. These sausages can be kept at room temperature for several months; they will firm up with age.

To cook fresh, raw sausages • Slowly pan-fry them to render their fat and cook them through to the center. Or poach fresh sausages to cook them through, then grill or sauté to create a crisp, well browned surface. Raw sausages are cooked through when they are no longer pink in the middle.

To cook sausages on a griddle • The key here is to take time and allow the sausages to cook slowly on a griddle, turning them occasionally until they are browned all over. This should take at least 30 minutes, if not longer.

To cook in a skillet • Another excellent way to cook sausages, especially Italian sausages or breakfast links, is to prick them several times with a fork and then cook them in a skillet with ¼ cup water, turning often. The water will cook away and the sausages will begin to sizzle in their own fat. Cook and turn until browned all over.

To prepare smoked sausages, such as kielbasa • These sausages are best when grilled, pan-fried, or broiled.

To get more browned surface area when pan-frying links sliced into coins • Slice on a diagonal.

S

HOMEMADE BREAKFAST SAUSAGE
Sauté **1 large finely chopped onion** in **2 tablespoons vegetable oil.** Add **1 large minced garlic clove; 1 tablespoon dried rubbed sage; ½ teaspoon** *each* **grated nutmeg, ground allspice, and dried thyme; ¼ teaspoon ground cloves; 2 teaspoons salt;** and **1 teaspoon ground black pepper.** Cook until fragrant, 1 to 2 minutes. Turn out into a large bowl and let cool. Crumble in **2 pounds ground pork** and add **¼ cup orange juice.** Mix well. Cover and refrigerate 12 to 24 hours. Use as bulk sausage, or shape into patties (which can be frozen). *Makes 2 pounds.*

PROBLEM SOLVERS
▼

To substitute for loose sausage • If you can't find loose or bulk sausage, simply remove the meat from inside the casings of link sausages.

To prevent pan-fried sausage casings from bursting • Fill a sauté pan with 1½" of water and add 1 tablespoon oil. Simmer the sausages over medium-low heat until the water cooks off. The oil will remain so that you can proceed to brown the sausages. Another way to avoid bursting is to prick the casings with the tines of a fork before cooking. This lets steam escape.

To reduce flare-ups when grilling sausages • Don't pierce the casings. This way, the fat will remain inside the casing.

TIME SAVERS
▼

To cook link sausage ahead • Brown link sausages in a skillet over medium-high heat until firm and no longer pink inside. Blot excess fat from the surfaces with several layers of paper towel. Place the sausages on a pan in a single layer and freeze them until solid. Seal them in a zipper-lock freezer bag and freeze up to 3 months. Reheat them over medium-low heat in a skillet until browned.

HEALTHY HINTS
▼

To reduce fat when cooking sausage • When purchasing sausages, look for highly seasoned sausages. These will provide the maximum amount of flavor to season a dish, which allows you to use less meat. You can also reduce fat by rinsing cooked sausage. Sauté sliced or crumbled sausages in a dry skillet (or with a little water) until they are no longer pink. Place cooked sausages on paper towels and blot them well to remove excess fat. Place the meat in a colander and pour boiling water over the top, rinsing off residual fat. Depending on the sausage used, this method can reduce up to 50 percent of the fat.

To replace pork sausages • Turkey sausages make a good substitute for Italian pork sausages. Like their fattier pork counterparts, they are available in both sweet and hot varieties. Be aware that chicken sausages are not necessarily lower in fat, since, like ground turkey, they can be made with ground skin and fat. Always check the nutrition label.

HOMEMADE TURKEY SAUSAGE Sauté **1 chopped onion** in **1 teaspoon olive oil** until soft, 6 minutes. Stir in **3 crushed garlic cloves** and **1¼ teaspoons poultry seasoning** or **ground sage.** Cook 1 minute more. Remove from heat and cool to room temperature. In a large bowl, combine **1½ pounds lean ground turkey, ¼ cup chopped fresh parsley, 1 teaspoon** *each* **ground ginger and red-pepper flakes, ½ teaspoon salt,** and **¼ teaspoon ground black pepper.** Stir in onion mixture until well-blended. Shape into twelve 2" patties, each about ¾" thick. To store, wrap individually and freeze for up to 3 months. Cook, unthawed, in a greased and preheated nonstick skillet until meat is no longer pink, 6 to 8 minutes per side. *Makes 12 patties.*

SAUSAGE AND CHICKPEA STEW In a deep nonstick skillet, cook ¾ **pound spicy sausages (such as chorizo or hot Italian sausage)** over medium-high heat until no longer pink inside, 6 minutes. Drain on paper towels to remove excess fat. Place sausages in a colander and pour boiling water over them. Drain well. Heat **2 teaspoons olive oil** in the same skillet over medium heat. Add **2 chopped onions** and cook until soft, 10 minutes. Stir in **1** *each* **chopped red and green bell pepper, 3 chopped garlic cloves,** and **1 teaspoon** *each* **oregano, herbes de Provence (or thyme), and paprika.** Cook 7 minutes. Stir in **2 cans (15 ounces each) diced tomatoes, with juice; 1 can (14½ ounces) fat-free chicken broth; 1 drained can (15 ounces) chickpeas; ¼ teaspoon hot-pepper sauce;** and the cooked sausage. Simmer 8 minutes. Stir in **¼ cup chopped fresh parsley** and serve.

Makes 6 servings.

Sautéing

A technique that cooks foods quickly in a small amount of fat over medium-high heat in an open pan, sautéing adds an enormous amount of flavor to almost any food. This method is often used with other cooking methods, such as braising and roasting. Sautéing can also be done on its own as a fast, simple way of giving food a crisp, well-browned exterior.

BASICS ▼ **To sauté perfectly** • Pat any excess moisture off of food before adding it to the pan, because wet ingredients will steam rather than brown. To keep the surface of very moist ingredients, such as fish or veal, dry, dust them with a powdering of flour:

Shake the ingredient in a zipper-lock plastic bag with 1 cup flour, remove the ingredient, and shake off any excess flour. It's equally important to heat the pan and the fat before adding any foods to be sautéed. Use a thin film (about ¹⁄₁₆") of oil in the pan. The oil transfers heat thoroughly and quickly to the food. Too little oil will limit the contact that a sautéing ingredient has with the heated surface, causing hot spots and slowing down the cooking; too much oil will take longer to reach the right temperature and prolong the cooking. Use more or less oil depending upon the size of your pan. Also, avoid crowding the pan: You should be able to see the bottom of the pan between pieces of food. Adding too much food to the pan will lower the temperature and create steam, which prohibits proper browning. Likewise, avoid using a pan that's too big: A pan with too much empty space will scorch, which could transfer a burnt flavor to a sauce made in the pan after the food is sautéed. A final tip: Let the food cook in the hot fat for several minutes without turning or tossing it. You'll get better browning if you leave the food alone for a few minutes before moving it.

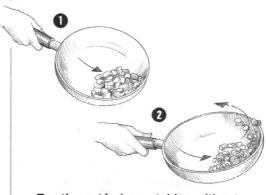

To stir sautéed vegetables without a wooden spoon • Use a nonstick pan with

S

sloped sides and an ample amount of fat. Lift the pan slightly off the heat and tilt it away from the handle so that the food begins to slide down away from you and gather at the farthest sloped side ❶ (see page 449).

As the food reaches the sloped side, jerk the handle down with a short, quick motion to flip the food back from the edge toward the center of the pan ❷ (see page 449). Repeat this process a few times to flip the food evenly. Shake the pan to even out the food in the center of the pan. This method also works for one-handed flipping of foods such as fried eggs and burgers.

SAUTÉED CHICKEN BREASTS IN BALSAMIC BROWN BUTTER SAUCE Pound **4 boneless, skinless chicken breast halves** between sheets of oiled plastic wrap to an even thickness of ⅛" to ¼". Mix **½ cup flour, 1 teaspoon salt,** and **½ teaspoon ground black pepper** in a bowl. Dust chicken with seasoned flour. Heat **1 tablespoon olive oil** in a sauté pan over medium-high heat. Add chicken and sauté until outside is browned, inside is no longer pink, and juices run clear, about 2 minutes per side. Remove to a warm plate and reduce heat to medium. Add **6 tablespoons unsalted butter** to the pan and cook until butter just starts to brown. Add **2 tablespoons capers** and **1 tablespoon balsamic vinegar** to pan. Pour over chicken. (You can also use pounded veal or thin fish fillets for this dish.) *Makes 4 servings.*

SAUTÉED FISH WITH ROSEMARY, GARLIC, AND SAGE Mix **½ cup flour, 2 teaspoons** *each* **ground rosemary and ground sage, ½ teaspoon salt,** and **¼ teaspoon ground black pepper** in a bowl. Dust **1½ pounds thin white fish fillets** with seasoned flour. Heat **1 tablespoon olive oil** in a sauté pan over medium-high heat. Add fish and sauté until outside is browned and fish flakes easily, about 1 to 2 minutes per side. Remove to a warm plate and reduce heat to medium. Add **2 tablespoons** *each* **butter and extra-virgin olive oil,** and **2 minced garlic cloves.** Cook until garlic softens, 4 minutes. Serve with lemon wedges. *Makes 4 servings.*

TIME SAVER ▼ **To sauté meat or fish faster** • Slice meat ¼" to ½" thick (freezing the meat for 30 minutes will make it easier to slice). Place the slices between 2 sheets of oiled plastic wrap and pound them with a smooth meat pounder to a thickness of ⅛" to ¼". Because fish is too delicate to pound, flatten the thicker sections of a fish fillet by pressing it with the heel of your hand until the fillet is an even thickness.

HEALTHY HINT ▼ **To sauté with less fat** • Use a nonstick pan. Nonstick pans allow you to greatly reduce the amount of fat needed to brown foods and prevent sticking. You'll need as little as ½ to 1 teaspoon oil in a 10" skillet. Also, preheat the pan and the fat. A hot pan and hot fat will quickly sear the food, allowing less oil to be absorbed. It helps to use room-temperature foods, too: They brown faster, cook more evenly, absorb less fat, and are less likely to stick to the pan than refrigerated foods. And add any salt at the end of the cooking, as salt impedes the browning of food during sautéing. To increase browning, you can add a sprinkle of sugar. This encourages caramelization, which will boost flavor in the food as well as create a browned residue in the pan, which can be deglazed and used to make a sauce.

Scallions *see also* Onions

This darling of the onion family goes by other names, such as green onions and spring onions. But true scallions have straight sides at the white base, whereas spring onions or green onions are actually immature onions that will eventually develop a rounded white bulb at the base.

BASICS ▼ **To choose** • Look for scallions with straight sides at the base. These have a milder flavor than immature (spring) onions. The bases should be firm and white, and the tops should be crisp and bright green.

To store • Keep them unwashed in a plastic bag in the refrigerator crisper drawer for up to 1 week. If the scallions are wet, dry them on paper towels before storing. Rinse them just before using.

To add scallions to a recipe • Sauté the white parts briefly with or in place of onions. The green tops are best added at the last minute.

Chef's Tip: One of the nicest things about scallions, besides their delicate onion flavor, is that you can use just one or two and have no leftover onion to deal with. Whenever you need a small amount of onion, consider using scallions instead.

To loosen scallion rings • Smash the scallion with the side of a chef's knife so that the ring layers separate when sliced.

To make clean slices through scallions • Rather than cutting straight down through the scallion, which tends to mash the delicate vegetable, position the tip of your knife on the cutting board and drag the knife so that it slices through the scallion. You can also slice scallions with kitchen shears.

To replace chives • The thin, delicate inner leaves of scallions can be used in place of chives.

SCALLION AND CORN SALSA Slice **1 small bunch scallions,** then rinse and drain well. Combine scallions, **1 cup frozen and thawed corn, 1 small chopped red bell pepper, 2 tablespoons chopped fresh cilantro, 1 tablespoon lime juice, 1 teaspoon olive oil, ½ teaspoon ground cumin,** and ¼ **teaspoon** *each* **ground cinnamon and salt.** Serve with grilled meats, poultry, or fish. Or use as a bruschetta topping.
Makes about 2¾ cups.

TROUT STUFFED WITH SCALLIONS Mix **1 thinly sliced bunch scallions (white part only), 2 ounces chopped Japanese pickled ginger,** and the **grated zest of 1 lemon.** Stuff into the interior of **4 cleaned and boned rainbow trout.** Close and douse with the **juice of 1 lemon.** Preheat broiler. Rub each fish with **1 teaspoon olive oil.** Broil 4" from heat until fish is opaque, about 4 minutes per side.
Makes 4 servings.

TIME SAVERS ▼ **To dice quickly** • Cut each scallion lengthwise twice. Line up the scallions in parallel rows and cut them crosswise into small squares.

To save prep time • Whenever you chop the white parts of scallions, chop extra and freeze them raw in an airtight container. Add them frozen to sautéed dishes whenever they're needed. Avoid freezing the delicate green scallion tops, which discolor and become limp.

S

Scallops *see also* Doneness Tests and Temperatures (page 572)

What most people think of as a scallop is actually the abductor muscle used to open and close the scallop shell. It's only one of several edible portions of this popular shellfish. The pale pink roe (eggs) is also quite tasty.

BASICS ▼ **To choose** • For the best flavor, choose scallops that are creamy white or slightly pink, rather than bright white (which indicates that they have been soaked and are probably less flavorful). Smell the scallops too: They will always have some odor, but choose those with the mildest scent. If you're lucky enough to find scallops in their shells, don't hesitate to buy them. Though they cost more than shucked scallops, their exceptionally fresh taste is well worth the expense. The shells usually gape open a bit. As long as they close slightly when tapped and smell fresh, they're fine. Quick-frozen scallops are another good option. Because they are frozen as soon as they are shucked, these scallops often have a better flavor than those that have grown old in a ship's hold for several days before they ever get to the market.

To store • Buy scallops the day you plan to serve them, and keep them refrigerated until ready to cook.

To clean • Run the scallops under cold water and, if desired, pull off the little white tendon that may be on one side of the scallop (not every scallop has one). This tendon is the "hinge" from the scallop shell. It isn't absolutely necessary to remove the tendon, but some cooks prefer to. If you see a little coral-colored pouch on some scallops, however, leave the pouch intact and cook as planned. The pale pink pouch is the scallop roe, and is delicious!

Chef's Tip: Be aware that some lesser-quality scallops are actually cut out of large pieces of fish fillets that have a similar texture, such as skate. For true scallops, it is best to shop at a reliable fish market.

To cook • Scallops take well to a wide range of cooking methods. They are wonderful fried, sautéed, grilled, steamed, poached, or baked. Scallops are also wonderful in seviche and other marinated salads. However you choose to prepare them, watch the cooking time carefully. Scallops cook through in just a few minutes, and if left on the heat for too long, they quickly turn rubbery and dry.

To brown sea scallops on one side • Chefs like this method of cooking sea scallops. Cut large sea scallops in half through the side to make two equal-size disks out of each. Pat the disks dry on paper towels. Combine 1 tablespoon *each* butter and olive oil in a large skillet over medium-high heat. When the pan is hot, add the scallops, leaving a little space between each, and cook on one side only until deeply browned and flesh is opaque, about 3 minutes. If the browning is taking too long, increase the heat to high. Serve with Lemon-Basil Mayonnaise (see page 273).

GRILLED SCALLOP APPETIZER Preheat a grill. Toss **1 pound cleaned sea scallops in a mixture of 2 tablespoons *each* olive oil, lemon juice, and prepared grated horseradish; ¼ teaspoon salt; and ⅛ teaspoon ground black pepper.** Cut **2 ounces prosciutto** into ½" × 4" strips. Wrap each scallop in a prosciutto strip and secure with a toothpick.

THE SCOOP ON SCALLOPS

Choosing among types of scallops is largely a matter of taste. All types can be quite good. As with other seafood, there is but one key to getting the best-tasting scallops: Choose what is freshest at the market.

Bay: The most prized of all scallops, bays have a sweet, delicate flavor and fetch a high price. Bay scallops are harvested from a small region of the Atlantic and are rarely found outside of East Coast fish markets. Their short season begins in October and runs through March.

Calico: These tiny scallops usually come at a very reasonable price. Because shucking the small shells is too expensive for most processors, the shells are steamed open, and the scallops arrive in the market partially cooked. If cooked correctly, calico scallops can be tender and flavorful, but they quickly turn rubbery and tough if exposed to heat for more than a few minutes.

Sea: The most common type of scallop, sea scallops are larger than other varieties but are still quite tender and have a sweet, rich flavor. Because scallop boats stay out at sea for weeks at a time, it is common practice to soak sea scallops in a solution of salts and water (sodium tripolyphosphate, or STP) to help preserve them. While soaking makes the scallops last longer, the meat absorbs much of the soaking water, which increases the weight (and the price) and dilutes the flavor. Wholesalers are required to label their scallops as "soaked" or "dry" (unsoaked), but retailers do not always pass this information on to their customers. Here's how to tell whether or not scallops have been soaked: If the scallops are bright and shiny, clinging together in clumps, they have most likely been soaked. Unsoaked scallops usually remain separate and range in color from pale ivory to pale coral.

Grill over a medium fire until scallops are opaque and firm, 2 minutes per side. *Makes 4 to 6 servings.*

SOUTH AMERICAN SCALLOP SALAD
Sauté **2 large, thinly sliced onions** and **2 minced garlic cloves** in ¼ **cup olive oil.** Add **1 pound cleaned sea scallops,** ½ **teaspoon ground ginger,** and ¼ **teaspoon dried thyme.** Cook until barely firm, about 2 minutes. Add **2 tablespoons wine vinegar** and the **juice of 1** *each* **orange, lemon, and lime.** Heat to simmering. Remove from heat and stir in ½ **teaspoon salt,** ¼ **teaspoon ground black pepper,** and **a pinch of ground red pepper (or more to taste).** Chill. Stir in **2 tablespoons chopped fresh parsley** and serve. *Makes 4 servings.*

Chef's Tip: Scallops are one of the safest shellfish to eat raw. Like all shellfish, scallops filter large amounts of seawater for the nutrients that they need to stay alive, accumulating some toxins in the process. But their filtration mechanism is discarded during processing, and only the abductor muscle, where few toxins are stored, is usually eaten. Raw scallops marinated in lime juice are excellent.

Scones *see also* Breads, Quick

A nifty Scottish quick bread, scones are usually eaten for breakfast or tea with butter or jam. They were originally made with Scotch oats and cooked on a griddle. Now, they are usually made with flour and baked in an oven. For Oat Scones, see page 310.

FLAVOR TIP ▼ **To add flavor and texture** • Toss in dried fruit, such as currants, raisins, or dried cranberries, and complementary flavorings, such as grated lemon peel, cinnamon, or grated orange peel.

CURRANT SCONES Preheat oven to 350°F. In a large bowl, whisk together **2 cups flour, ¼ cup sugar, 1 teaspoon** *each* **baking powder and cream of tartar,** and **½ teaspoon salt.** Make a well in the center. Add **¾ cup buttermilk, 2 tablespoons melted butter,** and **⅔ cup dried currants.** Gradually stir in dry ingredients just until combined. Scrape onto a floured surface and pat into a ¾"-thick circle using floured hands. Cut into 8 wedges using a floured knife, and place on a greased baking sheet. Bake until golden, 15 to 18 minutes. *Makes 8.*

Scoops *see also* Measuring

In a professional kitchen, scoops are used for everything from measuring and portioning to filling and forming. Because they perform so many functions so easily and so well, chefs generally have an arsenal of scoops of various sizes at their disposal. Even if your kitchen has just one scoop, take advantage of its many timesaving uses.

SCOOP SIZES

Numbered according to their volume, scoops with a large number have a smaller volume, and vice versa. Here's the breakdown.

Scoop Size	Tbsp	Fluid oz
#30	2	1
#24	2¾	1½
#20	3	1¾
#16	4	2
#12	5	2½
#10	6	3
#8	8	4
#6	10	5

TIME SAVERS ▼ **To portion muffins with a scoop** • Grease a muffin pan or line the cups with paper liners. Portion the batter with a #8 scoop. For standard muffins, scrape the batter flat to the rim of the scoop. For extra-large muffins, mound the batter in the scoop.

To portion cookies with a scoop • Use #8 scoop for large cookies, #16 for standard cookies, and #30 for small, dainty cookies. Scoop cookie dough directly onto a lined baking sheet, leaving enough room between cookies for spreading. Flatten the tops of the batter with moistened fingers.

To portion meatballs with a scoop • Use a #16 scoop to scoop the meat mixture onto a lined baking sheet. Wet your hands with cold water and form each mound into a ball. Cook as desired.

To fill a pastry bag using a scoop • Place the pastry bag in a jar or bowl and fold the top of the bag over the rim of the jar or bowl to make a cuff. Fill the bag using a large scoop such as #8.

Searing *see also* Braising; Roasting; Sautéing

Browning food quickly over high heat, usually to prepare it for a second cooking method such as braising, is known as searing. For years, cooks believed that searing sealed juices in and kept meat from drying out, but food scientists have proved that searing has the opposite effect and draws juices to the surface, releasing them into the pan or fire. Searing does add flavor, however. Cooking over high, dry heat sets off a series of reactions between the sugars and proteins in meat, caramelizing the natural sugars, which results in a richer and more complex flavor. The crisp, browned surface of a seared piece of meat is also more appetizing than the dull, gray look of meat that hasn't been properly browned.

BASICS ▼ **To give seared foods a well-browned color and rich flavor** • Pat meat dry with paper towels before searing. Also, avoid overcrowding the pan, which reduces the temperature of the pan and creates steam, both of which will prevent the meat from searing properly.

Sea Vegetables

Sea vegetables (seaweed) have been used for centuries in Asian cuisines. Their briny flavor makes an excellent seasoning, especially in soups, and they are high in iodine, which may help prevent goiter (hyperthyroidism). The most popular form is nori, which is often used to roll up sushi.

BASICS ▼ **To rinse** • Briefly rinse all dried sea vegetables under cool running water to remove excess salt and any tiny shells. Rinse only for a short time; many of the nutritious trace minerals are near the surface.

To toast • Bring out the flavor of seaweed by toasting it before using. Toast it in a 350°F oven until just fragrant, 1 to 2 minutes, watching carefully so that it doesn't burn. Sheets of nori can also be toasted by holding the sheets one at a time with tongs about 1" over a flame until they change color, about 2 minutes. Toasted nori can be cut or torn into strips for garnishing stir-fries, salads, or rice.

FLAVOR TIP ▼ **To make a toasted nori snack** • Dip strips of toasted nori into a mixture of ¼ cup reduced-salt soy sauce, 1 teaspoon lemon juice, and a dash of chili powder.

INSTANT MILD SEAFOOD BROTH OR POACHING LIQUID Combine **1 quart cold water** and **1 ounce dried kelp** or **kombu.** Heat to simmering. Remove kelp and add **1 ounce dried bonito flakes** (a type of dried tuna available at Asian markets). Heat to boiling without stirring. Immediately remove from heat. Allow bonito flakes to settle, about 2 seconds. Strain. *Makes 1 quart.*

Fascinating Fact: Seaweed is a common ingredient in cookies, candies, ice cream, jams, syrups, and salad dressings. Look for "algin," "agar," and "carrageenan" on food product labels. These substances come from seaweed and are used as stabilizers, thickeners, and emulsifiers in many foods.

HEALTHY HINT ▼ **To get maximum nutrients from sea vegetables** • Use sea vegetables in soups and stocks to receive the full benefit of their

S

S

COMMON SEA VEGETABLES

Here's a guide to the five most common types of seaweed. These are usually sold dried in packages in health food stores and Asian markets.

Kelp: Similar to Japanese kombu, kelp is sold in wide, dark green strips. It is popular simmered in soups and stews as a salt substitute. To reduce the saltiness, rinse kelp briefly before using. Toasted kelp makes a crunchy addition to salads, stir-fries, and casserole toppings (see "To toast" on page 455). Or add it to soups for rich mineral flavor and body, cooking it until softened. You can also add kelp to cooking beans to thicken them and to promote easier digestion.

Dulse: Used raw, maroon-colored dulse cuts or tears easily and is chewy and slightly moist. For a crisper, more brittle texture, roast or fry it briefly. When cooked in liquid, dulse becomes very tender and will dissolve if cooked longer than 5 minutes. Use it in fish or clam chowders, fish cakes, and Caesar salads, or fry it in oil and use it in place of bacon in a BLT.

Nori: Also known as laver, these dark green-black sheets are most often used to make sushi. Nori is also available in flakes, which dissolve immediately in liquid, thicken slightly, and lend a greenish color to soups. Try adding nori flakes to breading or savory pie crusts for a nutty flavor. Or use them to season salads or to add flavor and color to salad dressings. To make nori broth, simmer 1 part nori in 6 parts water.

Wakame: These long, dark green strips are often added to soups and salads in Japan. Dried wakame strips, sold in the United States, should be soaked in warm water before using.

Hijiki: Dried into thin, green-black strips, hijiki is wonderful scattered over salads or stir-fries for savory crunch.

---

nutrients. Their minerals are released into the broth, and the solids provide valuable fiber and unique phytochemicals such as the alginate in kelp, which may help fight cancer.

Seitan

This meat substitute, pronounced "SAY-tan," is made of concentrated wheat gluten, which is high in protein (almost double that of meat) yet contains one-third less fat and no cholesterol. Used in many vegetarian dishes, seitan can be found in the refrigerator or freezer sections of health food stores and large supermarkets. Also called wheat gluten, seitan is a key ingredient in many vegetarian convenience foods such as veggie hot dogs, burgers, and cutlets.

HEALTHY HINTS ▼

To use • Use refrigerated or frozen seitan in any manner that you would use meat. Slice it to use in a stir-fry, chop or shred it to use in ground meat dishes, or cube it to use in casseroles or stews.

To cook • For seitan with a chewy texture, oven-braise and simmer it. For a lighter texture, bake it (an especially good choice for ground or shredded seitan). For a somewhat softer texture, cook seitan in a pressure cooker. And for a very soft, slippery texture, which is perfect for absorbing flavorful sauces, deep-fry seitan.

Sesame

Perhaps the oldest condiment on earth, sesame seeds have been processed into various forms since 1600 B.C. This familiar topping for hamburger buns is also pressed to make sesame oil and crushed to make sesame paste. Asian sesame paste and sesame oil are made from toasted sesame seeds, while Middle Eastern sesame paste (tahini) and cold-pressed sesame oil are made from untoasted sesame seeds.

BASICS ▼ **To choose** • For the best price, buy sesame seeds in bulk rather than in tiny jars. While ivory-colored seeds are the most common, you can also buy black, brown, or red sesame seeds. When buying sesame oil for cooking, be sure to look for "pure" toasted sesame oil. It should be dark amber in color. Some supermarkets carry toasted sesame oil that is mixed with less-expensive oils such as canola oil, which dilutes the toasted sesame flavor. Japanese brands of pure toasted sesame oil are consistently delicious.

To store • Keep sesame seeds in a tightly sealed jar in the refrigerator up to 6 months. Likewise, keep all forms of sesame oil in the refrigerator, as sesame oil tends to become rancid easily. Don't worry if the oil becomes cloudy from the cold temperatures; it will clear up again upon reaching room temperature. Tahini can be refrigerated for up to 1 year after opening.

To toast sesame seeds • Place them in a dry skillet and toast over low heat, shaking the pan often, until the seeds are fragrant and golden brown, 2 minutes. Transfer to a plate so that the seeds do not continue cooking in the hot pan, which could make them dark and bitter-tasting.

Fascinating Fact: Toasted sesame seeds are so appreciated in Japan that the Japanese invented a special little skillet with a screened lid for toasting them. Sesame seeds sometimes pop out of the pan during toasting, so the screened top is handy. An inverted large-mesh sieve will also do the trick. Avoid using a solid pan lid, which would trap steam in the pan and turn the seeds soggy.

To use toasted sesame seeds • Toss them freely over steamed broccoli, green beans, asparagus, grilled chicken, green salads, stir-fries, rice, and most any other dish. If using sesame seeds to top baked goods, add them raw rather than toasted. The seeds will toast in the oven.

To use toasted sesame oil • For the most flavor, add it at the end of the cooking time. If heated too long, toasted sesame oil loses much of its nutty flavor. Also, avoid using too much toasted sesame oil, which can cause a cloying sensation at the back of the tongue. For a stir-fry that serves 4, about ½ teaspoon is plenty.

To use tahini • Ground sesame paste, or tahini, is used in some Greek and many Middle Eastern dishes, the most famous of which is hummus (see page 237). It is also a main ingredient in sauces for falafel. You may need to stir tahini before using, as it tends to separate.

TARATOR SAUCE Combine ½ **cup tahini, ⅓ cup water, ¼ cup lemon juice, 1 pressed garlic clove, ¾ tea-**

spoon salt, and ¼ **teaspoon ground black pepper.** Usually spooned over falafel, but also perfect for dipping cooked chicken and raw vegetables. *Makes about 1 cup.*

COLD SESAME NOODLES In a small skillet, combine **1 tablespoon vegetable oil, 2 tablespoons finely chopped fresh ginger,** and **2 minced garlic cloves.** Cook gently over low heat until fragrant and soft, 4 minutes. Remove from heat. In a bowl, mix ¼ **cup** *each* **tahini and smooth peanut butter; 2 table-spoons** *each* **soy sauce and dry sherry; 1 tablespoon** *each* **toasted sesame oil, rice vinegar, and sugar; 1 to 2 table-spoons cold water;** and ¼ **teaspoon ground red pepper.** Stir in the ginger-garlic mixture. (This sauce can be made days ahead and refrigerated.) In a large pot of salted boiling water, cook ½ **pound thin linguine** or **spaghetti (or 12 ounces fresh Chinese noodles)** until tender but firm to the bite, 6 to 8 minutes for linguine or spaghetti, and 2 to 3 min-utes for fresh Chinese noodles. Drain and rinse under cold water. Toss with sauce. Sprinkle with ¼ **cup chopped toasted peanuts** and **2 tablespoons chopped fresh cilantro.** If desired, serve with crunchy vegetables such as bean sprouts and cucumber slices. Serve cool or at room temperature. *Makes 4 modest servings.*

Shallots

A member of the allium family, shallots taste like a mild cross between garlic and onions. They look similar to garlic, with a head com-posed of large cloves covered with a brown, papery skin.

BASICS **To choose** • As with onions and garlic, look for firm shallots with dry skin. Avoid moist, wrinkled shallots or those that have begun to sprout.

To store • Keep in a cool, dry place up to 1 month.

To peel • Trim off both ends and cut a slit in the skin from end to end. Roll the shallot on its sides to loosen the skin, then peel off the skin.

To use • If a recipe calls for 1 shallot, use 1 clove from the head.

SHALLOT AND HERB STUFFED CHICKEN LEGS In a food processor, combine **2 coarsely chopped shallots,** ⅓ **cup packed fresh parsley leaves, 3 thin slices peeled fresh ginger, 1 tea-spoon dried tarragon,** and ¼ **teaspoon salt.** Pulse until finely chopped. Add **3 ta-blespoons lemon juice** and **1 table-spoon** *each* **water and olive oil.** Process until smooth. Loosen the skin from **4 whole chicken legs.** Rub the paste under the skin, spreading it over the chicken meat, and pulling the skin back over the meat to cover. Place in a greased 11" × 7" baking dish and bake at 400°F until internal temperature registers 170°F on an instant-read thermometer and juices run clear, 40 minutes. *Makes 4 servings.*

TIME SAVER **To quickly peel a large amount of shal-lots** • Break them into cloves and drop them into a pot of rapidly boiling water. Immediately remove the pot from the heat and let it stand 1 minute. Drain the shal-lots and run them under cold water. Slice off the pointed ends and remove the peels, leaving the root ends intact. This blanching technique will soften the outer-most layer of skin, making it more flexible and easy to remove.

Sherbet *see also* Sorbet

Basic sherbet contains only sweetened fruit juice and water. Fancier versions can include wine, liqueur, flavor extracts, milk, egg whites, or gelatin.

TIME SAVER ▼ **To save prep time** • Use canned fruit and freeze the can. Then dig out the contents and puree in a food processor with other flavorings.

EASY PEACH SHERBET Freeze **1 unopened can (28 ounces) peaches in heavy syrup** until solid. Open the can, dig out the frozen contents, and puree in a food processor along with ⅛ **teaspoon almond extract, 1 tablespoon finely chopped crystallized ginger,** and/or ¼ **teaspoon raspberry vinegar.**
Makes 4 servings.

EASY LITCHI SHERBET Freeze **1 unopened can (15½ ounces) litchis in heavy syrup** until solid. Open the can, dig out the frozen contents, and puree in a food processor along with **1 tablespoon dry sherry, 1 tablespoon finely chopped ginger preserves,** and/or ¼ teaspoon sweet rice wine vinegar.
Makes 4 servings.

Sherry

Originating in Spain, sherry is a fortified wine that includes brandy or another spirit to boost the alcohol content. Most sherries are excellent for sipping.

BASICS ▼ **To choose** • Spanish sherries are good for both sipping and cooking. Dry and very dry sherries (called fino and manzanilla) are light in flavor. They are often used in cooking along with mushrooms, in paella, and in many sauces. Medium-dry sherry (amontillado) is slightly sweeter and darker-colored. It is equally delicious in both savory and sweet dishes. Medium-sweet sherry (oloroso) and sweet sherry (cream sherry) are best for desserts.

To store • Store sherry in a cool, dark place. Opened bottles of fino and manzanilla will keep up to 1 week, and opened oloroso and cream sherries will keep up to 1 month.

Shrimp *see also* Doneness Tests and Temperatures (page 572)

Most of the shrimp eaten in the United States is harvested from relatively warm, shallow tropical waters. Though there are literally hundreds of species of shrimp, only a few varieties appear in our markets, where they are usually labeled by size rather than by their species name.

BASICS ▼ **To choose** • Most shrimp is frozen at sea right after it is caught. The fish markets then buy it frozen and usually thaw it before selling. Shrimp freezes well, so frozen shrimp is generally the best buy. Of course, if you can find very fresh shrimp (sometimes called day boat shrimp) that have never been frozen, or better yet, live shrimp, the flavor and texture will be a revelation. When buying frozen shrimp, press on the bag or box. If you hear a crunchy covering of ice crystals, the shrimp has thawed partially and been refrozen. Look for a box or bag without a crunchy sound. It also helps to feel around for areas that are soft or empty, a sign that the box is beginning to thaw or may have been refrozen. When buying thawed

S

shrimp, always smell before you buy: It should smell sweetly of the ocean. A stale ammonia scent indicates that the shrimp has begun to deteriorate. Black spots along the sides of shrimp are another sign that the shrimp is past its prime. Also avoid shrimp with a pinkish cast, which have been sprayed with a fine mist of hot water for purely cosmetic reasons. Go for the gray shrimp instead, which will turn pink when cooked. Buy unpeeled shrimp whenever possible. The peels help keep the shrimp moist and flavorful. When buying cooked shrimp, make sure that it looks plump, moist, and succulent.

To store • Store fresh or thawed shrimp in a colander that is filled with ice and set over a bowl to provide for drainage. Thawed shrimp will keep for up to 1 day. Wrap frozen shrimp in plastic wrap and then in aluminum foil, and freeze up to 2 months.

To prepare • Shrimp need only to be rinsed and dried before cooking. It's true that leaving the shells intact will help keep shrimp moist while they cook and will give them a bit more flavor. But the added flavor is so minimal that, for most dishes, it's better to peel shrimp before cooking.

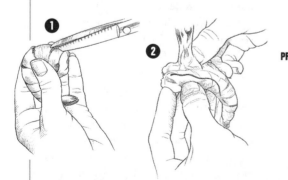

To peel and devein at the same time • With kitchen shears or a small knife, cut the shrimp shell along its outer curve, just deep enough into the flesh to expose the dark vein ❶.

Peel back the shell under running water, loosening the vein (the intestine) with your fingertips ❷. If it's really stuck, use the tip of the shears or knife to pull it out. If the vein is light in color, it is empty, and there is no reason to bother pulling it out.

To butterfly • Peel and devein the shrimp in one step as described above, but cut about three-fourths of the way into the flesh, without cutting all the way through. Lay the shrimp on a flat surface and flatten it.

To poach • This method is sometimes referred to as boiling or steaming. Bring a large pot of salted water to a boil. Add the juice of 1 lemon and drop in peeled or unpeeled shrimp. Stir briefly. Remove from the heat and cover. Allow to steep 1 minute for small shrimp, 1½ minutes for medium shrimp, and 3 to 4 minutes for large to jumbo shrimp. When the shrimp are cooked, they will be pink, firm, and opaque in the center; cut one to check. If they still look translucent, cover for another 30 seconds, then check again. When the shrimp are done, drain them.

PROBLEM SOLVER ▼ **To prevent shrimp from curling during cooking** • Shell and devein large shrimp. Insert a small bamboo skewer lengthwise through the center of each shrimp, starting near the tail and pushing through to the wide end. Cook as desired.

TIME SAVER ▼ **To save prep time** • Buy small shrimp, which need only peeling and not deveining. To quickly peel small shrimp, start at the wider end and pull off as many of

SIZING UP SHRIMP

Shrimp are usually sold by "count" or size. The count, such as 16/20, refers to the number of shrimp you'll get per pound according to their size. It can be a little confusing; here's how to make sense of it.

Size	Shrimp per lb
Small	40–50
Medium	31–40
Large	26–30
Extra large	21–25
Jumbo	16–20

the legs as you can grasp with 2 fingers. Wedge a finger up under the shell and push back toward the tail. The shell should come off in one piece. Leave the tail on for recipes in which the shrimp will be picked up by hand. If using shrimp in a stew or sauce, remove the tail by pinching it and pulling the body of the shrimp away from it with the other hand. The tail meat will come out in one piece.

MARINATED SHRIMP APPETIZER In a saucepan, combine **12 peeled and deveined jumbo shrimp, 2 thinly sliced garlic cloves, ½ bunch sliced scallions (white part only), 2 tablespoons white wine,** and **1 tablespoon extra-virgin olive oil.** Bring to a simmer over medium heat. When shrimp are opaque, immediately remove from heat and add **another 1 tablespoon extra-virgin olive oil, 2 tablespoons lemon juice,**

¼ teaspoon salt, ⅛ teaspoon ground black pepper, and **a pinch of ground red pepper.** Transfer to a serving bowl and refrigerate until cold. Serve with toothpicks as finger food. *Makes 4 servings.*

QUICK SHRIMP SCAMPI In a skillet, sauté **1½ pounds peeled and deveined large shrimp** in **2 tablespoons extra-virgin olive oil** until shrimp just begin to become firm, about 1 minute. Remove shrimp with a slotted spoon. Add **6 minced garlic cloves** and **1 cup white wine** to pan. Boil until wine reduces to ½ cup. Return shrimp to the pan and add the **juice of ½ lemon, 1 tablespoon chopped fresh parsley, ½ teaspoon salt,** and **¼ teaspoon ground black pepper.** When shrimp are opaque, remove from heat and stir in **½ stick (¼ cup) unsalted butter.** *Makes 4 servings.*

SMOKED SHRIMP Toss **2 pounds peeled and deveined large shrimp** with the **juice and finely grated zest of 2 lemons, 1 dried chile pepper (such as chipotle),** and **2 tablespoons** *each* **soy sauce and cider vinegar.** Set aside. Mix **½ cup loose hibiscus tea** with **½ cup sugar.** Line a heavy wok, skillet, or Dutch oven with 2 layers of heavy foil. Place tea mixture on the foil and set a rack over top. Heat over high heat until the tea smokes. Place reserved shrimp on the rack. Cover and smoke shrimp until opaque, 5 minutes. Serve with bottled teriyaki sauce for dipping. *Makes 4 servings.*

FLAVOR TIPS ▼ **To flavor poached shrimp** • Poach the shrimp (see "To poach" on opposite page). In a large bowl, combine about 3 cups ice cubes with 3 tablespoons dry white wine and 1½ teaspoons salt. Add the shrimp, toss, and let it chill for about 15 minutes. Drain the shrimp, cover, and chill until needed. Great for shrimp cocktail!

SHRIMP CHIPS Mix ½ **cup cornstarch** with **1 teaspoon ground red pepper.** Butterfly 20 large shrimp and dredge well in cornstarch mixture. Place each between 2 sheets of plastic or waxed paper and pound gently with a mallet until shrimp are paper-thin (less than ⅛" thick). Lift shrimp carefully from the plastic or paper and dredge again in cornstarch. Heat ½" of vegetable oil in a deep skillet or deep fryer to 375°F. Add shrimp and fry until firm, 15 to 30 seconds. Remove to paper towels to drain. Serve immediately, seasoned with **1 teaspoon salt.** Or refrigerate up to several hours; just before serving, fry again for a few seconds to crisp, then season with the salt. *Makes 4 servings.*

BACON-WRAPPED GRILLED SHRIMP Preheat a grill. In a shallow glass dish, combine **2 tablespoons lemon juice, 1 tablespoon** *each* **sugar and olive oil,** and ½ **teaspoon** *each* **paprika, ground red pepper, curry powder, ground cumin, ground coriander, salt, and ground black pepper.** Add **1½ pounds peeled and deveined jumbo shrimp,** tossing to coat. Marinate at room temperature 30 minutes. Cut **10 slices bacon** in half to make 1 piece for each shrimp. Wrap a piece of bacon around each shrimp, securing ends with a toothpick. Toss in the dish to coat with remaining marinade. Grill over a medium-hot fire until shrimp are opaque and firm, 2 to 3 minutes per side. Serve hot or warm. *Makes 6 servings.*

Sieves

These bowl-shaped mesh strainers come in various sizes, the largest of which is often called a colander. Sieves are used for everything from draining pasta and straining stock to dusting desserts with cocoa or confectioners' sugar.

BASICS ▼ **To choose** • If buying a colander, choose a metal one with strong handles. Plastic ones are more likely to break. When buying a mesh sieve, look for a sturdy frame and handle. Dishwasher-safe sieves can save on cleaning time.

To clean easily • Wash sieves as soon as you are finished with them. Otherwise, food dries up in the holes, making cleaning more difficult. To clean a clogged sieve, soak it in hot, soapy water, then scrub it with a vegetable brush.

To use a large-holed colander as a fine sieve • Line the colander with a double thickness of cheesecloth.

TIME SAVER ▼ **To quickly remove liquid from a pot of solids and liquids** • Insert a sieve into the pot (a cone-shaped sieve works best). The solids will remain on the outside of the sieve so that the liquid can be quickly removed with a ladle. This technique is useful for removing stock from a pot without straining the whole pot, or for removing excess water from an ice-water bath in which the ice has melted too much.

Sifting

Sifting dry ingredients through fine mesh performs two basic functions: removing lumps for even distribution and aerating for an increase in volume. Confectioners' sugar is often sifted over baked goods so that it can be evenly distributed. And flour is often

S

sifted to aerate it, which produces a greater volume in baked goods. Sifting, however, is not the most efficient method for mixing dry ingredients. If you're sifting only to mix ingredients, but not to aerate them or remove lumps, save time and use a whisk instead.

BASICS ▼ **To measure sifted ingredients properly** • If a recipe calls for "1 cup flour, sifted," measure 1 cup flour, then sift it. If a recipe calls for "1 cup sifted flour," sift the flour first, then measure it.

To remove lumps • Soft pastry and cake flours clump easily and should be sifted to remove any lumps. Mashing lumps later in the mixing process can result in overmixing and can toughen a dough. Likewise, powdered sugar often clumps, and sifting offers an easy way to eliminate lumps. If your recipe does not call for sifting, sift after measuring.

To sift ingredients without a sifter • Use a fine-mesh sieve.

Slicing

Sliced food is usually cut into strips or rounds of uniform thickness. Slicing provides a lot of surface area for cooking, yet the cut is large enough that food retains its shape and flavor. Strips of bell peppers and onions are great for stir-fries or fajitas, while thin slices of potatoes are perfect for scalloped potatoes.

BASICS ▼

To slice • Steady the food with your hand and slice down through it, starting with the tapered end of the knife and pushing

forward slightly so that the slice ends with the heel of the knife.

To slice large amounts • Use a mandoline, a hand-operated slicing machine that streamlines the process. Mandolines can also be used for julienning, french-fry cutting, and waffle cutting. You can also use a food processor with the slicing disk.

Slow Cookers *see also*

Braising; Stews

Slow cookers, such as Crock-Pots, run contrary to the axiom that speed equals convenience. Instead, these appliances simplify cooking by slowing it down so much that the cook no longer needs to be present.

TIME SAVER ▼ **To save attended cooking time** • Instead of using the stove top or oven for long-cooking dishes, use a slow cooker instead. Slow cookers make excellents stews and braised dishes such as pot roast.

SLOW-COOKED POT ROAST Rub **1 beef bottom round** or **rump roast (4 to 5 pounds)** with **1 tablespoon oil.** Brown under a broiler on both sides. In a 4-quart slow cooker, combine **2 chopped onions, 4 minced garlic cloves, ½ cup cider vinegar, 6 tablespoons brown sugar,** and **2 cups** *each* **ketchup and beef broth.** Add the browned beef and **4 to 5** *each* **peeled and quartered carrots and celery ribs.** Cover the cooker and cook until meat is fork-tender, on low for 8 hours or high for 5 hours. *Makes 10 to 12 servings.*

SLOW-COOKED CREAMY POT ROAST Rub **1 beef bottom round** or **rump roast (4 to 5 pounds)** with **1 table-**

spoon oil. Brown under a broiler on both sides, then transfer meat to a 4-quart slow cooker. Mix together **2 cans (10 ounces each) condensed mushroom soup, 1 can water,** and **1 packet (1 ounce) dry onion soup mix.** Pour over pot roast. Cover the cooker and cook until meat is fork-tender, on low for 8 hours or high for 5 hours. *Makes 10 to 12 servings.*

SLOW-COOKED CHICKEN CACCIA-TORE Mix ¼ **cup flour** and ½ **teaspoon** *each* **salt and ground black pepper.** Place **3 pounds bone-in chicken legs** and **chicken thighs** in a slow cooker with the seasoned flour and **2 tablespoons olive oil.** Add **1 large sliced onion, ½ pound sliced mushrooms, 1 cup** *each* **chicken broth and white wine, 2 chopped tomatoes, 2 minced garlic cloves, ½ teaspoon** *each* **hot-pepper flakes and salt,** and ¼ **teaspoon** *each* **dried oregano and ground black pepper.** Cook on low until a thermometer inserted in the thickest portion registers 170°F and juices run clear, 6 hours. Stir in **1 tablespoon** *each* **finely chopped anchovy fillets and finely chopped fresh parsley.** *Makes 4 to 6 servings.*

Smoked Fish

Though the qualities of texture and flavor may vary, just about any kind of fish can be smoked. The most commonly available commercial varieties include salmon, trout, cod, and sturgeon.

BASICS ▼ **To choose** • There are two basic methods of smoking fish: hot smoking and cold smoking. Hot-smoked fish is processed at gradually increasing temperatures, starting at around 120°F and increasing to about 180°F over a 6- to 8-hour period. In general, hot-smoked fish has a stronger smoke flavor and firmer texture. Cold-smoked fish is processed at temperatures of 70°F to 90°F for anywhere from 1 day to 3 weeks. Cold-smoked fish is both milder and more tender. Regardless of the smoking method, avoid any smoked fish that looks overly dry.

To store • Wrap smoked fish well in plastic wrap and foil to prevent the flavor from spreading to other foods. Refrigerate it for up to 3 days.

To easily remove skin and bones • Do the job while the fish is cold.

To help separate thin slices • Separate them while the fish is still cold. After separating the slices and arranging them on a platter, cover the fish with plastic wrap and allow it to sit at room temperature for at least 10 minutes.

To best enjoy the flavor • Serve smoked fish at room temperature.

FLAVOR TIP ▼ **To flavor tuna salad** • Add 2 ounces crumbled smoked trout or whitefish to tuna salad made from 1 can (6 ounces) tuna.

SMOKED-FISH MOUSSE Mix together **6 ounces softened cream cheese; 2 tablespoons light cream; 2 ounces finely chopped or crumbled smoked salmon, smoked trout,** or **smoked whitefish; 1 teaspoon chopped fresh dill;** ¼ **teaspoon salt;** and ⅛ **teaspoon ground black pepper.** Serve with cherry tomatoes, celery sticks, and carrot sticks. *Makes 6 to 8 servings.*

SMOKED-FISH DEVILED EGGS Cut **4 peeled and chilled hard-cooked eggs** in half lengthwise. Mash the yolks with **1** teaspoon mustard, **1 tablespoon pre-pared horseradish, 2 tablespoons mayonnaise,** and **1 small minced garlic clove.** Mix in **¼ pound finely chopped** or **crumbled smoked salmon, smoked trout,** or smoked whitefish. Mound into the hollow of each half of egg white. *Makes 4 servings.*

Sorbet *see also* Sherbet

A light and refreshing frozen dessert, sorbet is usually made with fruit puree or juice and sometimes flavored with coffee, chocolate, wine, or other flavorings. Sorbet differs from sherbet and ice cream in that it is made without milk products, eggs, or gelatin. It is generally smoother than granita or water ice, both forms of granular sorbet.

BASICS ▼ **To choose fruit** • Look for the ripest, most fragrant fruit you can find. Overripe, mushy fruits are perfect for using in sorbets.

To prepare less-than-ripe fruit for sorbet • Poach the fruit in sugar syrup (2 parts water to 1 part sugar) before pureeing it. This step will develop the fruit's flavor and break down its flesh, which makes it easier to puree.

To make creamy and smooth • Stick to the amount of sugar specified in your recipe. Sugar helps create smaller ice crystals and a better texture. Too little sugar could mean that the ice crystals will be too big, while too much sugar could prevent the sorbet from ever freezing beyond a slush. Also, try adding a bit of vodka to the base (just a teaspoon or two). Like sugar, alcohol interferes with the formation of ice crystals and creates a smoother sorbet.

To store • Transfer sorbet to a plastic container and press a sheet of plastic wrap directly onto the surface of the sorbet. Cover and freeze for up to 2 weeks.

PROBLEM SOLVERS ▼ **To fix a sorbet that doesn't freeze** • If your sorbet looks like slush, it probably contains too much sugar or too much alcohol. The practical fix is to add additional amounts of all the other ingredients (except the sugar or alcohol) to, in effect, "lower" the sugar or alcohol content.

To make sorbet without an ice cream maker • Pour the sorbet mixture into a shallow metal baking pan and freeze until ice crystals form. Break up the ice crystals with a fork about every 30 minutes or so, until the mixture forms frozen granules that can be scooped into a ball. This method produces a more granular sorbet that is closer in texture to granita.

TIME SAVER ▼ **To help a sorbet base freeze more quickly** • Chill the base for several hours before processing it in an ice cream maker.

STRAWBERRY SORBET Puree **1 quart sliced strawberries** with **1 can (14 ounces) sweetened condensed milk** and **2 teaspoons lemon juice.** Freeze in a shallow metal pan, stirring occasionally to break up and form crystals. (You can use 1 can sweetened condensed milk to replace the sugar and milk in any recipe that calls for 4 cups fruit.) *Makes 6 servings.*

Soufflé *see also* Eggs

Made from sweet or savory custards lightened with beaten egg whites, soufflés are one of the standard-bearers of classic French cuisine. Most are served hot, but some are served cold.

S

BASICS ▼ **To choose a dish** • Use a tall, straight-sided, ovenproof dish. The straight sides help the soufflé rise.

To ensure a flavorful soufflé • Over-season the base mixture (the sauce). Since the base will be diluted by the beaten egg whites, it should be intensely flavorful.

To ensure a light soufflé • Use two-thirds more egg whites than yolks. The volume of beaten whites should at least double the volume of the base (the sauce).

To ensure a high-rising soufflé • Lightly grease the soufflé dish, then dust it with an even layer of fine bread crumbs, grated Parmesan cheese, corn-meal, nuts, cookie crumbs, or unsweet-ened cocoa powder. Or skip greasing and dusting the sides of the dish altogether. Too much grease on the pan can weigh down a soufflé. Also, when folding in any additional ingredients, do it as gently yet as quickly as possible. Make sure that ad-ditional ingredients are very finely chopped so that they don't sink in the soufflé and weigh it down. Avoid over-beating the egg whites, too, which can cause them to deflate. Likewise, check the consistency of the base (the sauce). It should be just soft enough to fall from a spoon. If it's too thin, the soufflé won't rise properly; if it's too thick, it will de-flate the egg whites rather than mix in with them. For the maximum rise, fill the soufflé dish to within ½" of its rim. Set the dish on a low rack in the oven, and allow plenty of room above it for the soufflé to rise.

To maximize caramelization on the top of a hot, sweet soufflé • Sprinkle with confectioners' sugar or superfine sugar during the last 5 minutes of cooking. Move quickly when doing this so that the soufflé does not collapse.

To freeze a soufflé • Fill the soufflé dish with the soufflé mixture. Cover with plastic wrap and freeze until solid. Wrap in foil and freeze up to 1 month. To bake a frozen soufflé, let it rest at room tempera-ture 30 minutes, then bake it at 350°F for about 1 hour, or twice as long as you would bake an unfrozen soufflé.

To make a chilled soufflé • Chilled dessert soufflés are mousses that are molded in soufflé dishes. Because they do not bake and rise, they are much less fragile than baked soufflés and can be as-sembled up to 24 hours ahead of serving. To prepare one, follow any recipe for mousse. Wrap a double layer of foil around the rim of the soufflé dish to form a collar that extends at least 2" up. Pour the mousse into the dish so that it fills the dish at least halfway up the collar. Refrigerate until firm. Carefully remove the foil, re-vealing a layer of mousse that will appear to have risen above the rim of the dish.

SWEET POTATO SOUFFLÉ Preheat oven to 375°F. Grease a 2-quart soufflé dish and dust with **2 tablespoons finely ground pecans.** Combine ½ **cup plain yogurt, 2 tablespoons brown sugar, a pinch of ground cloves, ½ teaspoon salt,** and **4 egg yolks.** Mix into **2 cups hot mashed sweet potatoes.** Cool. **Beat 6 egg whites** with **a pinch of salt** until soft peaks form when the whisk or the beaters are lifted. Fold into potatoes and pour the mixture into the prepared dish. Bake until puffed and browned, about 30 minutes. *Makes 4 servings.*

CHOCOLATE SOUFFLÉ Preheat oven to 375°F. Grease a 2-quart soufflé dish and dust with **2 tablespoons unsweetened**

cocoa powder. Combine **7 ounces melted semisweet chocolate,** ¼ **cup sugar, a pinch of salt, 1 tablespoon instant coffee granules, 6 egg yolks,** and **3 tablespoons cognac.** Cool. Beat **6 egg whites** with **a pinch of salt** until soft peaks form when the whisk or the beaters are lifted. Fold into chocolate and pour the mixture into the prepared dish. Bake until puffed and slightly dry on top, about 15 minutes. *Makes 6 servings.*

PROBLEM SOLVERS ▼

To make without a soufflé dish • Use a saucepan, a straight-sided casserole dish, or even ovenproof mugs.

To provide added height to a dish that is too small • Make a collar on the rim of the dish with a double layer of parchment paper or aluminum foil, overlapping the dish by a couple of inches. Tie the collar with kitchen twine to secure it.

To prevent overflowing • Leave enough room for the uncooked mixture to double or triple in size.

To prevent shrinking • Watch the cooking time and avoid overbaking.

To prevent a soufflé from falling • Protect it from drafts as it cooks by keeping the oven door shut. Open the door only when the soufflé is at least 75 percent cooked. Also, serve the soufflé immediately. A soufflé will start to fall immediately upon contact with cool air.

To fudge a fallen soufflé when serving it to guests • First, peek inside to see whether the soufflé is undercooked. If so, return it to the oven to cook through. Then, top a savory soufflé with grated Parmesan cheese or finely chopped herbs. Top a sweet soufflé with a sauce, whipped cream, berries, and/or chocolate shavings.

To mask any cracks on the top of a soufflé or mousse • Cover it with a sauce or dust it with confectioners' sugar.

To prevent a chilled soufflé from turning out heavy and dense • Gently fold in the whipped cream and beaten egg whites. Avoid stirring.

To cover up a chilled soufflé or mousse that is overly stiff • Slice it extremely thin and serve it in layers between whipped cream and slices of fruit or a fruit puree. Drizzle with a caramel sauce. Or, top the soufflé with fresh fruit, crushed wafers, or thin chocolate shavings. You could also spoon the soufflé or mousse over ice cream or pound cake. Or spoon it into fluted glasses. Layer whipped cream and/or fruit between the spoonfuls and refrigerate. Just before serving, insert a crisp, light wafer into the top layer for some textural contrast.

HEALTHY HINT ▼

To avoid salmonella when making a chilled soufflé or mousse • According to the American Egg Board, all eggs should be cooked to 160°F before eating. If you are making a chilled soufflé or mousse, combine the egg whites and sugar from the recipe with water and cream of tartar (use about 2 tablespoons sugar, 1 teaspoon water, and a pinch of cream of tartar per egg white used). Cook the mixture in a double boiler or a metal pan over simmering water, beating constantly with a handheld mixer on low speed until the whites reach 160°F. Remove the whites from the heat and beat them until soft peaks form when the beaters are lifted.

RASPBERRY SOUFFLÉS Preheat oven to 375°. Grease six 8-ounce soufflé dishes and dust with ¼ **cup sugar.** In a large bowl using an electric mixer, beat **4 egg whites** with **a pinch of salt** until

S

S

SAVORY SOUFFLÉS

To make any of the soufflés below, prepare the All-Purpose Sauce, choose a flavor variation, then bake. To make a soufflé ahead, prepare the sauce, add the flavoring, and refrigerate for up to 24 hours. Then follow the "To Bake" directions just before putting the soufflé in the oven. Serve immediately. Each recipe makes 4 servings.

All-Purpose Sauce for a Soufflé: Sauté **½ small chopped onion** in **3 tablespoons oil** or **butter** until tender, 4 minutes. Stir in **¼ cup flour** and cook 1 minute. Add **1¼ cups hot milk** and whisk until smooth. Season with **½ teaspoon salt, ¼ teaspoon ground black pepper, ⅛ teaspoon dry mustard,** and **a pinch of ground red pepper.** Cook until the mixture is as thick as porridge, about 5 minutes, stirring constantly. Remove from heat and beat in **6 egg yolks.** Cool.

Ham and Blue Cheese Soufflé: Into the cooled **All-Purpose Sauce,** mix **½ cup** *each* **finely chopped ham and crumbled blue cheese.**

Spinach and Feta Soufflé: Into the cooled **All-Purpose Sauce,** mix **¾ cup** chopped cooked spinach (or frozen and thawed spinach), **1 minced garlic clove,** and **½ cup crumbled feta cheese.**

Crab Soufflé: Into the cooled **All-Purpose Sauce,** mix **½ pound cleaned crabmeat** and **a pinch of nutmeg.**

Mushroom Soufflé: Into the cooled **All-Purpose Sauce,** mix **9 ounces finely chopped mushrooms** that have been sautéed in **1 tablespoon olive oil** with **1 finely chopped small onion** and **1 minced garlic clove.**

To Bake: Preheat oven to 375°F. Grease a 2-quart soufflé dish and dust it with **2 tablespoons dry bread crumbs** or **grated Parmesan cheese.** Beat **8 egg whites** and **a pinch of salt** until soft peaks form when the whisk or the beaters are lifted. Stir one-fourth of this mixture into the cooled and flavored **All-Purpose Sauce** until the sauce is lightened. Gently fold remaining egg white mixture into the sauce, trying to maintain as much air in the mixture as possible. Pour into the prepared dish. Bake until puffed and browned, about 30 minutes.

---

soft peaks form when the beaters are lifted. Gradually beat in **¼ cup sugar,** beating until stiff peaks form. In a medium bowl, whisk about one-fourth of the egg whites with **¼ cup strained raspberry jam** just until blended. Gently fold back into remaining egg whites just until combined. Spoon into the prepared dishes and bake until lightly browned, 10 minutes. Serve immediately. *Makes 6 servings.*

Soups *see also* Broth; Stews; Stock

Just about any combination of meat, fish, and/or vegetables cooked in a liquid can qualify as a soup. Though most soups are served hot, some, such as gazpacho, vichyssoise, and fruit soups, are traditionally served cold.

BASICS To make flavorful soup • Start with a rich, deeply flavored homemade stock. No canned stock can match the flavor of homemade. See the recipe for Basic Chicken Stock on page 471.

To thicken a soup • Puree some of the soup and stir it back into the soup pot. If you are using a food processor, transfer only the solid ingredients to the work bowl. A handheld immersion blender simplifies this process because you can puree right in the soup pot. To prevent a gummy texture, avoid pureeing potato soup and other soups with a lot of starch. Mash the potatoes with a potato masher instead, or pass them through a food mill. Another thickening method is to puree some of the soup's liquid with a small amount of cooked rice or potatoes, then add it back into the soup. Or, try adding instant mashed potato flakes a tablespoon at a time. Stir, and wait a few minutes before adding more. This is a particularly good way to thicken creamy vegetable soups. You can also whisk one or two egg whites in a bowl and add 1 cup of hot broth per white, whisking constantly to combine smoothly. Just before serving, whisk the egg mixture back into the soup. Bread makes a good thickener too: Add plain, crustless bread cubes to soup, mashing the cubes with the back of a spoon to break them up. Or puree the bread cubes with some of the soup's broth in a blender. Use about ⅓ cup bread cubes for 2 cups broth. If you have fresh bread crumbs, stir them right into the soup and cook until thickened. Start with ¼ cup bread crumbs for 2 cups broth, adding more bread crumbs for a thicker texture.

To transform a hot soup into a cold soup • Many soups, such as tomato, potato, broccoli, and squash soups, can serve double duty by being served either hot or cold. To serve them cold, slightly increase the salt and seasoning and thin the consistency with broth, milk, or juice (depending on the flavor of the soup) after the soup has cooled.

To store • Most soups freeze beautifully. If the soup will contain a dairy product such as milk, cream, or cheese, freeze it without the dairy component because these ingredients can separate when thawed. Transfer cooled soups to airtight plastic containers or even to heavy-gauge zipper-lock freezer bags, label them, and freeze up to 3 months. If you are using zipper-lock freezer bags, the easiest filling method is to line a large bowl with the opened bag. Ladle in the soup, leaving some extra space for expansion. Suck out excess air with a straw, and seal the bag. Place bags in a single layer on a baking sheet and freeze them until solid. Then, stack frozen bags of soups in the freezer. To reheat, place a bag in a pot of simmering water and simmer until the contents are hot.

To make an edible soup bowl • Cut a thin slice from the bottom of a small pumpkin, Hubbard squash, or acorn squash. (If using acorn squash, cut it in half lengthwise, then cut a thin slice from the bottom of each half to make 2 bowls.) Cut off the top and scoop out the insides, leaving at least ½" of shell intact. The bowl may be cooked or raw; if it's cooked, you can eat it when you've finished the soup. For a decorative garnish, swirl sour cream or pureed vegetables into the soup. Or sprinkle it with chopped fresh herbs or seasoned croutons.

PROBLEM SOLVERS ▼ **To boost flavor in a lacking soup** • Add the rind from Parmesan cheese and simmer it to release its flavor, then remove

S

it before serving. Or garnish the soup with finely chopped chives, parsley, or other fresh herbs. You can also sprinkle the soup with grated Parmesan cheese or top it with a dollop of sour cream.

To avoid curdling when adding yogurt or sour cream • Use low heat only. Never raise the heat beyond a simmer once you have added yogurt or sour cream.

To repair a milk-based soup that has curdled • Strain it through a sieve.

To clear up cloudy broth-based soup • Stir in 2 to 3 egg whites for each 6 to 8 cups of soup. The whites will attract the cloudy-looking particles and float to the top. Then, skim off the top and discard the skimmings. The soup must be hot for the whites to coagulate and rise to the top.

To avoid making a soup with over-cooked, mushy rice or pasta • Cook the pasta or rice separately and add it to the soup shortly before serving, to rewarm it.

To stretch a pot of soup that is slightly short for your number of guests • Serve it in wide, shallow soup bowls. They can only hold a ladle or two.

To avoid a mess when cooking thick soups • Pureed soups and other thick soups tend to splatter when they bubble. Protect your stove top by using a splatter screen or by partially covering the pan with a lid. Or loosely cover the pan with foil that has been punctured in a number of places so that steam can escape.

To cure an oversalted soup • Dilute it with more broth (homemade or low-sodium). If it's appropriate, add an extra can of tomatoes, another method for diluting. Or add a pinch of sugar to help counteract the saltiness. You can also float a few slices of raw potato on top and simmer for 5 to 10 minutes. The potato slices will absorb excess salt. Remove them before serving the soup.

TIME SAVERS ▼

To encourage soup to cook more quickly • Cut ingredients into small pieces.

To speed prep time • Of course, canned broth saves loads of time. Whenever possible, use reduced-sodium broths; fully salted canned broths can be overpoweringly salty. To save chopping time, you can use a food processor to chop and slice vegetables. To get a more even chop from a food processor, chop vegetables of similar hardness together and chop the hardest vegetables first. For instance, chop carrots and turnips together, remove them, and then chop tomatoes. There is no need to wipe out the work bowl between vegetables. You can also save time by using precut or frozen vegetables. Because frozen vegetables are already partially cooked, they will cook the most quickly.

CORN AND BEAN SOUP FROM LEFT-OVER HAM In a soup pot, sauté **1 finely chopped onion** in **1 tablespoon oil** until soft, 4 minutes. Add **2 cups cubed cooked ham, a pinch of red-pepper flakes,** and **½ cup long-grain rice.** Stir to coat rice with oil. Add **6 cups chicken broth** and cook until rice is tender, 12 to 15 minutes. Add **1 bag (10 ounces) frozen succotash (corn and lima beans), 1 teaspoon cider vinegar,** and **¼ teaspoon** *each* **salt and ground black pepper (or more to taste).** Heat through. Garnish with **2 tablespoons chopped fresh parsley.** *Makes 4 servings.*

SWEET-AND-SOUR BEEF BORSCHT Sprinkle **1½ pounds beef short ribs** all over with **½ teaspoon** *each* **salt and ground black pepper.** Brown in a soup pot with **2 tablespoons vegetable oil.** Add **1 pound rinsed and drained**

sauerkraut and **3 cups** *each* **vegetable cocktail juice and water.** Heat to boiling and simmer until meat is fork-tender, about 45 minutes. Remove short ribs from soup. Cut meat from bones and finely chop. Return meat to soup and discard bones. Taste and add more water, salt, and pepper, if necessary. *Makes 4 servings.*

FLAVOR TIPS ▼

To doctor up canned soup • Mask the canned taste by adding a splash of wine or dry sherry, or even a bit of brandy. Also, a pinch of chopped fresh herbs on top will give great aroma and flavor.

To "beef up" onion soup • Add ¼ teaspoon instant coffee granules for each 4 cups of broth.

Basic Chicken Stock

When making this stock, if you want some of the chicken meat for use in a soup, remove the breast and thigh meat after 1 hour. Return all the trimmings to the pot and continue simmering.

4 pounds chicken parts

4 quarts cold water

2 onions, quartered

2 celery ribs, sliced

2 small carrots, sliced

6–8 parsley sprigs

4 whole peppercorns

4 cloves

2 bay leaves

1 teaspoon dried thyme

1 tablespoon vinegar

½ teaspoon salt

1. Cut a few gashes in the chicken parts. Place in a large stockpot or Dutch oven over medium heat. Add the water and bring to a simmer. Reduce the heat to low and cook 15 minutes, skimming any foam from the surface.

2. Add the onions, celery, carrots, parsley, peppercorns, cloves, bay leaves, thyme, vinegar, and salt. Simmer gently 3 to 5 hours, adding more water, if necessary, to keep the chicken covered.

3. Scoop out the largest pieces of chicken with a slotted spoon and transfer them to a large colander set over a large bowl. Drain and discard the pieces (the chicken meat will be dried out and flavorless). Strain the stock and discard all solids. If desired, strain again through a finer sieve. Refrigerate the stock overnight. Skim off and discard the fat on the surface. For double-strength stock or a glaze, return the stock to a saucepan and simmer until reduced by half (for double-strength stock) or by three-quarters (for glaze).

Makes about 2 quarts

S

Chicken Noodle Soup

For the best flaver, cook the noodles separated, then add to the soup.

2 **quarts Basic Chicken Stock (page 471) or canned broth**

2 **onions, chopped**

2 **carrots, peeled and chopped**

2 **celery ribs, chopped**

1 **bay leaf**

2 **tablespoons chopped fresh parsley**

4 **ounces wide egg noodles**

1. If using homemade stock, remove some of the breast and thigh meat after the stock simmers 1 hour. If using canned broth, poach 1 chicken breast or thigh so that you can add chicken pieces to the soup.

2. In a soup pot or large saucepan over medium heat, combine the stock or broth with the onions, carrots, and celery. Add the bay leaf and bring to a boil. Simmer until the vegetables are tender, 15 minutes.

3. Finely chop the cooked chicken. Add to the pot along with the parsley.

4. Meanwhile, cook the noodles according to package directions. Add noodles to each serving. Remove the bay leaf before serving.

Makes 6 to 8 servings

Italian Chicken Soup: Add 1 cup chopped spinach, 8 quartered mushrooms, and 4 peeled and chopped plum tomatoes along with the stock or broth. Before serving, add ¼ cup shredded fresh basil and ¼ cup grated Parmesan cheese.

Chinese Chicken Soup: Add 5 slices fresh ginger and 2 cups sliced bok choy with the stock or broth. Replace the parsley with fresh cilantro. Before serving, remove the ginger slices and garnish each serving with sliced scallion and a few drops of toasted sesame oil. If desired, stir in a splash of soy sauce (it will darken the color).

To add more flavor to tomato-based soups • Just before serving, sprinkle grated Parmesan cheese over the top. Excellent with minestrone.

Fascinating Fact: The two classic styles of clam chowder are New England, made with cream and potatoes, and Manhattan, made with tomatoes and celery. There is also a fairly popular third type that's favored in Rhode Island, made with both cream and tomatoes. Take your pick.

To add flavor to New England clam chowder • Replace the salt pork or fatback with sautéed smoked bacon. A few drops of Worcestershire sauce will boost the flavor too.

To add more flavor to Manhattan clam chowder • Add sautéed smoked bacon and a generous amount of white wine (¾ cup for each large can of tomatoes used).

PUREE OF BUTTERNUT SQUASH SOUP In a soup pot, sauté **2 chopped leeks (white parts only), 1 chopped parsnip, ½ pound chopped carrots,** and **1 teaspoon grated fresh ginger** in **2 tablespoons butter,** 5 minutes. Add **2 pounds peeled and chopped butternut squash, 1 teaspoon dried thyme, a pinch of ground mace, 1½ quarts chicken broth, ½ teaspoon salt,** and **¼ teaspoon ground black pepper.** Bring to a boil and simmer until squash is tender, 20 to 30 minutes. Puree in batches in a blender or food processor until smooth. Return to the pot, taste, and add more salt and pepper if necessary.
Makes 8 servings.

POTATO-LEEK SOUP In a soup pot, sauté **1 chopped onion** and **3 chopped leeks (white parts only) in 3 tablespoons butter** until soft, 6 minutes. Add **2 pounds peeled and sliced russet potatoes, 6 cups chicken broth, 1 teaspoon salt, ¼ teaspoon ground white pepper,** and **a pinch of nutmeg.** Simmer until potatoes are tender, 20 minutes. Force the solid ingredients and half the liquid through a food mill. Return to the soup pot and add **1 cup *each* light cream and milk.** Heat through. Serve hot or chilled, garnished with **2 tablespoons chopped fresh chives.** To served chilled, thin with a little bit of milk or buttermilk before serving.
Makes 6 servings.

SUMMER MINESTRONE Warm **2 tablespoons olive oil** in a large soup pot over medium heat. Add **2 peeled and thinly sliced carrots, 2 chopped celery ribs,** and **1 large chopped onion.** Sauté until soft, about 5 minutes. Add **2 large minced garlic cloves, 2 bay leaves,** and **1 teaspoon dried oregano.** Cook 1 minute longer. Pour in **6 cups chicken stock** or **vegetable stock (or canned broth)** and **1 cup dry white wine.** Bring to a boil. Add **3 small peeled and chopped boiling potatoes; 1 cup green beans (cut into ½" pieces); 2 peeled and chopped tomatoes (or one 14-ounce can, drained); 2 small zucchini, halved lengthwise and cut into ¼" crescents;** and **½ small head (2 cups) shredded green cabbage.** Simmer until vegetables are tender, about 20 minutes. Remove bay leaves. Add **½ cup chiffonade of fresh basil (or chopped fresh basil)** and **1 teaspoon salt.** For deeper flavor, let cool and reheat. Top each serving with **1 tablespoon grated Parmesan cheese.** You can easily vary the vegetables to your liking in this recipe.
Makes 6 to 8 servings.

HEALTHY HINT ▼ **To draw fat out of a soup** • Place the soup in the freezer for 30 minutes, and the fat will congeal on the top. Skim off and discard the fat with a spoon or spatula. Or siphon the fat off the surface of the warm soup with a bulb baster. When only a thin layer remains, use a paper towel to absorb the rest. You can also place a couple of ice cubes in a slotted spoon or in cheesecloth and drag it over the top of the soup. The fat will cling to it.

S

Sour Cream *see also* Cream

Sour cream is simply cream that has been deliberately soured. By adding a bacterial culture to the cream, producers can control the souring process as the lactose in the cream converts to lactic acid.

BASICS ▼ **To choose** • Try a few brands to find the one you like best. The best-tasting reduced-fat sour creams are "one-third reduced fat" varieties, which are made with half-and-half rather than with a lot of thickeners and stabilizers.

To store • Refrigerate sour cream and use it within 1 week of its sell-by date.

To use to enrich a soup or sauce • Bring the sour cream to room temperature and add it at the very end of the cooking time. Sour cream will curdle if exposed to high heat, so avoid simmering or boiling once it has been stirred in. Keep in mind that sour cream and other milk products won't separate as easily in flour-thickened mixtures. To avoid curdling, you can also temper the sour cream before adding it to a hot mixture. Place the sour cream in a small bowl, then stir in some of the hot mixture and add the whole thing back to the hot mixture. Again, avoid simmering or boiling after the sour cream is added. If the mixture does separate, blend it in a food processor or blender to restore its smooth texture.

To replace • Replace sour cream with an equal amount of yogurt. Or use fat-free evaporated milk mixed with lemon juice, using 1 tablespoon lemon juice per cup of evaporated milk.

CHILLED CUCUMBER SOUP In a food processor, combine **2 peeled, seeded, and chopped cucumbers; 2 peeled and chopped celery ribs; 3 chopped scallions (white parts only);** and **1 minced garlic clove.** Process until finely chopped. Mix the chopped vegetables into **2 cups chilled chicken broth (with fat removed), 1 cup sour cream, 2 tablespoons white wine vinegar, 1 tablespoon chopped fresh dill, 2 teaspoons finely grated lemon zest, ½ teaspoon salt, ¼ teaspoon ground black pepper,** and **a dash of hot-pepper sauce.** *Makes 4 servings.*

Soy Milk

Made from boiled and ground soybeans, soy milk is higher in protein than cow's milk, and it's cholesterol-free. It makes an excellent substitute for those who are lactose-intolerant or who choose not to drink cow's milk.

BASICS ▼ **To choose** • Soy milk is available in whole, low-fat, and enriched versions as well as in plain, vanilla, and chocolate flavors. Often, the best-tasting soy milk is sold in the refrigerated section of the supermarket. You can also buy soy milk in aseptic containers.

To store • Refrigerated soy milk keeps in the fridge until 1 week after the sell-by date. Aseptically packaged soy milk will keep at room temperature until the expiration date. Once it is opened, use it within 1 week.

To use • Soy milk can replace cow's milk in most cooking applications. Use it for cereals, shakes, soups, custards, puddings, and baked goods. Keep in mind that soy milk tends to curdle when mixed with acidic ingredients such as lemon juice, wine, and even coffee.

BASMATI RICE AND SOY PUDDING Preheat oven to 300°F. In a large bowl, combine **2 cups soy milk, 2 beaten** eggs, ⅓ cup brown sugar, 2 teaspoons vanilla extract, 1 teaspoon grated lemon zest, ½ teaspoon ground nutmeg, and ¼ teaspoon salt. Stir in 2 cups cooked basmati rice and ⅓ cup golden raisins. Pour into a greased, shallow, 1½-quart baking dish. Bake until a knife inserted in center comes out clean, 60 to 70 minutes. *Makes 4 servings.*

CHERRY-SOY OVEN PANCAKE Preheat oven to 350°F. Scatter 2 cups pitted cherries (a scant pound cherries with pits) in a greased 9" pie plate. In a blender, combine 1 cup soy milk, 3 eggs, 2 teaspoons vanilla extract, ½ cup flour, ⅓ cup sugar, ½ teaspoon baking powder, and ¼ teaspoon salt. Process until smooth. Pour into the prepared dish over cherries. Bake until puffed and golden, 35 minutes. Cool slightly, dust with 2 teaspoons confectioners' sugar, and serve warm. *Makes 4 servings.*

Soy Sauce

A fermented blend of roasted soybean meal and ground wheat, salty-tasting soy sauce is a ubiquitous Asian condiment.

BASICS ▼ **To choose** • China and Japan produce several different types of soy sauce. Light soy sauce is a thinner, saltier-tasting soy sauce. Don't confuse it with "lite" soy sauce, which is the reduced-sodium variety. Dark soy sauce is thicker and richer-tasting. And Japanese tamari, the by-product of making miso (a fermented soy food), has the darkest color and the richest flavor. When buying soy sauce, look for the words *naturally brewed* on the label, and avoid artificially produced soy sauces made with corn syrup, salt, and caramel color. These have a harsh salty flavor and lack the complexity and rich taste of authentic soy sauces.

To store • Soy sauce will keep indefinitely at room temperature.

Spices *see also specific spices*

The dried aromatic parts of certain plants, including the seeds, berries, buds, roots, flowers, and bark, spices add a dynamic range of flavors to both savory and sweet foods.

BASICS ▼ **To choose** • Whenever possible, buy whole spices instead of ground. The seed coatings and hulls help protect the flavors of whole spices, which helps them keep longer. The volatile character of a spice begins to fade once spices are ground, and it deteriorates entirely within a few months. It helps to shop in a store that sells a lot of spices and turns over its inventory rapidly. Many mail-order sources offer fresher spices than you can find in supermarkets. Also, because their flavor fades fast, buy spices in small quantities and replace them after 1 year. If you are buying spices from a bulk bin, give them a good sniff to make sure that they are highly aromatic. Don't buy spices that look faded or have an uneven color.

Fascinating Fact: It's been said that Connecticut is the Nutmeg State because early 19th-century peddlers whittled whole nutmeg replicas from wood and sold them to unsuspecting housewives as real nutmegs. Nutmeg must have been very expensive, considering how long it would have taken to carve a wooden nutmeg replica. The nickname stuck. And, for the record, nutmeg grows in tropical climates, not on the Northeast coast.

To store • Keep spices in airtight containers away from heat, moisture, and light. A cool cupboard or drawer is ideal.

S

S

SPICE RUBS

Applied to food to infuse it with flavor, spice rubs are ideal for rubbing into meats that will be grilled, broiled, or even baked. To add flavor without fat, rub the dry spice mix into the meat (a dry rub). Or make a paste by combining the spice mix with a little bit of oil, which helps the seasoning adhere to the meat. Rub any of the following seasoning blends into beef, pork, lamb, or chicken. Wrap the meat in plastic and refrigerate for several hours before cooking.

Carolina Spice Rub: Combine **2 tablespoons paprika, 1 tablespoon brown sugar, and ½ teaspoon** *each* **celery salt, ground** black pepper, dry mustard, and onion powder. *Makes about ¼ cup.*

Tropical Spice Rub: Combine **2 teaspoons** *each* **dried cilantro, garlic powder, and salt, and 1 teaspoon** *each* **ground black pepper, ground cumin, and ground oregano.** *Makes 3 tablespoons.*

Mid-East Spice Rub: Combine **2 teaspoons ground black pepper, 1½ teaspoons ground cumin, 1 teaspoon** *each* **ground coriander and salt, ½ teaspoon ground cardamom, and ¼ teaspoon ground cloves.** *Makes about 2 tablespoons.*

To keep track of age and freshness • Mark the date on the label upon purchasing.

To find spices quickly • Organize them alphabetically. Or, if you use a few spices regularly, store them separately with other primary cooking staples, such as oils and vinegars. It may also help to store important baking spices, such as cinnamon, nutmeg, and ground ginger, near your other baking staples (baking soda, baking powder, and salt).

To grind whole spices • Place about 1 tablespoon of spice in an electric spice grinder or clean coffee mill. Grind to a fine powder and use immediately. You can also grind spices in a mortar with a pestle.

CURRY POWDER Mix together **¼ cup ground coriander; 1½ tablespoons ground turmeric; 1 tablespoon** *each* **ground fenugreek and ground cumin; 1 teaspoon** *each* **ground cardamom, ground ginger, ground cinnamon,** **and ground allspice; and ⅛ teaspoon ground red pepper (or more to taste).** *Makes about ½ cup.*

Spinach *see also* Greens, Cooking; Salads

Brought to the United States from Spain, spinach is notorious for being gritty because it grows on short stems close to the ground.

BASICS **To choose** • Look for spinach with crisp, dark green leaves. For the most delicate flavor and tender texture, choose small, "baby" spinach leaves. Older, larger spinach leaves tend to be more bitter in flavor and chewier in texture.

To store • Keep refrigerated in a plastic bag up to 3 days.

To trim • Fold large spinach leaves in half vertically. Pinch the sides together just where the leaf meets the stem. Pull the stem, and it will tear away from the leafy part. Save the stems for flavoring a broth, or discard them.

To clean • Swish the leaves around in a bowl of cold water to loosen grit and dirt. Lift the leaves out of the bowl to a strainer to dry, so that you aren't disturbing the sediment in the bowl bottom.

To cut into thin strips (chiffonade) • Stack 4 or 5 spinach leaves and roll from the short end into a cigar. Slice across the cigar into thin strips.

To steam • In a large, deep skillet with a tight-fitting lid, bring ¼" of water to a boil. Add 20 ounces trimmed and cleaned spinach, tossing it to distribute it evenly. Cover and steam 2 minutes. Toss the spinach to push any uncooked leaves to-ward the bottom, cover the skillet again, and steam the spinach just until it wilts, another 30 seconds to 1 minute. Drain the spinach through a strainer and season it with 1 teaspoon oil or butter, ½ teaspoon salt, and ¼ teaspoon ground black pepper.

PROBLEM SOLVERS ▼

To prevent discoloration • Cut spinach with a stainless steel knife. A carbon steel blade will cause discoloration.

To avoid a soggy mess • Drain and squeeze out excess liquid from cooked spinach before adding it to other foods.

TIME SAVERS ▼

To save prep time • Buy baby spinach, which has tender stems that do not need to be removed.

THREE QUICK SPINACH SAUTÉS

From fridge to table in less than 5 minutes, spinach is one of the fastest-cooking fresh vegetables. These easy sautés keep spinach from getting soggy because the moisture evaporates in the open pan. Each recipe makes 4 servings.

Garlic Spinach: Sauté **2 tablespoons finely chopped onion** and **1 minced garlic clove** in **2 tablespoons butter** until tender, 2 minutes. Add **20 ounces trimmed and cleaned spinach.** Cook, tossing once or twice, just until wilted, 1 minute. Season with **½ teaspoon salt** and **¼ teaspoon ground black pepper (or more to taste).**

Spinach Boursinaise: Sauté **2 table-spoons finely chopped onion** and **1 minced garlic clove** in **2 tablespoons butter** until tender, 2 minutes. Add **20 ounces trimmed and cleaned spinach.** Cook, tossing once or twice, just until wilted, 1 minute. Stir in **2 ounces (¼ cup) herbed cream cheese, 1 teaspoon sour cream, ½ teaspoon salt,** and **¼ teaspoon ground black pepper (or more to taste).**

Curried Spinach: Sauté **2 tablespoons finely chopped onion** and **1 minced garlic clove** in **2 tablespoons butter** until tender, 2 minutes. Add **¼ teaspoon *each* ground coriander and curry powder,** and **a pinch *each* ground black pepper, ground red pepper, and grated nutmeg.** Cook 10 seconds. Add **20 ounces trimmed and cleaned spinach.** Cook, tossing once or twice, just until wilted, 1 minute. Season with **½ teaspoon salt** and another **¼ teaspoon ground black pepper (or more to taste).** Remove from heat and stir in **⅓ cup plain yogurt.**

Spanakopita

Spinach-cheese pie is a classic Greek entrée. This lightened version uses fat-free cottage cheese to replace some of the traditional feta cheese. Fresh dill complements the flavors of the spinach and cheese.

2   **tablespoons olive oil, divided**

1   **large onion, chopped**

4   **scallions, sliced**

3   **packages (10 ounces each) frozen spinach, thawed and squeezed dry**

¾   **cup fat-free cottage cheese**

¾   **cup finely crumbled feta cheese**

2   **tablespoons fresh dill or 1 teaspoon dried**

½   **teaspoon + a pinch of salt**

¼   **teaspoon ground black pepper**

3   **egg whites + 1 tablespoon egg white**

1   **tablespoon butter, melted**

8   **sheets (11" × 17" each) phyllo dough, at room temperature**

8   **teaspoons plain dried bread crumbs, divided**

1. Heat 1 teaspoon of the oil in a medium nonstick skillet over medium-low heat. Add the onion and cook until softened, 10 minutes, stirring occasionally. Stir in the scallions. Cook 2 minutes.

2. Meanwhile, coarsely chop the spinach. Add to the skillet and cook until any liquid cooks off, 2 minutes. Place in a large bowl and let cool for 10 minutes. Add the cottage cheese, feta cheese, dill, ½ teaspoon of the salt, and the pepper to the bowl. (The recipe can be made ahead up to this point. Refrigerate, covered, for up to 1 day.) Stir in 3 egg whites.

3. Preheat the oven to 350°F. Coat a 12" × 8" baking dish with cooking spray. In a small bowl, combine the remaining 5 teaspoons oil and the butter. Whisk in the remaining 1 tablespoon egg white until combined. Add the pinch of salt.

4. Place the phyllo sheets on a work surface with the short side facing you. (Cover the sheets not in use with a damp cloth to prevent drying.) Lightly brush the bottom half of one of the phyllo sheets with the egg white mixture. Sprinkle with ½ teaspoon of the bread crumbs. Fold the unbrushed side toward you on top. Brush it lightly with the egg white mixture. Place in the prepared baking pan. Sprinkle with ½ teaspoon of the remaining bread crumbs. Repeat with 2 more sheets, layering them in the pan.

5. Evenly spread the spinach mixture into the pan. Repeat layering with the remaining phyllo, egg white mixture, and bread crumbs. Do not sprinkle bread crumbs on the top layer. Cut three 1" slits down the center of the phyllo, opening them a bit with the knife.

6. Bake until golden brown, 40 to 45 minutes.

Makes 6 servings

To quickly cook prewashed bagged spinach • Poke a hole in the bag with a small, sharp knife and place the bag in a microwave oven, hole side up. Cook on high power until the spinach is wilted, 3 minutes. Season as desired.

To quickly thaw and cook frozen spinach • Place the spinach, in its box, in a microwave oven and cook on high power until the spinach is wilted, 4 minutes. Open the box and press out excess moisture in a strainer.

To use frozen spinach without cooking • Place the spinach, in its box, in a bowl in the refrigerator overnight or at room temperature for 2 hours. Squeeze out excess moisture before using.

To use leftover cooked spinach • Lightly toast 2 pieces leftover bread and spread with ½ cup chopped leftover spinach. Top the spinach with ¼ teaspoon dried oregano and ¼ cup crumbled feta cheese. Broil the spinach toasts until heated through, 2 minutes.

FLAVOR TIP ▼ **To boost flavor** • Nutmeg makes an exceptional flavor complement to spinach. Add freshly grated nutmeg to spinach dishes near the beginning of cooking time.

LINGUINE WITH SPINACH SAUCE In a large pot of salted boiling water, cook ½ **pound linguine** until tender yet firm to the bite, 7 to 9 minutes. Meanwhile, place **1 pound trimmed and cleaned spinach** in a large saucepan. Cover and cook over medium-high heat until just wilted, 1 to 2 minutes. Drain, cool slightly, and squeeze out excess liquid. Coarsely chop. Add **2 minced garlic cloves** to the saucepan and sauté in **2 tablespoons olive oil** until tender, 30 seconds. Return spinach to the pan and add ½ **teaspoon dried basil (or**

¼ **cup fresh whole basil leaves).** Toss to mix. Transfer to a food processor and add ½ **cup sour cream,** ¼ **cup grated Parmesan cheese,** ½ **teaspoon salt,** and ¼ **teaspoon ground black pepper.** Puree until smooth. Drain pasta and toss with sauce. *Makes about 4 servings.*

Squash, Summer *see also*
Zucchini

Squash can be divided into two huge categories: winter and summer squash. Summer squash includes all of the softer, more fragile immature squash such as zucchini, crookneck squash, and pattypan squash. These have a high water content, which makes them more perishable than winter squash.

BASICS ▼ **To choose** • Look for firm, glossy-looking summer squash with brightly colored skin. Small to medium-size squash are always the best choice for texture and flavor. Larger ones tend to be watery and have more seeds.

To store • Keep summer squash in a perforated bag in the vegetable drawer of your refrigerator up to 5 days.

PROBLEM SOLVER ▼ **To salvage overcooked, soggy summer squash** • Drain out excess liquid and serve the squash with a crunchy topping, such as toasted bread crumbs.

FLAVOR TIP ▼ **To use squash blossoms** • Summer squash blossoms are an offbeat edible flower. Nip the orange male blossoms, which appear first. Female blossoms, which produce the squash, contain a bulbous swelling flower and a 4-part pistil in the center. The male blossoms can be added to salads or stuffed with soft cheese, cooked and crumbled sausage, or burgers, and then breaded and fried or baked.

Squash, Winter *see also*

Pumpkin

The varieties of winter squash are countless. Some of the more popular types include pumpkin, acorn, butternut, and Hubbard. These thick-skinned vegetables have large seeds and a dense, sweet flesh that can be used in both savory and sweet dishes.

BASICS ▼

To choose • Look for firm winter squash that feels heavy for its size. Avoid squash with soft, spongy spots.

To store • Keep winter squash in a cool, dry place with plenty of ventilation. Use within 3 weeks of purchase. Once winter squash is cut, cover the exposed flesh with plastic wrap, refrigerate it, and use it within a day or two.

To cut • Slice off the stem with a heavy knife. Then, cut through the squash with heavy pressure on a sturdy surface. It may help to use a meat cleaver and a rubber mallet or a hammer wrapped in a thick kitchen towel to hammer the cleaver through the squash like a wedge.

To peel butternut squash • Prick the squash several times with a fork and warm it in a microwave oven on high power until the skin is more tender, about 2 minutes. Slice off the two ends and cut the squash in half near the center, where the neck meets the bulb. Place each half on its widest cut side and use a thin knife or vegetable peeler to remove the peel in strips running from top to bottom.

To remove seeds and strings • Use a melon baller. Or, if the squash will be pureed, remove only the seeds, then cook the flesh as desired. Puree with a handheld mixer and the strings will wrap themselves around the beater necks.

To roast • If you are roasting whole winter squash, pierce the squash a number of times with a fork or the tip of a paring knife to allow steam to escape. Or cut medium squash such as acorn or butternut in half lengthwise, and scoop out the seeds. If you are using a large squash such as pumpkin, calabaza, or banana squash, cut it into large (4" to 6") pieces. Arrange the squash, skin side up if cut, in a large, shallow roasting pan containing ½" of water. Bake at 400°F until the squash is very soft when pierced with a fork or knife tip, 45 minutes to 1 hour. Serve it with butter, salt, and pepper, or cool and puree it to use in recipes.

Fascinating Fact: Squash got its name from the Narraganset Indians, who called summer squash *askatasquash*. That was too big a mouthful for Colonists, so they simplified it to "squash."

PROBLEM SOLVER ▼

To rescue overcooked winter squash • Serve it as a puree. Or add broth to the puree, as well as a touch of cream and spices, to make cream of squash soup.

TIME SAVERS ▼

To cook quickly • Peel and seed the squash, then shred the flesh on the large teeth of a grater or in a food processor with the shredding disk. Shredded squash can be sautéed in oil with seasonings or boiled until tender in just a few minutes.

To microwave • Slice off both ends of the squash. Stand the squash on one of its cut ends and slice it in half from top to bottom. Scoop out the seeds and strings. Season as desired and wrap each half in microwaveable plastic wrap. Cook on high power 7 minutes (for 1 pound squash) or 12 minutes (for 2 pounds). If you are using very large squash, such as Hubbard or pumpkin, cut it into chunks rather than in half, and cook it the same way.

To save prep time • When a recipe calls for pureed squash, save time by using canned or frozen pureed squash, which is available in most grocery stores.

FLAVOR TIP ▼ **To flavor desserts and soups** • Use pureed butternut squash in place of pumpkin in desserts and soups. It has a sweeter flavor and is less watery. To make puree, microwave chunks of peeled butternut squash on high power, 15 minutes. Mash the flesh and use it immediately or freeze it until needed. Eight ounces peeled squash equals about 1 cup puree.

BUTTERNUT SQUASH RISOTTO In a medium saucepan, bring **4 cups chicken broth** to a simmer. In a large nonstick skillet, sauté **1 small chopped onion** in **2 teaspoons olive oil** until soft, 4 minutes. Add **2 cups cooked butternut squash,** mashing in the pan. Cook 2 minutes. Stir in 1¼ **cups Arborio rice** and 1 cup of the simmering broth. Simmer until almost all of the liquid is absorbed, stirring constantly. Repeat adding and stirring remaining broth, 1 cup at a time, until rice is tender yet firm to the bite, about 20 to 25 minutes. Stir in ¼ **cup chopped fresh parsley, 3 tablespoons grated Parmesan cheese,** and ¼ **teaspoon ground black pepper.** Serve immediately.
Makes 4 servings.

SOUR CREAM SQUASH PIE Whisk together **1 pound (2 cups) canned or frozen and thawed butternut squash puree, 1 cup sour cream,** ¾ **cup light brown sugar, 1 teaspoon** *each* **ground cinnamon and ground ginger,** ½ **teaspoon salt,** ¼ **teaspoon allspice,** and **2 lightly beaten eggs.** Pour into a prepared 9" pie crust and bake at 350°F until crust is browned and center of filling is set,

45 minutes. Cool before slicing. Serve with additional sour cream, if desired.
Makes 8 servings.

HEALTHY HINT ▼ **To get maximum beta-carotene** • When choosing winter squash, look for the darkest skin, which indicates a higher concentration of beta-carotene. Also, storing winter squash in a cool, well-ventilated place increases its beta-carotene content. Store up to 1 month.

Squid *see also* Doneness Tests and Temperatures (page 572)

It wasn't too long ago that most Americans were squeamish about squid. But today, calamari is an increasingly popular restaurant dish, particularly when it is fried. A mild, sweet flavor and reasonable price have helped make squid more popular.

S

BASICS ▼ **To choose** • Trust your nose. A delicate ocean scent is the most reliable indicator of freshness. Looks count too: Fresh squid looks firm and shiny. If the squid in your market is limp and dull, pass it by. Also, if it has not been cleaned, check the color of the mottled membrane covering it; it should be gray but not pink or purple. Squid freezes well, so if the fresh squid doesn't measure up, check the freezer section of your market. Purchasing cleaned squid will save you time, but remember that uncleaned squid is often half the price.

To store • Squid is extremely perishable. Refrigerate it on a bed of ice until ready to use, and try to use it the same day you buy it.

To clean • Reach under the hood and pull out the innards, including the plasticlike quill. Cut off the tentacles just beneath the eyes, and discard the quill, head, and innards.

Rinse out the hood under cold running water. Use the back of a paring knife to scrape the gray membrane off the hood. Cut off the 2 small wings on either side of the hood and reserve them. The cleaned hood can be sliced into rings or left whole for stuffing.

To cook • Deep-fry, grill, or stir-fry squid very quickly over high heat (no longer than 2 minutes), or braise it slowly over low heat for at least 1 hour for optimum tenderness. Any cooking time in between will make the squid tough.

QUICK, YOU'VE SPILLED!

Most stains on clothing are removable—if you act fast. The treatments vary depending upon whether you have, for instance, poured wine down your shirt front or skimmed your cuff across a gravy boat. The treatments below start with a "Quick Fix" and end with "If All Else Fails." Be sure to rinse the garment between treatments if you try each treatment.

Stain Removal Ground Rules

• Read your garment's care instructions. Some delicate fabrics and "dry-clean only" garments are best treated by a professional cleaner.

• Act immediately. The longer you wait, the more likely the stain is to set.

Spilled Substance	Quick Fix	Backup Plan
Chocolate	Blot with cold water. Rinse.	Blot with a mild laundry detergent and cold water, or treat with an enzyme presoak product or prewash spray. Rinse thoroughly with cool water.
Coffee	Blot with cool water. Rinse.	Saturate with a pretreatment stain remover and rinse. Or blot with a solution of water and laundry detergent. Rinse.
Eggs	Soak in cold water for several hours.	Soak in a solution of mild laundry detergent, cold water, and a splash of ammonia.
Gravy	Soak in cold water for several hours.	Treat with an enzyme presoak product or prewash spray. Launder.
Grease, cooking oil, or mayonnaise	Sprinkle with a little cornstarch, allow cornstarch to absorb oil, and lightly brush off.	Treat with a spot remover, allowing a few minutes for it to penetrate. Rub with liquid laundry detergent and launder.
Juice	Blot with warm water.	Soak in warm water and an enzyme presoak product. Launder.
Red wine	Cover with a thick layer of salt. Follow with a cold-water rinse.	Blot with liquid laundry detergent and rinse with cold water.

S

Stains *see also* Burnt Foods; Cleaning

The best way to prevent stains is to clean them up before they set. This is particularly true for tomato juice or berry juice stains on cutting boards and countertops. See also "Quick, You've Spilled!"

BASICS ▼ **To clean stains from glass electric-drip coffeepots** • Wash the pot in a solution made of 3 tablespoons baking soda mixed

---

- Scrape off whatever you can with a dry edge, such as a spoon or a butter knife. Why rub in whatever has not yet soaked into the fabric?
- Never rinse with hot water. Heat tends to seal in stains.
- Use a gentle hand and avoid scrubbing, which may grind the stain more deeply into the fabric.

- Place something absorbent, such as a napkin or a clean rag, on top of the stain as you blot with cold water or a spot remover from behind the stain. That way, the stain is repelled out instead of being driven deeper into the fabric.
- Work from the stain's edges inward to avoid spreading the stain farther outward.

Last-Ditch Effort	If All Else Fails
For milk chocolate, blot with a solution of mild laundry detergent, a few drops of ammonia, and cold water. For dark chocolate, blot with a solution of laundry detergent, white vinegar, and cold water. Rinse.	Soak colorfast garments in a diluted solution of liquid chlorine bleach and water. Take non-colorfast or highly valued garments to a dry cleaner.
For a black coffee stain, try blotting with hydrogen peroxide. Rinse. For a coffee-with-milk stain, blot with a solution of water, laundry detergent, and a few drops of ammonia.	If the garment is colorfast, soak the whole item in a diluted solution of liquid chlorine bleach and water. If it is not colorfast, or if it is a valued garment, take it to a dry cleaner.
Treat with an enzyme presoak product or prewash spray. Then, launder.	Take it to a dry cleaner.
If the garment is colorfast, soak in a solution of liquid chlorine bleach diluted with water.	Take it to a dry cleaner.
If you can't launder immediately, blot with a towel and then dab with nail polish remover. Rinse. (*Caution:* Not recommended with rayon fabrics.)	Take it to a dry cleaner.
If the garment is colorfast, soak in a solution of liquid chlorine bleach diluted with water. Or try pretreating with a solution of 1 tablespoon vinegar and ½ cup warm water. Then launder.	Take it to a dry cleaner.
Soak in cold water and an enzyme presoak product. Launder.	Take it to a dry cleaner.

with 1 quart water. To clean the machine itself, run this solution through the coffee-making cycle.

To prevent stains in plastic storage containers • Acidic ingredients such as tomatoes can leave a stain on plastic containers. To avoid the stains, coat the containers with cooking spray before using.

Steaming *see also* Microwave Cooking; Pressure Cookers

One of the simplest cooking techniques, steaming calls for food to be placed on a rack over simmering water, covered with a tight-fitting lid, and cooked. This moist-heat cooking method is an excellent way to prepare vegetables, fish, some meats, and even desserts. Steaming is also among the most nutritious cooking methods because the nutrients remain in the food instead of leaching out into the cooking water.

BASICS **To steam** • Set up a steamer, which could be a set of bamboo racks to be placed in a large wok or the steamer insert basket that often comes with pots or saucepans. You can also set up a steamer by purchasing an inexpensive steamer basket or by propping a small wire rack or metal colander on top of some ramekins or crumpled foil balls set in the bottom of a pot with a tight-fitting lid. Add a few inches of water to the pot, making sure that it doesn't rise above the level of the steamer rack. Bring the water to a boil, then reduce it to a rapid simmer. Place the food on the rack. Cover and begin timing. If you open the steamer either to add more water or to see whether the food has finished cooking, increase the heat to bring the water back to a boil, then reduce it to a simmer, replace the lid, and continue timing.

To help foods steam evenly • Stir or use tongs to bring foods on the bottom to the top and vice versa.

To steam a whole fish • Place the fish on a wire rack that fits inside of a roasting pan. Prop the rack up on balls of aluminum foil so that the fish does not sit in the water. Add a few inches of water, cover the pan with foil, and heat by setting the pan over 2 burners. When the fish is done, the top fillet will easily pull away from the backbone. Avoid baking until the fish is very flaky and falls apart, a sign that it's overdone.

SALMON STEAMED OVER ORANGE-BASIL TOMATO SAUCE Provided that there is not too much liquid, food can be steamed directly on a simmering sauce. In a large, deep skillet over medium heat, cook ½ **chopped onion, 2 minced garlic cloves,** and **1 tablespoon finely grated orange zest in ½ cup** *each* **orange juice and white wine** until liquid is reduced to ¼ cup. Add **4 chopped canned plum tomatoes, ½ teaspoon salt,** and ¼ **teaspoon ground black pepper.** Sprinkle **4 pieces skinless salmon fillet (¼ pound each)** with another ½ **teaspoon salt** and ¼ **teaspoon ground black pepper,** and **1 teaspoon extra-virgin olive oil.** Top each piece of fish with **1 basil leaf** and place on the simmering sauce. Cover and steam until fish is opaque, 8 minutes. *Makes 4 servings.*

PROBLEM SOLVERS **To avoid steam burns** • Always lift pot lids with the open side away from you to allow steam to escape.

To secure a loose pan lid when steaming • A tight-fitting lid is essential to proper steaming. If your lid is loose, line the interior of the lid with foil, folding the edges up so that they stick outside of the pan lid. Fit the lid snugly over the pot.

To ensure that water does not run out during steaming • Place a heatproof fork or spoon in the pan of water. If there's ample water in the pot, it should rattle.

Stevia

Native to South America, stevia is an herb used since pre-Colombian times to sweeten medicines and beverages. It is now grown and cultivated throughout the world, including the United States, Canada, China, Ukraine, and the United Kingdom. In Japan, stevia sweeteners have been approved and commercially used in food products and soft drinks since the 1970s.

BASICS **To choose** • Stevia is available in both powdered and liquid forms. The white powder tastes the best. Look for it in health food stores.

To use • Often used as a replacement for sugar or artificial sweeteners, stevia is noncaloric and contains no carbohydrates. It is up to 300 times as sweet as sugar, so a little goes a very long way. It can be used hot or cold to sweeten fruits, cereals, shakes, beverages, and yogurts, but it works best in dishes with strong flavors such as cranberry because it tends to have a bitter aftertaste. When baking with stevia, keep in mind that it will not caramelize and dissolve like sugar. This means that baked goods made with stevia will not develop a browned crust and may require additional liquid to keep the interior moist. Stevia is usually added to the dry ingredients in baked goods. Use just a small pinch ($\frac{1}{32}$ teaspoon) of stevia to sweeten a cup of tea; use $\frac{1}{8}$ teaspoon for a 4-serving batch of pancakes or waffles; and

use $\frac{1}{2}$ teaspoon stevia for a typical muffin or quickbread recipe that contains $1\frac{1}{2}$ to 2 cups of flour.

Stews *see also* Braising; Browning; Chili; Slow Cookers; Soups

Usually made from a combination of meat and vegetables, stews employ the same cooking principles as braising: long cooking in a covered pot over low heat to create a rich, satisfying meal.

BASICS **To stew** • Begin by browning any meat in a small amount of fat in the stew pot. Once the meat is evenly browned, remove it from the pot with a slotted spoon and pour off some of the fat if necessary. Sauté any firm, aromatic vegetables, such as carrots and onions, along with seasonings such as garlic and fresh herbs in the remaining fat. When the vegetables are tender, return the meat to the pot and add the cooking liquid (such as broth, wine, beer, or water). Bring to a boil, reduce to a simmer, then cover the pot and cook until the ingredients are tender. If using more-tender vegetables, add them in the middle of the cooking process rather than at the beginning.

To choose a stew pot • Use a thick, heavy-bottom pot that will hold heat and distribute it evenly. Make sure that the pot has a lid so that you can cover the pot as the stew cooks.

To choose stew meat • Tougher cuts of meat, such as chuck, round, brisket, and shank, are excellent for stewing. The long, slow cooking in liquid helps tenderize these tougher cuts.

To cook stew meat to a rich brown color • Sear meat cubes in batches with ample space between them so that they brown properly rather than steam-cook.

S

Also, blot the meat with paper towels before browning. Dry meat browns better than moist meat. Avoid tossing meat cubes in flour before browning, however. The flour tends to burn while the meat is searing, and it lends an undesirable raw flour taste to the stew.

MAKE-AHEAD SEAFOOD BOUILLA-BAISSE In a large pot, sauté **1 large chopped onion** and **2 minced garlic cloves** in **2 tablespoons olive oil** until tender, 5 minutes. Add **2 chopped celery ribs, 1 teaspoon *each* ground fennel seeds and dried basil leaves, ½ teaspoon dried thyme, 1 bay leaf, ¼ teaspoon crumbled saffron threads, 1 cup white wine,** and the **finely grated zest and juice of 1 large orange.** Heat to boiling. Add **4 peeled, seeded, and chopped tomatoes; 3 cups water;** and **2 fish bouillon cubes.** Simmer 5 minutes. (At this point, the recipe can be held in the refrigerator for 48 hours). Ten minutes before serving, reheat the stew to simmering. Add **12 cleaned littleneck clams** and simmer 3 minutes. Add **16 scrubbed and debearded mussels** and simmer 2 minutes. Add **½ pound trimmed sea scallops** and **¾ pound peeled and deveined large shrimp.** Simmer 1 minute. Add **¼ cup chopped fresh parsley** and simmer 1 minute more. Scallops and shrimp will be opaque when done, and clam and mussel shells will be opened. Discard any unopened shells, and remove bay leaf. Serve soup with crusty bread. *Makes 6 to 8 servings.*

MEXICAN BEEF STEW In a Dutch oven, heat **2 teaspoons olive oil** over medium-high heat. Add half of **3 pounds beef round** or **chuck,** cut into 1" pieces. Cook until browned on all sides. Remove and repeat with **another 2 teaspoons oil** and remaining beef. Pour off any oil. To Dutch oven, add **1 cup *each* chunky salsa** and **beef broth, ¼ teaspoon salt,** and reserved meat. Bring to a simmer. Cover tightly and cook over low heat until beef is fork-tender, 1¼ hours. Stir in **2 zucchini, sliced into half-rounds; 1 can (15 ounces) rinsed and drained black beans; and ½ cup frozen corn.** Return to a simmer, cover, and cook until vegetables are tender, 15 minutes. Mix **2 tablespoons cornstarch** and **3 tablespoons water** in a small bowl. Stir into stew and cook until thickened, 1 to 2 minutes. Garnish each serving with **1 tablespoon *each* chopped fresh cilantro and sour cream** (optional).

Makes 8 to 10 servings.

SLOW-COOKED PORK AND PEANUT STEW In a slow cooker, combine **4 boneless trimmed pork chops (½ pound each), 1 red bell pepper cut into strips, 1 sliced leek, ⅓ cup bottled teriyaki sauce, 2 tablespoons red wine vinegar, 2 large minced garlic cloves,** and **⅛ teaspoon ground red pepper.** Cover and cook on low until pork is fork-tender, 8 hours. Remove pork and shred with a fork. Stir **¼ cup chunky peanut butter** into cooking liquid along with **1 tablespoon lime juice** and the shredded pork. Serve over **1 pound cooked egg noodles** and garnish with **½ cup chopped fresh cilantro.**

Makes 6 to 8 servings.

PROBLEM SOLVERS ▼ **To serve a stew that will not feed all of your guests** • Spoon it over noodles, rice, or potatoes to add bulk. This trick also helps draw attention away from an over-cooked stew.

To avoid mushy vegetables in stew • Add them later in the cooking process. If any vegetables become inedible from over-cooking, fish them out and serve the stew as described above.

To rescue a burning stew • Immediately pour the stew into a new pot. Do not scrape any of the burned stew from the bottom of the first pot. If necessary, add more liquid to the new pot.

HEALTHY HINT ▼ **To stretch the meat in stews** • Add chewy, meaty vegetables such as porto-bello or shiitake mushrooms, eggplant, sun-dried tomatoes, or hominy. For a single portion, reduce the meat amount by one-half, adding ½ cup of raw vegetables, such as mushrooms or eggplant. If using sun-dried tomatoes, add 2 tomato halves per serving. If using hominy, add 3 table-spoons per serving.

Stir-Frying

One of the fastest cooking methods, stir-frying consists of quickly cooking foods over very high heat, tossing and stirring all the while to prevent sticking or burning. Stir-frying is often associated with Asian cuisine, but the flavor possibilities are endless.

BASICS ▼ **To stir-fry over an electric burner** • Use a flat-bottom wok or a large, flat-bottom skillet. Avoid round-bottom woks or pans, which will result in hot spots and cause food to cook unevenly.

To stir-fry over a gas flame • Use a round-bottom wok. The flames will reach up around the bottom of the wok to heat it evenly. If your gas stove has high, flat grates that prevent the flames from nearing the pan, try removing the grate and setting the wok directly over the flame.

To break down a stir-fry into steps • First, prepare all of your ingredients and put them in one spot within arm's reach of where you will be cooking. Everything should be prepped and ready to go before you turn on the heat. That includes all in-gredients, sauces, and garnishes. Next, heat the pan over high heat. When the pan is hot, add the oil and swirl quickly to coat the pan with an even glazing of oil. When the oil is hot (about 15 seconds of heating), add the main ingredients, such as meat or vegetables. Stir briskly to prevent scorching. If necessary to avoid over-crowding, cook these ingredients in batches, grouping together ingredients that cook at the same rate (such as carrots and celery). Let the pan become hot again be-tween batches. Next, add any aromatic in-gredients, such as garlic, ginger, chile peppers, or scallions, and cook, stirring, until fragrant. Finally, add any seasonings or sauces, such as soy sauce, salt, or sugar. If you are using a sauce that contains a thickener such as cornstarch or arrowroot, push the ingredients to the sides of the pan and pour the sauce in the center. Stir the sauce until thickened, 30 seconds to 1 minute, then stir in the other ingredients to coat with the sauce. Remove from the heat and serve topped with any garnishes.

To prepare foods for stir-frying • Cut them into thin strips or slices so that they cook quickly. It also helps to slice foods such as carrots and celery on a diagonal to expose more surface area, which helps create a tender-crisp texture.

To choose stir-fry oil • Use an oil with a high smoke point, such as peanut, canola, or soybean, so that it can withstand the high temperatures of stir-frying without burning.

S

To test the pan • Sprinkle a little water into the hot pan. If it evaporates on contact with the pan, you're ready to add the oil to the pan and begin stir-frying.

To thicken a stir-fry sauce • Many recipes call for cornstarch or other thickeners to be mixed right into the sauce. If the cooked sauce is still not thick enough, dissolve 1 teaspoon cornstarch in 1 tablespoon cold broth, soy sauce, or water. Add this mixture to the pan and stir until thickened, 30 seconds to 1 minute.

To thin a stir-fry sauce • Add broth, soy sauce, or water, 1 tablespoon at a time, until the sauce reaches the desired consistency. If you accidentally add too much, cook until the excess liquid evaporates and the sauce thickens again.

PROBLEM SOLVERS ▼

To stir-fry without a wok • Use a large, flat-bottom skillet.

To spruce up an overcooked stir-fry • Add crunchy texture with sesame seeds, crushed peanuts, cashews, fresh bean sprouts, shredded raw carrot, or thinly sliced and coarsely chopped cabbage.

To add color to a muddy-looking stir-fry • Sprinkle with chopped fresh parsley or fresh cilantro.

To avoid discoloring other ingredients when stir-frying red cabbage • Cook red cabbage separately and add it to the other ingredients just before serving.

TIME SAVERS ▼

To speed stir-frying time • Avoid using a nonstick pan, which slows down stir-frying. Also, be sure to use very high heat, which is essential for searing the food so that it cooks quickly.

To quickly stir-fry tough ingredients • Firm foods such as broccoli stems, cauliflower, potatoes, and turnips will not cook through in the few minutes allotted for most stir-frying. To stir-fry these ingredients, either precook them slightly before adding them to the stir-fry, cut them into very thin slices (julienne works well), or plan to cook them in some liquid at some point in the stir-frying. You can also steam-cook tough ingredients in the stir-fry. Sear them first, then add a little broth or water to the pan, cover, and steam-cook just until tender-crisp.

FLAVOR TIP ▼

To get the best flavor • Keep the stir-fry simple. Choose one meat or seafood and just one or two vegetables. For example, chicken or beef with asparagus or green beans is perfect. Rely on other ingredients, such as ginger, garlic, scallions, and sauce, to flavor the stir-fry.

BASIC STIR-FRY SAUCE In a small bowl, whisk **⅓ cup chicken broth; 1 tablespoon *each* soy sauce, rice vinegar or sherry, and cornstarch;** and **½ teaspoon *each* toasted sesame oil and sugar.** After stir-frying meat and/or vegetables, pour in sauce and stir until thickened. Add more broth or cornstarch to achieve desired consistency. *Makes about ½ cup.*

STIR-FRIED BARBECUED BEEF In a wok or large skillet, stir-fry **1½ pounds thinly sliced trimmed flank steak** and **¼ teaspoon red-pepper flakes** in **1 tablespoon vegetable oil** over high heat until meat is no longer pink, 2 to 3 minutes. Remove with a slotted spoon and set aside. Add **1 minced garlic clove, 1 tablespoon grated fresh ginger,** and **½ grated onion** to the pan. Stir-fry 10 seconds. Add **¼ cup ketchup, 2 tablespoons cider vinegar, 1 tablespoon Worcestershire sauce,** and **1 teaspoon brown sugar.** Simmer until thickened, 2 minutes. Return the reserved steak to the pan and toss with the sauce. Drizzle with the **juice of 1 lime.** *Makes 4 servings.*

Stock *see also* Broth; Soups

The terms *broth* and *stock* are somewhat interchangeable, but *stock* usually refers to the homemade variety, whereas *broth* often connotes a canned or store-bought version. Both are the result of cooking meat, fish, or vegetables in water and straining out the solids. *Brown stock* is made with bones, which add flavor as well as body to the liquid. Stocks form the basis of countless soups, sauces, and other dishes.

BASICS
▼
To make a basic chicken stock • Use a larger stewing chicken rather than a young roasting bird. The older chicken will have more flavor and more natural gelatin to enrich and thicken the stock. Put the meat (and bones, if using) in a tall, narrow, heavy-bottom pot that will hold the ingredients snugly. Add just enough cold water to cover the ingredients by 1". Adding too much water will make a weak-tasting stock. Also add a pinch of salt to help extract flavor from the meat and bones. Heat this mixture over low heat to gently draw out the impurities in the meat, which will float to the top of the pot. Skim off and discard the impurities with a spoon, then add aromatic vegetables and seasonings, such as onions, carrots, celery, and parsley, to the pot to give the stock a more rounded and complex flavor. Cook the stock at a bare simmer for 3 to 5 hours. Avoid boiling, which could cause the solid ingredients to disintegrate and turn the stock cloudy. Strain the cooked stock though a cheesecloth-lined colander set over a large pot. Discard the solids and

let the stock cool. If you are using the stock right away, blot any fat from the surface with a paper towel. Or transfer the stock to a covered container and refrigerate it. The fat will congeal on the surface and can be easily removed.

To make a basic beef stock • Follow the directions for making a basic chicken stock (at left), but use a flavorful cut of beef that can stand up to long cooking, such as chuck. Tougher cuts of beef that can withstand longer cooking have enough natural gelatin to enrich the stock with both flavor and texture.

To make a basic fish stock • Follow the directions for making basic chicken stock (at left), but use the carcass and trimmings of lean fish, or use leftover shells from peeled shrimp to make shrimp stock. Reduce the simmering time to 40 minutes.

To make a basic vegetable stock • Follow the directions for making basic chicken stock (at left), but use a combination of aromatic vegetables, such as carrots, onions, celery, and cabbage along with herbs such as parsley, bay leaf, and thyme. Avoid very strong-tasting vegetables, such as broccoli.

To freeze stock flat • Pour cooled degreased stock into heavy-duty zipper-lock freezer bags, leaving a small amount of empty space for expansion. Press out the excess air, seal the bag, and wipe off any moisture on the outside of the bag. Lay the bags on a sheet of waxed paper on the freezer floor or on a baking sheet so that they freeze flat. Then, stand the bags on edge for space-efficient storage. Stock stored this way also defrosts faster than stock stored in plastic tubs.

To easily ladle stock into a freezer bag • Prop the bag in a bowl with the edges folded over the rim of the bowl.

S

To measure stock ladled into a freezer bag • Use a liquid measuring cup as a ladle, and mark the plastic bag with the amount before filling.

To avoid oversalting stock • Add only a small amount (about ½ teaspoon) of salt during simmering. The salt flavor will become concentrated as the broth reduces. Add more salt at the end of cooking if necessary.

To save an oversalted broth • Add 1 thinly sliced potato and simmer until the slices are translucent (15 to 20 minutes), which means that the potato has absorbed its fill of salt. Strain the potato along with the other solids.

To prevent stock from turning cloudy • Cover the solid ingredients (especially bones) with cold water instead of hot water. When covered with cold water, the blood and other impurities in the bones will dissolve, rising to the surface when the water is heated. If covered with hot water, these impurities will coagulate and disperse throughout the stock, turning it cloudy. Skim off any impurities that float to the surface of the stock as it simmers. Also, avoid boiling the stock, which can cause the solids in the broth to break down and muddy the liquid. Instead, cook the stock at a bare simmer. Be sure to strain the broth through a strainer lined with a double layer of wet cheesecloth to filter out any small particles of solids.

To clarify cloudy stock • Stir in 2 to 3 egg whites for each 6 to 8 cups of stock while the stock is still hot. The egg protein will attract the particles that are clouding the stock and trap them as it coagulates. Remove the egg white with a handheld sieve, or by straining the stock.

To save prep time • Whenever you cook chicken, set aside necks, backs, and other unused parts and freeze them in zipper-lock freezer bags. Thaw them before using to make stock.

To make a quicker-cooking stock • Cut all the solid ingredients into small pieces. When more surface area is exposed, the ingredients yield their flavors to the liquid more quickly. By preparing ingredients in this way, you can make a stock in 1 hour instead of 5.

To make easy-to-use portions of stock • Freeze the stock in a muffin pan. Once the portions of stock are frozen, pop them out and store them in a zipper-lock freezer bag. When making a sauce, add a cube or two of frozen broth to a hot pan and heat to boiling.

To quickly thaw frozen stock • Immerse frozen bags or containers of stock in a bowl of warm water until enough stock has melted that the entire contents can be slipped out and into a pan. Proceed to melt the stock completely in the pan over medium-low heat.

To replace fish stock • In a pinch, when 1 to 2 cups of fish stock is required, use 1 to 2 bottles (8 ounces each) clam juice instead. Bottled clam juice is high in sodium, so taste the dish before adding any salt recommended in the recipe.

To make stock from leftover roasted chicken • When making roasted chicken, save the bones, skin, and trimmings and place them in a deep saucepan. Add 1 halved onion, 1 quartered carrot, 1 bay leaf, 1 teaspoon dried thyme, and just enough water to cover. If desired, add any leftover vegetable trimmings. Bring the mixture to a simmer and cook 1 hour, adding additional water if needed to keep the ingredients covered. Strain and cool.

FLAVOR TIPS ▼ **To double-boil stock for more flavor** • After making and degreasing a stock, simmer it gently until the liquid reduces by half.

To reduce stock to a glaze • Continue simmering meat or poultry stock until the liquid becomes a syrupy consistency. Refrigerate for up to several months. Or pour it into ice cube trays or a muffin pan and freeze until solid. Pop out the frozen portions of glaze and freeze them in a zipper-lock freezer bag up to 1 year. Add 1 to 2 portions frozen glaze to any dish requiring a richly flavored stock. Or reconstitute by adding it to 2 to 3 tablespoons boiling water.

To make a richer-tasting vegetable stock • Roast the vegetables before adding them to the stockpot. The natural sugars will caramelize and deepen the flavor of the stock.

FRAGRANT CHICKEN STOCK Place 2 quarts prepared **Basic Chicken Stock** (page 471) in a large saucepan and bring to a simmer. Add **10 thin slices fresh ginger, 2 sliced garlic cloves, 2 bay leaves,** and **several sprigs of fresh herbs (such as parsley, dill, or cilantro).** Simmer 15 minutes. Strain before serving. *Makes 2 quarts.*

Stoves *see also* Ovens

An essential part of any kitchen, a stove can be nothing more than a single-coil hot plate or an elaborate 6-burner professional range.

BASICS ▼ **To choose** • The main decision to make when purchasing a stove is whether to buy gas or electric. Most cooks prefer gas because the heat can be adjusted more quickly. With gas, you can take the heat from its very highest setting down to a low simmer in seconds simply by turning the knob. Electric coils, on the other hand, retain heat and take longer to cool down. Gas stoves are also preferred because they have the ability to cook foods faster than electric stoves. Gas heat is measured in BTU, or British thermal units. Gas stoves with higher BTU will deliver more heat, thereby boiling water faster and searing meat more quickly. Whichever stove you choose, make sure that the burners are far enough apart to accommodate your largest pans. Measure the distance between the centers of the burners. A distance of 12" will allow you to cook with several big pans at one time.

Strawberries *see also* Berries

The beloved strawberry descends from the rose family and is unrelated to raspberries and blackberries, which grow from canes.

BASICS ▼ **To choose** • As with other berries, it's best to buy strawberries with your nose. The ones that smell the best will have the best flavor. Also, look for a deep, even, red color. Pick up the basket and look at the bottom, too, to make sure that there are no squished or moldy berries inside.

To store • Refrigerate unwashed strawberries between layers of paper towels for 3 to 4 days.

To freeze • Spread unwashed berries in an even layer on a baking sheet and freeze until solid. Transfer the berries to a zipper-lock freezer bag and freeze up to 3 months.

To rinse • Rinse whole berries briefly with cold water just before using. Be sure to rinse strawberries before hulling them. If hulled strawberries are rinsed, they will absorb water like a sponge.

To hull • Slice off the stem end and pluck out the stem and green leaves with a huller, or dig out the hull with the pointed end of a vegetable peeler. You can also push a sturdy drinking straw through the fruit from the bottom to the stem end. The hull will pop right out. If you are hulling a large amount of strawberries, plan on using several straws.

STRAWBERRY SAUCE FROM STRAW-BERRY TRIMMINGS In a heavy medium saucepan, combine **2 cups stems, tops,**

Chocolate-Dipped Strawberries

So simple. So satisfying. You don't even need to hull the strawberries. These are best eaten right away, but they can be kept chilled for up to 8 hours and served cold.

¾ **cup chocolate chips**
1½ **teaspoons canola oil**
1 **quart fresh strawberries**

1. In a small, microwaveable cup, combine the chocolate chips and oil. Microwave on high power, 30 seconds. Stir. Repeat just until the chocolate melts and can be stirred into a smooth glaze.

2. Place a large piece of waxed paper on a work surface. Dip each strawberry into the melted chocolate. Lift the strawberry, allowing any excess chocolate to drip back into the cup. Place the dipped strawberries on the waxed paper and allow the chocolate to harden. To avoid smudging the chocolate as it hardens, place the strawberries, chocolate side up, in an empty egg carton. Or use the following method.

Use a wooden pick to horizontally skewer across the top of the berry as close to the stem as possible. Rotate the berry one-quarter turn and skewer it with a second wooden pick in the same manner, to make an X.

Dip the berry and place it, dipped side up, on waxed paper, with the X as a flat base to prevent tipping.

Makes 8 servings

and hulls from washed and hulled strawberries; ¾ cup sugar; the juice of ½ lemon; 2 tablespoons orange liqueur (such as Grand Marnier); and a pinch of salt. Heat to boiling. Reduce heat to medium-low and simmer 10 minutes, skimming any impurities that rise to the surface. Strain and chill. Use as a sweet dessert sauce, a bread spread, or a glaze for poultry. *Makes 1 cup.*

STRAWBERRY CREPES Toss **1 pint hulled and sliced strawberries** with **2 tablespoons sugar** and **1 tablespoon orange liqueur (such as Grand Marnier).** Use to fill **8** store-bought crepes. Drizzle the top of each crepe with **1 teaspoon melted strawberry jam** and **1 tablespoon sour cream** or **crème fraîche** (see page 148). *Makes 4 servings.*

PROBLEM SOLVERS
▼
To save less-than-perfect strawberries • Slice them horizontally. You'll expose more surface area, which will bring out more juice. You can also add a bit of extra sugar to enhance the sweetness. Or boost the strawberry flavor by adding ⅛ teaspoon wild strawberry essence to each pint of lackluster strawberries. See page 183 for more on flavor essences.

To hold strawberries together for strawberry shortcake • Mash a few berries and blend the mashed berries with the sliced or whole berries to bind them.

Stuffing

Also called dressing, stuffing is usually made with a base of well-seasoned bread cubes or bread crumbs. It can be baked separately or inside food such as chicken or turkey.

TIME SAVER
▼
To save cooking time • Bake the stuffing separately. Stuffing poultry makes both the poultry and the stuffing take longer to cook.

QUICK CRAB AND CORNBREAD STUFFING Mix **6 chopped scallions, 2 minced garlic cloves, 1½ pounds cleaned back-fin crabmeat, the grated zest and juice of 1 large lemon, 1 bottle (8 ounces) clam juice, 1 pound crumbled cornbread** or **cornbread stuffing mix, ¼ teaspoon salt,** and **⅛ teaspoon ground red pepper (or more to taste).** Bake in a 1- to 1½-quart casserole at 350°F until heated through, about 30 minutes. Or use to stuff 2 chickens or 1 turkey. *Makes 8 servings.*

FLAVOR TIP
▼
To get the best flavor in oven-baked stuffing • Cover the baking dish with foil to keep the stuffing moist during cooking. If you like a crunchy top on your stuffing, bake it uncovered for the last 5 to 10 minutes, or run it under the broiler briefly.

CHESTNUT STUFFING In a large, deep skillet, sauté **2 chopped onions, 4 chopped celery ribs, 1 chopped carrot, ¼ cup chopped fresh parsley, 1 teaspoon dried rosemary,** and **¼ teaspoon ground black pepper** in **2 tablespoons olive oil** until vegetables are soft, 5 to 7 minutes. Remove from heat and stir in **3 cups roasted and peeled** or **canned chestnuts, 6½ cups bread cubes, 1¼ cups chicken broth,** and **2 eggs.** Scrape into a 13" × 9" baking dish and bake at 325°F until heated through and internal temperature reaches 165°F, about 45 minutes. Or use to stuff 2 chickens or 1 turkey. *Makes 8 servings.*

S

S

SAFE STUFFING

It's safer and faster to bake stuffings outside the bird. If, however, you prefer the traditional method of baking the stuffing in the bird, follow these safety tips.

- Stuff the chicken or turkey just before roasting, rather than the night before, to help prevent bacteria from migrating from the meat to the stuffing.

- For birds weighing up to 10 pounds, use ½ cup stuffing per pound. For birds weighing more than 10 pounds, use ¾ cup stuffing per pound.

- Stuff both cavities loosely. Stuff the neck cavity first, then turn the wings back to hold the neck skin in place (or skewer it with toothpicks if the skin is too short).

Then, stuff the body cavity. There is no need to truss a stuffed bird.

- Make sure that the stuffing is moist, rather than dry, because heat destroys bacteria more rapidly in a wet environment.

- The bird is done when an instant-read thermometer registers 180°F in the breast meat and 165°F in the stuffing.

- Allow the bird to stand for 20 minutes after it is removed from the oven before carving. This allows the internal temperature of the stuffing to continue to rise and also makes it easier for the bird to be carved.

- Just before carving, scoop the stuffing from the bird into a bowl. Avoid storing leftover stuffing inside the bird.

HEALTHY HINT ▼ **To reduce fat** • Skip the giblets (organ meats), which are sometimes added to traditional stuffings. Also, moisten the stuffing with broth, juice, or wine rather than butter or oil. Boost flavor with herbs, nuts, and dried fruit.

Sugar, Brown *see also* Sugar, Granulated

Brown sugar is granulated sugar combined with molasses. It has a softer, moister consistency than granulated sugar and a distinctive, molasses-like flavor. Light brown sugar has a more delicate molasses flavor, while dark brown sugar is more intense. In a pinch, the two types are interchangeable.

BASICS ▼ **To store** • Keep brown sugar in a thick plastic bag in a cool, dry place.

To measure accurately • Always pack it firmly into the measuring cup.

To use in baking • The molasses in brown sugar gives it an acidic quality, which is one reason why it is often combined with granulated sugar in baking. The acid in brown sugar reacts with baking soda (an alkali) to make carbon dioxide bubbles and help baked goods rise.

To make • Stir together 1 cup granulated sugar with 3 to 4 tablespoons unsulphured molasses. Store in a zipper-lock plastic bag in a cool, dry place.

To replace granulated sugar • Using brown sugar to replace granulated sugar will result in moister baked goods with a hint of butterscotch flavor. Use 1 cup firmly packed brown sugar to replace 1 cup granulated sugar.

To replace light brown sugar with dark • To replace 1 cup light brown sugar, use ½ cup dark brown sugar mixed with ½ cup granulated sugar.

PROBLEM SOLVERS **To prevent drying or hardening** • After opening a bag or box of brown sugar, add a ribbon of orange zest (1" × 3"). Keep the bag tightly sealed and store it inside a zipper-lock plastic bag.

To salvage hardened brown sugar • Place a wedge of fresh apple or a slice of bread in the bag with the sugar. Seal it for up to 48 hours. Or soften the brown sugar in a microwave or conventional oven. To microwave, transfer to a microwaveable container, cover with vented plastic wrap, and heat on high power 30 seconds. Continue with 30-second increments, breaking up the sugar occasionally. To use a conventional oven, place the brown sugar on a rimmed baking sheet and bake at 225°F until softened, 5 to 10 minutes.

Sugar, Confectioners'

see also Sugar, Granulated

Granulated sugar ground to a fine powder is known as confectioners' sugar, powdered sugar, or icing sugar. The "X" designation on the label indicates the degree of fineness to which the sugar was ground. For instance, XXXX sugar is finer than XXX sugar, and 10X sugar is the finest. Because the powdery sugar tends to clump, about 3 percent cornstarch is usually added to minimize lumps. It dissolves almost instantly and is used most often in uncooked frostings and for decorating cakes and cookies. The added cornstarch also helps stiffen meringues and harden royal icings.

BASICS **To remove lumps** • Sift before measuring.

To dust cakes or cookies • Wait until the baked goods have cooled completely. If the cakes or cookies are too warm, the sugar will melt into a paste. For very moist baked goods, dust with confectioners' sugar at the last minute. Use a sifter to dust the confectioners' sugar over the baked goods. Or use a fine-mesh sieve, tapping the sides lightly. If you do not have a sieve, place sugar in a cup, cover it with foil or plastic wrap, secure it with a rubber band, and puncture holes in the cover with a fork or a toothpick. Voilà! A homemade powdered sugar shaker.

To replace granulated sugar • Use 1¾ cups confectioners' sugar to replace 1 cup granulated sugar.

Sugar, Granulated *see also*

Sugar, Brown; Sugar, Confectioners'; Sugar Syrup

Aside from its importance as a sweetener, sugar helps keep baked goods moist and gives many cooked foods a rich, golden color. It also helps stabilize beaten egg whites when making meringue. Sugar even helps prevent some foods from spoiling. Most forms of sugar are highly refined products that originate in sugar cane or sugar beets.

BASICS **To use** • Granulated sugar is an all-purpose sugar that can be used in most types of cooking. Superfine sugar is simply granulated sugar that has been pulverized to make very fine, uniform crystals. These ultra-fine crystals dissolve readily in liquid, making superfine a popular sugar for bartenders. The tiny grains of sugar can also improve the texture of cakes and cookies because the crystals have more sharp edges to cut into the butter when creamed, making more air pockets and thus lighter baked goods.

To make superfine sugar • Process regular granulated sugar in a food processor or blender, about 1 minute for 1 cup.

To store • Keep granulated sugar or superfine sugar in a cool, dry place, and it will last indefinitely.

To caramelize • When heated, granulated sugar or brown sugar will melt into a liquid, which eventually turns golden (about 320°F on a candy thermometer) and then deep brown (about 350°F on a candy thermometer). The darker the color, the more intense the flavor. Some recipes that call for caramelized sugar specify the addition of water, but this isn't really necessary. To caramelize sugar, simply place it in a saucepan over medium heat. Avoid stirring until most of the sugar melts. Once the sugar is melted, stir it occasionally until the desired color is reached, 1 to 4 minutes. Watch carefully, as caramelizing sugar darkens fast and can quickly become burnt. Use caramelized sugar to coat molds for crème caramel, to make nut brittle, or to flavor mousses or ice creams. Be careful to not touch hot caramel. It can cause severe burns.

PROBLEM SOLVERS ▼ **To break up small clumps** • Use your fingers, a fork, or a potato masher.

To salvage a block of hardened white sugar • Place it in a paper bag or a sealed zipper-lock plastic bag and pound it with a rolling pin, a flat stone, or a brick. You can also pulse large chunks in a food processor until separated into crystals.

Fascinating Fact: Turbinado sugar is raw sugar that has been cleaned by a steaming process, resulting in coarse, light brown sugar

crystals with a touch of molasses flavor. Because it is purified, this and most other raw sugars have the same nutritive value as granulated sugar.

Sugar Syrup

Cooking sugar and water together to dissolve the sugar makes what is known as sugar syrup or simple syrup. This syrup is the basis of most candies and is also used to moisten and glaze cakes and to poach fruit.

BASICS ▼ **To make** • Combine water and sugar in a saucepan. Cook over low heat, stirring gently, until the mixture is warm and the sugar has dissolved. Stop stirring once the sugar has dissolved, or crystals may form. Also, brush down the sides of the pan with a wet pastry brush to prevent crystals from forming. Bring the syrup to a simmer, cover, and let cook about 2 minutes. Remove the syrup from the heat and let cool before using.

To make a thin sugar syrup • Use 3 parts water and 1 part sugar.

To make a medium-density sugar syrup • Use 2 parts water and 1 part sugar.

To make a heavy sugar syrup • Use equal parts water and sugar.

To store • Sugar syrup can be stored at room temperature for up to 3 weeks and refrigerated for up to 6 months.

Sweetened Condensed Milk *see also* Milk

When sweetened whole milk is cooked to evaporate 60 percent of the water, sweetened condensed milk is created. It has a slightly caramelized flavor and a darker color than regular cow's milk. Sweetened condensed

milk is used to make candies, puddings, and pies. Don't confuse sweetened condensed milk with evaporated milk. Evaporated milk is unsweetened milk that has been reduced by half. The two are not interchangeable.

BASICS **To store** • Unopened cans of sweetened condensed milk can be kept at room temperature for up to 6 months. Once the can is opened, refrigerate condensed milk and use within 5 days.

FLAVOR TIP **To make an easy glaze for baked pears or apples** • Drizzle 1 tablespoon sweetened condensed milk over the fruit about 10 minutes before the end of baking time.

MILK CARAMEL Remove the label from **1 can (14 ounces) sweetened condensed milk.** (If it's stubborn, place it in a medium bowl, cover with hot water, and let stand 10 minutes.) Place the unopened can in a large, deep saucepan. Cover with water by 5" and bring to a boil over high heat. Reduce heat to medium and simmer 2 hours. Add water, if necessary, to keep the can covered. Remove with tongs and let cool. Open the can and enjoy. Wonderful over bananas, crepes, or ice cream. *Makes about 1¾ cups.*

EASY COCONUT MACAROONS Preheat oven to 350°F. Mix together **1 pound (4 cups) sweetened shredded coconut** or **½ pound (2¾ cups) unsweetened shredded coconut, a pinch of salt, 2 teaspoons grated orange zest,** and **1 can (14 ounces) sweetened condensed milk.** Stir in **1 teaspoon vanilla extract** and **2 egg whites.** Line 2 baking sheets with foil or parchment paper and scoop batter in 2-tablespoon portions onto the lined pans, about 1½" apart. Bake until golden brown on top and well-browned on the bottom, about 20 minutes, switching positions of sheets halfway through baking. Slide the foil or parchment with its cookies onto a rack and cool 5 minutes. Peel liner off cookies and cool on rack completely. *Makes about 30 small cookies.*

Sweet Potatoes

A member of the morning glory family, sweet potatoes are a root vegetable native to the tropics. Although they share a name, sweet potatoes are not related to white baking potatoes.

BASICS **To choose** • The two most common varieties are white sweet potatoes and dark sweet potatoes, often mislabeled as yams. White sweet potatoes are much like regular baking potatoes. They have a thin skin and pale yellow flesh, which becomes dry, crumbly, and not at all sweet after cooking. The more popular dark sweet potatoes have a thicker, darker skin and bright orange flesh that cooks up moist and sweet. Use white sweet potatoes anywhere you would use regular baking potatoes. Likewise, dark sweet potatoes can be baked, boiled, roasted, sautéed, or fried as chips. Whichever variety you choose, look for sweet potatoes with smooth, firm skins and no blemishes or bruises. Small or medium sweet potatoes generally taste better than large ones.

To store • Keep sweet potatoes in a cool, dry, dark, and well-ventilated place up to 2 weeks.

To bake • Scrub 1 or more sweet potatoes (about 8 ounces to 12 ounces each) and pat dry. Prick several times with a fork. Bake at 350°F directly on an oven rack (or in a shallow pan) until soft when pierced with a fork, about 1 hour. Add butter, salt, and ground black pepper.

PEANUT AND SWEET POTATO STEW Heat **2 teaspoons olive oil** in a large nonstick skillet or saucepan over medium-low heat. Add **1 sliced leek (white part only), 1 chopped green bell pepper, 1 tablespoon** *each* **chopped garlic and chopped fresh ginger,** and **1 chopped jalapeño chile pepper.** Cook 8 minutes. Stir in **2 peeled and finely chopped sweet potatoes, 1 cup vegetable broth, 1 tablespoon chili powder,** and **2 teaspoons ground cumin.** Cover and simmer until potatoes are tender, 45 minutes. Stir in **3 tablespoons peanut butter** and garnish with **2 tablespoons chopped peanuts.** *Makes 4 servings.*

PROBLEM SOLVERS ▼ **To prevent darkening** • Toss cut sweet potatoes with lemon juice, or drop them into acidulated water until ready to use. Drain and pat dry before using.

To remove fibrous strings • Larger, tougher sweet potatoes sometimes produce fibrous strings when mashed. Use electric beaters, and the strings will wrap around the beaters so that they can be discarded.

TIME SAVERS ▼ **To easily peel boiled sweet potatoes** • Drain them and submerge them in cold water. The peels will blister off.

To cook quickly • Scrub 2 large sweet potatoes (about 1 pound each) and prick with a fork. Place the sweet potatoes on paper towels and microwave on high power until tender, 12 to 14 minutes.

Chef's Tip: There is great confusion about what's a yam and what's a sweet potato. In the early part of the 20th century, a sweet potato with yellow-orange flesh was marketed as a "Louisiana yam" to help it stand out from whiter-fleshed sweet potatoes. Now, many people call sweet potatoes yams, which they are not. True yams (called *ñame* in Spanish) are tropical tubers. So, the "Louisiana yam" is a sweet potato unrelated to the yam. Sweet potatoes with light-colored flesh also go by the names *boniato, batata, batata dulce, camote,* white sweet potato, and Cuban sweet potato.

HEALTHY HINT ▼ **To obtain the maximum amount of beta-carotene** • Choose sweet potatoes with the brightest skin, which indicates a higher concentration of beta-carotene in the flesh. Also, keep in mind that beta-carotene requires a little bit of fat in order to be absorbed by the body. Eating baked sweet potatoes with a little bit of oil or butter or with other foods that contain some fat will do the trick. Whenever possible, eat sweet potatoes with the skins on for additional nutrients.

SWEET POTATO CHEESECAKE Preheat oven to 250°F. Line a 9" springform pan with a **Cookie Crumb Crust** made with graham crackers (see page 361). In a food processor, combine **1 cup part-skim ricotta cheese, 12 ounces softened Neufchâtel cheese, 1 tablespoon flour, 2 teaspoons ground cinnamon,** and **½ teaspoon ground ginger.** Puree until smooth. Scrape into a large bowl. In the food processor, combine **1¼ cups cooked, peeled, and chopped sweet potatoes; ⅓ cup** *each* **brown sugar and granulated sugar; 2 eggs;** and **2 egg whites.** Add to the bowl, stirring to mix. Pour into the pan and bake 80 minutes. Cool completely on a rack. Cover with foil and refrigerate overnight. *Makes 16 servings.*

T

Tacos *see also* Tortillas

A type of Mexican sandwich, tacos are made by folding corn tortillas over a filling of meat, poultry, seafood, vegetables, or cheese. Traditionally, soft corn tortillas are briefly heated and folded over the filling. The popular fried, crisp taco "shells" are an American variation on the Mexican dish.

BASICS **To soften corn tortillas for tacos** • The quickest way is to stack them on a paper towel, cover with another paper towel, and microwave on medium power until soft and pliable, 1 to 2 minutes. You can also spritz a piece of foil with water, stack the tortillas on the foil, then wrap and warm in a 300°F oven for 5 minutes. For the most flavorful softening method, heat the tortillas directly over a flame (or in a skillet, if you have an electric stove). Place a corn tortilla directly over high heat for 3 seconds, then turn and heat the other side 3 seconds. Spritz with a little bit of water, turn, and heat 2 seconds. Spritz again, turn, and heat 2 seconds more. Continue spritzing and turning every 2 seconds until the tortilla is soft and pliable. Stack the softened tortillas and cover to keep warm.

SIMPLE BEEF TACO FILLING In a skillet, brown **1 pound lean ground beef** with **1 large minced garlic clove** and **1 teaspoon** *each* **ground cumin and dried oregano.** When meat is no longer pink, add **1 tablespoon** *each* **flour and chili powder** and **½ cup chicken or beef broth.** Cook until slightly thickened, 5 minutes. *Makes 4 servings.*

BEEF AND POTATO TACO FILLING Follow the recipe for **Simple Beef Taco Filling** (above). But before adding beef to the skillet, sauté **2 finely chopped potatoes (peeled or unpeeled)** in **2 tablespoons vegetable oil** until tender and golden brown, 5 to 7 minutes. Push potatoes to one side and crumble in beef and seasonings. Proceed as directed. *Makes 4 servings.*

Tamarind

Also called Indian date, tamarind is the fruit of a tropical tree. The long, dark tamarind pods are filled with small seeds and a sweet-and-sour pulp that is dried and used in Indian and Middle Eastern kitchens, much the

t

same way that cooks in the West use lemon juice. Tamarind is also used in Southeast Asia, Mexico, and the Caribbean. Tamarind's natural acidity helps tenderize tough cuts of meats, making it excellent for marinades. It's also one of the key flavors in Worcestershire sauce.

BASICS ▼ **To choose** • Tamarind is available in several forms: whole pods, blocks of compressed tamarind paste (which may contain seeds), frozen pouches of paste, frozen tamarind nectar, sweetened tamarind syrup, and tamarind concentrate. Dark and thick tamarind concentrate is the easiest to use; simply stir a small amount (½ teaspoon) into a liquid, then add the liquid to a dish. Look for different forms of tamarind in large supermarkets or Indian and Middle Eastern grocery stores. If buying fresh whole pods, make sure that they bend easily in your hands.

To store • Keep pods and unopened packages of tamarind pulp in a cool, dry place. They will keep indefinitely. Opened packages of pulp or concentrate can be refrigerated for about 3 months.

To make tamarind paste from whole dried tamarind pods • Peel 4½ ounces pods and remove the fruit. Combine the fruit with 1 cup warm water and let soak 20 minutes. Pour through a fine sieve, pressing the pulp through the sieve with your hands or a wooden spoon. Stir to mix, and refrigerate in a tightly sealed glass jar for up to 1 week. Makes 1 cup.

To make tamarind paste from compressed blocks of tamarind • Cut off 2 ounces of the tamarind from the block and combine with ½ cup warm water. Soak for 20 minutes and strain before using. Makes ¾ cup.

MEXICAN TAMARIND DRINK (LICUADO DE TAMARINDO) In a large bowl, combine **4 cups boiling water** and **1 compressed block (8 ounces) tamarind paste with seeds,** breaking up tamarind with a spoon. Add about ¾ **cup sugar** and mash to dissolve sugar and tamarind. Let cool. Force through a sieve and discard seeds and fibers. Add **4 to 6 cups cold water.** Taste and add more sugar, if necessary. Serve over ice in tall glasses. *Makes 4 servings.*

Tapenade *see also* Olives

This classic olive paste from the Provence region of southern France is made from a blend of capers, olives, anchovies, and olive oil. The ingredients and proportions vary from cook to cook, but capers are essential (the name *tapenade* comes from the word *tapeno,* which means capers). Tapenade can be used as a dip for bread or as a sandwich spread, pizza topping, pasta sauce, or flavoring for chicken, lamb, pork, or beef. It is available in most grocery stores but simple enough to make at home.

BASICS ▼ **To store** • Keep tapenade refrigerated in a covered container up to 2 weeks.

BLACK OLIVE TAPENADE In a large mortar and pestle or a food processor, combine **2 cups pitted niçoise** or **kalamata olives, 2 anchovies, 2 tablespoons capers,** and **2 teaspoons lemon juice.** Mash or process to a coarse paste. Add about ⅓ **cup olive oil** (with the machine running, if using a food processor) and mash or process to a thick, spreadable paste. Taste and add **salt,** if desired. Other

optional seasonings include 1 minced garlic clove, ½ teaspoon dry mustard, ¼ teaspoon ground black pepper, or ½ cup finely chopped fresh parsley.
Makes about 2½ cups.

Tapioca

A cooking starch derived from the cassava plant, tapioca can be used to thicken soups, sauces, and fruit fillings for pies, and to make the popular tapioca pudding.

BASICS ▼ **To choose** • Tapioca comes in several forms, but the most common type is the finely textured, quick-cooking tapioca found in many supermarkets. Usually used as a thickener for soups, and for fruit fillings, quick-cooking tapioca requires no presoaking. Tapioca flour is also used as a thickener for sauces and gravies, much like cornstarch. A third type, old-fashioned pearl tapioca, must be soaked for several hours and requires long cooking. Pearl tapioca is often used to make pudding.

To store • Keep tapioca in a dark, cool spot, and it will last indefinitely.

To get the best texture when using tapioca as a thickener • After adding tapioca to a hot liquid mixture, avoid letting the mixture boil, which could make the tapioca stringy. Remove the mixture from the heat while it is still a little thin, as tapioca continues to set as it cools. Resist stirring while the mixture is cooling. Overstirring may cause the mixture to become too gelatinous.

To test for doneness • Quick-cooking and pearl tapioca are done when the grains are translucent and no longer gritty.

To replace flour or cornstarch with quick-cooking tapioca • To thicken stews, gravies, soups, and fruit fillings, use equal amounts of quick-cooking tapioca.

to replace cornstarch. To replace flour, use slightly less tapioca. Unlike flour- or cornstarch-thickened mixtures, tapioca-thickened mixtures do not need stirring and do not get cloudy. Tapioca-thickened mixtures can also be frozen and reheated without breaking down or separating.

To replace quick-cooking tapioca with tapioca flour • Increase the tapioca flour by one-half. For instance, to replace 1 tablespoon quick-cooking tapioca, use 1½ tablespoons tapioca flour.

To replace quick-cooking tapioca with pearl tapioca • Crush pearl tapioca in a heavy-duty zipper-lock plastic bag with a hammer until finely ground. Replace quick-cooking tapioca with an equal amount of crushed pearl tapioca.

CREAMY TAPIOCA PUDDING Separate **1 large egg** and set aside yolk. With an electric mixer, beat egg white on high speed until foamy. Gradually add **3 tablespoons sugar,** beating until soft peaks form when beaters are lifted. Set aside. In a medium saucepan, combine **2 cups milk** and **3 tablespoons** *each* **quick-cooking tapioca and sugar.** Let stand 5 minutes. Bring to a boil over medium heat, stirring constantly. Whisk in reserved egg yolk and remove from heat. Quickly stir beaten egg white mixture into hot tapioca until well-blended. Stir in **1½ teaspoons vanilla extract.** Cover with plastic wrap touching the surface of the pudding and cool 20 minutes. Stir and serve warm or chilled. *Makes 4 servings.*

COCONUT TAPIOCA PUDDING Follow the recipe for **Creamy Tapioca Pudding** (above). Replace milk with **canned coconut milk**. *Makes 4 servings.*

t

MAPLE-WALNUT TAPIOCA PUDDING
In a medium saucepan, combine **2½ cups milk**, **½ cup maple syrup**, **3 tablespoons quick-cooking tapioca**, **1 tablespoon honey**, and **1 beaten egg**. Let stand 5 minutes. Bring to a boil over medium heat, stirring constantly. Remove from heat. Stir in **3 tablespoons chopped toasted walnuts** and **1 teaspoon vanilla extract**. Cool 20 minutes. Pudding will thicken as it cools. Stir and serve warm or chilled. *Makes 4 servings.*

PROBLEM SOLVER ▼ **To avoid small, cooked bits of quick-cooking tapioca in thickened mixtures** • Use tapioca flour instead. Or run quick-cooking tapioca through a food processor or blender until it is ground to a powder. You can also soak quick-cooking tapioca for approximately 5 minutes in the recipe's liquid prior to heating. This brief soaking allows the tapioca beads to soften, maximizing their thickening quality.

Tea, Hot *see also* Tea, Iced

Made from the dried leaves of the tea plant, tea is one of the world's oldest and most popular beverages. There are three main styles of tea: green, black, and oolong. All three begin with the same plant and are then processed in different ways to give each a unique flavor. Specialty teas are made by adding flavorings to one of the three main types of tea. Herb tea is not related to true tea made from the tea plant; rather, it is an infusion of herbs, spices, and flavorings.

BASICS ▼ **To choose** • Look for tea sold loose rather than in bags. Loose tea is likely to be fresher, making it a better choice than tea bags, which are often stale.

To store • Store tea in a tightly sealed container and keep it in a cool, dark place for up to 1 year.

To choose a teapot • Look for one made of either glass or ceramic. Metal can adversely affect the flavor of tea.

To help keep hot tea warm longer • Warm the teapot by filling it with boiling water. Let the pot stand filled with the hot water for a few minutes. Then, pour out the hot water and filled the warmed pot with hot tea. You can also warm teacups the same way.

To make a pot of tea using loose tea leaves • Use 1 heaping teaspoon of tea and 6 ounces water per teacup, plus 1 additional teaspoon of tea for the pot.

To get the most bang for your bag • Squeeze tea bags before removing them.

To keep tea from tasting bitter • Let it steep in hot water for at least 3 minutes but no longer than 5 minutes.

PROBLEM SOLVERS ▼ **To prevent tea stains** • Rinse teapots and tea cups as soon as possible.

To remove tea stains • Scrub with a paste of baking soda and water. Wash and rinse thoroughly.

FLAVOR TIP ▼ **To flavor loose tea** • Store it with citrus peels, whole cloves, vanilla beans, or other whole spices.

EARL GREY SHALLOT SAUCE In a medium saucepan, sauté **⅓ cup chopped shallots** in **1 teaspoon olive oil**, 3 minutes. Add **1 cup chicken broth**, **¾ cup orange juice**, and **2 Earl Grey tea bags**. Bring to a boil and cook until liquid is reduced to ¾ cup, about 15 minutes. Whisk in **1½ teaspoons honey** and **1 tablespoon**

butter. Remove and discard bags. Serve with poultry or pork. *Makes about ¾ cup.*

THAI TEA RICE WITH PEANUTS Steep **2 jasmine tea bags** in **1¼ cups boiling water,** 5 minutes. Remove and discard bags. Set tea aside. In a large saucepan, sauté **1 chopped green bell pepper, 1 small chopped jalapeño chile pepper, 1 tablespoon grated fresh ginger,** and **2 teaspoons curry powder** in **2 teaspoons peanut oil** or **olive oil** until pepper is tender, 4 minutes. Stir in **1½ cups jasmine rice or long-grain rice** and stir until well-coated, 2 minutes. Add **1 can (14 ounces) vegetable broth,** reserved jasmine tea, and ½ teaspoon salt. Bring to a simmer, cover, and cook until liquid is absorbed, 18 minutes. Stir in **4 thinly sliced scallions** and ⅓ **cup chopped fresh cilantro.** Top with ¼ **cup chopped roasted peanuts.** Serve with lime wedges. *Makes 4 servings.*

TEA-SPICED PRUNES AND ORANGES In a medium saucepan, combine **2 cups boiling water, 2 Earl Grey tea bags (or other tea),** and **the peel of 1 orange.** Steep 5 minutes and discard tea bags. Add ⅓ **cup sugar, 8 halved cardamom pods,** and **3 whole cloves,** stirring until sugar is dissolved. Boil until liquid is reduced to about 1½ cups. Pour into a large bowl and add **12 prunes.** Cool mixture completely and discard orange peel. (At this point, mixture can be refrigerated for up to 5 days). Remove pith from the pared orange and slice crosswise. Peel and slice another **3 oranges** crosswise. Add to the bowl, cover, and chill at least 2 hours or up to 1 day. Bring to room temperature before serving. *Makes 4 servings.*

JASMINE SORBET In a small saucepan, bring **3 cups water** to a boil. Add **2½ tablespoons jasmine tea leaves.** Cover, remove from heat, and steep 5 minutes. Stir in ½ **cup sugar** and ¼ **cup honey** until dissolved. Strain through a fine sieve into a bowl. Cover and refrigerate until cold. Freeze in an ice cream maker according to the manufacturer's directions. (Can be made up to 2 weeks in advance.) *Makes 4 servings.*

HEALTHY HINTS ▼ **To reap the healing benefits of tea •** When drinking tea for its beneficial antioxidants, choose tea blends that contain real tea leaves, as opposed to herbal teas. Tea aficionados will choose loose tea, but tea bags are the wiser choice for a healthy cup of tea. The tea in bags is pulverized, exposing more surface area so that the tea's healing compounds can be released.

To help reduce tooth decay • The polyphenols and tannin in tea act as antibiotics, fighting bacteria in the mouth that could lead to tooth decay. Tea also contains fluoride, which helps ward off damaging bacteria.

Tea, Iced *see also* Tea, Hot

Americans popularized iced tea at the St. Louis World's Fair in 1904.

BASICS ▼ **To make •** For the best-tasting iced tea, use about twice as much tea as you would use for hot tea. If using loose tea, use about 2 heaping teaspoons tea per cup, plus 2 additional teaspoons for the pot. If using tea bags, use 2 bags per cup. Cover the tea with boiling water (6 ounces per cup) and cool to room temperature. Then, refrigerate for at least 24 hours. Strain before serving.

SUN TEA Place **6 tea bags (or 2 table-spoons loose tea)** and **2 strips lemon zest (each 1" long)** in a jar. Add **4½ cups cold water** and **2 tablespoons sugar.** Cover the jar and place in the sun for at least 4 hours. Remove tea and add **1 tablespoon lemon juice.** Chill and serve over ice. *Makes 6 servings.*

EASY LEMONADE ICED TEA Mix **1 can (12 ounces) frozen lemonade concentrate** with **1½ cans water.** Add to **1 quart prepared iced tea** or **sun tea.** *Makes 6 servings.*

PROBLEM SOLVERS
▼

To prevent cloudy iced tea • Avoid placing hot tea in a cold fridge. Allow the tea to cool to room temperature before chilling. Or, pour cold water over the tea before brewing, then cover and refrigerate for at least 24 hours before straining.

To clear up cloudy iced tea • Stir in some boiling water.

To easily remove multiple bags • Tie the bags together by their strings.

To cut bitterness • Add a pinch of salt to the tea.

To avoid diluting iced tea • Make ice cubes out of tea. Pour 2 cups cooled steeped tea into an ice cube tray and freeze. Serve with iced tea.

Texture *see also* Flavor

Whereas *consistency* refers mostly to the mouthfeel of moist foods, *texture* is a broader term that covers both moist and dry foods. The amazing thing about texture is just how much it can change with different cooking techniques. A potato slice can have a soft and tender texture when baked into a gratin or a crisp and crunchy texture when fried into a chip. Likewise, the exact same set of ingredients can turn out a soft and delicate cake or a crunchy and brittle cookie.

FLAVOR TIP
▼

To boost the taste of a meal • Include a variety of different textures. The exciting thing about texture is in contrasts. Think of a napoleon: This dessert owes its fabulous taste to the contrast of crisp, flaky layers of puff pastry separated by rich, luscious pastry cream. When planning a menu, include several contrasting textures, such as soft mashed potatoes, crisp-tender asparagus, grilled meat that is toothsome on the inside yet crisp on the edges, and perhaps a smooth sauce or crunchy garnish.

Thermometers

There are four basic types of thermometers for use in the kitchen: meat thermometers, candy or deep-fat frying thermometers, oven thermometers, and refrigerator or freezer thermometers. Each one is essential kitchen equipment. Thermometers eliminate guesswork by accurately measuring the doneness of foods and ensuring that ovens, refrigerators, and freezers are working properly.

BASICS
▼

To choose a meat thermometer • You have two choices here: a regular meat thermometer or an instant-read thermometer. A regular meat thermometer is inserted into the meat at the beginning of cooking time and left there during cooking; an instant-read thermometer is inserted during cooking. Instant-read thermometers are inexpensive and easy to use, and they will perform accurately for several years. Whichever type you choose, make sure that it has a reader-friendly scale that clearly shows the temperatures at which different meats are cooked. Look for one with a thin probe, which will make a narrower hole in the meat and allow fewer juices to escape.

To use a meat thermometer • Both regular and instant-read thermometers should be inserted into the thickest part of the meat, preferably near the center, without touching bone or gristle. For a regular meat thermometer, insert about half of the probe into the meat and leave it there throughout cooking. For an instant-read thermometer, insert about 2" of the probe into the meat and let it stand for at least 20 seconds. Instant-read thermometers can also be used to test the internal temperature of foods such as lasagna. For the most accurate reading, measure the food in several spots. Rotate the food if it is not cooking evenly.

To use an instant-read thermometer to estimate total cooking time • Check the internal temperature of the food before you cook it. A roast that is 55°F will cook a lot faster than one that is only 35°F.

To choose a candy or deep-fat frying thermometer • Most of these thermometers are in the shape of a clear glass tube with a bulb at the end. Look for one with a clear readout and an adjustable clip so that it can be attached to the side of the pan.

To use a candy or deep-fat frying thermometer • Stand it upright in the candy syrup or fat so that the bulb is completely immersed in the liquid but not touching the bottom of the pan. Clip the thermometer to the side of the pan.

To check the accuracy of a meat or candy thermometer • Insert it into boiling water for 20 seconds (for an instant-read thermometer) or 3 minutes (for a regular meat thermometer or a candy thermometer). It should read 212°F, the temperature at which water boils. If it doesn't, you can adjust an instant-read thermometer: Grip the hexagonal nut be-

neath the dial face with a pair of pliers or a small wrench and twist the face of the dial until it registers 212°F. For a regular meat thermometer or candy thermometer, if you get a reading other than 212°F, calculate the difference and adjust recipes accordingly. For instance, if your thermometer reads 207°F in boiling water, it is 5°F too low; when using it with a recipe that specifies cooking to 245°F, cook until your thermometer reads 240°F.

To choose an oven thermometer • There are two basic types: mercury-style glass tubes and spring-operated dial thermometers. The glass tubes are more expensive but more accurate.

To use an oven thermometer • Position the oven rack in the middle position and place the thermometer on it. Preheat the oven to 350°F for 15 minutes, after which time the thermometer should read 350°F. If it doesn't, calculate the difference and adjust recipes accordingly. For instance, if the thermometer reads 375°F, your oven runs 25°F hot; when a recipe specifies 350°F, set your oven to 325°F.

To use a refrigerator or freezer thermometer • Proper refrigerator and freezer temperatures are crucial for preserving the quality of foods and for food safety. Test your appliances by placing a thermometer near the top and front of the refrigerator or freezer. Let it sit for 6 hours or overnight. Refrigerators should read 40°F, and freezers should read 0°F or below. If the temperature is off, adjust your appliance's temperature regulator and test again.

Timing *see also* Entertaining; Mise en Place

In cooking, as in comedy, timing is everything.

TIMING THE HOLIDAY MEAL

For the home cook, holiday meals are like juggling acts. You have to coordinate multiple courses, cope with limited refrigerator and oven space, and play host to a house full of expectant guests, all while running against the clock. Here's how to orchestrate Thanksgiving and Christmas meals with minimal stress. Remember the key to timing any meal: Don't try to do it all at once. Prioritize, plan, prep, and, most important, have fun.

The Big Thanksgiving Meal

Two Weeks in Advance: Write out your menu, a shopping list, and a to-do list. As you make standard trips to the market, start collecting components on your shopping list that will keep well.

The Weekend Before: Make your pie crusts. Homemade pie pastry is worth the effort (see the recipe on page 362). Prepare the dough, roll it out, fit it into the pan, and freeze. Keep in mind that frozen pie doughs do not require thawing before baking. Also, apple pies can be completely prepared and frozen in advance.

Three to Four Days in Advance: Begin defrosting your frozen turkey. See the chart on page 522 to see exactly how much defrosting time you'll need. Complete all your last-minute shopping. Start setting aside 30 minutes in the mornings and/or evenings to start prepping the meal. Even in 10 minutes, you can finish simple things like measuring out the amount of sugar and pecans for a pie or chopping up carrots and storing them in a zipper-lock plastic bag. These little pockets of prep time can make all the difference when time gets tight later on. Some dishes, such as cranberry sauce and dips, can also be fully prepared a couple of days in advance.

The Day before Thanksgiving: This tends to be the real crunch day or night, a valuable period of intense cooking that will make Thanksgiving day a breeze. Focus your energy on baking the pies. That's one task that you do not want to be tackling on Thanksgiving day. If you are in need of refrigerator space, place the turkey in a large cooler and cover it with ice water. If you are brining the turkey, add salt and sugar to the ice water and remove the turkey from its wrapper. With a full shelf in your refrigerator, you can now finish more advance prep: Wash and store salad greens, scrub potatoes, and chop onions and other vegetables. If you are baking some kind of potato casserole or other baked vegetable dish, assemble it now, or even bake it now if you can. With a big turkey occupying your oven all day before the meal, there may not be room or time to bake other

TIME SAVERS ▼ **To get all the elements of a meal on the table at once** • Plan menus that allow you to do multiple tasks simultaneously. For instance, while dessert is baking, potatoes can be baking on another rack in the same oven. Fifteen minutes before the potatoes are done, you can start a fish grilling, and while the fish is cooking, you can assemble the salad. Begin by cooking the dishes that take the most time and the least attention, which frees you up to prepare other dishes that do require your presence.

To save more time with make-ahead dishes • Build make-aheads into your dishes. When baking a bean or sweet potato casserole ahead, just leave off the topping at first. Add the topping when reheating, so that the topping will be fresh and crisp.

Thanksgiving Day: It's the big day. Almost everything should be either cooked, assembled, or ready for assembly or last-minute touches. Of course, a few dishes are best when made fresh that day. For instance, mashed potatoes are ideally made within an hour of mealtime (a good task to delegate while you are attending to the turkey). If casseroles need reheating, pull them from the refrigerator 30 minutes before the turkey is scheduled to be done. After the turkey is out of the oven, put the casseroles in to reheat. If you've made soup, keep it warm in a slow cooker. This way, your stove top will be freed up for making gravy or other last-minute vegetable dishes.

The Christmas Meal Two Ways

An Easy Christmas at Home: In many households, the Christmas meal is less formal than the Thanksgiving meal. Why not serve a stew, which takes only 1 pot and benefits in flavor from being prepared a couple of days in advance? Spooned into wide, shallow bowls over a bed of rice or egg noodles or alongside warm, crusty bread, this kind of meal is homey and flavorful, and it easily nourishes a crowd with little effort other than reheating. Start with a simple salad of mixed greens, and finish with a fresh-baked apple pie that you assembled and froze days beforehand (or even a month prior, when making pies for Thanksgiving).

An Elegant Christmas to Remember: If the Christmas meal is a more formal affair in your household, prepare as much as you can in advance, including soups, salads, and desserts. A number of sophisticated desserts can be prepared in advance. Crème brûlée holds well in the refrigerator; all you need to do is caramelize the top before serving. A fallen chocolate cake or flourless chocolate cake can be mixed ahead of time, held in the refrigerator, and baked off at the last minute. As for the main course, the best choice is a roast, such as beef tenderloin, because it does not require constant fussing as it cooks. Partner the roast with root vegetables that also roast well, such as beets, carrots, or potatoes. If you want to serve homemade rolls, proof, knead, and shape the dough in the morning, then set the dough in the refrigerator for up to 24 hours. Remove the shaped dough balls about 1 hour before you are to bake them; bake them after the roast is pulled from the oven and is left to rest before carving.

menus. Most soups and stews get better if they are made the day before and rewarmed. Cakes and cookies can be frozen for weeks without compromising their quality. Pie crusts can be frozen, then filled and baked fresh the day they are served. Casseroles can be assembled ahead and baked just before serving. And vegetables can be chopped and blanched ahead, then sautéed briefly just before you put the meal on the table. You can even precook pasta ahead of time: Cook it until it's slightly underdone, cool it to room temperature in a bowl of ice water, drain it and toss it with oil to prevent sticking, then refrigerate it until needed. It reheats in boiling water in seconds. Make-ahead and precooked dishes help prevent last-minute disasters.

To save time by serving cold dishes • Whenever possible, work cold dishes into your menus. Most cold dishes can be stored without losing quality. Salads can be assembled hours ahead and dressed at the last minute. Roasted meats can be served at room temperature with pungent sauces. Potato salad can take the place of baked or mashed potatoes. Chilled asparagus or broccoli in a vinaigrette goes just as well with roasted chicken as a hot vegetable, and it saves you from having to do a lot of last-minute cooking. Better yet, store cold dishes such as salads and desserts on their serving plates for the ultimate in easy service.

Tofu *see also* Soy Milk

The process of making tofu is similar to that of making cheese. Soy milk is curdled, drained, and pressed into blocks. Depending upon how much whey has been pressed out, tofu can be soft, firm, or extra-firm. Tofu, also known as bean curd, has a very mild flavor that readily takes on the flavors of other foods, particularly marinades and sauces. It is usually sold packed in tubs of water. The custardlike "silken" tofu is sold in small, aseptic boxes.

BASICS **To choose** • There are two basic types of tofu: regular and silken. If a recipe doesn't specify silken tofu, use the regular type. Each type comes in soft, firm, or extra-firm varieties. Regular tofu is usually sold in tubs of water, while silken tofu comes in small, shelf-stable aseptic boxes. Regular tofu has a firmer texture than silken tofu and is best when marinated and grilled, broiled, baked, browned, sautéed, or stir-fried. You can also mash regular tofu with seasonings and use it in casseroles like you would use ricotta cheese. The custardlike texture of silken tofu works best when cubed and served in broth or when pureed to use in creamy soups, dips, sauces, and dressings. Pureed silken tofu makes a good substitute for sour cream or yogurt in baking as well. More processed forms of tofu are also available. Premarinated and baked or smoked tofu can be eaten right out of the package or used in recipes.

To store • Once opened, submerge tofu (regular or silken) in water in an airtight container and refrigerate up to 5 days, changing the water once or twice. Tofu spoils easily, so handle it as you would a fresh meat product. Marinate it in the refrigerator and keep it cold or bring it to room temperature just before cooking.

To freeze • When frozen, tofu becomes slightly darker in color and chewier in texture. It also has a more spongelike appearance, with many small holes throughout, which allows it to absorb more liquid flavorings. Regular tofu works best when frozen, then thawed, crumbled, and browned like ground beef. Simply remove regular tofu from the packaging, drain the liquid, wrap the tofu in plastic, and freeze it until solid. Thaw and press out excess liquid before using. To thaw tofu quickly, wrap it in foil and submerge it in hot tap water for 15 minutes, adding more hot water if the water gets too cool. Freezing silken tofu is not recommended.

To press tofu • Some recipes call for tofu to be drained and pressed. Pressing out excess liquid gives the tofu a firmer texture and allows it to absorb more flavors. Drain the packing liquid, then place the block of tofu on a plate lined with paper towels. Cover the tofu with more paper towels and top with a weight, such as a cast-iron skillet, a water-filled saucepan, or an un-opened heavy can. Let it sit for 15 minutes or up to overnight for a very firm texture. When pressing tofu for more than 30 minutes, do so in the refrigerator.

To quickly press tofu • When tofu will be crumbled in a recipe, skip the step of pressing out the water. Instead, place the tofu in a clean, nonterry dish towel, twist the ends, and firmly wring out the moisture. The tofu will be pressed and crumbled in one step.

EASY BAKED TOFU Mix **¼ cup bottled teriyaki sauce, 1 tablespoon water,** and **⅛ teaspoon Chinese five-spice powder** in a glass baking dish or zipper-lock plastic bag. Press **1 cake extra-firm tofu (1 pound),** then cut in half through the side to make 2 slabs, each about ½" thick. Add to marinade and refrigerate up to 5 days, if desired. Bake at 350°F, 30 minutes, turning once halfway through. *Makes about 4 servings.*

EGG-FREE TOFU MAYONNAISE Drain **1 pound soft tofu.** In a food processor or blender, combine tofu, **⅓ cup** *each* **olive oil and lemon juice, ¾ teaspoon** *each* **Dijon mustard and salt,** and **⅛ teaspoon ground black pepper.** Process until smooth. If mixture is too thick, add **2 tablespoons water.** Store in the refrigerator up to 1 week. *Makes 2 cups.*

TOFU BLUE CHEESE DRESSING In a food processor or blender, combine **½ cup drained firm tofu, ¼ cup crumbled**

TOFU MARINADES

Use any of these marinades to flavor 1 pound of tofu. Press the tofu to remove excess liquid, then cut through the side to make two ½"-thick slabs. Marinate for 15 minutes or up to 5 days in the refrigerator. Then bake at 350°F for 30 minutes, turning halfway through. These marinades can also be used with 1 pound of chicken, beef, or pork.

French Herb Marinade: Mix **¼ cup lemon juice, 3 tablespoons** *each* **olive oil and white wine vinegar, 2 teaspoons** *each* **honey and Dijon mustard, 1 crushed garlic clove,** and **1½ teaspoons herbes de Provence** (see page 233).

Sesame-Soy Marinade: Mix **¼ cup** *each* **rice vinegar, soy sauce, and vegetable broth; 3 tablespoons lime juice; 1 tablespoon sesame oil;** and **1 teaspoon ground coriander.**

Sweet-and-Sour Marinade: Mix **½ cup** *each* **ketchup and crushed pineapple, ⅓ cup** *each* **white vinegar and brown sugar, 2 minced garlic cloves,** and **3 sliced scallions.**

Barbecue Marinade: In a small saucepan, combine **1 cup ketchup, ⅓ cup** *each* **molasses and sherry, ¼ cup soy sauce,** and **2 tablespoons brown mustard.** Bring to a simmer, partially cover, and cook 10 minutes.

blue cheese, **2 tablespoons lemon juice, 1 tablespoon** *each* **white wine vinegar and olive oil,** and **1 teaspoon Worcestershire sauce.** Process until smooth. Stir in ¼ **cup chopped fresh parsley.** *Makes 1 cup.*

MEXICAN CHOCOLATE-TOFU PUDDING Drain **2 packages (10 ounces each) silken tofu** and place in a food processor. Add ⅔ **cup brown sugar, 5 tablespoons unsweetened cocoa powder, 2 teaspoons vanilla extract, 1 teaspoon instant coffee granules** dissolved in **2 teaspoons boiling water,** ¼ **teaspoon ground cinnamon,** and ⅛ **teaspoon ground allspice.** Process until smooth. Spoon into dessert dishes and chill until set, 30 minutes. *Makes 4 servings.*

TOFU-PUMPKIN PIE Preheat oven to 400°F. In a blender or food processor, combine **1½ cups drained firm tofu cubes, 1 can (15 ounces) pumpkin puree,** ½ **cup brown sugar,** ¼ **cup honey, 1 egg, 2 teaspoons** *each* **vanilla extract and ground cinnamon,** and ¼ **teaspoon** *each* **ground nutmeg and ground allspice.** Blend until smooth and pour into an unbaked 9" pie crust. Bake until a knife inserted in center comes out clean, 50 minutes. Cool completely on a rack and serve at room temperature. *Makes 8 servings.*

Tomatillos

Looking a bit like green tomatoes wrapped in parchment, tomatillos are an essential ingredient in Mexico's classic green salsas. Tomatillos have a lemony, herbal flavor that is sharply tart when raw and somewhat tem- pered by cooking. Most traditional recipes call for tomatillos to be either poached in gently simmering water or roasted in a skillet. Raw tomatillos are occasionally used in guacamole, salads, and sandwiches.

BASICS **To choose** • Though most commonly found in markets that specialize in Latin American foods, tomatillos are increasingly available in supermarkets. Look for firm, unblemished tomatillos that completely fill their husks. Canned tomatillos, available in many Latin American food stores, lack the spark of fresh but make an acceptable substitute in a pinch. Use 1 can (13 ounces) whole tomatillos to replace ½ pound fresh.

To store • Wrap tomatillos loosely in a paper or plastic bag and refrigerate for up to 3 weeks.

To husk • Peel off the brown, papery husk under warm, running water. The husk and the sticky, resinous substance that coats the fruit will rinse right off.

To poach • Place tomatillos in a saucepan and cover with cold water. Bring to a gentle simmer over medium heat and cook until tender, 5 to 15 minutes, depending on the size of the fruit.

To roast • Heat a skillet over medium heat. Add husked tomatillos and cook, turning frequently, until they are softened and blackened in spots, about 10 minutes.

Fascinating Fact: Although called *tomate verde* ("green tomato") in Mexico, tomatillos are more closely related to Cape gooseberries and ground cherries.

SALSA VERDE In a saucepan, combine **1 pound husked fresh tomatillos (12 to 15 medium)** and **1½ cups water.** (If using canned tomatillos, skip this poaching step and place 2 drained cans, 13 ounces each, whole tomatillos in a blender as directed below.) Bring to a boil and cook until tomatillos are soft, 8 to 10 minutes. Drain and reserve ¾ cup cooking liquid. In a blender, combine tomatillos, **½ cup cooking liquid (or water, if using canned),** and **1 to 2 finely chopped jalapeño chile peppers.** Puree until smooth. In a large skillet, sauté **2 minced garlic cloves** in **1 tablespoon corn oil or canola oil,** 15 seconds. Add the sauce, increase the heat to medium-high, and cook without stirring, 2 minutes. Stir and cook 2 to 3 minutes longer. Remove from heat and stir in **3 tablespoons chopped fresh cilantro** and **1 teaspoon salt.** If making ahead, cover and chill. When cold, tomatillo salsa will set up slightly, like gelatin. Bring to room temperature before using. Thin with **1 to 2 tablespoons water** if necessary. *Makes about 4 cups.*

Tomatoes, Dried *see also*

Tomatoes, Fresh; Tomato Paste

When dried by the sun, in a conventional oven, or in special dehydrators, fresh tomatoes develop a dense, chewy texture and intense tomato flavor. Sun-dried tomatoes make a wonderful addition to pizzas, pastas, sandwiches, salads, braises, or stews.

BASICS **To choose** • Sun-dried tomato halves are
▼ sold dry, chopped into bits, or packed in jars of olive oil. The ones packed in oil tend to be sweeter and have more flavor than dry-packed sun-dried tomatoes. Plus, you can add the flavorful oil to whatever you're making. When buying sun-dried tomatoes from a bulk-foods bin, look for ones that are soft, not brittle. They should have a deep, dark color.

To store • Refrigerate open jars of oil-packed sun-dried tomatoes up to 2 weeks. Don't worry if the oil gets cloudy; it will clear up as it reaches room temperature. Dry-packed sun-dried tomatoes will keep in a cool, dry place indefinitely.

To rehydrate • Drypack sun-dried tomatoes must be rehydrated before using. To rehydrate them, cover the tomatoes with hot water and let stand until softened, 10 to 15 minutes. You can also rehydrate by covering the sun-dried tomatoes with oil and letting them stand overnight.

To chop through the tough skins • Place sun-dried tomatoes in a cup or jar and snip them with kitchen shears. Or use a food processor to mince them.

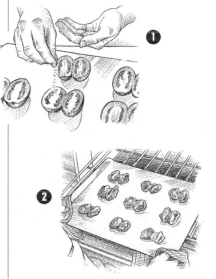

To oven-dry fresh tomatoes • Slice plum tomatoes lengthwise almost in half so that they lie open, cut side up, like a book. Arrange them on a nonstick baking sheet and sprinkle lightly with salt ❶.

Place the sheet in a 120° to 140°F oven and let the tomatoes dry until shriveled, about 10 to 12 hours ❷. They should feel dry but still be pliable. Oven-dried tomatoes will not be as dry as commercially dried ones. Store oven-dried tomatoes in an airtight container in the refrigerator for up to 6 months.

Tomatoes, Fresh *see also*

Tomatoes, Dried; Tomato Paste; Tomato Sauce

Almost every American kitchen contains some form of tomatoes. One of the most ubiquitous and best-loved vegetables, they are used to make ketchup, salsa, pasta sauce, tomato paste, and countless other products. Tomatoes are enjoyed fresh in salads and sandwiches and are delicious baked, fried, or stewed.

BASICS ▼

To choose • Tomatoes don't ship well, so the best places to shop for them are farmers' markets and local produce stands. The best time to shop is in the warm summer months, when they are at the peak of their growing season. Look for tomatoes that are firm, but not hard, and heavy for their size. They should have a sweet tomato aroma. If using tomatoes for sauce, choose plum or Roma tomatoes, which are less watery and have more pulp. Yellow tomatoes tend to have a sweeter, less acidic flavor than red varieties, making them excellent for salads.

To store • Keep fresh tomatoes in a cool but not cold spot. Never refrigerate a tomato. Temperatures below 55°F make tomatoes spongy and destroy their flavor.

Fascinating Fact: There are more than 4,000 varieties of tomatoes. Some are as small as marbles. The Ponderosa is the giant, weighing more than 3 pounds.

To ripen end-of-the-season green tomatoes • Layer them, stem end down, between sheets of newspaper in a box. Store the box in a cool location.

To core • Run a paring knife around the stem end to remove the inner white core.

To slice • Use a serrated knife, such as a steak or bread knife.

To peel several tomatoes • Cut a small X at the base of several tomatoes and drop them into a pot of boiling water just until the skins begin to loosen, 10 to 15 seconds. Remove them with a sieve or a pair of tongs, and hold each tomato under cold running water. The peel will slip off easily. See the illustrations on page 47.

To peel just a few tomatoes • Rub with the dull edge of a paring knife. If the tomato is ripe enough, the skin will buckle up and then readily peel off. You can also char each tomato by holding it over a flame with tongs or a long-handled fork until the skin is blistered and loosened all over. This method adds a wonderful smoky aroma. If what you want is tomato pulp, coarsely chop the tomatoes and run them through a food mill. Or slice off the stem ends and grate the tomatoes over a bowl on the coarsest teeth of a box grater. The flesh will scrape away from the skins, leaving you with a bowl of tomato pulp.

To seed • Cut the tomato in half crosswise. Hold one half in your hand, gently squeeze, and remove the seeds and gel with your fingers or the tip of a paring knife. Repeat with the other half. Or seed and peel a tomato in one step by chopping it and running it through a food mill.

To hollow out a cherry tomato • Slice off the stem end and scoop out the insides with the small end of a melon baller.

To preserve leftover fresh tomatoes • Freeze the tomatoes whole. Run under warm water to remove the peels, then use the whole frozen tomatoes to make sauce. You can also make fresh tomato sauce and freeze it. Or make a big batch of salsa and freeze it in zipper-lock freezer bags. Homemade salsa (even frozen and thawed) beats the jarred varieties any day.

BROILED TOMATOES WITH PARMESAN CRUST Spread **1 teaspoon extra-virgin olive oil** on a broiler pan. Arrange **4 thick slices tomato** in the pan and drizzle with another **1 teaspoon extra-virgin olive oil**. Combine **2 tablespoons** *each* **bread crumbs and freshly grated Parmesan cheese** and ¼ **teaspoon** *each* **fresh onion powder, garlic powder, salt, and ground black pepper.** Sprinkle a thick layer of this mixture on the top of each tomato and drizzle with another **1 teaspoon extra-virgin olive oil.** Bake at 450°F until golden brown, 10 minutes. *Makes 4 servings*

FRIED GREEN TOMATOES Core and cut **3 green tomatoes** into ¼"-thick slices. Combine in a shallow dish with ⅔ **cup milk.** In another shallow dish, combine ⅓ **cup** *each* **flour and cornmeal** and ½ **teaspoon** *each* **salt, ground black pepper, and ground red pepper (optional).** Remove tomato slices from milk and dredge in cornmeal mixture to lightly coat. Dip back into milk, then again into cornmeal mixture. Place slices on a rack as they are coated. Heat ⅛" **of bacon fat** or **vegetable oil (or half of each)** in a large skillet over medium-high heat. Add tomato slices without crowding the pan and fry until crisp and golden, 2 to 3 minutes per side. Drain on paper towels. Serve hot. *Makes 4 to 6 servings.*

PROBLEM SOLVERS ▼ **To make slices that are less prone to fall apart** • Slice vertically from top to bottom.

To prevent stuffed baked tomatoes from losing their shape • Place each one in a greased ramekin, a small ovenproof bowl, or one of the cups of a muffin pan.

Fascinating Fact: Ketchup was sold in the 1830s as medicine.

TIME SAVERS ▼ **To quickly chop up whole canned tomatoes** • Leave them in the opened can and snip them with kitchen scissors.

To save peeling time • Quickly peel tomato skins by microwaving the tomatoes on high power for 25 seconds. Let stand 30 seconds, then peel. Or skip peeling altogether. There is no reason to peel tomatoes for dishes that have a relatively short cooking time (under 1 hour). Peeling is necessary only when cooking tomatoes for a long time, as they will completely lose their shape and the skins will separate out.

To save seeding time • Skip seeding. Seeding tomatoes reduces a small amount of bitterness, but wastes much of the bulk of the tomatoes and it also drains away the flavorful tomato gel along with the seeds.

To make sauce faster • Freeze tomatoes whole, then peel them under warm running water (the peels will slip right off).

t

Place the peeled frozen tomatoes in a saucepan whole. Cook them until thawed, then pulse them in a food processor until chopped. Return the chopped tomatoes to the saucepan and finish cooking. Frozen tomatoes give up their liquid faster and will create a thick sauce in less time than fresh tomatoes.

QUICK TOMATO AND RED-PEPPER SAUCE In a small pot of boiling water, cook **3 peeled garlic cloves,** 3 minutes. Remove garlic and place in a food pro-

cessor along with **2 slices toasted and torn sandwich bread, 2 drained jars (7 ounces each) roasted red peppers, ¾ cup tomato sauce, 1 tablespoon olive oil, 1 teaspoon sugar,** and **⅛ teaspoon ground red pepper.** Process until smooth. Place in a saucepan and heat through. Use to top grilled chicken, pork, or fish. *Makes about 2 cups.*

FAST FRESH TOMATO SAUCE Sauté **2 small chopped onions, 2 minced garlic cloves,** and **1 dried chile pepper (such**

Fresh Tomato Soup

If you have only ever had the canned stuff, get ready for enlightenment.

2 tablespoons olive oil

1 tablespoon butter

2 large onions, chopped

2 garlic cloves

2 celery ribs, chopped

2 tablespoons all-purpose flour

10 large, very ripe tomatoes, coarsely chopped, juice reserved

2–3 teaspoons sugar

2 large fresh basil branches

¾ teaspoon salt

¼ teaspoon ground black pepper

⅛ teaspoon red-pepper flakes

2 tablespoons chopped fresh basil

1. Heat the oil and butter in a large stockpot over medium heat. Add the onions, garlic, and celery. Cook until very soft but not brown, 6 to 8 minutes. Add the flour and cook 1 minute more, stirring frequently.

2. Add the tomatoes, reserved tomato juice, sugar, basil branches, salt, black pepper, and red-pepper flakes. Bring to a gentle boil. Skim the surface of the soup and discard any foam. Simmer 10 minutes.

3. Run the soup through the fine blade of a food mill or press it through a coarse strainer, discarding the solids. Return the soup to the pot to rewarm. Stir in the choped basil just before serving.

Makes 8 to 10 servings

as cayenne; wear plastic gloves when handling) in **2 tablespoons olive oil** until onion is soft, 4 minutes. Add **12 peeled and coarsely chopped fresh plum tomatoes** and **1 roasted and chopped bell pepper.** Cook until tomatoes begin to release their liquid, 15 to 20 minutes. Stir in **1 tablespoon tomato paste, ½ teaspoon salt,** and **¼ teaspoon ground black pepper.** Cook 2 minutes. Add **⅓ cup chopped fresh herbs (basil or parsley is good)** and heat 1 minute. Remove and discard chile pepper. *Makes 4 servings.*

EASY CHILLED TOMATO SOUP In a food processor, combine **2 large cored tomatoes, 3 ice cubes, 1 roasted and peeled red bell pepper, ¼ chopped onion, 1 minced garlic clove, 3 tablespoons olive oil, ½ teaspoon salt,** and **¼ teaspoon ground black pepper (or more to taste).** Process until finely chopped. Stir in another **3 ice cubes, 1 tablespoon chopped fresh parsley,** and **¼ cup jarred basil pesto.** *Makes 4 servings.*

HEALTHY HINT ▼ **To benefit from tomato's lycopene •** There is no need to buy fresh tomatoes to reap the benefits of lycopene, an antioxidant that may help prevent heart disease and certain cancers. Lycopene can withstand the high heat used in processing and cooking, so all canned and bottled tomato products include the health benefits of lycopene. However, lycopene will be more readily absorbed by the body when tomatoes are eaten with a small amount of fat, such as olive oil.

Tomato Paste

Made from tomatoes that have been slowly cooked for hours until they are very thick, tomato paste has a deep, concentrated taste and is used to add rich tomato flavor to a wide range of dishes.

BASICS ▼ **To choose •** Look for imported brands of tomato paste. Those from the Parma region of Italy tend to have a deeper and truer tomato flavor. Tubes of tomato paste are more convenient to use and last longer than canned tomato paste.

To store • Store opened tubes of tomato paste in the refrigerator for up to 8 months.

To save leftover canned tomato paste • Place tablespoon-size mounds on a pie pan lined with plastic wrap. Freeze until firm. Lift the plastic and pop off the tomato paste mounds. Store in a zipper-lock freezer bag and use as needed. No need to defrost.

FLAVOR TIP ▼ **To get a richer-tasting tomato paste •** Buy sun-dried tomato paste in a tube.

SIMPLE SUN-DRIED TOMATO SAUCE Whisk together **2 tablespoons sun-dried tomato paste, ⅓ cup extra-virgin olive oil, 3 tablespoons red wine vinegar,** and **¼ teaspoon *each* salt and ground black pepper.** Serve with fish or chicken. *Makes about ⅔ cup.*

TOMATO-BASIL CONSOMMÉ Soften **1 tablespoon unflavored gelatin powder** in **½ cup canned defatted chicken broth.** Place in a heavy saucepan and add another **5½ cups chicken broth.** Stir until blended. Stir in **¼ cup tomato paste, 1 finely chopped celery rib, ¼ small finely chopped onion, 2 teaspoons dried basil, 6 peppercorns, 1 crumbled bay leaf,** and **¼ teaspoon salt (or more to taste).** Bring to a simmer and cook 15 minutes. Strain and stir in **2 tablespoons shredded basil leaves** just before serving. *Makes 4 servings.*

Tomato Sauce *see also* Sauces;

Tomatoes, Fresh

Top-quality tomatoes, either fresh or canned, and a few aromatic ingredients are all that is needed to make an excellent tomato sauce.

BASICS **To choose fresh tomatoes for sauce •** Make sure that the tomatoes are ripe and have a well-balanced flavor. Plum or Roma tomatoes, which have a larger ratio of flesh to seeds, are a good choice.

To choose canned tomatoes for sauce • Look for good-quality whole tomatoes. Crushed or pureed tomatoes are often too watery for sauce.

To make meaty, rustic tomato sauce • Blanch the tomatoes briefly in a pot of boiling water, peel them, and cut them into coarse pieces before cooking.

To preserve the shape of chopped tomatoes for sauce • Cook them quickly over high heat.

To make smooth tomato sauce • Cut the tomatoes in half and cook them in a covered saucepan over medium heat for about 10 minutes. Then, pass the tomatoes through a food mill fitted with the disk with the largest holes.

To make tomato sauce that has a rich, concentrated flavor • Cook it uncovered.

To store • Transfer cooled tomato sauce to a covered container and refrigerate up to 4 days or freeze up to 6 months.

PROBLEM SOLVERS **To prevent an off taste or color when cooking tomato sauce •** Avoid using an aluminum or cast-iron pan.

To avoid a bitter taste in homemade tomato sauce • Remove seeds from tomatoes before cooking.

To balance overly tart tomato sauce • Add ½ teaspoon sugar to each 2 cups of sauce. Taste and, if desired, add more sugar, ½ teaspoon at a time, to reach the desired balance.

To salvage watery tomato sauce • Cook it further to reduce the liquid. Or use a bulb baster to spoon off and discard excess liquid. You can also strain the sauce through a fine wire-mesh sieve. Catch the liquid in a bowl in case you want to add some back in.

To avoid staining a plastic container when storing leftover tomato sauce • Lightly coat the container interior with cooking spray.

TIME SAVER **To easily thaw frozen tomato sauce •** Float the sauce container in the pasta water as it comes to a boil. Or microwave on high power for 3 to 5 minutes, occasionally breaking up the chunks with a fork.

FLAVOR TIP **To add smoky flavor and aroma •** Cook 4 slices chopped bacon until crisp. Drain off all but 1 tablespoon of the fat, and use the fat to start your tomato sauce. Add the bacon, if desired.

Tortillas *see also* Tacos

These flat, unleavened breads are one of the cornerstones of the Mexican kitchen. Traditionally made from either ground corn or wheat flour, tortillas form the basis of countless classic Mexican dishes, such as tacos, enchiladas, and corn chips.

BASICS **To choose •** You'll find the best tortillas freshly made in Mexican bakeries. If there are none near you, look for those made with the least amount of preservatives. Flour tortillas are best for burritos and quesadillas, while corn tortillas work best for chips, tacos, and enchiladas.

To store • Keep tortillas well-wrapped in the refrigerator for up to 1 week.

To warm • Stack the tortillas on top of one another and wrap the stack in foil. Heat in a 350°F oven until warm. If the tortillas are dry, sprinkle them with a little bit of water before wrapping. You can also heat flour or corn tortillas one by one directly over a stove-top flame, turning them quickly to prevent burning. Avoid heating tortillas in a microwave oven, which ruins their texture.

To keep tortillas warm at the table • Wrap the warm tortillas in a towel and serve them in a covered basket.

THREE VERSATILE TORTILLA FILLINGS

These fillings can be used with both corn and flour tortillas to make tacos, burritos, or enchiladas. Each makes enough for 4 to 6 servings.

Shredded Beef Filling: Pat dry about **1 pound well-trimmed beef chuck cubes (1½" each).** In a large, deep skillet or wide saucepan, heat **2 tablespoons vegetable oil** over medium-high heat. Add beef and brown well on all sides, 3 to 5 minutes. Add **1 large minced garlic clove** and **1 bay leaf.** Sauté 10 seconds, then add **2½ cups water,** stirring to deglaze the pan. Reduce heat to low, cover, and simmer until beef is very tender and easy to shred, about 2 hours. Remove beef with a slotted spoon. Discard bay leaf. When beef is cool enough to handle, tear it into shreds and place in a bowl. Add ⅓ cup of the braising liquid and **1 teaspoon salt.** Toss to mix.

Shredded Chicken Filling: In a saucepan, combine **1½ pounds halved bone-in chicken breasts, 1½ cups water, 2 large sliced garlic cloves, 1 bay leaf,** and **½ teaspoon salt.** Partly cover, and simmer until center of thickest chicken piece registers 170°F on an instant-read thermometer and juices run clear, 15 to 20 minutes. Remove from heat and let cool to room temperature in the broth. Remove chicken and simmer broth until reduced to ⅓ cup. Remove and discard bay leaf. Remove and discard chicken skin and bones. Tear meat into shreds about ¼" to ½" wide and place in a bowl. Add the reduced broth and **½ teaspoon** *each* **salt and ground black pepper.** Toss to mix.

Scrambled Egg and Chorizo Filling: Heat a large nonstick skillet over medium heat. Slit the casings of **½ pound soft Mexican chorizo** and crumble the meat into the pan. Cook until liquid evaporates and chorizo is sizzling and no longer pink, 8 minutes. Remove chorizo with a slotted spoon and drain off fat. Wipe out the skillet with a paper towel and add **1 tablespoon vegetable oil.** Place over medium heat. If desired, sauté **1 small chopped onion** in the hot oil. In a bowl, whisk **8 large eggs (or 4 eggs plus 6 whites)** with **1 tablespoon water** and **¼ teaspoon salt.** Pour into the hot skillet and reduce heat to low. Cook 30 seconds, then push with a spatula to gently scramble. Fold in chorizo.

t

TORTILLA CHIPS Stack **5 tortillas** and cut the stack into 8 wedges, like a pizza, to make a total of 40 wedges. Arrange on 2 baking sheets and coat with cooking spray. Sprinkle evenly with **½ teaspoon** *each* **salt and chili powder (optional).** Bake at 350°F until crisp, 7 to 10 minutes. Serve warm, or let cool and store in a zipper-lock plastic bag at room temperature up to 5 days. *Makes 40.*

EASY QUESADILLAS Coat a nonstick skillet with cooking spray and heat over medium heat. Place **1 flour tortilla** (8" diameter) in the skillet. Scatter **1 ounce (¼ cup) shredded cheese (any type)** over the tortilla. Top with **1 tablespoon salsa** and **another tortilla.** Cook until golden brown and cheese melts, 4 minutes per side. Cool slightly, cut into quarters, and serve. *Makes 1 serving.*

t

Trussing *see also* Poultry

Trussing ties up roasting poultry so that it keeps a tightly compacted shape for presentation at the table. If speed is an objective, trussing poultry for roasting is not only unnecessary but also counterproductive. When the legs are secured around the breast, heat circulation is greatly reduced and roasting can take 50 percent longer. If you're in a hurry, don't truss.

Tuna *see also* Fish; Doneness Tests and Temperatures (page 572)

A member of the mackerel family, tuna is usually sold precooked and canned. It has firm flesh and rich flavor.

BASICS ▼ **To choose** • Albacore tuna is the mildest available and the only type that can be called white meat tuna. Yellowfin tuna (also called *ahi*) has a stronger flavor and light meat. Bluefin tuna has a fairly strong flavor and dark flesh. When buying canned tuna, look for "solid" or "fancy" tuna, the highest grade with the largest and best-tasting pieces. The other grades are "chunk," which has smaller pieces, and "flaked," which consists of very small pieces. Water-packed tuna tends to have a fresher and cleaner flavor than oil-packed tuna.

To easily crumble canned tuna • Use a pastry blender.

FLAVOR TIPS ▼ **To get the best-tasting canned tuna** • Use a combination of solid white tuna and chunk light tuna.

To boost flavor in tuna salad • Mix 2 teaspoons *each* anchovy paste and lemon juice. Stir into your favorite tuna salad.

To add a niçoise flavor to tuna salad • Add 1 chopped hard-cooked egg and 1 tablespoon *each* capers and lemon juice to your favorite tuna salad.

QUICK TUNA CROQUETTES Crumble the fish from **3 drained cans (6 ounces each) water-packed tuna.** Mix with **½ cup condensed cream of mushroom soup, 2 egg yolks, ½ cup seasoned bread crumbs, ¾ minced scallion, 2 tablespoons finely chopped fresh parsley, 2 teaspoons lemon juice, 1 teaspoon spicy brown mustard,** and **½ teaspoon hot-pepper sauce.** Form into 12 patties. Roll patties in another **1 cup seasoned bread crumbs** until well-coated. Brown in ¼" of hot oil in a large skillet, about 3 minutes per side. Serve with lemon wedges. *Makes 4 to 6 servings.*

Tuna–Noodle Casserole

This version of the American favorite combines solid white tuna and chunk light tuna for more flavor. Mushrooms add another flavor dimension.

½ **pound wide egg noodles**

1 **tablespoon olive oil or butter**

½ **pound white or brown cremini mushrooms, sliced**

1 **teaspoon dried oregano**

2 **cans (10¾ ounces each) condensed cream of mushroom soup**

⅓ **cup half-and-half or milk**

1 **can (6 ounces) solid white water-packed tuna**

1 **can (6 ounces) chunk light water-packed tuna**

¼ **cup dry white wine**

¼ **teaspoon ground black pepper**

½ **cup finely crushed potato chips**

1. Preheat the oven to 425°F. Grease a shallow 8" × 8" or 2-quart baking dish.

2. Cook the noodles according to package directions.

3. Meanwhile, coat a medium skillet with the oil or butter and place over medium-high heat. Add the mushrooms and cook, without stirring, until brown, 1 to 2 minutes. Add a splash of water and the oregano. Cook and stir until soft, 1 minute longer.

4. In a large bowl, combine the soup and half-and-half or milk. Add the tuna (with liquid) and wine. Stir together, breaking the tuna into large chunks. Stir in the mushrooms and pepper.

5. Add the noodles to the tuna mixture. Stir to mix. Spoon into the prepared baking dish. Sprinkle with the potato chips. Bake until golden, 25 to 30 minutes.

Makes 4 to 6 servings

t

MAIN-DISH TUNA SALAD In a large bowl, mix **2 tablespoons** *each* **olive oil, orange juice, and red wine vinegar;** ½ **teaspoon** *each* **red-pepper flakes and salt;** and ¼ **teaspoon freshly ground black pepper.** Add **2 drained cans (6 ounces each) water-packed white tuna, 1 rinsed and drained can (15 ounces) black beans, 1 finely chopped red bell pepper, 4 thinly sliced large scallions, 2 teaspoons** **grated orange zest, 1 finely chopped small red onion,** and **1 minced garlic clove.** Mix well and chill. *Makes 4 servings.*

BALSAMIC TUNA STEAKS Marinate **2 tuna steaks,** each about ¾" thick, in ¼ **cup olive oil** mixed with **3 tablespoons lemon juice, 1 large sliced garlic clove,** and **2 teaspoons dried oregano** for 1 hour. Heat a large, heavy skillet over high heat. Remove fish, brushing off marinade, and place in the hot skillet. Cook until fish is just opaque, 3 to 4 minutes per side. Remove to a plate. To the skillet, add ¼ **cup dry white wine, 1 tablespoon white wine vinegar,** and **1 tablespoon balsamic vinegar.** Deglaze pan, scraping up browned bits as sauce comes to a boil over medium-high heat. Place hot tuna steaks on a bed of **arugula,** top with the sauce, and sprinkle with **parsley.** *Makes 2 servings.*

EASY LOW-FAT TUNA SALAD Crumble the fish from **2 drained cans (6 ounces each) water-packed tuna.** Mix with **1 can (10 ounces) condensed cream of celery soup, 1 small finely chopped celery rib, 1 teaspoon lemon juice,** and ¼ **teaspoon** *each* **onion powder and ground black pepper.** *Makes 4 servings.*

Turkey *see also* Poultry; Stuffing; Doneness Tests and Temperatures (page 572); Holiday Hotlines (page 574

Native to America, turkey was domesticated by the Aztecs. The turkeys that are most commonly eaten today come from a Dutch breed that is noted for its plumpness.

BASICS **To choose** • For the best flavor and texture, look for fresh (not frozen), organic or free-range turkeys. Avoid self-basting turkeys, which have been injected with butter, vegetable oil, or broth and sometimes other seasonings to help keep the bird moist and add flavor. They are usually of very poor quality. When buying a whole turkey, plan on about 1 pound per person. Buy a few extra pounds if you want to be sure to have leftovers.

To cook a whole turkey perfectly • Turkey breasts (white meat) cook faster than turkey legs and thighs (dark meat). To keep breast meat from overcooking and drying out before the dark meat is done, place ice packs over the turkey breasts while defrosting the bird. When the bird is defrosted, remove the ice packs and cook as normal. The ice packs keep the breast meat cooler so that it cooks in the same amount of time as the dark meat.

To roast whole • Choose a bird that weighs 12 to 15 pounds. Defrost it with ice packs over the breasts as described above. Roast the bird, breast side up, at 425°F until a thermometer inserted into the breast registers 180°F and the stuffing, if any, reaches 165°F in the center, about 2 hours. Do not rely on pop-up timers. You can wait forever for them to pop, and frequently, they do not work at all. Test for doneness with an instant-read thermometer instead. If you don't have ice packs, massage 4 to 5 tablespoons unsalted butter into the breast before roasting. Roast the bird, breast side down, for most of the cooking time. Turn it breast side up toward the end of the cooking time to brown and crisp the skin. Baste the breast frequently with pan juices during roasting.

To keep roasted turkeys moist and add flavor • Soak them in a brine for several days before cooking. See page 64 for more on brining.

To brine an extra-large turkey without using all your refrigerator space • Place it in a large cooler and add ice water to the brine to keep the turkey cold. A food-safe bucket will also work as long as you periodically replenish it with ice. If you live in a cold climate, you can leave the brining turkey outside on a porch or in a garage if the temperature is 40°F or cooler.

To keep the turkey well-submerged in brine • Place a heavy pan or another clean, relatively heavy object on the bird to keep it under the salted water.

To estimate amounts • See "Estimating Food for a Crowd" on page 168.

To ensure a crisp, golden skin • Brush the skin periodically with melted butter as the turkey cooks.

To lift a hot, heavy turkey onto a carving board • Wad up 2 thick kitchen towels and use them to grab each end of the turkey. Before transferring it, tilt the turkey so that excess juices in the cavity drain into the pan for making gravy (and to protect you from burns). If the turkey is light enough, you can also lift it by inserting large wooden spoons into the carcass through each opening.

TURKEY SLOPPY JOES Sauté **¼ pound chopped mushrooms, ½ chopped onion, 1 chopped celery rib,** and **1 small chopped green bell pepper** in **3 tablespoons oil** until tender. Add **1 pound ground turkey** and cook until turkey is no longer pink. Add **¼ cup** *each* **beef broth and ketchup,** and **1 teaspoon hot-pepper sauce.** Simmer 1 minute and serve on **4 toasted hamburger buns.** *Makes 4 servings.*

TURKEY CUTLETS IN APPLE BUTTER SAUCE Season **1 pound turkey cutlets (each ¼" thick)** all over with **½ teaspoon salt** and **¼ teaspoon ground black pepper.** Brown in **1 tablespoon vegetable oil** in a large skillet, about 1 minute per side. Remove and set aside. Add **2 tablespoons finely chopped onion** to the pan and cook until lightly browned, 1 minute. Add **1 cup apple juice, 2 tablespoons cider vinegar,** and **1 teaspoon brown sugar.** Return turkey to the pan and simmer until turkey is firm and no longer pink and liquid is slightly thickened, 2 to 3 minutes. Remove from heat and transfer turkey to a platter. Swirl **2 tablespoons butter** into sauce and pour over turkey. *Makes 4 servings.*

HERB-CRUSTED TURKEY CUTLETS Dredge **1 pound turkey cutlets (each ¼" thick)** in **½ cup seasoned bread crumbs.** Sauté in a large skillet in **2 tablespoons olive oil** until crust is browned and turkey is firm and no longer pink, 3 to 5 minutes per side. Remove to a platter. Add **2 tablespoons butter, 1 small minced garlic clove,** and **1 tablespoon** *each* **chopped fresh rosemary and fresh sage** to the pan. Cook 10 seconds and pour over turkey. *Makes 4 servings.*

CAJUN DEEP-FRIED TURKEY Combine **¼ cup kosher salt; 1½ tablespoons** *each* **onion powder, garlic powder, ground black pepper, and ground white pepper; 1 tablespoon chopped fresh basil; 2 teaspoons** *each* **ground red pepper and paprika;** and **1 teaspoon** *each* **filé powder** (ground sassafras leaves) **and ground bay leaves.** Remove giblets and neck from a **10- to 12-pound turkey.** Rinse turkey with cold water and pat dry (especially both inside cavities). Place in a large pan and rub inside and out with the seasoning mix. Cover the pan and refrigerate overnight.

Do not stuff turkey. Place an outdoor gas burner outside in an open area on level dirt or grass. Add **4 to 5 gallons peanut oil** to a 7- to 10-gallon pot with a basket or rack. Heat the oil to 375°F, which will take 20 to 40 minutes. Wearing oven mitts, place turkey in a basket or on a rack, neck down, and slowly lower into hot oil. The oil level will rise due to the frothing and will stabilize in 1 minute. Adjust heat to maintain an oil temperature of 350°F. If the temperature drops to 340°F or below, oil will begin to seep into the turkey. Fry until a thermometer inserted into a breast registers 180°F, about 3 to 4 minutes per pound (35 to 40 minutes for a 10- to 12-pound turkey). Carefully remove turkey from hot oil and drain a few minutes. Remove from rack and place on a serving platter. Let rest for 20 minutes before carving. Cool the oil completely before storing or disposing. *Makes 12 servings.*

PROBLEM SOLVERS
▼
To avoid slowing the rate at which a turkey cooks • Cook the stuffing separately instead of in the bird.

To cover up turkey meat that is excessively dry and overcooked • Serve it with lots of gravy or cranberry sauce to add moisture.

TIME SAVERS
▼
To reduce roasting time • Remove a defrosted whole turkey from the refrigerator about 1 hour before roasting it.

To roast turkey quickly • Roast turkey parts rather than a whole turkey. The parts roast in half the time that the same weight of a whole bird would roast. Because the pieces are smaller, turkey parts can be roasted at a higher temperature, and because they can be spread out, heat will permeate each piece faster. Another option, if you prefer breast meat anyway, is to roast a whole turkey breast (a turkey "London broil") instead of a whole turkey. Turkey breast will roast in much less time than a whole bird, and there is less chance of dry meat because you won't have to wait for the legs to finish cooking. Yet another time saver: Oven-roasting bags (sold in most grocery stores) will cut roasting time by about 25 percent.

TURKEY TIMETABLE

Here's how long it will take to defrost and roast a whole turkey. When defrosting in cold water, change the water occasionally. When roasting, cook until a thermometer registers 180°F when inserted into a breast and the stuffing, if any, reaches 165°F in the center.

Weight of Turkey (lb)	Defrosting Time, Fridge (hr)	Defrosting Time, Cold Water (hr)	Roasting Time Unstuffed (hr)	Roasting Time Stuffed (hr)
5–7	16–22	3–5	1½–2	2–2½
7–9	18–24	4–6	2–2½	2½–3
9–11	24–36	8–10	3–3½	4–4½
12–15	36–48	10–14	3½–4	4½–5½
16–20	48–64	16–20	4–6	5½–7

CARVING THE BIRD

Carving a turkey (or chicken) can be a nerve-racking experience, particularly when you're the one at the head of the table. Master a few cuts, and you'll do it right every time.

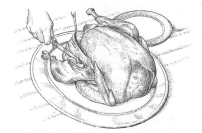

❶ Remove the leg-and-thigh section by cutting straight down between the leg and the breast, cutting through the joint that holds the thigh to the carcass. To remove the thigh from the drumstick, wriggle the leg to find the joint between the two, then cut straight down through it.

❷ Bend a wing out to find the joint, then cut straight down to remove it.

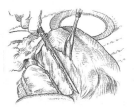

❸ Make a long incision through one side of the breast near the bottom, right along the breastbone.

❹ Now, you can slice breast meat right off the carcass by carving lengthwise in smooth, even slices.

❺ Or remove the breast entirely from the carcass by making a deep cut along the top of the breast, between the breast and backbone.

❻ Then, slice the breast as you would a boneless roast, by carving crosswise in smooth, even slices.

t

To slow-roast a turkey • Season a cleaned 15- to 20-pound turkey inside and out with 1½ teaspoons salt and ½ teaspoon ground black pepper. Place it on a rack in a roasting pan. Roast at 450°F, 1 hour. Reduce the oven temperature to 180°F and roast until a thermometer inserted into a breast registers 180°F, or at least 1 hour for every pound of turkey being roasted. Because the oven is set at the desired internal temperature of the meat, slow-roasting will not cause overcooking. The initial cooking at a high temperature kills any surface bacteria.

TURKEY: THE SEQUEL

This buxom bird seems destined for a repeat performance. Leftover turkey provides infinite possibilities: Stir-fry it with scallions and green apples or toss it in a spicy-hot sweet-and-sour dressing for a warm winter salad. Here are a few other ideas. Each makes 4 servings.

Turkey Vinaigrette: In a mixing bowl, combine ¼ cup *each* cider vinegar, olive oil, and vegetable oil; 2 tablespoons *each* orange juice and chopped fresh parsley; 2 minced scallions; 1 minced garlic clove; ½ teaspoon salt; ¼ teaspoon ground black pepper; and a pinch of ground red pepper. Toss with 4 cups finely chopped roasted turkey meat, 2 finely chopped celery ribs, ¼ finely chopped small red onion, 2 ounces sliced mushrooms, and 1 cup cooked rice, potatoes, or pasta.

Hot Turkey Sandwiches: In a large skillet, combine 1 can (15½ ounces) turkey gravy, 1 cup milk or half-and-half, ¼ teaspoon *each* dried poultry seasoning and salt, and ⅛ teaspoon ground black pepper. Heat until simmering. Add 8 to 10 slices roasted turkey breast and cook until warmed through, 3 to 4 minutes. Serve over 4 slices toast or 4 fresh biscuits.

Sweet-and-Sour Turkey Salad: In a large bowl, mix ½ cup mayonnaise, 3 tablespoons maple syrup, 2 tablespoons *each* sweet orange marmalade and cider vinegar, 1 tablespoon mild hot-pepper sauce, ½ teaspoon salt, and ¼ teaspoon ground black pepper. Add 4 cups finely chopped roasted turkey meat, 1 cup halved orange sections, 2 finely chopped celery ribs, and ¼ finely chopped small red onion. Toss to mix.

Turkey-Cranberry Turnovers: In a small saucepan over medium heat, combine ⅔ cup cranberries, 2 tablespoons sugar, and the juice and grated zest of ½ orange. Cook until the berries soften and pop, 5 minutes. Mash lightly with a fork. (You could substitute about 1 cup leftover cranberry sauce for these ingredients.) In a skillet, sauté ¼ small finely chopped onion in 1 teaspoon butter until soft, 3 minutes. Add 1 cup finely chopped roasted turkey meat, the cranberry mixture, ½ teaspoon salt, and ¼ teaspoon ground black pepper. Using 2 frozen puff pastry sheets, form turnovers according to package directions, using the turkey-cranberry mixture as the filling. Bake at 400°F until golden brown, 25 minutes.

CHUTNEY CREAM CHEESE AND SMOKED TURKEY SANDWICH Mix together **2 teaspoons jarred mango chutney, ¼ teaspoon chopped jalapeño** or **cayenne pepper,** and **1 tablespoon cream cheese.** Spread over **2 slices rye bread.** Add **2 ounces sliced smoked turkey** and **4 thin cucumber slices.** Assemble sandwich. *Makes 1.*

MAKE-AHEAD TURKEY CUTLETS In a shallow bowl, beat **1 egg** with **1 teaspoon dried Italian herb seasoning.** In another shallow dish, combine **1 cup fresh whole wheat bread crumbs, ¼ cup grated Parmesan cheese,** and **3 minced scallions.** Dip **1 pound turkey cutlets (each ¼" thick)** in the egg, then in crumbs. Place coated cutlets on waxed paper–lined baking sheets. Freeze until solid, 45 minutes. Place in zipper-lock freezer bags and freeze up to 4 months. To cook, place frozen cutlets on a greased baking sheet. Coat the tops of the cutlets with **oil** or **cooking spray** and bake at 400°F until no longer pink in the center, 9 to 12 minutes. *Makes 4 servings.*

Turnips

A cruciferous root vegetable, turnips are round and white-fleshed with a purple-colored top. Turnip greens, the leafy top of the vegetable, have a slightly bitter flavor and can be used like a stronger form of spinach.

BASICS
▼

To choose • Look for small, young turnips with unblemished skins that feel heavy for their size. Young turnips have the most sweet and mild flavor. As they age, turnips develop a stronger flavor and woody texture. If buying turnip greens, take home those that are tender and fresh-smelling without wilting or bruising.

To store • Remove turnip greens (if attached). Wash the greens, pat them dry with a paper towel, and store them wrapped in paper towels in a zipper-lock plastic bag up to 3 days. Or spin them dry in a salad spinner and refrigerate in the spinner. Turnips themselves keep best in a cool, dark, well-ventilated place. Or refrigerate them in a plastic bag for up to 2 weeks.

To trim • If the turnips are very small (less than 1" diameter), scrub and cook them whole. For larger turnips, remove the stem and root ends, then peel and cut as desired before using.

To use • Raw young turnips cut into julienne add wonderful crunch to salads and stir-fries. You can also boil turnips and mash them like potatoes (or along with potatoes). Or sauté them with other vegetables, or add to soups and stews. Turnip greens can be sautéed or stir-fried like any other bitter green.

PROBLEM
SOLVER
▼

To avoid an off taste when cooking turnip greens • Use a stainless steel pan. Avoid aluminum pans, which will turn the greens a dark color and impart an unpleasant metallic taste.

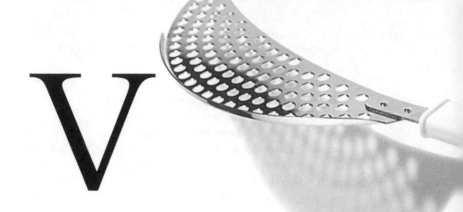

V

Vanilla

America's most popular flavor for ice cream, vanilla comes from bean pods that grow on tropical orchid vines. Many people are so accustomed to tasting vanilla that its complex, aromatic flavor is often referred to as "plain."

BASICS ▼ **To choose vanilla beans** • Look for Bourbon vanilla beans from Madagascar and the Comoro Islands in the Indian Ocean. These beans are generally regarded as having the smoothest flavor and highest moisture content.

To store vanilla beans • Wrap the beans tightly in plastic wrap and keep them in an airtight jar in the refrigerator for up to 6 months.

To use vanilla beans • Vanilla beans are used primarily for making infusions. Steep the beans in warm milk or custard, or even in wine to use for poaching fruit. For a more intense flavor, split the bean open and scrape out the tiny seeds inside to use as a flavoring.

Fascinating Fact: Vanilla orchids must be hand-pollinated because the birds and bees that once pollinated the flowers are now extinct. Hand-pollination and a very labor-intensive fermentation and drying process make vanilla one of the most expensive flavorings in the world.

To reuse vanilla beans • Once the beans have been used for an infusion, they can be rinsed, dried, and reused as long as they retain their scent.

To choose vanilla extract • Read the label and make sure that you are buying pure vanilla extract, not imitation vanilla flavoring.

To store vanilla extract • Keep the bottle tightly sealed and store it in a cool, dry place. It will keep indefinitely.

VANILLA EXTRACT In a large glass jar, combine **1 bottle (750 milliliters) inexpensive vodka, 6 split vanilla beans,** and **½ to 1 cup commercial vanilla extract** (to get the flavor started). Let sit in a cool, dark place at least 6 weeks to develop flavor (the color may be light, but flavor is what counts). If desired, remove vanilla beans as necessary, scraping out the seeds to use in recipes; then, return the pods to the extract. Use the extract as needed and continue strengthening it by occasionally adding a fresh vanilla pod or two, or additional vodka. *Makes about 4 cups.*

VANILLA SUGAR Bury **2 vanilla beans** in **1 pound granulated or confec-**

tioners' sugar. Keep at room temperature in an airtight container for at least 1 week, stirring occasionally. Remove beans and store, use for another recipe, or reuse to make more vanilla sugar. Use the flavored sugar to sweeten fruit, desserts, or coffee, or for decorating cookies or cakes. *Makes 1 pound.*

TYPES OF VANILLA

Indigenous to the Papantla region of southeastern Mexico, vanilla orchids are now grown in Java, Madagascar, Mexico, and Tahiti. The flavor of vanilla can vary dramatically, depending upon the region in which the orchids were grown.

Amazingly, the bean pod produced by vanilla orchids has no fragrance or flavor when freshly picked. It took the Totonac people of Papantla to unlock vanilla's hidden treasure of aroma and flavor.

Vanilla bean pods grow between 4" and 8" in length and must be picked just as they begin to turn from green to golden. If picked too late, the pods will burst and their minute seeds will be lost to the wind. If picked too early, the flavor will be inferior. After the harvest, the plump bean pods go through a series of fermentation and drying periods for 4 to 6 months. The pods then turn from light brown to dark brown, shriveling into pencil-thin, brownish black vanilla beans that contain the world's most precious sweet aroma and flavor. Each vanilla bean houses a rich, concentrated paste, made up of thousands of tiny dotlike seeds (you may have seen these bean flecks in "real vanilla" ice cream). When steeped in liquid or in sugar, these seeds create an aromatic infusion of vanilla flavor. The flavor of vanilla is so essential to desserts, sweets, and other baked goods that most of these foods would taste bland without it.

Here's a guide to common types of vanilla and their distinctive flavors and uses.

Vanilla Type	Characteristics and Uses
Java	These are the least flavorful and least expensive vanilla beans. The beans are often small. Usually, when vanilla extract does not state the country of origin, it is from Java.
Madagascar	Sometimes called Bourbon vanilla, these beans have a heavy, robust aroma and a deep, complex, sweet flavor that is almost winey and fermented compared with other vanillas. Madagascar vanilla is a good choice for baking, as its flavor tends to withstand heat better than other varieties.
Mexican	Highly fragrant, with a sweet floral bouquet and hints of chocolate, this is perhaps the best all-purpose vanilla for both hot and cold preparations. While whole beans from Mexico are perfectly safe, some Mexican vanilla extracts have been found to contain coumarin, which has been banned by the FDA. When buying extract, choose a bottle that states that it does not contain coumarin.
Tahitian	This most fragrant and most expensive vanilla was originally developed for the perfume industry. The exotic, sweet floral aroma and flavor dissipates during baking. Tahitian vanilla is best used in cold preparations such as pastry creams, mousses, custards, and ice creams.

Veal *see also* Beef; Meat; Doneness Tests and Temperatures (page 572)

The meat of calves between the ages of 8 and 12 weeks, veal is extremely lean, with a much subtler flavor than beef.

BASICS
▼

To choose • Look for veal that is very pale, with creamy white fat, a sign that the calf was milk-fed rather than grass- or grain-fed. It will have a more delicate texture. The meat should be firm and dense, with an even color. Veal bones should be white on the outside and bright red in the middle. A reddish tinge to the meat indicates that it came from an older calf and was partially grain-fed. Veal from older calves has a stronger flavor and is not as tender as the meat from younger animals.

To store • Remove veal from its wrapping and rewrap it loosely in waxed paper. Keep it in the coldest part of the refrigerator and use within 2 days.

To prepare • Veal neck and chuck are the best cuts for braising and stewing. Shoulder cuts can be roasted or braised. The sirloin should be braised or stewed, or pounded thin and used for scallops. The top round can also be used for scallops. The foreshanks are best cut into sections and braised. Veal breast is quite tough but very flavorful and can be stuffed and roasted or cut into pieces and stewed. Rib and loin cuts are the most tender and should be grilled, roasted, or sautéed. When using ground veal, be sure to add a bit of fat to prevent it from drying out.

To make veal scallops • Pound veal cutlets to ⅛" thickness between sheets of plastic wrap.

To test for doneness • Veal cooks quickly, due to its low fat content. Because its texture is so delicate, avoid overcooking any cut of veal. Generally, veal should be cooked until no longer pink in the center. Veal roasts, however, should be cooked until they are faintly pink in the center and until a thermometer inserted into the meat registers 145°F for medium-rare, 155°F for medium, or 165°F for well-done. Let the roast rest for 15 minutes before carving, during which time the temperature can rise as much as 10°F.

FLAVOR TIPS
▼

To flavor • Veal has a very delicate flavor that can be easily overpowered. Seasonings that enhance veal's mild flavor include butter, olive oil, white wine, sherry, garlic, onion, celery, parsley, oregano, marjoram, thyme, rosemary, sage, bay leaf, mustard, and nutmeg.

To seal in moisture and flavor • Bread cutlets and chops before cooking.

VEAL PICCATA Pound **1 pound veal leg cutlets** to ⅛" thickness between sheets of plastic wrap. On waxed paper, combine **3 tablespoons flour, ½ teaspoon salt,** and **¼ teaspoon *each* paprika and ground white or black pepper.** Coat both sides of veal with flour mixture. Heat **2 teaspoons olive oil** in a large nonstick skillet over medium heat. Add half of veal and cook until no longer pink in center, 1 to 2 minutes per side. Remove veal and keep warm. Repeat with another **1 teaspoon oil** and remaining veal. Add **⅔ cup white wine** and **2 tablespoons lemon juice** to the empty skillet. Bring to a boil, stirring to dissolve any browned bits. Cook and stir until slightly thickened, 2 minutes. Remove from heat. Stir in **2 teaspoons capers** and **1 teaspoon butter.** Spoon sauce over veal. *Makes 4 servings.*

VEAL SCALLOPS WITH HERBES DE PROVENCE Pound **1½ pounds veal cutlets** to ⅛" thickness between sheets of plastic wrap. On waxed paper, combine **⅓ cup flour, ¾ teaspoon salt,** and **½ teaspoon** *each* **paprika and ground white or black pepper.** Coat both sides of veal with flour mixture. Heat **2 tablespoons olive oil** in a large, heavy skillet over medium heat. Add veal and cook until meat is no longer pink in center, 1 to 2 minutes per side (work in batches if necessary). Remove to a platter. Add **2 teaspoons herbes de Provence (see page 233), 1 finely chopped shallot,** and **2 minced garlic cloves** to the pan. Cook 30 seconds. Add **1 cup white wine** and **2 tablespoons white wine vinegar.** Cook, stirring occasionally, until liquid is reduced to ¼ cup. Add juices from veal platter. Bring to a boil. Remove from heat and swirl in **2 tablespoons unsalted butter.** Pour over veal. *Makes 6 servings.*

MUSTARD GRILLED VEAL CHOPS Preheat the grill. Combine **3 tablespoons dry mustard, 1 tablespoon olive oil, 1 large minced garlic clove, ¾ teaspoon salt,** and **¼ teaspoon ground black pepper.** Coat **4 veal chops (each 1" thick)** with mustard mixture. Grill over a medium-hot fire until an instant-read thermometer inserted in centers registers 145°F (medium-rare), 160°F (medium), or 165°F (well-done), 4 to 5 minutes per side. *Makes 4 servings.*

HEALTHY HINT ▼ **To choose lean cuts** • The leanest cuts of veal are well-trimmed chops, rib roasts, arm roast, round steak, arm steak and cutlets.

VEAL SCALLOPS WITH MUSHROOM SAUCE Cut **1½ pounds boneless veal round steak** into 6 even pieces. Pound each to ⅛" thickness between sheets of plastic wrap. Heat **1 tablespoon olive oil** in a large nonstick skillet over medium-high heat. Add veal, two pieces at a time, and cook just until browned outside and no longer pink in center, 1 to 2 minutes per side. Remove to a platter and keep warm. Add **⅓ cup red wine** and **½ pound sliced mushrooms** to the skillet. Increase heat to high and cook, stirring up browned bits in the skillet, until mushrooms are tender and liquid is almost evaporated, 3 to 5 minutes. Add **2 cups canned chopped tomatoes (drained well), ⅓ cup shredded fresh basil leaves,** and **1 tablespoon balsamic vinegar.** Cook until heated through, 1 minute. Spoon over veal. *Makes 6 servings.*

Vegetable Juice

Stock isn't the only basis for a sauce. Vegetable juices make wonderful sauces. Sweet potatoes, for instance, can be juiced to make a rich-tasting sauce with a hint of sweetness. If you don't have a juicer, ask your local health food store to make vegetable juice blends for you. Or use low-sodium vegetable cocktail juice.

FLAVOR TIPS ▼ **To use in soup** • Replace half of the broth or water with vegetable juice.

To flavor polenta • Replace 1 to 2 cups of the broth with vegetable juice.

To perk up spaghetti sauce • Add 1 to 2 cups vegetable juice to your favorite spaghetti sauce when simmering.

BASIC VEGETABLE JUICE BLEND In a juicer, combine **1 pound carrots, 1 pound fresh tomatoes, 2 celery ribs, and 1 medium leek (white part only).** *Makes 3 cups.*

VEGETABLE JUICE SAUCE In a saucepan over medium-high heat, boil **3 cups Basic Vegetable Juice Blend (above)** until reduced to about ¾ cup, 8 to 10 minutes. For a richer texture, swirl in **¼ cup heavy cream** and boil 1 minute longer; whisk in **2 tablespoons butter** and **⅛ teaspoon salt (or more to taste).** Use as a sauce with meat, poultry, fish, or vegetables. *Makes about 1 cup.*

Vegetables *see also* Roasting; Vegetable Cooking Times (page 569); *and specific types*

A source of varied and abundant nutrients, vegetables are among the most diverse of all food groups. This broad food category includes tender leafy greens and soft mushrooms as well as sturdy cabbages, beans, corn, tubers, and roots. It also includes vegetables that are technically fruits, such as peppers, tomatoes, and eggplant.

BASICS **To choose** • In general, look for vegetables that are plump, without blemishes or bruises. Ones that are heavy for their size can be counted on to have the most succulent flesh.

To store • The flavor and texture of vegetables are best if enjoyed soon after harvest. Discard any vegetables that show signs of rot, because spoilage tends to spread quickly among vegetables stored together. Most vegetables keep best in the refrigerator. A few, such as tomatoes, potatoes, onions, eggplants, garlic, and winter squash, do better when stored at room temperature.

To prepare • Avoid washing and cutting vegetables until you're ready to prepare them. Vegetables with thick peels, such as potatoes, other root vegetables, and winter squashes, will retain more vitamins and be easier to peel if cooked with their peels intact. If boiled or steamed with their peels on, they'll absorb less water, too, which means that they'll have a better, less diluted flavor.

To boil • Boiling is particularly effective for long-cooking vegetables such as potatoes, carrots, and squash. When boiling green vegetables, avoid covering the pot, which could muddy the vegetable's color. Test boiling vegetables frequently for doneness. Pull a vegetable out with a pair of tongs. Then, either taste it or use the tines of a fork to check it for the desired doneness. Once cooking is complete, drain the vegetables immediately. When boiling quicker-cooking vegetables such as green beans, ever-so-slightly undercook the beans because they will continue to cook from residual heat after they are drained.

To preserve color when boiling • Boil vegetables in an uncovered pot with plenty of salt.

To blanch • Also known as parboiling, this is a shortened form of boiling. It is used to set a vegetable's color or to precook the vegetable in preparation for another cooking method (or freezing). Blanching can also reduce the bitter taste of vegetables such as broccoli rabe and kale. Simply drop the vegetables into boiling water just until brightly colored— usually, only 15 to 30 seconds. Remove them with a slotted spoon, or lower the vegetables into the water with a pasta insert or large sieve for easy removal. When blanching vegetables for freezing or to set their color for a raw vegetable platter, immediately plunge the blanched vegetables into ice-cold water after draining. This step prevents them from cooking further.

To steam • This cooking method is popular with delicate vegetables because it is a gentle form of heat that retains flavor and nutrients. Place the vegetables in a steamer basket or metal colander over simmering water, cover, and cook until tender. Make sure that the vegetables are up above the water rather than sitting in it. You can also "pan-steam" vegetables by adding a few tablespoons of water to a hot sauté pan or wok, cov-

---

GUIDE TO GRILLING VEGETABLES

A hot grill brings out the best in many vegetables, infusing them with a sweet, smoky flavor. Start with a medium-hot fire. Toss vegetables with oil (seasoned, if desired) before grilling. For even cooking, leave space between vegetables on the grill (or grill screen if using small vegetables). If any vegetables cook too quickly, move them to the side of the fire (known as indirect heat) and bunch them together. Cook all vegetables until tender and lightly charred.

Vegetable	Preparation	Type of Heat
Artichokes	Trim, blanch, and cut in half	Direct
Asparagus	Snap off tough ends	Direct
Baby carrots	Wash but don't peel; blanch	Direct
Beets	Blanch and cut into wedges	Indirect
Bell pepper, sliced	Core, seed, and cut into strips	Direct
Corn	Grill whole; peel back husk and silk after cooking	Direct
Eggplant, sliced	Cut into ½"-thick slices; slice Japanese eggplant lengthwise	Direct
Eggplant, whole	Pierce in several places with a fork	Indirect
Fennel	Trim tops and peel fibrous strings; cut into wedges	Direct
Garlic	Slice off top of head	Indirect
Leeks	Trim, rinse, and remove tough outer leaves; halve lengthwise; blanch large leeks	Direct
New potatoes	Blanch; cut in half or quarters	Direct
Onions	Slice; secure slices with toothpicks	Direct
Portobello mushrooms	Wipe clean and remove stems; grill caps gill side up	Indirect
Scallions	Trim root ends	Direct
Zucchini	Trim and slice lengthwise	Direct

V

ering them, and cooking until tender. Whenever you steam vegetables, periodically check that the pan has enough water in it. If all of the water steams off, a pan can be permanently damaged. For even cooking, steam the vegetables in a single layer.

To use leftover trimmings • Store all those bits of vegetable trimmings in a container or freezer bag. Freeze and add more scraps as they accumulate. When making stock, simply add the frozen leftovers and cook as directed in your stock recipe.

TIME SAVERS ▼ **To save peeling time** • Cook vegetables with their peels intact whenever possible. You'll get more vitamins and minerals, too.

To save thawing time • Small frozen vegetables such as peas and corn don't require thawing before they are added to soups, stews, or stir-fries. Likewise, when using a frozen vegetable in a salad, there is no need to cook it. Just thaw it to room temperature and toss it with dressing.

To save prep time • Whenever you chop vegetables, prepare more than you need. This single act can save you loads of

Vegetable Moussaka

Steaming the vegetables makes them remarkably tender in this vegetarian rendition of the classic Greek casserole made with lamb. Lower in fat but not short on taste, the flavors here remain surprisingly true to the original. To slice the vegetables easily, use a mandoline (a hand-operated slicing machine) or the thin slicing disk on a food processor. You can easily make this dish ahead. After assembling, just cool and refrigerate for up to 24 hours.

¼ **cup bulgur**	2 **onions, chopped**
¾ **cup boiling water**	½ **pound mushrooms, chopped**
1 **pound russet or all-purpose potatoes, sliced ⅛" thick**	1 **teaspoon dried oregano**
1 **teaspoon salt, divided**	¼ **cup tomato paste**
¾ **teaspoon ground black pepper, divided**	¼ **teaspoon ground cinnamon**
1 **eggplant (1 pound), peeled and cubed ½" thick**	2 **cups low-fat soy milk or low-fat cow's milk, divided**
2 **zucchini (1 pound), trimmed, halved crosswise, and sliced ⅛" thick**	¼ **cup all-purpose flour**
2 **teaspoons olive oil**	1 **egg, beaten**
	6 **tablespoons grated Parmesan cheese, divided**

time in the kitchen. All but the most perishable prepared vegetables will stay fresh in a zipper-lock plastic bag in the refrigerator for 24 hours. And cooked vegetables can be refrigerated for 3 days. Grilled or roasted vegetables can also be frozen. Cool grilled or roasted vegetables and spread them out on a baking sheet, leaving some space between them. Freeze until solid. Bend the pan slightly, and the frozen vegetables will pop off. Store in zipper-lock freezer bags. To rewarm frozen grilled or roasted vegetables, bake at 375°F for 10 minutes.

To get different vegetables done at the same time • If tough vegetables such as carrots and turnips will be sautéed with more-tender vegetables such as mushrooms or tomatoes, blanch or lightly pan-steam the tough vegetables first. For instance, toss ½ pound trimmed green beans, broccoli stalks, finely chopped turnips, or julienned carrots in 2 tablespoons water in a deep dish; then, cover the dish with plastic wrap and microwave it on high power for 4 minutes.

1. Grease an 11" × 8" baking dish.

2. In a small bowl, combine the bulgur and water. Let stand until softened, 30 minutes. Drain if needed.

3. Preheat the oven to 375°F. Bring 1" of water to a boil in a large pot. Set a steamer basket in the pot. Place the potatoes in the basket, cover, and cook just until tender, 8 minutes. Spread in a single layer in the prepared baking dish. Sprinkle with ¼ teaspoon of the salt and ¼ teaspoon of the pepper.

4. Add the eggplant to the basket. Cover and cook until tender, 8 minutes. Remove and set aside. If necessary, add more water to the pot. Add the zucchini to the basket. Cover and cook until just tender, 3 minutes. Remove and set aside.

5. Heat the oil in a large nonstick skillet over medium heat. Add the onions and cook until softened, 6 minutes. Add the mushrooms and oregano. Cook until the liquid has evaporated, 4 minutes. Stir in the eggplant,

tomato paste, ¼ teaspoon of the remaining pepper, the cinnamon, and ½ teaspoon of the remaining salt. Cook 1 minute. Remove from the heat and stir in the bulgur. Spoon evenly over the potatoes in the baking dish. Arrange the zucchini slices in an even layer on top.

6. In a small saucepan, whisk together ½ cup of the milk and the flour until smooth. Stir in the remaining 1½ cups milk, ¼ teaspoon salt, and ¼ teaspoon pepper. Bring to a simmer over medium-low heat, whisking until thickened.

7. In a small bowl, beat the egg with some of the hot milk mixture. Whisk the egg mixture into the saucepan. Cook just until thickened, 1 minute. Do not boil. Stir in 3 tablespoons of the cheese. Spoon onto the casserole, spreading in an even layer. Sprinkle with the remaining 3 tablespoons cheese.

8. Bake until heated through, 35 minutes (55 minutes, if refrigerated).

Makes 6 servings

To roast vegetables quickly • Chop them into ½" pieces and toss with oil and seasonings. Roast at 450°F until browned at the edges, 10 to 25 minutes (depending upon the vegetable), turning once during roasting.

QUICK DIP FOR RAW VEGETABLES Beat together **1 cup** *each* **sour cream and cottage cheese, 1 packet dried vegetable soup mix,** and **1 finely sliced scallion.** *Makes 6 to 8 servings.*

QUICK GRILLED VEGETABLES Preheat the grill. Combine **6 to 8 cups chopped mixed vegetables, 2 to 3 tablespoons extra-virgin olive oil, 2 minced garlic cloves, ¾ teaspoon salt,** and **½ teaspoon ground black pepper (or more to taste)** on a large piece of heavy-duty foil. Wrap up the foil and grill over a hot fire until tender, 10 to 12 minutes. To serve, open the foil and sprinkle on **1 teaspoon balsamic vinegar.** Toss to coat. *Makes 4 to 6 servings.*

STIR-FRIED VEGETABLE CURRY Stir-fry **1 finely chopped large onion, 1 small minced garlic clove, 2 teaspoons** *each* **finely chopped fresh ginger and curry powder, 1 teaspoon** *each* **ground coriander and ground cumin,** and **a pinch of red-pepper flakes** in **1 tablespoon vegetable oil** over high heat until onion is soft, about 1 minute. Transfer to a bowl and stir in **1 tablespoon lemon juice** and **¼ cup chopped fresh cilantro.** Set aside. Add **another 1 tablespoon vegetable oil** to the pan and stir-fry **1 teaspoon mustard seeds** in the oil until the seeds color, 15

seconds. Add **1 cup** *each* **broccoli florets and cauliflower florets; about ¼ pound green beans, sliced;** and **1 sliced carrot.** Stir-fry until vegetables are brightly colored, 2 to 3 minutes. Add **½ cup water.** Cover and steam another 2 minutes. Add the curried onion mixture, toss, and simmer 2 to 3 minutes. *Makes 4 servings.*

EASY RATATOUILLE On a large rimmed baking sheet or roasting pan, toss **½ pound chopped eggplant, 1 chopped onion, 1 chopped green bell pepper, 2 chopped celery ribs, 6 chopped plum tomatoes, 2 sliced zucchini, ¼ cup olive oil, 1 tablespoon finely chopped anchovies, 1 teaspoon dried basil,** and **¼ teaspoon dried oregano.** Roast at 450°F, 15 minutes. Remove from the oven and toss with **¼ cup chopped green olives; 2 tablespoons** *each* **white wine vinegar, extra-virgin olive oil,** and **chopped fresh parsley; 1 tablespoon capers; ¾ teaspoon salt;** and **½ teaspoon ground black pepper (or more to taste).** *Makes 6 to 8 servings.*

FLAVOR TIPS ▼ **To dress up simple cooked vegetables** • To each pound of cooked vegetables, add ¼ cup toasted pine nuts, almonds, or pecans. Or melt 1 tablespoon butter in a medium skillet, add 1 minced clove of garlic, and cook until golden, 5 minutes; then stir in 3 tablespoons grated Parmesan cheese and sprinkle the mixture over the vegetables. You can also toss 1 pound cooked vegetables with ¼ cup chopped ham or prosciutto and 3 tablespoons "fried" canned onions. Another idea: Sauté 2 thinly sliced cloves of garlic in ¼ cup olive oil until golden to make garlic

FOUR SIMPLE SAUCES FOR STEAMED VEGETABLES

Turn those same old weeknight vegetables into something special with these simple ideas. Each recipe makes about 4 servings, or enough to sauce approximately 1 pound of steamed vegetables.

Dijon-Walnut Sauce: In a small bowl, whisk together **2 tablespoons walnut oil, 3 tablespoons** *each* **red wine vinegar and strong brewed tea, 2 teaspoons Dijon mustard,** and **¼ teaspoon** *each* **salt and ground black pepper.** Stir in **1 tablespoon toasted chopped walnuts.**

Creamy Goat Cheese Sauce: In a blender or mini food processor, combine **⅓ cup buttermilk** or **low-fat plain yogurt, 2 ounces mild goat cheese, 2 teaspoons olive oil, ¼ teaspoon** *each* **dried thyme and ground black pepper,** and **½ crushed garlic clove.** Blend until smooth.

Sesame-Orange Sauce: In a small saucepan over medium-high heat, combine **1 cup orange juice, 2 large chopped shallots, 1 tablespoon red wine vinegar,** and **1½ teaspoons** *each* **grated orange zest and soy sauce.** Cook until liquid reduces to ½ cup, 5 minutes. Stir in **1 teaspoon toasted sesame oil** and **1 tablespoon toasted sesame seeds.**

Rosemary-Garlic Sauce: Flatten **1 garlic clove** on a cutting board with the broad side of a knife. Sprinkle with **½ teaspoon kosher salt** and mash to a paste. Place in a small bowl and add **2 tablespoons** *each* **olive oil, red wine vinegar, and apple juice; 2 teaspoons** *each* **chopped fresh rosemary and Dijon mustard;** and **½ teaspoon** *each* **anchovy paste and ground black pepper.** Whisk until smooth.

chips; toss them with 1 pound cooked vegetables and 2 tablespoons bottled vinaigrette or lemon juice. Or serve 1 pound cooked vegetables with a quick dip made from ¼ cup sour cream mixed with ½ teaspoon lemon juice.

To serve a whole head of broccoli or cauliflower • Cut off the stem from 1 head of broccoli or cauliflower so that the vegetable sits at the base where its branches join together. Steam, covered, in a steamer basket over simmering water until tender in the center, about 8 minutes (for broccoli) or 10 minutes (for cauliflower). Sprinkle the top with ½ cup grated Cheddar or Swiss cheese, cover, and steam until the cheese melts, 1 minute. Remove to a serving platter and carve individual servings at the table. Makes 4 servings.

HEALTHY HINT ▼ **To retain the maximum nutrients in vegetables** • Avoid boiling, which causes nutrients to leach out into the cooking water. Instead, bake or roast vegetables to seal in juices, flavors, and nutrients. Steaming vegetables will also retain their nutrients, but it won't caramelize their natural sugars, which helps boost flavor.

Vermouth *see also* Wine

A fortified white wine flavored with various spices, herbs, and fruits, vermouth is best known as an essential part of a martini.

To choose • Dry vermouth, which contains just 2 percent to 4 percent sugar, can be served as an aperitif and is a key ingredient in many cocktails. Sweet vermouth, also called Italian or red vermouth, is colored with caramel and has a minimum of 14 percent sugar. Sweet vermouth is used for sweet cocktails such as manhattans and can also be enjoyed alone over ice. A less common type of sweet vermouth is white vermouth or vermouth bianco.

To store • Because it is fortified, vermouth will last at room temperature for 1 week or in the refrigerator for 6 weeks, unlike regular wines.

To replace white wine in cooking • Use dry vermouth in any recipe that calls for white wine. The dish will have a more herbal flavor if vermouth is used; you may want to reduce the amount of herbs called for, or use part vermouth and part broth.

CHOOSING VINEGAR

Matching vinegar with other ingredients is simple. Just keep in mind that most vinegars are made from wine. Use red wine vinegar and other intensely flavored vinegars with hearty, rich-flavored foods such as beef stew. White wine vinegar and other lighter-flavored vinegars go well with more-delicate foods such as chicken and salad greens.

Balsamic Vinegar: This very distinctive Italian vinegar is aged in wooden barrels for at least 10 years. Some have been aged 50, even 100 years, but these are generally family heirlooms handed down in wills. True balsamic is made from concentrated Trebbiano white grape juice and is aged by transferring from barrel to barrel, each made from a different kind of wood that imparts flavor and color. When you see the words *aceto balsamico tradizionale* on a bottle of balsamic vinegar, you know that you have the real thing. To enjoy it at its best, don't heat balsamic vinegar. You might not even want to combine it with other ingredients. Savor it, instead, in its purest form, drizzled over grilled steaks or tossed with ripe red berries. For intense flavor and a light color, try

white balsamic vinegar. Commercial balsamic vinegars are made from red wine vinegar that has been fortified with concentrated grape juice and, sometimes, caramelized sugar. While they lack the complexity of true *balsamico,* these vinegars can have a sweet, pungent quality that works quite well when used to make a deglazing sauce or when used in salad dressings or to season slow-cooked meats and stews.

Cider Vinegar: Look for cider vinegar that is unfiltered and unpasteurized. It will have the fruitiest apple flavor. Use cider vinegar to make a deglazing sauce for a pork roast or in a vinaigrette for a salad garnished with bacon and bits of hard cheese. Its mild flavor also makes it a good vinegar to use for pickles.

Distilled Vinegar: Made from commercially processed grain alcohol, distilled vinegar has a harsh, pungent flavor. Though it is widely used in processed foods and preserves, in the home kitchen, it's best reserved for washing down counters and cutting boards.

Flavored Vinegars: These are made from wine vinegars (usually white wine) infused with

Vinegar *see also* Salad Dressings

Though most vinegars are made from fermented wine, other ingredients such as rice wine, sugar cane, and fruit are also used. The high acid content of vinegar makes it a great preservative and a key flavoring in dressings, dips, and sauces.

BASICS ▼ **To store** • Keep vinegar in a cool, dry place. Unopened bottles of vinegar will last indefinitely. Once opened, vinegar should be used within 8 months.

QUICK FRUIT VINEGAR In a saucepan, combine **1 pint blueberries, raspberries,** or **blackberries** and **1 cup white wine** or **red wine vinegar.** Heat over medium heat just until the surface of the liquid shimmers, about 180°F. Remove from the heat, cover, and steep 1 hour.

fruits and/or fresh herbs. Use them to add a subtle herbal or fruit flavor to your salads, chicken, or fish. Raspberry vinegar is one of the most flavorful fruit vinegars and has a particular affinity for beets. In Mexico, many home cooks make pineapple vinegar. If you're looking for an herb vinegar, tarragon vinegar is one of the best. It lends fabulous flavor to salad greens, potato salad, and fish.

Malt Vinegar: A classic condiment for fish and chips, malt vinegar is traditionally made from beer. It has a mild flavor that makes it a good choice for pickles and salad dressings.

Red Wine Vinegar: The best wine vinegars are produced in the world's great wine-making regions, such as France, Italy, and California. Deglaze a roasting pan with red wine vinegar to make a sauce for beef or lamb, or combine it with mustard and shallots for a boldly flavored vinaigrette.

Rice Vinegar: There are three main types of rice vinegar: white, red, and black. White rice vinegar has a pale, golden color and delicate flavor and is by far the most versatile. Use white rice vinegar in Asian-inspired sauces for chicken, fish, and vegetables. When buying white rice vinegar, keep in mind that Japanese brands tend to be milder and sweeter than the sharper, more acidic Chinese versions. Red rice vinegar is used mainly as a dipping sauce. The more esoteric black rice vinegar is used most often as an ingredient in Chinese pickled pigs' feet.

Sherry Vinegar: Sweeter and more complex than ordinary wine vinegar, sherry vinegar is aged for a minimum of 6 years in a network of barrels known as a solera. The best sherry vinegars come from southern Spain and bear the words *Xeres* or *Jerez* on the label, Spanish terms for sherry. Sherry vinegar makes an extraordinary vinaigrette and can also be used to deglaze a roasting pan or sauté pan when making a pan sauce for pork, chicken, or beef.

White Wine and Champagne Vinegar: Use these subtle-flavored vinegars with more delicate foods. They're great with seafood salads or in a sauce for chicken or fish. They can also be used for pickles.

V

Strain vinegar and store it in a tightly closed jar with a few berries in it. *Makes about 1 pint.*

LEMON-GARLIC VINEGAR In a saucepan, combine **1 head garlic (broken into cloves)**, **¼ cup finely chopped lemon zest**, and **1½ cups white wine vinegar.** Heat over medium heat just until the surface of the liquid shimmers, about 180°F. Remove from the heat, cover, and steep 1 hour. Strain and stir in the **juice of 2 lemons.** Store in a tightly closed jar. *Makes 1 pint.*

PEAR-VANILLA VINEGAR In a saucepan, combine **3 finely chopped ripe pears** and **2 cups white wine vinegar.** Heat over medium heat just until the surface of the liquid shimmers, about 180°F.

Remove from the heat, cover, and steep 1 hour. Meanwhile, place **1 large, perfect pear** and **1 vanilla bean** in a wide-mouth jar. Strain vinegar and pour into the jar. Seal tightly. *Makes 1 quart.*

QUICK HERB VINEGAR In a saucepan, combine **1 cup chopped fresh herbs (basil, tarragon, rosemary, chervil, oregano, cilantro, or other herbs)** and **2 cups white or red wine vinegar.** Heat over medium heat just until the surface of the liquid shimmers, about 180°F. Remove from the heat, cover, and steep 1 hour. Strain and store in a tightly closed jar with **1 fresh herb sprig.** *Makes 1 pint.*

PROBLEM SOLVER ▼ **To save an oversweetened dish** • Stir in a small amount of vinegar to balance the sweetness.

V

W

Waffles *see also* Pancakes

Made from a quick bread batter much like the one used for pancakes, waffles make a great breakfast or brunch dish. Their honeycombed surface is just the right shape for holding syrup and other sweet liquids.

BASICS ▼ **To create light, rather than leaden, waffles** • Separate the eggs and beat the whites to stiff peaks. Then, fold the beaten whites into the batter.

To make thin, crisp waffles • Add a bit of sugar to the batter. It also helps to increase the amount of oil or butter. When spooning batter onto the waffle iron, use just enough to coat the bottom. Wait until the edges of the waffle iron stop steaming, then continue to cook the waffles for 2 to 3 minutes.

To make thick, soft waffles • Add a thick layer of batter to the waffle iron and cook just until no more steam appears at the edges.

To remove from the waffle iron • Lift waffles out of the iron with a fork. If your waffle iron has a nonstick coating, be careful not to scratch it.

To keep warm • Arrange the waffles in a single layer on a cooling rack. Or put them directly on an oven rack and keep warm in a 225°F oven. Avoid stacking or wrapping hot waffles; the steam will make them as soggy as wet dishrags.

To store • Cool cooked waffles, then seal them in a zipper-lock freezer bag or wrap them well in a double layer of plastic wrap and foil. Freeze for up to 6 months.

To reheat frozen waffles • Put the frozen waffles directly in a toaster or on a baking sheet in a 325°F oven and heat until warmed through, about 5 minutes.

To clean a waffle iron • Wait until the waffle iron has cooled completely, then wipe it with a soft cloth. If any bits are stuck to the grid, remove them with a soft brush such as an old toothbrush. Avoid using a scouring pad or an abrasive cleaner.

To protect the surface of a waffle iron • Store it with waxed paper between the grids.

PROBLEM SOLVERS ▼ **To prevent sticking** • If possible, use a waffle iron with a nonstick surface. Also, before preheating, make sure that there are no crumbs adhering to the waffle iron. If there are any crumbs, use a clean toothbrush to wipe them away. After the waffle iron is preheated, brush the waffle grids with oil or coat them with cooking spray.

To salvage a waffle that splits open when the waffle iron lid is lifted • Serve with fruit, whipped cream, or a fried egg sandwiched in between.

W

To save cleanup time • Arrange paper towels beneath the waffle iron to catch drips.

To save portioning time • Mix up the batter in a wide-mouthed pitcher or very large glass measure, and pour directly from the pitcher.

To use leftover waffles • Use them instead of bread to make bread pudding.

BUTTERMILK WAFFLE MIX Mix together **3 cups cake flour, ⅓ cup sugar, 1 tablespoon baking powder, 1 tablespoon baking soda,** and a **pinch of salt.** Store in a sealed container at room temperature for up to 3 weeks. When it comes time to make waffles, preheat a waffle iron. Separate **3 eggs.** Combine the entire portion of mix with the egg yolks, **2 cups buttermilk,** and **3 tablespoons melted butter.** Whip the egg whites to soft peaks and fold into batter. Coat the hot iron with oil and ladle about 1 cup batter onto it. Close the lid and bake until brown and crisp, about 5 minutes. Repeat with remaining batter. *Makes 12.*

YEAST-RAISED WAFFLES In a large bowl, combine ½ **cup warm water** and **1 package (2¼ teaspoons) active dry yeast.** Let stand 5 minutes. Add **2 cups warm milk, 6 tablespoons melted butter, 1 teaspoon** *each* **sugar and salt,** and **2 cups all-purpose flour.** Whisk until smooth. Cover with plastic wrap and refrigerate overnight. When it comes time to make waffles, preheat a waffle iron. Beat **2 eggs** and ¼ **teaspoon baking soda** into the batter (it will be runny). Coat the hot iron with oil and ladle about ¾ cup batter onto it. Close the lid and bake until brown and crisp, about 5 minutes. Repeat with remaining batter. *Makes 8.*

Walnuts *see also* Nuts

English walnuts are by far the most common variety of this popular nut. Other varieties include white walnuts, also called butternuts, and black walnuts. Widely used in both sweet and savory dishes, walnuts are also used to make highly aromatic walnut oil.

To choose • Walnuts in the shell should be free of any holes or cracks. When buying shelled walnuts, make sure that they are plump and crisp with no signs of softening or shriveling.

To store • Walnuts in the shell will keep at room temperature up to 3 months. Shelled walnuts can be refrigerated in a zipper-lock plastic bag up to 6 months or frozen up to 1 year.

WALNUT BUTTER In a food processor, combine **1 pound walnut pieces, 2 teaspoons light brown sugar,** and ⅛ **teaspoon salt.** Process in short pulses until finely chopped. Then, process continually until smooth, about 3 minutes, scraping down the sides of the bowl as necessary. Stir in **1 tablespoon oil** to make a smooth paste. *Makes 2 cups.*

WALNUT CUPCAKES Preheat oven to 350°F. Into a bowl, sift **2 cups flour** with **1 teaspoon baking powder** and ⅛ **teaspoon salt.** Stir in ¾ **cup finely chopped walnuts.** In another bowl, beat ½ **cup butter** with **1½ cups sugar** and ½ **teaspoon** *each* **vanilla and almond extracts** until fluffy. Beat in **3 extra-large eggs,** one at a time, beating until smooth. Beat in the dry ingredients in two additions, alternately with **1 cup milk.** Scrape into two 12-cup muffin pans that have been lined with paper liners. Sprinkle tops with **another ½ cup finely chopped walnuts.** Bake until a toothpick inserted in center of a muffin comes out clean, 25 minutes. Cool in the pan 10 minutes. Remove and cool until warm. Dust with ½ **cup confectioners' sugar.** *Makes 2 dozen.*

PROBLEM SOLVER ▼ **To prevent walnuts from sinking to the bottom of a batter** • Toast them first, which makes them lighter.

TIME SAVERS ▼ **To crack easily** • Place them in a saucepan, cover them with water, and bring to a boil. Remove from the heat, cover, and let stand 15 minutes. Pat the nuts dry before cracking them.

To chop quickly • Place them in a food processor and process in 2- to 3-second pulses until the desired fineness is reached. Avoid processing too long, as the natural oiliness of the nuts may cause clumping. If clumping occurs, add 1 teaspoon of sugar or flour, which will absorb some of the oil.

Wasabi

A vegetable that grows in the wet earth near cold mountain streams in Japan, wasabi is often mistakenly referred to as a type of horseradish. The two roots are unrelated. Wasabi is extremely pungent and is most often served in little green dabs to accompany sushi and other Japanese foods.

BASICS ▼ **To choose** • Fresh wasabi is not available in most parts of the United States. Instead, look for tins of powdered wasabi, and use it to make wasabi paste (see below). Tubes of wasabi paste are a poor second choice because they lack the bite of the powdered version. Unless you use wasabi a lot, buy wasabi powder in the smallest-size can. Like any spice, its flavor will deteriorate over time.

To store powdered wasabi • Keep the tins in a cool, dry place and use within 1 to 2 years.

To make wasabi paste • Mix equal parts powdered wasabi and hot water. Let stand 10 to 15 minutes to develop flavors.

FLAVOR TIP ▼ **To enliven hamburgers** • Spread ½ teaspoon wasabi paste over a grilled burger. Add 2 tablespoons mayonnaise and 2 tomato slices, and serve.

Water Bath

Known in France as a *bain marie,* a water bath is used to cool or warm anything placed in it with a gentle but steady change of temperature. Egg-based dishes such as custards, soufflés, and cheesecakes are often baked in a warm water bath, to provide a layer of insulation that surrounds the food with gentle heat and helps prevent curdling and overcooking.

BASICS ▼ **To set up a water bath for baking** • Choose a roasting pan or other shallow, ovenproof dish. Just make sure that it's big enough to hold whatever dish you are baking in. There should be at least 1" of space between the baking dish and the larger dish that holds the water bath. Place the baking dish or custard cups in the larger dish, and place it on the rack set in the bottom third of the oven. Bring a kettle of water to a boil and slowly pour enough water into the larger dish for the water line to come at least halfway up the sides of the smaller baking dish or custard cups.

W

To prevent splashing • Pour the water slowly down the back of a spatula and into the larger pan.

To provide an extra layer of insulation • Place a thick dish towel in the bottom of the larger dish before adding the smaller baking dish and the water. Make sure the towel is completely submerged.

To prevent discoloration • If your water bath pan is aluminum, dissolve a large pinch of cream of tartar in the water before adding to the pan.

Water Chestnuts

Once you have tasted fresh water chestnuts, you will find that canned are no comparison. Canned water chestnuts retain some of their natural crunch, but the flavor is the same as the brine in which they are packed. Freshly cooked water chestnuts have sensational crunch, with subtle flavor nuances of coconut and raw corn.

To choose fresh water chestnuts • Fresh water chestnuts look somewhat like squat gladiola bulbs. They grow in water and will probably be muddy. They are highly perishable, and some may have soft brown spots. Look for the firmest ones.

To prepare fresh water chestnuts • Using a paring knife, slice off the top and bottom, then trim off the skin in thick slices as you work around each bulb. Expect to lose about half the weight after trimming. As they are peeled, drop them into acidulated water to prevent browning. Drain them and place them in a small saucepan. Cover them with cold water and bring it to a boil over medium heat. Simmer until tender, 3 to 5 minutes. Drain and cover with cold water. Let stand until cool, then slice and add to stir-fries, sautés, or salads.

To replace fresh water chestnuts • Use an equal amount of sliced fresh jicama (page 244). Of course, you could use canned water chestnuts, but they will not have nearly as much flavor as fresh.

Watermelon *see also* Melons

A sure sign of summer, watermelons comes in all shapes, sizes, and colors, from round to football-shaped and from the size of a cantaloupe to the size of a medicine ball. The flesh of a watermelon can be red, pink, yellow, or cream-colored.

To choose • It is said that a perfectly ripe watermelon will sound a perfect B-flat note when thumped. But some of us are tone-deaf, and there are other ways to buy a ripe melon. See page 279 for the essentials.

To store whole • Refrigerate up to 1 week. Or keep in a cool, dark place for up to 4 days.

To store cut • Wrap in plastic and refrigerate for no more than a day or two.

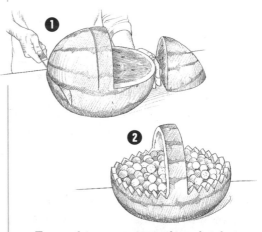

To make a watermelon basket • Choose a somewhat round watermelon rather than a very oblong one. Cut a small slice off the bottom of the melon so that it lies flat. Using a large, sharp knife, make 2 parallel cuts along the top of the melon, leaving a 2" "handle" of melon between the cuts. Make each cut halfway down the short sides of the melon. Then, starting from one of the short sides, make a lengthwise cut into the center of the melon to meet the first cut that was made. Remove a quarter-wedge of melon from that side. Repeat on the other side, removing the opposite quarter-wedge ❶.

Cut the melon flesh from the handle, leaving a 1" to 2" thickness of rind. Using a melon baller, scoop out the remaining melon flesh, leaving a 1" to 2" thickness of rind to make the basket. If desired, cut the sides of the basket into a crown shape ❷. Fill the basket with melon balls or fruit salad. When picking up the basket, lift it from the bottom instead of the delicate handle.

TIME SAVER ▼ **To quickly peel, seed, and cut** • Using a large knife, cut the melon into round slices, as thick as you like. Using a paring knife or large biscuit cutter, cut out the seedless center and set it aside. With a paring knife, cut out and discard the concentric ring of seeds remaining on the slice of watermelon. Then, cut just inside the white part of the rind to remove the rind. Cut the nearly seedless ring of watermelon and the seedless center as desired.

FLAVOR TIPS ▼ **To make "rummy" watermelon** • Cut a small hole through the rind in the top of the melon, saving the plug that you cut out. Pour rum into the melon until it is full (the total amount depends on the size and age of the melon). Reinsert the plug and refrigerate overnight. The melon will absorb the rum, flavoring the fruit with a tropical taste that won't be overly alcoholic.

To make watermelon juice • A large watermelon can yield up to ½ gallon of juice. The easiest way to extract the juice is to cut thick slices and cut off the rind. Put the pieces in a food processor, and process until pureed. Strain the puree through a sieve and drink it as is or add it to fruit drinks or punches.

WATERMELON POPS In a blender or food processor, combine **3 cups seeded and chopped watermelon (3 pounds whole)**, ½ **cup fresh or frozen raspberries, 3 tablespoons** *each* **honey and sugar,** and 1½ **tablespoons lemon juice.** Puree until smooth. Strain into a medium bowl, pressing on solids. Pour into 8 frozen-pop molds or small drink cups, dividing equally. Freeze overnight. (If using drink cups, freeze 1 to 2 hours or until slushy, insert wooden craft sticks, and then freeze solid). *Makes 8.*

WATERMELON GAZPACHO In a food processor or blender, combine half of **6 cups seeded watermelon cubes (6 pounds whole);** all of **1 peeled, seeded, and cubed cucumber;** ½ **chopped yellow bell pepper; 3 chopped scallions; 1½ chopped garlic cloves; 2 tablespoons lemon juice; 2 teaspoons olive oil;** and ½ **teaspoon hot-pepper sauce.** Process until finely chopped. Add remaining watermelon, **1 cup chilled cranberry juice,** and **3 tablespoons chopped fresh mint.** Process with pulses until just chopped. *Makes 4 servings.*

FROZEN WATERMELON SLUSH Freeze **2 cups seeded watermelon cubes (2 pounds whole)** until solid. Place half the cubes in a blender or food processor and

W

add **1 cup white grape juice** and **1 tablespoon** *each* **lime juice and honey.** Blend until smooth. With the machine running, add remaining cubes and **2 tablespoons rum (optional).** Blend until slushy. Pour into chilled glasses and serve. *Makes 4 servings.*

WATERMELON, ORANGE, AND PROSCIUTTO SALAD Line 4 salad plates with **2 bunches arugula** or **watercress.** In a medium bowl, combine **3 cups seeded and cubed watermelon (3 pounds whole),** the **segments from 3 oranges, 4 thin slices red onion,** and **2 tablespoons shredded mint.** Spoon over greens and top with **2 ounces thinly sliced prosciutto.** Serve with **Citrus Vinaigrette (page 422).** *Makes 4 servings.*

HEALTHY HINT ▼ **To retain maximum nutrients** • Buy melons whole. When melons are cut and exposed to light, their vitamins will start to break down. Also, buy the smallest melons you can find. After cutting melons, cover and refrigerate them, cut side down, to help retain nutrients.

Waxed Paper

Both nonstick and moistureproof, wax-coated paper is used primarily to wrap food for storage.

PROBLEM SOLVERS ▼ **To keep a cake platter clean during icing** • Line the rim of the platter with strips of waxed paper. After the cake is iced, slip the strips out from under the cake. Any drips of icing will be removed with the paper.

To help keep jars or pitchers from dripping • Rub a piece of waxed paper around the rim of the jar. The wax that transfers to the jar will lubricate it and keep food from clinging to the lip.

To prevent splattering in a microwave oven • Cover foods such as oatmeal, or foods such as butter that will be melted, with a sheet of waxed paper.

TIME SAVERS ▼ **To save mixing time** • When mixing a small amount of dry ingredients for bread coatings, skip the bowl and mix the ingredients with your hands on a sheet of waxed paper.

To save cleanup time • Place a sheet of waxed paper under a measuring cup when sifting dry ingredients into the cup; or under a grater to catch grated cheese, chocolate or citrus zest; or on the counter when rolling out pastry dough (wet the back of the paper to keep it from slipping). You can even place a sheet of waxed paper on the floor of a microwave oven for easy cleanup.

Wheat Germ

The heart of the wheat berry cut into flake form, wheat germ is a concentrated source of vitamins. It has a wonderfully nutty flavor and a variety of uses in uncooked and cooked dishes.

BASICS ▼ **To choose** • Although you can purchase wheat germ in health food stores, jarred wheat germ is toasted and has more flavor and more crunch.

To store • Wheat germ has a high oil content that makes it prone to rancidity. For the longest storage, keep wheat germ in the refrigerator and use it by the expiration date.

CRISPY FISH FILLETS WITH WHEAT GERM In a shallow dish, combine ¼ **cup toasted wheat germ, 2 tablespoons** *each* **finely chopped hazelnuts** or **wal-**

nuts and chopped fresh parsley, and ¼ **teaspoon** *each* **salt, paprika, and ground red pepper.** Dip **4 tilapia** or **catfish fillets (¼ pound each)** in the mixture to coat. Place fish on a greased baking sheet and bake at 425°F until fish flakes easily, 12 to 15 minutes.
Makes 4 servings.

PEACHY WHEAT GERM MUFFINS Preheat oven to 400°F. In a large bowl, combine **1⅔ cups flour, ½ cup toasted wheat germ, 2 teaspoons baking powder, 1 teaspoon baking soda,** and **½ teaspoon** *each* **ground cinnamon and salt.** Make a well in the center of dry ingredients and pour in **1 cup fat-free plain yogurt, 1 egg, ¼ cup packed brown sugar,** and **1 teaspoon grated lemon zest.** Stir together liquid ingredients until blended. Add about **2 chopped medium peaches (2 cups)** and stir together all ingredients just until combined. Spoon into a greased 12-cup muffin pan. In a small bowl, combine another **2 tablespoons** *each* **wheat germ and brown sugar.** Sprinkle on tops of unbaked muffins. Bake until lightly browned and a wooden pick inserted in center of a muffin comes out clean, 15 to 17 minutes. Serve warm. *Makes 12.*

Whisk

Made of thin wires bent into loops and joined together at a long handle, whisks are primarily used for beating air into liquid ingredients such as eggs, cream, and sauces.

BASICS **To choose** • No matter what type of whisk you're buying, always look for one with stainless steel wires that will not corrode or react to acidic ingredients.

To choose a whisk for making smooth sauces • Use a straight whisk, also known as a French whisk. These elongated whisks have relatively stiff wires. Aside from smoothing out sauces, straight whisks are also good for stirring heavy batters.

To choose a whisk for whipping egg whites or cream or for stirring light batters • Use a balloon whisk. Its thin wires and large, bulb-shaped head are designed to beat the maximum amount of air into thin liquids.

To choose a whisk for stirring a roux or deglazing a pan • Use a flat whisk, designed to get into the corners of a pan so that no lumps of flour or caramelized juices remain stuck to the pan.

TIME SAVER ▼ **To save mixing time** • When mixing dry ingredients, use a whisk instead of a spoon. It does the job much more efficiently.

Wild Rice *see also* Rice

A type of aquatic grass, wild rice is only distantly related to regular rice. While most wild rice is cultivated in man-made paddies, true wild rice is available at some specialty stores and has a cleaner, lighter taste than the cultivated varieties.

BASICS ▼ **To choose** • Grains of natural wild rice have a range of colors from dark brown to

W

tan to light green. Look for the word *natural* on the label, which indicates truly wild rice, not cultivated wild rice.

To store raw • Keep wild rice in an airtight container away from heat and light. Because it is low in moisture and fat, wild rice will keep for up to 3 years.

To rinse • Put the wild rice in a bowl and cover it generously with cold water. Stir the grains with your hands to loosen any bits of hulls. After the debris floats to the surface, pour off the water.

To cook • Use 1 part rice to 3 parts liquid (water or broth). Different batches of rice absorb different amounts of liquid, so you may need to add more liquid as the rice is cooking, or drain some once it's done. Simmer the rice and liquid in a covered pan over medium heat until chewy, 15 to 20 minutes for natural wild rice, or up to 1 hour for cultivated wild rice. Be careful not to overcook wild rice, or it will become mushy and lose both its flavor and its color.

To store cooked • Transfer cooked and cooled wild rice to a sealed container and refrigerate up to 5 days.

To reheat • Warm it with 1 to 2 tablespoons water in a pan over medium-low heat, 4 to 5 minutes. Or microwave it on medium power for 1 to 3 minutes.

FLAVOR TIP ▼ **To add nutty flavor to quick breads** • Grind wild rice in a blender or mini food processor until powdered into wild rice flour. Replace up to one-fourth of the all-purpose flour in muffins, pancakes, or other quick breads with wild rice flour.

Wine *see also* Champagne; Sherry; Vermouth

Fermented grape juice is a rather unromantic term for a beverage as rich in lore and history as wine. Produced around the world, wine is made in many different styles and from a broad range of grapes.

BASICS ▼ **To store** • Keep wine in a dark place that is free of vibrations and that has a consistent temperature of about 55°F. Store wine bottles on their sides to keep the cork from drying out. A dry cork can shrink, allowing air into the bottle, which can ruin a wine.

To serve white or rosé wine • Chill it before serving.

To serve red wine • Serve at a temperature of about 65°F.

To serve several different styles of wine at one meal • Serve light wines before dark ones, young before old, and dry before sweet.

To avoid drips when pouring wine • Give the bottle a slight twist just as you finish pouring.

To store an opened bottle of wine • Transfer the wine to a smaller container to minimize airspace. Seal tightly and try to use it within a day or two.

To use leftover wine • Whatever you do, don't throw it away! Freeze it in ice cube trays, then freeze the cubes in a zipper-lock freezer bag. Use it for flavoring sauces, stews, and casseroles. Or add leftover wine to vinegar to make simple wine vinegar; use ½ cup wine for every 2 cups vinegar.

PROBLEM SOLVER ▼ **To remove bits of cork from wine** • Strain the wine through a sieve or double layer of cheesecloth into a decanter.

TIME SAVER ▼ **To chill wine quickly** • Put the wine in an ice bucket filled with ice and cold water. The wine should be at serving temperature in about 20 minutes.

WINESPEAK: A GLOSSARY OF BASIC WINE TERMS

The world of wine has a language of its own. Here are some definitions of common wine terms that will help you read a wine list, buy a bottle of wine, or better understand what's in your glass.

Acidity: One of the basic elements of wine that brings a crisp, sharp flavor to the drink.

Big: Describes powerful, alcoholic wines with the potential to develop further with time.

Body: The consistency of a wine. Acidity, tannin, and the level of alcohol all contribute to a wine's body.

Bouquet: The aroma of a wine.

Dry: Lacking in sweetness.

Earthy: The taste or aroma of soil in wine.

Fat: Describes wines that are full of flavor.

Finish: The last impression that a wine leaves in your mouth.

Flabby: Describes wines that are weak and without character.

Fruity: Refers to a variety of fruitlike aromas and tastes in wine, aside from grapes. Apple, apricot, blackberry, cherry, citrus, and plum are some of the fruit flavors used to describe a wine.

Herbal: Describes the herb flavors of some wines, such as lavender, mint, rosemary, thyme, or savory.

Legs: The rivulets of wine that drip down the inside of the glass after the wine has been swirled or a drink has been taken. Legs indicate a wine's richness.

Mature: Wines that are aged to the point at which they are ready to drink.

Nose: The aroma of a wine.

Oak: An aroma and flavor found in wines aged in new oak barrels.

Round: Describes mellow, full-bodied wines.

Sparkling: These are wines that have tiny bubbles that rise to the surface when the wine is uncorked.

Tannin: A bitter, astringent substance that acts as a preservative during the aging process, tannin can be identified by its mouth-puckering effect. Tannins soften over time as the wine matures.

Young: Describes immature, fresh wines meant to be drunk early in their lives.

W

Chef's Tip: *Zinfandel* refers to the most widely planted red wine grapes in California. They produce wine with a fine ruby color and a bouquet as fruity as French Beaujolais. Including flavor nuances of wild blackberries, red Zinfandel is best enjoyed young. It enhances many fruit desserts and often finds its way into poaching liquids for pears and other fresh fruit. White Zinfandel has a pink blush and less complex flavor.

FLAVOR TIPS ▼ **To cook with wine** • Match the flavor of the wine to the dominant flavors of the food (see "Pairing Wine and Food" on page 549). Start by adding just a tablespoon or two to avoid overpowering the dish. You can always add more. After adding wine to a recipe, turn the heat to medium-high to help evaporate the alcohol; then, cook the dish until there are

THE RIGHT WINEGLASS

It may come as a surprise, but the shape and size of a wineglass affects the flavor of wine. To appreciate wine at its best, serve it in a glass that best showcases its colors, aromas, and flavors. Look for wineglasses made of clear, untextured glass. Cut-glass goblets and tinted stemware may look good, but they dampen a drinker's ability to examine and appreciate the color of a wine. Make sure that the glass is big enough. A 12- to 15-ounce glass is a good size, allowing enough room to swirl the wine without risk of spills. Fill wineglasses no more than two-thirds full to allow room for swirling, which helps to release a wine's aromas and flavors.

Balloon-shaped glasses showcase red Burgundies. The rounded sides and large bowl of these glasses gives the delicate, complex aromas of these wines room to develop. And since drinking from these glasses requires drinkers to tilt their heads back, the wine lands on the back of the tongue, where the earthy, herbal flavors of these wines are best perceived.

Tulip-shaped glasses are best for dry white wines. The relatively straight sides of these glasses emphasize both the aroma and the fruit in wines such as Sauvignon Blancs and Chardonnays. The shape of these glasses brings the wine right to the tip of your tongue, where fruit flavors are best appreciated.

Flutes, with their tall, slender bowls, are designed to show off the bubbles in champagne and other sparkling wines. Since the bouquet of a sparkling wine develops from bubbles bursting on its surface, these wines are not swirled and the glasses are filled almost to the top.

Chimney-shaped glasses combine a large bowl with straight sides to focus the rich flavors of robust red wines such as red Bordeaux and other Cabernet Sauvignons. Because these wines are sometimes overly tannic, the glasses direct the wine to the front of the tongue, where the tannins are not as easily noticed.

---

no sharp alcohol vapors left. When choosing wine to cook with, avoid buying so-called cooking wines. These are essentially inferior wines with plenty of added salt to discourage anyone from sipping them. In fact, that is how "cooking wine" got its start; salting the wine kept the cook from taking a sip. It is best to cook with a good wine, per– haps the same wine that you will be serving.

To add to long-simmered dishes • When cooking a stew or braise, add a small amount of wine near the beginning of cooking time, perhaps to deglaze the pan. Then, add a bit more near the end of cooking time to help bolster the flavor. Cook for 15 to 20 minutes before serving.

PAIRING WINE AND FOOD

The key to successfully choosing wine for food is not in any rule book. It is in your taste-buds.

Match like with like. Match the flavor of the wine with the dominant flavors in the food and you can't go wrong. For example, acidic wines such as Vinho Verde or red Sancerre pair well with acidic foods such as tomatoes. Sweet wines like Sauternes taste best with sweet foods such as pound cake.

Balance one flavor with another. You can also choose a wine that will temper or balance the flavor of food. For example, the acidity of a dry German Riesling will perfectly balance the saltiness of oysters (much like the way lemon juice works on fish).

Keep in mind tannin, oak, and fruit. Tannin is a bitter-tasting substance in wine that pairs well with bitter foods such as grilled meats. Oak flavor in wine is imparted by new oak barrels in which the wine is aged. In general, very oaky wines do not pair well with food. Fruit encompasses a wide variety of flavors, which can be extremely helpful when choosing wine to complement food.

Ask questions. How will you know when a wine is acidic, sweet, tannic, or oaky, or what fruit flavors it has? The label or wine list may be of some help. Or ask a good wine merchant or knowledgeable waiter. After a few wine-and-food pairings, your tastebuds will also help light the way.

Use a fail-safe method. If all else fails, choose white wines to go with light sauces and mild dishes and red wines to go with dark sauces and robust dishes. Or simply pick a young, fruity red wine that isn't too oaky. It will go with practically anything but dessert. Try a young Beaujolais or a young California Pinot Noir.

To use as a baste • Mix ¼ cup wine with 2 tablespoons oil or melted butter. Brush over grilled or roasted meats during cooking to flavor and moisten the meat.

Wok *see also* Stir-Frying

An essential tool in the Asian kitchen, the wok is designed to cook food quickly over very high heat.

BASICS ▼ **To choose** • Use a round-bottom wok on a gas stove and a flat-bottom wok on an electric stove. Spun steel, the traditional material used for woks, offers excellent heat conduction and is heavy enough to heat oil quickly, yet light enough for easy handling.

To clean a new wok • Woks are often sold covered with a layer of grease that is intended to protect the wok from rust. Clean the wok before using it for the first time by washing it inside and out with soap and an abrasive pad.

To season • After washing a new wok, season it before using. Heat the wok over high heat until a bead of water evaporates upon contact with the hot pan. When the pan is hot, wipe it evenly with a thick wad of paper towels dunked in corn or peanut oil. The oil will begin to

W

smoke, and the center of the wok will blacken. Once the wok is completely coated with oil, remove it from the heat. Let it cool at least 10 minutes. Wipe off any oil left on the surface. Reheat the wok and coat it with fresh oil. Let the wok cool another 10 minutes. Repeat this process 2 more times. After applying the last coat of oil and heating briefly, wipe the wok dry so that the surface is not left with a gummy residue when it cools.

To clean a seasoned wok • Rinse the wok with hot water and use a rag or soft sponge to remove any bits of food stuck to the pan. Avoid using soap or abrasive pads on a seasoned wok. Once the wok is clean, wipe it dry and heat it over high heat. Wipe the hot pan with oil-soaked paper towels, then let it cool, wiping off any oil that remains on the surface. It's a good habit to clean a wok immediately after using, while it is still hot. Then, dry it over high heat before storing.

To store • Keep your wok in a dry spot where it won't be easily scratched.

W

Yeast *see also* Breads, Yeast

The preferred leavening of most bread bakers, yeast is a single-celled living microorganism that occurs naturally.

BASICS ▼ **To choose** • Yeast is most frequently sold as active dry yeast or compressed cake yeast. Most supermarkets carry active dry yeast, a granular powder available in ¼-ounce foil packets (equal to a scant tablespoon). Active dry yeast is also sold in small jars. Many health food stores carry active dry yeast in sacks of varying weights, which is great for people who bake a lot of bread. Compressed cake yeast works as well as active dry yeast, but because it's considered old-fashioned and rarely called for in recipes, there is little reason to use it. Quick-rising yeast looks like active dry yeast but it has been genetically engineered to cut the rising time of the dough almost in half. It cannot be used interchangeably with active dry yeast. Use quick-rising yeast only when a recipe specifically calls for it.

To store • Keep yeast in the refrigerator and use it by the date marked on the package.

To proof yeast • Sprinkle it over warm water (105° to 115°F) mixed with a tiny bit of sugar, honey, or another natural sweetener, which will feed the yeast. In a few minutes, the mixture will bubble and foam, a clear indication that the yeast is active and more than capable of raising your loaf. Proofing is not necessary for most recipes because dry yeast does not need to be moistened before it is used. You can simply mix the yeast in with the dry ingredients. As for testing or "proving" the yeast's freshness, smell it instead. If it smells fresh and yeasty, it will work properly. If it smells like alcohol, the yeast is dead and will not raise your loaf.

TIME SAVER ▼ **To save prep time** • You can have yeast ready for bread baking at any time by saving some dough from a previous batch of bread. Refrigerate the dough in a covered bowl, and keep the yeast active by stirring the dough down every day, which will keep excess carbon dioxide from building up.

Chef's Tip: Quick-rising yeast is not formulated for refrigerated doughs. If you are making a recipe for a dough that will be refrigerated overnight or made ahead, use regular active dry yeast.

Yogurt

Made from milk fermented with bacterial cultures, yogurt is thick and tart, with a custardlike texture. Yogurt can be full-fat, low-fat, or fat-free, depending upon the milk

y

used to make it. Available in a wide range of flavors, yogurt can be made from goat's milk, sheep's milk, or soy milk, as well as from cow's milk.

To choose • Check the sell-by date, and make sure that the yogurt is the freshest available.

To store • Yogurt does not improve with age, so enjoy it soon after purchase. It will keep in the refrigerator up to 10 days after the sell-by date on the container.

To cook with yogurt • The bacteria cultures in yogurt give it tenderizing properties that make it useful as a marinade for meats. It also adds body and flavor to salad dressings, sauces, and soups. For a tender crumb, use yogurt to make quick breads and cakes. When using yogurt in a recipe that includes other acidic ingredients, such as wine or lemon juice, slightly reduce the amount of those acidic ingredients to compensate for the tartness of the yogurt.

To replace milk with yogurt in baking • Add ½ teaspoon baking soda for each cup of yogurt used.

To prevent curdling when added to a hot mixture • Bring the yogurt to room temperature before using. To temper or help stabilize the yogurt, you can also stir 1 teaspoon cornstarch into every ⅓ cup yogurt. For the best results, gently stir yogurt rather than beating it, and add it over low heat at the end of cooking time. Never boil yogurt, or it will separate.

YOGURT Place **4 cups milk** in a large, heavy-bottom pot (use fat-free, 1%, 2%, whole, or flavored milk, or a combination of whole milk and half-and-half, depending upon desired richness). Bring to a boil, stirring constantly to prevent a skin from forming. As soon as milk boils, remove from heat and let cool until slightly warm (ideally, between 110° and 115°F). If a skin forms on the surface during cooling, skim it off with a spoon. Add **2 tablespoons plain yogurt** to the warm milk and stir well. Cover loosely with cheesecloth or a kitchen towel and set in a warm place with a constant temperature between 80° and 115°F. Let it rest undisturbed until thickened, 10 to 15 hours. The longer the yogurt stands, the thicker and tarter it will be. Once it is thickened to the desired consistency, refrigerate up to 1 week. *Makes 1 quart.*

To fix a yogurt mixture that has separated • For each cup of yogurt used, dissolve 1 teaspoon cornstarch or 2 teaspoons all-purpose flour in 2 teaspoons cold water. Stir into the separated mixture over low heat until recombined.

To benefit from yogurt's live cultures • Use the freshest yogurt available because the active cultures will start to dissipate after a few weeks. Also, avoid overheating yogurt, as high temperatures will kill the live cultures. The most healthful way to enjoy yogurt is to eat it cold. When heating yogurt in a recipe, remove the mixture from the heat before stirring in the yogurt, or stir it in very gently over low heat.

To use as a low-fat substitute • Use fat-free plain yogurt instead of mayonnaise or sour cream in dressings, dips, and baked goods. For a richer texture, use **Yogurt Cheese** (see page 554).

MULTIGRAIN YOGURT PANCAKES In a large bowl, combine **1 cup flour, ½ cup oat flour, 3 tablespoons corn-**

HEALTHY MIX-INS FOR FROZEN YOGURT

Why stick with supermarket flavors? It's incredibly easy to create customized frozen yogurt flavors at home. Soften 1 pint of frozen vanilla yogurt in the refrigerator for 20 to 30 minutes. Or microwave it on medium-low power for 20 to 50 seconds. Then, use the suggestions below to make your own combinations.

Peach-Bourbon Frozen Yogurt: Combine **2 chopped peaches, 2 tablespoons bourbon,** and **1 tablespoon dark brown sugar.** Add softened yogurt and mash until blended. Freeze at least 15 minutes before serving.

Piña Colada Frozen Yogurt: Combine **1 well-drained can (8 ounces) crushed pineapple packed in juice, 2 tablespoons dark rum, 1 tablespoon dark brown sugar,** and **⅛ teaspoon coconut extract.** Add softened yogurt and mash until blended. Freeze at least 15 minutes before serving.

Malted Chocolate Frozen Yogurt: Combine **2 tablespoons crème de cacao** and **1 tablespoon grated chocolate.** Add softened yogurt and **⅓ cup chopped malted milk balls.** Mash until blended and freeze at least 15 minutes before serving.

Toasted Hazelnut Frozen Yogurt: Combine **⅓ cup chopped toasted hazelnuts, 2 tablespoons hazelnut liqueur (such as Frangelico),** and **1 tablespoon honey.** Add softened yogurt and mash until blended. Freeze at least 15 minutes before serving.

Ginger-Honey Frozen Yogurt: Combine **¼ cup chopped crystallized ginger, 1 tablespoon honey,** and **¼ teaspoon ground ginger.** Add softened yogurt and mash until blended. Freeze at least 15 minutes before serving.

---

meal, **1½ teaspoons baking powder, ½ teaspoon baking soda,** and **¼ teaspoon salt.** Make a well in the center of dry ingredients and add **1 cup low-fat plain yogurt, 2 tablespoons** *each* **applesauce and honey,** and **1 tablespoon canola oil.** Mix wet ingredients until well-blended. In a medium bowl, beat **2 egg whites** until stiff (but not dry) peaks form when beaters are lifted. Stir together the liquid ingredients and dry ingredients just until combined. Fold in egg whites just until blended. Preheat a large, greased nonstick skillet over medium heat. Drop batter by ¼-cup portions onto the skillet. Cook until bubbles form on the surface, 3 to 4 minutes. Flip and cook until golden on the bottom. *Makes about 12.*

CHOCOLATE-MOCHA FONDUE In the top of a double boiler or in a metal bowl, combine **6 ounces semisweet chocolate, ½ cup fat-free vanilla yogurt,** and **1 teaspoon instant coffee granules** dissolved in **2 teaspoons boiling water.** Heat over simmering water until chocolate is melted and mixture is hot, stirring occasionally. Stir in **2 tablespoons coffee liqueur (such as Kahlúa) or strong brewed coffee.** Serve with **sliced fruits** and **cubed angel food cake** for dipping. *Makes 4 servings.*

y

YOGURT CHEESE Line a sieve or colander with cheesecloth and set it over a deep bowl or other container. Stir **3 cups yogurt** and spoon it into the sieve (use yogurt without gum, starch, or gelatin, as these thickeners inhibit draining). Cover loosely with plastic wrap and refrigerate until thickened, 6 hours or overnight. For the thickest yogurt cheese, fold the cheesecloth over yogurt and weight it down with a bag of beans or another weight. Discard drained liquid or reserve it for another use. Refrigerate yogurt cheese up to 1 week. Use in place of sour cream or cream cheese in fillings. Or use it for rich-tasting spreads, dips, and toppings. *Makes about 1½ cups.*

SMOKED SALMON AND DILL DIP In a medium bowl, combine **1 cup Yogurt Cheese (above)**, **¼ cup low-fat sour cream**, **2 ounces finely chopped smoked salmon**, **2 tablespoons chopped fresh dill**, **1 teaspoon lemon juice**, **¾ teaspoon grated lemon zest**, and **¼ teaspoon ground black pepper.** Serve with rye toasts and crudités. *Makes about 1½ cups.*

PASTA PRIMAVERA SALAD In large pot of salted water, cook **½ pound radiatore pasta** according to package directions. During the last 3 minutes of cooking, add **1 cup small broccoli florets** and cook 1 minute. Add **½ cup frozen peas** and **½ chopped red onion.** Cook 2 minutes more. Drain, rinse under cold water, and set aside. In a large bowl, whisk together **1½ cups low-fat plain yogurt, ⅓ cup low-fat mayonnaise, 3 tablespoons white wine vinegar, 2 teaspoons Dijon mustard,** and **½ teaspoon salt.** Add pasta mixture and **2 shredded carrots, 1 chopped celery rib,** and **⅓ cup chopped fresh parsley.** Toss and serve cold. *Makes 4 servings.*

FETA–YOGURT CHEESE PHYLLO TRIANGLES In a medium bowl, combine ⅔ **cup Yogurt Cheese (at left), ½ cup crumbled feta cheese, 1 egg white, 3 tablespoons** *each* **chopped fresh parsley and grated Parmesan cheese, 1 tablespoon plain dried bread crumbs,** and **5 drops hot-pepper sauce.** In a small dish, stir together **1 tablespoon** *each* **melted butter and olive oil;** this will be used to moisten **8 frozen and thawed sheets phyllo dough.** One at a time, brush 2 sheets of phyllo very lightly with oil mixture, stacking one sheet on top of the other. Working from a long side of the stack, cut parallel to the short side of the stack to make 6 equal-size strips. Place 1 heaping teaspoon of filling at the bottom of each strip. For each strip, fold one corner up in a triangular shape, continuing to fold up like a flag. Repeat stacking, filling, and folding 3 more times with remaining phyllo and filling. Make a small slit in the top of each triangle for steam to escape. (Triangles can be made ahead up to this point and frozen up to 2 months.) Place triangles (fresh or frozen) on a baking sheet, brush lightly with any remaining oil, and bake at 350°F, 25 to 30 minutes. Serve warm. *Makes 24.*

y

Zest *see also* Citrus Fruits

The thin, brightly colored portion of a citrus peel, known as the zest, is rich in essential oils that can bring tremendous flavor to all sorts of foods. Just underneath the zest lies a bitter white membrane know as the pith. Be sure to remove only the zest and not the bitter white pith when zesting citrus fruits.

BASICS ▼ **To remove and grate citrus zest** • When zesting and juicing a single piece of citrus fruit, always remove the zest first. A juiced fruit is nearly impossible to zest. The easiest zesting method is to use a rasp or a citrus zester with several small holes. When pulled across the fruit's rind, these kitchen tools will remove only thin, wispy strips of zest and none of the bitter pith underneath (these small strips can be used whenever grated zest is called for). You can also remove citrus zest by gently rubbing the fruit on the fine or rasplike teeth of a handheld cheese grater. To make the grater easier to clean, press a sheet of plastic wrap over the teeth before grating the fruit. Or clean the grater with a clean toothbrush. Another zesting method: Use a vegetable peeler to remove the zest in long strips, then chop the zest with a sharp knife.

To remove a ribbon of zest • Use a vegetable peeler to cut off strips of zest, taking care not to cut down into the bitter white pith.

To store • Put the zest in a bottle or jar with some vodka. It will keep for several months. You can also freeze citrus zest in zipper-lock freezer bags for several months.

Zipper-Lock Bags

How did we ever live without these? Zipper-lock bags have a perfect, leakproof seal that has become indispensable in the kitchen. They can be used for much more than just food storage.

BASICS ▼ **To crush crumbs** • Place dried bread, nuts, cookies, potato chips, or other crispy food in a zipper-lock plastic bag and seal. Roll with a heavy rolling pin until the crumbs reach the desired fineness.

To coat foods with batter, flour, or crumbs • Place the coating in a zipper-lock bag and add the food to be coated. Seal the bag and shake until thoroughly coated.

To marinate foods • Zipper-lock bags are ideal for marinating because the marinade remains in constant contact with the food. Mix the marinade directly in the bag, then add the food and suck out excess

Z

air. Seal the bag and place it on a platter or in a glass dish (just in case there are any leaks). Refrigerate, turning the bag once in a while.

To roll out pastry without making a mess • Place a chilled round of pastry in a large zipper-lock plastic bag, squeeze out excess air, and seal. Place the bag on a work surface and roll the pastry right in the bag. If air bubbles develop, open the bag to release the air.

To improvise a disposable pastry bag • Fill a zipper-lock bag with the mixture to be piped. Then, seal the bag and snip off one of the bottom corners. Pipe the mixture through the opening.

To toss salad with dressing • Mix salad ingredients in a zipper-lock bag, add the dressing, seal, and shake to coat.

To freeze liquid ingredients • Use heavy-duty freezer bags to freeze soups, sauces, or other liquids. Line a large bowl with the opened bag. Ladle in the liquid, and leave a little extra space for expansion. Suck out excess air with a straw, and seal. Place the bags flat in a single layer on a baking sheet and freeze them until solid. Frozen bags can be stored upright in the freezer to save space. To reheat, place a bag in a pot of simmering water, and simmer until the contents are hot.

To remove excess air • After filling a bag, close it almost all of the way and insert a straw in the opening. Suck out the air through the straw. Quickly remove the straw and seal the bag. If there is solid food or raw meat in the bag, you can press out excess air with your hands instead.

Zucchini *see also* Squash, Summer

With their thin, green skins and soft, white flesh, zucchini are among the fastest-growing squash.

Z

BASICS ▼ **To choose** • As zucchini grows and matures, the skin thickens and the seeds become large. Small to medium zucchini (about 6" long and 2" in diameter) tend to have the best flavor. The skin should be vividly colored and free of blemishes.

To store • If it will be used in a day or two, zucchini can be stored at room temperature. Otherwise, refrigerate it in a plastic bag for up to 5 days.

To shred • If shredding large batches, use the shredding disk of a food processor. Or shred smaller amounts on the large teeth of a handheld cheese grater. To shred the flesh of zucchini and avoid the waterlogged core of seeds, cut off the ends of the zucchini and shred the zucchini lengthwise against the large teeth of a cheese grater. Shred until you reach the core of seeds. Stop and turn the zucchini a quarter-turn, then shred that side. Keep turning and shredding until all you have left is the core of seeds, which can be discarded.

FLAVOR TIP ▼ **To grill** • Medium-large zucchini are great for grilling. And since they soften and shrink, consider starting with twice as many as you think you want. Trim the ends from 2 pounds zucchini. Cut them lengthwise into ¼"-thick slabs and toss with ½ cup bottled Italian salad dressing. Remove them from the dressing and grill over a medium-hot fire until they are soft and slightly charred, turning once, 2 to 3 minutes per side.

GIANT STUFFED ZUCCHINI Place **1 large zucchini (about 2 pounds)** on a surface with the long side facing you. Cut out a lengthwise lid from the top, angling inward as you cut (like cutting the top of a jack-o'-lantern). Using a melon baller or a spoon, dig out and discard the seeds and

THE ZUCCHINI ARE COMING!

If you've ever grown zucchini or lived near someone who does, you've probably witnessed an onslaught of either several small zucchini or one giant zucchini. The trick to handling such an invasion with the coolness of a cucumber is to create a simple zucchini base that can be used in a variety of recipes.

All-Purpose Zucchini Base In a large saucepan, sauté **1 finely chopped onion** and **1 minced garlic clove** in **2 tablespoons vegetable oil.** Add **5 pounds shredded zucchini.** Cook and stir until soft, 4 to 5 minutes. Cool and drain. Squeeze cooked zucchini through a clean towel or press in a colander to remove most of the moisture. Use to make any of the recipes below. Refrigerate up to 3 days. *Makes 8 cups.*

Zucchini Soup: In a large saucepan, sauté **1 finely chopped onion** and **1 minced garlic clove** in **2 tablespoons butter.** Add **3½ cups All-Purpose Zucchini Base, 1 teaspoon curry powder, ⅛ teaspoon ground red pepper,** and **3 cups chicken** or **vegetable broth.** Simmer 10 minutes. Add **1 cup light cream** and heat through.
Makes 4 to 6 servings.

Chilled Zucchini Soup: Follow the recipe for **Zucchini Soup,** but use **2 teaspoons curry powder, ¼ teaspoon ground red pepper,** and **3½ cups chicken broth.** Add **1 teaspoon ground coriander** along with the curry powder. Replace the light cream with **plain yogurt.** Chill and garnish with **¼ cup chopped walnuts.**
Makes 4 to 6 servings.

Zucchini Pasta Primavera: In a large pot of salted boiling water, cook **¾ pound shaped pasta (such as rotelle)** according to package directions. Meanwhile, in a large saucepan, sauté **1 halved and thinly sliced onion** and **1 minced garlic clove** in **2 tablespoons olive oil** until soft, 4 minutes. Add **2 chopped medium tomatoes, 3 cups All-Purpose Zucchini Base,** and **1 tablespoon finely chopped fresh basil.** Cook 2 minutes. Drain pasta and toss with sauce. Top with **¼ cup grated Parmesan cheese.**
Makes 4 modest servings.

Stuffed Zucchini: Follow the recipe for **Zucchini Pasta Primavera,** but omit pasta. Split **2 zucchini** lengthwise and hollow out the centers. Stuff with the sauce and top with the cheese. Bake on a baking sheet at 350°F until tender and heated through, 20 minutes.
Makes 4 servings.

Zucchini Burgers: In a large skillet, sauté **1 finely chopped onion, 2 minced garlic cloves, 1 shredded carrot,** and **1 chopped roasted red bell pepper** in **2 tablespoons olive oil.** Transfer to a bowl. Add **2 cups All-Purpose Zucchini Base, 2 beaten extra-large eggs, ½ cup seasoned bread crumbs,** and **a pinch of ground red pepper.** Refrigerate 30 minutes. In a pie plate, combine **6 tablespoons** *each* **all-purpose flour and seasoned bread crumbs.** Form ¼-cup portions of zucchini mixture into patties. Dredge in crumbs to coat both sides. Cook in another **1 tablespoon olive oil** over medium-high heat until browned and cooked through, 3 to 4 minutes per side. Drain on paper towels. *Makes 6 to 8.*

Z

fiber from the center, or reserve them for another use. Follow the recipe for Classic Meat Loaf (page 279). Fill the hollowed squash with the meat mixture. Press the lid into place and secure with toothpicks. Place in a roasting pan and cover with **4 cups spaghetti sauce.** Cover and bake at 375°F until zucchini is tender, internal temperature of meat registers 160°F, and meat is no longer pink, about 1 hour. Cut into thick slices and serve with ⅓ **cup grated Parmesan cheese.** *Makes 6 to 8 servings.*

ZUCCHINI BREAD Preheat oven to 350°F. Shred about **1 medium zucchini** to make 1½ cups shredded zucchini. Pat dry with paper towels. In a medium bowl, combine ⅔ **cup sugar,** ¼ **cup milk, 1 egg, 2 tablespoons oil, 2 tablespoons honey, 1 teaspoon** *each* **vanilla extract and ground cinnamon,** and ½ **teaspoon ground cloves. In a large bowl, whisk together 1⅓ cups all-purpose flour,** ¾ **teaspoon baking powder,** ½ **teaspoon baking soda,** and ⅛ **teaspoon salt.** Add the zucchini and the milk mixture. Stir just until moistened (lumps are okay). Scrape into a greased 9" × 5" loaf pan and bake until a wooden pick inserted in center comes out clean, 35 to 45 minutes. Cool in the pan 10 minutes. Remove and cool completely on a rack. *Makes 1 loaf; 10 slices.*

CHOCOLATE ZUCCHINI BREAD Follow the recipe for **Zucchini Bread** (above), but stir ½ **cup unsweetened cocoa powder** in with the flour and add ½ **cup mini chocolate chips** along with the zucchini. *Makes 1 loaf; 10 slices.*

Z

Useful Tables and Charts

Converting To and From Metric

Use the following formulas to convert U.S. measurements to metric. To convert from metric measurements to U.S. measurements, use the same formulas but work backward, dividing by instead of multiplying by the number in the center column. For instance, teaspoons multiplied by 4.93 will give you milliliters. And vice versa, milliliters *divided* by 4.93 will give you teaspoons. When making conversions, be sure to convert the measurements for all of the ingredients in your recipe to maintain the same proportions as the original recipe.

When This Is Known . . .	Multiply It By . . .	To Get . . .
tsp	4.93	ml
Tbsp	14.79	ml
fluid oz	29.57	ml
cup (liquid)	236.59	ml
cup (liquid)	0.236	liter
cup (dry)	275.31	ml
cup (dry)	0.275	liter
pt (liquid)	473.18	ml
pt (liquid)	0.473	liter
pt (dry)	0.551	liter
qt (liquid)	946.36	ml
qt (liquid)	0.946	liter
qt (dry)	1,101.22	ml
gal	3.785	liter
oz	28.35	g
lb	0.454	kg
in.	2.54	cm

Ingredient Guide and Equivalents

Food	Weight or Amount	Approximate Equivalent
Almonds, in shell	1 lb	⅓ cup ground almond meal
Almonds, shelled	1 lb	1 cup
Almonds, shelled, blanched	1 lb	3 cups whole; 4 cups slivered
Apples, fresh	1 lb	3 medium; 3 cups chopped or sliced; 3½ cups shredded; 1¼ cups applesauce
Apples, dried	1 lb	4⅓ cups finely chopped; 8 cups cooked
Apricots, fresh	1 lb	8–12 whole; 2½ cups sliced; 2 cups chopped
Apricots, dried	1 lb	2¾ cups; 5½ cups cooked
Artichokes	1 lb	2 large
Artichokes, Jerusalem	1 lb	3 cups cut in 1" pieces
Asparagus, frozen cut	10 oz	2 cups
Asparagus spears, fresh	1 lb	16–20 spears; 2⅔ cups cut in 1"–1½" pieces
Asparagus spears, canned	14–16 oz	12–18 spears
Avocados	1 lb	2 small; 2½ cups chopped; 1 cup mashed
Bananas, fresh	1 lb	3 medium; 2 cups sliced; 1½ cups mashed
Bananas, dried	1 lb	4½ cups sliced
Barley	1 cup	3½ cups cooked
Beans, canned	16 oz	2 cups
Beans, chickpeas, dried	1 lb	2 cups; 6 cups cooked
Beans, green, fresh	1 lb	3½ cups whole; 4–5 cups 1" pieces raw
Beans, green, frozen	9 oz	1½ cups
Beans, green, canned	16 oz	1¾ cups
Beans, kidney, dried	1 lb	2½ cups; 5½ cups cooked
Beans, lentils, dried	1 lb	2¼ cups; 5 cups cooked
Beans, lima, dried	1 lb	2⅔ cups; 6 cups cooked
Beans, navy, dried	1 lb	2⅓ cups; 5½ cups cooked
Beets, fresh, without tops	1 lb	1¾ cups shredded; 2 cups chopped or sliced
Beets, canned	16 oz	2 cups
Blueberries, fresh	1 pt 1 qt	2 cups 3½ cups
Blueberries, frozen	10 oz	1½ cups
Blueberries, canned	14 oz	1½ cups
Bread, dry	1 slice	⅓ cup dry bread crumbs
Bread, fresh	1 slice	½ cup soft bread crumbs
Broccoli, fresh	1 lb	1 large head; 2 cups florets + 2 cups stems

Food	Weight or Amount	Approximate Equivalent
Broccoli, frozen	10 oz	1½ cups chopped
Broth, beef or chicken	1 cup	1 tsp instant bouillon or 1 envelope or cube bouillon dissolved in 1 cup boiling water
Brussels sprouts, fresh	1 lb	4 cups
Brussels sprouts, frozen	10 oz	18–24 sprouts
Bulgur	1 lb 1 cup	2¾ cup; 3¾ cup cooked 3 cups cooked
Butter or margarine	¼ lb ½ lb 1 lb	½ cup; 8 Tbsp; 1 stick 1 cup; 16 Tbsp; 2 sticks 2 cups; 32 Tbsp; 4 sticks; 3 cups whipped
Cabbage, napa	1 head	6 cups shredded
Cabbage, red, green, or savoy	1 lb	1 small head; 5 cups shredded; 3 cups cooked
Cantaloupe	1 lb	½ medium cantaloupe; 1½ cups cubed
Carrots, fresh, without tops	1 lb	4–6 medium; 3 cups chopped or sliced; 2¾ cups julienned; 2½ cups shredded or grated
Carrots, frozen	1 lb	2½–3 cups sliced
Carrots, canned	16 oz	2 cups sliced
Cashews, shelled	6 oz 1 lb	1 cup 2⅔ cups
Cauliflower, fresh	1½ lb	1 head; 6 cups florets; 1½ cups chopped
Cauliflower, frozen	10 oz	2 cups chopped or sliced
Celeriac	1 lb	1 medium root; 2 cups chopped or shredded
Celery	1 medium rib 1 lb	½ cup chopped or sliced 3 cups chopped or sliced
Cheese, blue or feta	4 oz	1 cup crumbled
Cheese, Cheddar or mozzarella	1 lb	4 cups shredded or grated
Cheese, cottage	8 oz	1 cup
Cheese, cream	8 oz	1 cup
Cheese, Parmesan	4 oz	1⅓ cups grated
Cheese, ricotta	1 lb	2 cups
Cherries, fresh	1 lb	3 cups pitted
Cherries, frozen	10 oz	1 cup
Cherries, canned	1 lb	1½ cups
Chestnuts, in shell	1 lb	35–40 large; 2½ cups cooked and shelled; 1 cup puree
Chestnuts, shelled	1 lb	3⅓ cups

(continued)

Ingredient Guide and Equivalents (cont.)

Food	Weight or Amount	Approximate Equivalent
Chicken breast halves, boneless, skinless	4 oz raw	1 piece; 2 cups cooked and chopped
Chocolate, chips	6 oz	1 cup
Chocolate, squares	8 oz	8 squares (1 oz each)
Coconut, shredded	1 lb	5⅔ cups
Coffee, ground	1 lb	5 cups; 80 Tbsp; 40 brewed cups (6 oz each)
Corn, fresh	2 medium ears	1 cup kernels
Corn, frozen	10 oz	1¾ cups kernels
Corn, canned, cream-style	16 oz	2 cups
Corn, canned, whole kernel	12 oz	1½ cups
Cornmeal	1 lb 1 cup	3 cups dry, 12 cups cooked 4 cups cooked
Cornstarch	1 lb	3 cups
Corn syrup, light or dark	16 fl oz	2 cups
Crackers (*see* Graham crackers; Soda crackers)		
Cranberries, fresh	12 oz	3 cups
Cranberry sauce, canned	1 lb	1⅔ cups
Cream, light or half-and-half or sour	½ pint	1 cup
Cream, heavy	½ pint	1 cup; 2 cups whipped
Cucumber	1 lb	2 medium; 4 cups cubed; 3 cups sliced; 2 cups shredded
Currants, dried	1 lb	3¼ cups
Dates, unpitted	1 lb	2 cups; 2½ cups pitted and chopped
Egg, whole, extra large	1 doz	3 cups
Eggs, whole, large	1 doz	2⅓ cups
Eggs, whole, medium	1 doz	2 cups
Eggs, whole, small	1 doz	1¾ cups
Egg whites, extra large	1 doz	1¾ cups
Egg whites, large	1 doz	1½ cups
Egg whites, medium	1 doz	1⅓ cups
Egg whites, small	1 doz	1¼ cups
Egg yolks, extra large	1 doz	1 cup
Egg yolks, large	1 doz	⅞ cup
Egg yolks, medium	1 doz	¾ cup
Egg yolks, small	1 doz	⅔ cup
Eggplant	1 lb	3½ cups chopped; 1½ cups cooked

Food	Weight or Amount	Approximate Equivalent
Fennel bulb	1 lb	1 large bulb; 2 cups sliced
Figs, fresh	1 lb	12 medium
Figs, dried	1 lb	2½ cups chopped
Figs, canned	1 lb	12–16
Filberts (*see* Hazelnuts)		
Flour, all-purpose or bread or self-rising	1 lb	3¾ cups unsifted, 4¼ cups sifted
Flour, buckwheat	1 lb	3½ cups unsifted
Flour, cake or pastry	1 lb	4 cups sifted
Flour, gluten	1 lb	3 cups sifted
Flour, rice	1 lb	3½ cups sifted
Flour, rye	1 lb	3½ cups sifted
Flour, soy	1 lb	4 cups unsifted
Flour, whole wheat	1 lb	3½ cups unsifted, 3⅔ cups sifted
Garlic	1 small clove	1 tsp minced
Gelatin, unflavored	¼ oz	1 envelope; 1 Tbsp granulated; 3½ (4" × 9") sheets
Graham crackers	15	1 cup crumbs
Grapefruit, fresh	1 lb	1 medium; 1½ cups segments; ⅔ cup juice
Grapefruit, frozen	13 oz	1½ cups segments
Grapefruit, canned	16 oz	2 cups segments
Grapes, seeded or seedless	1 lb	75 grapes; 2½–3 cups
Greens, collards	1 lb	10 cups pieces; 2 cups cooked
Greens, Belgian endive	1 lb	5½ cups sliced into rounds
Greens, escarole	1 lb	12 cups torn leaves; 8 cups shredded
Greens, general, fresh	1 lb	2 cups cooked
Greens, general, frozen	10 oz	1½–2 cups
Grits	1 lb 1 cup	3 cups, 10 cups cooked 3⅓ cups cooked
Hazelnuts, shelled, whole	1 lb	3½ cups
Herbs, fresh, chopped	1 Tbsp fresh	1 tsp dried
Hominy	1 lb 1 cup	2½ cups, 16¼ cups cooked 6½ cups cooked
Honey	1 lb	1⅓ cups
Horseradish, bottled	1 Tbsp	1½ tsp freshly grated
Ice cream, ice milk, sherbet	1 qt	4 cups
Jicama	1 lb	3 cups chopped or shredded

(continued)

Useful Tables and Charts

Ingredient Guide and Equivalents (cont.)

Food	Weight or Amount	Approximate Equivalent
Ketchup	16 oz	1⅔ cup
Kiwifruit	1 medium	½ cup sliced or chopped
Leeks, white parts only	1 lb	2 leeks; 4 cups chopped; 2 cups cooked
Lemons	1 lb 1 medium	4–6 medium; 1 cup juice 2–4 Tbsp juice; 2–3 tsp zest
Lentils	1 lb	2¼ cups dry; 5 cups cooked
Lettuce, Bibb	1 medium head	4 cups leaves
Lettuce, iceberg	1 lb	1 medium head; 10 cups leaves; 8 cups shredded
Lettuce, leaf	1 medium head	8 cups leaves
Lettuce, romaine	1 medium head	8 cups leaves
Limes	1 lb 1 medium	6–8 medium; ½ cup juice 1–2 Tbsp juice; 1–2 tsp zest
Macaroni	1 cup dry 1 lb	2 cups cooked 4 cups dry; 9 cups cooked
Mango	1 medium	1½ cups chopped; 1 cup pureed
Maple syrup	16 fl oz	2 cups
Marshmallows, large	1 lb 1 cup	About 60 marshmallows 6–7 marshmallows
Marshmallows, miniature	10½ oz 1 cup	400 marshmallows 85 marshmallows
Meat, ground	1 lb	2 cups raw
Melon	1 lb	1 cup cubed
Milk, dry	1 lb	3⅔ cups; 14 cups reconstituted
Milk, evaporated, whole or fat-free	14½ oz	1⅔ cups; 3⅓ cups reconstituted
Milk, fat-free or whole, or buttermilk	1 qt	4 cups
Milk, sweetened condensed	15 oz 14 oz	1⅓ cups 1¼ cups
Millet	1 lb	2⅛ cups; 5½ cups cooked
Mixed vegetables, frozen	10 oz	2 cups cut
Mixed vegetables, canned	16 oz	2 cups cut
Molasses	16 fl oz	2 cups
Mushrooms, fresh	1 lb	35 medium; 4 cups sliced; 2 cups sautéed
Mushrooms, dried	4 oz	1 lb fresh
Mushrooms, canned	4 oz	⅔ cup sliced or chopped
Nectarines	1 lb	3 medium; 2½ cups chopped
Noodles, Chinese, dry	¾ lb	5 cups cooked
Noodles, fine width	½ lb	5½ cups cooked

Food	Weight or Amount	Approximate Equivalent
Noodles, linguine	1 lb	5 cups cooked
Noodles, pappardelle	½ lb	3¼ cups cooked
Noodles, 1" pieces	1 lb	6–8 cups; 8 cups cooked
Nuts (*see* individual nuts)		
Oats, rolled	3 oz 1 lb	1 cup dry; 1¾ cups cooked 5 cups dry; 9 cups cooked
Okra, fresh	1 lb	2¼ cups chopped
Okra, frozen	10 oz	1¼ cups chopped
Olives	6 oz	4 oz pitted
Onions, green (*see* Scallions)		
Onions, white, fresh	1 lb	4 medium; 3–4 cups chopped
Onions, white, frozen	12 oz	3 cups chopped
Oranges, fresh	1 lb 1 medium	3 medium; 1 cup segments; 1 cup juice; ¼ cup zest ⅓ cup segments; ⅓ cup juice; 1–2 Tbsp zest
Oranges, mandarin, canned	11 oz	1¼ cups fruit and juice
Orzo	4 oz	⅔ cup dry; 1½ cups cooked
Oysters	1 qt 1 dozen	50 shucked 1 cup meat after shucking
Papaya	1 lb	2 medium; 2 cups cubed; 1 cup pureed
Parsley, fresh	4 oz	1 bunch; 4 cups packed; 2 cups chopped
Parsnips	1 lb	4 medium; 2 cups chopped
Pasta (*see* Macaroni; Noodles; Orzo; Spaghetti)		
Peaches, fresh	1 lb	4 medium; 2¾ cups sliced; 2½ cups chopped; 1 cup puree
Peaches, frozen	10 oz	1⅛ cups sliced with juice
Peaches, dried	1 lb	2¾ cups; 5½ cups cooked
Peaches, canned	1 lb	6–10 halves; 2 cups sliced
Peanuts, in shell	1½ lb	1 lb shelled; 3½–4 cups nuts
Pears, fresh	1 lb	3 medium; 2 cups sliced
Pears, dried	1 lb	2¾ cup; 5½ cups cooked
Peas, black-eyed, fresh	1 lb	2⅓ cups
Peas, black-eyed, frozen	10 oz	1½ cups cooked
Peas, dried, split	1 lb	2¼ cups; 5 cups cooked
Peas, green, fresh, in pod	1 lb	1 cup shelled
Peas, green, frozen	10 oz	2 cups
Peas, green, canned	1 lb	2 cups

(continued)

Ingredient Guide and Equivalents (cont.)

Food	Weight or Amount	Approximate Equivalent
Peas, snow	3 oz 1 lb	1 cup 5–6 cups
Pecans	1 lb	4 cups halves; 3¾ cups chopped
Peppers, bell	1 lb	3 medium; 2 cups chopped
Peppers, chile	1" segment	2 tsp finely chopped
Pimientos	1 jar (4 oz)	½ cup chopped
Pineapple	3 lb	1 medium; 2½ cups chopped
Pistachios	1½ lb	1 lb shelled; 3½–4 cups
Plantains	1 lb	2 cups 1" pieces
Plums, fresh	1 lb	6 plums; 2½ cups pitted and sliced; 1½ cups puree
Plums, canned, whole	1 lb	Six to eight 2" plums; 3 cups sliced
Pomegranates	1 lb	3 medium; 1½ cups seeds; ¾ cup juice
Popcorn	½ cup kernels	4 cups popped
Potatoes, sweet (*see* Sweet potatoes)		
Potatoes, white	1 lb	2–3 medium russet or 6–8 new; 3–3½ cups chopped, sliced, or cubed; 1¾–2 cups cooked and mashed
Prunes, pitted	1 lb	2½ cups chopped; 4 cups cooked
Prunes, dried	1 lb	2½ cups; 4–4½ cups cooked
Prunes, canned	1 lb	10–14 prunes
Pumpkin, fresh	1 lb	1 cup cooked and mashed
Pumpkin, canned	16 oz	2 cups mashed
Pumpkin seeds, hulled	1 lb	3¼ cups
Radishes	½ lb	1⅔ cups sliced
Raisins, seedless	1 lb	3–3¼ cups
Raspberries	½ pint	Scant 1½ cups
Rhubarb, fresh	1 lb	3 cups chopped; 2 cups cooked
Rhubarb, frozen	12 oz	1½ cups chopped and sliced
Rice, brown	1 cup	4 cups cooked
Rice, converted	1 cup	3½ cups cooked
Rice, quick-cooking	1 cup	2 cups cooked
Rice, white	1 cup	3 cups cooked
Rice, wild	1 cup	4 cups cooked
Rutabaga	1 lb	2½ cups cubed
Sausage, Italian link	1 lb	4 links

Food	Weight or Amount	Approximate Equivalent
Scallions, fresh	1 bunch	9 with tops; 1 cup sliced; ¾ cup minced
Sesame seeds	1 lb	3¼ cups
Shortening, vegetable	1 lb	2 cups
Shallots	½ oz	1 medium; 1 Tbsp finely chopped
Shrimp, in shell	1 lb	40–50 small 31–40 medium 26–30 large 21–25 extra large 16–20 jumbo
Soda crackers, saltines	28 crackers	1 cup fine crumbs
Spaghetti, 12" pieces	1 lb	About 7 cups cooked
Spinach, fresh	1 lb	10 cups torn pieces; about 1 cup cooked
Spinach, frozen	10 oz	1½ cups
Spinach, canned	15 oz	2 cups
Split green peas (*see* Peas, dried, split)		
Sprouts, mung bean	½ lb	1½ cups
Squash, acorn	1½ lb	1 medium; 2 cups cooked and mashed
Squash, spaghetti	5 lb	1 medium; 6–6½ cups strands
Squash, summer, fresh	1 lb	3 medium; 3½ cups sliced; 3 cups shredded
Squash, summer, frozen	10 oz	1½ cups sliced or chopped
Squash, winter, fresh	1 lb	2 cups cooked; 1½ cups mashed
Squash, winter, frozen	12 oz	1½ cups
Strawberries, fresh	1 pint 1 quart	1½–2 cups sliced or chopped 3–4 cups sliced or chopped
Strawberries, frozen, sliced	10 oz	1 cup
Strawberries, frozen, whole	1 lb	1⅓ cups
Sugar, brown, light or dark	1 lb	2¼ cups packed
Sugar, confectioners'	1 lb	3½–4 cups unsifted; 4½–5 cups sifted
Sugar, granulated	1 lb	2–2¼ cups
Sugar, superfine	1 lb	2⅓ cups
Sugar, turbinado	1 lb	3⅛ cups
Sunflower seeds	1 lb	3¼ cup
Sweet potatoes, fresh	1 lb	3 medium; 3 cups shredded; 3½ cups chopped or sliced
Sweet potatoes, canned	16 oz	1¾ cups
Tangerines	1 lb 1 medium	4 medium; 2 cups sectioned 3–4 Tbsp juice; 3–4 tsp zest

(continued)

Useful Tables and Charts

Ingredient Guide and Equivalents (cont.)

Food	Weight or Amount	Approximate Equivalent
Tea leaves	1 lb	About 200 cups brewed
Tofu	1 lb	1 cake; 2 cups cubed; 1½ cups mashed
Tomatillos	1 lb	12 medium; 1¼ cups chopped
Tomatoes, fresh	1 lb	3–4 medium; 2 cups chopped
Tomatoes, canned	15 oz	1¾ cups drained pulp
Tuna, canned	6 oz	⅔ cup drained and flaked
Turnips	1 lb	3 medium; 2½ cups chopped
Vegetables, mixed (*see* Mixed vegetables)		
Wafer cookies, chocolate	18 wafers	1 cup crumbs
Wafer cookies, vanilla	22 wafers	1 cup fine crumbs
Walnuts	1 lb	3¾ cups halves; 3½ cups chopped
Watercress	¼ lb	1 bunch; 1 cup loosely packed
Wheat germ	1 lb	4 cups
Yeast, active dry	¼ oz	1 pkg; 1 scant Tbsp; 1.6 oz compressed fresh yeast
Yogurt	½ pint	1 cup

Stages of Cooked Sugar for Candymaking

Use a candy thermometer to test the temperature of sugar syrup. You can also use a visual test by dropping a small amount of sugar syrup into ice water.

Stage	Temperature	When dropped into ice water, a small amount of sugar syrup will:
Thread	223°–234°F (106°–112°C)	Spin a soft 2" thread
Soft ball	234°–240°F (112°–116°C)	Form a soft, flat ball
Firm ball	242°–248°F (118°–120°C)	Form a firm but pliable ball
Hard ball	250°–265°F (121°–129°C)	Form a hard, compact ball
Soft crack	270°–290°F (132°–143°C)	Separate into hard but not brittle threads
Hard crack	300°–310°F (149°–154°C)	Form hard, brittle threads
Caramel	320°–338°F (160°–170°C)	Form hard, brittle threads, and the liquid will turn brown

Vegetable Cooking Times

Vegetable	Amount	Microwave, High (min)	Steamer (min)	Pressure Cooker (min)
Artichokes	4 medium	20–25	30–35	9–11
Asparagus	1 lb, trimmed	5–6	6–7	1–2
Beets	1 lb	12–15	30–35	20–22
Broccoli	1 lb, cut into florets	8–12	5–7	2–3
Brussels sprouts	1 lb	7–11	11–12	4–5
Cabbage	1 medium, cut into wedges	9–13	12–15	3–4
Carrots	1 lb, sliced	8–10	7–10	4–5
Cauliflower	1 lb, cut into florets	4–7	8–10	2–3
Corn on the cob	4 ears	10–14	10–12	3–4
Eggplant	1 medium, cubed	7–10	5–7	3–4
Green beans	1 lb	10–12	7–9	2–3
Kale	1 lb, 2" pieces	8–10	5–6	3–4
Leeks	1 lb, ½" slices	4–6	8–10	2–3
Mushrooms	1 lb, sliced	6–8	3–4	1–2
Onion, small whole	1 lb	6–8	15–20	4–5
Peas, green	1 lb, shelled	5–7	8–10	Not recommended
Peas, snap	1 lb	6–10	8–10	Not recommended
Potatoes, small whole	1 lb, pricked with fork	9–11	25–30	6–7
Spinach	1 lb	5–7	3–4	2–3
Squash, spaghetti	3 lb, halved and seeded	7–9	25–35	14–17
Squash, summer	1 lb, sliced	4–6	8–10	2–3
Squash, winter	1 medium, halved and seeded	8–10	25–30	6–7
Sweet potatoes	2 lb, pricked with fork	13	30–35	8–10
Turnips	1 lb, peeled and cut	7–9	10–12	3–4
Zucchini	1 lb, sliced	4–6	8–10	2–3

Useful Tables and Charts

Healthy Substitutions

Replace This . . .	With This . . .
DAIRY	
1 cup whole milk	1 cup fat-free, 1%, or 2% milk 1 cup buttermilk (for baking)
1 cup fat-free milk	⅓ cup nonfat dry milk mixed with ¾ cup water
1 can sweetened condensed milk (14 oz)	1 can fat-free sweetened condensed milk (14 oz)
1 can evaporated milk (12 oz)	1 can fat-free evaporated milk (12 oz)
1 cup heavy cream	1 cup 1% milk + 1 Tbsp cornstarch 1 cup fat-free evaporated milk
1 cup whipped cream	1 cup frozen light nondairy whipped topping, thawed
1 cup buttermilk	1 cup low-fat or fat-free plain yogurt
1 cup sour cream	1 cup fat-free plain yogurt 1 cup fat-free sour cream 1 cup fat-free evaporated milk + 1 Tbsp lemon juice
1 cup shredded Cheddar cheese (4 oz)	1 cup shredded reduced-fat or fat-free Cheddar cheese
4 oz blue cheese, feta cheese, or goat cheese	2 oz appropriate cheese + 2 oz fat-free cream cheese
8 oz cream cheese	8 oz fat-free ricotta cheese 8 oz dry-curd cottage cheese 8 oz fat-free cream cheese (block-style or tub-style) 4 oz fat-free cream cheese + 4 oz reduced-fat cream cheese 8 oz reduced-fat cream cheese (block-style or tub-style) 8 oz mascarpone cheese 4 oz mascarpone + 4 oz fat-free cream cheese
FAT	
½ cup oil	½ cup fat-free chicken broth (for salad dressings and marinades) ¼ cup unsweetened applesauce + ¼ cup buttermilk (for baking) ½ cup unsweetened applesauce or baby food prunes (for baking) ⅓ cup vinegar + ¼ cup fat-free chicken broth + ¼ cup pineapple juice + 2 Tbsp strong-flavored oil (to make 1 cup salad dressing or marinade)
½ cup margarine or butter (1 stick)	½ cup unsweetened applesauce (for baking)
1 cup butter	⅞ cup vegetable oil ¼ cup unsweetened applesauce + ¼ cup buttermilk (for baking) ½ cup baby food prunes (for baking) ½ cup marshmallow creme (for frostings and fillings) ½ cup light butter
2 Tbsp oil	2 Tbsp wine or fat-free broth (for sautéing)
Olive oil	Equal amount of any vegetable oil
1 cup chopped walnuts	½ cup chopped walnuts, toasted

Replace This . . .	With This . . .
FAT (cont.)	
1 cup chopped pecans	½ cup chopped pecans, toasted
1 cup slivered almonds	½ cup sliced almonds, toasted ½ cup slivered almonds, toasted

PROTEIN

6 oz pork sirloin, cooked	6 oz pork tenderloin, roasted
6 oz flank steak, cooked	6 oz round steak, roasted
6 oz chicken thigh, no skin, cooked	6 oz chicken breast, no skin, roasted
6 oz dark turkey meat, cooked	6 oz turkey breast, roasted
1 whole egg	2 egg whites 3 Tbsp liquid egg substitute
6 oz tuna in oil, drained	6 oz tuna in water, drained
1 lb ground beef	1 lb ground turkey breast 1 lb chopped pork tenderloin 1 lb chopped chicken breast 1 lb ground turkey 1 lb extra-lean ground beef (15 percent fat)
6 oz pork sausage, cooked	6 oz turkey sausage, cooked

MISCELLANEOUS

1 cup frozen nondairy whipped topping	1 cup frozen light nondairy whipped topping
1 cup chocolate chips	½ cup chocolate chips ½ cup mini chocolate chips
1 cup flaked coconut	1 tsp coconut extract ½ cup flaked coconut
1 cup sliced olives	½ cup sliced olives
1 oz baking chocolate	3 Tbsp unsweetened cocoa powder
Single pie crust	3 sheets phyllo dough (6 half-sheets)
1 can condensed cream of mushroom soup (10.7 oz)	1 can condensed reduced-fat cream of mushroom soup (10.7 oz)
1 cup sugar	¾ cup sugar
1 small package flavored gelatin mix (4 servings)	1 small package sugar-free gelatin mix (4 servings)
1 cup basic white sauce (1 cup whole milk + 2 Tbsp flour + 1 Tbsp butter)	1 cup basic white sauce (1 cup 1% milk + 1 Tbsp cornstarch)

Useful Tables and Charts

Doneness Tests and Temperatures

For the most accurate doneness test, use an instant-read thermometer to get a temperature reading. Insert the thermometer into the center or thickest portion of the meat. After roasting meats, let the roast rest 10 minutes before carving to allow the juices to seep back into the meat.

This food . . .	Is done when . . .
BEEF	
Ground (loose)	No longer pink
Ground (in loaf or patties)	160°F, no longer pink
Roasts, steaks	145°F (medium-rare) 160°F (medium) 165°F (well-done)
Long-cooking pot roasts	Fork-tender
Cutlets	No longer pink
Calf's liver, sliced ¼" thick	Just pink in the center
Veal, roasts	145°F (medium-rare) 155°F (medium) 165°F (well-done)
PORK	
Chops, ribs	160°F, juices run clear
Roasts, tenderloin	155°F, juices run clear
Ham, country	160°F
Ham, precooked	140°F
LAMB	
Chops	160°F, juices run clear
Roasts, leg steaks	145°F (medium-rare) 160° (medium) 165°F (well-done)
CHICKEN AND CORNISH GAME HEN	
Boneless breasts	160°F, juices run clear
Bone-in parts	170°F, juices run clear
Whole or butterflied	180°F for breast, juices run clear; 165°F for stuffing
Ground (loose)	No longer pink
Ground (in loaf or patties)	165°F, no longer pink
Cutlets	No longer pink, juices run clear
Livers	No longer pink

This food . . .	Is done when . . .
TURKEY	
Breasts	170°F, juices run clear
Whole	180°F for breast, juices run clear; 165°F for stuffing
Ground (loose)	No longer pink
Ground (in loaf or patties)	165°F, no longer pink
DUCK AND GOOSE	
Whole	175° to 180°F for thigh
Breast	Still slightly pink
GAME MEATS	
Bison tenderloin steaks	145°F (medium-rare) 155°F (medium) 165°F (well-done)
Emu steaks	145°F (medium-rare)
Venison chops	145°F (medium-rare)
VARIOUS CUT-UP MEATS	
Cubed or crumbled meats	No longer pink
Long-cooking stew and other meats	Fork-tender
FISH	
Fillets (salmon)	Fish is opaque
Fillets (other)	Fish just flakes easily
Steaks	Fish is just opaque
SHELLFISH AND MOLLUSKS	
Clams, mussels, oysters	Shells open (discard any unopened shells)
Shrimp, scallops, lobster, crabs	Flesh is opaque
Octopus	Until tender
Squid	Until tender

Holiday Hotlines

Holidays can sometimes be hectic, but don't panic. There are people just a phone call away who can help you get through it with aplomb. Some of these hotlines are answered by experienced home economists; a few have tape-recorded messages. For additional tips, see Entertaining (page 167) and Turkey (page 520).

American Dietetic Association's Consumer Nutrition Information Hotline: (800) 366-1655. Call anytime to hear timely food and nutrition messages recorded by registered dietitians. Dietitian referrals are available Monday through Friday, 9:00 A.M. to 4:00 P.M. Central Time and on their Web site: www.eatright.org.

Butterball Turkey Talk-Line: (800) 323-4848 (Bilingual: English and Spanish) Great for questions about thawing, preparing, carving, and storing turkey and leftovers. Web site: www.butterball.com. Talk-Line operators can provide a personalized answer to your e-mail questions (allow 48 hours for a response). Lines are open in November and December; for information year-round, call (800) BUTTERBALL.

Fleischmann's Yeast Baker's Help Line: (800) 777-4959. This Help Line is for yeast baking questions only. Lines are open 8:00 A.M. to 6:00 P.M. Central Standard Time, 365 days a year, including holidays. Extended hours continue through Easter from 7:00 A.M. to 8:00 P.M. Monday through Saturday and 11:00 A.M. to 8:00 P.M. on Sunday. Visit their Web site at www.breadworld.com for recipes and information.

Foster Farms Consumer Helpline: (800) 255-7227. Open Monday through Friday, 8:00 A.M. to 5:00 P.M. Pacific Standard Time, except holidays. Live representatives and voice mail. Answers are available for a variety of cooking questions. Special Turkey Holiday help line with live operators is available 24 hours a day starting the week before Thanksgiving through the Monday after Thanksgiving, including Thanksgiving Day. Visit their Web site at www.fosterfarms.com for helpful information and to send questions by e-mail.

General Mills: (888) ASK-BETTY. Company employees fully trained in Betty Crocker products offer new recipe ideas and help you find lost recipes using their products. Callers may listen to recordings of the most popular recipes from a recipe database or opt for a live agent. Open all year 7:30 A.M. to 5:30 P.M. Central Standard Time, except holidays.

Land O' Lakes Holiday Bakeline: (800) 782-9606. Home economists and baking experts find recipes and answer baking questions. Callers receive a free copy of holiday recipes called "Share the Secrets." Lines are open 9:00 A.M. to 9:00 P.M. Central Standard Time from November 1 to December 24. Holiday recipes are also available on their Web site: www.landolakes.com. You can also e-mail questions to the Web site.

Nestlé Bakeline: (800) 637-8537. Get help with chocolate baking recipes from well-trained consumer representatives from 8:00 A.M. to 8:00 P.M. weekdays year-round. For Libby's Pumpkin, call (800) 854-0374 for automated responses to frequently asked questions. For Nestlé Consumer Services, call (800) 854-8935. Visit their Web site at www.verybestbaking.com.

People for the Ethical Treatment of Animals: (888) VEGFOOD. There are no live operators or taped information, but you can leave your name and address anytime to request vegetarian recipes and a free Vegetarian Starter Kit. You can also visit their Web site at www.goveg.com to request the starter kit.

Reynolds Kitchens Tip Line: (800) 745-4000. Prerecorded message for recipes and tips. Visit their Web site at www.reynoldskitchens.com for turkey tips.

USDA Meat and Poultry Hotline: (800) 535-4555. Operators answer questions about meat and poultry handling, cooking, and safety. Talk to live operators 10:00 A.M. to 4:00 P.M. Monday through Friday; listen to taped information at other times.

Index

Underscored page references indicate boxed text and tables. *Italic* references indicate illustrations.

Emergency Substitutions

If You're Out of This . . .	Use This . . .
Allspice, ground, 1 tsp	½ tsp cinnamon + ½ tsp ground cloves
Apple pie spice, 1 Tbsp	2 tsp cinnamon + 1 tsp nutmeg + a pinch of allspice
Arrowroot, 1 Tbsp	1 Tbsp all-purpose flour OR 2¼ tsp cornstarch or potato starch
Baking powder, 1 tsp	¼ tsp baking soda + ½ tsp cream of tartar OR ¼ tsp baking soda + ½ cup buttermilk or soured milk (reduce liquid in recipe by ½ cup) OR ¼ tsp baking soda + 6 Tbsp molasses (reduce liquid in recipe by ¼ cup and adjust sweetener)
Bread crumbs, dry, 1 cup	3–4 slices oven-dried bread, crushed, OR ¾ cup cracker crumbs OR 1 Tbsp quick-cooking oats
Broth, beef or chicken, 1 cup	1 cup boiling water + 1 bouillon cube, 1 envelope bouillon, or 1 tsp instant bouillon granules
Butter, 1 stick (½ cup)	½ cup (8 Tbsp) margarine OR 7 Tbsp vegetable oil
Buttermilk, 1 cup	1 cup plain yogurt OR 1 Tbsp vinegar or lemon juice + enough milk to equal 1 cup (let stand 5–10 min before using)
Chives, chopped, 1 Tbsp	1 Tbsp minced scallion tops
Chocolate, semisweet, 1 oz (1 square)	½ oz unsweetened chocolate + 1 Tbsp sugar
Chocolate, semisweet, 6 oz chips, melted	9 Tbsp unsweetened cocoa powder + 7 Tbsp sugar + 3 Tbsp butter, shortening, or vegetable oil
Chocolate, unsweetened, 1 oz (1 square)	3 Tbsp unsweetened cocoa powder + 1 Tbsp butter, shortening, or vegetable oil
Coconut milk, fresh, 1 cup	1 cup canned coconut milk
Coconut, grated, 1 cup	1⅓ cups flaked coconut
Corn syrup, dark, 1 cup	¾ cup light corn syrup + ¼ cup light molasses OR 1 cup packed brown sugar + ¼ cup water or liquid used in recipe
Corn syrup, light, 1 cup	1 cup sugar dissolved in ¼ cup water or liquid used in recipe
Cornstarch, 1 Tbsp, for thickening	2 Tbsp all-purpose flour OR 2 tsp arrowroot OR 1⅓ Tbsp quick-cooking tapioca
Cracker crumbs, 1 cup	1¼ cups bread crumbs
Cream, half-and-half, 1 cup	½ cup light cream + ½ cup whole milk OR 1 Tbsp melted unsalted butter + enough whole milk to equal 1 cup
Cream, heavy, 1 cup	⅓ cup melted unsalted butter + whole milk to equal 1 cup
Cream, light, 1 cup	3 Tbsp melted unsalted butter + whole milk to equal 1 cup
Cream, sour, 1 cup	1 cup plain yogurt OR 1 cup plain yogurt + 1 Tbsp cornstarch OR ⅓ cup melted unsalted butter + ¾ cup buttermilk, soured milk, or plain yogurt OR 1 cup evaporated milk + 1 Tbsp vinegar or lemon juice OR 1 cup cottage cheese blended with 2 Tbsp milk and 1 Tbsp lemon juice

(continued)

Emergency Substitutions (cont.)

If You're Out of This . . .	Use This . . .
Egg, whole, 1 egg	2 egg whites OR 2 egg yolks + 1 Tbsp cold water OR 3½ Tbsp frozen and thawed egg OR ¼ cup egg substitute OR 2½ Tbsp powdered whole egg + 2½ Tbsp water
Egg white, 1 white	2 Tbsp frozen and thawed egg white OR 1 Tbsp powdered egg white + 2 Tbsp water
Egg yolk, 2 yolks	1 whole egg (for thickening sauces) 2 Tbsp frozen and thawed yolk OR ¼ cup powdered yolk + 4 tsp water (for baking)
Flour, all-purpose, 1 Tbsp (for thickening)	½ Tbsp cornstarch, potato starch, or rice starch OR 2 tsp arrowroot OR 1 Tbsp quick-cooking tapioca OR 2 egg yolks
Flour, all-purpose, sifted, 1 cup	1 cup minus 2 Tbsp unsifted all-purpose flour
Flour, cake, sifted, 1 cup	1 cup minus 2 Tbsp sifted all-purpose flour OR 1 cup minus 2 Tbsp sifted all-purpose flour mixed with 2 Tbsp cornstarch
Flour, potato, 1 Tbsp	2 Tbsp all-purpose flour OR 1 Tbsp cornstarch or arrowroot
Flour, self-rising, sifted, 1 cup	1 cup sifted all-purpose flour + 1½ tsp baking powder + pinch of salt
Garlic, minced or pressed, 1 clove	½ tsp jarred minced garlic OR ⅛ tsp garlic powder
Ginger, fresh, grated, 1 Tbsp	⅛ tsp ground ginger (for baking) OR 1 Tbsp rinsed chopped candied ginger (for baking)
Herbs, fresh, chopped, 1 Tbsp	1 tsp dried herb OR ¼ tsp powdered or ground
Honey, 1 cup	1¼ cups sugar + ¼ cup liquid called for in recipe
Hot-pepper sauce, 3 drops	Pinch of ground red pepper
Italian herb seasoning, 1 Tbsp	1½ tsp dried oregano + ¾ tsp dried basil + ¾ tsp dried thyme
Ketchup or chili sauce, ½ cup	⅓ cup tomato sauce + 2 Tbsp sugar + 1 Tbsp vinegar
Lemon juice, fresh, 1 Tbsp	1 Tbsp bottled or frozen lemon juice OR 1½ tsp white wine vinegar
Lemon zest, grated, 1 tsp	½ tsp lemon extract
Lime juice, fresh, 1 Tbsp	1 Tbsp bottled or frozen lime juice or lemon juice
Lime zest, grated, 1 tsp	1 tsp grated lemon zest
Liqueur, almond-flavored, 2 Tbsp	2 Tbsp water + ½–¾ tsp almond extract
Liqueur, chocolate-flavored, 2 Tbsp	2 Tbsp water + ¾ tsp chocolate extract
Liqueur, coffee-flavored, 2 Tbsp	2 Tbsp water + ¾ tsp instant coffee granules
Milk, fat-free, 1 cup	⅓ cup nonfat dry milk + ¾ cup water
Milk, sour, 1 cup	1 Tbsp lemon juice or distilled vinegar + enough milk to equal 1 cup (let stand 5–10 min before using)
Milk, whole, fresh, 1 cup	1 cup fat-free milk + 2 Tbsp butter or margarine OR ½ cup evaporated whole milk + ½ cup water OR ⅞ cup water + ¼ cup dry milk OR ⅞ cup water + ¼ cup nonfat dry milk + 2½ tsp butter or margarine OR 1 cup soy milk